The British Isles

Shetland Islands

Atlantic Ocean

Orkney Islands

The Hebrides

Scotland

Braemar

Fort William ▲ *Ben Nevis*

The United Kingdom of Great Britain and Northern Ireland (UK)

Edinburgh
Glasgow

North Sea

Northern Ireland

Belfast

Hadrian's Wall
Vindolanda ● Newcastle upon Tyne
River Wear ● Durham

Lake District

The Isle of Man

Irish Sea

Republic of Ireland

Dublin

Liverpool ● Manchester

Bethesda ● Chester
Caernafon ● *River Dee*
Mount Snowdon ▲ Llangollen ● Whitchurch
Chirk

● Ennis

Wales

River Towy

England

● Birmingham

● Cambridge

● Oxford

London
River Thames

Celtic Sea

Cardiff

Bristol ●
Bath

Portsmouth ● Brighton
The Solent

● Devon

■ capital cities of the UK and the Republic of Ireland
● capital cities of the countries
● important cities/places in On Track 1, 2 and 3
● cities in On Track 4

● Plymouth

English Channel **France**

0 ___ 50 ___ 100 miles
0 ___ 100 km

How to use this book

On Track 4 starts with a *Welcome* double-page spread. Then there are four regular workshops. Every workshop has the same three parts. Parts one and two teach you new things, and part three helps you practise what you've learned. The activities and exercises have numbers and letters. Sometimes they have symbols, too.

Here is an explanation of the symbols:

Symbols in *On Track 4*

audio	🔊	Listen to a dialogue, a text, song or story.
video	🎞	Watch a film.
partner work	👥	Work with a partner.
group work	👥	Work with two or more partners.
whole class work	👥	Work with the class.
bus stop	(BUS)	Work with a new partner.
mingling	⟳	Go around the classroom and ask your partner / partners questions.
placemat	✉	Think about a topic and share your ideas in groups.
First track, On track, Fast track	⟫⟫⟫	Do the First track, On track and Fast track exercises.
Extra track	＋	Do the extra exercise.
American English	🇺🇸	American English (specific vocabulary or spelling).
revision	*	Grammar revision
step 1, 2, 3, …	S1	Activities with this symbol help you with a more complex task – step by step.
grammar	→ G11	There is more information about this grammar point in the *Appendix*.
webcode	@ WES-40324-002	There is a webcode on the left-hand page of every workshop. This webcode helps you to find all the audio and video material. You will also find transcripts of the audios and videos as well as extra material.

How to use the webcodes

A webcode is like a small website. All the *On Track* audio and video material that you need for class or homework is here: www.westermann.de/webcodes. There is also extra material. You can listen and watch online or download everything. Type in the code for the workshops (**WES-40324-001**) without the @ and click "Aufrufen" and you will find the page for *Workshop 1*. There are webcodes in your workbook, too.

These are the webcodes in *On Track 4*:

Welcome: @ WES-40324-000   Workshop 2: @ WES-40324-002   Workshop 4: @ WES-40324-004

Workshop 1: @ WES-40324-001   Workshop 3: @ WES-40324-003

Contents

* grammar revision

PART 2 / PART 3

PART 1 / PART 2

* grammar revision

Vocabulary	Grammar	Skills focus	
careers, jobs, the future of work, humans vs. robots, skills and qualities	Gerund after prepositions (G 28)	Reading: Humans versus robots Video 14: Spotlight on: marine biologist	
part-time jobs, advantages and disadvantages, job ads, balancing school life and part-time jobs, volunteering	Statements in reported speech (G 29)	Viewing: Video 15 – 17: Job talk	
jobs, curriculum vitae, working life, skills, preferences	Questions, requests, advice and orders in reported speech (G 30)	Speaking: Volunteering abroad	
rights of children, working conditions, legal requirements, child labour, biography	Quantifiers (G 31)	Writing: Young heroes: Malala Yousafzai Video 18: Craig Kielburger's story	

What do you know about the USA?

1 Do the quiz to find out how much you already know about the USA. The pictures can help you.

2 How many questions did you get right? What have you learned?

1 What's the population of the United States?
A over 1 billion
B over 300 million
C over 130 million

A

B

2 Who arrived in North America first?
A the Vikings
B the Native Americans
C the Pilgrims from England

3 What's the most common language in the US after English and Spanish?
A German
B Navajo Indian
C French

4 On what date does America celebrate its independence from Britain?
A 4th June
B 4th July
C 14th July

C

5 Who was the first president of the United States?
A Abraham Lincoln
B Thomas Jefferson
C George Washington

D

6 What's the most popular sport in the US?
   A baseball
   B basketball
   C American football

E

7 Which American city is known as 'The Big Apple'?
   A Atlanta
   B New York City
   C Chicago

8 Which country gave the Statue of Liberty to the US as a gift?
   A France
   B England
   C Canada

F

9 Which of these popular American foods actually comes from the US?
   A pizza
   B potato chips (or, in the UK, crisps)
   C burgers

10 Which country is in the south and shares a border with the US?
   A Canada
   B Cuba
   C Mexico

G

@ WES-40324-001

Dreaming USA

Hey there! I'm Emily, from San Francisco. I love the outdoors, and this region has lots of it. The state of Washington has rainforests, Nevada has hot deserts, and Colorado has snowy mountains. California has all of these – and sunny beaches, too. But earthquakes and forest fires are a real danger.

Hi, I'm Germaine. I'm from Nashville, Tennessee. They call this place Music City. Music is a big part of life in this region. Country, blues, jazz and rock & roll music all started here. What else makes this region special? The warm, wet weather is good for growing cotton and tobacco. And the Florida beaches are great in the winter!

USA REGIONS

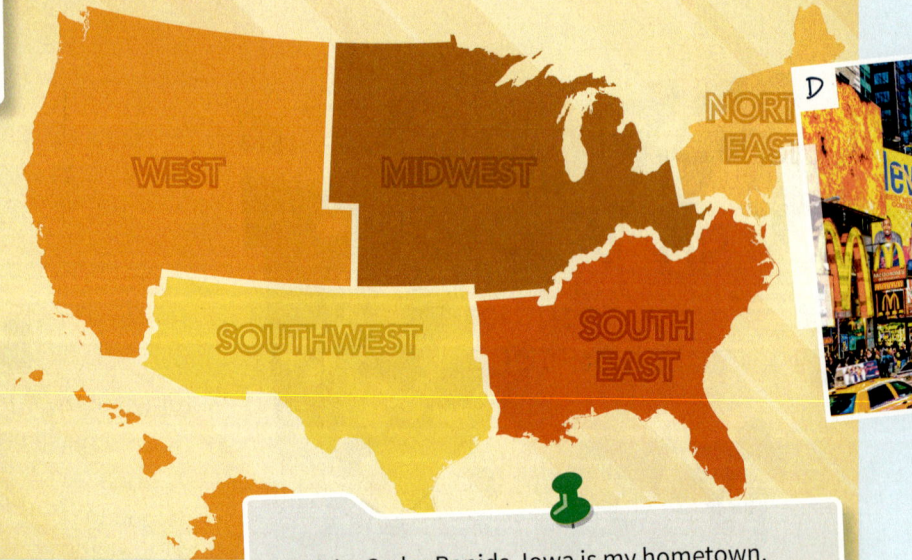

WEST

MIDWEST

NORTH EAST

SOUTHWEST

SOUTH EAST

1 **a** There are five regions in the USA. Look at the map and the photos around it. Then read and listen to what each person says about their region. Match the photos (A – E) to the regions.

b Imagine you have applied to be an exchange student in the USA. Which part of the country would you like to go to and why?

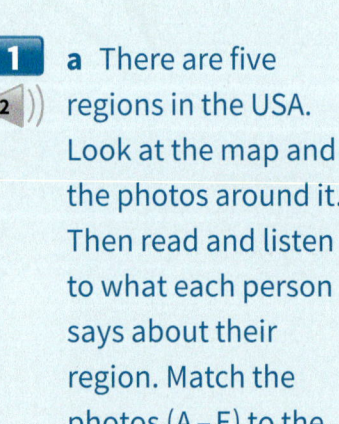

I'm Eric. Cedar Rapids, Iowa is my hometown. People like to call this part of the country 'America's Heartland'. It's a huge region with endless farmland. If you drive east from here, you come to the Mississippi River. Further east and to the north are the Great Lakes. Chicago and Detroit are two of the main cities in the region.

C

My name is Luis. I live near Tucson, Arizona. It's very hot and dry here, but I don't mind. Most people in this region live in bigger cities like Phoenix or Houston because of the desert climate. I love the natural beauty here and the awesome landscapes like the Grand Canyon.

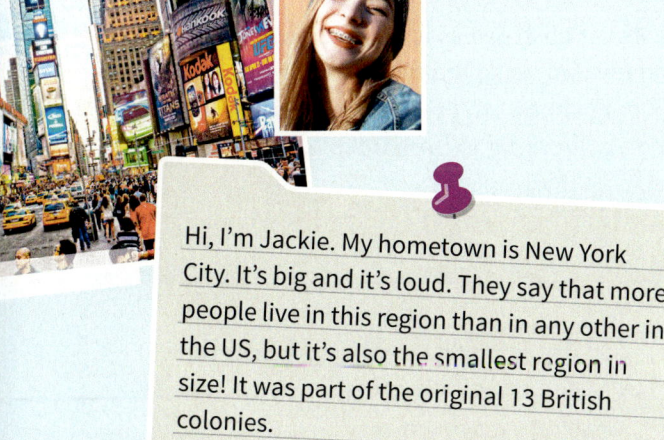

Hi, I'm Jackie. My hometown is New York City. It's big and it's loud. They say that more people live in this region than in any other in the US, but it's also the smallest region in size! It was part of the original 13 British colonies.

2 Ellie Quinn is a 15-year-old student from Glasgow, Scotland. Her dream for the next school year is to go to the USA as an exchange student. Discuss how you think she could benefit from a student exchange.

3 **a** A student exchange organization invites Ellie to take part in a live web conference. In this part of the conference, three exchange students in the USA talk about their experiences. Listen and decide which US regions the three students are living in. Compare your answers.

4 **b** Copy the table. Now listen to the three students answer more questions. Complete the table.

	enjoys …	is surprised that …	misses …
Mina			
Conor			
Joshua			

YOUR TRACK

After this workshop you will be able to:
- talk about chores.
- compare life today to life in the past.
- talk about national holidays and celebrations.
- discuss issues related to immigration.
- research and write a short article. (Workshop task)

Words and phrases

cotton   a material used to make clothes such as T-shirts

heartland   the central part of a country

Living in the USA

1 **A different place.** Ellie Quinn is now living with an American family in Lexington, Massachusetts, and is going to high school there. Read Ellie's blog. Match the topics in the box to paragraphs 1 – 4. There is one extra topic.

> a friendly community ■ American lifestyle ■ walk or drive ■ my American family ■ far from home

MY YEAR IN AMERICA

1 Last week I told you about some cool places in Lexington and Boston. I like exploring my new neighbourhood, but it's not always easy. Walking can be dangerous here. Sometimes there's a pavement (or 'sidewalk', as Americans call it), but often there isn't. Driving is a lot more popular.
5 People use their cars to go to the shop down the road!

2 I like seeing how people live here. Most houses are made of wood and they're quite nice. There's often a porch at the front of each house. It looks like a cool place to hang out. And there's usually a garden (they call it a 'yard') with grass and plants at the front
10 and the back of the house. Nice! I see a lot of American flags, too. Nearly every house has one.

3 Most of the neighbours are open and friendly. Mrs Dodd from next door hugged me when she heard my accent. She's got Scottish relatives in Dundee! The family across the road comes from Jamaica, another family is from Ukraine, and the people at the local food shop are Korean. And they've all got American
15 flags in front of their houses, too, like they all want to belong here.

4 My host family are Polish-Americans. Eating pierogi and other Polish dishes is totally normal for them. I feel very lucky – they're all so relaxed and easy-going. And my American brother and sister, Alex and Nina, are lots of fun. I already feel like part of their family. Doing chores isn't my favourite activity, but it's what they do on Saturdays. I don't mind sweeping the porch. Working in the garden isn't bad either.

20 That's it for this week. Write a comment and tell me what you think! I'll have a mobile phone (or 'cell phone') number soon – I promise!

❗ page 146, Writing skills

2 **Living in Lexington**

a Look at how Ellie uses *-ing* forms (gerunds) in her blog. Then answer the questions in the box.

1 *Walking can be dangerous here.* (line 2)
2 *Driving is a lot more popular.* (line 4)

3 *I like* **seeing** *how people live here.* (line 6)
4 *I don't mind* **sweeping** *the porch.* (line 19)

> - Do the gerunds in the first two examples function as (a) a verb, (b) a noun or (c) an adjective?
> - Is the gerund the subject or the object in each sentence?

🔊 **Words and phrases**

Housework

to **empty**	to take out everything in a container
porch	a small area with a roof outside a home
to **sweep**	to clean a floor with a brush or broom
to **vacuum**	to use a vacuum cleaner to clean something

American English vs. British English

sidewalk	pavement
sneakers	trainers
to stand in line	to queue

b Complete Ellie's thoughts with a gerund.

1 I really enjoy **g▓▓▓** to Boston.
2 **W▓▓▓** a blog is my new hobby.
3 I love **w▓▓▓** in the garden.
4 **M▓▓▓** pierogi is quite a chore!
5 **M▓▓▓** new people here isn't so hard.

3 One language, two worlds

a Read Alex Kominiski and Vivian Wang's messages. What are their two main topics?

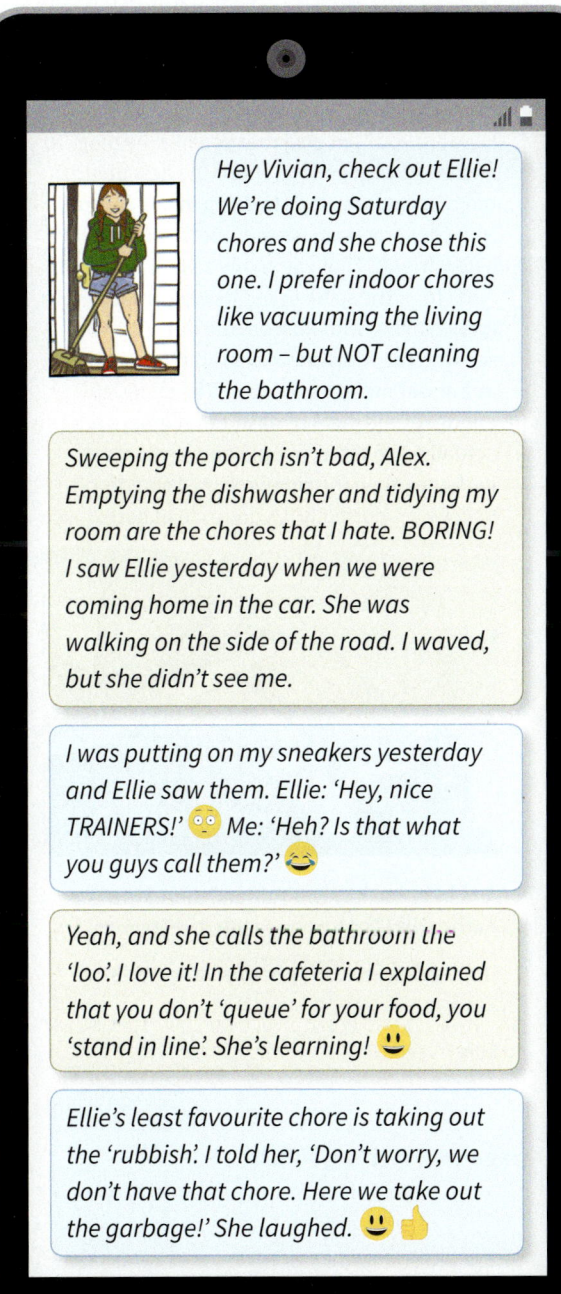

> *Hey Vivian, check out Ellie! We're doing Saturday chores and she chose this one. I prefer indoor chores like vacuuming the living room – but NOT cleaning the bathroom.*

> *Sweeping the porch isn't bad, Alex. Emptying the dishwasher and tidying my room are the chores that I hate. BORING! I saw Ellie yesterday when we were coming home in the car. She was walking on the side of the road. I waved, but she didn't see me.*

> *I was putting on my sneakers yesterday and Ellie saw them. Ellie: 'Hey, nice TRAINERS!' 🙄 Me: 'Heh? Is that what you guys call them?' 😂*

> *Yeah, and she calls the bathroom the 'loo'. I love it! In the cafeteria I explained that you don't 'queue' for your food, you 'stand in line'. She's learning! 😃*

> *Ellie's least favourite chore is taking out the 'rubbish'. I told her, 'Don't worry, we don't have that chore. Here we take out the garbage!' She laughed. 😃👍*

b Answer the questions.

1 Which chore do Ellie and Vivian prefer?
2 What was Ellie doing when Vivian saw her?
3 What did Alex learn from Ellie?
4 Why did Ellie laugh?

c Vivian says:
*I **saw** Ellie yesterday when we **were coming** home in the car.*
Find another example of a sentence with the simple past and the past progressive. Then choose the correct alternatives in the box.

> ● We use the **simple past / past progressive** to focus on the length of an action or to show that it wasn't finished.
> ● We use the **simple past / past progressive** to focus on the action itself or to show that it was finished.

d Complete these sentences with the simple past and past progressive.

1 Ellie ▓▓▓ (*sweep*) the porch when Alex ▓▓▓ (*take*) the photo.
2 Alex's text message ▓▓▓ (*arrive*) while Vivian ▓▓▓ (*read*) her emails.
3 Ellie ▓▓▓ (*queue*) for lunch when Nina and Vivian ▓▓▓ (*come*) into the cafeteria.

❗ page 146, Writing skills

4 Doing chores

a List the chores in the blog and in the messages.

🔊 6 **b** Now listen to Alex and his sister Nina. Who is doing which chore?

5 YOUR TURN: My chores. Compare your chores at home. Which do you prefer? Explain why.

> don't like ▪ don't mind ▪ enjoy ▪
> hate ▪ like ▪ love ▪ quite like

I enjoy talking the dog for a walk, but I don't like going out in the dark.

Grammar and structures

Gerund as subject → G1
Doing chores isn't so bad.

Gerund as object → G2
She enjoys **writing a blog**.

Simple past and past progressive (revision) → G3
When Leo **rang**, I **was tidying** my room.

Practice: Away from home

1 GET STARTED! Think about the area that you call home. What are the first thoughts and feelings that you have? Describe them to a partner.

2 Ellie's neighbourhood project

a Ellie is interviewing three of her Lexington neighbours as part of a project for her social studies class. She wants to know how they feel about their neighbourhood. Copy the table. Then listen and complete it.

name	likes	dislikes	wants to see changed
...			

b Compare your answers. Which answers do you find surprising? Why?

c Think about your own neighbourhood. Write your answers to Ellie's questions. Then ask your partners. Discuss your answers.

3 An interesting afternoon. Ellie is telling her host family about her project. Complete her story with the simple past or the past progressive.

> be ■ cook ■ ~~find~~ ■ get ■ go ■
> not have ■ interview (2x) ■ plant ■
> smell ■ step ■ talk ■ understand

The Reeds were first on my list. I *found* Mrs Reed in her flower garden. She [1] roses. While I [2] her, I nearly [3] on one of the roses. That was embarrassing! After that I [4] to see Mr Kim in his shop. Mr Kim is very nice. He has a strong accent, but I [5] everything that he [6] about. My next person was Daisy Clarke. She [7] much time for me because she and her mum [8] dinner. It was Jamaican food and it [9] great. Anyway, I [10] her quickly in the kitchen while they [11] dinner ready. The chat with her [12] very interesting!

»» page 36

4 Hi, cousin. Ellie's email to her cousin is a bit mixed up: she's used some American words and phrases. Rewrite the email in British English.

From:	Ellie
To:	Ryan
Subject:	RE: Hi, cousin

Hi Ryan,

Yes, I got your mail. Sorry! There is so much happening here. The reason you can't text me is because I don't have a **cell phone** (1) number. I'm working on that!
How are you? I'm glad that you like my blog. To answer your questions about the new photos: the two girls who are **standing in line** (2) are Nina, my American 'sister', and Vivian, a new friend. That was in my school cafeteria. And I took the selfie in our lovely **yard** (3) while I was playing with Roscoe, the dog. Can you see my crazy new **sneakers** (4)? I bought them at a street market in Boston. The shoes are good, but the market wasn't that great, actually. Too many people and so much **garbage** (5) on the **sidewalk** (6). I couldn't believe it – normally it's quite clean here.

And because it was outdoors, there wasn't a **bathroom** (7). I had to go into a restaurant.

Hope you're well. Say hi to your **mom** (8)!
See ya,

Ellie

! page 146, Writing skills

Words and phrases

Jobs
garbage collector  person who takes away rubbish
mail carrier  person who delivers the post

5 Away from home

a Ellie and Vivian are talking after school. Read their conversation. How does Ellie feel about being away from home? How does Vivian's situation compare?

Vivian   How are you, Ellie? You don't look so happy today.

Ellie   Oh, I'm fine. Maybe I'm just tired. It was a big day. Lots of things were 5 new for me.

Vivian   Oh, I know what that's like. Two years ago I was new at this school, too. It was hard learning how everything works.

Ellie   10 I think it's also harder coming here as an exchange student. I feel a bit lonely sometimes, and I really miss my parents and my brother and the people I know.

Vivian   15 I totally understand. Moving here from Rochester, New York, was different because I was with my family. But I sometimes felt homesick like you. I didn't have any 20 friends and I missed our old house and our old neighborhood.

Ellie   My dad says, 'feeling homesick is normal'. I'm sure he's right. I mean, it's so cool going to school here. 25 Living with my host family and making new friends like you, Vivian, is really special, too.

Vivian   Aw, thanks.

Ellie   I read somewhere that homesickness 30 is part of being an exchange student. I just need to remember all the good parts about it, too!

❗ **page 146, Writing skills**

b Answer these questions.

1   What was hard for Vivian? What has been hard for Ellie?

2   What has Ellie heard and read about homesickness?

c Think of a time when you were away from home and you felt lonely or homesick. Share with your partner. Discuss the reasons why you felt that way.

I missed having my favourite breakfast every morning.

6 WRITING FOCUS: A letter to a host family

a Imagine you're applying to be an exchange student in the US. An important part of your application is a letter to your host family in which you introduce yourself.
Write your own introductory letter to your host family.

> **TIP**
>
> **When you write your introductory letter:**
> - Begin by introducing and describing yourself (your name, your age, where you're from and your personality). Be positive!
> - Include short paragraphs about the following topics:
>   - your family and your family life
>   - where you live and what it's like there
>   - your interests and hobbies
>   - your classes at school
>   - why you are excited about being an exchange student
> - Thank your host family and conclude your letter.

 b Form small groups. Take turns reading your letters aloud in your group. Give feedback on each letter. What do you think is good? What could be improved?

Think about:
- the structure
- the amount of detail
- whether the language is clear

New England: Birthplace of America

PART 1

PART 2

PART 3

1 **Living history museums**

a Ellie wants to find out about New England's colonial history, so her host family are going to take her to a 'living history' museum. Look at the website. What is a living history museum?

b What information does Ellie find out from the website about:
- the Pilgrim Fathers
- why they emigrated to New England
- how they got there
- the Wampanoags

🔍	NEWS	CALENDAR	CONTACTS	BLOG	GALLERY	✉	🖨	🔊

New England living history museums

New England is one of the most historic regions of the USA. This is the place where it all began.
5 The region was home to one of the earliest European settlements in the 1600s when the Pilgrim Fathers arrived from England in search of religious
10 freedom. Thousands more English settlers followed the Pilgrims, ready to start a new life in America. The War of Independence, which led to the founding of the United States, took place here in the 18th century.
Go back in time at one of New England's 'living history'
15 museums, where staff dress in period costumes and are ready to answer all your questions about life in the past.

Plimoth Plantation: The real thing

The first community the
20 Pilgrims built when they arrived in 1620 was in Plymouth. Visit a re-creation of their 17th century village to see
25 how they lived. You can also visit the homesite of the Wampanoag tribe, whose land this was. Talk to Native Americans who are descendants of that nation. It was the

Wampanoags that taught the settlers how to plant corn, where to hunt and fish, and how to survive the cold winter.
30 Find out about the feast the Pilgrims shared with the Wampanoags, which is often called the 'First Thanksgiving'.

Mayflower II – The Voyage that changed the world

Step aboard a replica of the
35 tiny ship which brought the Pilgrims to the New World in 1620. Find out what life was like during the voyage for the passengers who
40 traveled aboard the *Mayflower*.

Boston Tea Party ships and museum

Relive the event which
45 started the American Revolution! Learn about the brave people that rebelled against the British Government. The British introduced many new taxes, which
50 the colonists thought was very unfair. When a tax on tea was introduced, a group of colonists, whose leader was called Samuel Adams, boarded three British tea ships in Boston Harbor. They threw 342 crates of tea overboard in protest.

2 **Information about the Pilgrims.** Identify the relative clauses in sentences 1–7. Then answer the questions in the box on page 19.

1 The War of Independence, which led to the founding of the United States, took place here in the 18th century.

2 The first community (which) the Pilgrims built when they arrived in 1620 was in Plymouth.

3 You can also visit the homesite of the Wampanoag tribe, whose land this was.

4 Talk to Native Americans who are descendants of that nation.

🔊 **Words and phrases**

descendant	somebody who is related to a person who lived long ago
period costume	the clothes people wore at a time in the past
to rebel	to fight against authority

5 It was the Wampanoags that taught the settlers how to plant corn.

6 Step aboard a replica of the tiny ship that brought the Pilgrims to the New World in 1620.

7 The British introduced many new taxes, which the colonists thought was very unfair.

Defining relative clauses give important information about a person or thing.
● What relative pronouns do we use
  – for people, for things?
  – to mean 'of who / of which'?
● When can we leave out the pronoun?

Non-defining relative clauses add extra information. We use commas to separate the extra information from the rest of the sentence.
● Can we leave out the relative pronoun?
● Which pronoun can't we use?
We sometimes use non-defining relative clauses to refer to a whole sentence.

---

3 **Asking questions**

a Make questions about the Pilgrims.

name | place | the Pilgrims settled in?

What was the name of the place (which) the Pilgrims settled in?

1 name | ship | brought the Pilgrims to Plymouth?
2 name | tribe of Indians | lived in the area?
3 name | holiday | Americans still celebrate in November?
4 name | protest | took place in Boston Harbor?

b Test your memory! Cover page 18. Take turns to ask and answer the questions in **a**. How much do you remember?

---

4 **Adding information**

a Join the sentences. Use non-defining relative clauses.

1 New England is where many early colonists settled. It is one of the most historic regions of the USA.
2 The voyage on the *Mayflower* was very uncomfortable. The *Mayflower* took the Pilgrims to Plymouth.
3 The Wampanoag tribe lived near the Pilgrims. They were very friendly towards the settlers.
4 The settlers only survived with the help of the Native Americans. The Native Americans taught them how to plant crops, hunt and fish.
5 The British Government introduced a tax on tea. This was the one of the main reasons for the American Revolution.

⟫⟫ **page 36**

b Compare your sentences. Did you join them in the same way?

---

5 **How much do you know?** Listen to Ellie and Alex doing a general knowledge quiz about the USA. How many answers can you get right?

---

6 **YOUR TURN: General knowledge class quiz**

a In teams, prepare your own general knowledge quiz. Think about famous people, places or events that you know about. Write at least 5 or 6 questions.

This person, who lived in ..., became the first ...
What's the name of a recent film that stars ... ?
What's the name of the (building/statue/...)
which you can see in ... ?
It's a holiday that we celebrate every year on ...

b Take turns to ask your quiz questions. The team with the most correct answers wins.

Grammar and structures

Relative pronouns (revision) → G4
who, which, that, whose
Defining relative clauses (revision) → G5
Talk to Native Americans **who** are real descendants of that Nation.

Non-defining relative clauses (revision) → G6
The British introduced many new taxes, **which** the colonists thought was very unfair.

Practice: Where it began

1 **GET STARTED!** Look at the photos taken at the Living History Museum. What do they show you about life at the Plimoth colony in the 1600s? What jobs do you think the men, women and children did? Use the phrases in the box to help you.

> chop wood ■ cook over an open fire ■
> fire a rifle ■ go hunting ■ grow their
> own food ■ keep chickens / goats ■
> lead a hard / simple life ■ live in a
> one-room house

2 **LISTENING FOCUS: At the Plimoth Plantation**

a Ellie and her host family are at the colony. They're asking a family of settlers, who are played by modern-day actors, about life in the settlement. Read the questions they ask Goodwife Tilley and her two children, Constance and Samuel. Can you predict some of their answers?

1 Why did you leave England?
2 What was life like for you at the beginning?
3 What kind of food do you eat?
4 What's your daily routine?
5 Do you go to school?
6 What do you do at the weekend?
7 What about entertainment – what do you do?
8 Do you miss your homeland?
9 What do you miss the most?

b Listen and check. How many of your ideas were right?

c Listen again and make notes of the answers. Then compare with a partner and, if necessary, complete your answers.

> **TIP**
>
> **Listening for details**
> While you are listening, make notes. Just write key words, not complete sentences.

3 **Life then and now**

a Compare your life today with how the children in the village of Plimoth lived. Think about food, daily routines, chores, school and weekend activities, and make a list of differences.

b Share your ideas with the class.

4 **Ellie's blog.** Complete Ellie's blog with relative pronouns. Which relative clauses contain necessary information and which contain extra information? When can you leave the pronoun out?

> Hello again everyone, I'm learning so much about American history. This weekend we went to the Boston Tea Party Ships and Museum. It's amazing! You take a tour `1` lasts about an
> 5   hour. Real actors, `2` wear the clothes of that time, guide you on the tour. It's a re-enactment of the Boston tea rebellion `3` took place in 1774 and led to the War of Independence. The colonists were very angry about a new tea tax
> 10 `4` the British had introduced. I actually role-played one of the townspeople `5` were there! You go on board one of the British tea ships `6` were anchored in Boston Bay (a replica of course!) and you throw crates of tea
> 15 overboard! At the end of the tour, we watched a film re-enactment of the first battle `7` started the war, the Battle of Lexington. It wasn't like anything `8` I've experienced before!

Words and phrases

to **capture**	to catch somebody
to **chop (wood)**	to cut (wood) into small pieces
dawn	the first light in the sky in the morning
to **fetch**	to bring
laundry	clothes or linen that need washing or have just been washed
to **worship**	to show respect for a god

Squanto

Folk Hero (c.1580 – c.1622)

Squanto, *who is famous for helping the Pilgrims survive their first winter*, was a Native American of the Wampanoag Nation.

He was born in 1580 and grew up near Plymouth
5 Bay. In 1605, an English explorer captured Squanto and took him to England. In England, Squanto lived with a man called Ferdinando Gorges. Squanto returned to North America in 1614, but another explorer captured him again and sold him
10 as a slave in Spain. Squanto finally escaped and returned to the Wampanoag region in 1619. However, when he arrived in his village, it was empty. This was because of a smallpox epidemic. So he went to live with another Wampanoag tribe.
15 When the Pilgrims arrived and built Plimoth Colony, Squanto became the interpreter between

them and the Wampanoag. He also taught the Pilgrims how to grow corn and catch fish in the rivers. He probably took part in the first
20 Thanksgiving feast.

---

5 **Squanto, folk hero**

a Read the information about Squanto. Why is he called a 'folk hero'?

b Add the extra information in sentences 1 – 6 to the text.

> ~~Squanto is famous for helping the Pilgrims to survive their first winter.~~

1 The English explorer's name was Captain Weymouth.

2 Ferdinando Gorges taught him English and used him as an interpreter.
3 The explorer hoped to make some money.
4 The epidemic had lasted three years and killed many Native Americans.
5 Squanto could speak English very well.
6 This helped the colony to survive.

>>> **page 36**

---

6 **Thanksgiving celebrations**

a Before you watch a video about how people celebrate Thanksgiving, make a mind map with the words in the box and your own ideas.

> bands ■ feast with friends / relatives ■ fireworks ■ float ■ giving food to the poor ■ parades ■ pumpkin pie ■ turkey ■ volunteering ■ watching sports on TV

Food

Family activities

THANKSGIVING CELEBRATIONS

Public events

Helping others

b **VIDEO TRACK: Thanksgiving Day.** Watch the video. Make notes on how many Americans celebrate Thanksgiving.

❗ **page 143, Speaking skills**

---

7 **National holidays in Germany**

a Make a list of important national holidays in Germany. What's your favourite?

b Choose one holiday. Make notes, then tell an American exchange student (your partner) how you celebrate it.

Method coach: Internet research

S1 Search tips: Using keywords

a Imagine you need to find out some information about the famous Native American folk hero Pocahontas for a school history project. Here are some things you want to know:

1 Who was Pocahontas?
2 When was she born?
3 Why is she a folk hero?
4 Where did she die?
5 How did she die?

Read the TIP box. What is the quickest / best way to find information on the internet?

 b List keywords for your search.

 c Compare your keywords. Which ones are the most useful?

> **TIP**
>
> **How to find information quickly on the internet**
> Enter as few words as possible – not full sentences.
> *When was the folk hero Pocahontas born? > Pocahontas born*
> If you get too many results, be more specific.
> *Pocahontas > Pocahontas folk hero*
> To limit your search, put quotation marks "…" round your search words.
> *"Pocahontas died"*
> Or if you have a question, just type in the question.
> *Why is Pocahontas a folk hero?*

S2 Using reliable / appropriate sources

a Information on the internet isn't always correct. It's important to choose websites that give you the right information. Look at the descriptions of different websites. Which kind:

1 is the most reliable?
2 is the least reliable?
3 can give helpful opinions and advice?
4 is mostly trying to sell something?
5 often has good information, but you should make sure it is correct?

b Which kind of website would be your first choice for the questions about Pocahontas?

Description
A) **.com** means this is a commercial website. It wants to sell a product, so the information might be factual, but it might only give you one side of the story.
B) **.org** means this is a non-profit organization. Non-profits are not trying to sell something, so in most cases you can trust their information.
C) Wikipedia is a useful website, but many of its volunteer writers are not experts. It's a good idea to check the information.
D) Personal blogs and online forums or message boards are not always reliable, but they're useful if you're looking for a personal opinion or an interesting anecdote.
E) **.edu** means this is an educational institution — usually a college or university. These are normally good sources of accurate information.
F) **.gov** is used by official government websites. They have up-to-date statistics and other reliable information.

S3 Bookmarking and noting your sources

a It's important to be able to save your sources. If you don't know how to 'bookmark' a website on your browser, find out. Then bookmark some websites that you often use.

b If you already use the bookmark function, make notes and explain to a partner how to do it.

🔊 Words and phrases

Facts and information

accurate   correct   **reliable**   can be trusted

PART 1

PART 2

PART 3

@ WES-40324-001

Workshop task: Find and evaluate sources

S1 Finding the right sources of information

a You and your family are planning to visit Boston in New England. You're interested in the city's history and you want to find out about:

1 Boston's role in the American Revolution
2 The Freedom Trail

You also want to check out:

3 fun things for teenagers to see and do in Boston
4 how to get around the city

b Write down keywords for your topic searches.

c Compare your keywords with a partner. Which ones did you decide on? Why? Do you want to change your keywords?

S2 Evaluating search results

a Use your keywords from **S1** to research Boston's role in the American Revolution.

b Which websites offer information from:

1 reliable factual sources?
2 a source that needs to be checked?
3 a personal blog?
4 a message board?
5 a commercial organization?

How do you know?

c Which websites do you think could be most useful for your research? Why? Choose three sources from your search. Bookmark them.

S3 Do your own research

a Now choose one of the other topics in **S1**. Use your keywords and, if necessary, refine your search. Then decide which websites are most useful for your research. Bookmark them.

b Tell a partner what you have found out. Which keywords worked best? Which websites did you choose to read?

A nation of immigrants

1 Emigrating to America

a During the 19th and 20th centuries millions of people left their home countries and went to the USA. Think of answers to these questions.

1 Why did they leave?
2 What attracted them to the USA?
3 How did they benefit their new country?

b Read the article and check your ideas. What new information did you find in the text? What is the writer's attitude towards the immigrants?

c Make notes under these headings. Then summarize what you have learned.
● Main reasons for emigrating to the USA
● Main ways immigrants benefit the US economy
● Main contributions immigrants have made to American culture

The American Dream

The United States has been a nation of immigrants from its earliest days. Some of the men who led the American Revolution in the 18th century were born far away from the Thirteen Colonies of New England. Alexander Hamilton, for example, was born on the island of St Kitts in the British West Indies.

5 As the country expanded westwards during the 19th century, German and Irish immigrants arrived in their millions. The biggest wave of immigration
was between 1880 and 1920 from Europe, the Middle East,
10 Canada, Mexico and China. Most European immigrants crossed the Atlantic by ship from ports like Liverpool or Hamburg. The Statue of Liberty in New York Harbor was a symbol of hope to these new arrivals.

Many immigrants were escaping from religious or political persecution. They were looking for
15 safety in America. Others, like the Irish, left to escape famine or poverty and unemployment. They hoped to build a better life in the New World for themselves and their families, and they were willing to work hard.

Since the mid 20th century, European immigration has slowed down. Today, most immigrants come from Central and South America, Asia and Africa.

20 Immigrants contributed to the wealth and culture of their new home in many different ways. The Irish built America's roads and bridges – and the Empire State Building in New York. German farmers settled in the valleys of the Mississippi, Ohio and Missouri rivers and helped to feed the
growing nation. Germans introduced the 'all-American' hamburger and hot dog. The French contribution was the
25 New Orleans Mardi Gras and the Mardi Gras pancake.

In the 20th century, German scientists helped build the rockets that took astronauts to the moon in 1969. Today, California's Silicon Valley wouldn't exist without highly skilled immigrants – around 70 percent of the Valley's
30 technology employees are foreign-born!

🔊 Words and phrases

to **contribute**	to give something
famine	when people don't have food for a long time
persecution	being treated badly because of your beliefs
wealth	a large amount of money

2 **Places and people.** Read the explanations, then find examples in the article to match the rules.

- Use *the* before
  - names of countries that include words like *States, Kingdom, Republic*: *the United Kingdom*
  - specific regions: *the Midwest*
  - most buildings and man-made or natural landmarks: *the Brandenburg Gate, the Grand Canyon*
  - names of oceans, seas and rivers: *the Baltic Sea*
  - names that refer to nationality groups with no plural form, mountain ranges, islands: *the British, the Alps*
- Use *a/an*
  - for one person or thing: *a nation*
  - with jobs: *a farmer, an engineer*
- Don't use an article before
  - names of continents, most countries, states or cities: *Asia, Turkey, New York*
  - individual lakes, mountains, islands: *Lake Michigan, Mount Everest*
  - nationality groups with a plural form and languages: *Americans, German*

3 **Famous immigrants.** Complete this information about three famous immigrants with the missing articles. Write 0 if no article is needed.

Levi Strauss was born in ▮1▮ Bavaria. He emigrated from ▮2▮ Germany to ▮3▮ United States at the age of 18 and arrived in New York in 1847. When he heard about the California
5 Gold Rush, he went out west to San Francisco to make his fortune. He did not work as ▮4▮ gold miner – he started the first company to make extra strong denim jeans for working men.

Steve Chen is ▮5▮ Taiwanese-American. Jawed
10 Karim is ▮6▮ Bangladeshi-German-American, who was born in ▮7▮ Merseburg, East Germany, but grew up in ▮8▮ West Germany. His mother is ▮9▮ scientist. Together the two men founded a famous video streaming platform.

15 Karim uploaded the first video ever in 2005. It was 19 seconds long and called 'Me at the zoo'. It has had over 26 million views.

Jan Koum was born in ▮10▮ Soviet Union. He emigrated to ▮11▮ California in 1992 with
20 his mother. He started off as ▮12▮ cleaner in a grocery store. But then he co-founded a messaging app with a friend, and the rest is history!

4 **Continents, countries and languages**

a Find the four continents in the *American Dream* article. How many countries in each continent can you write down in two minutes?

b Complete the sentences with your own ideas.

1 I would like to be able to speak …
2 The countries I would most like to visit are …
3 The capital city of my state / country is …
4 I was born in …
5 My brother / sister / father / mother is …
6 Some famous buildings in my town / city / country are …
7 Some famous geographical landmarks in my country are …

c Compare your ideas. How many are the same?

5 **YOUR TURN: What will you pack?** Many early immigrants to the US carried their belongings with them. Imagine you need to leave your home in an hour. You can only take what you can carry.

a **Think:** Think about how much you can carry and what you will need on your journey.

b **Pair:** Compare your choices with a partner and explain why you have chosen those items.

c **Share:** Compare your ideas with another pair.

d **Gallery walk:** Take photographs of the belongings you have decided to take and make a wall poster. Stand by your poster and explain your choices to your classmates.

Grammar and structures

The definite, indefinite and zero article → G7
the Brandenburg Gate, **a** farmer / **an** engineer, Mount Everest

Practice: The American Dream

PART 1

PART 2

PART 3

1 GET STARTED!

a What difficulties do immigrants often face when they arrive in a new country? Think about: language, accommodation, work, school, cultural differences and misunderstandings, unfriendly people.

b Which do you think might be the most difficult?

2 Immigrant stories

 a Listen to three immigrants. Copy the table and complete the information.

	Person 1	Person 2	Person 3
Name	???	???	???
Country of origin	???	???	???
Age at immigration	???	???	???
Place entered in US	???	???	???
Status*	???	???	???

* (legal / illegal immigrant, refugee / asylum seeker, green card / visa winner)

 b Listen again. Make notes to answer the questions.
- Why did they leave their country?
- What difficulties have they faced / do they face now?
- How do they feel about living in the US?

 c Compare and complete your notes.

 d How did each story make you feel? Explain your reactions.

3 SPEAKING FOCUS: Describing and interpreting photos

 a Each person in your group chooses one photo.

1 Describe what the people are doing.
2 Speculate which country the photo was taken in and explain why you think so.

 b Share your ideas about your photo with the class. Which photo do you find the most interesting? Explain why. You can use the phrases in the TIP box on page 27.

 c Write a description of your photo, using the ideas you discussed.

Words and phrases

Immigration

to **deport somebody**	to force a person to leave the country
diversity	different groups of people in a society
green card	a permit that allows immigrants to live and work legally in the US

4 Tourist information

a Read part of a website for tourists about German-American towns. Why are there so many? What do you find especially interesting or surprising?

b Complete 1–8 with the missing articles. Write 0 if no article is needed.

DESTINATIONS	TRIP IDEAS	FORUMS	BOOKING

TRAVEL USA

Kutztown, Pennsylvania

Helen, Georgia

Best German towns in the USA

It's easy to find interesting German-American destinations in ⬛1 USA. That's thanks to the waves of immigrants who settled there. During the 17th and 18th centuries, they came in search of religious freedom. Many small religious groups like ⬛2 Mennonites and ⬛3 Amish settled in ⬛4 Pennsylvania. They founded towns with German names like ⬛5 Manheim and ⬛6 Berlin. ⬛7 Amish still speak ⬛8 German and follow the same simple way of life as their ancestors. During the 19th century new immigrants spread out to other states, such as Georgia and as far west as California.

5 **YOUR CHOICE: Tourist attractions.** In groups, choose task A or task B.

A Best towns in Germany to visit

A travel organization has invited people to nominate the best town to visit in their region / country. Decide which town you will nominate and give reasons.

Present your nomination to the class. Then take a class vote on the best choice.

B Create your own tourist attraction

Make a list of the different things that attract visitors to your hometown / area. Then come up with a new idea to attract more tourists and make your town one of the top visitor attractions.

Present your idea to the class, then take a class vote on the best idea.

Going west

PART 1

PART 2

PART 3

1 A road trip

a The Kominski family is driving across the American West. At the moment, they are in the state of Wyoming. Talk about the photos and what they tell you about their trip.

18)) **b** Listen to the Kominskis' conversation. Where are they going and why? What do they find there?

18)) **c** Listen again and make notes on these questions. Discuss your answers.

1 What were conditions like on the Oregon Trail?
2 What did the government promise the pioneers?
3 Why is the name 'Independence Rock' the perfect name?
4 Who do they see on the rock and what is this person doing?

2 On the Oregon Trail

a Alex and his sister Nina find an information display. Look at the map and find Independence Rock. Where did the Oregon Trail begin and end?

b The display also shows an entry from a settler's diary. Read and answer these questions.

1 What were the settlers celebrating? How did they celebrate?
2 How many wagon train members didn't arrive? What happened to them?
3 What was their experience with Native Americans?
4 What do you learn about the settler's wife and children?

c List three interesting facts that you learned from the diary. Then complete this sentence: *What surprised me most in the diary was …*

Independence Rock, July 4th, 1856

A happy day! Our wagon train arrived safely yesterday. We had hoped to reach this place sooner, but the bad weather slowed us down. To celebrate today, we ate and sang together, then we climbed the great rock to give our prayers and thank the Lord.

We are halfway to Oregon with another 1,000
5 miles ahead. We've come far, but we still have far to go. The journey here was much harder than we had imagined. Six members of our group died of cholera. The poor Parsons' boy had just had his 8th birthday when he fell and died under
10 a wagon wheel. And Mrs White and her baby son drowned, sadly, while crossing the Platte River. I thank God that I still have my health and that Martha and the three children are well.

For all the dangers along the trail, there are
15 many long, boring days. On such days we're glad when we meet Indians who ask us for flour and sugar in exchange for their goods. The children complain a lot. They have no school, lots of chores and few chances to play. Martha is
20 pregnant again and she is not happy about it. She says the days are hard enough. I believe the Lord will watch over our family.

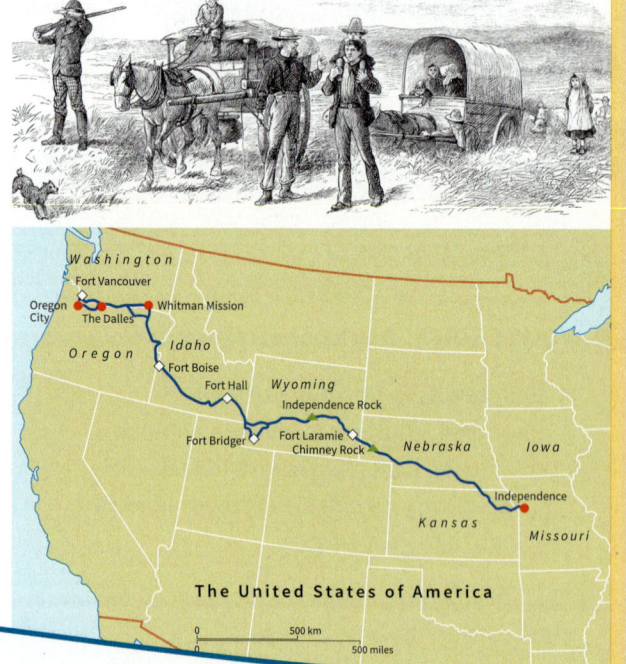

---

17)) ### Words and phrases

herd	a group of animals of the same type (e.g. cows, buffalo)
pioneer	one of the first people to go and live in a region
pregnant	having a child developing in your body
wagon train	a long line of wagons and animals used to travel in the 19th century

3 **Before and after the journey**

a Look at how the settler described past events and answer the questions in the box.

*We **had hoped** to reach this place sooner, but the poor weather **slowed** us down.* (lines 1 – 2)

- Which event happened first: (a) *we had hoped* or (b) *the poor weather slowed us down*?
- Which tense is event (b) in?
- Event (a) is in the past perfect. We form this tense with *had* and the ▬▬.

b Find two more examples in the diary of how the two tenses are used together.

c Complete these sentences with the simple past and the past perfect.

1 When they ▬▬ (*arrive*) at the campground, the other wagon train ▬▬ (*already leave*).
2 They ▬▬ (*just start*) on the trail when he ▬▬ (*begin*) to feel ill.
3 Years later, she ▬▬ (*think*) about all the difficulties they ▬▬ (*have*) along the trail.

≫ **page 36**

4 **A young pioneer**

🔊19 **a** Listen to Alex and Nina's conversation with an old woman. Where is the woman from and why has she come to Independence Rock?

🔊19 **b** Read the sentence beginnings. Then listen again and take notes. Complete the sentences.

1 Bessie's journey changed after five weeks when …
2 The camps along the trail were not healthy because …
3 In South Dakota, they saw herds of buffalo and also …
4 The river water was high because …
5 The men on horses rushed into the river and …

5 **Time on the trail**

a Look at these two sentences from the old woman's story. Answer the questions in the box.

*Settlers **had been camping** along the trail for many years before they came.*
*It **had been raining** a lot and the water was very high.*

The highlighted verb tense is called the past perfect progressive.
- How is the tense formed?
- The sentences describe two events or situations. What happened first over a period of time in each sentence?

TIP

We use the **past perfect progressive** to focus on the length of an action or to suggest that the action wasn't finished. We use the **past perfect** to focus on the action itself or to suggest that the action is complete.

b Complete the sentences with the past perfect progressive and the simple past.

1 Native Americans ▬▬ (*live*) there for centuries before the first wagons ▬▬ (*come*).
2 The kids in the wagon train ▬▬ (*be*) tired because they ▬▬ (*travel*) all day.
3 The wheel ▬▬ (*break*) because the wagon ▬▬ (*carry*) too much weight.
4 He ▬▬ (*drink*) dirty water before his stomach pains ▬▬ (*begin*).

6 **YOUR TURN: Memories.** Think about some events in your life and answer these questions.

1 Where were your parents living when you were born? How long had they been living there?
2 Has a good friend ever moved away from your area? How long had you known each other when he / she left?
3 What's the longest journey you remember? How long had you been travelling when you reached your destination?

Grammar and structures

Past perfect and simple past (revision) → G8
Many pioneers **had died** by the time they **reached** Oregon.
Past perfect progressive → G9
It **had been raining** for a long time and the river was high.

Practice: This land is our land

1 **GET STARTED!** What do you know about Native Americans and their culture and lifestyle today? Look at the photos and make notes. Then compare with a partner.

2 **VIDEO TRACK: Young on the reservation**

a Watch a video about how one Native American teenager tries to find meaning on South Dakota's Cheyenne River reservation. Watch until minute 2:45 and make notes on these questions:

1 Who is Genevieve?
2 What do you learn about life on the Cheyenne River reservation?

b Compare notes with a partner. Then talk about how you felt after you had watched the first part of the video. Were your feelings similar or different?

c With your partner, decide on three questions that you would like the film to answer. Now watch until minute 6:30 and make notes. Which of your questions did the film answer?

d What was the effect of the second part of the video? Compare this with your feeling after the first part.

+ e Look again at your questions that the film didn't answer. Research the questions (see *Method coach* and *Workshop task* on pages 22–23 for help) and report your findings to the class.

3 **Bessie on the Trail.** The old woman who talked to Alex and Nina knew a lot about her great-great-grandmother's journey. Complete these sentences using the simple past and the past perfect.

1 They ▓▓▓ (*not rest*) all day because they ▓▓▓ (*want*) to reach Independence Rock before dark.
2 They ▓▓▓ (*see*) some Native Americans a few days before, so they ▓▓▓ (*know*) that they were near.

3 When Bessie's father ▓▓▓ (*become*) ill, she knew that he ▓▓▓ (*probably drink*) some bad water.
4 Bessie ▓▓▓ (*never drive*) the wagon before, but she ▓▓▓ (*decide*) that it was time to start.
5 Before they reached Independence Rock, she ▓▓▓ (*feel*) weak, but then she ▓▓▓ (*have*) more strength.

Words and phrases

pipeline	a series of underground pipes used for carrying oil
sacred	very important and treated with respect
to supply	to give somebody something they need or want

PART 1
PART 2
PART 3

4 **Travel photos.** Alex took some photos on their trip. He wants to put them on his social media page with captions. Complete the captions with the past perfect progressive and the simple past.

1 Nina ▨ (*sleep*) in the car. I took this when she ▨ (*wake up*).

2 Poor Granddad ▨ (*need*) a drink after he ▨ (*drive*) for four long, hot hours!

3 After we ▨ (*look for*) a motel for hours, we ▨ (*give up*) and ▨ (*decide*) to camp.

4 I ▨ (*be*) exhausted because Nina and I ▨ (*race*) up and down Independence Rock.

5 **READING FOCUS: Letter to the editor**

a The letter below is a comment in a US newspaper. Skim it and answer these questions.

1 Who is the writer and where does he or she come from?
2 What is 'Dakota Access'?
3 How does the writer feel about Dakota Access?

b What's the main argument of the letter? Choose the statement that sums it up best.

1 We Native Americans will always protect our culture and Mother Earth.
2 As in the past, the government is ignoring Native American rights and destroying the earth, but we won't let them.
3 The government helps the oil companies and not the Native Americans, but our culture is strong.

! page 146/147, Writing skills

History is repeating itself

Dear Editor,
I grew up on an Indian reservation in the Midwest. Many of my people still got their food from the soil, the plants and the wildlife. But Native American
5 traditions were disappearing because of modern pressure on our lifestyle and culture.
Today this pressure is more real than ever. The Dakota Access Pipeline – the project by big oil companies to transport oil underground across four
10 Midwestern states – shows how little has changed in our country's history. Many people, including Native Americans, protested against this project. The oil companies built the pipeline across land that is important and sacred to the Native American
15 tribes in the area. The pipeline is also a danger to the water quality in the Missouri River, which supplies clean, safe water to thousands of residents on the Standing Rock and Cheyenne River reservations, and also to 17 million Americans
20 further down the river.

The US government showed little interest in the arguments of Native Americans and others
25 who were against this project. Instead they allowed the construction of the pipeline. Since the early 1800s when white
30 settlers first began pushing Native Americans off their land and onto reservations, the US government has ignored our rights and wishes and has tried to destroy our culture and way of life.
35 Today history is repeating itself.
We are still the keepers of this beautiful land. Although it was taken from us, it is still part of us. We want the US government to respect this land and water and look after it, and we will fight until
40 they do.
Sincerely yours,
John Walker Bear

TIP

To find the main argument: Look first at the title. If you can't find it in the title, look at the introduction. If you can't find it in the introduction, look at the conclusion.

Method coach: Research and select information

S1 **Choose relevant information.** Your teacher asks you to write an informative article about the Amish way of life in modern-day America. Read the extracts below from a website and answer these questions.
- Where do the Amish come from?
- What are their values and beliefs?
- How would you describe their way of life?

1 The Amish are an American Protestant religious group that were formed in Europe during the Reformation. The first Amish arrived in Pennsylvania in the 1730s to escape religious persecution.

2 Although the Amish and Mennonites are very similar, there are some differences. The Mennonites worship God in meetinghouses, but the Amish worship at home.

3 The Amish believe in family and community above all. To protect their way of life and identity, they limit interaction with American society and don't marry non-Amish. They use modern technology for work and to communicate, but don't have things such as TVs or cars.

2

Values and beliefs
- family and community more important than individuals
- believe hard work, simple lifestyle keeps them close to God

Lifestyle
- wear plain clothing, dark colours, no jewellery – known as 'Plain People'
- don't allow TV, radios, phones at home – believe may be bad influence and break up the community

Young people
- children usually attend private Amish schools, leave end 8th grade
- at age 16, teenagers can start 'rumspringa' (running around) period – helps them choose if want to join the church and stay in their community – most teenagers choose to stay

S2 **Make notes**

a Compare extracts from two sets of notes for the article. Which set is better and why?

b Look at the TIP box, then do research to find more information for your article. Make notes.

1 Amish roots are in Europe. Amish came to Pennsylvania in 1730s. Their main occupation is farming. Amish don't use modern technology like TV, phones or internet at home because they think it can be a bad influence on young people. Horse and buggy = main method of transport. They don't wear modern clothes. Family life is very important, families are big — often have 7 or 8 children. Children learn to be hard-working, responsible, care about other people.
The best way to find out about Amish way of life — visit the Amish settlement in Lancaster Pennsylvania. You can buy traditional hand-made products like quilts as well.

TIP

In your research, follow these guidelines.
- Use more than one source – and at least one English source.
- Skim a text for the main ideas.
- Choose relevant information (e. g. *Who*, *What*, *When*, *Where*, *Why*).
- Don't copy and don't cut and paste from the website.
- Write short notes in your own words.
- Record the website details of your source.
- Give your source if you use a direct quotation.
Don't forget to bookmark or write down your sources, so you can refer to them again.

21)) **Words and phrases**

plain   simple, with no decorations

WES-40324-001

Workshop task: Research, write and evaluate a short article

S1 **Choose a research topic.** Look at the photos. Choose one of the topics. You are going to research and write an informative article about the topic for your school magazine.

A

A popular tourist destination in a region in the USA

B

High school student exchange experiences in the USA

C

Life for an Amish teenager

D

A famous modern Native American

S2 **Collect information**

a Choose the keywords you will use for your search. Find the most useful websites. Follow the TIP box on page 22.

b Read and take notes. Follow the research tips on page 32.

S3 **Write your article**

a Read the two TIP boxes.

> **TIP**
>
> Think of a **title** that catches the reader's attention.
> The **opening paragraph** should introduce the main point of the article and get the reader interested, for example by using a question.
> The **middle paragraphs** should contain the main information. You can use **sub-headings** to show the content of each paragraph.
> Summarize your main points again in the **final paragraph**.

b Write your first draft. When you have finished, check through your draft for mistakes. Then rewrite it.

> **TIP**
>
> Does the article have a clear structure?
> Does the writer use linking words to connect ideas, e. g.:
> - adding ideas: *and, also*
> - contrasting ideas: *but, although, However*
> - introducing causes and reasons: *so, because (of), as a result, That's why …*
> - introducing examples: *for example*
>
> Is the grammar and spelling correct?

S4 **Evaluating**

a When you have finished, form groups of three or four. Take turns to describe your topic and how you researched it. What difficulties did you have? What new research strategies did you try? How successful were they?

b Share your articles in your group and give feedback.

Mediation

1 **Boudin at the Wharf.** You're spending some days with your parents in San Francisco. At the moment you're making plans for the next few days. You have found the website of a bakery, but you aren't sure yet if you should have lunch there the next day. Your parents don't understand everything. Answer their questions.

Home of our mother dough – flagship of our brand. This beautiful building is the place to see the bakers at work, dine with a view or in a casual café, and learn the full story of our famous sourdough bread

5 and the city that made it possible.

We bring you delicious, made-to-order meals at a reasonable price. Join us for breakfast, lunch, and dinner in a casual, family-friendly atmosphere, or place an order for to-go or catering […].

Who We Are

10 We are The Original San Francisco Sourdough™. Today, we still bake our sourdough fresh every day using the same mother dough cultivated from a gold miner's sourdough starter. We have extended our love of San Francisco and our place in its culinary history to

15 offer a full range of […] dining options – from specialty breads and casual breakfast, lunch and dinner – to a full service dining experience at Fisherman's Wharf.

Heritage

We are San Francisco's oldest continuously operating business. Much has changed since our boomtown

20 beginnings, but one thing hasn't: our commitment to honor and preserve the art and science of The Original San Francisco Sourdough™ […].

Demonstration and Production Bakery

Watch our bakers busy at work crafting batches of bread by hand through our 30-foot observation

25 window. Have a question? Ask it directly to our bakers through a two-way intercom system. They are sure to have an answer.

Menu

| Hot and cold soups | Salads | Pizzas | Sandwiches | Cereals and desserts |

© 2019 Boudin Bakery, San Francisco; www.boudinbakery.com [06.10.2020]

Deine Mutter Das scheint eine spezielle Bäckerei zu sein, die ihr Brot mit Sauerteig macht. Ich dachte, wir könnten dort mittags etwas essen. Aber auf der Webseite steht etwas von *breakfast*. Kann man da nur morgens essen?

Du …

Deine Mutter Aber morgen ist ja Sonntag. Backen die da überhaupt? Ich möchte eigentlich kein altes Brot essen.

Du …

Dein Vater Also ich hätte mittags gerne etwas Warmes zu essen, nicht nur Brot.

Du …

Deine Mutter Meinst du für mich als Vegetarierin gibt es dann auch etwas Warmes?

Du …

Dein Vater Dann ist ja für alle etwas dabei. Aber was macht diese Bäckerei neben den speziellen Sauerteigbroten denn so besonders? Da steht was von *demonstration*.

Du …

Deine Mutter Das klingt alles gut. Meinst du, das Essen dort ist recht teuer?

Du …

Deine Mutter OK. Dann essen wir da morgen, bevor wir Alcatraz besuchen.

2 **The most popular German towns.** Jason, your friend from America, contacts you via email. After he'd seen a TV programme about the competition 'Most liveable towns in Germany', Jason got interested in this topic. He has found an article and asks you some questions. Answer them in an email.

Schönste Stadt der Welt – Hoher Wohlfühlfaktor in Hamburg

Als hätten wir es nicht schon immer gewusst: Hamburg ist nicht nur die schönste, sondern auch die lebenswerteste Stadt Deutschlands. Gleich mehrere
5 Studien zeigen, dass die Menschen in der Hansestadt zu den glücklichsten in Deutschland gehören. [...]
Alljährlich listet *The Economist* in seinem Ranking zur „Most liveable city" die
10 lebenswertesten Städte der Welt auf und 2017 gelang Hamburg erstmals der Sprung unter die Top Ten. [...] Entscheidende Faktoren im Ranking sind das subjektive Sicherheitsgefühl der Bewohner einer Stadt, die öffentliche Ordnung und die Kriminalitätsrate, die in Hamburg im Vergleich zu anderen Städten gering ist. Überzeugend seien zudem das reichhaltige und vielfältige Kultur- und Freizeitangebot, die Vielfalt des
15 Arbeitsmarktes, die Gesundheitsversorgung und die breit aufgestellten Bildungsmöglichkeiten. 2019 wurde erstmals die Umweltsituation in die Bewertung miteinbezogen. [...]
[Christoph] Drösser untersuchte im Auftrag des Meinungsforschungsinstituts YouGov „Wie wir Deutschen ticken" und stellt fest: Hamburg ist die beliebteste Stadt Deutschlands. Dieses Ergebnis wird von einer Anfang 2016 durchgeführten YouGov-Studie zu den beliebtesten Städten
20 Deutschlands bestätigt. 16 Prozent der Befragten gaben als Lieblingsstadt Hamburg an – das verwundert natürlich nicht. Die Hansestadt wird dabei durchweg positiv gesehen, [...].
Bei einer Umfrage unter 180 Architekten zum Städteranking, [...] wurden [diese] gebeten, die architektonisch schönsten Städte Deutschlands aufzuzählen. Dabei wurde Hamburg von den meisten Architekten (52 Prozent) spontan als schönste Stadt Deutschlands bezeichnet. [...] Vor allem
25 die HafenCity mit ihren architektonischen Besonderheiten trägt dazu bei, dass Hamburg auch in diesem Ranking den ersten Platz einnimmt. [...]

www.hamburg.de [06.10.2020]

From: Jason
To: [your name]
Subject: Hamburg

Hi!
How are you? I'm looking forward to seeing you in the summer and I have done some research. I understood some aspects of the article, but not everything. Could you answer my questions, please?
– Why is Hamburg one of the most liveable cities in the world?
– What is YouGov? And what has Christoph Drösser found out?
– I understood the word 'architects'. What do they say about Hamburg?
– What do you think about Hamburg? Do you think it's a good idea to visit it in the summer?

Yours
Jason

››› First track

3
p.16
Ellie is telling her host family about her project. Complete her story with the simple past or the past progressive.

The Reeds were first on my list. I *found* Mrs Reed in her flower garden. She ▢**1** (*plant*) roses. While I ▢**2** (*interview*) her, I nearly ▢**3** (*step*) on one of the roses. That was embarrassing! After that I ▢**4** (*go*) to see Mr Kim in his shop. Mr Kim is very nice – he has a very strong accent, but I ▢**5** (*understand*) everything that he ▢**6** (*talk*) about. My next person was Daisy Clarke. She ▢**7** (*not have*) much time for me because she and her mum ▢**8** (*cook*) dinner. It was Jamaican food and it ▢**9** (*smell*) great. Anyway, I ▢**10** (*interview*) her quickly in the kitchen while they ▢**11** (*get*) dinner ready. The chat with her ▢**12** (*be*) very interesting!

4
p.19
a Use the correct relative pronoun to complete the sentences.

1 New England, ▢ is one of the most historic regions of the USA, is where many early colonists settled.
2 The voyage on the *Mayflower*, ▢ took the Pilgrims to the New World, was very uncomfortable.
3 The Wampanoag tribe, ▢ lived near the Pilgrims, were friendly to the settlers.
4 The settlers only survived with the help of the Native Americans, ▢ taught them how to plant crops, hunt and fish.
5 The British Government introduced a tax on tea, ▢ was one of the main reasons for the American Revolution.

5
p.21
b Read about Squanto. Then join the sentences where there is an asterisk (*) as in the example.

Squanto

Folk Hero (c.1580 – c.1622)

Squanto * was a Native American of the Wampanoag Nation.
He is famous for helping the Pilgrims to survive their first winter.
Squanto, who is famous for helping the Pilgrims to survive their first winter, was a Native American of the Wampanoag Nation.

1 He was born in 1580 and grew up near Plymouth Bay. In 1605, an English explorer * captured Squanto and took him to England.
The English explorer's name was Captain Weymouth.
2 In England, Squanto lived with a man called Ferdinando Gorges. *
Ferdinando Gorges taught him English and used him as an interpreter.
3 Squanto returned to North America in 1614, but another explorer * captured him again and sold him as a slave in Spain.
The explorer hoped to make some money.
4 Squanto finally escaped and returned to the Wampanoag region in 1619. However, when he arrived in his village, it was empty. This was because of a smallpox epidemic. *
The epidemic had lasted three years and killed many Native Americans.
5 So he went to live with another Wampanoag tribe. When the Pilgrims arrived and built Plimoth Colony, Squanto * became the interpreter between them and the Wampanoag.
Squanto could speak English well.
6 He also taught the Pilgrims how to grow corn and catch fish in the rivers. * He probably took part in the first Thanksgiving feast.
This helped the colony to survive.

3
p.29
c Choose the right tenses – the simple past or the past perfect – to complete the sentences.

1 When they **arrived / had arrived** at the campground, the other wagon train **already left / had already left**.
2 They **just started / had just started** on the trail when he **began / had begun** to feel ill.
3 Years later, she **thought / had thought** about all the difficulties they **had / had had** along the trail.

Extra reading

Woody Guthrie's song *This Land is Your Land* says the USA belongs to everybody who lives there – and not just to people who own property.

Woody Guthrie (1912 – 1967)
Woody Guthrie was a famous American folk singer-songwriter. Guthrie had a tough childhood and as a teenager sang on the streets for food and money. In 1935, the Great Depression, ten years of high unemployment and poverty, hit the Mid-West. Like thousands of others, Guthrie became a 'Dust Bowl Refugee[1]'. One of Woody Guthrie's greatest admirers was Bob Dylan.

🔊 22)) *This Land is Your Land* (1940)

This land is your land, this land is my land
From California to the New York island;
From the red wood forest to the Gulf Stream waters
This land was made for you and me.

₅ As I was walking that ribbon of highway,
I saw above me that endless skyway;
I saw below me that golden valley:
This land was made for you and me.

Congress Trail, Sequoia National Park, California

I've roamed and rambled and I followed my footsteps
₁₀ To the sparkling sands of her diamond deserts;
And all around me a voice was sounding:
This land was made for you and me.

When the sun came shining, and I was strolling,
And the wheat fields waving and the dust clouds rolling,
₁₅ As the fog was lifting a voice was chanting:
This land was made for you and me.

As I went walking I saw a sign there
And on the sign it said 'No Trespassing.'
But on the other side it didn't say nothing,
₂₀ That side was made for you and me.

Crazy Kanne Point, Grand Canyon National Park, Arizona

In the shadow of the steeple I saw my people,
By the relief office I seen my people;
As they stood there hungry, I stood there asking
Is this land made for you and me?

₂₅ Nobody living can ever stop me,
As I go walking that freedom highway;
Nobody living can ever make me turn back
This land was made for you and me.

by Ludlow Music, Ltd., D / A / CH: Essex Musikvertrieb GmbH, Hamburg

Seven Miles Bridge, Key West, Florida

---

[1] A 'Dust Bowl Refugee' was a resident of the Midwestern United States who relocated as a result of the 'Dust Bowl', a drought that devastated most of the farmland in the Midwest in the 1930s.

My review

What can I do?

Look at these sentences about Workshop 1.
Are the sentences true for you? Choose the right symbol for each sentence.

1 I can talk about chores.
2 I can compare life today to life in the past.
3 I can talk about national holidays and celebrations.
4 I can discuss issues related to immigration.

>>>   = 'I'm great at this!'
>>>   = 'I'm good at this.'
>>>   = 'I'm OK at this.'

What do I know?

1   About chores. Ellie and Vivian are talking about chores. Complete the conversation with the correct form of the verbs in brackets and with the words from the box.

> bin ■ chore ■ dishwasher ■
> rubbish ■ yard

Vivian   Hi Ellie! I see ■1■ (*take out*) the garbage is your job.
Ellie   The garbage. Oh, yes – I keep forgetting you say 'garbage' and not ■2■ .
Vivian   Yes, there seem to be lots of words that are different.
Ellie   Well this is definitely one ■3■ I hate ■4■ (*do*).
Vivian   I don't know. I think there are worse chores.
Ellie   Really?
Vivian   Yes, ■5■ (*clean*) the bathroom and ■6■ (*vacuum*) the living room. Are there any chores you like doing?
Ellie   ■7■ (*walk*) the dog is fun.
Vivian   Yes, but not in the rain.

Ellie   No, if the weather is bad, then it's not so great. What about you?
Vivian   I love ■8■ (*sweep*) the ■9■ .
Ellie   What?
Vivian   Oh yes, you say 'garden', don't you?
Ellie   Right, I'd better put this in the ■10■ and go back inside. Alex is ■11■ (*empty*) the ■12■ and he asked me to help him.
Vivian   OK, see you later.
Ellie   Bye.

■ / 12

Talking about chores, pp. 14–15
Gerund as subject and object → G1, G2 ; pp. 14–15

2   About life in the past. Ellie writes an email to her cousin Ryan in Scotland. Complete the missing words and phrases.

From: Ellie
To: Ryan
Subject: The Plimoth Plantation

Hi Ryan,

I'm having a great time here with the Kominskis. When I first arrived, I was really homesick, but I'm starting to get used to things here. Yesterday we went to a living history museum called the Plimoth Plantation. It's all about the Pilgrims. I think they led a really h_____ l_____ (1).
After they arrived in America, most families lived in o_____-r_____ (2) houses, so it must have been really crowded inside. They also had to do lots of chores. I know we have chores like t_____ (3) our bedroom and e_____ (4) the dishwasher, but those are easy compared to what they had to do. They didn't have any h_____ (5), so the only way to stay warm was to light a fire. They also had to cook over an o_____ f_____ (6). So, two of the chores they had to do, which we don't do today, were c_____ w_____ (7) and f_____ w_____ (8).
The Pilgrims also g_____ (9) their own v_____ (10) as well as k_____ (11) chickens and goats and sometimes they would go h_____ (12). Today, we go shopping at the supermarket or go out to a restaurant to eat. Life must have been really difficult for the Pilgrims.
Right, I have to go now as I need to help Alex with some of the chores.
Write soon.

Ellie

■ / 12

Life in the past, pp. 20–21

3 **About national holidays and celebrations.**
Ellie is talking to Alex about national holidays and celebrations in the USA. Choose the correct phrases to complete the conversation.

Ellie   I'm really looking forward to July 4th.

Alex   Me too. Come on, let's see how much you can remember from the Boston Tea Party Ships and Museum. When did the original thirteen colonies declare independence?

Ellie   That's easy! They **declared / were declaring / had declared** (1) independence after they **fought / were fighting / had been fighting** (2) against Britain for just over a year.

Alex   Right. So, **did the war finish / was the war finishing / had the war been finishing** (3) then?

Ellie   No, they **carried on / were carrying on / had been carrying on** (4) fighting until 1783, so for another seven years.

Alex   Wow! I'm impressed. And what can you remember about the Boston Tea Party?

Ellie   I know it was something to do with taxes, right?

Alex   Yes, the British **collected / were collecting / had been collecting** (5) taxes for years and the colonists weren't happy about paying so much, so in December 1773 a group of people **threw / were throwing / had thrown** (6) 342 crates of tea into the harbor.

Ellie   But I bet that **didn't make / wasn't making / hadn't made** (7) us very happy!

Alex   No, it didn't.

Ellie   So has America celebrated Independence Day ever since?

Alex   No, it **didn't become / wasn't becoming / hadn't become** (8) an official holiday until 1941.

Ellie   And so what do you normally do on July 4th?

■ / 8

American history, pp. 18 – 21
Past tenses → G3, G8, G9 **; pp. 14 – 15, pp. 28 – 29**

4 **About immigration.** Complete the article with *a, the* or no article. Write 0 if no article is needed.

Since the Pilgrims first landed in **1** USA, millions of people have emigrated there from around the world. In the early years, most immigrants were from **2** Europe. They arrived by ships that crossed **3** Atlantic Ocean. For many of these people, the first thing they saw when they arrived was **4** Statue of Liberty in **5** New York Harbor. The statue had been a gift from **6** France. Many famous people were originally immigrants to the country. For example, Sergey Brin, who started the most famous search engine with Larry Page, moved with his family from **7** Moscow in 1979 because of religious persecution. His dad was **8** university professor and his mom worked as **9** NASA researcher. Another famous immigrant is Arnold Schwarzenegger. He was born in **10** Austria in 1947 and moved to **11** California in 1968. From the age of ten, it had been his dream to move and to make his fortune. When he arrived, he didn't speak very good **12** English, but it didn't stop him becoming one of the most well-known actors in **13** Hollywood.

■ / 13

Immigration, pp. 24 – 27
The definite, indefinite and zero article → G7 **;**
pp. 24 – 25

■ / 45

What's my score?

Check your answers to the review (Workbook, p. 32). What are your scores for each question?

What was your total score?	
⟫⟫⟫	score 36 – 45
⟫⟫⟫	score 21 – 35
⟫⟫⟫	score 0 – 20

Do you want to change your answers to the 'What can I do?' statements on page 38?
Look at the tasks on pages 40 – 41: ⟫⟫⟫**,** ⟫⟫⟫ **and**
⟫⟫⟫**. Choose the tasks to help you.**

My practice pages

Talking about chores

1 **Chores, chores, chores.** Chris writes a blog entry about the chores he and his sister Megan have to do. Complete his blog with the words from the box.

> doing (2x) ▪ emptying ▪ sweeping ▪ taking ▪ tidying (2x) ▪ vacuuming ▪ walking ▪ washing

On weekends Megan and I help our parents with the chores. I hate ▢**1** chores, but I know they are important. I usually do the outdoor chores, so things like ▢**2** the yard and ▢**3** the car. One chore I do almost every day is ▢**4** out the garbage. The chore I really love is ▢**5** the dog. We don't have a dog but our neighbor does, so I offer to help on weekends. Megan usually does the chores in the house. I don't think she likes ▢**6** chores either. However, when she's ▢**7** the living room, she listens to music and sometimes she sings along. It's terrible! The other chore she does every day is ▢**8** the dishwasher. I think that's the easiest one. The only chore I don't mind is ▢**9** my room. I'm quite organized, so it doesn't take me long. Megan's room is always really messy so she spends ages ▢**10** it up.

2 **Helping out.** Nina is busy with some chores and Ellie offers to help. Complete the conversation between Ellie and Nina.

Nina   Phew!
Ellie   What's wrong?
Nina   I just hate d ▢**1** chores.
Ellie   Do you want me to help you?
Nina   Sure, if you don't mind.
Ellie   What do you want me to do?
Nina   If you carry on v ▢**2** the living room, I can do the bathroom. I don't enjoy c ▢**3** it, but somebody has to. After that, I can start t ▢**4** my room.

Ellie   Oh, I could help you with that.
Nina   No, it's okay, thanks. But would you mind e ▢**5** the dishwasher and can you check if Alex has finished s ▢**6** the porch?
Ellie   Okay, and what's next on his list?
Nina   T ▢**7** the garbage out. Then we can all take Joe's dog for a walk.
Ellie   Great! W ▢**8** the dog is great fun when it isn't raining.

3 **Your chores.** Write a short description of the chores you (and your brothers and sisters) have to do at home and how you feel about them.

Comparing life now and in the past

4 **Life in the past.** While the Kominskis and Ellie were at Plimoth Plantation, one of the actors gave them some background information. Complete it with the phrases from the box.

> chopping wood ▪ cooked over open fires ▪ keep animals ▪ one-room house ▪ simple life ▪ went hunting

Welcome to Plimoth Plantation Living History Museum. While you are here, you will learn all about how the first Pilgrims lived after they arrived on the *Mayflower* in 1620. First of all, it's important to realize that life was very different for them than it is today. They lived quite a ▢**1**, often living in a ▢**2**. There were no shops, so they had to grow their own food and ▢**3** like chickens and goats. They also ▢**4** and if they were lucky, they shot something like a rabbit or wild turkey. One of the most important chores was ▢**5**. This was important as they ▢**6**, so they needed plenty of firewood.

5 **Life for the Pilgrims.** Look at the pictures on page 20 and write sentences about these topics: where the Pilgrims lived, cooking, chores, food, general living.

6 **Comparing your life with the Pilgrims.** Look at the pictures on page 20 and write a short essay comparing your life with the life of the Pilgrims.

PART 1
PART 2
PART 3

Describing national holidays and celebrations

7 **An email to Ryan.** Ellie writes another email to Ryan telling him about a conversation with Alex. Choose the correct verbs to complete the email.

Hi Ryan,

I'm really enjoying my stay here with the Kominskis. Last night after we **were having / had had** (1) dinner, Alex **told / had told** (2) me all about his favourite holiday, Independence Day. I can hardly wait until July 4th as it sounds amazing.
Last year Alex's family **planned / had been planning** (3) a big party for weeks, but then they **had to / were having to** (4) cancel it.
Everyone was so disappointed because they **were spending / had spent** (5) ages preparing special food to eat and Alex's grandpa **was buying / had bought** (6) fireworks. They **had also invited / had also been inviting** (7) lots of neighbours.
Just before the party **started / was starting** (8), Nina, Alex's sister, **was falling / had fallen** (9) downstairs and she **had to / was having to** (10) go to hospital. Let's hope there are no problems this year! I'll let you know how it goes.

Ellie

---

8 **A trip to Mardi Gras.** Read Vivian's blog entry about a trip to New Orleans. Complete the blog with the correct form of the verbs in brackets.

Last year, my family and I **_1_** (*go*) to New Orleans to celebrate Mardi Gras. My father **_2_** (*plan*) the trip for a long time and he **_3_** (*buy*) some guidebooks so he could do some research. Anyway, he **_4_** (*decide*) we would drive down all the way from Lexington. It's a long journey of over 1,500 miles. Unfortunately, he **_5_** (*not plan*) the route very well and we **_6_** (*have to*) stop twice overnight. By the time we finally **_7_** (*arrive*), the Mardi Gras celebrations **_8_** (*almost finish*)!

---

9 **Your story.** Have you ever been to a festival or celebration? Write a short blog or an email describing what happened.

Talking about immigration

10 **A famous immigrant.** Complete Alex's notes about a famous immigrant with the correct articles. Choose 0 for no article.

Jerry Yang was born in a / the / 0 (1) Taipei in 1968. He emigrated to a / the / 0 (2) USA at the age of ten with his family. When he arrived, the only word he knew in a / the / 0 (3) English was 'shoe'. He went to school in a / the / 0 (4) San Jose, California and studied electrical engineering at Stanford University. While he was at university, he started a / the / 0 (5) website that later became a famous search engine.

---

11 **Another famous immigrant.** Read the conversation and complete it with *a, an, the* or zero article (*0*).

Ellie   Hi Alex, what are you doing?

Alex   Hi Ellie, I'm working on **_1_** school project. We have to find out about famous immigrants to **_2_** USA and write a short biography about them.

Ellie   Who are you writing about?

Alex   Well, I've just finished writing about Jerry Yang who's one of the people who started a search engine, but he's originally from **_3_** Taiwan. Now I want to write about Mila Kunis.

Ellie   I know a lot about her. She's **_4_** actress. I love all her movies.

Alex   Wow! Can you help me then?

Ellie   Sure. So she was born in **_5_** Chernivtsi in Ukraine, but she moved to Los Angeles at **_6_** age of seven.

Alex   That's why she speaks great English.

Ellie   Yes, but life was hard for her family until her dad found a job as **_7_** cab driver.

Alex   Thanks, that's **_8_** really useful information.

12 Write a short biography about Khaled Hosseini.

Name: Khaled Hosseini
Place of birth: Kabul, Afghanistan
1976 moves to France with parents
1979 moves to California
First job: doctor
Now: famous author; first book:
The Kite Runner

23)) Marcus Sedgwick

Edgar and the terrible kidnappers

➤ ONE ➤

'What is the point of children?'
This is a question I have often asked myself, and when I say 'children', I mean, in particular: *small* children. Now, I know that someone reading this will

5 say – Edgar! Behave yourself! It's obvious; small children become big children, and with a little luck and a lot of food, big children become adults. And then the same person might talk about how from adults we get more small children, and they may even

10 mention something to do with the survival of the human species[1], and so on. But I'm not convinced that's such an important thing. So, I ask again: what is the point of small children? However, one day last year, something happened that made me see things

15 differently.

It all began on what we call Open Sunday. Every first Sunday of the month, we open the castle to visitors. We do not do this because we are nice. We do not do this because we like sharing history with people. We

20 do this because we are broke. Hard-up. What the man in the street might call 'skint'. In short, these are all ways of saying: we don't have much money. We are, I have to confess, poor. And we open the castle up to charge[2] people a little money to look at the suits of

25 armour[3], or inspect[4] the tapestries on the walls.

Heaven knows[5] why anyone would want to do that, but they do. They even pay for it.
There is a reason why we are poor, despite the fact[6] that we live in a castle. We only live in a castle

30 because it came into the possession[7] of the Otherhand family some 300 years ago following an 'incident'. The 'incident' went like this: once upon a time, the castle was owned by a family called the Deffreeques. Then, the third Lord Otherhand came

35 along, and decided he really wanted to live in the castle. Then there was a short battle, and some 'nasty business'[8]. Since then, the Otherhands have lived in the castle, with an ever decreasing fortune. Not one penny has been spent on repairing the place since

40 the third Lord Otherhand moved his family in. So that's why we live in a castle, but I didn't tell you why we are poor. We are poor because Valevine and Minty, the parents of Solstice and Cudweed, Fizz and Buzz, the latest Lord and Lady Otherhand, are stupid.

45 Really, really stupid.

---

[1] **human species** Menschen – [2] **to charge sth.** etwas verlangen – [3] **suit of armour** Rüstung – [4] **to inspect** untersuchen – [5] **Heaven knows** weiß der Himmel – [6] **despite the fact** obwohl – [7] **possession** Besitz – [8] **nasty business** schmutzige Angelegenheit

I may have told you before that Valevine is an inventor. And I may have told you before that his inventions come in two kinds: first, there are the things that might be a good idea, but simply don't

50 work. Then, there are the things that *do* work, but which are totally useless. Actually, now I think about it; there is a third type of invention that he makes – things that don't work *and* are also totally useless. Actually, now I think about it, *most* of his inventions

55 are of this third kind. For example, at the time this story starts, he was up in the tower where he has his laboratory. He was working on a machine that could clean itself. Needless to say[9]; it wasn't working; this machine to clean itself, and (this is important) since

60 it had *no other function*, you may wonder what the use of it would be, even if it *did* work. Solstice tried pointing this out to her father and was sent to her room for the rest of the day for saying so.
Then there's Minty. Now, once upon a time, she had

65 been a witch, but she was no longer a witch, and people remembered that she was a bad witch, even

70 when she was one. By 'bad', I don't mean she was *evil*[10], or that she cast wicked spells[11] on people to turn them into post boxes,

75 or anything like that. I mean she was bad, as in, she was really, really terrible at making spells.
Since then, she has had a lot of children, of course,

80 and children are very time-consuming[12] things. Minty has four children, namely[13] Solstice, then Cudweed, and then, a bit later, the twins, Fizz and Buzz. Minty sometimes refers to the twins as 'my little accident' (I have no idea what that means) and this is where I

85 started, isn't it, because it is small children that I really have trouble understanding. I mean, what is the point? Not only that, but Fizz and Buzz are quite unusual. Even compared with other small children. They are always getting into mischief[14] of some kind

90 or other, and often get into dangerous situations, even though they themselves always survive unharmed[15]. They have, it's called, 'a charmed life'[16].

Anyway, this story starts (at last! I hear you cry) with the twins. It began on one of the Open Sundays. The

95 castle was open to visitors, who had each paid the ludicrously[17] small sum of £1.50 to look around. I keep trying to tell Minty she should charge more, but I think she feels guilty[18] charging anyone at all, since her family stole the castle from the Deffreeques in

100 the first place.
On days like this, I like to hide. I go up to my cage in the Red Room which is in a part of the castle we never open, so we can have some peace even on Open Sunday. The day wore on[19], boring and slow as

105 Open Sunday always is, and finally, at five o'clock, the last of the visitors left the castle and the gardens, and we were alone again.

Minty counted up the day's takings[20]; it was barely[21] enough to pay for the electricity for another week,

110 but while Valevine and Minty were talking about that, Solstice came in.
'Er,' she said, 'er, has anyone seen the twins?'
'Fizz and Buzz?' said Valevine, as if he had many sets of twins.

115 'Exactly,' said Solstice. 'I've asked everyone and I've looked everywhere. I think …'
(Here she looked worried and her lip began to wobble[22].)
'… I think they might be missing.'

120 Minty blinked twice.
Valevine said, 'what, what?'
Cudweed said, 'I think so, too.'
And it was true. The twins were indeed missing.

---

[9] **needless to say** selbstverständlich – [10] **evil** böse – [11] **to cast a wicked spell** einen bösen Zauber anwenden – [12] **time-consuming** zeitaufwendig –
[13] **namely** und zwar – [14] **mischief** Unfug – [15] **unharmed** unversehrt – [16] **a charmed life** einen Schutzengel haben – [17] **ludicrously** lachhaft –
[18] **guilty** schuldig – [19] **to wear on (wore, worn)** sich hinziehen – [20] **takings** Einnahmen – [21] **barely** kaum – [22] **to wobble** wackeln

Youth culture USA

1 Look at the topics in the box below. For each one, think of some aspects that this workshop might include.

> clothes & fashion ■ music ■ friends & relationships ■ media & entertainment ■ school & sports ■ city & country life

2 Now read and listen to the quotes from teens around the US. What are they interested in? What do they care about?

3 **a** Form small groups. In your group, choose one topic. Discuss the questions for three minutes. Formulate a short statement about the topic that you all agree on. Your teacher will tell you when to move on to the next topic.

b When you have discussed all the topics, share your statements with the class. In what ways are you similar to or different from US teens?

CLOTHES & FASHION

It's important to have your own style.

There's too much pressure to keep up with the latest trends.

Thrift stores and recycling have become really popular.

- How important is fashion to you?
- Do you have a favourite brand?
- Do you worry about bad effects on the environment?

FRIENDS & RELATIONSHIPS

For me there's a difference between friends and social media 'friends'. I want to talk to my friends face-to-face.

Looks are not everything – personality counts too!

- How do you define a good friend?
- What do you and your friends do when you get together?
- Is it important – or even possible – to have a best friend?

MUSIC

I'm into lots of music genres and artists. I listened to jazz and hip-hop on the school bus this morning.

I like making music, not just listening to it.

- What kind of music do you prefer?
- Which artists are on your playlist?
- Do you play an instrument?

MEDIA & ENTERTAINMENT

There's so much good stuff on the internet. I watch films on my phone, but I also play online games with my friends.

Many kids are into having their own video-sharing channels. There's a lot of content creation going on.

- Where do you usually get your entertainment?
- How active are you in creating and sharing content online?
- Do you play video games? If so, what kind?

CITY & COUNTRY LIFE

The last time I was in a big city, it stressed me out. If I can avoid it, I don't go there.

Whenever we go somewhere different, I feel like I learn something new about the world.

- What do you or don't you like about cities?
- Do you like living where you live? Why or why not?
- Do you enjoy travelling and sightseeing? Why or why not?

SCHOOL & SPORTS

After-school activities are the best thing about school.

Sports are really important to me. I think it's because kids my age generally like competing in everything – school, sports, life.

- Which subjects do you like best and which are the most useful?
- What after-school activities does your school offer?
- How important is sport at your school?

24 🔊 Words and phrases

brand	a product by a particular company
genre	style (of music, literature)
to keep up with fashion	to buy the latest fashion
thrift store 🇺🇸	a shop that sells second-hand clothes and other items

YOUR TRACK

After this workshop you will be able to:
- talk about relationships.
- talk about fashion.
- compare different school systems.
- compare city life and country life.
- carry out a survey. (Workshop task)

Making friends

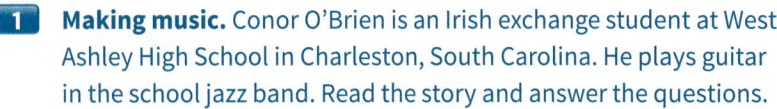

1 **Making music.** Conor O'Brien is an Irish exchange student at West Ashley High School in Charleston, South Carolina. He plays guitar in the school jazz band. Read the story and answer the questions.

1 What does the band director tell Conor?
2 Who does Conor meet and why does he find this person interesting?
3 How does Conor feel after the concert. Why?

! **page 144, Reading skills**

The last note of the song 'Autumn Leaves' hung in the air. Jordan looked up from his drums to Conor and gave him a thumbs up. 'That was better,' said Mrs Withers, the jazz
5 band director. 'Trumpets, you sounded great but a bit too loud,' she said to Alisha and the other two trumpet players.
'Mr O'Brien, the guitar solo was better. But try to put more feeling into it,' she said. Conor
10 nodded. Then Mrs Withers clapped her hands. 'That's all, everybody. Same time tomorrow!'
...
The school cafeteria was busy and loud. Conor and Jordan were eating lunch.

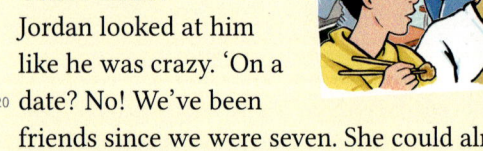

15 'Have you ever gone out with Alisha?' Conor asked. Jordan looked at him like he was crazy. 'On a
20 date? No! We've been friends since we were seven. She could almost be my sister.'
Just then Alisha arrived with her friend Meg. 'Hey, guys,' Alisha said. The two girls put their
25 lunch trays on the table and sat down.
'Meg, you haven't met Conor yet,' Jordan said. 'He's been playing in our band since October.' Meg smiled. 'Hi. Alisha has already told me about you. You're from Ireland.'
30 'That's right. I'm here for a year,' Conor said.

'That's so cool,' she said, 'but isn't it hard?' 'It was at first, but now I've been here for a couple of months, I love it,' Conor said. 'He's an awesome guitar player,' Jordan said to
35 Meg. He turned to Conor. 'Meg is an expert. She's been listening to jazz guitar all her life.' Conor looked at Meg.
'My dad plays. He's in the jazz scene,' Meg said. Conor sat up. 'Really?' He had never met
40 anyone whose dad was a jazz guitarist.
'Meg is musical, too – she sings,' Alisha said. 'In the drama club, that's all,' Meg added. Conor was impressed. 'Cool!'
...
On Friday evening, the school jazz band's
45 concert ended and Mrs Withers was all smiles. There was loud applause from the audience. After the concert Conor saw Meg. She was talking to Alisha. Conor joined them. 'You sounded really good!' Meg said.
50 'Thanks,' Conor said. 'Hey, we're going to the Sunday Jazz Series this weekend at Folly Beach. Would you like to come?'
Before Meg could answer, Dan Sykes, a tall senior, stepped in. He smiled at Alisha but
55 ignored Conor. Then he turned to Meg. 'I've been waiting over there for you,' he said. Meg looked at Dan and then at the others. 'Dan is driving me home,' she said. Meg gave a small wave and the two left.
60 Conor watched them go. 'You didn't tell me about those two,' he said.
'I'm sorry,' Alisha said. 'I didn't know that you wanted to ask her out.'
'Never mind, it's OK.' Conor tried to smile.

26)) **Words and phrases**

Never mind.	That's all right.

Relationships

to **ask somebody out**	to invite somebody on a date
to **be in love**	to have a strong feeling
(with somebody)	or attraction (for somebody)
to **break up**	to end a romantic relationship

to **go out (with somebody)**	to go on a date
to **have a crush on somebody**	to be interested in somebody in a romantic way

2 Who's who?

a Match each character in the story with the statement that best describes him or her.

1 Conor   4 Mrs Withers
2 Alisha   5 Meg
3 Jordan   6 Dan

a … is going out with a girl.
b … has a family connection with jazz.
c … leads the school jazz band.
d … plays trumpet in the band.
e … is an old friend of Alisha's.
f … wants to ask somebody out.

b Write at least three more sentences about Conor.

3 A question of time

a Answer the questions in the box.

> When Conor asks about Alisha, Jordan says:
> *We've been friends since we were seven.*
> ● When did Jordan first meet Alisha? Are they still friends now?
> Later he says about Meg:
> *She's been listening to jazz guitar all her life.*
> ● When did Meg listen to jazz the first time? Does she listen to jazz now? How is this sentence different from the first sentence?

b Find more examples of the present perfect and the present perfect progressive in the text.

> **TIP**
>
> Generally we use the present perfect with **state verbs** like *be, know, remember, love, see* and *understand* and the present perfect progressive with **action verbs** like *go, listen, make, talk* and *play*.
>
> *He's **known** this band for a long time.*
> *He's **been listening** to their music for years.*

4 How long? Complete the questions. Then complete the answers with *since* or *for*.

1 How long ▨ (*the band / practise*) for the concert? ▨ the last two months.
2 How long ▨ (*Jordan / know*) Alisha? ▨ he was in elementary school.
3 How long ▨ (*Conor / like*) Meg? ▨ he met her in the cafeteria.
4 How long ▨ (*Meg and Dan / go out*) together? ▨ a week.

5 Jazz on the beach

 a Conor, Alisha and Jordan are at the concert at Folly Beach. Listen. Which is the best heading for this part of the story and why?

1 A missed chance
2 Music and text messages
3 Music brings people together

 b Listen again. True or false?

1 Jordan thinks Conor has a crush on Meg.
2 Alisha, Jordan and Conor have been at the beach since about 2 p.m.
3 Dan's last girlfriend broke up with him because he only thought about himself.
4 Gus has been playing the guitar for 15 years.

> **6 YOUR TURN: How long?**
> Talk about your friendships, past and present:
> ● how long you've known each other,
> ● when and where you first met,
> ● what you like about your friends,
> ● your friends' hobbies and interests and how long they have been doing them.

Grammar and structures

Present perfect (revision) → G10
I**'ve heard** that song three times today.
Present perfect progressive (revision) → G11
They**'ve been playing** it on the radio all afternoon.

Time words → G12
He's had that trumpet **for** a long time.
They've been practising **since** 2 o'clock.
She's been listening to jazz guitar **all** her life.

Practice: Media and entertainment

PART 1
PART 2
PART 3

1 **GET STARTED!** Are free-time activities today different from when your parents were young. How?

2 **Media habits**

a Describe in your own words what this infographic from 2012 shows.

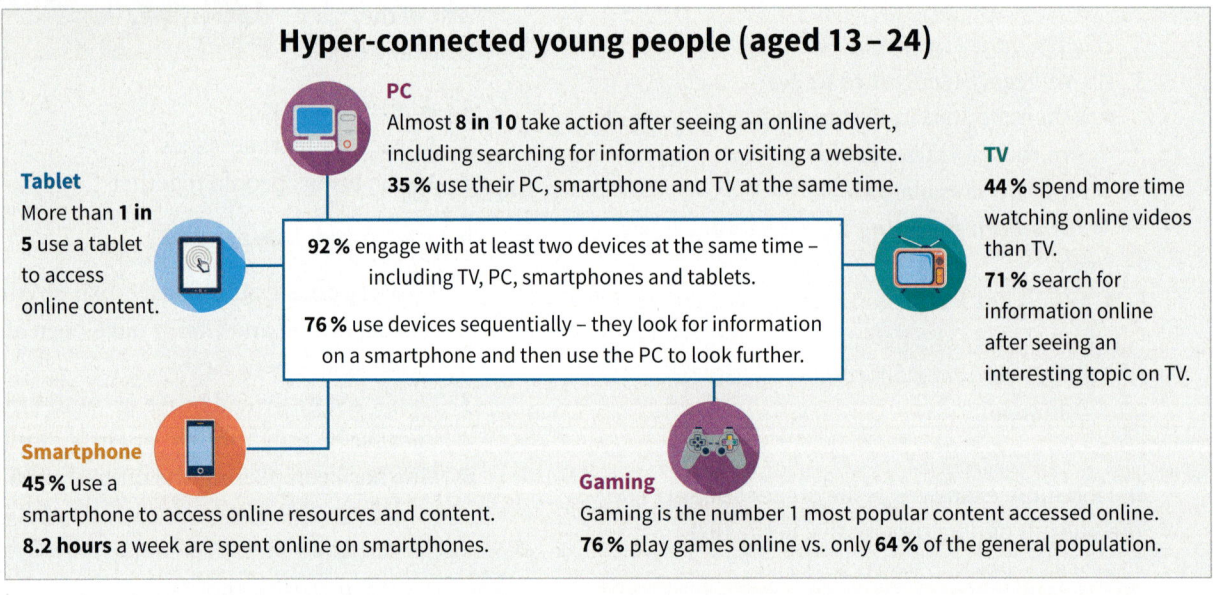

Hyper-connected young people (aged 13 – 24)

PC
Almost **8 in 10** take action after seeing an online advert, including searching for information or visiting a website.
35 % use their PC, smartphone and TV at the same time.

Tablet
More than **1 in 5** use a tablet to access online content.

92 % engage with at least two devices at the same time – including TV, PC, smartphones and tablets.

76 % use devices sequentially – they look for information on a smartphone and then use the PC to look further.

TV
44 % spend more time watching online videos than TV.
71 % search for information online after seeing an interesting topic on TV.

Smartphone
45 % use a smartphone to access online resources and content.
8.2 hours a week are spent online on smartphones.

Gaming
Gaming is the number 1 most popular content accessed online.
76 % play games online vs. only **64 %** of the general population.

Data: Ipsos / Google 2012 Teens & Twenty-Somethings Research Study

b Discuss your media habits:
- how you access online content,
- what kind of content you access online,
- what your primary source of information is,
- how much time you spend watching videos online and how much time watching TV,
- …

c Discuss whether the statistics in the infographic are still true today. Think about:
- the different devices that are used today,
- the most popular content accessed today,
- how devices are used to find information,
- …

d In groups, discuss your findings from **c**. Agree on a short statement about what has changed since 2012.

3 **Digital Saturday.** Complete with the present perfect or the present perfect progressive.
1 Jordan, ▭ (*you / check*) your messages yet? I ▭ (*text*) you twice.
2 I ▭ (*watch*) videos since lunchtime, but I think I ▭ (*watch*) enough now.
3 He ▭ (*not have*) his phone very long, so he ▭ (*not understand*) some of the apps yet.
4 Conor ▭ (*chat*) with his sister for an hour!

 page 68

4 **An awesome game.** Conor has read an online review of a new video game. He tells Jordan about the review, but he gets some things wrong. Read the review and correct his statements (1 – 6).

Hey gamers, today I'm going to talk about *Crashplanet*. I know what you're all going to say: 'We've already played that game!' 'It's been on the market for nearly two years!' Well, yes and no. Yes, *Crashplanet* is about two years old and it's been popular since it was presented at the last Dreamhack Festival. But have you experienced the NEW *Crashplanet* yet? I don't think so because it's only been on the market for about five days. I've been playing it since it arrived in my mailbox three days ago and I haven't got bored with it yet. It is awesome. If you've already played the old *Crashplanet*, then get ready – the new *Crashplanet* is so much better.

1 A lot of gamers haven't heard of *Crashplanet*.
2 They've been playing the old *Crashplanet* for at least three years.
3 It's been popular since it came on the market.
4 Most gamers have already played the new *Crashplanet*.
5 The blogger has been enjoying the new version for the last five days.
6 It's so boring that he's already stopped playing it.

5 **Just friends.** Tom and Amy, two West Ashley High School students, are texting. Read their text messages and complete the sentences.

1 Amy thinks that Lara …
2 Tom is sure that Jordan will never …
3 The reason Tom gives is that …
4 Amy doesn't think Jordan and Alisha have ever …
5 Amy is not surprised that Meg …
6 Tom has a good idea. He suggests that …

Hey Tom. Have you noticed how Lara looks at Jordan? I think she has a crush on him.

Maybe, Amy, but he'll never ask her out. He's in love with Alisha.

What!! 😂 Have you ever seen Alisha and Jordan on a date? They're just friends!

Well, have you heard about Meg and Dan? Meg broke up with him last Friday night.

😔 I don't think they were ever 'together'. She only went out with Dan once or twice.

Are you sure? Hm. Well, maybe Lara and Dan should get together!

6 **VIEWING FOCUS: A film trailer**

a Look at this photo from a trailer. What do you think the film is about?

 **b** Watch the trailer and find out what the film is about.

Think: Make notes individually.
Pair: Compare your notes with a partner. Then write a short summary of the plot.
Share: Find another pair and share your summaries. Does the trailer do its job? Explain.

TIP

The idea behind a film trailer is to get people interested in a film by showing short clips from the most interesting or exciting parts, usually together with music. A good trailer should tell you what the film is about, without saying too much about the plot.

 c Compare two film trailers. Follow these steps:

1 Go to an online video site to choose and watch a trailer of a film for teenagers.
2 How does it try to 'sell' the film? Compare the techniques with those used in the trailer in **b**.

Shopping challenge

1 **Free-time activities**

a What do you like doing with your friends after school or at the weekend? Make a list.

 b Compare your list with a partner. Is shopping on one or both of your lists? Why (not)?

2 **A survey**

a Read the introduction to a survey of US teenagers' shopping habits and do the tasks.

1 Explain who Generation Z is.
2 Describe how Generation Z is different from older generations.
3 Discuss whether you think the description is correct and if you would add anything.

b Read the rest of the survey. Make notes about teen shopping habits and key trends.

c Compare your notes from **b**. How similar or different are US teens and teens in Germany?

Teen shopping habits in the US

Generation Z – those born between the mid 1990s and early 2010s – will soon become the largest generation in the US. Today's teenagers are the first generation to grow up with the internet and smartphones. They're better informed than ever before. They're also interested in social justice. According to the experts, this influences their shopping habits. A survey of high school students shows some key trends.

5 **Natalie, 16, San Francisco**
How do I decide what clothes to buy? I usually just look at what the people at my school are wearing, and if I think something's cool, I'll go out and buy it. Sometimes I see something on social media and get inspired by it. If I want a second opinion when I'm in the store, I
10 message my friends with a photo and ask them what they think.

Alisha, 15, South Carolina
I think there's a lot of pressure on teenagers to follow fashion trends. There are so many adverts telling us to buy, buy, buy. They try to make you think that if you're not wearing the latest fashion, nobody will like you. But I'm not into buying lots
15 of stuff anymore. If we didn't buy so much, it would be better for the environment. Thrifting has really become a trend recently. It's cheaper and it helps you stand out from the crowd, too.

Jeff, 17, Boston, Massachusetts
When my friends and I are hanging out, we usually go to a park, or someone's home, or watch a movie. I think shopping is boring. If I want something, I order it online because it's convenient. I have the apps
20 for the stores I like on my phone and I ask my mom to pay with her credit card.

---

28)) **Words and phrases**

Fashion

convenient	without trouble or effort	to **influence**	to have an effect on somebody or something
to **exploit**	when you don't pay somebody enough for their time and work	**social justice**	when society treats people well / fairly
habit	something you do regularly	to **thrift**	to buy clothes at a flea market or a second hand shop

Mia, 17, Portland, Oregon

I'm not into fast fashion. In my social studies class, we watched a documentary that showed how fast fashion companies exploit clothing workers in developing countries. I really don't want to
25 support that. I often buy second-hand clothes from a thrift shop like *Goodwill*. It's a way to look a bit different. And if we recycled more, there would be less waste.

David, 18, New York City

I work part-time at the local mall. I won't buy anything unless I have
30 enough money, so I have to save up. I always look for bargains in stores or special offers online. When I'm shopping in-store, I use my phone to compare prices. Even if I had lots of money, I'd still look for sales.

3 **Who do you agree with?**

a Read the examples and complete the explanations in the box below. Then find more examples in the survey.

*If I **think** something's cool, I**'ll go out** and buy it.* (line 8 – 9)
*If we **didn't buy** so much, it **would be** better for the environment.* (lines 15 – 16)

- We use *if*-sentences type 1 to talk about situations that are likely to happen. The verb in the *if*-clause is in the ▆▆▆. In the main clause, we use ▆▆▆ + the infinitive.
- We use *if*-sentences type 2 to talk about impossible or unlikely situations. The verb in the *if* clause is in the ▆▆▆. In the main clause, we use ▆▆▆ + the infinitive.

TIP

- 'unless' means 'if not'
  *I won't buy anything **unless** I **have** enough money.*
  *I won't buy anything **if** I **don't have** enough money.*

b Read these comments and complete them with the correct form of the verbs.

1 We wouldn't know what to buy if we ▆▆▆ (*not have*) advertising.
2 If we had less advertising, there ▆▆▆ (*be*) less pressure to buy things we don't need.
3 We would be much happier if we ▆▆▆ (*not buy*) so much stuff.
4 If everyone looked the same, we ▆▆▆ (*get*) bored looking at each other.

 c Which comments in **b** do you agree with? Discuss and compare your ideas.

4 **YOUR TURN: What would you do?**
Discuss each question with a different person.

1 What would you wear if someone you like invited you out on a date?
2 If you won 250 euros in a competition, what would you do with it?
3 How would your life be different if you didn't have a phone?

Grammar and structures

If-sentence type 1 (revision) → **G13**
If I **find** a nice dress, I**'ll buy** it.

If-sentence type 2 (revision) → **G14**
If I **didn't buy** so many clothes, I **would have** more money.

Practice: The cost of fast fashion

1 **GET STARTED!** Discuss the questions. Then compare answers with another pair.

1 Where are your favourite clothes made?
2 What do you do with clothes you don't want any more?

2 **The cost of fashion**

a Scan the interview and find the missing numbers in the graphics.

We buy more than .... items of clothing every year.

.... people work to make our clothes.

.... are women aged 18 – 24.

Many workers in clothes factories earn less than .... a day.

Only .... of clothing donated to thrift stores ever get sold.

It takes .... litres of water to make one pair of jeans.

b Read the interview. Make notes about how the fast fashion industry harms people and the environment.

c Use your notes to discuss why 'fast fashion is bad for our health and bad for the planet'. Correct or complete your notes.

d Amy says, 'We have to change how we shop.' Make two suggestions.

! **page 147, Writing skills**

The real cost of fast fashion
by Oliver, Pine Ridge High School

I was going through my closet last weekend trying to decide what to wear to a party. I realized that it's full of clothes I never wear! I started to ask myself: 'Why do I buy so many clothes?' So I decided to talk to Amy Rice, a Fashion Design student in 12th Grade, who's been investigating the fashion industry.

Q Amy, why do we buy so many clothes?!
A That's a good question. I found out that we now buy more than 80 billion items of clothing every year. The main reason is the fast fashion industry. Now everyone can keep up with the latest fashion trends because clothes are so cheap – $5 for a T-shirt or $19 for a dress, for example.

Q So we buy more and more because we think we're getting a good deal?
A Right. And the styles change every few weeks – that's why it's called 'fast fashion'. If we go into a store and see something we like, we're under pressure to buy it at once because it won't be there the next time we come. But cheap clothes don't last long because they're poor quality. So we throw them away or give them to charity. But thrift stores can only sell 10 – 20% of the clothes they get. Most of the rest goes to landfill.

Q How do companies make clothing so cheaply now?
A The main reason is cheap labor in developing countries. Just imagine – 75,000,000 people work to make our clothes, mainly in countries like Bangladesh, Cambodia, Indonesia or China. 80% of workers are young women. And most of them earn less than $3 for a 14-hour day. Working conditions are often dangerous. This puts workers under terrible stress.

Q What about the effect on the environment?
A OK, take denim jeans, for example. Two billion pairs of jeans are made every year. But it takes around 3,800 liters of water to produce just <u>one</u> pair. Cotton production for clothing causes up to 25% of global pollution. Most of it is from pesticides. Workers can get cancer from the dyes they use to produce bright colours. And, finally, when clothes go into landfill, toxic chemicals escape into the air.

Q So fast fashion is bad for our health and bad for the planet. What can we do?
A We have to change how we shop.

3 **Meet the makers.** Rifa works in a clothes factory. Read what she says, then complete the sentences to tell a friend about her.

1 'Fast fashion means we have less time to make the clothes which the fashion companies order. I have to make an arranged number of items every day. I only get paid if I make enough clothes.' *Unless Rifa makes …*

2 'My husband is ill. I have to work so my family can eat.' *If she didn't …*

3 'I want to send my daughter to school but I don't earn enough money.' *If she …, she could …*

4 'I dream about having a good job so I can go on holiday to faraway countries.' *If …, she …*

5 'Women like me must be strong. Then we can make a difference for women who work in this industry.' *If women like her …*

 **page 68**

4 **Taking action for social justice**

30 **a** Amy Rice gives a talk to 9th grade students at an after-school debating club. Listen to the introduction.

1 What's Amy going to talk about?
2 What facts do you think she will mention at the start?

31 **b** Listen to the first part of her talk.

1 Were your predictions correct?
2 Predict what three ideas she will suggest next.

32 **c** Listen to the next part of the talk. What are Amy's three suggestions? Compare them with your predictions.

32 **d** Listen again. What are the benefits of each suggestion? Make notes and discuss in class.

! **page 147, Writing skills**

5 **Invitation to a meeting.**
Write a notice for your school noticeboard inviting people to come to a meeting about the negative aspects of fast fashion. Include this information:
- a big headline to attract attention,
- what the meeting is about,
- why it's important,
- when and where it will be.

6 **SPEAKING FOCUS: A short talk about fast fashion**

a Brainstorm ideas. You can use the information in **2** and **5** to help you or find out more yourself.

b Think about how you can get the audience's attention from the start, for example with a question: *Did you know …?* And, if possible, use some visual aids to make your talk more interesting.

c Prepare and practise your talk.

d Give your talk to the class. Ask for questions.

> **TIP**
> - Structure your talk:
>   **Introduction** – tell the audience what you're going to talk about
>   **Middle** – three to five main points
>   **Conclusion** – summarize your main points
> - Write notes on cards. Use keywords, not sentences.

29 ## Words and phrases

Clothes production
cancer a serious disease

dye something which changes the colour of something
synthetic not natural
working conditions work hours, breaks, pay, equipment

Method coach: Prepare to write a questionnaire

PART 1

S1 **What do you want to know?** You want to carry out a survey about young people's shopping habits. Start by brainstorming what you want to find out. Look at these questions and think of more.

1 What do they spend their money on?
2 How do they decide what to buy?
3 Where do they buy products?
4 …

PART 2

S2 **Survey question types.** Look at the following question types. Write your own answers to the questions. Then compare with other students.

RANKING
What do you like to spend your money on? Rank from 1 (= least important) to 5 (= most important).
☐ clothes ☐ food
☐ entertainment ☐ books and magazines
☐ computer games

On a scale of 1 (= not important) to 5 (= very important), how important is fashion to you?

SELECT ALL THAT APPLY
How do you find out about new products?
☐ Social media ☐ Friends / Classmates
☐ E-commerce websites ☐ None of the above
☐ Online ads

MULTIPLE CHOICE
Where do you shop more often?
☐ in-store ☐ online

How often do you buy second-hand clothes?
☐ always ☐ often ☐ sometimes
☐ occasionally ☐ never

YES / NO
Do you like shopping?
☐ YES ☐ NO

TEXT BOX
What's the name of your favourite fashion brand?
_____

RATING
It's important to keep up with the latest trends.
☐ Strongly agree ☐ Agree ☐ Disagree
☐ Strongly disagree ☐ Don't know

TIP

How to write good questions:
Do
● Write short simple questions.
● Make sure the questions will give you the exact answers you want.
● Make sure the questions allow people to answer honestly (e.g. by giving enough options).
Don't
● Use biased language – this can influence people's answers.
● Ask questions that are really two questions but only allow one answer.

S3 **Bad questions**

a Read the TIP box. Why are these bad questions?

> **1 Do you always shop online?**
> ☐ YES ☐ NO
>
> **2 What's your favourite second-hand shop?**
> _____
>
> **3 Should shoppers who care about the environment avoid fast fashion brands?**
> ☐ YES ☐ NO
>
> **4 How many times a month do you shop in-store or online on average? Enter a number.** ☐

b Suggest changes to improve the questions. Then rewrite them.

S4 **More questions.** Choose three of the question types in **S2** and write another question for each.

 Words and phrases

Questionnaires
biased   not neutral

PART 3

@ WES-40324-002

Workshop task: Write a short questionnaire for a survey

S1 **Brainstorm the topic.** You want to find out how students in your school spend their time and use media outside school. Brainstorm some questions for your survey. For example:

- What kind of activities do you like to do for fun?
- What kind of activities do you do competitively?
- What activities do you enjoy doing most?
- How much time do you spend on social media every day?

S2 **Write some questions.** Refer to the list of question types in **S2** on page 54. Decide the best question types to find out what you want to know. Write at least five questions.

S3 **Write your questionnaire.** Discuss your questions and choose the best ones. Then write a clean copy of your questionnaire.

S4 **Edit a questionnaire.** Exchange your questionnaire with another pair. Are their questions good or do they need improvement? Refer to the TIP box on page 54. Give feedback on each other's questionnaires.

S5 **Revise your questionnaire.** Revise your questions if necessary.

S6 **Circulate your questionnaire.** Decide how you want to circulate your questionnaire – as a photocopied handout or digitally (e.g. in an email). Try to get results from at least six people. Keep your results. You will need them for the next Method coach.

TIP

It can be useful to ask for some personal information at the beginning of your survey, for example gender or age. This can help you identify differences of opinion between boys and girls, and between different age groups.

Gender	???	???
Age	???	???

Going to school in the USA

1 **Our school.** What do you know about high schools in the USA? What similarities and differences are there between your school and high schools in the US?

2 **Joshua's American school**

a Joshua, an exchange student from Manchester, England, is attending high school in Santa Fe, New Mexico. Read his blog. Then list the similarities and differences between Joshua's US school and your school.

b Match American English words in the blog to their British English equivalents:
- year
- timetable
- optional subject

c Write a comment for Joshua's blog.

3 **About Joshua.** Look at the sentences. Complete the explanations in the box with 'gerund' or '*to*-infinitive'. Then find more examples in the blog.

1 I **want to talk** about a typical school day.
2 I **enjoy being** an exchange student.
3 I **love going** to school. / I **love to take** photos.

> - Some verbs, e.g. *want, hope,* are followed by a ▮▮.
> - Some verbs, e.g. *enjoy, miss,* are followed by a ▮▮.
> - Some verbs, e.g. *love, hate,* are followed by a ▮▮ or a ▮▮ with no change in meaning.

4 **Joshua's school life**

a Complete with the correct form of the verbs in brackets. Sometimes two forms are possible.

Joshua can't stand 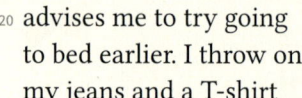 (*get up*) early. He enjoys ▮2▮ (*go*) to school by bus. He's started ▮3▮ (*take*) photography classes. He doesn't want ▮4▮ (*join*) the Math Club. He prefers ▮5▮ (*do*) sport. He's hoping ▮6▮ (*become*) a member of the baseball team.

≫ **page 68**

Joshua in the USA

I'm Joshua Garfield. I'm from Manchester, UK, and I'm a high school exchange student in New Mexico, USA.

A day in my American life
Hi everyone!
5 I usually write about special or fun things I do, but in this blog post I want to talk about a typical school day. I enjoy being an exchange student, but it isn't just fun – I have to study, and the school expects you to do homework and take tests as well! But, still, I love going
10 to school here. There are so many people from different backgrounds and cultures (there are 1,500 students). And the teachers are very friendly – they even allow us to call them by their first names! I remember feeling really nervous before I started here, but not anymore. I
15 don't miss being at my old school either.

7.00 Rise and shine! I hate getting up this early because I need lots of sleep. My host mom
20 advises me to try going to bed earlier. I throw on my jeans and a T-shirt (they don't force us to wear uniforms here!), eat breakfast, then run for the school bus. Taking the bus is
25 fun because it helps me to meet other students. But lots of students in 11th and 12th grade stop taking the bus as soon as they start driving.

> **TIP**
>
> Some verbs, e.g. *want, expect, would like* can be followed by an object + *to*-infinitive. They are never followed by *that* in English.
>
> *My English teacher **wants** / **expects** / **would like me to do** my homework alone!*

b Write what people want or expect Joshua to do.

Joshua's school: The students don't have to wear uniforms at Joshua's school. *(not expect)*
Joshua's school doesn't expect the students to wear uniforms.

1 Joshua's parents: Please call us every week. *(want)*
2 Joshua's grandma: Could you send me some photos of your host family? *(would like)*

So here's my regular schedule – it's easy to remember because it's the same every day! (I forgot to tell you I'm in 9th grade – that's the first year of high school.) Some classes are required, like math, English and science, but students can choose their other classes – they're called electives. I decided to take photography because I love to take photos.

8.05 Social Studies
9.05 Math
10.05 – 10.20 break
10.20 Photography
11.20 Science
12.20 – 12.55 Lunch
12.55 Contemporary American literature
1.55 PE

The last period ends at 2.55 p.m., so the school day is pretty much the same as my school back home. But the day isn't over yet! The school encourages all students to get involved in after-school activities. Sports like soccer and basketball are very popular. There are lots of clubs, too. Some of my classmates want me to join the Math Club with them, but I prefer doing sport. My PE teacher has persuaded me to try out for the baseball team – he says I'm a natural!

That was a normal day in my American life! I hope you enjoyed reading it!

3 Joshua's host mother: You should go to bed earlier so you're not tired in the morning. (*advise*)
4 The school: The students should be punctual for lessons. (*expect*)
5 Joshua's teachers: It's a good idea for the students to take part in after-school activities. (*encourage*)
6 Joshua's friends: Why don't you join the Math Club, Joshua? (*would like*)
7 Joshua's PE teacher: You should try out for the baseball team, Joshua. (*want*)

 **page 68**

Grammar and structures

Verb + gerund or *to*-infinitive → G15, G16, G18
I **enjoy playing** in the band.
We **hope to give** a concert soon.
Verb + object + *to*-infinitive → G17
My classmates **want me to join** the Math Club.

---

5 **About you**

a Look at the examples in the box. Then choose the correct option in sentences 1 – 4.

> • Some verbs can be followed by a gerund or an infinitive, but the meaning changes. What's the difference?
>
> I'm **trying to learn** Spanish.
> **Try going** to bed earlier so you aren't tired in the morning.
>
> I must **remember to do** my homework.
> I **remember feeling** really nervous.
>
> I **forgot to tell** you – I'm in 9th grade.
> I'll never **forget arriving** in the US.
>
> I **stopped to talk** to a friend.
> The teacher told me to **stop talking**.

1 I often forget **to do / doing** my homework.
2 I remember **to cry / crying** on my first day at school.
3 To improve my English, I want to try **to watch / watching** films in English.
4 My parents want me to stop **to play / playing** video games.

b Are the sentences true or false for you?

c Complete the sentences so they are true for you.
1 I often forget …
2 On my first day at school, I remember …
3 To improve my English, I want to try …
4 My parents want me to stop …

---

6 **YOUR TURN: Your life.** Think about the topics below, then tell your partner about them. How similar or different are your answers?

About you
• something you've decided to do soon
• something you'd like to do next summer
• something you hate doing

About you and others
• something a friend has helped you to do
• something your parents don't allow you to do
• something your parents expect you to do

Practice: The school year

PART 1

1 GET STARTED! The first day at school is a special event. Do you remember how you and your family celebrated it?

2 Homecoming. Read the website and look at the photos about homecoming, a special event at American schools. What do you learn about it?

PART 2

September 21st–22nd
WEST HIGH SCHOOL
HOMECOMING

Wednesday 09·19
Wacky Day
Mismatched, backwards, crazy colors

September 21st and 22nd
HOMECOMING
WEST HIGH SCHOOL

School spirit days:

Monday: Sports Day
Tuesday: Pajama Day
Wednesday: Wacky Day
Thursday: Class Color Day
Friday: Pride & Spirit (wear blue and gold)

Friday, September 21st

Homecoming Parade on campus
from 1.20 – 2.25 p.m.
Homecoming Rally in the Jefferson Gym
from 2.25 – 3.40 p.m.
Homecoming Football Game at Parkland Stadium vs. Tigers at 7.00 p.m.

Saturday, September 22nd

Homecoming Dance in the Gym at 7.30 p.m.

PART 3

3 VIDEO TRACK: Homecoming

a You're going to watch Toni talking about homecoming week on her video sharing channel. What does she tell you about homecoming and the events listed on the website? What extra information does she talk about?

b Note down what you remember. Watch again and check your notes. Write a summary of the main points.

! page 143, Speaking skills

4 Special events in the German school year

a What special events take place during the year at your school? Make a list. What's your favourite?

+ b Choose an event on your list in **a**. Write a blog describing how you celebrate it at your school.

5 The school dance

a Complete the conversation with the correct form of the verbs in brackets.

Mom   Hi Dan, why are you home from the school dance so early? I didn't expect ▢1 (*see*) you back before midnight.

Dan   Oh, I'd hoped ▢2 (*meet*) Emma in town. We'd arranged ▢3 (*go*) to the dance together. I waited for ages, but she didn't come.

Mom   That's very strange. Why didn't you call her?

Dan   Because she'd promised ▢4 (*go*) to the dance with me. That's why. I don't mind ▢5 (*wait*), but if someone is going to be late, I expect them ▢6 (*let*) me know! I didn't want ▢7 (*go*) on my own so I decided ▢8 (*come*) home.

Mom   Well, I would like you ▢9 (*call*) her and find out if she is OK. Perhaps something has happened.

Dan   It has. I texted her and said I don't plan ▢10 (*see*) her anymore!

b What do you think? Do you agree with Dan? What would you do in this situation?

 Words and phrases

dress code	rules about what to wear
pride	the feeling of being proud
wacky	crazy

6 Doing things differently

a Read about some unusual schools. What's special about them?

b Write two or three sentences about each school, but don't write the name of the school. Start your sentences like this:

The teachers help … .
The school allows / doesn't allow …
The school doesn't force …
The school expects / doesn't expect …
Students need / don't need …
The school wants …
Teachers try …
The school encourages …
Students can choose (not) …

Brooklyn Free School, New York

At Brooklyn Free School there isn't a timetable that all students have to follow. The teachers work with students to develop a personal learning plan. Students can choose to study any topics they are interested in. They can attend teacher-led classes or work alone or together on their own projects. There are no grades and no homework, and students don't have to take exams. Students have a say in the running of the school through weekly Democratic Meetings.

c Exchange your sentences with a partner. Match your partner's sentences to the right school.

7 WRITING FOCUS: School and education

Imagine you are a student at your perfect school. Describe your school and explain why you like it.

School of the Future, Philadelphia

At the School of the Future it isn't necessary to buy pens, paper or books. All the students have a laptop, and the teachers use computerized smart boards. Students receive their tasks, comments, and grades through a learning management system (LMS). Everyone has to follow the school dress code and be clean and tidy at all times. Students mustn't wear ripped jeans, sleeveless tops or sandals. The school wants the students to get good jobs when they leave, so they have to dress and behave well.

Lumiar schools, Americas

At the Lumiar schools there are no classrooms, schedules and lessons. The idea is that students learn for themselves by doing project work. Instead of traditional teachers, there are tutors and part-time masters. The tutors help the students to choose their projects. The masters may be engineers, business people, chefs, etc. They help the students to design their projects and learn the skills they need, such as how to use technology. Students of different ages can work together and learn from each other. If students don't want to do a project, they can study on their own in the library.

> **TIP**
>
> Write three paragraphs:
> **Introduction:** Introduce your perfect school.
> **Middle paragraph / s:** Describe a typical school day.
> **Conclusion:** Say why you like your school.

Weekend in the city

1 **Small-town life and city life.** Mina, the exchange student from Frankfurt, is living in Sterling, Illinois. She is planning a weekend trip to Chicago with her friend Alma. Look at the photos. How do you think life in Sterling is different from life in Chicago?

2 **Making plans**

36 **a** Read and listen to Mina and Alma making plans for their trip. What do they need to decide?

Mina	I'm so excited about going to Chicago! How far is it from here? Do you know how to get there?
Alma	It's only about a two-hour drive. If I ₅ had my driver's license, we could take my mom's car.
Mina	But you won't have it until next semester, Alma. We need to decide whether to go by train or by bus.
Alma ₁₀	Well, that's easy. There isn't a train service between Sterling and Chicago.
Mina	Oh, so that means the bus.
Alma	Yes, we can check the times online and decide when to leave.
Mina ₁₅	OK. Let's talk about where to stay. We have to think whether to book a hotel or a hostel. I read about a popular hostel in downtown Chicago called Tramper's Inn. In the online reviews, ₂₀ people say it's clean and it isn't very expensive. What do you think?
Alma	A hostel sounds cool. But we would save money if we stayed with my grandma. She lives in an area called Hermosa. It's ₂₅ not too far from downtown.
Mina	That's a great idea!
Alma	I'll call her. She likes having visitors. And she knows the city well. I'm sure she'll show us where to go and what to do.
Mina ₃₀	That would be perfect!

b Look at the sentences from **a**. Complete the information in the box. Then find more examples in the conversation.

*Do you know **how to get** there?*
*We need to decide **whether to go** by train or bus.*

> - We can use a question word followed by a ▆▆▆ after verbs like *ask, decide, explain, forget, know, show, tell, understand* and *wonder,* and phrases like *I'm not sure* and *I have no idea.*
> - ▆▆▆ can also be followed by a *to-*infinitive.

3 **Decisions.** What does Mina want to say to Alma? Write sentences with a phrase from the box and a question word or *whether* and a *to*-infinitive.

What should I take with me?
I can't decide what to take with me.

> I can't decide ▪ I'm not sure ▪ Let's talk about ▪ I'm wondering ▪ Do you know …?

1 How do we book the tickets?
2 Should I take some sandwiches for the bus trip?
3 What time will we meet at the bus station?
4 Where do we get off the bus in Chicago?
5 What should we get Alma's grandmother?

35 **Words and phrases**

block		group of buildings with streets on all sides
driver's license	🇺🇸	driving licence
pier		a structure that is built from land over water

4 Out and about in Chicago

a Listen to the girls. What activities do they talk about? What order do they want to do them in?

b Match each place (1–3) with two of the descriptions (a–f).

1 The Art Institute
2 The 606
3 Navy Pier

a There are shops there.
b It's downtown.
c It's not far.
d Bus number 65 goes there.
e It's quiet on Sunday mornings.
f There were once trains there.

5 Giving advice

a Look at these sentences from the conversation in **4a** and choose the correct words in the box.

*Sunday morning is **the quietest time to visit**.*
*Chicago was **the first city to have** a Ferris wheel.*

> We use a **_to_-infinitive** after superlative adjectives and after numbers like *first, second*.

b Give advice to somebody visiting your town.

> *I'm looking for a good place to stay.*

> *The best place to stay is …*

1 What about a cheap place to eat?
2 I'd like to visit some interesting sights.
3 Are there any nice parks around here?
4 What's a quick way to get around town?

6 Big or small?

a Listen to Mina and Alma. Which does each girl prefer – big-city life or small-town life?

b Listen again. True or false?

1 Mina feels that Frankfurt is like Chicago.
2 Alma likes the mall in Sterling.
3 Alma's grandmother wants to leave Chicago because of the city's problems.
4 Both Mina and Alma like the community feeling in Sterling.

c Look at the questions and choose the correct words to complete the information in the box.

*Chicago's great, **isn't it**?*
*You **haven't** ever lived there, **have you**?*

> - We often use question tags to check information, or when we ask someone to agree with us.
> - If the verb in the main sentence is positive, we add a **positive / negative** question tag.
> - If the verb in the main sentence is negative, we add a **positive / negative** question tag.

d Add questions tags. Then listen and check.

1 You probably feel homesick now, ▬▬ ?
2 Yes, she mentioned the prices, ▬▬ ?
3 She'll never leave there, ▬▬ ?
4 There aren't very many trees, ▬▬ ?

7 YOUR TURN: City life and country life.

Think about city life and country life. Then discuss each topic with a different person.

> cafés ▪ cool shops ▪ lake ▪ museums ▪ parks ▪ public transport ▪ river ▪ sports centres ▪ swimming pool ▪ traffic ▪ zoo

Grammar and structures

Infinitives after question words and _whether_ → G19
I have no idea **how to get** there.
I don't know **whether to take** the train or bus.

Infinitives after superlatives and numbers → G20
It's **the easiest** way **to find** it.

Question tags (revision) → G21
We're on the right bus, **aren't we**?

Practice: City and country

1 **GET STARTED!** '*Home is where your heart is.*'
Discuss what you think this saying means.

2 **VIDEO TRACK: Are you happy?**

5 **a** An interviewer in the US wants to know where people are happier: in rural areas or in cities. What do you think he'll find out? Discuss with a partner. Then watch the video. Compare your answers.

b Match the words and phrases from the video (1–6) with the definitions (a–f).

1	the right fit		**a**	very sad and without hope
2	dive in		**b**	general health and happiness
3	depressed		**c**	think about or do something with energy and concentration
4	rural dweller		**d**	a collection of statistics about a subject
5	well-being		**e**	the best match
6	index		**f**	a person who lives in the countryside

c Answer these questions.

1 The interviewer says, 'It's not really a debate between rural and city life.' What does he mean?

2 What does the Well-Being Index show?

d What is the interviewer's conclusion? Do you agree or disagree with him? Discuss.

3 **A new place.** You and your family have moved to a new town. You're texting with a friend. Complete the sentences with a question word or *whether* and a verb from the boxes. The question words can be used more than once, the verbs only once.

what ■ where ■ when ■ how ■ whether

be ■ do ■ find ■ go ■ join ■ play

> Hey, how's it going? Have you made any new friends yet?

> No, not yet. I'm not sure how to meet other teenagers. So the weekends have been pretty boring so far. I don't know **1** with my time!

> That's a shame. You should just ask people. They'll know **2** – you know, where young people hang out.

> I've done that, actually. Someone suggested sport clubs, so I'm trying to decide **3** a volleyball club. I've never played, but it looks like fun.

> You should do it! I'm sure they'll show you **4** . Last week you wanted to explore the town and you were wondering **5** information about the buses. Have you got any further with that?

> Yes! I've got a great new app. It tells me which bus I need to take and shows the timetable so that I know **6** at the bus stop.

> Sounds good!

39)) **Words and phrases**

harvest	picking and gathering food
income	the money that you earn or get
nutrition	eating a healthy diet

4 Tourists!

a At the tourist centre in downtown Chicago the assistants get all kinds of questions. Complete the tourists' questions with the correct question tags.

1 We can walk from here to the lakeside, [____] ?
– No, you can't. You need to take the bus.
2 You don't know a nice pizza place, [____] ?
– Yes, I do. It's called Lucky's Pizza.
3 The trains run all night, [____] ?
– Yes, some trains have a 24-hour service.
4 Those bikes over there aren't for hire, [____] ?
– They are, actually. They're very cheap.
5 Lincoln Park Zoo has got penguins, [____] ?
– Yes, it's got lots of penguins.
6 The Ferris wheel doesn't go very fast, [____] ?
– No, don't worry. It goes very slowly.

page 68

b Write down three or more questions that a tourist might ask about your area. Use question tags. Then ask each other your questions.

5 READING FOCUS: Urban gardening in Chicago.
Read the article: true, false or not in the text?

1 Chicago is the only US city with an urban gardening programme.
2 Urban gardening in Chicago started over 100 years ago.
3 The local community paid the residents to help set up the first gardens.
4 Today some of the local residents still help take care of the gardens.
5 Young people are also involved in the urban gardening programme.

Making Chicago's inner city more liveable

Chicago is a place of skyscrapers, heavy traffic and big social problems. But it's also full of beautiful urban gardens. In community gardens, plant-loving residents are thankful to have a peaceful green space to cultivate and to look after.

5 The first community gardening program in Chicago began in the 1940s when there was no money to build on empty city land. With help from hard-working volunteers, the Victory Gardens program cleaned up overgrown, garbage-filled lots between buildings and transformed them into gardens where low-income residents could grow food. Today many of the

10 community gardens are in parks and are supported by the non-profit Community Gardens in the Parks.

Urban gardening helps Chicago's young people, too. The Windy City Harvest Youth Farm is a youth development program that teaches valuable skills and employs teens from low-income areas. They learn to grow food, work as a team, eat in a healthy way, and

15 be responsible and helpful community members. The program has also built oases of vegetable and fruit gardens in low-income neighborhoods where health and nutrition are big issues. Youth gardener Jarvis White, 17, says, 'I've learned a lot about problem-solving and about community responsibility. And the

20 transformation that I've seen in other kids is unbelievable. The support we get here is amazing.'
The Windy City Harvest Youth Farm shows how urban gardening helps make cities more liveable.

6 YOUR CHOICE: Urban gardens. Research urban gardening in your area. Make notes. Then choose task A or task B.

A Write a report about what you found out.
B Give a three-minute talk in class.

PART 1

PART 2

PART 3

Method coach: How to collect and present survey results

S1 **Collect information.** We can record the results of a survey quickly and easily in a table. Look at the table and answer the questions.

1 What was the survey about?
2 How many people were interviewed?
3 How many people prefer sport?
4 What percentage prefer English?

Favourite school subjects	Tally (running total)	Totals	Totals %
Sport	𝍷𝍷𝍷𝍷 𝍷𝍷𝍷𝍷 IIII	14	47%
History	𝍷𝍷𝍷𝍷 IIII	9	30%
English	𝍷𝍷𝍷𝍷	5	16.5%
Maths	II	2	6.5%
???	???	30	100%

S2 **Ways of presenting information.** The information in **S1** can be presented in a pie chart or a bar chart. Which chart do you think presents the information more clearly? Explain your answer.

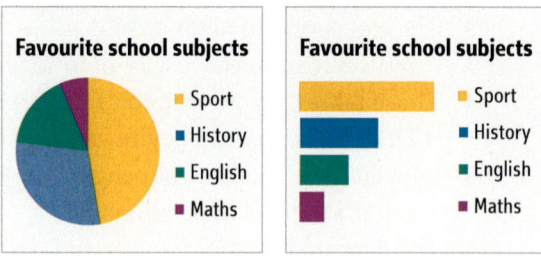

S3 **Interpret charts.** Look at the bar chart below and complete the sentences.

1 Generation Z most often discover products on ▆▆▆.
2 Millennials most often discover products on ▆▆▆.
3 44% of ▆▆▆ discover products on e-commerce websites, compared with 46% of ▆▆▆.
4 Only 24% of millennials discover products through ▆▆▆, compared with 32% of Generation Z.

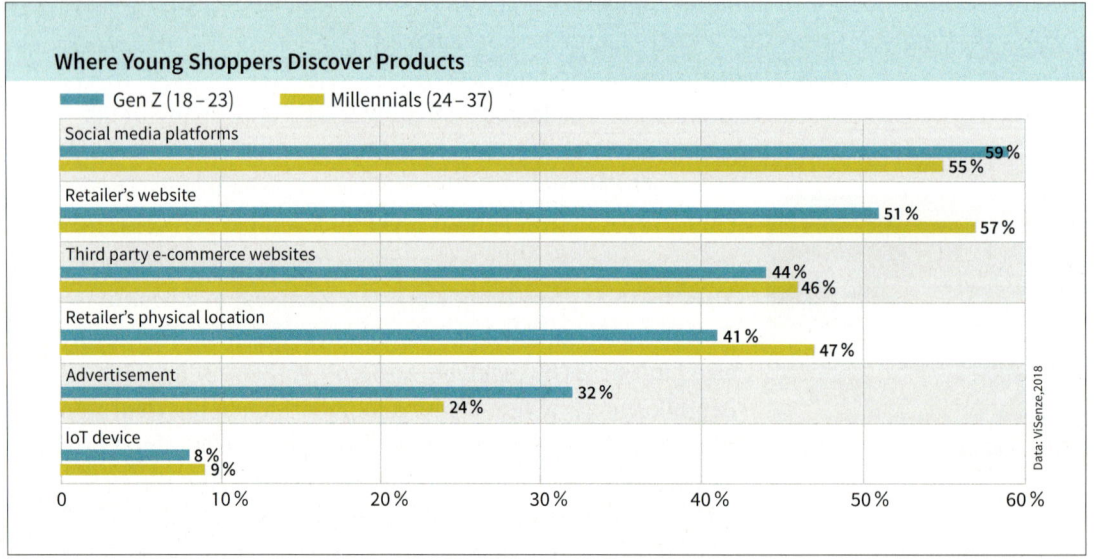

S4 **Present results**

🐾 **a** Choose a question from your questionnaire on page 55 and record the answers in a table.

b Put the results in a chart. Write a few sentences to summarize the results.

TIP
- Remember to include a title.
- If you use a bar chart, write labels along the horizontal axis and use a suitable scale up the vertical axis.
- If you use a pie chart, use colours and a key.

Workshop task: Carry out a survey

S1 **Choose a topic.** You are going to carry out a survey on a topic of your choice. You can prepare a questionnaire about one of these topics, or choose your own topic.

The shopping habits and preferences of today's teenagers

I like to buy my clothes from thrift stores. Fast fashion is bad for the planet.

I have a part-time job on Saturdays so I can buy things I want.

The attitudes and values of today's teenagers

In my opinion, social media has a positive effect on people my age. It helps us connect with friends and make new friends.

I think everyone has to take care of the environment by doing things like recycling and buying less stuff.

S2 **What do you want to know?**

a Brainstorm what you want to find out.

b Write your questions. Refer to the list of question types in **S2** on page 54.

c Check and edit. Refer to the TIP on page 54.

d Write a final draft.

S3 **Carry out the survey**

a Decide how to conduct your survey:
- interviews face-to-face or
- circulate the questionnaire using email or social media and give a time limit for completing and returning it

b Conduct the survey. Make sure you get results from at least six people.

S4 **Collect the information.** Record your results in a table. Refer to the example on page 64.

S5 **Prepare your survey report**

a Decide what kind of chart you will use to present the results for each question.

b Write a few sentences to summarize the results for each chart. You will need these in your presentation.

S6 **Present your results.** If possible, prepare a PowerPoint presentation. Use a new slide for each chart and be ready to summarize the most important information.

Mediation

1 **Teenage media use.** Olivia, a member of a school magazine in Seattle, has contacted schools in different countries to find out about media use in these countries. Your principal has asked you to write an English article for the school magazine in Seattle. Use the information below to answer Olivia's questions. Write about 100 words.

Hi!

Could you please include the following information in your article?
Which media do German teenagers use most frequently and how long are they online every day? Has time spent on the internet changed compared to previous years? What do teenagers use the internet for?
And what about the role of newspapers and books? Are they still read by young people?
It would be great if you could add a short statement about yourself.
Looking forward to your reply. Thank you!

Olivia

Statistiken zur Mediennutzung von Jugendlichen
von Matthias Kemmerich

Von allen Medien nutzen Jugendliche das Handy bzw. das Smartphone am häufigsten. Laut einer Umfrage zur Mediennutzung
5 von Jugendlichen in Deutschland gaben rund 94 Prozent der Befragten im Alter von 12 bis 19 Jahren an, ihr Smartphone täglich zu verwenden. Beim täglichen
10 Medienkonsum folgen das Internet (91 Prozent) und das Musik hören (84 Prozent). Online-Videos schauen insgesamt 65 Prozent der Jugendlichen täglich.
15 Digitale Spiele nutzen ein knappes Drittel der Befragten jeden Tag. Bücher lesen immerhin noch 19 Prozent der Jugendlichen täglich, Tageszeitungen hingegen deutlich weniger (10 Prozent). Die Internetnutzungsdauer von Jugendlichen lag 2018 bei 214 Minuten pro Tag. Zehn Jahre zuvor lag dieser Wert noch bei 117 Minuten. Die tägliche Sehdauer bei der Fernsehnutzung der 14- bis 19-Jährigen in Deutschland lag 2017 mit 70
20 Minuten unter dem Vorjahreswert (81 Minuten).

Den größten Anteil an der Nutzungszeit im Internet von Jugendlichen nimmt der Bereich Kommunikation ein. Unter den regelmäßig ausgeführten Aktivitäten im Internet mit dem Schwerpunkt Kommunikation liegt im Jahr 2018 die Nutzung des Messaging-Dienstes WhatsApp mit Abstand vorn (95 Prozent), gefolgt von den Online-Diensten Instagram (67 Prozent) und Snapchat (54 Prozent). Die tägliche Nutzungsdauer
25 von Games liegt im Jahr 2018 laut dem Medienpädagogischen Forschungsverbund Südwest (mpfs) bei insgesamt 103 Minuten (Montag bis Freitag) bzw. 125 Minuten (Wochenende). Besonders bei den Jungen sind digitale Spiele sehr beliebt. Dagegen ist der Anteil der Jugendlichen, die regelmäßig Tageszeitungen und Zeitschriften in Form von Printmedien nutzen, in den letzten Jahren zurückgegangen. Das regelmäßige Lesen von Büchern erfreut sich hingegen einer relativ konstanten Beliebtheit.

Quelle: „Statistiken zur Mediennutzung von Jugendlichen", statista.de, 2019

2 **A 'future' school.** Sam, who goes to an American 'future' school, is visiting you as part of an exchange. One of your teachers who doesn't speak English very well, Mrs Lammert, asks about Sam's school. You mediate between Sam and Mrs Lammert.

You	Hallo, Frau Lammert. Darf ich Ihnen meinen Austauschpartner Sam vorstellen?
Mrs Lammert	Hi, Sam!
Sam	Hello.
Mrs Lammert	Ich habe gehört, dass Sam auf eine besondere Schule geht.
You	Ja, er geht auf eine sogenannte „future school".
Sam	What did she say?
You	She already knows that … and I told her …
Mrs Lammert	Ich würde gern etwas über diese Schule erfahren. Aber mein Englisch ist nicht so gut. Kannst du Sam fragen, was an dieser Schule besonders ist?
You	…
Sam	At our school, all lessons are multidisciplinary. This means that we study one topic from the viewpoint of different subjects.
You	…
Mrs Lammert	Das hört sich interessant an. Wir haben hier ja auch immer mal wieder fächerübergreifende Projekte. Kann Sam mir vielleicht ein konkretes Beispiel dafür geben, wie fächerübergreifender Unterricht bei ihm an der Schule umgesetzt wird?
You	…
Sam	When we worked on the Olympic Games, we all chose a country that regularly takes part in the Olympic Games and created a map of the country in geography and art lessons, in math we measured the parade route for the Opening Ceremony, in our writing lessons we created poems for the winners, in PE we tried out new disciplines, and in science we created meals for the athletes using the information from food pyramids.
You	…
Mrs Lammert	Ich dachte immer „future schools" unterscheiden sich von unseren Schulen vor allem durch die technische Ausstattung.
You	…
Sam	That's also true. At our school, all teachers and students have laptop computers. Students often get individual learning plans, which have been created by our teachers. And when we learn individually, we use a special telephone system. So we can send voicemail to our teachers, who then answer our questions. We also often use smartphones to find information or to talk to experts when we study a topic.
You	…
Mrs Lammert	Das hört sich alles toll an. Aber ich weiß nicht, ob ich dazu technisch in der Lage wäre.
Sam	What did she say?
You	…
Sam	Teachers take part in special further training courses. So they learn all the skills they need.
You	…
Mrs Lammert	Bei uns in Deutschland gibt es auch schon Schulen, die ein ähnliches Konzept ausprobieren. Ich bin gespannt, wie sich das weiterentwickelt. Danke, Sam!

First track

PART 1 · PART 2 · PART 3

3
p. 48 Complete what the friends say with the present perfect or the present perfect progressive.

1 Jordan, **have you checked / have you been checking** your messages yet? **I've texted / I've been texting** you twice.
2 **I've watched / I've been watching** videos since lunchtime, but I think **I've watched / I've been watching** enough now.
3 He **hasn't had / hasn't been having** his phone very long, so he **hasn't understood / hasn't been understanding** some of the apps yet.
4 Conor **has chatted / has been chatting** with his sister for an hour!

3
p. 53 Complete the sentences about Rifa with the correct form of the verbs.

1 Unless Rifa makes enough clothes, she ▮ (*not get*) paid.
2 If she didn't work, her family ▮ (*can not eat*).
3 If she ▮ (*earn*) more money, she could send her daughter to school.
4 If she ▮ (*have*) a good job, she could go on holiday to faraway countries.
5 If women like her ▮ (*be*) strong, they could make a difference for women who work in this industry.

4 a Choose the correct form of the verbs.
p. 56 Sometimes both forms are possible.

Joshua can't stand **to get up / getting up** (1) early. He enjoys **to go / going** (2) to school by bus. He's started **to take / taking** (3) photography classes. He doesn't want **to join / joining** (4) the Math Club. He prefers **to do / doing** (5) sport. He's hoping **to become / becoming** (6) a member of the baseball team.

b What do these people want Joshua to do? Complete the sentences with phrases from the box.

> to be punctual ■ to call them every week ■ to go to bed earlier ■ to join the Math Club ■ to send her some photos ■ to take part in after-school activities ■ to try out for the baseball team ■ to wear uniforms

Joshua's school doesn't expect the students *to wear uniforms*.

1 Joshua's parents want him ▮.
2 Joshua's grandma would like him ▮ of his host family.
3 Joshua's host mother advises Joshua ▮ so he's not tired in the morning.
4 The school expects the students ▮ for lessons.
5 Joshua's teachers encourage the students ▮.
6 Joshua's friends would like him ▮.
7 Joshua's PE teacher wants him ▮.

4 a At the tourist centre in downtown Chicago the
p. 63 assistants get all kinds of questions. Complete them with the correct question tag.

1 We can walk from here to the lakeside, **can we? / can't we? / can't I?**
 – No, you can't. You need to take the bus.
2 You don't know a nice pizza place, **don't you? / do I? / do you?**
 – Yes, I do. It's called Lucky's Pizza.
3 The trains run all night, **don't they? / do they? / have they?**
 – Yes, some trains have a 24-hour service.
4 Those bikes over there aren't for hire, **are we? / are they? / aren't they?**
 – They are, actually. They're very cheap.
5 Lincoln Park Zoo has got penguins, **doesn't it? / has it? / hasn't it?**
 – Yes, it's got lots of penguins.
6 The Ferris wheel doesn't go very fast, **does it? / do they? / doesn't it?**
 – No, don't worry. It goes very slowly.

Extra reading

Simon Mason, *Hey Sherlock!*

Hey Sherlock! is the third novel in Simon Mason's Garvie Smith crime series. The hero, Garvie, is a math genius and very smart, but also very lazy and very awkward when it comes to people skills. As in the novels before, he becomes involved in a crime that Inspector Singh is trying to solve – the disappearance of Amy Roecastle. Garvie, who has recently left school, gets involved while he is working at Amy's family home putting up fences.

! page 144, Reading skills

The van went slowly now along a single-track lane, rocking slightly, [...]. Turning by an ornamental bus shelter with a thatched roof into a recess, it pulled up in front of the gates of 'Four Winds', home of
5 Dr Roecastle FRCS. [...]
A silence descended, a moment of contemplation of the day's fencing ahead. And into this silence, Garvie said calmly: 'Something's wrong.' Smudge looked at him blankly. [...] Even as he spoke, a squad car came
10 into view round the drive behind them.
Getting out of the vans, the men stood there warily, watching it approach. [...] a policeman got out. [...] As he went, he glanced over at the eight men standing awkwardly by their vans in their sloppy
15 sweatpants and creosote-smeared hooded tops – and stopped in surprise, staring at Garvie.
'What are you doing here?' he asked.
'The fencing.'
For a moment Inspector Singh's mouth remained
20 open, but it seemed that he could find nothing else to say, and at last he collected himself, gave a curt nod and made his way to the front door, which was abruptly opened as he was approached by Dr Roecastle, still wearing her clothes from the night
25 before, who said in a critical voice, high-pitched with emotion, 'At last!' [...]
'So,' he [Inspector Singh] said, in his usual careful manner, 'tell me what has happened.'
She told him her daughter had disappeared.
30 Speaking with emotion, [...], she described Amy coming in after midnight, their conversation, and how she'd waited for Amy to continue it.
'At first I didn't realize she'd left,' she said. 'I'd just put the alarm on, I would have heard her if she'd
35 deactivated it, so I searched here for an hour before it became clear. How she left the house I don't know. Then I waited for her to return for two more hours before calling the police. I haven't been to bed at all.'

40 [...] 'I'm furious. I'm extremely busy and I frankly don't have time for this.' [...] he asked about Amy's movements the night before.
'She spent the evening in town with a friend,' she said. 'When she got in, frankly I thought she was drunk.'
45 'She's sixteen, you said?' 'Seventeen next February. She's at Alleyn's studying for her A levels.'
'She's very young to be drinking in town, isn't she?' 'I can tell you don't have children of your own,' she said drily.
50 He hesitated, then went on, 'Who was the friend she was with?' 'Sophie Brighouse. ... You'll want to talk to her, I assume.'
He nodded. 'I'll go there on my way back to the station.' He thought for a moment. 'Has anything
55 happened recently to prompt Amy to leave? [...]' An argument with a boyfriend? 'She doesn't date.'
'An argument with you?'
'She argues with me all the time. Little things.'
He thought about that. 'Has she left home before?'
60 he asked.
Tight-lipped, Dr Roecastle said, 'In February she disappeared for three days.' [...] That's when my marriage was falling apart.'
Singh nodded sympathetically. 'And Amy's father
65 lives elsewhere now?'
'He does.'
'Could she have gone to him last night?'
'Amy's relationship with her father is even worse than with me. They don't talk.' [...]
70 Singh nodded. 'Thank you for being so frank. We'll check the hotels, of course.' He paused. 'Is there anything else that might be relevant?'
'I think I've said all that needs to be said. I'm handing this over to you.'
75 He got to his feet. 'May I look upstairs?'
'Why?'
'I'd like to see Amy's room.'

Mason, Simon. *Hey, Sherlock!* (The Garvie Smith Mysteries). David Fickling Books Ltd. Kindle-Version.

My review

What can I do?

Look at these sentences about Workshop 2.
Are the sentences true for you? Choose the right symbol for each sentence.

1 I can talk about relationships.
2 I can talk about fashion.
3 I can compare city life and country life.
4 I can compare different school systems.

> ⫸ = 'I'm great at this!'
> ⫸ = 'I'm good at this.'
> ⫸ = 'I'm OK at this.'

What do I know?

1 **About relationships.** Conor writes an email to his best friend back in Ireland. Complete it with the correct form of the verbs in brackets and the correct time words.

From: Conor O'Brien
To: Rory
Subject: News from Charleston

Hi Rory,

I hope the weather is as good over there as it is here. As you know, I __1__ (be) here __2__ a few months now. In the last few weeks, I __3__ (play) guitar in the school jazz band, which is great. And I __4__ (make) lots of new friends. There's one girl in particular, Meg, I guess I've got a bit of a crush on her, but I __5__ (not speak) to her much __6__.
On Sunday we went to a jazz concert at a place called Folly Beach. While we were there, Meg came over with her dad. He's a jazz musician. Apparently, he __7__ (play) for more than 35 years! I found out that Meg went out with Dan on Friday, but it wasn't a great date. All weekend I __8__ (hope) they'll break up soon. Then I'm going to ask her out. Hopefully she'll say 'yes'! It's the first time I __9__ (meet) such a great girl __10__ I got here! I'll write again soon.

Conor

■ / 10

Present perfect and present perfect progressive
→ G10, G11 ; pp. 46 – 47
Time words → G12 ; pp. 46 – 47

2 **About fashion.** Meg and Alisha talk about shopping habits and fast fashion. Complete their conversation with the words from the box and *if*-sentences type 1 or 2.

allowance ■ bargain ■ exploited ■ fast ■ in-store ■ label ■ online ■ second-hand ■ thrift ■ trends

Meg   Hi Alisha, I like your top. Did you buy it __1__?
Alisha   No, this comes from the __2__ store downtown.
Meg   Really? It looks new, it certainly doesn't look __3__.
Alisha   I know. If you __4__ (look) carefully, you can pick up some really good stuff. This only cost $5.
Meg   Wow! That was a real __5__.
Alisha   If you want, I __6__ (give) you a call next time and we can go together.
Meg   Thanks, but I like to keep up with the latest fashion __7__.
Alisha   Who doesn't? I guess if I __8__ (have) a bigger __9__, I would as well. However, __10__ fashion really isn't very good.
Meg   What do you mean?
Alisha   Well, many of the people who make the clothes are __11__. I won't buy anything unless I know where it was made.
Meg   How do you do that?
Alisha   If you check the __12__, you can see where the item was produced. That's another reason I like to shop __13__. Then if I __14__ (not know), I can ask someone.
Meg   Wow! I guess it would be better if we all __15__ (think) about where the clothes are made. Next time you go shopping, give me a call and we can go together.
Alisha   Great. Will do.

■ / 15

Fashion, pp. 50 – 53
***If*-sentences type 1 and 2 →** G13, G14 : pp. 50 – 51

3 **About city and country life.** Emily is thinking about moving to the country. Complete her blog with the words from the box. There are two you don't need.

cultural ■ dangerous ■ diverse ■ friendly ■ happy ■ hectic ■ interesting ■ laid-back ■ noisy ■ peaceful ■ rural ■ safe

Our family has been trying to decide where to live: in the city or the country? Our experience is that life in the city can be quite ▪1▪ with
people always rushing around! In contrast, people who live in the country are often more relaxed and ▪2▪. Some people might find that boring, but I like the quiet – for me it's ▪3▪ and much nicer than living in a ▪4▪ city with all the traffic. Some people say that cities can be quite ▪5▪ especially at night. On the other hand, they offer a lot of ▪6▪ activities, for example you can go to museums, theatres, cinemas and so on. And, of course, there are so many ▪7▪ sights to see. Cities are also more ▪8▪ with lots of different people living there. Many of my friends say that people in the country are more ▪9▪ as they often stop to chat with each other. So, I think I'd prefer to live in a ▪10▪ area.

■ / 10

City or country, pp. 60 – 63

4 **About school systems.** Choose the correct form of the verbs to complete the interview with Conor.

Brad   Thanks for agreeing **to do / doing** (1) this interview.

Conor   Alisha was the one who persuaded me **to talk / talking** (2) to you.

Brad   OK. So, how do you feel about school here?

Conor   Well, it's so big! The first week I managed **to get lost / getting lost** (3) every day.

Brad   Yes. I'll never forget **to feel / feeling** (4) totally lost when I started high school.

Conor   Exactly. So I decided **to ask / asking** (5) some of the others for help. One of them invited me **to spend / spending** (6) the weekend at his house. And he suggested **to join / joining** (7) the school jazz band.

Brad   And what things are different here?

Conor   Well, I enjoyed **to go / going** (8) to homecoming. We don't have that.

Brad   Really? Was that fun?

Conor   Yes! I remember **to think / thinking** (9) what a great idea it is. It allows you **to get to know / getting to know** (10) other students better.

Brad   And are there any other differences?

Conor   Yes. In Ireland we have a uniform. I didn't mind **to wear / wearing** (11) it. You don't have to think about what to put on in the morning! Now I can't afford **to buy / buying** (12) much stuff, so it isn't a problem!

Brad   And is there anything you don't like?

Conor   Sure, I miss **to see / seeing** (13) my friends, but I try **to focus / focusing** (14) on the positives. I certainly don't regret **to come / coming** (15) here!

■ / 15

Verb + gerund or *to*-infinitive → [G15, G16, G18]; pp. 56 – 57
Verb + object + *to*-infinitive → [G17]; pp. 56 – 57

■ / 50

What's my score?

Check your answers to the review (Workbook, p. 57). What are your scores for each question?

What was your total score?
⋙   score 38 – 50
⋙   score 23 – 37
⋙   score 0 – 22

Do you want to change your answers to the 'What can I do?' statements on page 70?
Look at the tasks on pages 72 – 73: ⋙, ⋙ and ⋙. Choose the tasks to help you.

My practice pages

Talking about relationships

1 **A new relationship?** Choose the correct words or phrases to complete the conversations.

Alisha   I've noticed / I've been noticing (1) that Conor has a crush on you.

Meg   Conor? But I've only met / I've only been meeting (2) him once!

Alisha   Yes, but he's stared / he's been staring (3) at you ever since we got here.

Meg   Well, he hasn't spoken to me already / yet (4).

Alisha   Perhaps he has waited / he has been waiting (5) for the right moment. Why don't you go over and talk to him?

…

Alisha   So, have you decided / have you been deciding (6) what to do?

Meg   I've been busy all / every (7) week. I've rehearsed / I've been rehearsing (8) for our new play since / for (9) days.

Alisha   Well, I've already / yet (10) spoken to Jordan and they're coming over later.

Meg   Alisha!

2 **Rory.** Jordan asks Conor about his best friend at home in Ireland. Complete the conversation.

Jordan   So, tell me about Rory. How long | you | know each other | ? (1)

Conor   We | be friends | nine years old. (2)

Jordan   Wow! So you | be | friends | six years. (3)

Conor   Yes, we have. He plays the guitar, too.

Jordan   How long | he | play | ? (4)

Conor   We | both | learn | about four years. (5)

Jordan   Always jazz?

Conor   No, I | only | be into jazz | a couple of years. (6)

3 **An interview.** You want to interview a celebrity for a teen magazine about relationships. Write eight questions using the present perfect or present perfect progressive and time words like *yet, already, for, since* and *all.*

Talking about fashion

4 **Shopping today**

a Make expressions connected to fashion.

1	fast	a	bargain
2	follow	b	fashion trends
3	look for	c	online
4	order	d	fashion
5	thrift	e	store

b Choose the correct form.

1 If Alisha **has / will have** time tomorrow, she will check out the new thrift store.
2 If she's lucky, she **finds / will find** a dress.
3 If Alisha **had / would have** more money, she would go shopping more often.
4 But **was she / would she be** happier?

5 **Shopping choice**

a Complete the blog with the correct words.

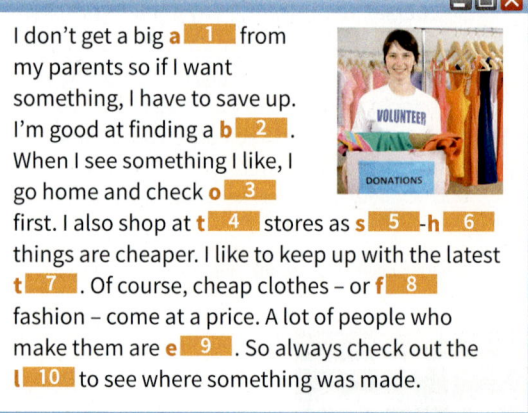

I don't get a big **a** 1 from my parents so if I want something, I have to save up. I'm good at finding a **b** 2 . When I see something I like, I go home and check **o** 3 first. I also shop at **t** 4 stores as **s** 5 -h 6 things are cheaper. I like to keep up with the latest **t** 7 . Of course, cheap clothes – or **f** 8 fashion – come at a price. A lot of people who make them are **e** 9 . So always check out the **l** 10 to see where something was made.

b Find the correct endings for these sentences.

> had more clothes ■ had the same problems ■ will go to the new thrift store ■ would have more money for vacations ■ wouldn't have so many clothes

1 If Alisha has time tomorrow, she …
2 If Meg had a smaller allowance, she …
3 If Meg didn't buy so many clothes, she …
4 Would Alisha be happier if she …?
5 Life would be boring if Alisha and Meg …

6 **A shopping survey.** Make a questionnaire from the prompts to find out about teenagers' shopping habits.

1 How often | check | labels?
2 prefer | shop | online | in-store?
3 If | have a choice | visit | a thrift store | a mall?
4 buy | fast fashion?
5 use | phone | compare prices?
6 keep up | latest trends?

Which of these sentences best describe you?
- If | want something | order | online.
- only buy something new | if | really need it.
- If | see | cool | buy | immediately.
- If | bigger allowance | still spend | everything.

Comparing city life and country life

7 **City or country?** Which words in the box are often connected to the city or to the country?

cultured ■ dangerous ■ hectic ■ laid-back ■
noise ■ not diverse ■ peaceful ■ rural

8 **Moving to the country.** Alisha's mom is talking to a friend. Complete the conversation with six of the words from the box in **7**.

Dana Just think how ▮1▮ it will be in the country.

Cindy I know, but I'm used to the ▮2▮ now. When it's quiet, I find it hard to sleep.

Dana Yes, most ▮3▮ communities are positively dead! Charleston is a really ▮4▮ place to live. There are so many places to visit.

Cindy That's true, but life in the city is so ▮5▮. I'm always rushing around.

Dana Well, I guess the country is quite ▮6▮, but I think I'd get bored.

9 **If you had the choice.** Where would you prefer to live – the city or the country – and why?

Comparing different school systems

10 **Another email.** Complete Conor's email with the correct form: gerund or *to*-infinitive.

Hi Rory,

So, school over here is different from back home. Firstly, we start at 8 a.m. You know I hate early mornings! My host family **offered to drive / driving** (1) me in, but one of my friends has a car, so every morning he stops **to pick me up / picking me up** (2). Of course, I enjoy not **to have to / having to** (3) wear a uniform! Most of the teachers allow us **to call / calling** (4) them by their first names, it's so relaxed. They expect us **to do / doing** (5) lots of homework, but I don't mind **to study / studying** (6) so that's OK. We can choose some subjects, so next semester I plan **to take / taking** (7) Spanish. A few students have asked me **to join / joining** (8) the soccer team and I'm quite excited.
Oh, I forgot **to say / saying** (9) that I won't be home for Christmas. My host family have asked me **to celebrate / celebrating** (10) it with them. Mum and Dad have agreed, so I'll be here until next summer.

Conor

11 **Advice from Santa Fe High School.** Read the advice for the students and complete it with the correct form of the verbs.

Dear students,
Here's some advice on trying ▮1▮ (*stay*) healthy and focused at school. We recommend ▮2▮ (*read*) these tips so you can concentrate better at school.
Avoid ▮3▮ (*drink*) coffee before bedtime.
Try ▮4▮ (*watch*) less TV in the evening.
Remember ▮5▮ (*set*) your alarm early to give yourself enough time in the morning.
Finish ▮6▮ (*do*) your homework before you start anything else.
Don't arrange ▮7▮ (*meet up*) with your friends on a school night.
Most doctors suggest ▮8▮ (*get*) at least eight hours sleep a night.

12 **Help your friend.** Your friend has a few problems with schoolwork. Write some advice.

TWO

What *is* the point of small children?
I understand (sort of) the point of the larger kind. For example: Solstice and Cudweed. I forget exactly how old they are now, but for some time I have had to
5 admit that they are actually quite fun. You can do things with them. For example, you can play games, like the game we play where they give me a rotten pear and then I fly high up into the air with the pear in my claws, and then drop it on whoever they point
10 at. I don't often hit anyone, but it's fun trying, and when I do, Cudweed and Solstice fall over from laughing too much. That's sweet.
And sometimes, large children, such as Solstice and Cudweed, can even be *useful*, which is a really
15 remarkable thing. For example, they sometimes clean my cage out (not that I ever spend much time in there – I don't like cages, and I only go in there when I am sulking, and on Open Sunday). And when we go on holiday, they carry my little suitcase. What does a
20 raven take on holiday, you ask? You'd be surprised!
Sunglasses, fancy[1] shirts, a book to read … In fact, anything *you* would take on holiday, with the
25 exception of sun cream. Ravens don't need sun cream.
Anyway, all this is
30 beside the point. The point is that I have never really understood the point of small children, and why adults seem to be so intent[2] on making new ones. So when the twins went missing[3], I really didn't see what all the fuss was
35 about.
First of all, everyone ran all around the castle (which takes a really long time) looking for Fizz and Buzz. And everyone was really upset, especially Minty, who kept bursting into tears. I even think Valevine
40 was a bit upset, too, because his eyebrows kept twitching and he said 'what, what?' about a hundred times every hour.

Because I know Fizz and Buzz well, I kept thinking that it was entirely possible that they were just having
45 a nap somewhere, probably inside a cannon. Or that they were hiding from us on purpose. But by dinnertime, even I had to admit it looked like they really were missing, because the twins do not miss dinner. Ever. That's one smart thing about them, at
50 least. As I said before, there is a way that big children become adults, and it is the same way that small children become big children. What you do is that you

give them food, and when you have done this for long enough, you will one day discover that they are big.
55 And the twins had really grown. They were no longer babies, only able to crawl about[4] on hands and knees. These days they could walk; and even run (sort of), and I liked them even less since then, because they could chase me and try to pull my tail feathers out
60 much more easily than when they could only crawl. That now meant there were *three* creatures trying to pull my tail feathers; the twins, and Cudweed's awful pet monkey, Fellah. Although Fellah wasn't around just then; he'd been sent away to monkey training
65 school. This is just like those places where they get dogs to behave better, only for monkeys. I don't know why they bothered[5], it was the fifth time he'd been sent there, it clearly wasn't working.

---

[1] **fancy** ausgefallen; originell – [2] **to be intent on** auf etwas bedacht sein – [3] **to go missing** verschwinden – [4] **to crawl about** herumkrabbeln – [5] **to bother** sich bemühen

Anyway, there was a big argument about what to do
70 next.
Valevine thought we should just keep looking, but
Minty said we should call the police. Cudweed
thought that was a very good idea (although mainly, I
think, because he thought it would be exciting if a
75 police car came to the castle). Solstice came over to
me and asked if I could organize a search party[6] of
ravens, crows and possibly other very much less
intelligent birds, (which is to say, all of them).
I said, 'Kronk', which meant 'well, I could do, but
80 maybe I could have dinner first?' because everyone
seemed to have forgotten all about eating. Everyone
ignored me.
There was even an argument about whether the
twins really were missing, and not just playing a
85 trick on us all[7]. But then everything changed.
Everything changed because Cudweed, who had
been searching for the twins in the kitchen came
back holding a letter. He also seemed to be chewing,
which made me suspicious about what he was really
90 doing in the kitchen.

'I was just walking back past through the hall, and I
saw this had been put under the front door,' he said,
waving the letter.
'What, what?' said Valevine, and Minty sighed.
95 She took the letter from her son and opened it.
Then she screamed, and then she fell backwards on
the floor.

Solstice grabbed the letter from her hand.
'It's a ransom note[8]!' she said. 'The twins have been
100 kidnapped! The kidnappers want a large amount of
money, and they say Edgar has to bring it to them,
alone, or we'll never see Fizz and Buzz ever again.'
Minty opened her eyes, sat up. Then she remembered
what had happened and fainted again.
105 Valevine's eyebrows rose up on his forehead as far as
I had ever seen them go.
'You say kidnappers,' he said to Solstice. 'What makes
you think there is more than one?'
Minty opened her eyes again, and sat up again.
110 'Do you think anyone could handle the twins on
their own?' she said.
'Good point,' said Valevine, and everyone nodded
thoughtfully.
Then Solstice said, 'Now we really have to call the
115 police!'
'Yes, you're right!'
Even Valevine agreed now, and went away to phone
the police, muttering[9] as he did, 'Scoundrels[10]!
Wicked villains[11]! Criminals!'
120 'Oh, what are we going to do?' cried Minty, and
Cudweed tried to comfort[12] her.
'Don't worry, Mother,' he said, 'The police will know
what to do. They *always* know what to do on TV.'
'Whoever the kidnappers are,' said Solstice, 'They
125 must have taken Fizz and Buzz during the time the
castle was open. Or maybe they were snatched[13] in
the gardens! It must have been some of the visitors
who did it!'
'Yes, you're right,' agreed Cudweed. 'If only we had
130 security cameras!'
'You know we couldn't afford them,' said Minty. 'And
now look what's happened! Oh! My poor little twins!
Will I ever see them again?'
Solstice said, 'Of course we will!'
135 And I said, 'Rork', which meant, 'Are we really sure it
wouldn't be okay to leave them with the
kidnappers?'
But everyone ignored me.
Then Cudweed said, 'I'm going to search in the
140 kitchen again. Just in case.'
Bless him, he always eats a lot when he's worried.

---

[6] **search party** Suchtrupp – [7] **to play a trick on sb.** jmd. einen Streich spielen – [8] **ransom note** Erpresserbrief – [9] **to mutter** murmeln – [10] **scoundrel** Schurke – [11] **villain** Bösewicht – [12] **to comfort** trösten – [13] **to snatch** schnappen

Science and technology

Great Modern Inventions That Changed the World

THE ELECTRIC LIGHT BULB

A

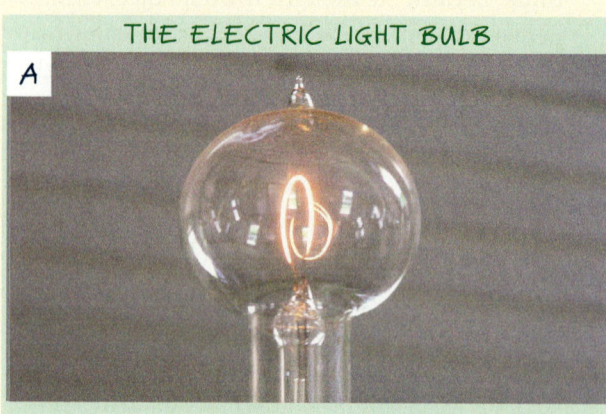

Thomas Edison patented the incandescent electric light bulb in ███.

SOCIAL MEDIA

C

The first social media platform was created as far back as ███.

SPACE ROCKETS

D

The Soviet Union launched Vostok 1 into orbit in ███. This was the first spacecraft to contain a person, Yuri Gagarin.

THE AUTOMOBILE

F

Karl Benz designed and built the first petrol car powered by an internal combustion engine in ███.

THE SMARTPHONE

G

The first smartphone was released in ███.

THE INTERNET

B

The internet first became available to the public in ▢ .

THE PERSONAL COMPUTER

E

The first personal computers were introduced in ▢ .

THE AIRPLANE

H

The American Wright brothers built and piloted the first powered airplane to fly successfully in ▢ .

1 Mina's class at Sterling High School has to present great modern inventions that have helped to change the world. Look at the inventions which Mina and her classmate Kate have chosen. Match the dates to the correct inventions. Then listen and check.

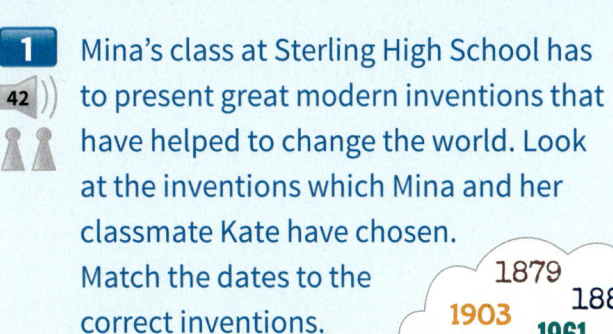

1879 1885
1903 1961
1991 1994 1977
1997

2 a Listen to Mina and Kate presenting 'their inventions'. What reasons do they give for their choices?

b Do you agree with their choices or do you have different opinions? Think of other important inventions.

c Share your ideas with the class and explain your reasons. Then take a class vote on the top five.

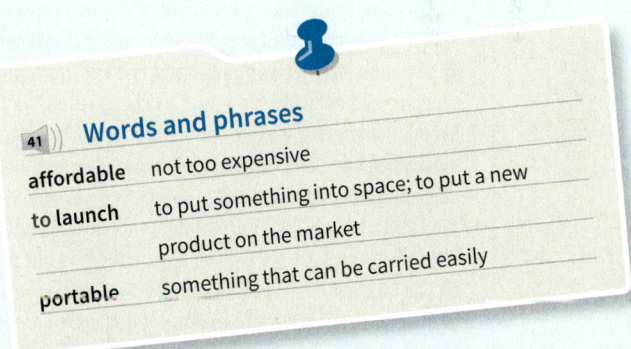

41 **Words and phrases**

affordable	not too expensive
to launch	to put something into space; to put a new product on the market
portable	something that can be carried easily

YOUR TRACK

After this workshop you will be able to:
- discuss past and future technological developments.
- talk about the climate debate and protecting resources.
- present arguments and discuss environmental issues.
- make predictions about the future.
- create and present a new product or service. (Workshop task)

Modern technology

1 Technology in everyday life

a Describe the picture and how technological developments have made life easier. Use words in the box to help you.

> dishwasher ■ drone ■ e-book reader ■ electric car ■
> flying taxi ■ game console ■ home robot ■ laptop/
> netbook ■ messaging apps ■ robot vacuum cleaner ■
> self-checkout machine ■ smart/digital TVs ■
> smart fridge ■ virtual reality headset

b List the items from the box under these headings: *Home, Entertainment, Communication/Information, Transport, Shopping*. Which ones already exist? Which haven't been developed yet?

2 The impact of technology

a Read the article. Match the paragraphs to the topics in **1b**. What inventions or innovations are mentioned?

How has technology changed our lives?

It's hard to imagine life before electricity was invented, before the automobile, the internet, the cell phone. Our lives today have been transformed by technology. But we take it all for granted!

5 ❶ Look around your home. Imagine taking away all the technology. Most homes didn't have electricity until the early 20th century, and household chores had to be done by hand. Today many household tasks are done by machines and appliances such as washing machines and dishwashers.

10 ❷ Since the internet was developed, the way we communicate, socialize and entertain ourselves has been revolutionized. Before the internet, people sent letters by post. Today email, messaging apps and video conferencing make communication quick and easy. Before the first search engines were launched in

15 the 1990s, people got information from books. People used to watch films on TV. Now, we can stream them to our phones! ❸ The internet has even changed the way we do our shopping. In the past, people went to real shops and were served by a shop assistant. Things were paid for in cash. Today, cashiers

20 have been replaced by automatic check-outs in many stores. Most goods are paid for electronically with a card or a phone app. And now we can shop online any time of the day or night.

Future trends

In the future, more and more devices will be connected to the internet and become part of the 'Internet of Things'. 25
❹ Our homes will be full of smart appliances that can be controlled remotely. Our smart fridge will tell us when to buy more food and order it online for us, our smart toothbrush will tell us if we've brushed our teeth properly.
❺ Developments in artificial intelligence (AI) will allow machines 30 to carry out many tasks that are now done by humans. Housework will be done by home robots. Autonomous drones will be used to deliver parcels to our doors. Human drivers will no longer be needed: self-driving cars and trucks will take over the roads. There is a downside, though. Many jobs will be lost as 35 more and more work is taken over by intelligent machines.

🔊)) **Words and phrases**

to **be on the move**	to go from one place to another
'**snail mail**'	the ordinary postal service, slower than email
to **socialize**	to spend time with people in your free time
to **take something for granted**	to accept something without questioning it

b Compare life in the past and present. Make notes and discuss with a partner.

	PAST	PRESENT
Home	people did chores by hand	machines / appliances make life easier

c Say how technology will change our lives.

1 Smart appliances will tell us …
2 Home robots will …
3 Drones …
4 Autonomous cars, trucks and flying taxis …
5 Intelligent machines …

3 **Past, present and future**

a Answer the questions. Find more examples in the article.

- How do we form the passive?
  Simple present and simple past
  Today many household tasks **are done by machines.**
  The first web search engines **were launched** *in the 1990s.*
  Present perfect
  Our lives today **have been transformed by** *technology.*
  Will-future and modal verbs
  Housework **will be done by** *home robots.*
  Many appliances **can be controlled** *remotely.*
- What happens in the passive when a verb is followed by a preposition?
  Verb + preposition
  People **paid for** *things in cash.*
  Things **were paid for** *in cash.*

TIP

- We use the passive when we don't know who or what does an action or when this information is not important.
- If we want to say who or what does the action in a passive sentence, we use a phrase with *by*.

b Rewrite the sentences using the passive to focus on the action. Use a *by* phrase if necessary.

Technology has changed the way we live.
The way we live has been changed by technology.

1 In the past, women did most of the housework.
2 The smartphone has replaced many older technologies such as cameras.
3 Today people pay for many things using a card or mobile phone app.
4 Thanks to advances in medical science, we can cure most diseases today.
5 In the future, robots will take over more jobs.

≫ page 100

4 **Then and now**

45 **a** Steven Price's grandmother is telling him about life when she was growing up. What does she talk about? Does she think life was better or not before?

45 **b** Listen again. Make a table and take notes.

Topic	Then	Now
Looking up information	???	???

c Check and complete your notes. Then compare your lives today with Steven's grandmother's life.

5 **YOUR TURN: The technology-free challenge**

a How can you do these things without using modern technology?
- find the way to a new place
- send a message to a friend
- check the spelling / meaning of a word
- watch a film / read a book / play a game

b Discuss which device or gadget you would find the most difficult to live without for a week.

I don't think I could give up …
If I gave up …, I wouldn't be able to / I'd have to …
I could probably live without … for a week.
I could … instead.

Grammar and structures

Passive: present, past, *will*-future and modals → G22
Today, most goods **are paid for** electronically.
The first web search engines **were launched** in the 1990s.

Our lives today **have been transformed by** technology.
Housework **will be done by** home robots.
Many appliances **can be controlled** remotely.

Practice: Technology – good or bad?

PART 1

PART 2

PART 3

1 **GET STARTED!** With a partner, make a list of all the things you couldn't do if you didn't have electricity.

2 **Living off the grid.** In the USA over two million people have chosen alternative off-the-grid lifestyles. Look at the pictures and what Lily Rae says. What does it mean 'to live off the grid'? Why did Lily's family choose to do it? Can you think of other reasons why people live off the grid?

Hi! My name's Lily. I'm fifteen years old and I live off the grid in Missouri with my Mom and Dad and my brother Tom, who's 12. We use solar power to generate our electricity, pump our water up from a well and use a composting toilet. Mom and Dad decided to go off the grid seven years ago. They wanted to live in a more sustainable way and become as self-sufficient as possible. So they quit their jobs in the city, bought an old barn with some land and started turning it into an off-grid home.

3 **VIDEO TRACK: Meet Lily**

6 **a** Watch Lily talking about her family's life off the grid. What's the purpose of her video? What topics does she talk about?

6 **b** How much do you remember? Write notes using the prompts. Then watch again to check and complete your notes.

lived in camper van before ...
use a hand pump to ...
also collect ...
don't have running water — carry ...
solar panels provide enough electricity to ...
heat and cook with ...
grow own ...; raise ... for food; stock up with ...
empty composting toilet ...
homeschooled: weekly lesson schedule ... school
subjects ...

7 **c** Watch the last part of Lily's video. How does she answer this question? What are the pros and cons?

So what do Tom and I think about living off the grid?

46 **Words and phrases**

Living off the grid

to **bring up children**	to look after children until they are adults	**running water**	water through pipes
to **generate**	to produce	**self-sufficient**	able to live without outside help
to **install**	to put something in so you can use it	to **stock up (with)**	to get a large amount of something to use later
to **raise animals**	to keep animals for food	**sustainable**	not causing harm to the environment

4 Website article

a You want to write an article about Lily's family and their way of life for your school's international website. Copy and complete the headlines to summarize the main information for your readers. Use your notes from **3b**.

Meet a family living off the grid in rural Missouri in a home they built themselves.

- Lily Rae's parents bought their Missouri land seven years ago.
- Water is pumped up from a well. Rainwater …
- They no longer have an electricity bill. Electricity …
- They eat what they produce on their land. Chickens and rabbits …
- Wood-burning stoves …
- Lily and brother Tom don't go to school. They …

By ontrack-gym.de REPORTER

b Now write the main part of your article. Start like this:

Lily Rae and her family are living their dream life off the grid in rural Missouri. Lily's parents bought … They wanted to have a more … The family lived …

 page 100

5 What do you think?

 **a** Discuss these questions in a small group.
- Is it fair to bring up kids off the grid far away from town or city life?
- Does this way of life prepare them for college / university / adult life / 'the real world'?

b Read the two comments, then write your own.

> **Comments**
> **Ruby from Boston**
> Those kids must be lonely without friends nearby. It'll be hard for them when they leave home to go to college or find a job.
>
> **Charlie from Chicago**
> I think the kids are learning how to think for themselves, how to analyse and solve difficult problems. They're really important skills for life.

6 Talking about changes

a Think about your school, neighbourhood or town. What changes have been made over the last few years? What improvements do you think should be made in the future? Make two lists.

Changes which have been made	Changes which should be made
The school buildings have been repainted.	The old school gym equipment should be replaced.

b What improvements do you think are most important / necessary? Rank your ideas in **a**.

c You want to convince the class that your top two or three improvements are important and necessary. Prepare and give a one-minute talk.

7 WRITING FOCUS: Life in the 20th century

a Interview a family member about life 30–40 years ago. How did they manage without modern technology? Look at your table in **4** on page 79 for ideas. Take notes.

b Use your notes to write another article in English for your school's international website.

c Exchange your articles and give each other feedback.

Inventions and innovations

1 Made in the USA – Three stories

a Here are three stories of American inventions and innovations. Look at the headings and pictures. What information do you get from them?

b Read story 1, do the tasks and compare your answers.

1 Outline the connection between the Frisbie Pie Company and Yale University.
2 Explain what students shouted and why.
3 Describe what happened to the first plastic flying disc after it was invented.

c One partner reads story 2, the other story 3. Write down three questions for your story.

d Read the other story and answer the questions.

2 A new thing

a Which story is the most interesting? Why?

b Compare how the inventions / innovations in the three stories were brought to the market. What similarities or differences do you see?

c No one had ever used polyurethane wheels on a skateboard before. Nasworthy's Cadillac Wheels were a new development – an *innovation*. Which of these technological developments was an invention and which was an innovation?

1 the car – the electric car
2 the laptop – the computer

d Think of further inventions and innovations.

3 The inside story

a Look at the sentence from the first story. It has two objects. Decide which is an indirect object and which is a direct object.

*A big toy company paid **him** a lot of money for his design.* (lines 15 – 16)

1 More than a pie tin

The story of the Frisbee began in 19th-century Bridgeport, Connecticut with the Frisbie Pie Company. The company's pies
5 were baked and sold in metal pie tins with the words 'Frisbie Pies' on the bottom. The company wanted the empty tins to be returned, but students at Yale University enjoyed playing catch with them. When a
10 student threw a pie tin to another student, he or she often shouted 'Frisbie!', because the flying tins could be dangerous. Years later, in the 1940s, William Morrison developed a flying disc made of
15 plastic. A big toy company paid him a lot of money for his design. The new toy was given the name 'Frisbee disc' in memory of the Frisbie pie tins. Of course, the rest is history.

2 Reinventing the wheel

Skateboarding didn't really become popular until the early 1970s. Before that skateboard wheels were made
5 of hard clay, so it was difficult and dangerous to do turns, jumps and other cool tricks with them. The smallest stones or gaps in the pavement needed to be avoided.
10 Frank Nasworthy was an 18-year-old who liked to skateboard. His friend's dad owned a plastics factory. On a visit one day, Nasworthy was shown some new roller-skate wheels made
15 of polyurethane, which is a flexible plastic material. His friend's dad offered him some of the wheels, and Nasworthy got an idea. He went home and put them on his skateboard. It was a eureka moment: with the new wheels he could move on his
20 skateboard better than ever before. Three years later he began selling his own Cadillac Wheels, the first polyurethane skateboard wheels. They soon became the standard for skateboards everywhere. Frank Nasworthy didn't invent polyurethane. He wasn't even the first to make wheels from
25 the material. However, thanks to his innovation, skateboarding was given a new breath of life.

- The passive form of a verb with two objects often begins with the indirect object.
  He was paid a lot of money for his design.
- Some other verbs with two objects are: *award, give, offer, send, show* and *tell*.
  Find one example in each story of similar passive sentences.

Words and phrases

clay	earth that becomes hard when dried
eureka moment	when a person gets a great idea or finds a solution to a problem
prototype	the first design of something
roller skate	a type of shoe with wheels on the bottom

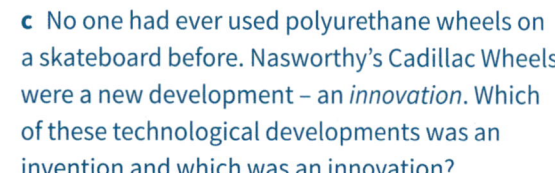

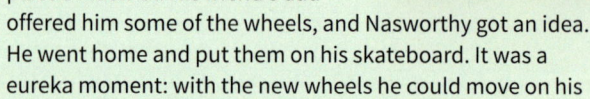

3 A bright idea

When disaster strikes somewhere in the world, people send food, water, medical
5 supplies, tents and clothing. Anna Stork and Andrea Sreshta, two design students at university in New York, saw another need: light. At night, disaster areas with no electricity become dangerous places,
10 especially for women. Hospitals also need light to function. The earthquake that struck Haiti in January 2010 left three million people without basic services. Stork and Sreshta wanted to design a product that could help. Their idea was an inexpensive, waterproof solar light that, when filled with air,
15 becomes a soft, bright lantern. The design is so simple, people don't need to be shown how it works.
Stork and Sreshta raised money for its development with an online campaign, and they tested their first prototypes in Indian villages. Since then, their solar lanterns have been used
20 in several disaster relief areas. Over 50,000 of them have been sent to social projects in 100 countries. The two young inventors have been awarded prizes for their bright idea which is helping to improve lives everywhere.

→ Workbook, pages 63/64

> **TIP**
>
> We sometimes use the **passive infinitive** construction after verbs like *hope, want, expect, need, like, love, hate* and *prefer*.
>
> *The company wanted the empty tins **to be returned**.*
> *The design is so simple, people don't need **to be shown** how it works.*

4 **At a technology museum.** Use these notes to complete part of a flyer for new museum guides.

Remember: students | need | give | time to explore the museum.
Remember: students need to be given time to explore the museum.

1 Most teachers | not need | remind | of this – they are happy if they can spend the afternoon in our museum café!
2 Some students | want | give | a guided tour of the museum – that is where we come in.
3 As guides, we | should expect | ask questions, so make sure you're prepared!
4 Don't forget: most students | not like | tell too many facts.
5 Other students | prefer | give | chance | look around on their own, but you should be there in case they have any questions.

b Look at these active sentences. Form passive sentences from them with the indirect object as the subject. Sometimes you have to change the form.

Our science teacher gave us a project –
to design something to help the elderly. →
We were given a science project – to design something to help the elderly.

1 Ms Rice showed the class a few projects from the previous year.
2 She offered the less creative students a list of project ideas.
3 After my presentation to all the science teachers, they told me the result.
4 They awarded me a prize for my design.

⟫⟫ **page 100**

5 **YOUR TURN: Tell me a story.** You are going to tell each other a story about a famous American inventor and his or her inventions.

8 **Student A:** Watch the video about Thomas Edison. Take notes to retell the story of this inventor. Watch a second time if necessary.

9 **Student B:** Watch the video about Hedy Lamarr. Follow the instructions as above. Then tell each other your stories.

Grammar and structures

Passive: verbs with two objects → G23
They showed an investor their new idea.
An investor was shown their new idea.
Their new idea was shown **to** an investor.

Passive infinitive → G24
They didn't **expect to be paid** so much for it.

Practice: The inventor's world

PART 1

PART 2

PART 3

1 **GET STARTED!**

a Many inventors and innovators share certain characteristics. Look at the characteristics in the box. Discuss the meaning of the words and phrases or look up any that you don't understand in a dictionary.

b Talk about why these characteristics are important in an inventor or innovator.

 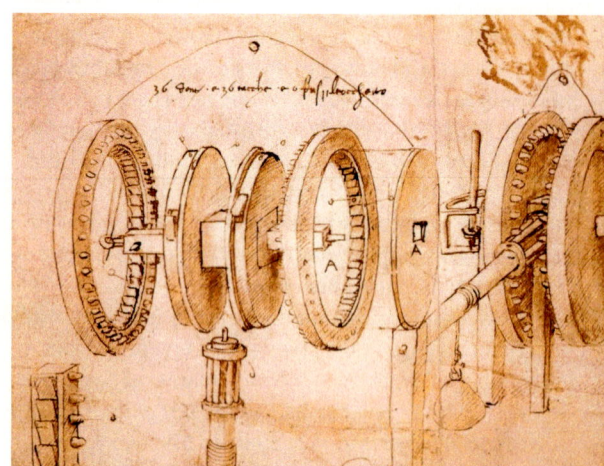

Leonardo Da Vinci (1452 – 1519) and one of his many inventions

can accept failure ■ creative ■ curious ■ innovative ■ problem-solver ■ self-motivated ■ team player ■ very energetic ■ willing to take risks

2 **VIDEO TRACK: Inspired by nature**

a Kavita Shukla is the inventor of a simple and natural product that offers an answer to one of the world's big food challenges. Look at the two images and say what they tell you about Shukla's invention.

10 **b** Watch the video, then discuss these questions.

- How did nature inspire Kavita Shukla as a young girl?
- What did she do with the inspiration?
- What was the final product?

c Which characteristics of an inventor (see **1**) do you think Kavita Shukla shows?

d Research and write a short biography of the inventor and businesswoman Kavita Shukla. Present your results to the class.

◄)) **Words and phrases**

48

curious interested in learning about things
failure not a success

3 **An inventor's dream.** Two young inventors have an exciting meeting with Mandy Lopez, a big investor. Write their story for the school's international website.

Ms Lopez's assistant sent us an invitation to meet her.

We were sent an invitation to meet Ms Lopez.

1 She asked us for our drawings and test results before the meeting.

2 When we arrived, her assistant showed us the new production site.

3 Then Ms Lopez invited us for lunch in a stylish restaurant.

4 Over lunch, she gave us the chance to explain our idea.

5 She asked us a lot of questions about the possible uses.

6 At the end, she offered us a fifty-thousand-dollar investment!

4 **LISTENING FOCUS: Invention Project**

a Listen to a talk about Invention Project, an educational programme in the US for middle-school students. Which of the adjectives below would you *not* use to describe it?

> challenging ■ creative ■ exciting ■
> expensive ■ fun ■ hands-on ■
> theoretical

b Listen again and answer the questions.

1 Who started the Invention Project?
2 How are the students helped when they're working?
3 What do students learn about in sessions 1 and 2?

c Look at the TIP box. Then listen again and note down the phrases from the box that you hear.

5 **Giving a talk about an inventor or innovator**

a Choose the person you want to talk about. The inventions on pages 76 – 77 will give you some ideas. Then do some research. Make notes about the person's life and most important work.

b Prepare your notes and materials. Use 'signal phrases' (see TIP box) to structure your talk. Make sure you include visuals (photos, pictures, etc.).

c Give your talk. Then give each other feedback.

> *I liked the part where you …*

> *You could also talk about …*

TIP

Identifying key parts of a talk
A well-structured talk has clear 'signal phrases' that help the listener understand the information. Here are some examples of signal phrases.

1 Introduce the topic
a My topic today is …
b I'd like to talk to you today about …

2 Describe how the talk is structured
a There are two main points I'd like to discuss: …
b I'll start by … Then I'll …

3 Introduce key information
a Let me first …
b First, let's …

4 Move to another main point
a Let's move on to …
b This brings me to my next …

5 Rephrase a main point
a To put that another way, …
b In other words, …

6 Introduce an example
a An example of this is …
b Let me give you an example of …

7 Conclude
a To sum up, …
b Finally, I want to say …

Method coach: Create a new product or service

S1 *Talented Teenagers*

 a The TV programme *Talented Teenagers* gives young people the chance to present their inventions and innovations. Listen to four adverts for new products or services. Match two of the ideas to the pictures. What problems do the other two ideas solve?

b Discuss how you think the other two ideas could work.

S2 **Choose an idea for *Talented Teenagers***

a Think: Think of a new product or service for the show *Talented Teenagers*. Start with these questions:

Is there …
- an everyday problem you or someone in your family has?
- a social or an environmental problem in your area?

Or do you need …
- help with something at home or at school?
- a new kind of game or other free-time activity?

 Pair: Go through your ideas with a partner. Inspire each other!

 Share: Share your ideas in a group. Talk about each one and think about these questions:
- Will other people want this product or service?
- Will they be willing to pay for it?
- Is there something similar on the market? How is your idea better?

 b Make a shortlist of the three best ideas. Discuss their strengths and weaknesses. Then agree on one idea that you think is the best.

TIP

Brainstorming effectively
- **Decide what your aim is.** What do you want to get out of your brainstorming?
- **Have a clear starting point.** In this case it can be the list of questions above, which focuses everyone's thoughts on the same input.
- **Think quantity, not quality.** Think of as many ideas as possible without analysing them. Be open to all ideas, even if they seem impossible or impractical. Evaluate them later.
- **Collect your ideas.** Have one person write all your ideas on an A3 sheet of paper. Or use sticky notes on a wall. Or do a placemat and collect the best ideas in the middle.

PART 1

PART 2

PART 3

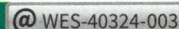
@ WES-40324-003

Workshop task: Write a plan for your idea

S1 **Two plans.** Look at the two plans below. Answer the questions for each product or service.

1 What problems or challenges does it solve?
2 Who will benefit from this idea?
3 Who will buy this product or service?

KEEPER

I Problem

When you are on the go, for example travelling to school or work or on holiday, there's always the danger that you will lose your bag or luggage. You might leave it somewhere or it might get stolen.

II Solution

Keeper is an electronic alarm system that protects your belongings. A small sensor alarm is attached to your bag or luggage. A special band on your wrist activates a GPS satellite connection. When you and your bag are separated, the alarm sounds and a GPS signal leads you to your bag.

III Market

This product is for all age groups because anybody can lose their bag. The wristband will come in different colours and styles for different fashion tastes.

FRIENDLY BOTS 4 HIRE

I Problem

Many elderly people are lonely and don't have enough contact with other people. This can lead to depression or other illnesses. Twenty per cent of the population is over 65 years old, and there aren't enough social workers to care for them.

II Solution

Intelligent robots that are small and cuddly are an effective alternative for elderly people who need a friend. The robots are programmed to react to human contact. But they are expensive, so most people can't afford them. Our solution is a low-cost rental service for homes for the elderly, hospitals, or private home visits.

III Market

Many elderly people live alone at home or in institutions. There is a large market for this service, which is cheaper than employing more social workers.

S2 **Write your plan**

a Divide the class into groups of at least three students. Each person in the group should write one of the three parts below. When you have finished, check each other's work.

I Problem: Describe the problem or need that you have identified.

II Solution: Describe your product or service and explain how it offers an answer to the problem or need.

III Market: Define who your customers are. How old are they? Are there a lot of them?

b **Gallery walk:** When you have finished, stick your plan on the classroom wall. Walk around and give feedback on the other groups' plans.

It's our planet, too!

1 **Join us!** At Sterling High School, the semester has just begun and the school clubs are presenting themselves. The first club is the Green Action Group. What could their focus be on?

2 **The Green Action Group.** Listen and decide if these statements are true or false.

1 This club was founded eight years ago to protest against river pollution.
2 The group sees no connection between local and worldwide problems.
3 The slogan 'Think and act globally' describes the Green Action Group.
4 The problems of climate change and plastic pollution have been solved.
5 The group needs more volunteers.

3 **A plan.** Read and answer the questions about the Green Action Group's second meeting.

1 According to Emilio, why didn't people come to the first meeting?
2 How does this week's meeting compare with the last one?
3 Why did they do an environmental review? What are the problem areas?

4 **Problems and solutions**

a The group discusses three aspects of the waste problem and how to deal with these. Copy and complete the table.

Problem	What to do about it
???	???

b Explain the German system Mina mentions.

Mina and Kate were walking to the science room after school. 'I hope this meeting goes better than the last one,' Kate said.
'Why do you think we only had one new member last week?' Mina asked.
5 'Emilio thinks our presentation was too serious,' Kate said. 'Maybe he's right. If our talk had been more fun, maybe more people would have come.'
'But how do we make pollution and waste fun?' Mina said.
Kate thought about it. 'Good question. When I think of a way,
10 I'll tell you.'
In the science room a group of noisy students was sitting and standing around. Kate and Mina looked surprised. 'Are we in the right room?' Kate asked.
'Yes!' Emilio called out from across the classroom. 'Can you
15 believe this?' he said. 'Eight new members!'
Mina turned to Kate. 'Maybe our presentation wasn't so bad.'
'We'll start as soon as everybody sits down!' Kate shouted.
Kate, the senior member in the group, was leading the meeting. 'Last semester we did something called an environmental
20 review. We wanted to identify what the school is already doing for the environment and what it could do better. We found two key problem areas where Sterling High School needs to become more sustainable. One area is energy – the school uses too much electricity. The other area is waste.'
25 'Waste. Do you mean like throwing away too much food?' one new member asked.
'That's one part of it,' Mina said. 'In October, when we did our review, the cafeteria threw away 400 pounds of food scraps.'
'Don't we have a compost bin?' another student asked.
30 'No. That's what we need,' Emilio said. 'If we'd had one, we could have used those food scraps for compost.'
'Another part of the waste problem is recycling. The school doesn't use the recycling bin enough. Too much paper and plastic and other food packaging lands in the garbage,' Kate said.
35 Mina shook her head. 'In Germany we have a system of different colored bins, one for each type of waste. It's very efficient. It's a shame the system in Sterling isn't more like that.'
'Wow,' said Kate, 'that sounds like a good system.'
40 'The third part of the problem is single-use plastic,' Emilio said. 'All the food packaging and the plastic forks and straws and stuff – it's all used once and then it's thrown away. Every day. And most of it can't be recycled.'
'Yeah, and too much of it goes into the Rock River, and then into
45 the Mississippi River and then into the ocean,' someone said.
'With food scraps and recycling it's clear what we have to do,' Mina said. 'But until we do something about single-use plastic, the waste problem won't go away.' Everyone in the meeting agreed.
50 'OK. We know where to start,' Kate said. 'Now we need an action plan.'

Words and phrases

The environment

environmental review	survey or report of how something affects the environment	**scraps** *(pl)*	food left after a meal
packaging	the material in which something is wrapped		

5 **An imperfect world**

a Look at the *if*-sentence type 3 that Kate uses to talk about the meeting and the presentation. Then answer the questions and find another *if*-sentence type 3 in the text.

*If our talk **had been** more fun, maybe more people **would have come**.* (lines 6 – 7)

- Think about what Kate says.
  – Was their talk fun? – **Yes / No**
  – Did many people come? – **Yes / No**
  – Did Kate describe something that happened? – **Yes / No**
- How do we form *if*-sentences type 3?
  – In the *if*-clause, we use the **present perfect / past perfect**.
  – In the main clause, we use ▬ + ▬ + the past participle.

b Kyle couldn't be at the first two meetings. Read what happened and what he thought later. Complete Kyle's other thoughts.

If I hadn't been ill last week, I could have gone to the meeting.

Kyle was ill last week, so he couldn't go to the meeting.

1 He missed the second meeting because he had band practice.
   I wouldn't have ▬ if I hadn't ▬.
2 Kyle wasn't at the meetings, so he wasn't able to ask any questions.
3 Kyle didn't talk to Emilio after their math class because he left quickly.
4 He met Mina in the corridor, so the group knew that he wanted to join.

 **page 100**

c Look at these situations. If you had been Mina, what would you have done?

1 Mina went for a walk. She didn't have a phone and couldn't find her way home.
   If I had been Mina, I would have …
2 Mina didn't enjoy her first football game because she didn't understand the rules.
3 On her first day, Mina went to the school cafeteria alone and sat at an empty table.

> **TIP**
>
> We use conjunctions like *when, while, until, before, after, as soon as* and *once* to introduce time clauses which describe a future activity without using the future tense.
>
> ***When** I think of a way, I'll tell you.*
> *We'll start the meeting **as soon as** everybody sits down!*

6 **Next steps.** Complete Mina and Kate's statements with the right verb form.

1 After we ▬ (*finish*) our written action plan, we ▬ (*show*) it to the principal.
2 We ▬ (*not be able to*) do anything until the school ▬ (*give*) us the green light.
3 I ▬ (*text*) the group as soon as I ▬ (*hear*) from the principal,
4 Before we ▬ (*start*) organizing things, Emilio ▬ (*talk*) to the kitchen staff.

7 **The Zero-Waste Lunch Challenge**

🔊 53 ** a** Kyle has joined the Green Action Group. Listen to him talk to Kate and Emilio. Why has the group chosen the Zero-Waste Lunch Challenge?

🔊 53 ** b** Look at the steps in the group's action plan. Listen again and put them in the correct order.

a Introduce the project to students and staff.
b Decide how big and how often.
c Measure how much waste there is.
d Build and improve composting and recycling systems.
e Inform the parents.
f Do the Zero-Waste Lunch Challenge.

Grammar and structures

If-sentences type 3 (revision) → G25
If Kyle **hadn't been** ill last week, he **would have gone** to the meeting.

Conjunctions with future time clauses → G26
We'll start the meeting **as soon as** everybody **gets** here.

8 **YOUR TURN: Your Zero-Waste Lunch Challenge.**
Discuss how you could reduce waste at home, at school or in your neighbourhood. Then present your ideas to the class.

Practice: Saving the earth

1 **GET STARTED!**

a Look at these three enviromental campaign slogans. Talk about the meaning behind each slogan.

b Which slogan do you like the most? Which one do you think is most effective? Explain why.

2 **Adults, wake up!**

a Read the article Kate wrote for the school newspaper and answer the questions.

1 What did the report by climate scientists in October 2018 say?
2 What sparked a wave of student action against climate change?

How we got here
by Kate Harris

In October 2018, a report by the world's top climate scientists warned that the world had to act in just 12 years to slow down global warming or face terrible consequences. Radical changes
5 were needed in areas such as energy, transport and food production.
A month later, a 15-year-old Swedish student named Greta Thunberg stood on a stage in Stockholm and spoke hard, uncomfortable truths
10 about the climate crisis. 'You would think the media and every one of our leaders would be talking about nothing else,' she said. 'But no one talks about it. There are no emergency meetings, no headlines, no breaking news. No one is acting
15 as if we were in a crisis.' Her tough message to the older generations, especially our leaders, was clear: *You've failed in the past. Now we need to act. Wake up and do your jobs.* Her words voiced the feelings of a whole generation.

Greta had already begun her own school strike 20 alone in front of the Swedish parliament to draw attention to the crisis. 'Why should I be studying for a future that soon will be no more when no one is doing anything to save that future?' she argued. 25
Student action against climate change had already been growing, but Greta sparked a fire. Soon students everywhere were organizing weekly demonstrations during school time to call for more action. Within a few months there 30 were demonstrations by hundreds of thousands of students in over 90 countries. This was the beginning of a new level of student action.

b Do these tasks.

1 Explain why the 2018 report had such an effect on Greta.
2 Describe how Greta succeeded in involving so many young people.

3 Compare her view of the future with your own.

 c Discuss these questions.

• How important is it for young people to speak out in the climate debate?
• How effective is it?
• What other forms of action do, could or should young people take?

54)) **Words and phrases**

consequence a result of something that has happened
to face to have to deal with

shortage when there is not enough of something

d Do you agree or disagree with this comment by a teacher? Write your own opinion. Then read out your ideas and discuss them in class.

It's good that students are active and demand more change, but this should never be done during school time. If students really want to make a difference, they should work hard in school and study for a job where they can help fight climate change. Students' voices should be heard, but school always comes first.

3 **Going green at home.** Mina's activism is having a positive effect on her host parents. Complete their statements with the right verb form.

We ▭ (*plant*) more vegetables when spring ▭ (*come*).
We'll plant more vegetables when spring comes.

1 Once we ▭ (*have*) our own vegetables, we ▭ (*eat*) less meat.
2 When we ▭ (*take*) our showers in the morning, we ▭ (*try*) to use less water.
3 Before we ▭ (*buy*) another appliance, we ▭ (*ask*) ourselves if we need it.
4 I ▭ (*buy*) a second-hand bike as soon as I ▭ (*get*) paid.
5 Until I ▭ (*get*) my bike, I ▭ (*drive*) less and ▭ (*take*) the bus more.

4 **Earth Day celebration**

a Read what happened when the Green Action Group organized a community event in Sterling to celebrate Earth Day. What went wrong?

On a warm Saturday morning in Kilgour Park, the Green Action Group members set up the stage and sound system. Mina organized the information table and Kyle helped with the food and drinks. The
5 group had posted flyers and asked their friends on social media to tell people about the event.
There were already a lot of visitors when the event began at 11 o'clock. A local band played music, then Kate made an announcement about
10 Earth Day activities. At 12.30 the small park was full and people were still arriving. Soon the last of the food and drinks were sold.
When the band got on stage again, Emilio turned up the sound.
15 The police arrived soon after the neighbors had complained about the noise. Kate apologized to the police. 'If we had been better prepared, this wouldn't have happened.'

b If you had organized the event, what would you have done?

I would have …
I wouldn't have …

5 **SPEAKING FOCUS: Stop global warming**

a Choose one of the posters and think of reasons why your poster is the most effective. Make notes. Discuss your findings with a partner.
● Discuss the strengths and weaknesses of the posters. The TIP box will help you.
● Agree on one poster that you could use for a global warming campaign.

b Explain your decision to the class.

> **TIP**
>
> **Discussing and presenting arguments**
>
> | **Agreeing or disagreeing** | **Taking turns** |
> |---|---|
> | I agree (but …) | Could I just say … |
> | I disagree. / I don't agree. | I'd just like to say that … |
> | I see what you mean, but … | Sorry to interrupt … |
> | That's a good point. | I'm not finished. |
> | You have a point, but … | Go ahead. |

Think of how much plastic ends up in the ocean. Use sustainable materials!

Say no to plastic! THINK – ACT – SAVE!

PART 1
PART 2
PART 3

Space adventures

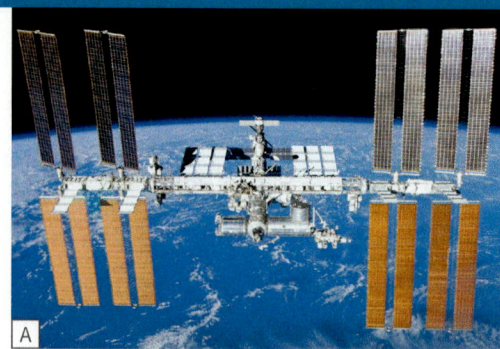

1 **Who wants to be an astronaut?**

a Look at the photos and match the captions to the images.

1 In 1969 Americans Neil Armstrong and Buzz Aldrin were the first men to walk on the moon.

2 The International Space Station (ISS) is a partnership between 16 countries. It was launched into orbit in 1998. It is used to carry out scientific research.

3 This Russian spaceship carries astronauts and passengers to the ISS. The cost is over $81 million per person.

4 Iranian-American Anousheh Ansari was the first woman space tourist to visit the ISS in 2006.

b Read the captions again. List all the vocabulary linked to space research. As you work through the rest of this section, add to your lists.

2 **The International Space Station.** Look at the questions about life in space. Then skim the extracts from Anousheh Ansari's space blog and find the answers. Which questions are not answered?

1 Where do you sleep in space?
2 How do you keep clean?
3 What do you eat?
4 How do you exercise and keep fit?
5 What do you do in your free time?
6 How do you stop things from moving?

Anousheh's Space Blog

September 25, 2006 Space Travel Details
Good hygiene in space is not easy! There is no shower or faucet with running water … There are wet towels and wet wipes and dry towels that are used for cleaning yourself.

September 25, 2006 Close Quarters
5 During the day everyone is pretty busy with specific tasks. At about 6.30 p.m. everyone gathers around the dining table. We heat up a few cans and hydrate some freeze-dried food and have a few laughs and share some space stories.

September 27, 2006 Thank God for Velcro
Weightlessness has wonderful advantages. You can fly and float around instead of walking, but everything
10 around you is floating, too. So God invented Velcro to keep things in place in weightlessness. Everything here has Velcro on it.

55)) **Words and phrases**

faucet	tap		
gravity	the force that makes objects fall to the ground	**to rotate**	to turn slowly
to hydrate	to add water	**weightlessness**	when there is no gravity pulling you down

3 VIDEO TRACK: A tour of the ISS

11 **a** As Commander of the ISS, Sunita Williams recorded a tour of the station. Watch the video to find the missing answers to the question in **2**.

b What else do you learn about life on the ISS? Ask and answer four more questions about life on the space station.

4 Space tourism.

Read this article and take a class vote. Will space travel have become a reality for most people by 2050? Are you interested in space travel? Why (not)?.

How to become a space tourist

In 2001, American businessman Dennis Tito became the first ever space tourist. His holiday cost $20 million. He was followed by six more private citizens. Although space tourism to the ISS ended in 2010, several private companies started developing spacecrafts. They predict that by 2050 attitudes will have
5 changed and people will have accepted space travel as normal.
However, according to a survey of US citizens, most people aren't interested in space travel because of the cost, danger and health risks. Fewer than half think space travel will have become a reality for ordinary people by 2050. In their opinion, space travel won't have happened before the end of the century as scientists won't have
10 solved the problems. It will remain an impossible dream for most of us.

5 Making predictions

a Read the example and answer the questions in the box.

*By 2050 attitudes **will have** changed and people will have accepted space travel as normal.*

- The verbs above are in the future perfect. How do we form this tense?
- We use it to talk about actions that will have been completed before a definite time in the future. What time phrases do we use?

b Use the notes to write predictions.

By the year 2050
- the Arctic ice sheet | melt
- humans | settle | on Mars
- the world's population | reach | 10 billion

By the year 2100
- many major cities | sink | under the sea
- robots | become | more intelligent than humans
- many of the world's languages | disappear

6 YOUR TURN: More predictions

a What else do you think will have happened by 2050? Copy the mind map and brainstorm ideas.

be banned ■ be cured ■ be replaced ■ become extinct ■ disappear ■ fly

b Now make a questionnaire and find out how many people in class agree with your predictions.

Grammar and structures

Future perfect → G27

One company **will have built** their own space station **by 2024**.
Space travel **won't have happened before the end of the century**.

Practice: Life on Mars

1 **GET STARTED!** How many planets are there? Can you name them all? This sentence can help you.

My **V**ery **E**ducated **M**other **J**ust **S**erved **U**s **N**uts

2 **What do you know about Mars?**

a Decide if these statements are true or false.

1 The nickname for Mars is the 'orange planet'.
2 Scientists have found proof of life on Mars.
3 It takes around eight months or 240 days to get to Mars.
4 The average temperature is – 81 °C.
5 Mars has rivers, lakes and streams and even an ocean.

57 **b** Listen and check. What else do you learn?

3 **Missions to Mars**

a Read the agendas of some government agencies and private companies. What have they already achieved? What will they perhaps have achieved by 2040?

NASA has already …
By … SpaceX / NASA / The Russians will have …

b Do you think these plans are likely to succeed in this time frame? Why / Why not?

4 **Martian pioneers**

58 **a** Listen to three young people who want to be Martian pioneers. Match the speakers to the correct reasons. There's one extra reason.

Dan

Sonia

Josh

Mars rover

The earth and Mars

2020: NASA launches Mars 2020 rover to test technologies necessary for human habitation.
5 **2022:** SpaceX lands cargo ship on Mars with equipment to prepare for human settlement.
2024: SpaceX lands four
10 vehicles on Mars, two with human crews to set up base.
2028: NASA sends crewed mission to moon to establish base for human
15 travel to Mars.
2030: China's space agency sends return rover to Mars to collect samples.
2033: NASA lands humans on Mars.
20 **2040:** Roscosmos, the Russian space agency, lands Russians on Mars.

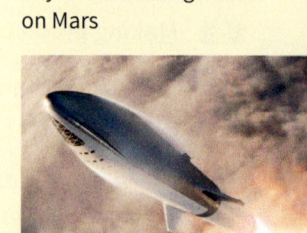
Sky crane landing a rover on Mars

SpaceX's Big Falcon Rocket

1 This person wants to improve life on Earth.
2 This person wants to be one of the first humans to live on another planet.
3 This person wants to make sure that the human race will survive if anything happens to Earth.
4 This person wants to set an example for other people and prove that Mars offers the chance of a new life.

56 **Words and phrases**

Success and failure

to **achieve**	to succeed in reaching an aim
to **establish**	to start or create
pointless	a waste of time

b Discuss the meaning of the words and phrases. Which characteristics are most important for pioneers? Can you think of others?

> adaptable ■ ambitious ■ have a sense of humour ■ optimistic ■ patient ■ resourceful ■ tolerant

c Listen again. Which of the characteristics in **a** does each speaker have?

d Discuss. If you had to choose just one of the volunteers, who would it be? Why?

5 **READING FOCUS: Should we explore space?**

a Read these statements and decide if you agree, disagree or are not sure.

A The money used for space exploration should be spent on more important things.
B Space research helps to improve our lives.
C It's better to send robots into space to do scientific research instead of humans.
D We should send people into space because it's human nature to explore new frontiers.

b Read the two articles. Which statements in **a** best summarize the opinions expressed?

c Are you for or against space research? Explain your point of view.

TIP

Recognizing degrees of certainty
We use various words and phrases to show how certain or uncertain we are (about something we write or say).

To show we are completely sure about something:
It's a fact that …
I strongly believe that …

To show we are almost sure:
It's likely that …

To show we are not completely certain:
It's (even) possible that …

---

6 **YOUR CHOICE: Interpreting a song.** Listen to two songs and choose one. Your teacher will give you the lyrics. In your group, discuss the message of the song. Present your ideas to the class.

In 1970, Dr Ernst Stuhlinger was researching the possibility of sending a crewed mission to Mars. A nun wrote to him asking how he could consider spending billions on such a project when children
5 were starving on Earth. In his reply, Stuhlinger told the story of a count who lived 400 years ago. The count gave most of his money to the poor. One day he met a man who had a little laboratory. He made small lenses from pieces of glass, put them in tubes
10 and used these gadgets to look at very small objects. The count invited the man to join his household and spend all his time perfecting his gadgets. The townspeople complained. They were absolutely sure that the count was wasting his
15 money. But he was right – the microscope has contributed enormously to the progress of medicine. There's no doubt that space exploration is playing the same role. It has already led to many new technologies and scientific discoveries.

Fran Bagenal, Professor of Planetary Science at Colorado University, thinks that sending crewed missions into space is unnecessary and pointless. She believes that scientific objectives can best be
5 achieved by using robots now that they are so advanced.
Bagenal is also totally against the idea of colonizing Mars. She argues that people will die on Mars and the entertainment industry could
10 even turn it into a reality TV show.
She points out that we can now explore the surface of Mars with Mars rovers using virtual reality. She's pretty sure that teenagers will find this more interesting than watching astronauts
15 moving around slowly in spacesuits.
According to Professor Bagenal, the only role left for humans in space is tourism. And the government should definitely not pay for that.

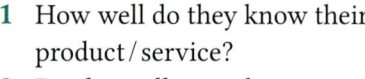
Method coach: How to present a product or service

S1 **VIDEO TRACK: Bad presentation, good presentation**

12 **a** You are going to watch a presentation for the product *Keeper* (see pages 86 – 87). First, look at the questions. Think about them while watching the video, then discuss the presentation and give your feedback.

13 **b** Now watch the second presentation for the service *Friendly Bots 4 Hire* (see pages 86 – 87). Think about the questions again. Compare the two presentations. Which one was better and why?

1 How well do they know their product / service?
2 Do they tell a good story about their product / service?
3 Do they use visual aids effectively?
4 Do they demonstrate their idea well?
5 Do they show how their idea is different?
6 Do they show how the customer will benefit?

S2 **Prepare your presentation**
You are going to present the product or service you created on page 87 to your class. Your presentation needs to be informative and entertaining, and it needs to 'hook' the audience. Look at the points in the TIP box. Are there any you wish to add?

> **TIP**
> **For a successful presentation, you should:**
> ● know your topic well.
> ● make it interesting, for example tell a story.
> ● keep it short (three minutes or less).
> ● use visual aids.
> **And if you're presenting a product or service, don't forget to:**
> ● demonstrate your product or service.
> ● show what makes it different.
> ● make it clear how the customer will benefit.

S3 **Practise your presentation.** Follow these steps when you practise your presentation.

> **STEP 1** Review your plan together. Make sure you know it well.
> **STEP 2** Decide on the roles in your group. Who will say what? Who will answer questions?
> **STEP 3** Look at the phrases in the TIP box.
> **STEP 4** Write cue cards. Prepare your visual aids and how you'll use them.
> **STEP 5** Practise your presentation, first with notes, then without. Work on speaking clearly and using positive body language.

> **TIP**
> **Useful phrases**
> *Have you ever …?*
> *Imagine that you …*
> *Picture this situation: …*
>
> *We want to show you how you can …*
> *We've come up with a solution: …*
>
> *Our plan is to …*
> *The best part about it is that …*
> *And that's not all, …*
>
> *People will want to buy our product / use our service because …*
> *Customers will love this because …*

 Words and phrases

Presentations
to **demonstrate**   to show how something works
to **hook**   to get somebody interested

Workshop task: Present your product or service

S1 Prepare to give feedback

a Look at this feedback checklist for the product idea *Keeper*. Then watch the video again.
Do you agree with the feedback?

Feedback checklist

Product / Service: **Keeper**

Presentation	0	+	++	+++
Knowledge of product / service		X		
Original / Creative presentation	X			
Visual aids			X	
Demonstration	X			
Speech			X	
Body language			X	
Timing		X		

Comments: *everybody spoke clearly; body language was good; shame they didn't prepare better; I like the product, I think people would buy it; the chip needs some work, but that's OK*

> **TIP**
>
> **Remember:**
> - keep eye contact.
> - speak loudly and clearly.
> - use positive body language.
> - be enthusiastic about your idea.

13 **b** Your teacher will give you a copy of the checklist in **a**. Then watch the second video again and complete the checklist for the product idea *Friendly Bots 4 Hire*.

S2 Present your product or service and give feedback

a Before you present your idea to the rest of the class, your teacher will give you another copy of the checklist to complete while you are watching the other presentations.

b Now give your presentation, remembering the advice in the TIP box.

c Talk about the presentations and give feedback. What did you like about them? What could have been better?

d Take a class vote. Which idea did you like the best? And was that also the best presentation?

> *I had the feeling you really know your product.*

> *The visual aids were very helpful. Maybe your demonstration would be better if …*

Mediation

1 **Marc Elsberg's novels.** Your English exchange partner Mandy is talking about the negative aspects of digitization at school. Her German teacher wants her to present a German book about this topic in class, but Mandy has no idea which book to choose. Your mother has four novels by Marc Elsberg. Read the information on each book and decide which book fits best. Tell Mandy in an email what this book is about and why she could use it for her presentation. You also tell her which of the other books you would like to read and why.

Helix – Sie werden uns ersetzen

Sie sind perfekt. [...] Sie werden dich ersetzen! Der US-Außenminister stirbt bei einem Staatsbesuch in München. Während der Obduktion wird auf seinem Herzen ein seltsames Zeichen gefunden –
5 von Bakterien verursacht? In Brasilien, Tansania und Indien entdecken Mitarbeiter eines internationalen Chemiekonzerns Nutzpflanzen und -tiere, die es eigentlich nicht geben kann. Zur gleichen Zeit wenden sich Helen und Greg, ein Paar Ende dreißig, die auf
10 natürlichem Weg keine Kinder zeugen können, an eine Kinderwunschklinik in Kalifornien. Der Arzt macht ihnen Hoffnung, erklärt sogar, er könne die genetischen Anlagen ihres Kindes deutlich verbessern. Er erzählt ihnen von einem – noch
15 inoffiziellen – privaten Forschungsprogramm, das bereits an die hundert solcher „sonderbegabter" Kinder hervorgebracht hat, und natürlich wollen Helen und Greg ihrem Kind die besten Voraussetzungen mitgeben, oder? Doch dann
20 verschwindet eines dieser Kinder, und alles deutet auf einen Zusammenhang mit sonderbaren Ereignissen hin – nicht nur in München, sondern überall auf der Welt ...

* Text verändert

Blackout – Morgen ist es zu spät [...]

An einem kalten Februartag brechen in Europa alle Stromnetze zusammen. Der totale Blackout. Der italienische Informatiker Piero Manzano vermutet einen Hackerangriff und versucht, die Behörden zu
5 warnen – erfolglos. Als Europol-Kommissar Bollard ihm endlich zuhört, tauchen in Manzanos Computer dubiose Emails auf, die den Verdacht auf ihn selbst lenken. Er ist ins Visier eines Gegners geraten, der ebenso raffiniert wie gnadenlos ist. Unterdessen
10 liegt ganz Europa im Dunkeln, und der Kampf ums Überleben beginnt ... *

* Text verändert

Gier – Wie weit würdest du gehen?

„Stoppt die Gier!", rufen sie und „Mehr Gerechtigkeit!".
Auf der ganzen Welt sind die Menschen in Aufruhr. Sie demonstrieren gegen drohende Sparpakete,
5 Massenarbeitslosigkeit und Hunger – die Folgen einer neuen Wirtschaftskrise, die Banken, Unternehmen und Staaten in den Bankrott treibt. Nationale und internationale Konflikte eskalieren. Nur wenige Reiche sind die Gewinner. Bei einem Sondergipfel in
10 Berlin will man Lösungen finden.
Der renommierte Nobelpreisträger Herbert Thompson soll eine Rede halten, die die Welt verändern könnte, denn angeblich hat er die Formel gefunden, mit der Wohlstand für alle möglich ist.
15 Doch dazu wird er nicht mehr kommen. Bei einem Autounfall sterben Thompson und sein Assistent – aber es gibt einen Zeugen, der weiß, dass es Mord war, und der hineingezogen wird in ein gefährliches Spiel. Jan Wutte will wissen, was hinter der Formel
20 steckt, aber die Mörder sind ihm dicht auf den Fersen ...

* Text verändert

Zero – Sie wissen, was du tust

[...] Wer sich im Netz bewegt, für den gibt es kein Entkommen. London. Bei einer Verfolgungsjagd wird ein Junge erschossen. Sein Tod führt die Journalistin Cynthia Bonsant zu der gefeierten Internetplattform
5 Freemee. Diese sammelt und analysiert Daten – und verspricht dadurch ihren Millionen Nutzern ein besseres Leben und mehr Erfolg. Nur einer warnt vor Freemee und vor der Macht, die der Online-Newcomer einigen wenigen verleihen könnte: ZERO,
10 der meistgesuchte Online-Aktivist der Welt. Als Cynthia anfängt, genauer zu recherchieren, wird sie selbst zur Gejagten. Doch in einer Welt voller Kameras, Datenbrillen und Smartphones kann man sich nicht verstecken ...

www.randomhouse.de

2 **The Soccket.** You belong to a school club which regularly produces podcasts about current issues. Today you are making a podcast about Jessica O. Matthews' invention the *Soccket*. Explain to your German audience how the *Soccket* works, its advantages, and how Jessica O. Matthews got the idea. Use the information from the article and the interview.

Jessica O. Matthews

Jessica O. Matthews has a degree in Psychology and Economics from Harvard University and an MBA from Harvard Business School. She is an inventor and the co-founder of *Uncharted Power*, an
5 award-winning company whose aim is to produce clean energy. The company has invented the *Soccket*, a soccer ball which can be used as a power generator. This ball uses the energy from being kicked to charge a battery. The power which is
10 generated in this way can, for example, be used to light a lamp for several hours. After being kicked for 30 minutes, the ball can produce three hours of light. This invention is a great help in developing countries where electricity is rare. At the moment,
15 the *Soccket* is produced in the US, but Matthews and her colleagues plan to move production to local companies in developing countries so that new jobs can be created there.
Matthews and her colleagues have invented
20 another eco-friendly toy for kids, which is called the *Pulse*. This is a jump rope, which also transfers kinetic energy that comes from movement into power. Matthews and her colleagues have used the same idea and technique from their other eco-
25 friendly products, for example sidewalk panels which harness energy from people who walk on them. In 2018, more than 500,000 *Soccket* and *Pulse* products were used in developing countries.
Jessica O. Matthews is a very successful business
30 woman. She has already been among the '10 Most Powerful Women Entrepreneurs' and was called

'Scientist of the Year' by Harvard University. She was invited to the White House by former President Barack Obama in 2012 and has appeared on the covers of various magazines and newspapers, 35 including *Forbes* and *The New York Times*. Our newspaper had the honour of interviewing this extraordinary woman. Here is the complete interview:

Journalist: Hello Jessica! Thank you for taking the 40 time to talk to us!

Jessica: No problem! I take every chance I get to spread my ideas about renewable energy.

Journalist: You use the fact that movement creates energy. What gave you the idea to invent a product 45 like the *Soccket*?

Jessica: I'm Nigerian-American and part of my family live in Nigeria. I was there at my aunt's wedding when I was 17 years old. Suddenly the electricity went off and diesel generators had to be 50 used instead. When I saw the fumes coming from the generators, I was sure that this couldn't be good for our health and I decided to do something about that.

Journalist: That's a great example of personal 55 experiences inspiring great solutions. What gave you the idea to create a soccer ball?

Jessica: I know that a lot of children in developing countries have to use eco-unfriendly kerosene lamps when they want to study in the evening. And 60 the same children often play soccer in their free time. So I asked myself whether we couldn't use some of this energy to provide a more eco-friendly and safer source of power for the children. In 2009, we invented the first ball which could store energy. 65

Journalist: That was a great idea! And you were able to solve a problem.

Jessica: That's right – isn't that what inventions should always do?

Journalist: I agree. Well, thank you for the 70 interview, Jessica. It was great to talk to someone who dedicates her time to solving electricity issues in developing countries.

Jessica: Thank you.

⫸ First track

3
p.79
b Find the direct object in the active sentence and identify the tense. Then rewrite the sentence using the passive to focus on the action. Use a *by* phrase if necessary.

Technology has changed **the way** we live.
(present perfect)
***The way** we live has been changed by technology.*

1 In the past, women did most of the housework.
2 The smartphone has replaced many older technologies such as cameras.
3 Today people pay for many purchases using a card or mobile phone app.
4 Thanks to advances in medical science, we can cure most diseases today.
5 In the future, robots will take over more jobs.

4
p.81
b Complete the report with the correct words.

> barn ▪ camper van ▪ groceries ▪
> homeschooled ▪ rainwater ▪
> self-sufficient ▪ solar panels ▪ stove ▪
> sustainable ▪ tank ▪ vegetables ▪ well

> Lily Rae and her family are living their dream life off the grid in rural Missouri. Lily's parents bought their land seven years ago. They wanted to have a more ⬛1 lifestyle and be as ⬛2 as possible. The family lived in a ⬛3 for a year while they were turning their ⬛4 into an off-grid home.
> They pump water up from a ⬛5 using a hand pump. They also collect ⬛6 from the roof in a big ⬛7 .
> They get their electricity from ⬛8 on the roof and they have a big wood-burning ⬛9 to provide them with heat. They want to be independent as much as possible for food, so they grow their own ⬛10 and they keep chickens and rabbits for food. But once a month they go to the nearest town and stock up with ⬛11 that they can't produce themselves, like rice, pulses and canned food.

> Lily and her brother Tom are ⬛12 . They have a regular lesson schedule during the week. They study the core subjects, including reading, math, social studies, languages and science.

3
p.83
b Look at these active sentences about a project. The indirect object is highlighted. Form a passive sentence with this object as the subject.

Our science teacher gave **us** a project – to design something to help the elderly.
We were given a science project – to design something to help the elderly.

1 Ms Rice showed **the class** a few projects from the previous year.
2 She offered **the less creative students** a list of project ideas.
3 After my presentation to all the science teachers, they told **me** the result.
4 They awarded **me** a prize for my design.

5
p.89
b Kyle couldn't be at the first two meetings. Read what happened and what he thought later. Complete his other thoughts.

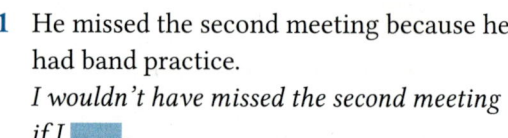

If I hadn't been ill last week, I could have gone to the meeting.

Kyle was ill last week, so he couldn't go to the meeting.

1 He missed the second meeting because he had band practice.
I wouldn't have missed the second meeting if I ⬛ .
2 Kyle wasn't at the meetings, so he wasn't able to ask any questions.
If I had been at the meetings, I ⬛ .
3 Kyle didn't talk to Emilio after their math class because he left quickly.
I would have talked to Emilio after math class if he ⬛ .
4 He met Mina in the corridor, so the group knew that he wanted to join.
If I hadn't met Mina in the corridor, the group ⬛ .

PART 1 PART 2 PART 3

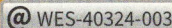 WES-40324-003

Extra reading

Extract from *Across the Universe* (2011) by Beth Revis

Amy is a teenager on a future Earth where plans are made to send space pioneers to a distant planet to start a new civilization. Amy's parents have been chosen for the mission. Amy has to make a huge decision: either join her parents in frozen sleep for the 300-year journey or say goodbye to her family and live on Earth without them. In this excerpt, Amy and her father are saying goodbye to her mother, who is being put to sleep by two workers, Ed and Hassan.

This was not the last image of Mom that I wanted. Her eyes sealed shut with yellow liquid, tubes crammed down her throat, a soft sky-blue color pumping through her veins. Daddy kissed her,
5 and Mom smiled a bit around the tubes. She gurgled something at me, and I leaned in closer. Three sounds. I knew the words she was trying to get past the tubes were, 'I love you.' [...] Ed and Hassan lifted up a large hose, and water
10 flecked with sky-blue sparkles filled the coffin-like chamber where she lay. [...] 'Just breathe it in,' Ed shouted over the sound of rushing liquid. 'Just relax.' The liquid covered her. Then Ed turned off the
15 hose. The water was still. She was still. Ed and Hassan lowered the lid over Mom. They pushed the box into the rear wall, and only when they closed it behind a little door on the wall, did I notice all the little doors in the wall, like a morgue. [...] One
20 second Mom was there, and the next, everything about her that made her Mom was frozen. She was as good as dead for the next three centuries until someone opened that door and woke her up. 'The girl's next?' Ed asked.
25 I stepped forward, balling my hands into fists so they wouldn't shake. 'No,' Daddy said. 'What?' I asked Daddy. 'I'm going next. Your mother wouldn't agree – she thought you'd decide not to come with us. Well,
30 I'm giving you that option. I'm going next. Then, if you'd like to walk away, not be frozen, that's okay. I've told your aunt and uncle. They're waiting outside; they'll be there until five. After they freeze me, you can just walk away.'
35 'But, Daddy, I –' 'No. It'll be easier for you to make an honest decision if you do it without facing us.' 'But I promised you. I promised Mom.' My voice cracked. Two hot trails of tears ran down my face.
40 'It doesn't matter. You have to make this choice yourself – if you want to stay here, I understand.'

'But you could stay here with me! You're not even important to the mission – you were with the military! How is a battlefield analyst going to help
45 on a new planet?' Daddy shook his head. His mind was made up. And it wasn't true, anyway. Daddy was sixth in command – that was pretty high up. Mom was important too; no one was better at genetic
50 splicing, and they needed her to help develop crops that could grow on the new planet. I was the only one not needed. Daddy undressed. He climbed into the cryo chamber and lay down. I stared at his face. I
55 watched them plug the two IVs in and then seal his eyes. Then Daddy squeezed my hand, once, hard, as they crammed the tubes down his throat, and I crumbled, inside and out. Before they filled his box with the blue-speckled
60 liquid, Daddy held up his hand, his pinky finger sticking out. I wrapped my own pinky around his. I knew that with it, he was promising everything would be okay. And I almost believed him. I cried so hard when they filled his cryo chamber
65 up. Then they lowered the lid, slammed him in his mortuary, and a path of light steam escaped through the cracks. 'So,' Ed said, 'are you going under, or are you leaving the party early?'
70 My eyes turned to the exit, past all the cryo equipment. Beyond that door were my aunt and uncle, who I loved, who I could be happy living with. And beyond them was Jason. And Rebecca and Heather and Robyn and all my friends. And
75 the mountains, the flowers, the sky. Earth. Beyond that door was Earth. And life. But my eyes drifted back to the little doors on the wall. Beyond those doors were my Momma and Daddy.

from *Across the Universe* by Beth Revis. London: Razorbill (Penguin Random House), 2011

My review

What can I do?

Look at these sentences about Workshop 3.
Are the sentences true for you? Choose the right symbol for each sentence.

1 I can discuss past and future technological developments.
2 I can talk about the climate debate and protecting resources.
3 I can present arguments and discuss environmental issues.
4 I can make predictions about the future.

> **»»** = 'I'm great at this!'
> **»»** = 'I'm good at this.'
> **»»** = 'I'm OK at this.'

What do I know?

1 **About technological developments.** Complete this talk about technological developments with the correct form of the verbs in brackets.

> Over the past thirty years or so our lives **1** (*transform*) by fast changes in technology. Nowadays, things such as heating and lights **2** (*control*) remotely using devices like our phones that **3** (*connect*) to the internet. Fridges that order our food **4** (*invent*), and, in the future, more and more chores **5** (*do*) using technology. Many jobs **6** (*already lose*) in places like big supermarkets as certain functions **7** (*take over*) by machines. When the first smartphones **8** (*launch*) in 1994, more than 50,000 **9** (*sell*) in just six months. However, these phones had black and white screens, batteries that lasted only one hour and they cost more than $1,000! Today phones **10** (*use*) for all sorts of things from connecting to the internet to paying for a coffee with an app.

■ / 10

Passive present, past, *will*-future and modals → G 22 ;
pp. 78 – 79

2 **About the climate.** Complete the sentences for each situation.

1 Mina didn't enjoy her lunch so she threw the food away.
If Mina **1** *her lunch, she* **2** *the food away.*
2 Kate forgot to say when the next meeting was. Nobody came.
If Kate **3** *to say when the next meeting was, lots of people* **4** .
3 Until recently people used a lot of plastic. They didn't know it is bad for the environment.
If people **5** *how bad plastic is for the environment, they* **6** *so much.*
4 Mina wanted to show a video about climate change at the meeting. Unfortunately, she left her laptop at home.
If Mina **7** *her laptop at home, she* **8** *a video at the meeting.*
5 Kate's last presentation to the Green Action Group didn't go well because she didn't prepare properly.
If Kate **9** *her presentation properly, it* **10** *better.*

■ / 10

***If*-sentences type 3 → G 25 ; pp. 88 – 89**

3 **About presenting and discussing arguments.**
Kate and Emilio are talking to a new member of the Zero-Waste group, Paul. Complete the conversation with the phrases in the box. There are two extra phrases you don't need.

> could I just say ■ exactly ■ go ahead ■
> I agree with ■ I don't agree ■ I'd just like to
> say ■ I'm not finished ■ sorry to interrupt,
> but ■ that may be, but ■ that might
> be true ■ you have a point

Kate	The most important thing is to stop using single-use plastics.
Paul	**1** you, but I don't see how it can be done. I mean it's so difficult to …
Emilio	**2** that's part of the problem.
Paul	What is?

Emilio	Negative attitudes. We need to be positive.
Kate	⬛ 3 ⬛. Emilio's right. The first thing we need to do is look at what single-use plastics we use in our daily lives …
Paul	I'm afraid ⬛ 4 ⬛. Will that really make a difference?
Kate	Sorry, but ⬛ 5 ⬛. Can I continue with my point?
Paul	Sure. ⬛ 6 ⬛.
Kate	When we go shopping, we try to buy products that aren't wrapped in plastic. It's not necessary.
Paul	⬛ 7 ⬛ it is so convenient and even if we stop buying packaged food, it isn't going to be enough.
Emilio	⬛ 8 ⬛, but we have to start somewhere.
Paul	OK. ⬛ 9 ⬛. Next time I go shopping with my parents, I'll ask them to do the same.
Kate	Great. That's a start.

■ / 9

Agreeing and disagreeing: pp. 90 – 91
Taking turns: pp. 90 – 91

4 **About the future.** Kate finds an article about climate change and predictions about the future on the internet. Read the article and choose the correct phrases to complete it.

Our planet is in crisis. If we don't do something immediately, then we **will face / will be faced** (1) with a completely different world. Unless we become carbon neutral, the situation **will be / will have been** (2) catastrophic.
Models show that by 2100 sea levels **will rise / will have risen** (3) by between 20 and 50 cm. Such a rise **will mean / will have meant** (4) that by 2100 cities such as Bangkok, Shanghai, Miami and London **will disappear / will have disappeared** (5) under water. Even by 2050 flooding **will have / will have had** (6) a terrible impact on many places. Some people say that experts are exaggerating the situation and that many of their predictions **won't happen / won't have happened** (7), but I'm not sure that we should risk it. After all, they are the experts!

We can already see that our weather is changing, and by 2050 most of us **will experience / will have experienced** (8) extreme weather conditions that we usually associate with places in Africa or the Arctic Circle. Today around a billion people fight against hunger, that's one in six people! By the end of this year around 36 million **will die / will have died** (9) because they didn't have enough food. By 2050 this situation **will become / will have become** (10) far worse, with many parts of the world not able to grow crops to feed people. Of course, some scientists say that by then we **will find / will have found** (11) new ways of producing food, but nobody can be sure.

■ / 11

Future perfect → ⬛ G 27 ⬛ **; pp. 92 – 93**

■ / 40

What's my score?

Check your answers to the review (Workbook, p. 82). What are your scores for each section?

What was your total score?
⟫⟫⟫ score 31 – 40
⟫⟫⟩ score 21 – 30
⟫⟩⟩ score 0 – 20

Do you want to change your answers to the 'What can I do?' statements on page 102? Look at the tasks on pages 104 – 105: ⟫⟫⟫, ⟫⟫⟩ and ⟫⟩⟩. Choose the tasks to help you.

My practice pages

Talking about technology

1 **Talking technology.** Choose the correct phrases to complete the sentences.

1 Millions of purchases **are made / have been made** using credit cards every day.
2 In recent years, a lot of jobs in this factory **are replaced / have been replaced** by robots.
3 One company says that in the future all their parcels **are delivered / will be delivered** by drones or driverless vehicles.
4 Smartphones **were invented / have been invented** in the 1990s.
5 The heating in our house **is controlled / has been controlled** by a phone app.
6 The electric car **was invented / has been invented** in 1884.

2 **Kids talk technology.**
Complete the conversations with the correct form of the verbs.

Kate   My dad bought an electric car last week.

Emilio   Aren't you worried about the battery going flat?

Kate   Not really. Over the last few years big improvements **1** (*make*).

Emilio   I still think it's better to wait a few years until the costs **2** (*reduce*) a lot.

Mina   Why did Emilio get zero for his assignment?

Kate   Because the text **3** (*download*) from the internet.

Mina   But how did the teacher know that?

Kate   Apparently the same text **4** (*already hand in*) by three other students this week!

Mina   What's 'snail mail'?

Emilio   That means letters, etc. that **5** (*send*) by post.

Mina   Can you imagine having to wait days for a reply to a message?

Emilio   No, I can't. All the messages I sent out this morning **6** (*already answer*).

3 **Technology changes.** Use the prompts to write sentences about how technology has changed and will change our lives.

1 Transport | by the invention of flying taxis
2 Communication | by the introduction of lots of messaging apps
3 Most household appliances | by remote controls
4 Shopping | easier by using a self-checkout system
5 Entertainment | when the first game consoles | introduced

Talking about the climate

4 **Action! Action!** Complete these sentences with the correct form of the verbs in brackets.

1 If you ▨ (*send*) me the petition yesterday, I would have signed it.
2 If people had known how harmful plastic was, they ▨ (*discuss*) banning it sooner.
3 If we ▨ (*not ignore*) the signs of global warming for so long, there wouldn't have been so many demonstrations in 2019.
4 If had known this bag was made of plastic, I ▨ (*not buy*) it.
5 If I had taken the train last summer, it ▨ (*be*) more expensive than flying.

5 **A Green Action Group meeting.** Complete the conversation with the correct form of the verbs.

Kate   Hi everyone, I'm so happy to see so many new people here today.

Mina   Yes, if we **1** (*know*) there would be so many new people we **2** (*book*) a bigger room.

Kate   Unfortunately, the action plan we discussed at our last meeting isn't ready yet. If we **3** (*finish*) it, we **4** (*bring*) it with us today and presented it.

Kyle   Okay, but we can't wait and do nothing. I have some questions which I **5** (*ask*) at the last meeting if I **6** (*be*) there.

Kate   That's fine. After this meeting, we're seeing the school principal.

Kyle   Oh. If I **7** (*realize*) that was the plan, I **8** (*email*) you my questions.

Kate   That's not a problem, Kyle. I'll make a note of your questions now.

6 **Life in the past.** Imagine you had been born fifty years ago. Write five sentences about what your life might have been like. Think about technology.

If I had been born fifty years ago, I wouldn't …
If I hadn't …

Presenting arguments

7 **My smartphone.** Choose the correct phrases to complete the conversation.

Emilio	I think the most important invention ever is the internet.
Kate	I'm sorry, but I **agree / don't agree** (1).
Emilio	Why not? It's great for finding out about things.
Kate	Yes, you **disagree / have a point** (2) but there are other ways to find information.
Emilio	That **might / might not** (3) be true, but the internet is so convenient.
Kate	I **agree / don't agree** (4), but there are more important inventions.
Emilio	What?
Kate	**Could I just say / I'm not finished** (5).
Emilio	Sorry, **go ahead / that's a good point** (6).
Kate	Don't you think electricity is a more important invention? Without electricity the internet wouldn't work.
Emilio	**I see what you mean / That may be** (7).

8 **Space adventure.** Complete the conversation with phrases presenting arguments.

Kyle	Why are we spending so much money on going into space?
Emilio	Because it's really important.
Kyle	I'm sorry, but I just **1** .
Emilio	We might have to live on the moon or another planet in the future.
Kyle	That **2** , but it's more important to spend money on saving our planet.
Emilio	That's **3** , but I still think we should invest in exploring space.
Kyle	I'm afraid I **4** . I think it's a complete waste of money. There are …
Mina	Sorry **5** , but I **6** with Emilio.
Kyle	I **7** . Surely there are lots more important things.
Mina	Can you give some examples?
Kyle	Sure, climate change, homelessness, …
Mina	I see **8** , but I still think Emilio is right.

9 **A conversation.** Kyle and Mina are discussing environmental slogans, but they don't agree. Complete the conversation with at least five exchanges.

Mina	I think we should use the slogan 'If you can't reuse it, refuse it'.
Kyle	I'm sorry, but I …

Talking about the future

10 **Predicting the future.** Complete the conversation between Kyle and Emilio with the correct form of the verbs in brackets.

Kyle	I'm fascinated by the future.
Emilio	I know, I think it'll be really exciting.
Kyle	So what do you think life will be like in 30 years' time?
Emilio	Well, by 2050 I think the population of the planet **1** (*reach*) 10 billion.
Kyle	True. Do you think people will live on the moon in the next 50 years?
Emilio	No, I don't think so. We **2** (*not invent*) the technology for that.
Kyle	Well, I hope that by then we **3** (*solve*) the problem of food supplies.
Emilio	Don't worry, by 2050 scientists **4** (*work out*) a way to feed the population.
Kyle	Really? I think by 2050 millions of people **5** (*die*) from hunger.
Emilio	Don't be so pessimistic!

11 **Into the future.** Use the prompts to write predictions about the future.

By 2050 …
1 special crops | develop | to feed everyone
2 humans | settle | Mars
3 space tourism | become popular
4 most jobs | replace | by robots
5 sea levels | risen | by more than 20 cm
6 more than 1 million driverless cars | sell

12 **Future predictions.** Choose three topics from the box and write three predictions for the future.

By 2030 … / By 2050 … / By 2100 …

communication / information ■ entertainment ■ food / shopping ■ home ■ transport

THREE

The kidnappers' note asked for a lot of money. This was a problem, because, as I said earlier, the one thing the Otherhands do not have much of, is money.

'But we're not going to pay them anyway, are we?'
5 asked Cudweed. 'That would be wrong.'

'It may be the *wrong* thing to do,' said his mother, 'but it might be the *only* thing to do! Just imagine if the police can't help.'

'I'm sure they can,' said Solstice, but I think she said
10 that more to make Minty feel better than because she believed it herself. As it turned out, she was probably right about the police.

Before they arrived, Valevine kept checking the amount of
15 money the kidnappers had asked for.

'One hundred thousand pounds ...' he said. 'Hmm. Minty, my dear, how
20 much do we have?'

£100,000 or else!

Minty blinked.

'You mean all the money we have in the world?'

'Yes, that's what I mean.'

'Well,' she said. 'We have today's takings from Open
25 Day.'

'And how much is that?'

'About sixty-two pounds.'

'So, we're a little short then?' asked Valevine.

'Yes, dear,' said Minty. 'About a hundred thousand
30 pounds short.'

'Children!' cried Valevine.

'Yes, father?' said Solstice and Cudweed.

'Go and check your piggy banks[1]. Right now! See if either of you have one hundred thousand pounds,
35 will you?'

Everyone ignored Valevine, because he was clearly losing his mind.

'Don't worry,' said Solstice, 'the police will be here soon.' And just as she said that, the doorbell rang and
40 it was, indeed, the police.

'Now everything will be all right,' she said, and went off to let them in.

A few minutes later Solstice returned with a policeman. Just one.

45 He was a short, skinny chap[2], so short that his uniform seemed to be too big for him. The bottoms of his trousers hung so low they dragged[3] on the floor, and his hat kept slipping down over his eyes.

'Where are the rest of you?' said Valevine.

50 'Hmm?' he said. It appeared that the police station had only sent one police officer. Not only that, they had sent one of their most stupid police officers. He took a notebook out of his pocket, and a pen, and began asking questions. But they were very stupid
55 questions.

'So,' he said, thinking hard, 'your twins have gone missing, am I right?'

'Yes, we told you that on the telephone!' said Minty.

'And you think they have been kidnapped? Why do
60 you think that?'

'Because we have had a ransom note from the kidnappers! We told you that, too!'

The policeman looked rather sternly[4] at Minty.

65 'And you don't think, for one minute, that perhaps your little twins are just playing a trick on you, and sent you the note themselves?'

Minty lost her temper[5].

70 'No, I do not! They are four years old! They can't even spell their own names. Do you think they can write a ransom note?'

75 The policeman looked unimpressed by this logic.

'When you've been a police officer as long as I have ...' he began, to which Valevine replied, 'Exactly how
80 long have you been a police officer?'

The policeman looked confused.

'What day is it?' he asked.

'Sunday,' said Cudweed. 'Why?'

'In that case, three weeks,' he said.

85 'Still waiting for the right size of uniform.'

Valevine looked as if he was about to explode.

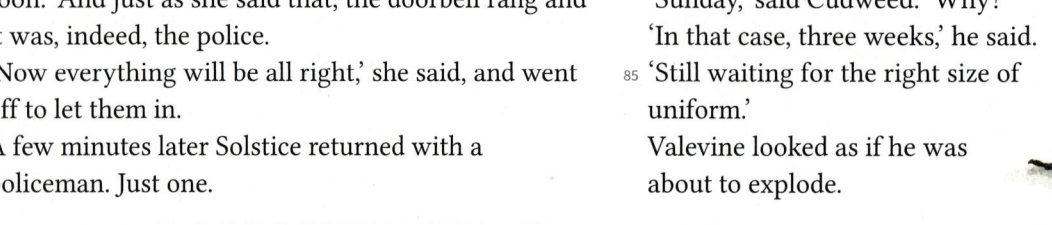

---

[1] **piggy bank** Spardose – [2] **chap** Kerl – [3] **to drag** schleifen – [4] **sternly** streng – [5] **to lose one's temper** die Geduld verlieren

'Three weeks! What use is this idiot?'

90 'Now, sir,' said the policeman, 'I will ask you to watch your behaviour towards an officer of the law.'

'Poppycock[6]!' declared Valevine. 'Officer of the law? A cabbage would be more useful!'

Now, at least someone was talking about food, which 95 seemed a good thing to me, even if ravens only eat cabbage in an emergency; the sort of emergency where there is nothing else to eat.

Anyway, at this point, I started paying attention again, because maybe we could turn 'cabbage' into 100 'dried mouse', and then I really would feel like eating something.

None of this happened however, because just then, as Valevine was talking 105 about cabbages, the doorbell rang again. Solstice ran off to see who it 110 was, and then five minutes later (it's a long way to the door), she came running back, with another letter in her hand.

'It must have been the kidnappers again!' she said. 115 'They were right here!'

She looked at the policeman.

'Well? Aren't you going to chase after them and see if you can arrest them?'

'Maybe,' he said. 'In a while.'

120 'But the longer you wait, the more time they –'

'What does the note say?' he asked, interrupting.

Solstice read it.

'Oh my God!' the note said. 'How do you put up with them for five minutes? It's unbearable[7]. You can have 125 them back. You don't need to give us one hundred thousand pounds after all.'

'Hooray!' shouted Cudweed, but Solstice hadn't finished reading the note.

'You can have them back,' the note added, 'on one 130 condition. We will swap your children for the big raven. He can meet us on the old scary bridge in the forest at midnight.'

'Krark?' I said, which meant 'Raven? *Big* raven? Do they mean me? I've been on a diet recently.'

135 'Let me get this right,' said Valevine. 'The kidnappers originally wanted one hundred thousand pounds. But now, they're happy to forget all that if we give them Edgar instead? That doesn't make any sense!'

'No,' said Minty, 'maybe not, but it seems like a pretty 140 good deal to me.'

And then, everyone turned to look at me.

They didn't say anything, but they didn't have to. It was clear what they were thinking.

What I was thinking was, 'are we sure we can't just 145 let them keep the twins?'

But it was no good[8].

Solstice came over to me and looked into my eyes for so long I thought I might melt.

'Kruk,' I said, very quietly, which meant, 'okay, but I 150 am really not happy about this.'

So that was how I found myself sitting on the old scary bridge in the forest at midnight, waiting to meet the kidnappers.

---

[6] **poppycock** Schnickschnack; Unsinn – [7] **unbearable** unerträglich – [8] **it was no good** es hat nichts genützt

Workshop 4

Looking forward

1 Name the jobs in the pictures. The words in the box can help you. Can you say what people in these jobs do?

An archeologist digs up and studies ancient buildings and objects.

> archaeologist ■ judge ■
> librarian ■ lifeguard ■
> photographer ■ surgeon ■
> video game designer

A

B

C

D

F

E

2 **63**)) **a** Listen to three people talking about their jobs. What subjects did they like at school and what jobs do they do now?

63)) **b** Listen again. Correct any of the statements below which are false.

1 Most of James' work now is at the theatre.
2 Jenny's company specializes in smaller buildings.
3 Travis has fulfilled his childhood dream.

 64)) **c** At the end of the interview, two of the speakers mention negative aspects of their jobs. Discuss what you think these could be, then listen and check.

d Explain why you could or couldn't imagine doing these jobs.

G

YOUR TRACK

After this workshop you will be able to:
- talk about your dream job.
- discuss part-time / summer jobs and interviews.
- decide what kind of volunteer work would suit you.
- give information about children's rights.
- make a short documentary film. (Workshop task)

PART 1

Dream big

1 **What do you want to be when you grow up?**

🔊 66

a Read and listen to some of the answers that American kids gave to this question.

b What's your answer to the question? Why do you dream of having that job?

> I love building things. I've always dreamed of becoming an architect.

> I'm really interested in helping animals that are treated badly.

> First, I had the idea of studying medicine, but then I changed my mind. Now I'm thinking about becoming a pilot because it'll give me the opportunity of travelling round the world.

> My schoolwork isn't great and I'm not very keen on studying. But I'm really good at drawing. Do you think I have any chance of getting a job as a comic book artist?

PART 2

2 **What do they do?**

👥

a Look at the people in the pictures. Decide what kind of jobs you think they do.

b Each read about one of the jobs. Then tell your partner what you have found out.

PART 3

Career Spotlight

This week's spotlight is on two very different career ideas.

Do you like to spend a lot of time by the ocean? You could think about becoming a professional surfer or a lifeguard. Or, if science is your thing, how about becoming a marine biologist? There are lots of good reasons for choosing this
5 career. Read on to find out more about this exciting job.

Marine biologists study the animals and plants that live in the ocean. In addition to becoming experts in aquatic plants and animals, they try to find solutions to different problems. They may specialize in studying plastic pollution in the oceans, or
10 be involved in creating special reserves for marine animals.
A big attraction of the job is that you have the chance of working outdoors. But marine biologists also spend a lot of time in the laboratory studying the results of a field trip.

If you're interested in becoming a marine biologist, you need to focus on science and maths at school. Also, look for volunteer jobs that will allow you to work with plants and animals. It's a popular career
15 choice because many people are passionate about saving the environment, so a volunteer job will help you to stand out from the crowd. Or would you prefer to be your own boss? What are the advantages and disadvantages of having your own business?

🔊 65 **Words and phrases**

Career choices

attraction	what makes people want to do something		
to **change your mind**	to make a new decision	**keen on**	very interested in
to **delegate**	to allow somebody else to make decisions	**passionate about**	feel strongly about
		to **range from … to**	to include several different things

If you have great ideas for new products or services, perhaps you could set up your own successful business one day. The possibilities
20 are endless and range from starting your own catering service to developing new apps.

Finding the right team is key to any successful business. As a manager it's important to be good at delegating. A monthly team meeting is a great way of motivating people and ensuring they're all working
25 together. To grow your company, you will probably have to spend a lot of time talking to customers or users, speaking at events, writing blogposts, etc. Most successful bosses work weekends and are never truly on vacation.

So if you have a vision, the right skills and qualities, don't mind working long hours, and think you could get used to working during your vacations, this could be the career for you!
30 We're looking forward to getting your feedback on this week's ideas. Could you imagine working as a marine biologist? Or do you like the idea of being your own boss? If so, we'd love to hear your ideas.

c Write your feedback for *Career Spotlight*.

3 Talking about jobs

a Complete the statements with help from **1** and answer the question. Find more examples in **2**.

> *I've always dreamed ▆▆ becoming an architect.*
> *I'm really interested ▆▆ helping animals.*
> *First, I had the idea ▆▆ studying medicine, but then I changed my mind.*
> - When a verb follows a preposition, what form of the verb do we use?

b Rewrite the sentences in the box about you.

 c Complete the questions. Then take turns to ask and answer them. What job do you think would be good for your partner?

1 What school subjects are you good …?
2 Are you interested …?
3 Would you enjoy …?
4 Would you like the chance …?
5 Have you ever thought … becoming a/an …?

4 VIDEO TRACK: Spotlight on a marine biologist

14 **a** Chris Meyer is a marine biologist and scientist. Watch him talking about his job.

1 Why did he become a marine biologist?
2 What does he like about his job?
3 According to him, what's 'the beautiful part about doing this job'?

b What advice does Chris give young people?

5 YOUR TURN: Your dreams

a 'Everyone should have a dream.' It's never too early to think about your plans for the future. What do you dream of?

- helping people
- inventing something
- making your hobby into your job
- living and working in another country
- becoming rich and famous
- …

b Find someone with the same ideas as you. Discuss your dreams and how realistic they are.

Grammar and structures

Gerund after prepositions → G 28

I'm really **good at drawing**.
I'm not very **keen on studying**.

Practice: Careers of the future

1 **GET STARTED!** Look at these statements and quotes.
Say which one(s) you can identify with.

> Don't live to work, work to live.

> A job for life is a thing of the past.

> The future depends on what you do today.
> *Mahatma Gandhi*

> Robots will harvest, cook, and serve our food. They will work in our factories, drive our cars, and walk our dogs. Like it or not, the age of work is coming to an end. *Gray Scott*

2 **Careers of the future**

a Imagine a future when robots do all the work. What's your first reaction? Why?

'That would be so boring!'
'Cool! We could just do what we want every day.'

b Which jobs do you think will be done by intelligent machines in thirty years' time? Which jobs will still be done by humans?

3 **READING FOCUS: Humans versus robots**

a Read the article and check your ideas in **2b**. What kind of jobs will disappear?

b Look at the TIP box, then read the article again.
Student A: find four facts about the future of work.
Student B: find four opinions.
Then share your information:
- Which facts did you find surprising?
- Think of more facts to support the opinions.

TIP

Facts and opinions
Information presented as facts is often supported by figures, dates and places.
Opinions are often introduced by verbs like *think*, *believe*, modal verbs like *could*, *might* and adverbs such as *(un)likely*, *probably*.

---

c How can you prepare for the future, according to the article? Can you think of more ideas?

The future of work

The world of work is changing fast. Millions of jobs that exist today will have disappeared by 2050. Most children starting school now will probably work in jobs that don't exist yet.

5 Routine jobs that only need a few simple, easy-to-learn skills are already disappearing. They range from supermarket cashiers, secretaries and bank tellers to construction, factory and farm workers. Thousands of

10 manufacturing jobs have already been taken over by robots. In the future, millions of farmhands could be replaced by intelligent machines. And it looks as if it won't be long until self-driving vehicles replace car and truck drivers.

15 What kind of jobs will remain? It will be harder to automate jobs that involve strategic planning, making important decisions, and managing and training people. Jobs where people need to interact with other people will

20 also remain. These include healthcare professionals – doctors, nurses, dentists – and teachers. These jobs require teamwork and good communication skills, which few people think machines can develop. Creative roles in

25 fields such as entertainment and fashion will always be important. Information technology and healthcare are two of the fastest growing areas in the US.

---

67)) **Words and phrases**

curiosity	the quality of being curious	**to put an animal to sleep**	to kill a sick animal in a way that isn't painful
to interact with other people	to talk to people	**to treat**	to help sick animals or people
to maintain	to keep in good condition	**vital**	very important

New jobs will also be created as technology
30 develops. There will be many new career
opportunities for computer programmers, cyber
security experts, engineers and scientists in the
future. The private space industry is growing in
the US, so space workers – astronauts, pilots
35 and engineers who can develop and maintain
equipment – will be in demand.

Young people will need to develop skills that
robots don't have, such as problem-solving and
creativity. In the future, many people are likely
40 to have 'portfolio' careers, doing several
part-time jobs at once. What personal qualities
will they need? They will have to be flexible
and adaptable, as well as self-motivated and
able to take on responsibility. Qualities such as
45 initiative, curiosity and leadership will be vital.

4 Selling yourself

a Make a list of skills and personal qualities
mentioned in *The future of work*.

b Write your own statement to show your skills
and abilities.

*I'm the captain of my school basketball team.
We practise hard to improve our skills as a team.
I love sport and I dream of becoming a
professional.*

5 Keep smiling! Describe the cartoon. Then explain how it is linked to the text in 3.

"We tried humans, but they weren't nice enough."

CartoonStock.com

6 Career Spotlight: veterinarian

a Complete the job description with the missing prepositions and the correct form of the verbs.

Career Spotlight

This week's spotlight is on being a vet.

This is a job many young animal-lovers dream ▨1▨
5 (*do*). A vet's duties range ▨2▨ (*diagnose*) and
looking after sick animals ▨3▨ (*carry out*)
operations. Sometimes they may have to put
very sick animals to sleep. Vets might work
with pets or large animals like cows. Some vets
10 do extra training and become experts ▨4▨ (*care
for*) zoo animals and wildlife. Others work in
laboratories and specialize ▨5▨ (*do*) research
into animal diseases. Vets must be good ▨6▨
(*solve*) problems and making decisions because
15 they have to identify what's wrong with an
animal and decide the best way to treat it. They
must also be excellent ▨7▨ (*communicate*) this
information to owners and staff.

To become a vet you need to be good at
20 sciences. High school students who are keen
▨8▨ (*get*) some hands-on experience with
animals should look for part-time or volunteer
work on farms, or in animal shelters or research
laboratories.

⟫⟫⟫ **page 132**

b Make two lists: things you would like about
being a vet and things you wouldn't like.

c Compare your lists with a partner. Explain your
reasons. Would the job be right for you?

*I would enjoy …
I'm good at …
I would worry about …
I couldn't get used to …
I wouldn't like to …*

My part-time job

PART 1
PART 2
PART 3

1 **Student jobs**

a Listen to the two descriptions of picture A. Which one is better? Together, make a list of features that you like about this description.

b Choose a different picture and describe it to your partner. Give each other feedback.

2 **Coast to coast**

a David Wang is 15 and lives in California. He's having an online video chat with his cousin Vivian in Lexington. Listen and decide which three statements sum up the conversation best.

1 David and Vivian both have part-time jobs.
2 David has a part-time job.
3 Vivian has a part-time job.
4 Part-time work can cause problems with schoolwork.
5 You shouldn't have a part-time job when you're still at school.
6 Part-time work can teach you some important skills.

b Listen again and complete the sentences. Then compare your answers.

1 David works part-time in a …
2 He wanted to get a job because he …
3 The school counsellor says that students shouldn't …
4 David likes where he works because he …

3 **The good and the bad**

a Listen again and take notes. Compare what you found out.
Student A: take notes on the arguments for having a part-time job.
Student B: take notes on the arguments against having a part-time job.

b Discuss whose arguments you agree with more – Vivian's or David's and explain why.

c Would you like to have a part-time job? What could you imagine doing and what would you do with the extra money? Use the jobs in the box or your own ideas to discuss with your partner.

babysitter ■ cleaner ■ dog walker ■ gardener ■ pizza deliverer ■ shop assistant

Words and phrases

American English vs. British English

takeout  **takeaway**	a restaurant that sells food to take and eat somewhere else	
	lawn	an area with short grass in a garden or park
	shift	a period of time when people work

4 **Job talk.** Answer the questions in the box.

> Vivian's dad (direct speech):
> *'David has a part-time job.'*
>
> Vivian (reported speech):
> *My dad said that you had a part-time job.*
>
> ● Name at least two differences between the two sentences.
> ● What happens to the verb in reported speech?

> **TIP**
>
> ● In reported speech, *tell* is followed by an indirect object (the person we are speaking to).
> *She **told me** that she was usually tired at school the next day.*
>
> ● We use *say* without an indirect object.
> *She **said** that she liked her job.*

5 **Busy days.** David told Vivian a lot about his daily life. What did Vivian share with her brother? Use the reporting verbs from the box.

> add ■ explain ■ mention ■ say ■ tell

1 I'm good at Ultimate Frisbee.

2 My favorite video games are *Surf City* and *Kingpin*.

3 I still write for the school newspaper.

4 I have a new mountain bike.

5 I go on bike hikes with my friends in the Oakland Hills.

6 **A hungry friend**

a David's friend Leo visited him at work. David is telling his mum about it now. What did David and Leo say exactly? Act out their dialogue.

> Leo came by the taco truck today. He asked about my boss and I told him that Juan **had just left** and that he **would be** back later. Then Leo asked for a free taco. He explained he **hadn't eaten** lunch yet. I told him I **couldn't just give** him a taco. I added Juan **wouldn't like** that. But he said he **hadn't brought** any money. So I told him that I **would lend** him the money.

b How do the verbs change in reported speech? Copy and complete the table.

direct speech		reported speech
simple present	→	???
simple past	→	???
present perfect	→	???
will	→	???
can	→	???

7 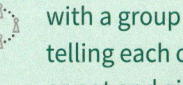 **YOUR TURN: At a concert.** You're at a concert with a group of friends. It's very loud. You're telling each other whether you like the concert or not and giving reasons.

Step 1: Walk around and find a partner. Take turns asking and answering.
How do you like the concert?

Step 2: Walk around again and find a new partner. Take turns to say who you were talking to before and what he or she said.
I was talking to Malik. He told me / said (that) he …

Grammar and structures

Statements in reported speech → G 29
My dad told me you **had** a part-time job.
Leo said he **was** hungry, but **didn't have** any money.

Practice: Student jobbing

1 **GET STARTED!** Statistics in the US show that fewer teenagers today have a part-time job than a generation ago. Why do you think this is? Do you think it is the same in Germany? Do you know of examples in your family?

2 **Job ads**

a Look at these job ads posted on a school bulletin board. Take turns to choose an ad, explain what the job is, and talk about the possible pros and cons.

b If you were looking for a part-time job, which of these job ads would you find the most interesting or attractive? Why? What questions would you have about the job? Discuss with your partner. Then share your ideas in class.

> **Help wanted**
> East Bay Car Wash is hiring part-time assistants.
> If you like working outdoors and you don't mind getting wet, apply now!
> Email: Dan@baywash.com

> **Hey animal lovers!**
> Do you want to be an animal care helper?
> The Oakland Animal Shelter needs volunteers.
> Call Ann at 235-4123.

> **Help wanted**
> We need an office cleaner for weekends. Minimum wage.
> Tel. 311-6020

> **Help wanted**
> Fenelli's Creamery is looking for part-time ice cream servers.
> No experience required.
> Call (265) 314-2222.

> **Digital archiving**
> Can you scan, upload and archive texts and photos?
> Earn 12 dollars an hour, 10 hours a week.
> Call McKee Law Offices: (265) 300-5150.

3 **VIEWING FOCUS: Job talk**

15
16
17

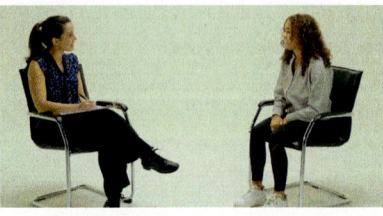  

a You are going to watch three videos. Stella, Lucas and Hailey are talking to their school counsellor about their part-time jobs. In groups of three, each focus on one student. Before you watch, copy the table, then complete it.

b Compare notes. What do the students have in common? How are they different?

How is it going with:	+ +	+	0	–	– –
the job?	???	???	???	???	???
school?	???	???	???	???	???
the work-school-life balance?	???	???	???	???	???

🔊 **71**)) **Words and phrases**

bulletin board 🖼 **noticeboard**	a board for notices
to **hire**	to give somebody a job
minimum wage	the smallest amount of money that a worker can legally be paid
rent	the money you pay to live somewhere

 **c** Find a partner from another group who also focused on your student. Compare notes. Then read the TIP box before you watch the video again. This time, pay attention to non-verbal communication.

1 Are your answers similar or different? Discuss the differences.
2 How did your student's non-verbal communication help you reach your conclusions?

TIP

Identifying attitudes through non-verbal communication
- **Tone of voice:** Does the person speak loudly or softly? Fast or slowly? Does the intonation go up and down or is it flat and monotone?
- **Eye contact:** Does the person look straight at you? Are his or her eyes fixed or do they move around a lot?
- **Facial expression:** Is the person's face relaxed or tense? Do his or her eyebrows or mouth move a lot? Are his or her expressions positive or negative?
- **Body language:** Are the person's shoulders relaxed or tense? Does he or she sit up or slump? With crossed arms or legs? Does the person use hand gestures? If so, what kind of gestures?

---

4 **A difficult balance**

a Read this article which David found on *Career Spotlight*. What is the 'difficult balance' the article describes?

A difficult balance

On a Tuesday morning, 17-year-old Beth Frazier prepared breakfast for her nine-year-old sister Rhonda. Their dad died when Rhonda was young, and their mom leaves for work early. So from Monday till Friday, Beth looks after her sister.

5 Like many teenagers who have only one parent at home or who come from a low-income family, Beth has to balance work, life and school. 'It's really hard,' said Beth. 'I'm trying to find out who I am and, at the same time, I'm trying to be the adult.'

She has an evening job in San Francisco to help with rent and food,
10 and she's like a part-time parent. Her day starts at 6.30 a.m. First school, then babysitting, then work, then home by midnight.

Beth wants to be the first in her family to graduate from university. That will be a challenge with her responsibilities at home. Beth doesn't get a fair chance to focus on school. But, for now at least, she knows what's most important.

15 'For a long time, I hated the responsibility at home, but now my perspective has changed. I can't just think about myself all the time. And this situation won't be forever.'

---

b Answer these questions.

1 Why does Beth look after her sister?
2 What is Beth's daily routine when she's working?
3 What is her goal?
4 How does Beth feel about her situation?

c This is what Beth told *Career Spotlight*. Put the direct statements into reported speech. Use the reporting verbs from the box.

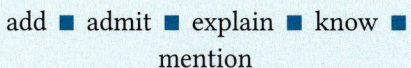

add ■ admit ■ explain ■ know ■ mention

1 It's really hard.
2 I'm trying to find out who I am and, at the same time, I'm trying to be the adult.
3 For a long time I hated the responsibility at home, but now my perspective has changed.
4 I can't just think about myself all the time.
5 This situation won't be forever.

 **page 132**

Method Coach: Choose an idea for a documentary film

S1 **Brainstorm a documentary film topic.** In groups of three or four, think about and discuss these questions to help you come up with ideas.

- What topics do you and your friends talk about a lot?
- What do you get excited or frustrated about?
- Are there any topics or issues that you'd like to find out more about?
- Is there something that you feel isn't right or fair and that you'd like to change?

You don't have to look far for ideas. You can find great stories in your own school, family or community. Some examples:

- Online learning versus school
- My first part-time job
- An unusual hobby
- How inclusive is our school?

You could also choose a concept as your topic. For example:

- Friendship
- Work

Follow the tips on how to brainstorm effectively on page 86. One group member takes notes. Collect your ideas.

An interview: My part-time job

S2 **Choose the best idea for your film**

a Go through your list of ideas. Talk about each topic and how you could make a film about it that is two to five minutes long.

b Make a shortlist of the three best ideas. Discuss their strengths and weaknesses. Agree on one idea that you think is the best.

> **TIP**
>
> There are different types of documentary films. The type that you will focus on is an **interview** with one or more people about a particular topic. Example: A student talking about her part-time job

S3 **Write a one-line summary**

a When film-makers are developing an idea, they often describe what their film will be about in a very short summary. Look at these two one-line summaries for the same documentary film. Discuss what makes an effective one-line summary.

> *An interview with a teenager who works to help her family and also wants to go to university.*

> *An ambitious student describes her conflict between following her dreams and helping the people she loves.*

b Why do you think it's a good idea to write a one-line summary when you want to make a film?

c Work in a group of four. Write a one-line summary for your film in your placemat section. Discuss your ideas in your group. Then agree on a one-line summary that best describes your film and write it in the middle of the placemat.

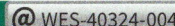
Workshop task: Create a storyboard

S1 **Describe a storyboard**

a A storyboard uses pictures – sketches or photos – to plan how each shot of the film should look. A storyboard is helpful during shooting because it gives you a visual overview of your story and the technical details about each shot. Look at the example. Choose one of the two shots and describe it.

Shot #2			
Image	Image description	Camera	Audio
	Zoe sitting at table or standing in snack bar, speaking to interviewer (off camera)	medium shot	interview

Shot #3			
Image	Image description	Camera	Audio
	Zoe serving customers at busy snack bar	long shot	Zoe and customer talking: other workers and general noise inside snack bar

b Describe what the camera shows in each shot and what kind of scene it might be good for.

S2 **Create your storyboard**

a Follow the steps.

Step 1: Copy the storyboard above or use the template your teacher gives you. Keep a blank copy for further pages. Or download and open one of the storyboard apps your teacher suggests.

Step 2: Discuss and visualize how you want to tell your story with each camera shot. Think about the role of elements like printed text and voice-over if you plan to use them.

Step 3: Agree on a plan for each shot. Add a picture and complete the information.

b Share your finished storyboard in class. Describe what happens and what the viewer sees in the film from one shot to the next. Make any changes or corrections.

TIP

These **film terms** will help you discuss a storyboard:
lighting: the type of light and how it is arranged (e. g. bright / dim, outdoor / indoor)
voice-over: spoken text in a film that is spoken by a person who is not seen on the screen

Summer jobs

1 **One student, two jobs**

a David Wang is looking for an extra summer job. He checks a movie theater website and finds three jobs. Describe each job in your own words.

Bay Movie Theater
Jobs in our theater include: <u>snack bar attendant</u>, <u>box office cashier</u> and <u>usher</u>.

Apply now!

73 b David fills in the online job application. A few days later, he is invited to an interview. Listen to his interview with the manager and answer the questions.

1 Which job do you think David has applied for and why?
2 What problem does the manager see?
3 What do you think of David's first question?
4 What day of the week do you think the interview is on and why?

2 **You said what?** David texts his friend Stacy. Look at their messages. In Stacy's view, what did David do wrong in his interview? Why?

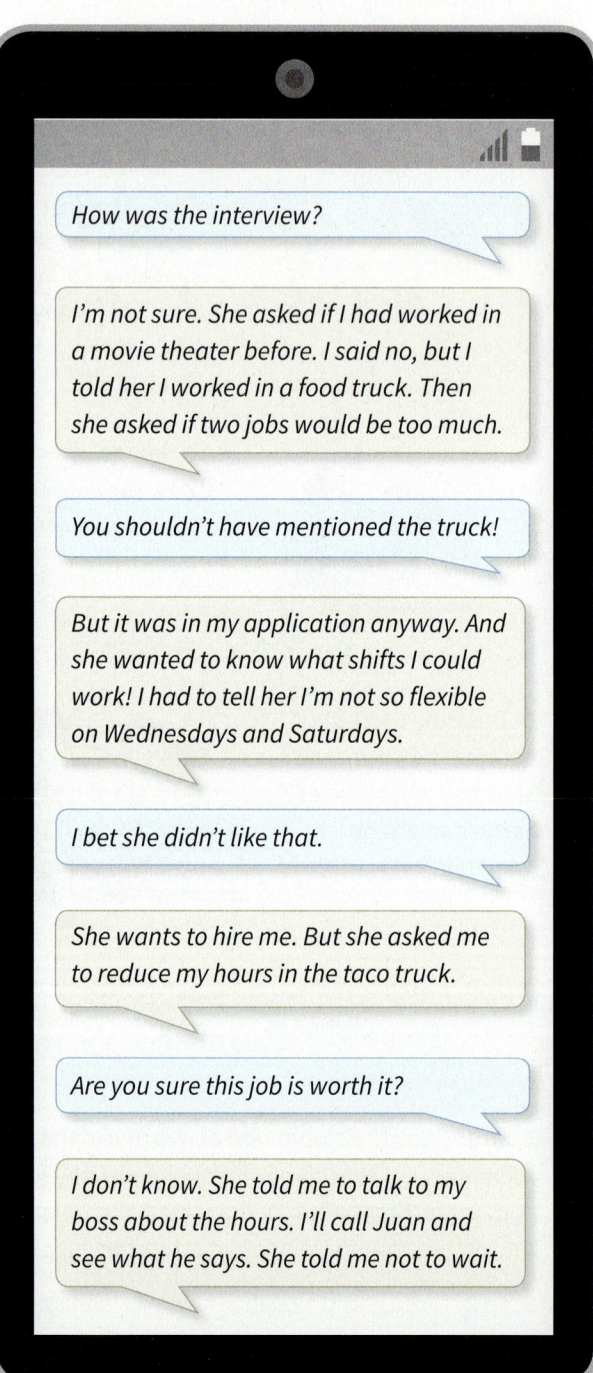

How was the interview?

I'm not sure. She asked if I had worked in a movie theater before. I said no, but I told her I worked in a food truck. Then she asked if two jobs would be too much.

You shouldn't have mentioned the truck!

But it was in my application anyway. And she wanted to know what shifts I could work! I had to tell her I'm not so flexible on Wednesdays and Saturdays.

I bet she didn't like that.

She wants to hire me. But she asked me to reduce my hours in the taco truck.

Are you sure this job is worth it?

I don't know. She told me to talk to my boss about the hours. I'll call Juan and see what he says. She told me not to wait.

72 Words and phrases

Jobs and work
applicant a person who applies for a job

(job) application the form that you fill in when you apply for a job
position a job

3 Hours and shifts

a Look at the box to see how David reports his interview to Stacy. Then complete the statements and answer the questions.

'Will two jobs be too much?'
She asked **if** two jobs would be too much.
● To report *yes-no* questions we add ▬▬ or *whether*.

'What shifts can you work for us?'
She asked what shifts I could work for them.
● In reported questions the subject comes **before / after** the verb.

'Could you reduce your hours?'
She asked me **to reduce** my hours.
● With reported requests, what happens to the form of the main verb?

'You should talk to him.'
She **told** me to talk to him.
'Don't wait until Saturday.'
She **told** me not to wait until Saturday.
● We report advice and orders with (*not*) and the ▬▬ .

---

b Is each of these quotes from the interview a question, a request, advice or an order. Rewrite them in reported speech.

1 Where did you see our ad?
   She asked him where …
2 Don't worry.
3 Do you have any questions about the job?
4 How much do you pay?
5 Could you be more flexible?
6 Call me as soon as possible.

>>> **c** What do you think David should do?

4 A summer to remember

74))) **a** David wants to hear about his dad's own experience with summer jobs when he was a teenager. Listen to the first part of their conversation and answer the questions.

1 What was Mr Wang's first summer job?
2 Explain what a paper route is.
3 What was difficult about the job?
4 What has changed about the job since Mr Wang was young?

75)) **b** Listen to the second part. How did Mr Wang get the summer job? Complete what he says.

1 I got paid more than the ▬▬ , so that was good.
2 It was a regular ▬▬ that he had during the school year.
3 My friend told me to ▬▬ before anyone else did.
4 They told me I didn't have to send in an ▬▬ .
5 I asked them if there had been other ▬▬ .
6 They ▬▬ me although they didn't know me.

5 YOUR TURN: Three-minute survey. You're interviewing young people on the street for a survey. You want to know about their job preferences, their opinions about student jobs in general and whether students should work.

Think: Write three questions that you'd like to ask.

Pair: Interview each other. Make notes.

Share: Share your results in your group. Explain who you interviewed, what you asked and what they told you. Compare your results.

Grammar and structures

Questions, requests, advice and orders in reported speech → G 30
The manager asked me **if** two jobs **would be** too much for me.
She asked me **what** shifts I **could work**.

She asked me **to reduce** my hours.
She told me **to talk** to Juan.
She told me **not to wait** until Saturday.

Practice: Into the world

1 GET STARTED!

a Volunteering is a great way to help others and get valuable work experience at the same time. Match the pictures (A – D) with some of the volunteering activities in the box.

> caring for elderly people ■
> cleaning up the environment ■
> helping homeless people ■ helping on a
> building project abroad ■ planting trees
> and plants ■ working in an animal shelter

b Think of other possible volunteering activities for students. Share your ideas in class.

2 A volunteer project for you

a Listen to the profiles of these four American teens and make notes. With a partner, agree on a volunteering activity from the box in **1a** or from your own ideas that matches each person best.

Abby

Trent

Aziz

Olivia

b Write your personal profile. Include any relevant experience, skills, interests and hobbies.

c Read your profiles aloud in your group. Agree on a suitable activity for each group member, either from **1a** or from your own ideas.

> You're good at …, so I think you should …

> As you …, why don't you …

3 David's dilemma

a David rings his boss and tells him about the job interview at the movie theater. Read part of their phone conversation. Summarize Juan's reaction.

Juan	What does that mean, David? Are you quitting?
David	No! I don't want to quit. But if I take that job, I can't work for you as much.
Juan	I see. How many hours a week is the other job?
David	It's about 25 hours.
Juan	Well, I don't mind if you come to work a little later. Does that help?
David	Not really. Do you need me on both Wednesdays and Saturdays?
Juan	Yes, I do. Listen, I don't want to lose you, David. But you have to choose – this job or the other one. Could you think about it and call me tomorrow?

b David tells his parents about the phone call with Juan.

1 *Juan asked me …*
2 *He wanted to know …*
…

⟩⟩⟩ **page 132**

 Words and phrases

Jobs and work

intern	a person working to get practical experience in a job
internship	practical experience in a job
mentor	a person who gives somebody help and advice
to mentor	to give somebody help and advice

supervisor	a person who leads workers and makes sure they do their work correctly

4 **A summer of service**

a Discuss with a partner what you think a volunteer at a nature reserve does.

b Read Stacy's article for the school newspaper about her experience as a summer volunteer. What was one of the first things that she learned?

My summer on the hill
by Stacy Pereira

When I first heard about volunteering with Sutro Stewards, I found out that
5 a steward is somebody who looks after something. Sutro Stewards volunteers
10 take care of and improve the nature trails on Mount Sutro. They also work to protect the native plants there. In case
15 you don't know, Mount Sutro is that big green hill in San Francisco. It's special because it's a nature reserve in the middle of the city. It has a beautiful forest and cool nature trails.

Sutro Stewards runs different volunteer
20 programs. I was part of the High School Summer Program, a five-week internship. My dream is to be a nature conservation officer, so this program was perfect. It was three days a week, about four hours each day. I was one of eight interns and
25 they gave us tools and gloves and a cool T-shirt. We were outdoors the whole time learning about plants and animals.

Our project supervisors showed us how to identify native plants, and together we worked to
30 restore the natural habitat. I learned so much, and I loved the forest. We worked in teams, which wasn't always easy, but we got things done. The summer is over now, but I know I'll volunteer with Sutro Stewards again.

c David wants to show Stacy that he's read her article. He collects some details on 1 – 4 below
Student A: summarize points 1 and 3.
Student B: summarize points 2 and 4.
Write down two or more details about each point. Then swap information.

1 Sutro Stewards
2 Mount Sutro
3 The High School Summer Program
4 Stacy's experience

d The project manager spoke to the volunteers about organizational matters. Look at 1 – 6. What did Stacy tell her parents later?

She told us to … / She asked us not to …

1 Please be on time.
2 Could you tell me your T-shirt sizes?
3 Could you give me your phone numbers, please?
4 Wear strong boots, please.
5 Do not wear sneakers.
6 Please don't leave the tools lying around.

5 **SPEAKING FOCUS: Volunteering abroad**

a You want to volunteer abroad in the summer. You take part in a webinar by a travel organization which offers two student projects. Before you listen, look at the TIP box.
 78 **Student A:** listen to Part 1 and take notes.
79 **Student B:** listen to Part 2 and take notes.

b Tell your partner about 'your' project. When listening, use the phrases in the TIP box.

TIP

Checking or confirming understanding

Asking for repetition
Could you repeat that, please?
I'm sorry, what did you say?
Sorry, I didn't catch that.

Asking for clarification
Did you say that …?
When you say …, what exactly do you mean?
What do you mean by …?

Rephrasing
In other words, … / So what you're saying is …

---

c Talk about the two projects and decide which one sounds most interesting. Explain your reasons.

Children's rights

1 **Do you know your rights?** Read the extracts from the United Nations Convention on the Rights of the Child and discuss the questions.

- Why is it important for children to have rights?
- Are any of these rights more important than others?
- Can you think of three more Rights of the Child?

- **Article 12:** Every child has the right to express their opinions and adults must listen.
- **Article 19:** Children have the right to be protected from any form of violence.
- **Article 24:** All children have a right to good health, including healthcare, clean water, nutritious food and a clean, safe environment.
- **Article 28:** All children have the right to an education.
- **Article 32:** Children should not be allowed to do work that is dangerous or might make them ill or stops them going to school.
- **Article 35:** Governments must make sure that children are not abducted, sold or trafficked.

2 **Child labour in the USA**

a Read the article. Did the owner of the Ohio egg farm follow the United Nations Convention on the Rights of the Child? Support your answers with information from the text.

b Choose two pieces of information that particularly surprised or shocked you in the article.

Trafficked in America

In recent years hundreds of thousands of unaccompanied minors have come to the United States. Most of them came from Central America to escape poverty and violence. Many
5 teens were trafficked from their homes into the US illegally.
This is the story of a major trafficking case which involved dozens of migrant workers, including eight teens from Guatemala. All of
10 them were forced to work against their will on an Ohio egg farm.
A trafficker promised them a better life in America if they paid him $15,000. But it was a lie: their dream turned into a nightmare.
15 In Ohio, they worked 12 hours a day, six days a week cleaning the hens' cages at the egg farm. The teenagers paid as little as $2 per day.

If they complained, the traffickers said they would kill them or their families.
20 Two of the victims spoke to investigators. Both of them told the same story. 'Every day, the work was the same. You start sweating, and your eyes burn because of all the dirt. Your clothes get dirty, completely filthy. We pick up
25 the chickens that have fallen from the cages. There are lots of dead chickens. It's really hard.'

80)) **Words and phrases**

to **abduct**	to take somebody away against their will
abuse	when somebody is treated badly
to **abuse**	to treat someone badly

debt	money that you must pay back to somebody
to **traffic**	to take someone to another place and force them to work

After a few months, one of the boys managed to call his uncle in Florida. The uncle informed the authorities, who rescued the boys. The
30 leader of the gang was sent to prison. But this case wasn't unusual. According to a high school educator in Iowa who works with immigrant teens, more than half of the students at her school have to work long shifts 35 at local food processing plants to pay off their debt to traffickers. The majority of them can't learn because they're too tired. Some kids miss school regularly.
Both Ohio and Iowa have high numbers of
40 immigrant workers. No one knows how many other victims of abuse there are in similar situations.

3 Facts and figures

a Read the TIP box. Find more examples of phrases that express quantity in the article in **2**.

TIP

- Talking about people or things in general:
  All children have the right to good health.
  Most farm workers in the US are migrants.

- People or things in a specific group:
  All (of) the minors were afraid.
  Most of the farm workers in Ohio are migrants.
  More than ***half (of) the students*** at an Iowa school have to work.

- Two people or things:
  Both boys / Both of the boys / Both of them told the same story.

- Note the expression 'both … and':
  Both Ohio ***and*** Iowa have high numbers of immigrant workers.

---

b Complete these facts using the information in brackets and words or phrases from the box.

> half of ■ majority of ■ many ■
> many of ■ most of ■ some of

More than ___1___ the nation's fruits and vegetable are grown in California. (60%) California produces ___2___ the strawberries that are grown in the US. (90%) ___3___ California's farmworkers are undocumented, or illegal migrants. (75%) There are around half a million children working in US fields. ___4___ children move with their families from farm to farm. (65%) The ___5___ agricultural workers under the age of 18 (85%) live in states where agriculture is an important industry such as Florida, California and Texas. ___6___ children are out of school and working full-time by the age of 11 or 12. (8%)

4 Child labour laws in the US. The bar chart is about migrant students at a high school in Central Valley, the main agricultural area in California. Explain what it shows.

All the students are aged 14 – 16.

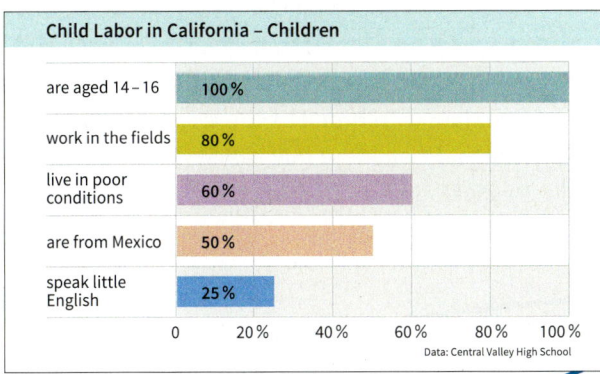

Child Labor in California – Children

are aged 14 – 16	100%
work in the fields	80%
live in poor conditions	60%
are from Mexico	50%
speak little English	25%

0   20%   40%   60%   80%   100%

Data: Central Valley High School

5 YOUR TURN: Being a child

a Copy and complete the sentences.

- The best thing about being a child is …
- The worst thing about being a child is …
- The most important thing to change for children in my country is …
- The worst thing for children in the world is …

b Discuss your sentences with a partner and give your reasons. Compare your answers.

Grammar and structures

Quantifiers → G31

All children should go to school.
All of the children at my school learn English.
Most children enjoy school.

Practice:
Stand up for children's rights

1 GET STARTED! Talk about the photos. What do you think is the connection between them?

2 A child rights hero

a David Wang's class was asked to write an essay about their hero. Skim David's essay and check your ideas in **1**. Why is Iqbal David's hero?

b Read and make notes about what happened to Iqbal.

1982 Iqbal Masik was born in Pakistan
1986 Iqbal was sold …

> 1986 – 1992 ■ 1992 ■ 1992 – 1994 ■
> 1994 ■ April 16, 1995

c Compare your notes and correct them if you need to. Then close your books. Use your notes to retell the main events of Iqbal's life.

MY HERO
Iqbal Masih
by David Wang

Iqbal Masih was born in Pakistan in 1982. When he was only four years old, his family sold him to a carpet manufacturer because they needed money. The working conditions
5 in the factory were terrible. Iqbal and the other children there had to work more than twelve hours a day without any breaks. The factory owner shouted at them and beat them all the time. They never had enough to eat.
10 In 1992, Iqbal and some other children escaped from the factory. They attended a Freedom Day celebration organized by the Bonded Labour Liberation Front. The children learned that they were 'debt slaves', forced to work to
15 pay off their parents' debts. Although there are laws against this in Pakistan, they are not enforced.
After that day, Iqbal refused to go back to his owner. The BLLF helped him to get his
20 freedom and he started attending their school for freed child slaves. He dreamed of becoming a lawyer because he wanted to fight for children's rights. While he was studying, he visited factories where children were working
25 and told them about their rights. Eventually he traveled all over the world telling people about child labor and his life experiences.
Iqbal won many awards. In 1994 he came to the United States to receive a *Human Rights*
30 *Youth Action Award*. Soon after receiving the award, he returned to Pakistan. He was shot and killed there on April 16, 1995. He was 12 years old. Many people think that the carpet manufacturers were responsible.
35 Iqbal is my hero because he was so brave and he spoke up for children against injustice and exploitation. Thousands of child slaves became free thanks to him. His life inspired a twelve-year-old Canadian boy called Craig Kielburger
40 to speak up for children, too.

🔊 **Words and phrases**

Making a difference

to **enforce a law**	to make people follow a law
fund	money for an activity or organization
illiterate	unable to read or write
injustice	when people are treated unfairly
to **speak out** (for / against)	to say your opinion in public
to **stand up for**	to defend or support somebody

3 **VIDEO TRACK: Craig Kielburger's story**

a Use the context to work out the meaning of the blue words below before you watch the video.

1 Iqbal **suffered** pain and hunger at work.
2 It is unfair and **inhumane** to treat children in this terrible way.
3 Young people have the **power** to change things: they are not **powerless**.
4 We must all work to **eradicate** child exploitation completely.
5 Many young people have signed **petitions** asking world leaders to end child labour.

b Craig was awarded an international Human Rights Award at the age of 14. Watch the first part of the video (until minute 2:01) to find out why. How did his story begin?

c Continue to watch until minute 3:18 and find out what action Craig and his friends took.

● Give the name of the organization they started.
● Explain what their organization set out to do.
● Describe one of their first projects.

d Watch the last part of the video (from 8:04 – 9:16). What was Craig's message to other children?

---

4 **WRITING FOCUS: Young heroes: Malala Yousafzai.** Use the notes to write a short essay about Malala Yousafzai. In your final paragraph, state your own opinion about her.

TIP

When you write about important events in someone's life, use time expressions and linking words to clearly show the sequence of events.
Read the essay about Iqbal again and find examples of these expressions.
When … ● *In 1992, …* ● *After that day, …* ●
While he …, he … ● *Eventually …* ● *Soon after …,*

5 **The right to education**

a Choose the correct word or phrase to complete this information about education.

1 **All the children / All children** should have the chance to get a good education.
2 Although **the majority / the most** of children in the world go to school, nearly **half / the half** who don't are girls.
3 **Many / Much** people around the world are still illiterate.
4 **Many / Much** of the crime involving young people is committed by teenagers who did not have a good education.
5 Some people say that unemployment and poverty are **the both / the two** main reasons for crime among young people.

b Discuss. Why is education important? How can education help children and improve their lives?

1997: born in the Swat Valley, Pakistan
2007: Taliban took control of the area — began attacking girls' schools — Malala started to speak out for girls' rights to education — started a blog for the BBC about life under the Taliban — used a false name
October 2012: shot and nearly killed by a Taliban gunman on way home from school, taken to hospital in England; recovered — started going to school in England
2013: published first book, *I Am Malala*, about her campaign for girls
2014: Malala's family moved to UK
2014: founded Malala Fund with her father — charity to help all girls get good education, give them a better future — received World's Children's Prize for her fight for girls' right to education
December 2014: age 17 awarded Nobel Peace Prize — youngest person to receive the prize
2017: accepted at Oxford University — continued to travel to different countries to talk to girls
Today: Malala Fund still campaigns for girls' right to education

Method Coach: Prepare to shoot your film

S1 Research and organize the shoot

a Information: To make your film informative and interesting, research any background information about your topic that you need.

b Location: Decide where you will shoot your film. If it's indoors, for example in the school canteen, find out if you need permission to film there.

c Subjects: Find people who you would like to be in your film. Make sure that they all agree to be filmed.

S2 Analyse a shooting schedule. Look at the example shooting schedule below. Answer the questions.

> **TIP**
>
> A **shooting schedule** is a plan that your group agrees on before you shoot. It's also a way to plan your shots according to location, time of day and when your subjects are available. This can save a lot of time and trouble.

1 In what order do the students film the shots? Why do you think they do this?
2 What do they have to watch out for when filming in the snack bar? Why?
3 When and where do they interview Zoe? What might be the reason?

Shooting order	Date	Scene	Shot	Location	What happens? How?	What to think about
1	16.03. 13.00 – 14.00	Scene 2: busy snack bar	Shot 3: long shot from behind customer	snack bar	Customer is ordering food, Zoe is taking order	permission to film from snack bar manager, agreement from customer
2	16.03. 13.00 – 14.00	Scene 2: busy snack bar	Shot 4: long shot from behind service counter, showing Zoe from side	snack bar	Zoe is taking order, getting food and drinks, taking money	permission to film behind service counter, stay out of way of workers
3	16.03. 14.00 – 15.00	Scene 1: interview	Shot 1: Zoe – close-up	snack bar (quieter area or back room)	Zoe is talking about how she found her part-time job	sound text: not too much noise?
4	16.03. 14.00 – 15.00	Scene1: interview	Shot 2: Zoe – medium shot	snack bar (ditto)	Zoe is talking about a typical work shift	

S3 Plan and write your shooting schedule

Step 1: Copy the table in **S2** or use the copy that your teacher gives you.

Step 2: Start planning.

Step 3: Complete your schedule. Make a copy for each group member.

> **TIP**
>
> **Important questions when planning your shooting schedule**
> - When will you begin shooting? Try to plan shooting dates when everybody in your group can be there.
> - What's the best order to film the shots you need? You don't have to shoot them in the order that they appear in your storyboard. Which shots depend on certain conditions, for example when a subject or a room is available?
> - What do you need to remember for each shot? For example: film equipment, conditions (e.g. lighting, sound, etc.).

Workshop Task:
Shoot and edit your film material

S1 **Shoot your film.** You've done all your preparation.
Now it's time to shoot. If you're shooting a video with a
mobile phone or tablet, think about the following points.

- Keep the camera horizontal and steady.
- Get as close to your subject as possible.
- Have the right light.
- Get a clear audio (this is probably more important than video quality).

S2 **Edit your film material**

a After shooting all your film material, look
through the material on your phone or tablet and
choose the shots that you want to use. Delete
those you don't need.

b If you don't already have a video editing app on
your phone or tablet, download one.

c Choose one person in your group to put
together a rough cut using the video editing app.

d Look through the rough cut together in your
group and discuss changes and improvements.
Then make your final cut.

> **TIP**
>
> Remember to shoot lots of film material so that you have
> more to choose from when you're editing. For example:
>
> - film a shot or scene two or more times
> - experiment with alternative shots
> - collect extra shots of, for example, objects and details
>   around the film location

> **TIP**
>
> These editing terms will help you discuss film
> material
> **cut:** the result of taking out a section of film
> material; the change from one shot or scene to
> another
> **rough cut:** when the material has been combined
> and edited to look like a film but isn't finished yet
> **final cut:** the finished version of a film

S3 **Watch your documentary film.** Download the finished film from your phone or tablet to a desktop computer
or to another device to show your film to the class. Give each other feedback.

> The sound quality is really clear.

> I like the way you added those extra shots.

> Maybe you could cut the last scene after the …

Mediation

1 **Summer jobs.** Marla, your 15-year-old American friend, is going to visit you during the summer holidays. You both want to earn some money for a holiday together, but Marla doesn't speak much German. In the local newspaper you find several job offers. Tell Marla in an email which jobs you could do and say which job you prefer and why.

Ferienjobs in unserer Stadt

Unsere Stadtverwaltung bietet unterschiedliche Ferienjobs für Schüler und Studenten (m/w/d) an. Bei Interesse melden Sie sich bitte telefonisch bei Frau Gebhardt im Rathaus. Frau Gebhardt kann Ihnen weitere Fragen, u. a. zur Bezahlung, beantworten.

Zeitungszusteller(innen) – Um die Urlaubs-
5 zeit zu überbrücken, brauchen wir für die Sommerferien Leute, die morgens die Zeitungen an
Privathaushalte verteilen. Die Zeitungen müssen im Zeitungsladen an der Hauptstraße abge-
holt und anschließend verteilt werden. Dafür
10 werden mehrere Leute eingesetzt, denen jeweils
ein Stadtbezirk zugewiesen wird. Handwagen
werden gestellt, so dass die Zeitungspakete
nicht getragen werden müssen. Bis 7 Uhr sollten
alle Zeitungen ausgeliefert sein.

15 **Helfer im landwirtschaftlichen Bereich** –
Die umliegenden Höfe sind auf der Suche nach
Schülern und Studenten (m/w/d), die die landwirtschaftlichen Betriebe im Sommer unterstützen möchten. Die Aufgaben sind abhängig von
20 der Art des Hofes und reichen vom Ernten von
Früchten und Gemüse sowie Weiterverarbeiten
dieser Produkte bis zur Mithilfe im Hofladen
oder dem Versorgen von Tieren.

Pizzaboten – Die Pizzeria am Marktplatz ist
25 auf der Suche nach Pizzaboten und -botinnen,
die Speisen mit dem Auto ausliefern können.
Voraussetzung sind ein eigenes Auto, ein siche-
rer Fahrstil sowie absolute Zuverlässigkeit. Die
Arbeitszeit ist unter der Woche am Abend und
30 am Wochenende sowohl mittags als auch
abends. Mitarbeiter/innen können kostenlos in
der Pizzeria essen.

Umfragen durchführen – Frau Graupner, die
bei der Stadtverwaltung für die Jugendarbeit
zuständig ist, ist auf der Suche nach jungen 35
Leuten, um eine Umfrage unter der jungen Bevölkerung durchzuführen. Umfragebögen werden gestellt. Wer hier mithelfen möchte, wird in
der Fußgängerzone Jugendliche ansprechen und
ihnen Fragen zum Angebot unserer Stadt stel- 40
len. Ziel der Befragung ist es herauszufinden, ob
die Stadt ausreichend Angebote für Jugendliche
bietet. Außerdem soll herausgefunden werden,
welche Angebote von den Befragten genutzt
werden und was sie sich zusätzlich wünschen. 45

Mitarbeit in Claudias Boutique – Claudia
Menges ist auf der Suche nach ein oder zwei
Personen, die sie in den Sommerferien in ihrer
Boutique unterstützen können. Die Boutique
hat sich auf klassische Mode und ausgefallene 50
Schuhe und Accessoires spezialisiert. Frau
Menges braucht Hilfe beim Auspacken und
Einräumen der Waren und der Dekoration
ihres Ladens. Die Arbeitszeit beträgt etwa fünf
Stunden in der Woche und ist flexibel. 55

2 **The Holy Apostles Soup Kitchen.** You and your sister are staying with your grandparents in New York for the summer holidays. Your grandmother shows you both the website of a charity she volunteers for. Answer your sister's questions about the website.

The Holy Apostles Soup Kitchen

Founded in 1982, the Holy Apostles Soup Kitchen is currently the largest emergency feeding program in New York City and in the Episcopal Church nationally. Housed within the nave of the Church, the Soup
5 Kitchen serves over 1,200 meals every weekday and offers counseling and other support services to help the guests break the cycle of hunger, poverty, and despair. [...]

Our Mission
10 Feed the hungry, comfort the troubled, seek justice for the homeless, and provide a sense of hope and opportunity to those in need. [...]

Volunteer
Make a difference to the lives of New York's hungry and homeless.
Every weekday at 10:30 a.m., hundreds of hungry and homeless New Yorkers walk through the
15 doors of the Holy Apostles Soup Kitchen to get a warm nutritious meal and seek help in finding their way on to a better way of life. But 45 minutes beforehand, another crowd is gathering: 50 – 60 volunteers who will make sure that happens.
From greeting guests to serving food, cleaning tables to handing out haircut vouchers, it is our volunteers who enable us to be here for our guests every day. One of the most important things we
20 do is to treat our guests with dignity and respect, and as a volunteer this is part of your job, too.
A warm smile or some friendly conversation can really help brighten our guests' days – and as a volunteer you might be surprised at how much this experience will brighten yours as well!
You can sign up to volunteer any weekday. You'll need to be available from 9:45 a.m. to 12:45 p.m.
Many volunteers stay for lunch afterwards and, just like our guests, enjoy the community to be
25 found here.
Sign up and make a difference today!

from: Church of the Holy Apostles and the Holy Apostles Soup Kitchen, New York

Your sister	Was liest du denn da?
You	Auf dieser Website sind Infos über …
Your sister	Das ist also die Organisation, zu der Oma zweimal in der Woche geht? Was genau macht diese Organisation denn?
You	…
Your sister	Und du meinst, dass du dort auch helfen kannst? Die haben doch bestimmt feste Angestellte, die dort immer arbeiten.
You	….
Your sister	Was sind die Aufgaben der Helfer?
You	…
Your sister	Ach, das ist ja interessant. Vielleicht können wir dann ja zusammen hingehen. Aber haben wir dann überhaupt Zeit, uns New York anzusehen, wenn wir den ganzen Tag da helfen müssen?
You	…
Your sister	Dann lass uns mal zu Oma gehen und ihr sagen, dass wir mitkommen.

⫸ First track

6
p.113

a Complete the job description with the correct prepositions from the box.

> at (2x) ▪ from ▪ in (2x) ▪ of ▪ on ▪ to

Career Spotlight

This week's spotlight is on being a vet.

This is a job many young animal-lovers dream ⬜1 doing. A vet's duties range ⬜2 diagnosing and looking
5 after sick animals ⬜3 carrying out operations. Sometimes they may have to put very sick animals to sleep. Vets might work with pets or large animals like cows. Some vets do extra training and become
10 experts ⬜4 caring for zoo animals and wildlife. Others work in laboratories and specialize ⬜5 doing research into animal diseases. Vets must be good ⬜6 solving problems and making decisions because
15 they have to identify what's wrong with an animal and decide the best way to treat it. They must also be excellent ⬜7 communicating this information to owners and staff.

20 To become a vet you need to be good at sciences. High school students who are keen ⬜8 getting some hands-on experience with animals should look for part-time or volunteer work on farms, or
25 in animal shelters or research laboratories.

4
p.117

c This is what Beth told *Career Spotlight* for the article. Put the direct statements into reported speech.

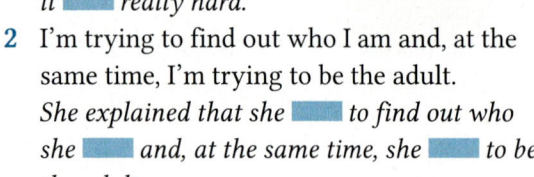

1 It's really hard.
Beth admitted that it ⬜ really hard.

2 I'm trying to find out who I am and, at the same time, I'm trying to be the adult.
She explained that she ⬜ to find out who she ⬜ and, at the same time, she ⬜ to be the adult.

3 For a long time I hated the responsibility at home, but now my perspective has changed.
Beth mentioned that for a long time she ⬜ the responsibility at home, but now her perspective ⬜.

4 I can't just think about myself all the time.
She knew that she ⬜ just think about herself all the time.

5 This situation won't be forever.
She also added that the situation ⬜ for ever.

3
p.122

b David needs some advice from his parents, so he reports what he and Juan talked about on the phone. Complete his sentences.

1 Juan asked me ⬜ that ⬜.
2 He wanted to know ⬜ I was quitting.
3 He ⬜ how many hours a week the other job ⬜.
4 He said he didn't mind if I came to work a little later. He asked ⬜ that ⬜.
5 I asked him ⬜ he ⬜ me on both days. He said I had to choose one job or the other.
6 He ⬜ me ⬜ about it and ⬜ him.

Extra reading

The soup kitchen

When 16-year-old Paul takes on a part-time job in a soup kitchen, he learns that there's more to making and serving soup than just filling people's bellies. This is an excerpt from Walter Dean Myers's novel *All the Right Stuff*.

I was late for my first day at the soup kitchen because I couldn't find the place. It wasn't marked SOUP KITCHEN or anything like that. It was on the basement floor of a brownstone on 144th Street, and there was a
5 small sign over the bell that read ELIJAH JONES'S SOUP EMPORIUM[1].

I rang the bell and a small, bright-eyed man with gray hair answered.

'My name is Paul Dupree,' I said. 'And I'm supposed
10 to be working here four days a week.'

'Welcome, Mr. Paul Dupree,' he said. 'I'm Elijah Jones. Please come in.'

I followed him in, through a room with six long tables set up and into a large, airy kitchen. Mr. Jones sat
15 himself down at one end of the table in the kitchen and gestured toward the other stool. I sat down.

'Hand me one of those vidalias over there, please.' He pointed in my direction, then started cutting up vegetables for the soup we were making.
20 I looked over to where he was pointing and didn't see what he was talking about. The only things sitting on the bench were some onions.

'Some what?' I asked him.

He turned toward me. 'Give me your particulars[2]
25 again?'

'Paul Dupree,' I said. 'Sixteen years old and just finished eleventh grade.'

'Did you want to add anything in there about not knowing what a vidalia was?' he asked.
30 'Not really,' I said.

'Well, a vidalia is a sweet onion,' Elijah said. 'I guess that's what the world is coming to today,' he said, turning back to his cutting board. 'We got wars going on, we got people robbing and shooting each other, and

we got young people like you don't even know what a 35 vidalia is. Do you think this might be the end of the world creeping up[3] on us?'

'No, sir, it's more about you dealing with onions and your vegetables, Mr. Jones,' I said. 'And if it was the end of the world, I don't think your onions would help too 40 much.'

'You'll call me Elijah,' he said.

'Sorry … Elijah,' I said.

'How about the soup? Do you think the soup would save the world? […],' he said.   45

Elijah told me he was eighty-four. He was dark, maybe five foot six or seven, and thin but not really skinny. He stood straight as an arrow and moved around his kitchen almost as if he was dancing.

'So you're saving the world with your soup?' I asked. 50

'I hear the smile in your voice, Mr. Dupree,' Elijah said. 'I'm not trying to save all of it, just my little corner here in Harlem. If we could get everybody to save their own little piece of this planet, then eventually we'd get the whole thing in pretty good shape.'   55

'Yes, sir.'

I watched Elijah make the soup of the day and get some vegetables ready for the next day's soup. At twelve o'clock, the first people started drifting in, and he had me serve them.   60

For most of the afternoon, I cleaned anything that could be cleaned. […] When everything was cleaned up, Elijah sat down at his cutting board and rolled an onion – okay, it was a vidalia – over to me.

'I want you to stop past the butcher's shop on your 65 way here tomorrow and pick me up ten pounds of veal bones. Do you think you can remember that?'

'Ten pounds of veal bones,' I repeated.

'The best soups start with a good liquid base,' Elijah said. 'The bones give some body to that base. People 70 like soup made from a good stock[4].'

'People like any soup that's free,' I said. 'You're making soup and giving it away for nothing. Naturally they like it.'

'I'm not just making soup,' Elijah said. 'I'm making 75 good soup for the senior citizens on this block. Now, don't pay more than five dollars for those bones,' Elijah said. 'And don't forget them because I'm running out of stock. And take that onion with you, Mr. Dupree, so you two can get acquainted[5].' […]   80

from: Walter Dean Myers, *All the Right Stuff*. New York: HarperCollins, 2012; pp. 13–17

---

[1] **emporium** Laden – [2] **particulars** Personalien – [3] **to creep up** hinaufschleichen – [4] **stock** Brühe – [5] **to get acquainted** sich kennenlernen

My review

What can I do?

Look at these sentences about Workshop 4. Are the sentences true for you?
Choose the right symbol for each sentence.

1 I can talk about my dream job.
2 I can discuss part-time / summer jobs and interviews.
3 I can decide what kind of volunteer work would suit me.
4 I can give information about children's rights.

>>> = 'I'm great at this!'
>>> = 'I'm good at this.'
>>> = 'I'm OK at this.'

What do I know?

1 **About my dream job.** Complete the job advert with the correct prepositions.

- Are you interested **1** helping us save the planet?
- We are looking for people who are passionate **2** making a difference.
- Our jobs range **3** working in a laboratory **4** doing fieldwork.
- Have you ever thought **5** becoming a scientist?
- Would you like to specialize **6** carrying out important research?
- Are you good **7** working under pressure?
- Would you like to be involved **8** saving endangered animals?

If you answered 'yes' to most of the questions and think you could get used **9** working irregular hours, then we are looking forward **10** hearing from you.
Contact us on …

■ / 10

Gerund after prepositions → G28 ; pp. 110 – 111

2 **About part-time jobs.** Vivian reports part of a conversation with David to a friend. Read the conversation, then complete what Vivian says. In the blue gaps add one of the reporting verbs from the box. Use each verb once.

David

> I've applied for another job because I'm saving to buy my first car.

> Be careful! A friend of mine, Lucy, has two jobs and she is often so tired and can't concentrate in school.

Vivian

David

> Don't worry. The new job doesn't start until the summer vacation, so it'll be OK.

explained ■ mentioned ■ said ■ told

David **1** that he **2** for another job. He **3** that he **4** to buy his first car. I warned him to be careful. I **5** a friend of mine – you know, Lucy. I **6** David that she **7** two jobs and she **8** often so tired and **9** concentrate in school. David told me **10** – the new job **11** until the summer vacation, so it **12** be OK.

■ / 12

Statements in reported speech → G29 ; pp. 114 – 115

3 **About volunteering.**

Rob listened to a phone-in radio programme about volunteering. Put the words in the correct order to report what he later told a friend. Be careful – in each sentence, there is one word or phrase you don't need.

1 said | there was | The expert | a wide range of opportunities | told | for young people | .
2 asked | people | She | to phone in | their questions | with | phone in | .

3 where they | could | the listeners | said | find more information | told | She also | .
4 did they select | the expert | volunteers | they selected | asked | how | A teenage boy | .
5 an age limit | was there | wanted to know | for volunteers | there was | A young girl | whether | .
6 asked | volunteers needed | any special training | Another caller | did volunteers need | if | .
7 her mind | what | changed | if | asked | A woman | will happen | she | would happen | .
8 don't apply | people | not to apply | advised | if they | The expert | weren't sure | .

■ / 8

Questions, requests, advice and orders in reported speech → G30 **; pp. 120 – 121**

Volunteering, pp. 122 – 123

4 **About children's rights.** Complete the text about children's rights in Germany with the correct quantifiers from the box. Use each quantifier once.

> a lot of ■ all ■ both ■ few ■
> half ■ majority ■ many ■ most ■
> most of ■ much

In Germany 1 children have to go to school until the age of 18. There are not 2 jobs which children under the age of 15 can do. The 3 of these jobs are considered as 'light' and 4 children do them because they don't get 5 pocket money. Babysitting and taking care of pets are two of the most popular jobs – 6 are done by girls and boys although 7 babysitters are girls.

Nearly 8 (48 %) of the teenagers interviewed in a recent survey said they had a part-time or summer job. 9 them said they were saving for something big like a holiday. A 10 said they thought the experience would also help them in the future and that this was one of the reasons they had got themselves a job.

■ / 10

Quantifiers → G31 **; pp. 124 – 125**

■ / 40

What's my score?

Check your answers to the review (Workbook, p. 107). What are your scores for each section?

> **What was your total score?**
> ⟫⟫⟫ score 31 – 40
> ⟫⟫⟫ score 21 – 30
> ⟫⟫⟫ score 0 – 20

Do you want to change your answers to the 'What can I do?' statements on page 134? Look at the tasks on pages 136 – 137: ⟫⟫⟫, ⟫⟫⟫ and ⟫⟫⟫.
Choose the tasks to help you.

My practice pages

Talking about your dream job

1 **When I grow up …** Complete with a preposition and the verbs in brackets in the correct from.

> about ■ at ■ for ■ in (2x) ■ of (3x)

1 I dream _____ (*become*) an astronaut.
2 I'm passionate _____ (*watch*) the stars.
3 That gave me the idea _____ (*study*) science.
4 I'm interested _____ (*visit*) Cape Canaveral.
5 I'd like the chance _____ (*travel*) in space!
6 My brother works for a start-up which is involved _____ (*create*) computer games.
7 He definitely doesn't want to be responsible _____ (*manage*) his own company.
8 He's really good _____ (*solve*) problems.

2 **My dream job.** Complete these sentences.

1 I love …
2 I'm really interested in …
3 I'm good at …
4 I've often dreamed of …
5 I'd like a job which gives me the chance …

3 **My dream job.** Describe your dream job. Use the prompts from **2** and the expressions below.

> keen on ■ look forward to ■ passionate about ■ responsible for ■ think about

Talking about part-time jobs

4 **What did he say?** Read the two conversations between Tony and Jane and Tony and Max.

Tony   I have a new job in a hotel kitchen. The work isn't well paid and I don't like it.
Jane   You should look for a better job.

Tony   I have a new job in a hotel kitchen. Are you interested in a job there?
Max   Thanks.

Now complete what Jane and Max say with the correct form of the verbs in brackets. In the blue gaps add one of the verbs from the box.

> advised ■ asked ■ said ■ told

Jane   Tony `1` me he `2` (*have*) a new job in a hotel kitchen.
Max   I know. He `3` me if I `4` (*be*) interested in a job there.
Jane   Really? But he `5` the work `6` (*not be*) well paid and he `7` (*not like*) it. I `8` him `9` (*look for*) a better job.

5 **A conversation.** Complete the conversation with the correct form of the verbs in brackets. In the blue gaps add one of the verbs from the box.

> advised ■ explained ■ mentioned ■ said ■ told

Kate   Last week, you `1` you `2` (*see*) an ad for a part-time job.
Hannah   Yes, I have an interview tomorrow. But my mum `3` me `4` (*wait*) until the summer holidays.
Kate   But our teacher `5` that it `6` (*be*) OK to work a few hours every week. Plus last week you `7` me you really `8` (*need*) the money.
Hannah   No, I `9` it would be nice to have some extra money. Let's see what they say at the interview. I promised mum that I `10` (*talk*) to her again before making a decision.

6 **She said …** Imagine you are telling a friend about what Emma said. Use different reporting verbs.

I've started a new part-time job. I'm working in an animal shelter. I've always loved animals, so it's the perfect job for me. I work three shifts a week: two after school and one on Saturday. I think this experience will help me in the future. My father told me about the job and suggested I apply. The interview was OK – they didn't ask too many difficult questions and I got the job!

Talking about volunteering

7 **What do you suggest?** Emily talks to a friend about volunteering. Later she tells her parents about the conversation. Complete what she says.

Emily	Please tell me about *Happy Helpers*.
Fred	It's a great place to work. All the helpers are very friendly.
Emily	How long have you been a volunteer?
Fred	I started in May.
Emily	And how many hours a week does a volunteer have to work?
Fred	Don't worry about the hours – it's up to you. Come for a day soon, then you'll see why I love it!

1 I asked Fred ▮▮▮ me about *Happy Helpers*.
2 He said it ▮▮▮ a great place to work and added that all the helpers ▮▮▮ very friendly.
3 I wanted to know how long he ▮▮▮ a volunteer.
4 Fred explained that he ▮▮▮ in May.
5 I asked him how many hours a week a volunteer ▮▮▮ work.
6 He told me ▮▮▮ about the hours – it ▮▮▮ up to me. He said ▮▮▮ for a day soon and then I ▮▮▮ why he ▮▮▮ it!

8 **A phone-in about volunteering.** Complete the report about a radio phone-in.

> Last week I listened to a part of a phone-in about volunteering. The expert, Rachel Harvey, explained that listeners ▮1▮ (*can*) ask questions. The first caller wanted to know what types of jobs there ▮2▮ (*be*). Rachel asked him ▮3▮ (*tell*) her how he ▮4▮ (*spend*) his free time. She said it ▮5▮ (*be*) important to volunteer in an area you ▮6▮ (*feel*) passionate about. Another person asked how old you ▮7▮ (*have to*) be. Rachel told her ▮8▮ (*check out*) the organization's website.

9 **Friendly advice.** You spoke to your parents last week about volunteering. Write a conversation between you and a friend explaining what you asked your parents and their advice.

Talking about children's rights

10 **Your rights.** Choose the correct quantifiers to complete the information.

While **a lot/most/much** (1) countries in the world have signed the UN Convention on the Rights of the Child there are still **a lot of/ both/few** (2) cases where these rights are ignored. **All/Majority/Most** (3) the articles in the declaration talk about the basic needs of children. **All/Few/Many** (4) people would disagree with these 'rights', but **a lot/many/ much** (5) children still suffer. According to the UN, over **all/half of/most** (6) the refugees in the world are children and **both/majority/many** (7) of these will spend the **majority/many/most** (8) of their lives away from home and their families.

11 **Facts and figures.** Choose the correct quantifier from the box to complete this report.

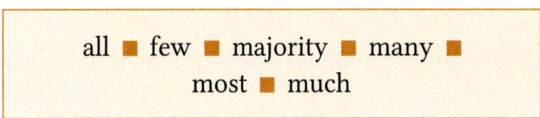

> all ▪ few ▪ majority ▪ many ▪
> most ▪ much

In the UK, ▮1▮ children should have the right to a healthy lifestyle. ▮2▮ people understand that having a healthy diet is important, but unfortunately very ▮3▮ children in the UK have a really healthy diet. Many of them don't eat enough vegetables or ▮4▮ fruit. In terms of exercise, the numbers are worse with ▮5▮ children not getting regular exercise. The ▮6▮ of children in the UK only take part in a sporting activity about once a month.

12 **Child labour.** Describe the infographic. Include as many quantifiers as you can.

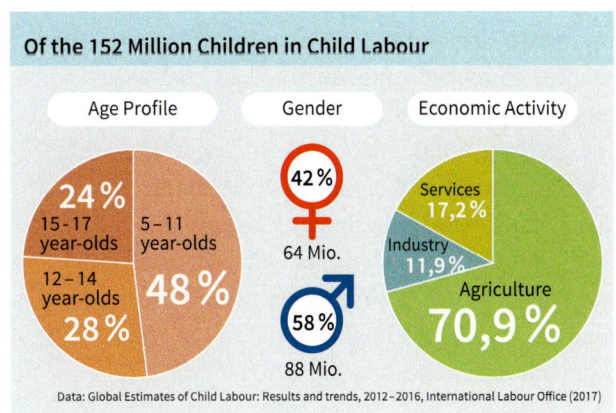

Of the 152 Million Children in Child Labour

Age Profile — Gender — Economic Activity

24% 15–17 year-olds
5–11 year-olds
12–14 year-olds 28%
48%

42% 64 Mio.
58% 88 Mio.

Services 17,2%
Industry 11,9%
Agriculture 70,9%

Data: Global Estimates of Child Labour: Results and trends, 2012–2016, International Labour Office (2017)

82))) → ⟶ FOUR ⟵ ←

The second note from the kidnappers said two final things:

1 'The raven must come alone!'

And:

5 2 'No funny business¹'

We weren't exactly sure what 'no funny business' meant, but we guessed it had something to do with 1; that I had to come on my own.

The policeman, whose name we finally found out

10 was Officer Slowfoot, had gone back to the police station. He didn't know what to do, and couldn't decide whether to do what the kidnappers said, or ignore them. He really was useless.

So, there I was, at midnight, sitting on the rail of the

15 old scary bridge in the middle of the forest. Waiting. They call it the 'old scary bridge', because that's exactly what it is. It's been there forever, and it looks as if it might fall down at any moment, but I had my instructions, so there I was: sitting on the bridge.

20 Solstice had told me I must do exactly what the kidnappers wanted. So I did.

Now, I would like to say that I wasn't very happy. Firstly, I still hadn't had anything to eat.

Secondly, I didn't see why I was being swapped for

25 the twins. I mean, I understood that the kidnappers were fed up with Fizz and Buzz. I mean, who wouldn't be? I can't spend more than three minutes in their company before I want to murder them. So that made sense. I just didn't see why the kidnappers

30 wanted *me* instead. And finally, I also didn't understand why the family thought it was just fine to hand me over to get the twins back. Solstice tried to explain that as soon as the twins were released², I would just be able to fly away, but something told me

35 it wouldn't be quite as simple as that. I wished they wanted Cudweed's monkey instead; that would solve another of my problems. But it seemed they wanted me, so there I was. I sat on the railing of the bridge, feeling grumpy and confused. And hungry.

40 And bored. Because although the kidnappers had said 'midnight', midnight had already come and gone. I know this because after a while Solstice and Cudweed suddenly appeared out of the forest. They ran up to me, looking worried.

_____

¹ **no funny business** keine faulen Tricks – ² **to release** freilassen

45 'Are you still here?' Solstice said.

'It's nearly one in the morning!' said Cudweed. As well as worried, he also seemed quite excited at being awake at one o'clock in the morning. His eyes were wide, and he looked sort of frantic.

50 'Kark!' I said, which meant: what are you doing here? If the kidnappers see you …

'Yes,' said Solstice, 'we know, but we're over there, in the bushes, with Mum and Dad, just waiting. If …' But she didn't finish what she was saying, because

55 we heard a vehicle approaching and saw headlights in between the trees.

'Kork!' I said, looking at the truck that was approaching, but when I looked back to the children, they had already disappeared again.

60 Then I heard a bush say something.

'Just remember to fly away!' said the bush, although I realized it was actually Solstice inside the bush. After a moment or two, the truck stopped on the bridge, but the engine stayed on.

65 At first, it was hard to see who was driving it, but then two figures climbed out of it.

They were a man and a woman, quite young. There was something odd about them, right from the start; they looked as if they didn't wash behind their ears

70 very often, for one thing. For another thing, they looked strange next to each other: the man was very short and round; the woman was very, very tall, and thin.

Also, they were arguing. Constantly[3].

75 'I told you we should turn left at the castle,' said the woman.

'Ha! You don't even know left from right[4],' said the man.

'At least I know how to drive,' said the woman.

80 'I could learn if I wanted to,' said the man.

'Oh, you just don't want to, that's all.'

And on and on it went, until finally the man saw me and said, 'Look! There it is!'

It! He called me it! Horrible person.

85 While I was still thinking about that, the woman came up to me. She stared at me.

'Do you think it bites?' she asked the man.

'Why don't you find out?' the man muttered under his breath.

90 'What?' she snapped.

'Nothing, sister. Nothing. Shall we get on with it?'

Sister! So they were brother and sister. But grown-ups.

95 I guessed they still lived together and had been arguing for approximately twenty-five years. They probably hated each other.

'Pull the truck forward,' said the man.

100 '*You* pull it forward,' said the woman, then added, 'Oh I remember now, you don't know how to drive.'

She got in the truck again and drove it another ten metres forward, so that I was looking at the back, which was open.

105 Inside, there were two large cages.

One of the cages was empty, but in the other …

'Gar-gar!' I heard two little voices, both speaking at once.

It was Fizz and Buzz! They seemed rather pleased to 110 see me, which was almost sweet. Almost. They were locked together in one of the cages. I should explain that they don't speak the way other people do. They seem to have invented their own language, that no one else understands, and although they can speak 115 English, mostly they speak in what we call 'twinnish'. For example, they don't say 'Edgar'. They say 'Gar-gar'. Stupid children.

Then I saw that the thin woman was looking at me.

'So apparently you can understand English … Is that 120 right?'

I ignored her.

'And you can speak English, too?' she asked.

I ignored her again.

The woman turned and looked at Fizz and Buzz.

125 'Are you lying about this?' she asked them, looking very mean.

'No, no!' they said together. In English for once. They say everything together, at exactly the same time. It's very weird. 'Edgar!' they said. 'What goes in the top 130 of a bottle?'

Well, I was not in the mood to play games and I told them so.

'Kork,' I said, which means 'please behave yourselves for once'.

135 However, I may have said the wrong thing, because the woman turned to the man and said, 'See! He said 'cork'! He does speak English!'

'Right,' said the man. 'Let's get on with this[5].'

He opened the door of the empty cage.

140 'You get in the cage. See? Then, we let the twins go.'

'And good riddance[6],' said the woman. 'What awful children.'

'Kark,' I said, because we were in agreement about that, at least. But I did not want to get in the cage. So 145 much for Solstice's idea about just flying away.

'Please, please, Gar-gar!' said the twins, and the woman pointed at the door of the empty cage.

'In you go,' she said, 'then we let the children go.'

Well, I didn't like it, but there was no choice.

150 I flapped off the railing and into the cage and the woman quickly shut the door behind me! I was not happy.

'Right,' said the man, 'Let's get out of here! Help me with the kids.'

155 He climbed into the back of the truck and opened the door of the cage in which Fizz and Buzz were sitting. The second the door opened, they jumped out.

Fizz bit the man's ankles, and Buzz started running towards the woman, who began screaming, 'Oh no! 160 Not again! Not again!'

There was a lot of fuss like this until finally the twins stopped attacking for long enough for the man and woman to jump into the truck and drive away. With me in the back!

---

[3] **constantly** ständig – [4] **to not know left from right** links und rechts nicht unterscheiden können – [5] **to get on with** weitermachen, fortfahren – [6] **good riddance** gut, dass wir sie los sind

165 As the truck pulled away into the darkness of the trees, I saw Minty and Valevine, Solstice and Cudweed run out of their hiding places towards Fizz and Buzz. The family was reunited[7]!

Apart, that is, from me, who was driven off in the 170 middle of the night, for hours.

For some time, I tried to look out of the back windows of the truck, to keep an eye on where we were going. But then, it was very late, and, well, I fell asleep. When I woke up, I was in a very strange place.

175 It was a large room. It didn't seem to have any windows, and was quite dark, and I guessed we were in a basement[8]. But I could see it was full of stuff. All kinds of stuff. Weird stuff. Strange things. There was a dead crocodile on top of a grand piano; there was 180 an old motorcycle with no wheels leaning against a grandfather clock[9]. There was a human skeleton, with a top hat on its skull, standing by the door. There were piles of books all around, and boxes and boxes of who-knows-what?

185 Just as I was trying to work out where I was, I heard arguing.

'This had better work,' said a voice, as a door opened and in came the man and the woman. I was still in the cage, but already looking for a way out. It seemed 190 there was only one door.

'Of course it will work,' said the man.

'Why do you say 'of course'? None of your other ideas have worked!'

'*My* ideas? What about *your* ideas? Look around you! 195 This room is full of things you said we'd be able to sell for a fortune!'

'What about the things you stole? That crocodile, for example...'

'It looked like it was worth a lot of money!'

200 'It looked like rubbish! It still does!'

And on and on they went, arguing again, without stopping.

So! Two things were obvious to me.

205 First: they were thieves, and they stole things that they thought they could sell again for money. And now they had me. And thought they could sell me for a lot of money.

Well, that was pretty clever, I admit, because I am an 210 extremely special bird.

The second thing that was clear was this; if I didn't find a way to escape within twenty minutes, their arguing would drive me mad. The kidnappers didn't seem that dangerous. In fact, they seemed mostly 215 harmless[10], and, apart from the idea about selling me, very stupid. In fact, there was a third obvious thing – if this pair were kidnappers, they were terrible kidnappers.

'Are you sure it can speak?' said the man, peering[11] 220 through the bars[12] of the cage at me. 'He only said 'cork'[13]. That could have been an accident.'

'If he can't speak, he's worthless[14]. We may as well get rid of him.'

Get rid of him? I didn't like the sound of that one 225 bit.

The woman came up to the cage. She stared at me again.

'Good birdy, good birdy. Say something, will you, birdy?' She had a horrible fake smile on her face. She 230 poked[15] her fingers through the bars of the cage a little, trying to encourage[16] me to speak. Then the nasty smile dropped from her face, and she added, 'Or you're in big trouble.'

'Futhork,' I said. I was starting to get worried. Maybe 235 they weren't as harmless as they appeared.

'What does that mean?' she said, turning to her brother. (It means something very rude, so rude I can't tell you what.) But while she wasn't looking, I took the chance to peck her fingers, very hard.

---

[7] **reunited** wiedervereinigt – [8] **basement** Keller – [9] **grandfather clock** Standuhr – [10] **harmless** harmlos – [11] **to peer** spähen – [12] **bars** Stäbe – [13] **cork** Korken – [14] **worthless** wertlos – [15] **to poke** durchstecken – [16] **to encourage** ermutigen

240 She screamed and I said 'kronk' – that's me laughing – which only made her more angry.

'I don't think this bird can speak at all!' she yelled at her brother. 'Another stupid idea of yours. We may as well put some stones in the cage and throw him in
245 the river, right now.'

Stones?! The river?! Aaaaark! They might look stupid, but they were dangerous after all. What evil people! I had to escape, and soon. Or I was going to be one drowned raven!

250 'Can't we just flush him down the toilet?' the man was saying.

'Don't be stupid, he's too fat.'

Fat! Well, now I was more angry than scared, and I decided to take matters into my own hands. Or claws.
255 You know what I mean.

As the woman tried to poke me again, I saw my chance! I grabbed her
260 finger in my beak and didn't let go.

'Help!' she screamed, 'it's got me! Get it
265 off me!'

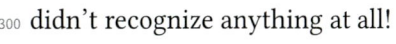

'Hang on!' said the man. 'I'll have to open the cage door.'

'Well, just be careful. Make sure it doesn't...'

But he was too slow.

270 The moment he opened the door of the cage, I flew out and began flying around the room at high speed, so they wouldn't catch me again.

'Now look what you've done!' said the woman.

'It was your fault, you shouldn't have poked it.'

275 Now, while I was flying around the room, I saw something. There was a log stove[17] in the corner of the room, and I noticed three things about it.

One, it wasn't alight[18]. (This was important for my plan.)

280 Two, the door was open.

And three, it had a chimney that led up through the ceiling and one thing I know about chimneys is that they always lead to open air.

The only problem was that the chimney pipe[19] was
285 quite narrow, but then, I told myself, no one has

given you anything to eat for at least 12 hours, you've probably lost a little weight.

So, while the man and woman were still arguing, I shot into the log stove and up the chimney like a
290 bullet in a gun.

I burst up into the air above a small house in the middle of the countryside.

I was free, but I had a
295 problem. I didn't know where I was. They must have taken me a long way in that truck, because I know all the forests around our castle and I
300 didn't recognize anything at all!

But then, just as I was worrying about how I was going to find the way home, I saw something. There! I looked down and saw three police cars, lots of police officers, and the whole family: Minty and
305 Valevine, Solstice and Cudweed, and Fizz and Buzz.

'Look!' shouted Solstice, 'I told you he'd free himself!'

I landed on the roof of the nearest police car.

'Yes, you were right,' said Valevine. 'But how clever of Fizz and Buzz to remember the way to the
310 kidnappers' house! Smart little things, eh?'

Fizz and Buzz had remembered the way? And told the police?

Well, I was dumbfounded[20].

And, as the police went inside and arrested the
315 terrible kidnappers, I looked at Fizz and Buzz.

'Krark,' I said. Perhaps small children do have a point. Sometimes.

I flapped over to them and, just to remind them who's in charge, gave each of them a friendly peck
320 on the top of the head.

THE END

---

17 **log stove** Holzofen – 18 **to be alight** brennen – 19 **chimney pipe** Kaminrohr – 20 **dumbfounded** verblüfft; sprachlos

Speaking skills

1 **VIDEO TRACK: Confusing sounds**

 a Some sounds in English can be difficult for German speakers to understand and produce. Watch Lena talking about some typical mistakes German speakers like her make when speaking English. What mistakes does she mention?

 b Listen to what Lena says again and repeat the examples.

When he started his Hollywood career, the Austrian actor Christoph Waltz played mostly German characters. Now he speaks almost without an accent.

2 **Tongue twisters**

 a Listen, then practise these tongue twisters to improve your pronunciation. Try saying them faster and faster.

1 /v/ /w/ /z/	Why isn't Vera feeling very well?
2 /v/ /w/ /ɔ:/	My verse is very bad but yours is much worse.
3 /ð/ /θ/	These three cats are thin but those over there are fat.
4 /ʃ/ /tʃ/	Sheila always chooses cheap sheep's cheese.
5 /ʃ/ /tʃ/ /dz/	Enjoy Gerry's German cherry pie with sherry.
6 /e/ /æ/	My pet cat sat on the wet mat.
7 /əʊ/	The lonely boy answered the phone on his own.
8 /ɔ:/ /əʊ/	John caught his coat in the door so he fell to the floor.
9 /ɜ:/	Shirley learned the German word for bird.
10 /d/ /t/	A he-toad who loved a she-toad tried hard to win her heart but the hard-hearted she-toad sent him away.

b Write your own tongue twisters to practise the sounds.

3 **VIDEO TRACK: How English is really spoken**

 a Watch the video to find out what happens in spoken English. Listen to the examples on the video and repeat.

b Search the internet and listen to authentic recordings and videos in British English. Identify as many features of natural English as possible.

> **TIP**
>
> When we write in English, each word is separate – there are spaces between the words. But that's not how we speak English. In spoken English, we usually string sounds together in different ways. Recognizing these features will help you understand native English speakers better.

4 **Up or down?**

 a Watch the video about intonation patterns in spoken English and repeat the examples.

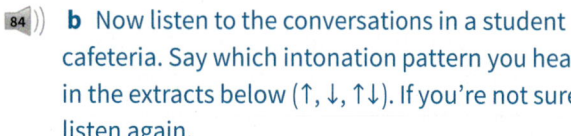 **b** Now listen to the conversations in a student cafeteria. Say which intonation pattern you hear in the extracts below (↑, ↓, ↑↓). If you're not sure, listen again.

c Listen again and repeat.

1 Excuse me. Is this seat free?
2 Sure. Sit down.
3 Koyomi, you're Japanese, aren't you?
4 Nice to meet you.
5 You're Irish, aren't you?
6 I'm going to get a hamburger, chips, a salad and a coke.
7 Did you go anywhere else?

d How does Koyomi feel about Dublin?

 e Roleplay a similar conversation in groups of three. You meet for the first time in a cafeteria. Introduce yourselves and find out more about each other.

5 **British or American?**

 a Listen to Josh and Emily talking about six big differences between British English and American English pronunciation. Listen to the examples they give. What are the differences?

b Take turns to say these sentences either in British English or American English. Your partner has to decide which pronunciation you used – and correct any mistakes.

1 My essay is due tomorrow.
2 Why did you park your car so far away?
3 I'll carry your bags, Harry.
4 I want to go to the shop to buy some pop.
5 I need to buy some water, some butter and some potatoes.
6 Let's go for a walk and talk.

c Watch the videos on page 21 and page 58 again. How many of the features in **a** do you notice? Can you identify any more?

6 **UK – US vocabulary challenge**

 a Match the British and American words / phrases with the same meaning. Take turns to test your partner. Try to pronounce the American words correctly. Then listen and check.

Student A *biscuit*
Student B *cookie*

> biscuit ■ break time ■ car park ■ chemist / pharmacy ■ chips ■ bin / dustbin ■ flat ■ holiday ■ jumper ■ lift ■ lorry ■ rubber ■ soft drink ■ shopping centre ■ tap ■ takeaway ■ underground

> apartment ■ cookie ■ drugstore ■ elevator ■ eraser ■ faucet ■ french fries ■ mall ■ parking lot ■ recess ■ soda ■ subway ■ sweater ■ takeout ■ trashcan ■ truck ■ vacation

b To help you remember the words, put them into categories in your notebook.

	Around the house	At school	Housing / buildings	Clothing	Food	Shopping	Travel / on the road
BE	???	???	???	???	???	???	???
AE	???	???	???	???	???	???	???

c Find more examples in WS 1, pages 14, 15 and 16. Add them to your lists. Continue to add to your lists as you come across more British or American English words.

Reading skills

1 **Making friends**

a Read the extract (ll. 34–40) from the story on page 46. Exchange student Conor O'Brien is introduced to Meg for the first time in the school cafeteria. The writer doesn't say directly that Conor finds her interesting. Which words tell you?

> 'He's an awesome guitar player,' Jordan
> 35 said to Meg. He turned to Conor. 'Meg is an expert. She's been listening to jazz guitar all her life.' Conor looked at Meg. 'My dad plays. He's in the jazz scene,' Meg said. Conor sat up. 'Really?' He had never
> 40 met anyone whose dad was a jazz guitarist.

b How does Conor feel when Meg leaves with Dan? The writer doesn't say directly. Read lines 57 to 64. Which words tell you?

> Meg looked at Dan and then at the others. 'Dan is driving me home,' she said. Meg gave a small wave and the two left.
> 60 Conor watched them go. 'You didn't tell me about those two,' he said.
> 'I'm sorry,' Alisha said. 'I didn't know that you wanted to ask her out.'
> 'Never mind, it's OK.' Conor tried to smile.

2 **Hey Sherlock!** Read the extract on page 69. What evidence is there in the text for these statements? Give line numbers where possible.

1 Dr Roecastle is well off.
2 The men who have come to put up fencing don't like the police.
3 Amy is a rebellious teenager who doesn't like being told what to do.
4 Dr Roecastle is impatient, sarcastic and has a bad temper.
5 She loves and cares about her daughter.

TIP

Sometimes it's very clear what a writer wants to say. Sometimes, however, the writer may *suggest* something indirectly rather than state it directly. When you are reading a fictional text – a story or a poem – you often need to make guesses to work out what the writer is saying about the characters, the setting or the plot. To do this, you can use clues and other information in the text and your own knowledge and experience as well.

3 **The Poet X.** Read the extracts from the verse novel by Elizabeth Acevedo. In the novel 16-year-old Xiomara (X) is attracted to Aman, whom she met at her school in Harlem in New York City. Both are from immigrant families from the Caribbean. What do you learn about X and Aman? Explain your ideas and conclusions with evidence from the text.

1 Describe the character of X and Aman and how the writer conveys the information.
2 Discuss why you think X 'never never' reads her work.
3 Say why you think reading a poem about Papi might be especially difficult for X.
4 Describe how Aman's feelings about his mother have changed since he left Trinidad. Speculate why Aman's mother 'never came'.
5 Analyse the relationship between X and Aman. How well do they know each other? How do they feel about each other?

About the author …
Elizabeth Acevedo is the youngest child and only daughter of Dominican immigrants. She grew up in New York. When she was 12, she wanted to be a rapper, but became more interested in poetry. At the age of 14, she competed in her first poetry slam. She has several university degrees and worked as a teacher. She wanted her students to read more and discovered that she could write books that interested her students. *The Poet X* is on the *New York Times* bestseller list and a *National Book Award* winner.

Friday, September 28
Listening

Today when Aman and I sit on the bench
l wait for him to pass me his headphones,
but he plays with my fingers instead.

'No music today, X.
5 Instead I want to hear you.
Read me something.'

And I instantly freeze.
Because I never, never read my work.
But Aman just sits patiently.

10 And with my heart thumping
I pull my notebook out.
'You better not laugh.'

But he just leans back and closes his eyes.
And so I read to him.
15 Quietly. A poem about Papi.

My heart pumps hard in my chest,
and the page trembles when I turn it,
and I rush through all the words.

And when I'm done I can't look at Aman.
20 I feel as naked as if I'd undressed before him.
But he just keeps fiddling with my fingers.

'Makes me think of my mother being gone.
You got bars[1], X. I'm down to[2] listen to them
anytime.'

————————
[1] **You got bars** You write well – [2] **I'm down to** I will

Mother Business

Aman and I don't really talk about our families
like that.
I know the rules. You don't ask about people's
parents.
5 Most folks got only one person at home,
and that person isn't even always the egg or the
sperm donor.
But I feel like I said too much and too little
about Papi.
10 And now I want to know more about Aman's
family.

'Can you tell me about your moms? Why is she
gone?'

His mouth looks zipped-up silent.
15 We are quiet for a while and there's no noise to
cover my shiver.
Even lost in his thoughts, Aman notices,
tucks my hand clasped with his inside his jacket
pocket.
20 I'm glad the cold breeze is a good excuse
for why my cheeks go pink. He finally looks at
me.
His eyes trying to read something in my face.

I don't expect him to ever answer.

And Then He Does

'My moms was a beautiful woman.
She and Pops married when they were teens.
He came here first, then sent for us.

I was old enough when I came here
5 that I can remember Trinidad:

the palm tree behind my grandma's house,
the taste of backyard mangoes,
the song in the voice every time someone spoke.

I was young enough to learn how my accent
10 could be rolled tight between my lips
until this country smoked it out
into that clipped 'good-accented English.'

My mother never came, you know.
She would call every day at first
15 and always tell me the same thing,
she 'was handling affairs.' 'We'll be together soon.'

She calls every year on my birthday.
I've stopped asking her when she's coming.
Pops and I get on just fine.

20 I've learned not to be angry.
Sometimes the best way to love someone
is to let them go.'

all three poems taken from Elizabeth Acevedo, *The Poet X*, New York: HarperTeen (Harper Collins Publishers), 2018, pp. 96 – 98

Writing skills

1 **Formal and informal writing**

a Find examples of formal and informal writing in the texts on page 14 (Ellie's blog), page 15 (Alex and Vivian's text message), and page 16 (Ellie's email).

b How do the writers start and end their text message and email?

c Compare the informal texts that you looked at in **a** to the formal letter to the editor on page 31. Identify the differences between informal and formal style.

TIP

When you write in English, it's important to use the right style depending on the audience and the purpose of the text. In personal blogs, text messages, emails and letters, you can use an informal style. You can:
- start a new sentence with linking words like *And*, *But*, *Because*.
- use dashes (–) instead of commas or full stops.
- use exclamation marks (!).
- use short forms like *Don't*, *they've*, abbreviations or emojis ☺.
- use informal / colloquial words and expressions like *cool*, *selfie*, etc.
- show a change of topic using *Anyway …*, *By the way …*
- ask direct questions.

---

2 **Structuring formal and semi-formal letters and emails**

a Although today most of our written communication is by informal email, text message or social media, there are still plenty of reasons why you might need to write a formal or semi-formal letter or email. Think of some examples of both.

TIP

A letter
Here are some tips on how to strucutre a letter:
- **Structuring the top of the letter:** Put your address in the top-right corner of the page. Below this, include the date. Below this, on the left-hand side, put the name and address of the recipient
- **Greeting / salutation:** You can use first name and surname, or title and surname: *Dear (John Doe), Dear (J Doe),* or *Mr/Mrs/Ms Doe*
  If you don't know the name of the recipient, you can use their job title or function: *Dear Editor, Dear Hiring Manager*
- **Structuring the body of the letter:**
  Opening paragraph: Introduce yourself and your reason for writing.
  Main body: Add further details / information.
  Final paragraph / conclusion: As in the diagram, thank the recipient for their time / help and say what action you expect from them, for example, you look forward to hearing from them.
- **Signing off:** If you used someone's name and title or function at the start, end with *Yours sincerely / Yours faithfully* (very formal), *Kind regards* (formal) or *Best wishes* (relaxed formal).
  Include your handwritten signature or a digital signature.

Opening paragraph

Main body

Closing statement

Sign off

---

b Read the instructions and TIP box to **6** on page 17. You don't know the name of the host family, as this is an application.

1 Decide what style to use: informal, semi-formal or very formal.

2 Choose the best way to start your letter.
Hi! / Dear Host Family / Dear Family

3 Decide how to conclude your letter.
Thanks a million. / Can't wait to meet you. / Thank you so much for giving me the chance to stay in your home. I really look forward to meeting you.

4 Choose the best way to sign off.
Yours sincerely / Kind regards / Best wishes / See ya!

3 **Writing a summary**

a A summary is a short account of the main ideas of a text: an article, a story or a video. It includes only important information, leaving out unnecessary details, examples and any direct speech. Follow these steps when summarizing narrative texts.

Step 1: Make sure you understand the text fully. Read the title and the first lines, then skim the rest of the text to get a general idea of the content. In an article, the topic sentence of each paragraph states the main point – usually the first and / or second sentence. Then read the whole text carefully.

Step 2: Note down the most important information in each paragraph / section. Use these Wh-questions to help you:
● WHAT / WHO is the text about?
● WHAT are the main points or arguments?
● WHAT are the main events?
● WHERE / WHY is it important?

Step 3: Write the introduction to your summary. Explain the topic and the main point of the article. Include the author, date and source if known.

Useful phrases
The article is about … In this article, …
The writer describes / believes / argues …

Step 4: Write the rest of the summary. Use the simple present. Don't copy whole sentences. Use your own words, though you can use some key words from the text.

b Read the letter to the editor on page 31. Then read this summary. Decide if the writer has followed steps 1 – 4 in **a**. Give examples of what he / she has done well and what could be cut or improved.

4 **Writing a comment.** Read the text on page 52 or listen to the talk on page 53. Write a comment.
Step 1: Read or listen to the text again. Make or add to your notes.
Step 2: Organize your notes into paragraphs.
Step 3: Write your comment, then edit it.

Useful expressions
● Giving opinions: *In my opinion / view … My own opinion about the matter is … I agree / don't agree with … Personally, I believe that …*
● Listing arguments: *First of all / Firstly / Secondly …*
● Introducing causes and effects: *As a result (of), so, because (of) …*
● Introducing contrasting ideas: *On the one hand … On the other hand …*
● Concluding: *To sum up … In conclusion … Therefore …*

TIP

In your comment, you give your personal opinion about a topic. You can use formal or informal language depending on who you are writing it to.
How to structure a comment
● **Introduction:** State the topic for discussion. State the view of the writer or speaker. Give your opinion briefly, for or against.
● **Middle:** Provide arguments / examples to support your opinion. You could include arguments both for and against your opinion.
● **Conclusion:** Briefly summarize your main points and your opinion.

In this letter to a US newspaper, the writer, a Native American called John Walker Bear, is protesting about the Dakota Access Pipeline, which was built to transport oil across the Midwest. The writer is angry that the US government allowed oil companies to build it in spite of protests by Native Americans and others. He claims that the government showed little interest in Native American
5 wishes. He points out that the pipeline crosses land that is sacred to local Native American tribes. It also threatens the supply of clean water from the Missouri River to Native American reservations and other residents. He argues that the US government is once again ignoring Native American rights, lifestyle and culture, as they have done since the 1800's. That's when white settlers first began pushing Native Americans off their land. He concludes that Native Americans will continue to fight
10 to save their land until the government listens to them.

Appendix

Grammatical terms

adjective	Adjektiv

adverb
   adverb of frequency
   adverb of manner
   adverb of place
   adverb of time
	Adverb
	   Adverb der Häufigkeit
	   Adverb der Art und Weise
	   Adverb des Ortes
	   Adverb der Zeit

adverbial	Adverbial

clause
   if-clause
   main clause
   subordinate clause
	Teilsatz
	   Konditionalsatz / Bedingungssatz
	   Hauptsatz
	   Nebensatz

comparative / superlative	Komparativ / Superlativ
conjunctions	Bindewörter

future
   future with *going to*
   future with *will*
	Futur
	   Futur mit *going to*
	   Futur mit *will*

gerund	Gerundium
infinitive	Infinitiv
negative / positive	negativ, verneint / positiv, bejaht
noun	Nomen, Substantiv
subject / object	Subjekt / Objekt

past
   simple past
   past progressive
   past perfect
   past perfekt progressive
	Vergangenheit
	   Imperfekt, Präteritum
	   Verlaufsform des Präteritum
	   Plusquamperfekt
	   Verlaufsform der Vergangenheit

possessive determiner	Possessivbegleiter

present
   simple present
   present progressive
   present perfect
   present perfect progressive
	Gegenwart
	   Präsens
	   Verlaufsform des Präsens
	   Perfekt
	   Verlaufsform des Perfekt

pronoun
   possessive pronoun
   reciprocal pronoun
   reflexive pronoun
	Pronomen
	   Possessivpronomen
	   Reziprokpronomen
	   Reflexivpronomen

quantifier	Zahlwort
question tag	Frageanhängsel
reported speech (indirect speech)	indirekte Rede
short answer	Kurzantwort
statement	Aussagesatz

Grammar

Do you have a question about grammar? The **grammar appendix** explains all the grammar that you learn in this book.

G 1 Gerund as subject
Workshop 1, pages 14 – 15

A gerund is the *-ing* form of a verb. A gerund followed by an object or adverbial is called a gerund clause.

We can use a gerund or a gerund clause as the subject of a verb. This is when the subject is an activity or action.

Walking can be dangerous here.
Doing chores isn't my favourite activity.
Going to the shopping mall is always fun.

To form the negative, we put *not* before the gerund.
Not going out on a Saturday evening is quite uncommon among teenagers in the USA.

We often use the gerund as a subject in signs and notices.

See also → G2 , G15 , G16 , G18 , G28

G 2 Gerund as object
Workshop 1, pages 14 – 15

A gerund is the *-ing* form of a verb. A gerund followed by an object or adverbial is called a gerund clause.

We can use a gerund or a gerund clause as the object of certain verbs. This is when the object is an activity or action.

*I love **cooking**.*
*I don't mind **sweeping the porch**.*
*I like **seeing how people live here**.*
*He doesn't enjoy **going to the gym**.*

To form the negative, we put *not* before the gerund.
*I regret **not going** to the school prom.*

See also → G1 , G15 , G16 , G18 , G28

I love cooking …

G 3   Simple past and past progressive (revision)   Workshop 1, pages 14 – 15

We use the simple past to talk about a completed action in the past.
*I **did** some chores this morning.*

We use the past progressive to talk about something in progress and unfinished at a specific time in the past.
*I **was doing** my chores at 10.00 this morning.*

We often use the simple past with the past progressive. This is when a shorter action happens at the same time as another action or 'interrupts' a longer action that is already in progress.
*Susan **called** round to see me while I **was doing** my chores.*

We often use *when* or *while* to link the actions. We use *when* before the simple past. We use *when* or *while* before the past progressive.

Examples

*I first **went** to America in 2010 when I **was studying** English at university.*
*I **saw** Ellie yesterday when we **were coming** home in the car.*
*My parents **were working** in New York when they first **met**.*
*Alex **phoned** me while we **were having** lunch yesterday.*

G 4   Relative pronouns (revision)   Workshop 1, pages 18 – 19

We use relative pronouns in defining relative clauses to identify people and things. We use them in non-defining relative clauses to give extra information about someone or something.

The relative pronouns are **who, which, that** and **whose**.
We use **who** for people and **which** for things.
In a defining relative clause, we can also use **that** for both people and things. We don't use *that* in a non-defining relative clause.

*Find out what life was like for the passengers **who / that** travelled aboard the Mayflower.*
*Relive the event **which / that** started the American Revolution!*
*Look! There are the people **who / that** we met yesterday.*
*The War of Independence, **which** led to the founding of the United States, took place in the 18th century.*

We use **whose** to show possession.
*Is that the man **whose** wallet you found?*
*You can also visit the homesite of the Wampanoag Indians, **whose** land this was.*

See also   → ,

G 5   Defining relative clauses (revision)

Workshop 1, pages 18 – 19

> A clause is a part of a sentence. A defining relative clause identifies a person, thing, place or time.
>
> A defining relative clause comes immediately after this person, thing, place or time.
>
> The relative clause begins with a relative pronoun (*who, which, that* or *whose*).
>
> *A descendant is related to a person **who lived a long time ago**.*
> *Is this the museum **that Alex recommended**?*
> *Step aboard a replica of the tiny ship **which brought the Pilgrims to the New World**.*
>
> A relative pronoun can be the subject or the object of a relative clause.
>
> | | RELATIVE PRONOUN / SUBJECT | VERB | OBJECT | |
> | --- | --- | --- | --- | --- |
> | *There's the man* | **who** | *helped* | *us* | *yesterday.* |
>
> | | RELATIVE PRONOUN / OBJECT | SUBJECT | VERB | |
> | --- | --- | --- | --- | --- |
> | *There's the man* | **who** | *we* | *helped* | *yesterday.* |

❗   We can leave out *who, which* or *that* when it is the object of the relative clause.

*There's the man (**who**) we helped yesterday.*
*The first community (**that**) the Pilgrims built when they arrived in 1620 was in Plymouth.*
*The book (**which**) you gave me is really interesting.*
*Is this the museum (**that**) Alex recommended?*

We don't leave out **who**, **which** or **that** when it is the subject of the relative clause.
NOT ~~There's the man helped us yesterday.~~

See also   →

G 6   Non-defining relative clauses (revision)

Workshop 1, pages 18 – 19

> We use a non-defining relative clause to give extra, non-essential information about someone or something.
>
> The relative clause begins with a relative pronoun (*who, which* or *whose*). Note that we don't use *that* in a non-defining relative clause.
>
> We always separate a non-defining relative clause from the main clause with commas.
>
> *George Washington**, who was born in 1732**, was the first president of the USA.*
> *I live in Concord, **which is the capital of New Hampshire**.*
> *A group of colonists, **whose leader was Samuel Adams**, boarded three British tea ships in Boston Harbor.*
>
> We can also use a non-defining relative clause to comment on the whole of the previous clause.
>
> *The British introduced many new taxes, **which the colonists thought was very unfair**.*
> *The museum was closed, **which meant we had to go back the next day**.*

❗   Note that non-defining relative clauses are used mostly in writing and in other more formal contexts.
Non-defining relative clauses that comment on a whole clause can be quite common in spoken English.

See also   →

G 7 The definite, indefinite and zero article

Workshop 1, pages 24 – 25

As well as the basic rules regarding the use of the definite, indefinite and zero article, there are a number of special cases. These include:

We use **the** before:
- countries with a plural element (including words like States, Kingdom, Republic):
  *I'm from **the Netherlands**.* • *She's from **the USA**.* • *Have you been to **the United Kingdom**?*
- certain geographical regions and island groups:
  *He's from **the Midwest**.* • *I'd love to go to **the Far East**.* • *We went to **the Galapagos Islands**.*
- some famous buildings and man-made or natural landmarks:
  *We went up **the Empire State Building**.* • *I'd love to go to **the Grand Canyon**.*
- oceans, seas and rivers, and mountain ranges:
  *We swam in **the Pacific Ocean**.* • *Lake Itasca is the source of **the Mississippi**.* •
  *We flew over **the Rockies**.*
- groups of people or nations:
  ***The British** ruled America until 1776.* • ***The Chinese** invented fireworks.*

We use **no article** (zero article) before:
- continents, most countries, states or cities:
  *Have you ever been to **Asia**?* • *I used to live in **Turkey**.* • *She's from **New York**.*
- lakes and mountains:
  *I live near **Lake Ontario**.* • *We flew over **Mount Everest**.*
- languages:
  *I'm learning **English**.* • *Do you speak **German**?*

We use **a / an** before:
- jobs:
  *He's **a farmer**.* • *I want to be **an engineer**.* • *She's **a lawyer**.* • *Are you **a student**?*

G 8 Past perfect and simple past (revision)

Workshop 1, pages 28 – 29

We use the past perfect to show that one event happened before another event in the past. We use the past perfect for the event that happened first and we use the simple past for the more recent event.

*A few hours after we **had started** along the trail, my father **fell** ill.*
*We **had hoped** to reach this place sooner, but the bad weather **slowed** us down.*

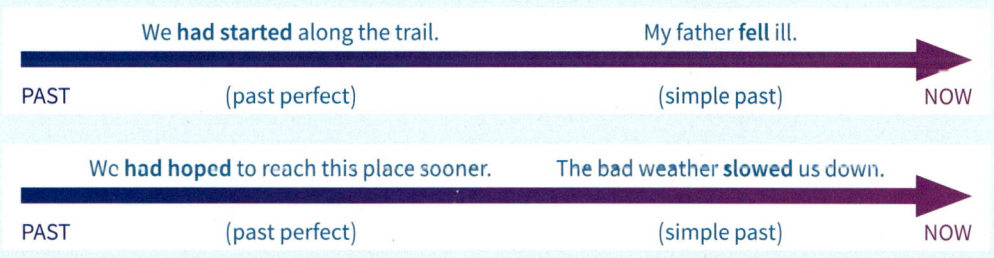

We also use the past perfect to show that something happened before a time in the past.
*We'**d travelled** over 200 miles **by 12 o'clock**.*

We often use sequence adverbs such as *when*, *before*, *after* and *until* to link the two events.
*The poor Parsons' boy **had** just **had** his 8th birthday **when** he fell and died.*

Examples *We **went** for a walk after we'**d eaten** lunch.*
*The train **left** before I'**d got** on it.*
*I **had** never **slept** in a tent until last summer.*

See also → G9

G 9 Past perfect progressive

Workshop 1, pages 28 – 29

We form the past perfect progressive with *had been* + verb + *-ing*.

Settlers **had been camping** *along the trail for many years before they came.*

We use the past perfect to show that one event happened before another event or before a specific time in the past.

We use the past perfect progressive to focus on the duration of the activity and / or to show that the activity was in progress or regularly repeated over a period of time.

It **had been raining** *a lot and the water was very high.*
They **'d been travelling** *for ten hours before they stopped to set up camp for the night.*

Examples

We **'d been waiting** *for over an hour before the bus arrived.*
I was tired because I **'d been driving** *all day.*
She **'d been feeling** *ill for a few days before she went to the doctor.*

See also   → G 8

G 10 Present perfect (revision)

Workshop 2, pages 46 – 47

We form the present perfect with *has / have* + past participle.

	Has / Have	Past participle	
I	**'ve**	**been**	*here for a few months.*
Morgan	**has**	**told**	*me about you.*
They	**haven't**	**arrived**	*yet.*

We form a question by putting the subject after the auxiliary verb *have*.

Have they arrived *yet?*
How long **have you lived** *here?*

We use the present perfect in two main ways.
● To talk about something in the past which is connected with or has a consequence in the present. We often use the present perfect in this way with *yet* and *already*.

   Mia, you haven't met Chris **yet**.
   I've **already** *booked the tickets.*
   He's lost his keys.
● To talk about something that started in the past and continues now. We use the present perfect in this way with *for* and *since* with *all* and in questions with *How long?*

   We've been friends **since** *we were seven.*
   He's known her **for** *ten years.*
   I've had problems with my computer **all** *day.* **How long** *have you known Mia?*

See also   → G 11 , G 12

G 11 Present perfect progressive (revision)

Workshop 2, pages 46 – 47

We form the present perfect progressive with *has / have been + -ing*.

	Has / Have been	*-ing*	
I	*'ve been*	*working*	*all day.*
It	*'s been*	*raining*	*since lunchtime.*
We	*haven't been*	*living*	*here for long.*

We form a question by putting the subject between *has / have* and *been*.
Has he been playing the drums for a long time?
How long have you been waiting?

We use the present perfect progressive to talk about a continuous or repeated activity, or a situation that continues to the present.
She's been listening to jazz guitar all her life.
I've been going to a lot of concerts recently.
It's been raining since I got up.

We've been living here for ten years … … and we still live here.

PAST   NOW

We use the present perfect in this way with *for* and *since* or with a time expression that connects the past with now (for example *recently, all her life, all afternoon, this week,* etc.).

! Remember that state verbs are generally not used in the progressive form.

*He's **had** a trumpet since 2019.* NOT ~~He's been having a trumpet since 2019.~~
*We've **known** each other for ten years now.* NOT ~~We've been knowing each other for ten years now.~~

See also → G 10 , G 12

G 12 Time words

Workshop 2, pages 46 – 47

We can use *for, since, already, yet* and *ever* with the present perfect and the present perfect progressive.

- We use the present perfect + *for* or *since* when an action or situation started in the past and continues to the present.

- We use *for* + a period in time (e. g. *for ten minutes, for three days, for ages, for a long time,* etc.):
  *He's had that trumpet **for a long time**.*
  *We've been living here **for twenty years**.*

- We use *since* + a point in time (e. g. *since 3 o'clock, since July, since 2019, since my birthday,* etc.):
  *I've had this book **since I was a child**.* • *They've been practising **since 2 o'clock**.*

- We use *already* to talk about something that happened previously. *Already* usually goes between *have* and the main verb.
  *We've **already** seen that film.*

- We use *yet* to talk about something that hasn't happened, but is expected to happen. *Yet* usually goes at the end of the sentence.
  *I haven't seen the film **yet**.*

- We can use *Have you ever …?* to ask about life experiences.
  *Have you **ever** been to Japan?*

See also → G 10 , G 11

G 13   *If*-sentences type 1 (revision) Workshop 2, pages 50 – 51

> We use *if*-sentences type 1 to talk about things that are possible or likely to happen.
> *If*-sentences type 1 have the form *if* + simple present, *will / won't* + infinitive.
>
> If I **think** something's cool, I**'ll go out** and buy it.
> If the phone **is** too expensive, I **won't buy** it.
>
> We use *unless* to mean *if not*.
> We'll go for a walk **unless** it **rains**. = We'll go for a walk **if** it **doesn't rain**.
>
> We use *when* for things which will definitely happen.
> **When** I get home, I'll call you.
>
> We can usually put the two clauses in any order. When the *if / when / unless* clause is first, there is a comma between the clauses.
> If I like it, I'll buy it.   I'll buy it if I like it.

Examples   If we **miss** the bus, we**'ll walk** home.
If you **see** Jenny, **will** you **say** hello from me?
I**'ll call** you when I **get** to the city centre.
I**'ll buy** this shirt unless I **see** a nicer one.

See also   → `G 14` , `G 25`

G 14   *If*-sentences type 2 (revision) Workshop 2, pages 50 – 51

> We use *if*-sentences type 2 to talk about things that are impossible, hypothetical or unlikely to happen.
> *If*-sentences type 2 have the form *if* + simple past, *would / wouldn't* + infinitive.
>
> If I **had** more money, I**'d buy** a new phone.
> If we **didn't buy** so much, it **would be** better for the environment.
> If we **recycled** more, there **wouldn't be** so much waste.
>
> We often use *could* or *might* in an *if*-sentence type 2.
> If I had more money, I **could** buy a new phone.
>
> We can usually put the two clauses in any order. When the *if* clause is first, there is a comma between the clauses.
> If I had more time, I'd read more books.   I'd read more books if I had more time.
>
> We can say *If I was …* or *If I were … .* However, we usually say *If I were you, … .*
> If I **was / were** richer, I'd travel round the world.
> If I **were** you, I'd start saving!

Examples   If I **had** more time, I**'d help** you.
I**'d go out** this evening if I **didn't have** so much homework.
What **would** you **do** if you **found** a wallet in the street?
If I **had** a credit card, I'm sure I**'d spend** a lot more!

See also   → `G 13` , `G 25`

G 15   Verb + gerund or *to*-infinitive   Workshop 2, pages 56 – 57

Sometimes we use two verbs together. The second verb adds information to what is expressed by the first verb. The second verb is usually the gerund (*-ing* form) or the *to*-infinitive.

We use the gerund after certain verbs. These include:
admit • avoid • can't stand • dislike • don't mind • enjoy • feel like • finish • give up • imagine • mention • miss • practise • recommend • suggest

*I **don't mind doing** chores in the house.*
*She **suggested having** some Italian food for dinner.*

We use the *to*-infinitive after certain verbs. These include:
agree • arrange • can afford • choose • decide • expect • hope • learn • manage • need • offer • plan • promise • refuse • seem • want • would like / love / hate / prefer

*I'**m planning to do** a student exchange in the US next year.*
*I **want to study** languages at university.*

See also   →

G 16   Verbs followed by gerund or infinitive
with no change of meaning   Workshop 2, pages 56 – 57

Some verbs can usually be followed by either *-ing* or the *to*-infinitive with no or little difference in meaning. These include:
begin • continue • hate • like • love • prefer • start

*I **prefer doing** sport. – I **prefer to do** sport.*
*He **started learning** French when he was six. – He **started to learn** English when he was six.*

See also   →

G 17   Verb + object + *to*-infinitive   Workshop 2, pages 56 – 57

Some verbs are followed by an object + *to*-infinitive. These include:
advise • allow • ask • choose • encourage • expect • help • invite • need • order • persuade • remind • tell • want • warn • would like

*My classmates **want me to join** the Math Club.*
*The teachers **allow us to call** them by their first names!*

When these verbs are in the passive, they are followed directly by the infinitive.
*We **are allowed to call** our teachers by their first names.*
*At school, I **was encouraged to study** languages.*

!   Note that we can use some verbs (e. g. *ask, choose, expect, help, need, want*) with or without an object.
*We **expect to arrive** at 8.30.*   *We **expect them to arrive** at 8.30.*
*He **helped to tidy** the room.*   *He **helped us to tidy** the room.*

See also   → G15 , G16 , G18 , G19 , G20

G 18 Verbs followed by gerund or infinitive with change of meaning

Workshop 2, pages 56 – 57

Some verbs can be followed by the gerund or the *to*-infinitive but there is a difference in meaning. These verbs include:

Try
We use *try* + *-ing* when we do something to see what the results will be.
Try going to bed earlier so you aren't tired in the morning.
I **tried turning** the computer on and off, but the program still didn't work.

We use *try* + *to*-infinitive when we attempt to achieve something.
We **tried to move** the box, but it was too heavy.
I'm **trying to learn** the drums, so that I can join a band.

Remember and *forget*
We use *remember* / *forget* + *-ing* to talk about memories.
Do you **remember going** to school for the first time?
I'll never **forget visiting** London. It was a great trip!

We use *remember* / *forget* + *to*-infinitive to talk about doing / not doing something.
Remember to phone Alex.
Oh no! I **forgot to invite** Anna to the party.

Stop
We use *stop* + *-ing* to talk about something ending or stopping.
I **stopped studying** French last year.
I hope it **stops raining** soon.

We use *stop* + *to*-infinitive to express the reason or purpose.
Sorry I'm late. I **stopped to get** something to eat on the way.
I was working, but I **stopped to watch** TV for a while.

See also   →

G 19 Infinitives after question words and *whether*

Workshop 2, pages 60 – 61

We can use some verbs + question word + *to*-infinitive. These include:

ask • decide • discover • discuss • explain • find out • forget • know • learn • remember • talk about • understand • wonder

Let's **talk about where to stay**.
I can't **decide who to invite** to the party.

We can also use certain phrases + question word + *to*-infinitive.
I'm **not sure** where to go.
I **have no idea** how to install the software.
Let me know what to buy.
Do you know how to get to the station?

We can also use a *to*-infinitive after *whether*.
We need to decide **whether to go** by train or by bus.
I'm not sure **whether to stay** here or go with them.

See also   →

G 20 Infinitives after superlatives and numbers

Workshop 2, pages 60 – 61

We can use a *to*-infinitive after a phrase with a superlative adjective.

*The **easiest way to get** there is by bike.*
*Where's **the most interesting place to go**?*
***The best time of year to visit** is September.*
*Who's **the oldest person to compete** in the Olympics?*

We can use a *to*-infinitive after a phrase with *last* or an ordinal number (*first, second, last,* etc.).

*Will **the last person to leave** please turn off the lights?*
*Chicago was **the first city to have** a Ferris wheel.*
*Who was **the second person to walk** on the moon?*

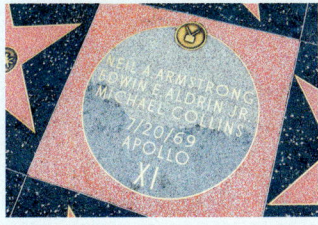

See also → G15 , G16 , G17 , G18 , G19

G 21 Question tags (revision)

Workshop 2, pages 60 – 61

We form a question tag with an auxiliary verb (*do, have, be* or a modal verb) + pronoun (*you, he, she, it, they,* etc.). We use the same auxiliary verb as in the first part of the statement. For the simple present and simple past, we use a form of *do*.

We use a negative question tag after a positive statement.
*You **remember** when we rode on that big Ferris wheel, **don't** you?*
*Samantha **has** been to the UK, **hasn't** she?*

We use a positive question tag after a negative statement.
*The museum **wasn't** open, **was** it?*
*Richard **can't** speak German, **can** he?*

We use a question tag in two main ways:
- When we expect someone to agree with us. In this case, the intonation on the question tag falls.

  Chicago's great, isn't it?

  You don't drink coffee, do you?

- When we ask a real question, often to check something. In this case, the intonation on the question tag rises.

  She's from New York, isn't she?

  They didn't go on the school trip, did they?

Examples
*He's studying English, **isn't he**?*
*You like Indian food, **don't you**?*
*It didn't rain much, **did it**?*
*He has a holiday job, **doesn't he**?*
*Sara can play the guitar, **can't she**?*

G 22 Passive: present, past, *will*-future and modals Workshop 3, pages 78 – 79

We use the passive when we are more interested in what happens than in who does the action. This is usually because who does the action is obvious, unknown or not important.

We form the passive with a form of *to be* + past participle:
- present tense: *is / are* + past participle
- past tense: *was / were* + past participle
- present perfect: *has / have been* + past participle

*Today, most goods **are paid** for electronically.*
*The first emails **were sent in** the 1970s.*
*Our lives today **have been transformed** by technology.*
Will: We use *will be* + past participle.
*Housework **will be done** by home robots.*
Modal verbs: We use *can be / might be / may be*, etc. + past participle.
*Our homes will be full of smart appliances that **can be controlled** remotely.*
*The new website **might be launched** soon.*

! We sometimes use the passive with *by* when we want to say who or what does the action (the agent).
*Today, many cashiers have been replaced **by** self-service check-outs.*

Examples *The internet **is used by** billions of people every day.*
*The film **was directed by** Christopher Nolan.*
*A lot of progress **has been made** in the field of medicine.*
*Many jobs **won't be done** by humans in the future.*
*In the future, human tour guides **may be replaced by** robots.*

See also → G 23 , G 24

G 23 Passive: verbs with two objects Workshop 3, pages 82 – 83

Some active verbs have two objects: a direct and an indirect object.

SUBJECT	ACTIVE VERB	INDIRECT OBJECT	DIRECT OBJECT
His friend's dad	*offered*	*him*	*some of the wheels.*

In the passive, the indirect object becomes the subject.

SUBJECT	PASSIVE VERB	DIRECT OBJECT
He	*was offered*	*some of the wheels.*

There is also another less common active structure.

SUBJECT	ACTIVE VERB	DIRECT OBJECT	TO	INDIRECT OBJECT
His friend's dad	*offered*	*some of the wheels*	*to*	*him.*

In the passive, the direct object becomes the subject. This passive structure is less common.

SUBJECT	PASSIVE VERB	TO	INDIRECT OBJECT
Some of the wheels	*were offered*	*to*	*him.*

! Note that we can use both passive structures with *by* + agent.
He was offered some of the wheels by his friend's dad.
Some of the wheels were offered to him by his friend's dad.

Examples *We were taught English by Ms Evans.*
First prize was awarded to David Jones.

See also → G 22 , G 24

G 24   Passive infinitive

Workshop 3, pages 82 – 83

The passive infinitive is formed with *to be* + past participle (e.g. *to be shown, to be met, to be invited*).

Some verbs (e.g. *arrange, ask, expect, hate, hope, like, need, plan, prefer, try, want, would like*) are followed by the *to*-infinitive. When there is passive meaning, these verbs are followed by the passive infinitive.

SUBJECT	VERB	PASSIVE INFINITIVE	
People	*don't need*	**to be shown**	*how it works.*
We	*hope*	**to be met**	*at the airport.*

Examples   *The company wanted the empty tins **to be returned**.*
*We have arranged for you **to be taken** to your hotel.*
*I expect **to be invited** to the ceremony.*
*The battery needs **to be charged** overnight.*

See also   →  G 22 , G 23

G 25   *If*-sentences type 3 (revision)

Workshop 3, pages 88 – 89

We use *if*-sentences type 3 to talk about something that didn't happen in the past. We talk about it in an imaginary or a hypothetical way.
If-sentences type 3 have the form *if* + past perfect, *would / wouldn't have* + past participle.

*If our talk **had been** more fun, more people **would have come**.*
*If you**'d got up** earlier, you **wouldn't have missed** the bus.*

We often use *'d* instead of *had* and *would*, especially in speaking and informal writing. We also often use *'ve* instead of *have*.
*If I**'d** known about the meeting, I**'d've** told you.*

We often use *could have* or *might* have in an *if*-sentence type 3.
*If I **hadn't been** ill last week, I **could have gone** to the meeting.*

We can usually put the two clauses in any order. When the *if* clause is first, there is a comma between the clauses.
If I had had more money, I would have bought it.
I would have bought it if I had had more money.

Examples   *If I**'d had** more time, I**'d have been able to** help you.*
*If we**'d left** earlier, we**'d have missed** the terrible traffic.*
*What **would** you **have done** if you **had been** in my situation?*
*If we **hadn't sat** next to each other on the bus, we **wouldn't have met** each other.*
*I**'d have gone out** last night if I **hadn't had** so much homework.*

See also   →  G 13 , G 14

G 26   Conjunctions with future time clauses
Workshop 3, pages 88 – 89

We often use conjunctions such as **when**, **while**, **until**, **before**, **after**, **as soon as** and **once** to introduce an action that is going to happen in the future.

When we are talking about the future, we usually use the simple present after a time conjunction.

When I **think** of a way, I'll tell you.
I'll let you know as soon as I **arrive**.

We can also use the present progressive after a time conjunction to express something in progress.
Let's meet **the next time** you**'re visiting** Berlin.
We can also use the present perfect after a time conjunction to emphasize that one action is completed before the other action.
When I**'ve finished** my presentation, I'll send it to you.

When we begin with the time conjunction, we put a comma between the clauses.
When we get to the station, I'll call you.
I'll call you when we get to the station.

Examples

Let's meet again before I **leave**.
I'll message you as soon as I **hear** any news.
I'll email you when I**'ve had** lunch.
As soon as we **get** the green light, we'll make a start.

! We do not use a future form with *will* after the time conjunction.
~~I'll call you as soon as I will arrive.~~
~~I'll email you when I will have had lunch.~~

G 27   Future perfect
Workshop 3, pages 92 – 93

We form the future perfect with **will have** + **past participle**.

SUBJECT	will have	PAST PARTICIPLE	
Space travel	will have	become	a reality by 2050.

We most commonly use the future perfect to talk about something completed at a point in the future.

Humans **will have visited** Mars by 2050.
I'm sure we**'ll have arrived** by midnight.

NOW   MIDNIGHT

We can also use the future perfect for something not completed or something still in progress at a specific time in the future.

I **won't have finished** the report by Friday.
We**'ll have lived** here for ten years next month.

We often use the future perfect with *by*.
We'll have finished the meeting **by** 10.30.

G 28   Gerund after prepositions

Workshop 4, pages 110 – 111

We use the gerund (-*ing* form) after a preposition or after a prepositional verb (verb + preposition).

*I've always dreamed **of becoming** an architect.*
*He's always been passionate **about cooking**.*
*We're thinking **of going** to the cinema tonight.*
*He apologized **for being** late.*
*My grandma thanked us **for helping** her.*

To form the negative, we put *not* before the gerund.
*She apologised **for not being** at the meeting.*

Useful prepositional verbs that are followed by a gerund include:

admit to • (dis)agree with • apologize for • be used to • benefit from • complain about •
concentrate on • dream of • feel like • focus on • forget about • look forward to • result in •
succeed in • talk about • think about • think of • use for • worry about

Examples   *We're **used to seeing** our families regularly.*
*Annie **is looking forward to having** dinner with her friends on Saturday.*

See also   →  G2 , G15 , G16 , G18

G 29   Statements in reported speech

Workshop 4, pages 114 – 115

We can use *say* and *tell* to report what someone says. We use an indirect object after *tell*.
We do not use an indirect object after *add*, *describe*, *explain*, *mention* and *say*.

*He **told me** he was teacher.*   *He **said** he was a teacher.*

NOT *He told he was a teacher.*   *He said me he was a teacher.*

We can use *that* when we are reporting. There is no rule about *that* and it is usually a personal choice.
*She **said that** she was hungry.*   OR   *She **said** she was hungry.*

When we report with a reporting verb in the past tense), we generally change the tense:
- present tense – *past tense*
  *I **work** in London – She told me she **worked** in London.*
- past tense / present perfect – past perfect
  *We **missed** the bus. – He admitted that they'**d missed** the bus.*
  *I'**ve** just **been** on holiday. – He mentioned he'**d** just **been** on holiday.*
- will – would
  *I'**ll** call you later. – She promised she'**d** call me later.*
- can – could
  *I **can't** fix it. – He explained he **couldn't** fix it.*
- must – had to
  *We **must** leave. – She said they **had to** leave.*

!   We do not always change the tense. This is usually to show that something is still true or important.

*Jim **left** about ten minutes ago. – He said that Jim **left** about ten minutes ago.*
*I'**ll be** back in ten minutes. – She added she'**ll be** back in ten minutes.*

See also   → G30

G 30 Questions, requests, advice and orders in reported speech

Workshop 4, pages 120 – 121

> **Questions**
> We can report a question with *asked*. We can use an indirect object or no indirect object after *asked*.
> *Where do you work? – He **asked me** where I worked.*
> *How much is it? – She **asked** how much it was.*
>
> For a *yes / no* question (without a question-word) we use *if or whether*.
> *Are you a student? – He asked me **if** I was a student.*
> *Does Peter speak Spanish? – She wanted to know **whether** Peter spoke Spanish.*
>
> **Requests**
> We can report a request with *asked* + indirect object + *to*-infinitive.
> *Could you help me? – Alex asked **me to help** him.*
> *Can you wait for me, please? – She asked **us to wait** for her.*
>
> **Orders and advice**
> We can report an order or advice with *told / advised* + indirect object + *(not) to*-infinitive.
>
> *Don't be late again. – He told **me not to be** late again.*
> *You should apologize to them. – She advised **me to apologize** to them.*

! Note that we generally, but not always, change the tense when we report questions with *asked*. → G 29

The word order is different from direct questions. The word order is the same as in a statement.
Where does he live? – She asked me where he lives.
When are we leaving? – He asked when we were leaving.
NOT ~~She asked me where does he live.~~ ~~He asked when were we leaving.~~

Examples
He asked me if I was OK.
She asked me where John lived.
Oliver asked me to phone him.
The receptionist asked us to wait a few minutes.
The teacher told the children to be quiet.
She told me to work harder.

See also → G 29

G 31 Quantifiers

Workshop 4, pages 124 – 125

We use quantifiers to express the quantity of something. Quantifiers are words such as *all*, *most*, *some*, *a few*, *both*, *none*, *no*, *each*, *every*.

To talk about things / people in general, we use *all / most / many / some / a few / no* + plural noun or uncountable noun (without *the*).
All children *have the right to an education.*
Most countries *have free education.*
Many people *don't have a job.*

We can also use *no* + singular noun.
Today, **no child** *should go hungry.*

To talk about things / people in a specific group, we use *all / most / many / some / a few / one / none* + *of* + *the / my / their /* etc. + plural noun or uncountable noun.
All of my friends *were surprised.*
All of my work *is interesting.*
One of his ambitions *is to be a model.*
None of the jobs *were interesting.*

We can also use *all / most / many / some / a few / one / none* + *of* + pronoun
Most of them *have a summer job.*
A few of us *are going to the meeting.*

We can also use *all* + *the / my / their / etc* + plural noun or uncountable noun (without *of*).
All my friends *were surprised.*
I spend **all my pocket money**.

We use *each / every* + singular noun.
Every child *has the right to express their opinion.*
I need to speak to **each person**.

To talk about two things, we use *both*. We use:
- *both* + plural noun
  I like **both colours**.
  Both jobs *were interesting.*

- *both (of)* + *the / my / these / etc* + plural noun
  Both of the jobs *were interesting.*
  Both my parents *speak English.*

- *both of* + pronoun
  Both of them *are teachers.*

We use a number of other expressions with *of* + plural or uncountable noun / pronoun, for example:
The majority of *people here don't have a passport.*
A large percentage of *them have never travelled abroad.*
A lot of *people didn't vote in the election.*
Three quarters of *the land is used for farming.*
A third of *the population lives in poverty.*
30 per cent of *18-year-olds go to university.*
Half of *the country is desert.*

We usually use these expressions without *the* to talk about things / people in general, but with *the* to talk about specific groups.
Over 50 % of people *don't have a passport.*
Over 50 % of the people *we interviewed don't have a passport.*

Irregular verbs

infinitive	simple past	present perfect	German
to **be**	**was / were**	**been**	sein
to **beat**	**beat**	**beaten**	schlagen
to **become**	**became**	**become**	werden
to **begin**	**began**	**begun**	beginnen, anfangen
to **blow**	**blew**	**blown**	blasen
to **break**	**broke**	**broken**	brechen
to **bring**	**brought**	**brought**	bringen
to **build**	**built**	**built**	bauen
to **burn**	**burned / burnt**	**burned / burnt**	(ver)brennen
to **buy**	**bought**	**bought**	kaufen
to **catch**	**caught**	**caught**	fangen
to **choose** [uː]	**chose** [əʊ]	**chosen** [əʊ]	auswählen
to **come**	**came**	**come**	kommen
to **cost**	**cost**	**cost**	kosten
to **cut**	**cut**	**cut**	schneiden
to **deal**	**dealt**	**dealt**	handeln
to **do**	**did**	**done**	tun
to **draw**	**drew**	**drawn**	zeichnen
to **dream**	**dreamed / dreamt**	**dreamed / dreamt**	träumen
to **drink**	**drank**	**drunk**	trinken
to **drive** [aɪ]	**drove** [əʊ]	**driven** [ɪ]	fahren
to **eat**	**ate** [et], [eɪt]	**eaten**	essen
to **fall**	**fell**	**fallen**	fallen, stürzen
to **feed**	**fed**	**fed**	füttern
to **feel**	**felt**	**felt**	(sich) fühlen, spüren
to **fight**	**fought**	**fought**	kämpfen
to **find**	**found**	**found**	finden

infinitive	simple past	present perfect	German
to **fly**	**flew**	**flown**	fliegen
to **forget**	**forgot**	**forgotten**	vergessen
to **forgive**	**forgave**	**forgiven**	vergeben
to **get**	**got**	**got / gotten**	bekommen, holen
to **give**	**gave**	**given**	geben, schenken
to **go**	**went**	**gone**	gehen, fahren
to **grow** [əʊ]	**grew** [uː]	**grown** [əʊ]	wachsen, anbauen
to **have (got)**	**had**	**had**	haben
to **hang**	**hung**	**hung**	hängen
to **hear** [ɪə]	**heard** [ɜː]	**heard** [ɜː]	hören
to **hide** [haɪd]	**hid** [hɪd]	**hidden** [hɪdn]	sich verstecken
to **hit**	**hit**	**hit**	schlagen
to **hold**	**held**	**held**	halten
to **hurt**	**hurt**	**hurt**	wehtun
to **keep**	**kept**	**kept**	(be)halten
to **kneel** [niːl]	**knelt** [nelt]	**knelt** [nelt]	knien
to **know** [nəʊ]	**knew** [njuː]	**known** [nəʊn]	wissen, kennen
to **lay**	**laid**	**laid**	legen
to **learn**	**learned / learnt**	**learned / learnt**	lernen
to **lead** [liːd]	**led** [led]	**led** [led]	führen, leiten
to **leave**	**left**	**left**	verlassen
to **lend**	**lent**	**lent**	leihen
to **let**	**let**	**let**	lassen
to **lie**	**lay**	**lain**	liegen
to **light**	**lit / lighted**	**lit / lighted**	anzünden, anmachen

infinitive	simple past	present perfect	German
to **lose** [uː]	**lost** [ɒ]	**lost** [ɒ]	verlieren
to **make**	**made**	**made**	machen, herstellen
to **mean** [iː]	**meant** [e]	**meant** [e]	bedeuten
to **meet**	**met**	**met**	(sich) treffen, kennen-lernen
to **pay**	**paid**	**paid**	bezahlen
to **put**	**put**	**put**	stellen
to **quit**	**quit**	**quit**	kündigen; verlassen
to **read** [iː]	**read** [e]	**read** [e]	lesen
to **ride**	**rode**	**ridden**	reiten, (Fahrrad) fahren
to **ring**	**rang**	**rung**	klingeln
to **rise**	**rose**	**risen**	wachsen, aufgehen
to **run**	**ran**	**run**	laufen, rennen
to **say** [eɪ]	**said** [e]	**said** [e]	sagen
to **see**	**saw**	**seen**	sehen
to **sell**	**sold**	**sold**	verkaufen
to **send**	**sent**	**sent**	schicken
to **set**	**set**	**set**	setzen, stellen, legen
to **shake**	**shook**	**shaken**	schütteln
to **shine**	**shone** [ɒ]	**shone** [ɒ]	scheinen
to **shoot**	**shot**	**shot**	schießen
to **show**	**showed**	**shown / showed**	zeigen
to **sing**	**sang**	**sung**	singen
to **sit**	**sat**	**sat**	sitzen
to **sleep**	**slept**	**slept**	schlafen

infinitive	simple past	present perfect	German
to **smell**	**smelled / smelt**	**smelled / smelt**	riechen
to **speak** [iː]	**spoke** [əʊ]	**spoken** [əʊ]	sprechen
to **spend**	**spent**	**spent**	verbringen, (Geld) ausgeben
to **spit**	**spat / spit**	**spat / spit**	spucken
to **spoil**	**spoilt**	**spoilt**	verderben
to **stand**	**stood**	**stood**	stehen
to **steal**	**stole**	**stolen**	stehlen
to **stick**	**stuck**	**stuck**	kleben
to **sting**	**stung**	**stung**	stechen
to **strike**	**struck**	**struck**	zuschlagen; streiken
to **swear**	**swore**	**swore**	schwören
to **sweep**	**swept**	**swept**	fegen
to **swim**	**swam**	**swum**	schwimmen
to **take**	**took**	**taken**	nehmen, dauern
to **teach** [iː]	**taught** [ɔː]	**taught** [ɔː]	unterrichten
to **tell**	**told**	**told**	erzählen
to **think**	**thought**	**thought**	denken
to **throw**	**threw**	**thrown**	werfen
to **understand**	**understood**	**understood**	verstehen
to **wake**	**woke**	**woken**	erwachen; wecken
to **wear** [eə]	**wore** [ɔː]	**worn** [ɔː]	tragen
to **win**	**won**	**won**	gewinnen
to **write**	**wrote**	**written**	schreiben

Vocabulary

Here are all the words from the workshops. They are in the same order as in the workshop.

There is the page number and the activity.

A ▨ at the side is for words from the listening text. A ▨ is for words from videos.

Words in **grey** are important for one text. They are only in this text and you don't have to learn them.

The phonetic transcription [ ] tells you how you say a word.

Sometimes there are irregular forms (shut, shut, shut).

The example sentence shows you how we use a word.

= shows words with the same meaning

≠ shows words with the opposite meaning

❗ shows words with the same meaning in French and Latin or it gives other interesting information about the word.

When you work with the *Vocabulary*, cover the German, look at the English word and the example or picture and say the German word. You can also cover the German and the example sentences to practise the English.

page	exercise	**Welcome Workshop**		
10	1	**common** [ˈkɒmən]	*What's the most common language in the US after English and Spanish?*	normal; gewöhnlich
		president [ˈprezɪdənt]	*Who was the first president of the United States?* ❗ *Fr. 'président, présidente' (m., f.)*	Präsident(in)

page	exercise	**Workshop 1**		
12		**to dream** [driːm]	*I dream about travelling around the world.*	träumen
		region [ˈriːdʒən]	*We will learn about five regions in the USA.* = *territory* ❗ *Fr. 'région' (f.)*	Region
	1a	**cotton** [ˈkɒtn]	*The warm, wet weather is good for growing cotton and tobacco.*	Baumwolle
		rainforest [ˈreɪnfɒrɪst]	*There is a rainforest in Washington.*	Regenwald
		snowy [ˈsnəʊi]	*Colorado has snowy mountains.*	verschneit
		to mind [maɪnd]	*It's very hot and dry here, but I don't mind.* = *be opposed*	etw. macht jmdm. etwas aus
		hometown [ˈhəʊmtaʊn]	*My hometown is New York City.*	Heimatstadt
		colony [ˈkɒləni]	*It was part of the original 13 British colonies.* ❗ *Fr. 'colonie' (f.), Lat. 'colonia, -ae' (f.)*	Kolonie
		heartland [ˈhɑːtlænd]	*People like to call this part of the country America's Heartland.*	Kernland
		endless [ˈendləs]	*It's a huge region with endless farmland.* ≠ *limited*	endlos; unendlich
		farmland [ˈfɑːmlænd]	*There is a lot of farmland in the USA.*	Ackerland

page	exercise	Workshop 1		
		further ['fɜːðə]	Further east and to the north are the Great Lakes.	weiter
	1b	**to imagine** [ɪ'mædʒɪn]	Imagine you have applied to be an exchange student in the USA. = envision	sich etwas vorstellen; sich einbilden; glauben
13	2	**to benefit** ['benɪfɪt]	Discuss how you think she could benefit from a student exchange. ≠ hinder	profitieren
	3a	**conference** ['kɒnfərəns]	Three exchange students in the USA talk about their experiences at the conference. ❗ Fr. 'conférence' (f.)	Konferenz
		web conference [web 'kɒnfərəns]	A student exchange organization invites students to take part in a live web conference.	Webkonferenz
		password ['pɑːswɜːd]	You need a password for the computer.	Kennwort; Passwort
		display [dɪ'spleɪ]	The display shows an entry from a settler's diary. = exhibit	Ausstellung
		let's [lets]	Let's get started.	lass / lasst uns
		relaxed [rɪ'læks]	People who live in the country are often relaxed and easy-going. ❗ Fr. 'relaxer'	entspannt
		photography [fə'tɒɡrəfi]	I'm taking a photography class at school.	Fotografie
		experience [ɪk'spɪəriəns]	A student exchange is a wonderful experience. ❗ Fr. 'expérience' (f.)	Erfahrung
		to move on [muːv ɒn]	Let's move on to the next topic.	weitergehen
	3b	**candidate** ['kændɪdət]	You can ask the candidates questions after the web conference.	Kandidat(in)
		microphone ['maɪkrəfəʊn]	Press the button on your microphone and speak clearly.	Mikrofon
		to go ahead [,ɡəʊ ə'hed]**, went, gone** [went, ɡɒn]	Go ahead and try some more. You're doing really well = continue	weitermachen
		paradise ['pærədaɪs]	I'm a music lover, and this is a music paradise.	Paradies
		shocked [ʃɒkt]	My mum was shocked when I told her that.	schockiert
		portion ['pɔːʃn]	I'm surprised at the size of portions in restaurants.	Portion; Menge
		container [kən'teɪnə]	The food containers are very big. = vessel	Behälter; Container
		to look lost [lʊk lɒst]	When I first arrived, I probably looked a bit lost at school.	verloren aussehen
		chore [tʃɔːr]	Grandma gave me this list of chores to do.	Hausarbeit

page	exercise	**Workshop 1**		
		national [ˈnæʃnəl]	*In school, we're talking about national holidays and celebrations.*	national
		issue [ˈɪsjuː]	*I can discuss issues related to immigration.*	Thema; Angelegenheit
		related to [rɪˈleɪtɪd tə]	*This issue is related to the environment.*	in Bezug auf
14	1	**lifestyle** [ˈlaɪfstaɪl]	*What do you know about Native Americans and their culture and lifestyle today?*	Lebensstil; Lifestyle
		neighbourhood [ˈneɪbəhʊd]	*I like exploring my new neighbourhood.* ⛌ neighborhood (AE)	Nachbarschaft
		pavement [ˈpeɪvmənt]	*There are a lot of stones on the pavement.* ⛌ sidewalk (AE)	Bürgersteig
		sidewalk [ˈsaɪdwɔːk]	*I ride my bike on the sidewalk.* ⛌ pavement (BE)	Bürgersteig
		porch [pɔːtʃ]	*There's a porch at the front of each house.* = veranda	Veranda
		to hang out [hæŋ aʊt]	*It looks like a cool place to hang out.*	abhängen; rumhängen
		flag [flæg]	*They've all got American flags in front of their houses.*	Fahne
		to hug [hʌg]	*My mother hugs me before I leave for school.*	(sich) umarmen
		accent [ˈæksənt]	*He has a strong accent, but I can understand him.*	Akzent
		to sweep [swiːp]	*I don't mind sweeping the porch.*	fegen
15	3a	**sneaker** [ˈsniːkər]	*You probably all have lots of jeans and sneakers.* = tennis shoe ⛌ trainer (BE)	Turnschuh
		trainer [ˈtreɪnər]	*I have some cool new trainers.* ⛌ sneaker (AE)	Turnschuh
		to queue [kjuː]	*In the cafeteria I explained that you don't queue for your food, you stand in line.* = to wait in line	anstehen; Schlange stehen
		thought [θɔːt]	*What are your thoughts about the movie?* = idea	Gedanke
		to vacuum [ˈvækjuːm]	*I prefer indoor chores like vacuuming the living room.*	staubsaugen
		to empty [ˈempti]	*Emptying the dishwasher and tidying my room are the chores that I hate.*	entleeren; leeren
		dishwasher [ˈdɪʃwɔːʃər]	*Please empty the dishwasher.*	Geschirrspülmaschine
		to take out [ˈteɪk aʊt], **took, taken** [tʊk, ˈteɪkən]	*Ellie's least favourite chore is taking out the rubbish.*	rausbringen

page	exercise	**Workshop 1**		
		garbage [ˈgɑːbɪdʒ]	*Too many people throw their garbage on the ground.* ❗ *rubbish (BE)*	Abfall
16	2a	**mail carrier** [ˈmeɪl kæriə]	*The mail carrier brings the snail mail.* *= postman, postwoman*	Postbote; Postbotin
		garbage collector [ˈgɑːbɪdʒ kəˈlektə]	*We bring the garbage cans down to the street on days when the garbage collectors come.*	Müllarbeiter(in)
		to mention [ˈmenʃn]	*What facts did she mention in her talk?*	erwähnen
		madman [ˈmædmən], **madmen**	*The madman who lives down the road puts his garbage in the street.*	Irrer; Verrückter
		teenage [ˈtiːneɪdʒ]	*You can see a teenage girl who is working in the shop.*	Teenager…
		anyway [ˈeniweɪ]	*I missed the movie, but I don't like that actor anyway.*	trotzdem; sowieso; jedenfalls
		trash [træʃ]	*They buy something, they open it outside and they leave the trash on the ground.*	Abfall
		Asian [ˈeɪʒn]	*There are people from all Asian countries in New York.*	asiatisch
		racist [ˈreɪsɪst]	*Accepting racist language and behaviour is bad for a society.*	rassistisch
		bike lane [ˈbaɪk leɪn]	*We need more bike lanes here, so that young people like us can move around easier.*	Radstreifen
	3	**to step** [step]	*Try not to step on the wet floor, I just cleaned it.*	treten
		rose [rəʊz]	*While I interviewed her I nearly stepped on one of the roses.*	Rose
	4	**to rewrite** [ˌriːˈraɪt], **rewrote, rewritten** [ˌriːˈrəʊt, ˌriːˈrɪtn]	*Rewrite the text in British English.*	neu schreiben; umschreiben
		selfie [ˈselfi]	*I took the selfie in our lovely yard and posted it online.*	Selfie
17	5	**homesickness** [ˈhəʊmsɪknəs]	*I read somewhere that homesickness is part of being an exchange student.*	Heimweh
	6	**application** [ˌæplɪˈkeɪʃn]	*David fills in the online job application.*	Bewerbung; Antrag
		introductory letter [ˌɪntrəˈdʌktəri ˈletə]	*Write your own introductory letter to your host family.*	Einführungsbrief
		personality [ˌpɜːsəˈnæləti]	*Looks are not everything – personality counts, too.*	Persönlichkeit
		to conclude [kənˈkluːd]	*= end* ❗ *Fr. 'conclure', Lat. 'concludere (concludo, conclusi, conclusum)'*	schließen (aus etwas); beenden
18		**birthplace** [ˈbɜːθpleɪs]	*New England is known as the birthplace of America.*	Geburtsort
	1a	**colonial** [kəˈləʊniəl]	*At the living history museum, you can learn about colonial history.*	kolonial

page	exercise	Workshop 1		
	1b	to **emigrate** [ˈemɪɡreɪt]	He emigrated to California with his mother. ≠ immigrate	auswandern
		settlement [ˈsetlmənt]	The region was home to one of the earliest European settlements.	Siedlung
		to **found** [faʊnd]	The War of Independence led to the founding of the United States. ≠ disestablish	begründen; gründen
		re-creation [ˌriːkriˈeɪʃn]	Visit a re-creation of their 17th century village to see how they lived.	Nachstellung; Neugestaltung
		descendant [dɪˈsendənt]	Talk to Native Americans who are descendants of the nation you are researching.	Nachkomme
		feast [fiːst]	Thanksgiving is mainly about having a feast with friends and family. = party	Fest; Festmahl
		aboard [əˈbɔːd]	What was life like for the passengers who travelled aboard the Mayflower?	an Bord
		replica [ˈreplɪkə]	Here you can step aboard a replica of the famous ship. = copy	Kopie
		to **relive** [riːˈlɪv]	At the museum you can relive historic events.	wieder erleben
		to **rebell** [ˈrebl]	The colonists rebelled against the British Government.	rebellieren
		tax [tæks]	The British introduced new taxes, which the colonists rebelled against.	Steuer
		to **board** [bɔːd]	When a tax on tea was introduced, a group of colonists boarded British tea ships in Boston Harbor. = to enter	an Bord gehen
		crate [kreɪt]	They threw 342 crates of tea overboard in protest.	Kiste
19	4a	**uncomfortable** [ʌnˈkʌmftəbl]	= comfortable ❗ Fr. 'inconfortable'	unbequem
		crop [krɒp]	They taught them how to plant crops, hunt and fish.	Ernte; Getreide
	5	**knowledge** [ˈnɒlɪdʒ]	Listen to Ellie and Alex doing a general knowledge quiz about the USA.	Wissen
		tricky [ˈtrɪki]	That is a tricky question. Let me think about it. = complex	kompliziert
		rap [ræp]	The musical is about his life and the music is all rap and hip hop.	Rap
	6	**recent** [ˈriːsnt]	= current ❗ Fr. 'récent'	neueste(r); jüngst
20	1	**goat** [gəʊt]	I get up at dawn and I feed the chickens and milk the goats.	Ziege

page	exercise	Workshop 1		
		rifle [ˈraɪfl]	*He took his rifle and left to go hunting.*	Gewehr
	2a	**to predict** [prɪˈdɪkt]	*= anticipate* **!** *Lat. 'prae' = before + 'dicere (dico, dixi, dictum)' = to say*	vorhersagen
		routine [ruˈtiːn]	*They've been practicing their routine for weeks.*	Routine; Tagesablauf
		homeland [ˈhəʊmlænd]	*Do you miss your homeland? It's so far away.*	Heimat
	2b	**to worship** [ˈwɜːʃɪp]	*They go to church on Sunday to worship God.*	eine Religion ausüben; anbeten
		God [gɒd]	*We wanted to have our own land and also to worship God in our own way.*	Gott
		ashore [əˈʃɔːr]	*This land was so wild and empty when we first came ashore.*	an Land
		butcher [ˈbʊtʃə]	*Here there are no shops, no butcher or baker, so we had to learn how to grow our own food.*	Fleischer(in); Metzger(in)
		cornbread [ˈkɔːnbred]	*We grow Indian corn and we make cornbread from that.*	Maisbrot
		eel [iːl]	*We catch eels in the river.*	Aal
		to gather [ˈgæðə]	*Gather your ideas.* *= collect*	sammeln
		mussel [ˈmʌsl]	*Sometimes I gather mussels from the beach.*	Muschel
		dawn [dɔːn]	*I get up at dawn and wait for the sunrise.* *≠ dusk*	Morgendämmerung
		laundry [ˈlɔːndri]	*On laundry days, I help her wash the clothes in the stream.*	Wäsche
		to fetch [fetʃ]	*First thing in the morning, I go to the spring to fetch water.* *= obtain*	holen; abholen
		firewood [ˈfaɪəwʊd]	*The winter was going to be cold, so they needed to chop plenty of firewood.*	Brennholz
		ripe [raɪp]	*The corn is ripe at the end of summer.*	reif
		harvest [ˈhɑːvɪst]	*When the corn is ripe, I help my father with the harvest.*	Ernte
		marbles [ˈmɑːblz]	*We play marbles and board games.*	Murmelspiel
		fair [feə]	*I miss the markets and the fairs and all the entertainment.*	Jahrmarkt
	4	**to contain** [kənˈteɪn]	*The middle paragraphs should contain the main information.* *= enclose*	etw. enthalten
		re-enactment [ɪˈnæktmənt]	*At the end of the tour we watched a film re-enactment of the first battle of the war.*	Nachstellung

page	exercise	Workshop 1		
		rebellion [rɪˈbeljən]	❗ *Lat. 'rebellio, -onis' (f.)*	Aufstand
		townspeople [ˈtaʊnzpiːpl]	*The townspeople complained that there was too much traffic.*	Stadtbewohner(innen)
		to **anchor** [ˈæŋkə]	*The British tea ships were anchored in Boston Bay.*	ankern
		battle [ˈbætl]	*At the end of the tour, we watched a film re-enactment of the first battle.*	Schlacht
21	5a	**folk hero** [ˈfəʊk hɪərəʊ]	*Pocahontas is a Native American folk hero.*	Volksheld
		to **capture** [ˈkæptʃə]	*In 1605, an English explorer captured Squanto and took him to England.* ≠ *release*	einfangen; festnehmen
		slave [sleɪv]	❗ *Fr. 'esclave' (m., f.)*	Sklave; Sklavin
		smallpox [ˈsmɔːlpɒks]	*A smallpox epidemic killed the entire Native American tribe.*	Pocken
		epidemic [ˌepɪˈdemɪk]	*The epidemic lasted three years and killed many Native Americans.*	Epidemie
		interpreter [ɪnˈtɜːprɪtə]	= *translator* ❗ *Fr. 'interpréter' (m.)*	Dolmetscher(in)
	5b	**captain** [ˈkæptɪn]	*I worked hard and got to be captain of my school team.*	Spielführer(in); Kommandant(in)
	6a	**firework display** [ˈfaɪəwɜːk dɪˈspleɪ]	*There are firework displays on the fourth of July in America.*	Feuerwerk
		float [fləʊt]	*The parade in New York City features large floats.*	Umzugswagen; Paradewagen
		parade [pəˈreɪd]	*There is a big parade in New York City on Thanksgiving.*	Umzug; Parade
	6b	**official** [əˈfɪʃl]	*Thanksgiving is an official holiday and is celebrated on the last Thursday in November.*	offiziell
		squash [skwɒʃ]	*Turkey is the traditional main course, with squash, cranberry sauce and a pumpkin pie.*	Kürbis
		sweet potato [ˌswiːt pəˈteɪtəʊ]	*We always eat sweet potatoes on Thanksgiving.*	Süßkartoffel
		cranberry [ˈkrænbəri]	*He picked some cranberries in the field.*	Cranberry; Moosberre
		to **base on** [beɪs ɒn]	*The menu is based on the first Thanksgiving meal that the Native Americans shared with the Pilgrims in 1621.*	auf etw. basieren
		goose [guːs]	*We don't know if they ate turkey at that first feast, but we know that they ate duck, goose, corn and plenty more.*	Gans
		percent [pəˈsent]	*Nearly 90 percent of Americans eat turkey on Thanksgiving.* ❗ *Fr. 'pour cent' (m.)*	Prozent

page	exercise			
		Workshop 1		
		to **be fond of** [bi fɒnd]	Families who are not so fond of sports find other things to do, like spending time in the outdoors.	etw. mögen
		oven [ˈʌvn]	The turkey is baking in the oven.	Ofen
		to **attract** [əˈtrækt]	It attracts up to three million spectators along the route. = to fascinate	anziehen
		to **feature** [ˈfiːtʃə]	Parades often feature marching bands.	aufweisen; präsentieren
		marching band [ˈmɑːtʃɪŋ bænd]	The marching band was playing during the parade.	Blaskapelle
		balloon [bəˈluːn]	There are giant balloons shaped like cartoon characters in the parade.	Ballon
		shaped [ʃeɪpt]	They make giant balloons shaped like cartoon characters.	geformt
		cartoon [kɑːˈtuːn]	My little brother watches cartoons on TV.	Zeichentrickfilm; Cartoon
		to **feast** [fiːst]	As well as feasting, Thanksgiving is a time for helping others.	feiern; schlemmen
		to **associate** [əˈsəʊsieɪt]	Most people still associate Thanksgiving with the Pilgrims' feast after the first harvest.	assoziieren

American history

battle [ˈbætl]	Schlacht	**persecution** [ˌpɜːsɪˈkjuːʃn]	Verfolgung
captain [ˈkæptɪn]	Kommandant	**pioneer** [ˌpaɪəˈnɪə]	Pionier(in)
to **capture** [ˈkæptʃə]	einfangen; festnehmen	to **rebell** [ˈrebl]	rebellieren
		rebellion [rɪˈbeljən]	Aufstand
colonial [kəˈləʊniəl]	kolonial	**reservation** [ˌrezəˈveɪʃn]	Reservierung;
colony [ˈkɒləni]	Kolonie		Vorbehalt; Reservat
famine [ˈfæmɪn]	Hungersnot	**sacred** [ˈseɪkrɪd]	heilig
folk hero [ˈfəʊk hɪərəʊ]	Volksheld	**settlement** [ˈsetlmənt]	Siedlung
to **found** [faʊnd]	begründen; gründen	**slave** [sleɪv]	Sklave; Sklavin
homeland [ˈhəʊmlænd]	Heimat	**westward** [ˈwestwəd]	westwärts
midwest [ˌmɪdˈwest]	mittlerer Westen		

page	exercise			
22	S1a	**keyword** [ˈkiːwɜːd]	Use your keywords and, if necessary, refine your search.	Stichwort
	S2a	**reliable** [rɪˈlaɪəbl]	Make a list of websites that are reliable sources of information.	verlässlich
		appropriate [əˈprəʊpriət]	Finding reliable and appropriate sources of information on the internet isn't always easy. ≠ inappropriate	angemessen
		commercial [kəˈmɜːʃl]	A website with '.com' at the end is a commercial website.	kommerziell
		factual [ˈfæktʃuəl]	Which websites offer information from a reliable factual source?	sachlich
		profit [ˈprɒfɪt]	They made a profit from advertising.	Profit; Gewinn

page	exercise	**Workshop 1**		
		non-profit [ˌnɒnˈprɒfɪt]	*Today many of the community gardens are supported by non-profit organizations.*	gemeinnützig
		blog [blɒg]	*A personal blog is not the best place to find reliable facts.*	Blog
		online forum [ˌɒnˈlaɪn ˈfɔːrəm]	*An online forum is not a reliable place to get information.*	Online-Forum
		anecdote [ˈænɪkdəʊt]	*Her blog is useful if you're looking for a personal point of view or an interesting anecdote.*	Anekdote
		institution [ˌɪnstɪˈtjuːʃn]	*The websites for educational institutions often have '.edu' at the end.*	Einrichtung
		accurate [ˈækjərət]	*They're normally good sources of accurate information.* *= correct*	genau; präzise
	S3	**to bookmark** [ˈbʊkmɑːk]	*Bookmark the sources you use online so that you can easily find them again.*	markieren
		browser [ˈbraʊzər]	*You can bookmark websites in your browser.*	Browser
		function [ˈfʌŋkʃn]	*If you already use the bookmark function, make notes and explain to a partner how to do it.* ❗ *Fr. 'fonction' (f.)*	Funktion
23		**to evaluate** [ɪˈvæljueɪt]	*Research, write and evaluate a short article.*	bewerten
	S3	**to refine** [rɪˈfaɪn]	*Use your keywords and, if necessary, refine your search.*	verfeinern
24	1b	**attitude** [ˈætɪtjuːd]	*What is the writer's attitude towards the immigrants?*	Ansicht; Einstellung
	1c	**contribution** [ˌkɒntrɪˈbjuːʃn]	*New immigrants have made many contributions to American culture.*	Beitrag; Mitwirkung
		to expand [ɪkˈspænd]	*As the country expanded German and Irish immigrants arrived.*	erweitern; expandieren
		westward [ˈwestwəd]	*They moved westward.*	westwärts
		political [pəˈlɪtɪkl]	*It's a political problem and it won't get better until our governments make stricter laws to protect the Earth.* ❗ *Fr. 'politique'*	politisch
		persecution [ˌpɜːsɪˈkjuːʃn]	*Many immigrants were escaping from religious or political persecution.*	Verfolgung
		famine [ˈfæmɪn]	*Many Irish immigrated to escape famine or poverty and unemployment.*	Hungersnot
		to be willing [bi ˈwɪlɪŋ]	*They are willing to work hard to build a better life.* *= want*	bereit sein

page	exercise	**Workshop 1**		
		mid [mɪd]	*Since the mid 20th century, European immigration has slowed down.*	in der Mitte; mittel
		to **slow down** [sləʊˈdaʊn]	*You have to slow down your car.*	(sich) verlangsamen
		to **contribute** [kənˈtrɪbjuːt]	*Immigrants contributed to the culture in many different ways.*	mitwirken
		wealth [welθ]	*Millionaires have great wealth.*	Reichtum; Vermögen
		pancake [ˈpænkeɪk]	*We make pancakes for breakfast on Sundays.*	Pfannkuchen
		rocket [ˈrɒkɪt]	*Rockets put satellites into space around Earth.*	Rakete
		astronaut [ˈæstrənɔːt]	*Astronauts travel in space.*	Astronaut(in)
		moon [muːn]	*The moon moves around the Earth.*	Mond
		skilled [skɪld]	*California's Silicon Valley wouldn't exist without highly skilled immigrants.*	geschickt; ausgebildet
		employee [ɪmˈplɔɪiː]	*He had many employees who helped him develop his inventions.*	Angestellte(r)
25	2	**kingdom** [ˈkɪŋdəm]	*A kingdom is a country with a king or queen.*	Königreich
		republic [rɪˈpʌblɪk]	*A republic is another kind of government, which is very different from a monarchy.*	Republik
		midwest [ˌmɪdˈwest]	*There are Indian reservations in the American midwest.*	mittlerer Westen
		landmark [ˈlændmɑːk]	*The Grand Canyon is a natural landmark.*	Wahrzeichen
		mountain range [ˈmaʊntən reɪndʒ]	*There are several sky resorts in the mountain range.*	Bergkette; Gebirgszug
	3	**gold rush** [ˈgəʊld rʌʃ]	*When he heard about the California Gold Rush, he went out west to San Francisco to make his fortune.*	Goldrausch
		miner [ˈmaɪnə]	*Adventurous settlers worked as gold miners.*	Bergarbeiter
		company [ˈkʌmpəni]	*A big toy company paid him a lot of money for his design.*	Unternehmen
		denim [ˈdenɪm]	*Levi Strauss made strong jeans out of denim.*	Denim; Jeansstoff
		Taiwanese [taɪˈwɑːnˈniːz]	*Steve Chen is Taiwanese-American and co-founder of a famous video streaming platform.*	taiwanisch
		Bangladeshi [ˌbæŋgləˈdeʃi]	*Jawed Karim is a Bangladeshi-German-American, who was born in Merseburg, East Germany but grew up in West Germany.*	Bangladescher(in)
		grocery store [ˈgrəʊsəri stɔː]	*He works at the cash register in the grocery store.*	Lebensmittelladen
		to **co-found** [kəʊfaʊnd]	*He co-founded a messaging app with a friend and the rest is history.*	mitbegründen

page	exercise	Workshop 1		
	4b	**geographical** [ˌdʒiːəˈgræfɪkl]	*There are some famous geographical landmarks in my country.*	geografisch
26	1a	**difficulty** [ˈdɪfɪkəlti]	*What difficulties do immigrants to a new country often have when they arrive?*	Schwierigkeit
		to **face** [feɪs]	*What difficulties will humans face in getting to Mars?*	begegnen
		misunderstanding [ˌmɪsʌndəˈstændɪŋ]	*How can we solve cultural misunderstandings when we travel?* 🛈 *Fr. 'malentendu' (m.)*	Missverständnis
		unfriendly [ʌnˈfrendli]	*I never go to that store. The employees are too unfriendly.*	unfreundlich
	2a	**status** [ˈsteɪtəs]	*What is their immigration status?*	Status; Stand
		legal [ˈliːgl]	*≠ illegal* 🛈 *Lat. 'lex, legis' (f.) = law*	rechtlich; legal
		illegal [ˈliːgl]	*≠ legal* 🛈 *Lat. 'lex, legis' (f.) = law*	illegal
		refugee [ˌrefjuˈdʒiː]	*The UN was dealing with thousands of Somali refugees. The situation was difficult.*	Flüchtling
		asylum seeker [əˈsaɪləm siːkə]	*Asylum seekers must try to build a new life in a foreign country.*	Asylbewerber(in)
		visa [ˈviːzə]	*Because I had my visa, I could get a job and a place to live.*	Visum
		to **transfer** [trænsˈfɜː]	*My family came to the US from Ukraine when my dad's job was transferred here.*	transferieren; übertragen
		beetroot [ˈbiːtruːt]	*Back home people eat things like borscht, that's soup made with beetroot.*	Rote Bete
		dumpling [ˈdʌmplɪŋ]	*Dumplings take a long time to prepare but are delicious!*	Kloß; Knödel
		current [ˈkʌrənt]	*I'm the president of the debate club, where we talk about current news topics.*	aktuell
		to **inform** [ɪnˈfɔːm]	*People are poorly informed by online media.*	informieren
		document [ˈdɒkjumənt]	*Are our travel documents ready?* 🛈 *Fr. 'document' (m.)*	Dokument
		to **deport** [dɪˈpɔːt]	*My mother is terrified that the government might deport her.*	ausweisen; deportieren
		helpless [ˈhelpləs]	*I feel so helpless when I can't solve a problem.* *= defenseless*	hilflos
		to **register** [ˈredʒɪstə]	*I registered for the class last week.*	(sich) anmelden; registrieren
		refugee camp [ˌrefjuˈdʒiː kæmp]	*I lived in a refugee camp for many months.*	Flüchtlingslager
		resettlement [ˌriːˈsetlmənt]	*I applied for resettlement to a third country.*	Umsiedlung

page	exercise	**Workshop 1**		
		many times [ˈmeni taɪmz]	I tried to call him many times.	häufig; oftmals
		hopeless [ˈhəʊpləs]	I feel hopeless and unhappy.	hoffnungslos; hilflos
		diversity [daɪˈvɜːsəti]	One day in 2012, I learned about the Diversity Immigrant Visa Lottery.	Vielfältigkeit
		lottery [ˈlɒtəri]	People who want to immigrate to America can enter a lottery.	Lotterie
	2d	**reaction** [riˈækʃn]	Explain your reaction to the movie. ⚠ Fr. 'réaction' (f.)	Reaktion
	3	to **interpret** [ɪnˈtɜːprət]	In art class, we learn to make and interpret art.	interpretieren
		to **speculate** [ˈspekjuleɪt]	Speculate which country the photo was taken in and explain why you think so.	spekulieren; nachdenken
27	4a	**destination** [ˌdestɪˈneɪʃn]	How long had you been travelling when you finally reached your destination?	Reiseziel
		ancestor [ˈænsestə]	Amish still speak German and follow the same simple way of life as their ancestors. ≠ descendant	Vorfahr(in)
		to **spread (out)** [spred]**, spread, spread** [spred, spred]	During the 19th century, new immigrants spread out to other states, such as Georgia and as far west as California.	verbreiten
	5	to **nominate** [ˈnɒmɪneɪt]	A travel organization has invited people to nominate the best town to visit in their region.	nominieren
		nomination [ˌnɒmɪˈneɪʃn]	Present your nomination to the class.	Nominierung; Ernennung

Immigration

asylum seeker [əˈsaɪləm siːkə]	Asylbewerber(in)	**refugee** [ˌrefjuˈdʒiː]	Flüchtling
		refugee camp [ˌrefjuˈdʒiː kæmp]	Flüchtlingslager
to **deport** [dɪˈpɔːt]	ausweisen; deportieren	to **register** [ˈredʒɪstə]	sich anmelden; registrieren
diversity [daɪˈvɜːsəti]	Vielfältigkeit		
document [ˈdɒkjumənt]	Dokument	**resettlement** [ˌriːˈsetlmənt]	Umsiedlung
to **emigrate** [ˈemɪgreɪt]	auswandern	**status** [ˈsteɪtəs]	Status; Stand
legal / illegal [ˈliːgl] / [ˈliːgl]	rechtlich; legal / illegal	**visa** [ˈviːzə]	Visum

page	exercise			
28	1b	**wagon** [ˈwægən]	They traveled with wagons that they pulled with horses or cows.	Wagen
		bumpy [ˈbʌmpi]	It was hot, dirty, bumpy and really slow.	holprig; uneben
		pioneer [ˌpaɪəˈnɪə]	This place was on the Oregon Trail, and the pioneers had to arrive here on or before July 4th.	Pionier(in)

page	exercise	Workshop 1		
		whoever [huːˈevə]	*There are different stories about that, but whoever named it, it was the perfect name.* = who	wer auch immer
		to **name** [neɪm]	*We named our dog Bob.* = call	benennen
	2b	**wagon train** [ˈwægən treɪn]	*The horses pulled the wagon train.*	Treck; Wagenzug
		prayer [preə]	*We climbed the great rock to give our prayers and thanked the Lord.* ⓘ *Fr. 'prière' (f.)*	Gebet
		halfway [ˌhɑːfˈweɪ]	*We are halfway to Oregon with another 1,000 miles ahead.*	halbwegs; halb
		cholera [ˈkɒlərə]	*Six people in the wagon train died of cholera.*	Cholera
		goods [gʊdz]	*We're glad when we meet Indians who ask us for flour and sugar in exchange for their goods.*	Güter
		pregnant [ˈpregnənt]	*Martha is pregnant and will have the baby in the spring.*	schwanger
29	3a	to **form** [fɔːm]	*You will learn to form new grammar tenses.*	gründen; bilden
	3c	**campground** [ˈkæmpgraʊnd]	*When they arrived at the campground, the other wagon train had already left.*	Zeltplatz
	4a	to **bother** [ˈbɒðə]	*Sorry to bother you. I just need to ask a question.*	stören
		curious [ˈkjʊəriəs]	*So, it looks like a lot of you have bright, curious minds – inventors' minds.*	neugierig; gespannt
		to **engrave** [ɪnˈgreɪv]	*Somebody probably helped her engrave it – it looks very neat for a 14-year-old.*	gravieren; eingravieren
		neat [niːt]	*Her room is very neat for a teenager!*	ordentlich
		herd [hɜːd]	*In South Dakota they saw herds of buffalo.*	Herde
		buffalo [ˈbʌfələʊ]	*While they were traveling through South Dakota, they passed huge herds of buffalo.*	Büffel
		gun [gʌn]	*She didn't know if the men were friendly, so Bessie grabbed a gun from the wagon.*	Schusswaffe
	5b	**weight** [weɪt]	*The wheel broke because the wagon carried too much weight.*	Gewicht
30	2	**reservation** [ˌrezəˈveɪʃn]	*Learn about how a Native American teenager tries to find meaning on South Dakota's Cheyenne River reservation.*	Reservat
	2a	**internship** [ˈɪntɜːnʃɪp]	*Students can do internships to learn about different jobs.*	Praktikum

page	exercise	Workshop 1		
		influence [ˈɪnfluəns]	*The Amish believe technology can be a bad influence on young people.* ⚠ *Fr. 'influencer'*	Einfluss
		within [wɪˈðɪn]	*Within a few months there were demonstrations by hundreds of thousands of students in over 90 countries.*	innerhalb
		facility [fəˈsɪləti]	*In our facility, we offer wellness programs and art classes.* ⚠ *Fr. 'facilité' (f.)*	Anlage
		wellness [ˈwelnəs]	*They offer wellness programmes for people who have been sick.*	Wellness; Wohlbefinden
		gymnasium [dʒɪmˈneɪziəm]	*We have a teen center, gymnasium, dance studio and computer lab.*	Sporthalle; Turnhalle
		mental [ˈmentl]	*We are talking about mental and physical health.*	geistig; mental
		to evolve [ɪˈvɒlv]	*As we've evolved, we've learned from our kids and from our community.*	(sich) entwickeln
		assimilation [əˌsɪməˈleɪʃn]	*Moving us to the reservations and the assimilation of our people – both of these things still impact us today.*	Assimilation; Anpassung
		to impart [ɪmˈpɑːt]	*We want them to impart that onto their children when the next generation comes.*	vermitteln
		generation [ˌdʒenəˈreɪʃn]	*Describe how Generation Z is different from older generations.* ⚠ *Fr. 'génération' (f.)*	Generation
	2e	**finding** [ˈfaɪndɪŋ]	*Research the questions and report your findings to the class.*	Ergebnis; Befund
31	4	**caption** [ˈkæpʃn]	*Look at the photos and match the captions to the images.*	Bildunterschrift; Bildtext; Untertitel
	5a	**access** [ˈækses]	*We have access to a lot of books.*	Zugriff; Zugang
	5b	**to ignore** [ɪgˈnɔː]	*As in the past, the government is ignoring Native American rights and destroying the Earth.*	ignorieren
		oil [ɔɪl]	*The government helps the oil companies and not the Native Americans.* ⚠ *Fr. 'huile' (f.)*	Öl
		soil [sɔɪl]	*Many of my people still gathered their food from the soil, the plants and the wildlife.*	Erde; Erdreich
		pipeline [ˈpaɪplaɪn]	*The pipeline is also a danger to the water quality in the Missouri River.*	Pipeline
		midwestern [ˌmɪdˈwestən]	*The project by big oil companies transports oil underground across four midwestern states.*	mittlerer Westen

page	exercise	Workshop 1		
		sacred [ˈseɪkrɪd]	*The oil companies built the pipeline across land that is sacred to the Native American tribes in the area.*	heilig
		resident [ˈrezɪdənt]	*The local community paid the residents to help set up the first gardens.* = *inhabitant*	Bewohner(in)
		construction [kənˈstrʌkʃn]	*They allowed the construction of the pipeline, which is bad for the environment.*	Bau
		keeper [ˈkiːpə]	*We are still the keepers of this beautiful land.* = *caretaker*	Hüter(in)
		sincerely [sɪnˈsɪəli]	*At the end of the letter, write 'Sincerely yours' and then sign your name.*	aufrichtig; mit freundlichen Grüßen
32		**to select** [sɪˈlekt]	= *choose* ≠ *reject*	wählen; auswählen
	S1a	**extract** [ɪkˈstrækt]	*Read the extracts from a website and answer these questions.* = *excerpt* ❗ *Fr. 'extrait' (m.)*	Auszug
		value [ˈvæljuː]	*The movie shows the attitudes and values of today's teenagers.* ❗ *Fr. 'valeur' (f.)*	Wert
		belief [bɪˈliːf]	*What are the values and beliefs in your family?* ≠ *disbelief*	Glaube
		reformation [ˌrefəˈmeɪʃn]	*The Amish are an American Protestant religious group that originated in Europe during the Reformation.* ❗ *Lat. 'reformare (reformo, reforma)'*	Reformation
		meetinghouse [ˈmiːtɪŋhaʊs]	*The Mennonites worship God in meetinghouses, but the Amish worship at home.*	Andachtshaus; Gebetshaus
		interaction [ˌɪntərˈækʃn]	= *communication* ❗ *Fr. 'interaction' (f.)*	Interaktion
		society [səˈsaɪəti]	❗ *Fr. 'société' (f.), Lat. 'societas, -atis' (f.)*	Gesellschaft
		to communicate [kəˈmjuːnɪkeɪt]	*It helps if you speak Spanish, but if you don't, you'll find ways to communicate with the people.*	kommunizieren; etw. vermitteln
	S1b	**relevant** [ˈreləvənt]	*Read the article and underline the most relevant information.*	wichtig; relevant
	S2	**root** [ruːt]	*The Amish have their roots in Europe.*	Wurzel
		occupation [ˌɒkjuˈpeɪʃn]	*Their main occupation is farming.*	Tätigkeit; Beschäftigung
		farming [ˈfɑːmɪŋ]	*Most parts of the land are used for farming.*	Landwirtschaft

page	exercise			
		Workshop 1		
		buggy [ˈbʌɡi]	*The main method of transport for the Amish is a horse and buggy.*	Pferdewagen; Kutsche
		quilt [kwɪlt]	*You can buy traditional hand-made products like quilts as well.*	Steppdecke
		individual [ˌɪndɪˈvɪdʒuəl]	*In his culture, family and community are more important than individuals.* ❗ *Fr. 'individuel, individuelle'*	Einzelne(r)
		plain [pleɪn]	*Their clothing is plain and simple.*	nicht Besonders; gutbürgerlich
33	S3a	**linking word** [ˈlɪŋkɪŋ wɜːd]	*Does the writer use linking words to connect ideas?*	Verbindungswort
		contrasting [kənˈtrɑːstɪŋ]	*If you use contrasting colours, the text will be easier to read.*	gegensätzlich
	S4	**strategy** [ˈstrætədʒi]	*What research strategies did you try?*	Strategie
36	5b	**asterisk** [ˈæstərɪsk]	*I put an asterisk by the most important points.*	Sternchen; Asterisk
39	3	**to declare** [dɪˈkleə]	*When did the original 13 colonies declare independence?* = *announce*	ausrufen; verkünden
		impressed [ɪmˈprest]	*He was so good, his teacher was impressed.*	beindruckt
	4	**professor** [prəˈfesə]	*His father was a university professor and his mother was a researcher.*	Professor(in)
		researcher [rɪˈsɜːtʃə]	*My mother works as a researcher at the university.*	Forscher(in)
41	7	**to cancel** [ˈkænsl]	*They planned the party for a year and then had to cancel it!*	absagen
	9	**festival** [ˈfestɪvl]	*Every year, there is a festival of flowers.* = *fair*	Festival; Festspiele; Fest
	10	**electrical** [ɪˈlektrɪkl]	*He studied electrical engineering at Stanford University.*	elektrisch
	11	**biography** [baɪˈɒɡrəfi]	*We have to find out about famous immigrants to the USA and write a short biography about them.*	Biografie
		cab [kæb]	*Life was hard for her family until her dad found a job as cab driver.*	Taxi; Fahrerkabine; Führerhaus

page	exercise			
		Workshop 2		
44	1	**aspect** [ˈæspekt]	*The group discusses three aspects of the waste problem and how to deal with them.*	Aspekt
	2	**style** [staɪl]	*It's important to have your own style.*	Stil
		trend [trend]	*There's too much pressure to keep up with the latest trends.*	Trend
		thrift store [ˈθrɪft stɔː]	*You can get really good quality stuff at thrift stores for much less than the original price.*	Secondhandladen

page	exercise			
		Workshop 2		
		brand [brænd]	*Do you have a favourite brand of trainers?*	Marke
		to define [dɪˈfaɪn]	*How do you define a good friend?*	definieren; bestimmen
		genre [ˈʒɒrə]	*I'm into lots of music genres and artists.*	Genre
		playlist [ˈpleɪlɪst]	*Which musical artists are on your playlist?*	Playlist; Wiedergabeliste
	3a	**to formulate** [ˈfɔːmjuleɪt]	*Formulate a short statement about the topic.* *= develop*	formulieren
45	2	**active** [ˈæktɪv]	*How active are you in creating and sharing content online?*	aktiv
		to avoid [əˈvɔɪd]	*It's so cold there! If I can avoid it, I won't go there.*	vermeiden
		whenever [wenˈevə]	*Come over whenever you're done with your homework.*	wann auch immer
		generally [ˈdʒenrəli]	*I think it's because kids my age generally like competing in sports.*	im Allgemeinen; hauptsächlich
46	1	**director** [dəˈrektə]	*The band director gave him some advice.* ■ *Fr. 'directeur' (m.), 'directrice' (f.)*	Leiter(in)
		leaf [liːf]**, leaves** [liːvz]	*The leaves fall from the trees in autumn.*	Blatt
		thumb [θʌm]	*Jordan looked up from his drums to Conor and gave him a thumbs up.*	Daumen
		trumpet [ˈtrʌmpɪt]	*She can play the trumpet well.*	Trompete
		solo [ˈsəʊləʊ]	*The guitar solo was the best part of the song.*	Solo
		series [ˈsɪəriːz]	*There's a series of jazz concerts. in the park.*	Serie
		senior [ˈsiːniə]	*The homecoming game celebrates the seniors on the football team.*	Oberstufenschüler(in); Senior(in)
		to step in [step ˈɪn]	*We stepped into the hall to talk in privacy.* *= enter*	eintreten
47	5	**to have a crush on** [həv ə krʌʃ ɒn]	*Jordan thinks Conor has a crush on Meg.* *= like romantically*	in jmdn. verknallt sein
		noon [nuːn]	*We've been hanging out here since about noon.*	Mittag
48	2a	**habit** [ˈhæbɪt]	*Discuss and make notes about your media habits.*	Gewohnheit
		hyper-connected [ˈhaɪpə kəˈnektɪd]	*Hyper-connected young people use digital devices hours per day.*	angeschlossen
		resource [rɪˈsɔːs]	*Almost half of the teenagers use a smartphone to access online resources and content.* *= means*	Ressource; Mittel

page	exercise	Workshop 2		
		to **engage** [ɪnˈɡeɪdʒ]	*Many teens engage with at least two devices at the same time.*	(sich) beschäftigen
		sequentially [sɪˈkwenʃəli]	*We use devices sequentially – we look for information on a smartphone and then use the PC to check the information.*	folgend; nacheinander
		gaming [ˈɡeɪmɪŋ]	*Gaming is the number one most popular content accessed online.*	Spielen
		to **access** [ˈækses]	*I don't want everybody on the internet to be able to access my photos.*	zugreifen auf
	3	**app** [æp]	*He hasn't had his phone very long, so he doesn't understand some of the apps yet.*	App
49	4	**gamer** [ˈɡeɪmə]	*Most gamers have already played the new Crashplanet.*	Gamer(in); Spieler(in)
		mailbox [ˈmeɪlbɒks]	*I've been playing it since it arrived in my mailbox three days ago.*	Briefkasten; Mailbox
		version [ˈvɜːʒn]	*The blogger has been enjoying the new version of the software.*	Version
	6	**trailer** [ˈtreɪlə]	*Have you seen the trailer for the new movie yet?*	Trailer
	6b	**individually** [ˌɪndɪˈvɪdʒuəli]	*We learn to work individually as well as with others.* = *alone*	einzeln
		freshman [ˈfreʃmən]	*I was a freshman in highschool when we met.*	Student im ersten Jahr; Studienanfänger(in)
		depressing [dɪˈpresɪŋ]	*If my English teacher is the only friend I make today, that would be sort of depressing.* ≠ *comforting*	deprimierend
		misfit [ˈmɪsfɪt]	*Welcome to the island of misfit toys! I'm a toy train with square wheels.*	Außenseiter(in)
		psycho [ˈsaɪkəʊ]	*He's acting crazy – is he a psycho?*	Psychopath(in)
		crime [kraɪm]	*Crime is high in some big cities.*	Verbrechen
		average [ˈævərɪdʒ]	*The average temperature is minus 81 degrees centigrade.*	durchschnittlich
		to **treat** [triːt]	*It is unfair and inhumane to treat children in this terrible way.*	behandeln
		alive [əˈlaɪv]	*Some day our stories will be history, but we are alive now!* ≠ *dead*	lebendig
		to **swear** [sweə]	*And in this moment, I swear we are infinite.*	schwören
		infinite [ˈɪnfɪnət]	*You have to get organized. Time is not infinite!*	unendlich
		plot [plɒt]	*A good trailer should tell you what the film is about, without saying too much about the plot.*	Handlung

page	exercise	**Workshop 2**		
	6c	**technique** [tekˈniːk]	*Compare the techniques used in each film.*	Technik; Methode
50	2a	**justice** [ˈdʒʌstɪs]	*They're also interested in social justice.*	Gerechtigkeit
		according to [əˈkɔːdɪŋ tə]	*According to the experts, this influences their shopping habits.*	gemäß; nach
		to influence [ˈɪnfluəns]	*New technology influences our shopping habits.* ▪ *Fr. 'influencer'*	beeinflussen
	2b	**to get inspired** [get ɪnˈspaɪəd]	*Sometimes I see something on social media and get inspired by it.*	inspiriert werden
		thrifting [θrɪftɪŋ]	*Thrifting is a good way to find interesting clothes.*	Secondhand shoppen
		convenient [kənˈviːniənt]	*If I want something, I usually order it online because it's more convenient.*	günstig; praktisch

Fashion and consumerism

bargain [ˈbɑːgɪn]	Schnäppchen	**production** [prəˈdʌkʃən]	Produktion; Herstellung
brand [brænd]	Marke		
company [ˈkʌmpəni]	Unternehmen	**sale** [seɪl]	Sale; Ausverkauf
deal [diːl]	Geschäft; Deal	**to supply** [səˈplaɪ]	versorgen; liefern
denim [ˈdenɪm]	Denim; Jeansstoff	**style** [staɪl]	Stil
factory [ˈfæktəri]	Fabrik	**trend** [trend]	Trend
fashion [ˈfæʃən]	Trend; Mode	**thrifting** [θrɪftɪŋ]	Secondhand shoppen
industry [ˈɪndəstri]	Industrie		
		thrift store [ˈθrɪft stɔː]	Secondhandladen

page	exercise			
51		**unless** [ənˈles]	*I won't buy anything unless I have enough money, so I have to save up.* = except	außer wenn
		bargain [ˈbɑːgən]	*I always look for bargains in stores or special offers online.*	Schnäppchen
		sale [seɪl]	*Even if I had lots of money, I'd still look for sales.*	Sale; Ausverkauf
	3a	**unlikely** [ʌnˈlaɪkli]	*It is very unlikely that I'll become famous!*	unwahrscheinlich
52	2a	**factory** [ˈfæktri]	*Robots will work in our factories, drive our cars and walk our dogs.*	Fabrik
	2b	**industry** [ˈɪndəstri]	*Make notes about how the fast fashion industry harms people and the environment.*	Industrie
		deal [diːl]	*We buy more and more because we think we're getting a good deal.*	Geschäft; Deal
		fashion [ˈfæʃn]	*Styles change every few weeks – that's why it's called 'fast fashion'.*	Trend; Mode
		labor [ˈleɪbə]	*There is cheap labor in developing countries.* ▪ *labour (BE)*	Arbeitskraft; Arbeit

page	exercise	**Workshop 2**		
		liter [ˈliːtə]	It takes around 3,800 liters of water to produce just one pair of jeans. ❗ *litre (BE)*	Liter
		production [prəˈdʌkʃn]	He started many companies and oversaw the mass production of his inventions. = *manufacture*	Produktion; Herstellung
		global [ˈgləʊbl]	Cotton production for clothing causes up to 25 % of global pollution.	global; weltweit
		pesticide [ˈpestɪsaɪd]	Pesticides are bad for the environment and our health.	Pestizid
		cancer [ˈkænsə]	Workers can get cancer from the dyes they use to produce bright colours.	Krebs
		dye [daɪ]	Dyes are used to make the bright colours. = *stain*	Färbemittel; Farbe
		toxic [ˈtɒksɪk]	When old clothes go into landfills, toxic chemicals escape into the air. = *harmful*	toxisch; giftig
53	3	**faraway** [ˈfɑːrəweɪ]	I dream about having a good job so I can go on holiday to faraway countries.	fern
	4a	**debating club** [dɪˈbeɪtɪŋ klʌb]	In our school's debating club, we talk about politics.	Debattierklub
	4b	**shopper** [ˈʃɒpə]	Should shoppers who care about the environment avoid fast fashion brands?	Käufer(in)
	4c	to **fall apart** [fɔːl əˈpɑːt]**, fell, felt** [fel, fel]	The clothes they produce are good quality and don't fall apart after five weeks.	auseinanderfallen
		synthetic [sɪnˈθetɪk]	Did you know that clothes that are made of synthetic materials can sit in landfills for up to 200 years.	synthetisch
	5	**invitation** [ˌɪnvɪˈteɪʃn]	We were sent an invitation to meet Ms Lopez last week.	Einladung; Aufforderung
	6b	**visual aid** [ˌvɪʒuəl ˈeɪd]	If possible, use some visual aids to make your talk more interesting.	Anschauungsmaterial
54	S2	**ranking** [ˈræŋkɪŋ]	We have a ranking of the best books of the year. = *hierarchy*	Rangfolge
		to **rank** [ˈræŋk]	Let's rank our favourite movies of the year. = *hierarchy*	in eine Rangfolge bringen
		e-commerce [ˈiː kɒmɜːs]	More people now shop via e-commerce than at the mall.	E-Commerce; Internethandel
	S3	**biased** [ˈbaɪəst]	Don't use biased language because it can influence people's answers. ≠ *unbiased*	parteiisch

page	exercise	Workshop 2		
55	S1	**competitively** [kəmˈpetətɪvli]	*What kind of activities do you do competitively?*	konkurrierend; wetteifernd
	S6	**to circulate** [ˈsɜːkjəleɪt]	*Decide how you want to circulate your questionnaire, as a photocopied handout or digitally.*	kursieren; zirkulieren
		to photocopy [ˈfəʊtəʊkɒpi]	*My teacher asked me to photocopy the handout.*	fotokopieren
		handout [ˈhændaʊt]	*She prepared a handout for her presentation.*	Handout; Flugblatt
		gender [ˈdʒendə]	*Before beginning your survey, ask for personal information, such as age and gender.*	Geschlecht; Gender
56	2a	**to advise** [ədˈvaɪz]	*My host mom advises me to try going to bed earlier.* ❗ Fr. 'aviser'	raten
	2b	**equivalent** [ɪˈkwɪvələnt]	*Match American English words in the blog to their British English equivalents.*	entsprechend
57	2a	**to require** [rɪˈkwaɪə]	= *need* ❗ Fr. 'require'	verlangen; fordern
		elective [ɪˈlektɪv]	*Some classes are required, like math, English and science, but students can choose other classes called electives.*	Auswahlfach
		contemporary [kənˈtemprəri]	*I like contemporary American literature better than older fiction.*	zeitgenössisch
		literature [ˈlɪtrətʃə]	*I take a contemporary American literature class in the afternoon.*	Literatur
	4b	**punctual** [ˈpʌŋktʃuəl]	*The students should be punctual for lessons.* = *on time*	pünktlich
58	2	**homecoming** [ˈhəʊmkʌmɪŋ]	*Read the website and look at the photos about homecoming, a special event at American schools.*	Absolvententreffen an Schulen oder Universitäten
		wacky [ˈwæki]	*On the school's wacky day I wear my clothes backward.*	verrückt; verdreht
		mismatched [ˌmɪsˈmætʃ]	*I love to wear mismatched, crazy clothes.*	nicht zusammenpassend
		spirit [ˈspɪrɪt]	*We show our school spirit during homecoming week.*	Geist
		pajamas [pəˈdʒɑːməs]	*One day, we all wore our pajamas to school!*	Schlafanzug; Pyjama
		pride [praɪd]	*During homecoming we show our pride in our school.*	Stolz
		rally [ˈræli]	*Some schools announce the winners during the rally before the football game.*	Treffen; Kundgebung
	3	**former** [ˈfɔːmə]	*At homecoming, we welcome former students back to the school.* = *previous*	ehemalig

page	exercise	**Workshop 2**		
		alumnus [əˈlʌmnaɪ]	*He is an alumnus of the school. He's returning with other alumni to visit the school.*	Absolvent; Ehemalige
		festivity [feˈstɪvəti]	*And, of course, there are lots of festivities to enjoy.*	Festlichkeit
		theme [θiːm]	*The school's band takes part and there are floats with a special theme.* ❗ *Fr. 'thème' (m.)*	Thema
		to aim [eɪm]	*Homecoming takes place in the school gym and aims to get everyone excited about the game.* = *intend*	zielen; beabsichtigen
		to elect [ɪˈlekt]	*The most important homecoming tradition after the football game is electing the King and Queen.*	wählen; auswählen
		formal	≠ *informal* ❗ *Fr. 'formel, formelle'*	förmlich; formell
		to socialize [ˈsəʊʃəlaɪz]	*It's a special evening when students can dress up, dance and socialize.*	Kontakte pflegen; unter die Leute kommen
		to decorate [ˈdekəreɪt]	*We will decorate the gym with balloons and streamers for homecoming.* ❗ *Fr. 'décorer'*	dekorieren; schmücken
		streamer [ˈstriːmə]	*The gym may be decorated with balloons and streamers and there's often a professional DJ.*	Luftschlangen
59	6a	**computerized** [kəmˈpjuːtəraɪzd]	*All the students have a laptop and the teachers use computerized smart boards.*	computerbasiert; computergesteuert
		smart [smɑːt]	*The teacher uses a smart board in class.*	intelligent; schlau
		virtual [ˈvɜːtʃuəl]	*We can now explore the surface of Mars with the Mars rover using virtual reality.*	virtuell
		dress code [ˈdres kəʊd]	*Everyone has to follow the school dress code and be clean and tidy at all times.*	Kleiderordnung; Dresscode
		ripped [rɪpt]	*Students mustn't wear ripped jeans, sleeveless tops or sandals.*	gerissen
		sleeveless [ˈsliːvləs]	*Sleeveless tops are not allowed in our school.*	ärmellos
		sandal [ˈsændl]	*I wear sandals every summer.*	Sandale
		democratic [ˌdeməˈkrætɪk]	*Students have a say in the running of the school through weekly democratic meetings.*	demokratisch
		tutor [ˈtjuːtə]	*The tutors help the students to choose their projects.*	Tutor(in)
		master [ˈmɑːstə]	*Instead of traditional teachers, there are tutors and part-time masters.*	Meister(in)

page	exercise	Workshop 2		
60	2a	**driver's license** [ˈdraɪvəz laɪsns]	*If I had my driver's license, we could take my mom's car.*	Führerschein; Fahrerlaubnis
		downtown [ˌdaʊnˈtaʊn]	*I read about a popular hostel in downtown Chicago called Tramper's Inn.*	Innenstadt
61	4a	**to rent** [rent]	*We rented bikes while on vacation.*	mieten
		ferris wheel [ˈferɪs wiːl]	*You remember when we rode on that big Ferris wheel, don't you?*	Riesenrad
		lakefront [ˈleɪkfrʌnt]	*We can walk from the holiday house to the lakefront.*	Seeufer
	6a	**stressful** [ˈstresfl]	*Life is stressful with both work and school.* = disturbing	stressig
		violence [ˈvaɪələns]	*There's a lot of crime and violence there and in other parts of the city.* = brutality	Gewalt
62	2a	**evenly** [ˈiːvnli]	*The world is pretty evenly divided between those that live in rural areas and those that live in cities.* = equally	ausgeglichen
		rural [ˈrʊərəl]	*We left the city for a rural home.*	ländlich
		depressed [dɪˈprest]	*This study says that rural people are less depressed.* ≠ cheerful	deprimiert
		dweller [ˈdwelə]	*This study concludes that rural dwellers are actually happier.* = inhabitant	Bewohner(in)
		elderly [ˈeldəli]	*Many elderly people are lonely and don't have enough contact with other people.*	älter
		to head out [hed aʊt]	*We headed out to the country to visit the farmer.* = set off	aufbrechen; losfahren
		old-fashioned [ˌəʊldˈfæʃnd]	*The Amish dress in old-fashioned clothing.* ≠ modern	altmodisch
		absolutely [ˈæbsəluːtli]	*They were absolutely sure that the count was wasting his money.*	absolut; wirklich
		to relax [rɪˈlæks]	*Listening to music helps me to relax.* = be at ease 🛈 Fr. 'relaxer'	sich entspannen
		index [ˈɪndeks]	*This index says liking where you live is one of the five things that are important for happiness.*	Index; Register
		indexer [ˈɪndeksə]	*Enjoying your work is one of the five main indexers for overall well-being.*	Indexer(in)
	2b	**concentration** [ˌkɒnsnˈtreɪʃn]	*When I'm tired, I have a problem with concentration.*	Konzentration

page	exercise	**Workshop 2**		
63	4a	**lakeside** [ˈleɪksaɪd]	*The best restaurant is on the lakeside.*	Seeufer
	5	**urban** [ˈɜːbən]	*Young people are also involved in the urban gardening programme.* *≠ rural*	städtisch; urban
		inner city [ˌɪnə ˈsɪti]	*To make inner cities better places to live, they need to have less traffic.*	Innenstadt
		liveable [ˈlɪvəbl]	*Urban gardening helps make cities more liveable.*	bewohnbar
		to **cultivate** [ˈkʌltɪveɪt]	*In community gardens, plant-loving residents are thankful to have a peaceful green space to cultivate.*	anbauen; bebauen
		overgrown [ˌəʊvəˈgrəʊn]	*The program cleaned up overgrown, rubbish-filled lots between buildings.*	überwuchert; überwachsen
		to **transform** [trænsˈfɔːm]	*Our lives today have been transformed by technology.*	verändern
		income [ˈɪnkʌm]	*Like many teenagers who have only one parent at home or who come from a low-income family, Beth has to balance work, life and school.*	Einkommen
		low-income [ləʊ ˈɪnkʌm]	*The youth development program teaches valuable skills and employs teens from low-income areas.*	einkommensschwach
		development [dɪˈveləpmənt]	*We will discuss past and future technological developments.*	Entwicklung
		nutrition [njuˈtrɪʃn]	*They plant gardens in low-income neighborhoods where health and nutrition are big issues.*	Ernährung
		gardener [ˈgɑːdnə]	*The gardener is planting new trees in the park.*	Gärtner(in)
		problem-solving [ˈprɒbləm sɒlvɪŋ]	*I've learned a lot about problem-solving and about community responsibility.*	problemlösend
		responsibility [rɪˌspɒnsəˈbɪləti]	*= duty* **ℹ** *Fr. 'responsabilité' (f.), Lat. 'responsalis, -e'*	Verantwortung
		transformation [ˌtrænsfəˈmeɪʃn]	*The transformation that I've seen in kids in the programme is unbelievable.*	Veränderung; Verwandlung
64	S1	**tally** [ˈtæli]	*Here is a tally of the hours I worked on the project.*	Gesamtliste
	S2	**chart** [tʃɑːt]	*What kind of chart will you use to present the results for each question?*	Diagramm; Chart
		bar chart [ˈbɑː tʃɑːt]	*The information can be presented in a bar chart.*	Balkendiagramm
		pie chart [ˈpaɪ tʃɑːt]	*He used a pie chart to present his information.*	Tortendiagramm; Kreisdiagramm
	S3	**millennial** [mɪˈleniəl]	*Millennials most often discover new products online.*	die Generation der Jahrtausendwende

page	exercise	**Workshop 2**		
		retailer [ˈriːteɪlə]	Retailers' websites are now more successful than their stores. = seller	Händler(in); Einzelhändler(in)
	S4	**horizontal** [ˌhɒrɪˈzɒntl]	If you use a bar chart, write labels along the horizontal axis and use a suitable scale up the vertical axis. ≠ vertical	horizontal
		axis [ˈæksɪs]	If you use a bar chart, write labels along the horizontal axis.	Achse
		suitable [ˈsuːtəbl]	Prepare a one-minute presentation explaining why you are a suitable candidate.	geeignet
		vertical [ˈvɜːtɪkl]	Label the vertical axis of the bar chart with numbers. ≠ horizontal	senkrecht; vertikal
70	1	**in particular** [pəˈtɪkjələ]	There's one girl in particular, Meg, I guess I've got a bit of a crush on her.	besonders
		apparently [əˈpærəntli]	He's very good. Apparently, he's played for more than 35 years. ❗Fr. 'apparemment'	anscheinend
		hopefully [ˈhəʊpfəli]	I'll ask my mom if I can go. Hopefully, she'll say yes. ≠ hopelessly	hoffentlich
71	4	**to focus** [ˈfəʊkəs]	I miss meeting up with my friends, but now I'm trying to focus on schoolwork.	fokussieren
72	3	**celebrity** [səˈlebrəti]	Teen magazines often feature interviews and photos of celebrities.	Prominente(r)
73	6	**prompt** [prɒmpt]	Use the prompts to write sentences about how technology has changed our lives.	Stichwort; Aufforderung
	7	**cultured** [ˈkʌltʃəd]	My parents are cultured and listen to classical music.	gebildet; kultiviert
		hectic [ˈhektɪk]	My work is hectic and that is stressful. = chaotic	hektisch
		laid-back [ˌleɪd ˈbæk]	Youth culture is laid-back and fun.	locker; entspannt
		diverse [daɪˈvɜːs]	Cities are more diverse than the countryside.	vielfältig; verschieden
	11	**focused** [ˈfəʊkəst]	The audience is focused and interested in the presentation.	fokussiert
page	exercise	**Workshop 3**		
76	1	**invention** [ɪnˈvenʃn]	What are the most important inventions or discoveries that changed the world?	Erfindung
		to patent [ˈpætnt]	Thomas Edison patented the incandescent electric light bulb.	patentieren
		airplane [ˈeəpleɪn]	It was the first time she flew in an airplane.	Flugzeug

page	exercise	**Workshop 3**		
		to **pilot** [ˈpaɪlət]	*The American Wright brothers built and piloted the first powered airplane.*	steuern
		powered [ˈpaʊəd]	*He built the first practical motor car powered by an internal combustion engine.*	angetrieben
		to **launch** [lɔːntʃ]	*Before the first search engines were launched in the 1990s, people got information from books.*	starten; auf den Markt bringen
		orbit [ˈɔːbɪt]	*The Soviet Union launched Vostok 1 into orbit.*	Orbit; Umlaufbahn
		spacecraft [ˈspeɪskrɑːft]	*Russians built the first spacecraft to contain a person, Yuri Gagarin.* = *spaceship*	Raumfahrzeug
		available [əˈveɪləbl]	*The internet first became available to the public in 1991.*	verfügbar; erhältlich
		to **release** [rɪˈliːs]	*The first smartphone was released in 1994.*	veröffentlichen; auf den Markt bringen
77		**automobile** [ˈɔːtəməbiːl]	*It's hard to imagine life before the automobile was invented.* = *car*	Automobil
		petrol [ˈpetrəl]	*The first petrol car was powered by an internal combustion engine.* = *gas*	Benzin
		internal combustion [ɪnˈtɜːnl kəmˈbʌstʃən]	*Karl Benz designed and built the first petrol car powered by an internal combustion engine.*	Verbrennungs-
		mass [mæs]	*He started many companies and oversaw the mass production of his inventions.*	Massen-
		to **contain** [kənˈteɪn]	*The first spacecraft to contain a person was launched into orbit by the Soviet Union.*	etw. enthalten
		portable [ˈpɔːtəbl]	*Portable computers weren't made until the 1990s.*	tragbar
		laptop [ˈlæptɒp]	*Modern computers – laptops – weren't developed until the 1990s.*	Laptop
		touchscreen [ˈtʌtʃskriːn]	*It has a touchscreen, can access the internet and does most of the things a computer can do.*	Berührungsbildschirm
	2a	**discovery** [dɪˈskʌvəri]	❗ *Fr. 'découverte' (f.)*	Entdeckung
		candlelight [ˈkændllaɪt]	*Imagine trying to do your homework by candlelight.*	Kerzenlicht
		aeroplane [ˈeərəpleɪn]	*There's an aeroplane, or airplane as you say, landing now!*	Flugzeug
		satellite [ˈsætəlaɪt]	*Rockets put satellites into space around Earth.*	Satellit

page	exercise	**Workshop 3**		
		affordable [əˈfɔːdəbl]	The first affordable smartphone was invented in 2007. = economical	bezahlbar
		technological [ˌteknəˈlɒdʒɪkl]	He gave a talk about technological developments.	technisch; technologisch
78	1a	**game console** [ˈgeɪm kənsəʊl]	He invented a game console that people with disabilities can use.	Spielekonsole
		robot [ˈrəʊbɒt]	This looks like a toy, but it's actually an intelligent robot.	Roboter
		netbook [ˈnetbʊk]	My parents bought me a netbook for my schoolwork.	Netbook
		self-checkout [ˌself ˈtʃekaʊt]	There are self-checkouts at the big grocery store.	Selbstzahlerkasse
		fridge [frɪdʒ]	❗ refrigerator	Kühlschrank
		vacuum cleaner [ˈvækjuːm kliːnə]	We have a robot vacuum cleaner that cleans the house while we're out.	Staubsauger
		reality [riˈæləti]	Do you think space travel will have become a reality for most people by 2050? ≠ imagination	Realität
		headset [ˈhedset]	I got a virtual reality headset for Christmas.	Headset
	2a	**innovation** [ˌɪnəˈveɪʃn]	What inventions or innovations are mentioned in the text? = modernization	Innovation; Neuheit
		to take for granted [teɪk fə ˈgrɑːntɪd], **took, taken** [tʊk, ˈteɪkən]	We don't have all the modern conveniences that other kids take for granted.	für selbstverständlich halten
		household [ˈhaʊshəʊld]	Most homes didn't have electricity and household chores had to be done by hand.	häuslich; Haushalts-
		to entertain [ˌentəˈteɪn]	= captivate ≠ bore	unterhalten
		to revolutionize [ˌrevəˈluːʃənaɪz]	Since the internet was developed, the way we communicate, socialize and entertain ourselves has been revolutionized. = change	revolutionieren
		video conferencing [ˈvɪdiəʊ ˈkɒnfərənsɪŋ]	Today email, messaging apps and video conferencing make communication quick and easy.	Videokonferenztechnik
		purchase [ˈpɜːtʃəs]	Today, people pay for purchases using a mobile phone app. = acquisition	Kauf; Ankauf
		cashier [kæˈʃɪə]	Cashiers have been replaced by automatic check-outs in many stores. ❗ Fr.'caissier' (m.), caissière (f.)	Kassierer(in)

page	exercise	Workshop 3		
		check-out [ˈtʃekaʊt]	*After finding everything on the shopping list, we went to the check-out.*	Kasse
		electronically [ɪˌlekˈtrɒnɪkli]	*Most goods are paid for electronically with a card or a phone app.*	elektronisch
		to control [kənˈtrəʊl]	*= command*	kontrollieren
		remotely [rɪˈməʊtli]	*Many appliances can be controlled remotely.*	aus der Ferne
		toothbrush [ˈtuːθbrʌʃ]	*Our smart toothbrush will tell us if we've brushed our teeth properly.*	Zahnbürste
		to brush [brʌʃ]	*I brush my teeth every morning and evening.*	bürsten; putzen
		artificial intelligence [ˌɑːtɪfɪʃl ɪnˈtelɪdʒəns]	*Developments in artificial intelligence will allow machines to perform many tasks.*	künstliche Intelligenz
		autonomous [ɔːˈtɒnəməs]	*Autonomous drones perform tasks without human involvement.* *= sovereign* ❗ *Fr. 'autonome'*	autonom; unabhängig
		to deliver [dɪˈlɪvə]	*When I was a kid, I delivered newspapers.* *= transfer*	liefern
		parcel [ˈpɑːsl]	*Autonomous drones will be used to deliver parcels to our doors.* *= package*	Paket
		downside [ˈdaʊnsaɪd]	*The downside of having a job is that I'll have less time to study.* *= disadvantage*	Nachteil
79	3b	**advance** [ədˈvɑːns]	*= progress*	Fortschritt
		medical science [ˈmedɪkl ˈsaɪəns]	*Thanks to advances in medical science, we can cure most diseases today.*	Heilkunde; Medizin
		to cure [kjʊə]	*Usually, a flu can be cured quite fast.*	heilen
	4a	**assignment** [əˈsaɪnmənt]	*If I need to know something for a school assignment, I look it up in an encyclopedia.*	Aufgabe
		folks [fəʊks]	*A lot of folks had a set of encyclopedias at home.*	Leute
		snail mail [ˈsneɪl meɪl]	*My grandmother likes me to send her snail mail.* *≠ e-mail*	Schneckenpost; traditioneller Brief
		landline [ˈlændlaɪn]	*When my parents first met, there was only snail mail and landlines and no internet or mobile phones!*	Festnetz
		kickball [ˈkɪkbɔːl]	*In the summer, we played baseball or kickball.*	Kickball
		competitive [kəmˈpetətɪv]	❗ *Lat. 'competitio, -onis' (f.) = competition*	konkurrenzorientiert

page	exercise	Workshop 3		
	5b	**gadget** ['gædʒɪt]	*Have you ever been curious about how a gadget or an app works?*	Gerät; technische Spielerei
80	2	**off the grid** [ɒf ðə grɪd]	*They quit their jobs in the city, bought an old barn and turned it into an off the grid home.*	vom Netz
		solar power [ˌsəʊlə 'paʊə]	*Solar power produces energy from the sun.*	Solarenergie; Sonnenenergie
		to generate ['dʒenəreɪt]	*We use solar and wind power to generate electricity for our home.*	erzeugen
		to **pump** [pʌmp]	*We pump our water up from a well and use a composting toilet.*	pumpen
		composting ['kɒmpɒstɪŋ]	*We chose a project that covers all the waste problem areas – single-use plastic, recycling and composting.*	Kompostierungs-
		sustainable [sə'steɪnəbl]	*We want to reduce single-use plastic at school and help find sustainable alternatives.* = continuous	nachhaltig
		self-sufficient [ˌself sə'fɪʃnt]	*They wanted to live in a more sustainable way and become as self-sufficient as possible.*	unabhängig; autark
		to **quit** [kwɪt]	*They quit their jobs in the city and bought an old farm.* = give up	kündigen; verlassen
	3a	**acre** ['eɪkə]	*We bought a few acres of land.* ❗ Flächenmaß	Morgen
		van [væn]	*We traveled around the country and slept in a van.*	Transporter; Lieferwagen
		camper van ['kæmpə væn]	*We had to live in this camper van for a whole year before our home was ready.*	Wohnmobil
		pond [pɒnd]	*Our land has a big pond on it.*	Teich
		rainwater ['reɪnwɔːtə]	*At first, we had to collect rainwater from the roof in big tanks.*	Regenwasser
		backup ['bækʌp]	*We still collect rainwater from the roof as a backup, just in case we run out of water.*	Backup; Unterstützung
		to install [ɪn'stɔːl]	= set up ❗ Fr. 'installer'	installieren
		lighting ['laɪtɪŋ]	*Wind power can generate electricity for lighting and appliances.*	Beleuchtung
		to provide [prə'vaɪd]	❗ Lat. 'providere (provido, providi, provisum)'	zur Verfügung stellen; versorgen (mit)
		to **charge** [tʃɑːdʒ]	*We use solar panels to power low-energy bulbs for lighting and to charge our phones and laptops.*	aufladen
		turbine ['tɜːbaɪn]	*My parents are planning to install a wind turbine as well.*	Turbine

page	exercise	Workshop 3		
		wood-burning [ˈwʊdˈbɜːnɪŋ]	*We heat our house with a wood-burning stove.*	holzverbrennend
		to **stack** [stæk]	*During spring and summer Dad spends a lot of time chopping and stacking wood.* *= pile*	stapeln
		coop [kuːp]	*The chickens live in a coop.*	Hühnerstall
		groceries [ˈgrəʊsəriz]	*Once a month, we go to the nearest town and stock up with groceries.*	Lebensmittel
		pulse [pʌls]	*Mom buys lots of dry goods like rice and pulses.*	Hülsenfrucht
		canned [kænd]	*We don't need to buy canned fruits. We grow most fruits ourselves.*	Dosen…
		heap [hiːp]	*It can be put on the compost heap and then used in the vegetable garden.* *= pile*	Haufen
		schooling [ˈskuːlɪŋ]	*I didn't go to school, my family lived too far away, so my schooling was by correspondence.*	Schulausbildung
		homeschooled [ˌhəʊmˈskuːld]	*We are homeschooled by our mother.*	zu Hause unterrichtet
		midday [ˌmɪdˈdeɪ]	*We eat lunch at midday.*	Mittag
	3c	**core** [kɔː]	*We have to study the core subjects: reading, math, social studies, language arts, and science.*	Kern; Haupt…
		convenience [kənˈviːniəns]	*We don't have all the modern conveniences that other kids take for granted.* *≠ inconvenience*	Bequemlichkeit; zweckmäßiges Gerät
		schoolmate [ˈskuːlmeɪt]	*I do miss having schoolmates and friends nearby but it's OK.*	Schulkamerad(in)
		purpose [ˈpɜːpəs]	*What's the purpose of this game?*	Zweck
81	6a	to **repaint** [ˌriːˈpeɪnt]	*The school buildings have been repainted and gym equipment has been replaced.*	übermalen
	6c	to **convince** [kənˈvɪns]	*If you want to convince your parents to let you go, show them you're responsible!* *= persuade*	überzeugen; überreden
82	1b	**tin** [tɪn]	*The first frisbees were made from pie tins.*	Dose; Zinn
	1c	to **reinvent** [ˌriːɪnˈvent]	*He is trying to reinvent the wheel using new materials.*	wieder erfinden
		to **skateboard** [ˈskeɪtbɔːd]	*I like to skateboard because it's fast.*	Skateboardfahren gehen
		skateboard [ˈskeɪtbɔːd]	*The skateboard moved better with the new wheels.*	Skateboard
		clay [kleɪ]	*Skateboard wheels used to be made of hard clay.*	Ton

page	exercise	Workshop 3		
		to own [əʊn]	*His friend's dad owned a plastics factory.*	besitzen
		roller skate [ˈrəʊlə skeɪt]	*He was shown some new roller skate wheels.*	Rollschuh
		polyurethane [ˌpɒliˈjʊərəθeɪn]	*Three years later he began selling the first polyurethane skateboard wheels.*	Polyurethan (Kunststoff)
		flexible [ˈfleksəbl]	*They will have to be flexible and adaptable in order to study in a foreign country.* *≠ rigid*	anpassungsfähig; flexibel
		eureka moment [juˈriːkə ˈməʊmənt]	*It was a eureka moment: with the new wheels he could move on his skateboard better than ever before.*	Heureka-Erlebnis
83		**to strike** [straɪk]**, struck, struck** [strʌk, strʌk]	*Disaster can strike any time.*	zuschlagen; streiken
		basic [ˈbeɪsɪk]	*The earthquake left three million people without basic needs.*	Grund-; grundsätzlich; einfach
		inexpensive [ˌɪnɪkˈspensɪv]	*Their idea was an inexpensive, waterproof solar light.*	billig; preiswert
		waterproof [ˈwɔːtəpruːf]	*I wear waterproof pants when I ride my bike in the rain.*	wasserdicht
		lantern [ˈlæntən]	*When we go camping we use lanterns for light at night.* *= lamp*	Laterne
		prototype [ˈprəʊtətaɪp]	*They tested their first prototypes in Indian villages.*	Prototyp
		relief [rɪˈliːf]	*Disaster relief areas can use solar lanterns for light at night.*	Erleichterung; Hilfe
		to award [əˈwɔːd]	*The two young inventors have been awarded prizes for their great ideas.*	vergeben; verleihen
	4	**flyer** [ˈflaɪə]	*Use these notes to complete part of a flyer for new museum guides.*	Flyer
	5	**to retell** [ˌriːˈtel]	*Take notes to retell the story of this inventor.*	nacherzählen
		businessman [ˈbɪznəsmæn]**, businessmen**	*Thomas Edison was an American inventor and businessman.*	Unternehmer; Geschäftsmann
		patent [ˈpætnt]	*He holds over 1,000 patents for his inventions.*	Patent
		phonograph [ˈfəʊnəɡrɑːf]	*One of Edison's most famous inventions is the phonograph.*	Phonograph
		gramophone [ˈɡræməfəʊn]	*It was able to record and play back sound, and it led to the development of the gramophone and later the record player.*	Grammofon
		motion picture [ˌməʊʃn ˈpɪktʃə]	*A third famous invention of Thomas Edison's is the motion picture camera.* *= film*	Film; Spielfilm

page	exercise	Workshop 3		
		colleague [ˈkɒliːg]	*Thomas Edison and his colleagues invented the motion picture camera in 1892.*	Kollege; Kollegin; Mitarbeiter(in)
		era [ˈɪərə]	*The camera he invented was the beginning of the motion picture era.* = age	Ära
		cellar [ˈselə]	*We store things like apples and potatoes in the cellar.* = basement	Keller
		telegraph [ˈtelɪgrɑːf]	*When he got older, he was trained as a telegraph operator and became interested in communications.*	Telegraf
		investor [ɪnˈvestə]	*With money from investors, Edison opened large research laboratories.*	Investor(in); Geldgeber(in)
		laboratory [ləˈbɒrətri]	*Marine biologists spend a lot of time in the laboratory studying the results of field trips.*	Labor
		to oversee [ˌəʊvəˈsiː]	*He started many companies and oversaw the mass production of his inventions.* = watch	überwachen; beaufsichtigen
		corporation [ˌkɔːpəˈreɪʃn]	*General Electric is one of the largest corporations in the world.*	Unternehmen
		award-winning [əˈwɔːd wɪnɪŋ]	*She acted in award-winning films.*	preisgekrönt
		misunderstood [ˌmɪsʌndəˈstʊd]	*This is the most misunderstood book in the world.*	verkannt; missverstanden
		Austrian [ˈɒstriən]	*In her early 20s, she married a rich Austrian businessman.*	Österreicher(in)
		glamorous [ˈglæmərəs]	*Lamarr once said, 'Any girl can be glamorous; all you have to do is stand still and look stupid.'*	glamourös
		military [ˈmɪlətri]	*She developed an idea she had for a secret communications system for the US military.*	Militär
84	1a	**innovator** [ˈɪnəveɪtə]	*Inventors and innovators share certain characteristics, such as creativity.* = groundbreaker	Innovator(in)
	1b	**failure** [ˈfeɪljə]	*I work hard but can accept failure.* ≠ success	Misserfolg
		innovative [ˈɪnəveɪtɪv]	*The innovative design won the competition.*	innovativ
		problem-solver [ˈprɒbləm sɒlvə]	*I am a very good problem-solver and work well with others.* ≠ solution	Problemlöser(in)
		self-motivated [ˌself ˈməʊtɪveɪtɪd]	*I am self-motivated and able to finish my work on time.*	motiviert
		energetic [ˌenəˈdʒetɪk]	*I am very energetic and get work done quickly.*	aktiv; energisch

page	exercise	**Workshop 3**		
	2	to **inspire** [ɪnˈspaɪə]	*How did nature inspire her to fight for the environment?* ≠ *discourage*	inspirieren; anregen
	2b	**inspiration** [ˌɪnspəˈreɪʃn]	*In the end, they learn new skills and get inspiration to become inventors themselves.*	Inspiration; Eingebung
		to **happen upon** [ˈhæpən əˈpɒn]	*As a kid, I thought I had happened upon something incredible.* = *discover*	zufällig entdecken
		garage [ˈgærɑːʒ]	*I never thought that these crazy experiments in my garage would lead to something.*	Garage; Werkstatt
		spoilage [ˈspɔɪlɪdʒ]	*We lose a lot of food to spoilage.*	Verderben; Abfall
		to **harvest** [ˈhɑːvɪst]	*Farmers harvest enough food to feed the planet, but we aren't able to distribute it efficiently.*	ernten
		to **distribute** [dɪˈstrɪbjuːt]	≠ *collect* 🛈 *Lat. 'distribuere (distribuo, distribui, distributum)'*	verteilen
		efficient [ɪˈfɪʃnt]	*If you're efficient, you'll be done with your work more quickly.*	effizient
		accidentally [ˌæksɪˈdentəli]	*I accidentally drank almost an entire cup.* 🛈 *Fr. 'accidentellement'*	zufällig; versehentlich
		murky [ˈmɜːki]	*My grandmother makes a murky brown spiced tea.* = *cloudy*	trübe
		spiced [spaɪst]	*My grandma makes spiced tea when it's cold outside.*	gewürzt
		sample [ˈsɑːmpl]	*I added the spices to samples of the pond water.*	Probe
		fuzz [fʌz]	*We couldn't eat the strawberries because there was fuzz on them.*	Fussel; Belag
		to **dip** [dɪp]	*Dip the chips in the sauce. That's delicious!*	tauchen
		berry [ˈberi]	*I dipped berries in my mixture and it was really good.*	Beere
	2d	**businesswoman** [ˈbɪznəswʊmən], **businesswomen**	*Write a short biography of the inventor and businesswoman Kavita Shukla.*	Unternehmerin; Geschäftsfrau
85	3	**stylish** [ˈstaɪlɪʃ]	*Ms Lopez invited us for lunch in a stylish restaurant.* = *modern*	schick
	4a	**challenging** [ˈtʃælɪndʒɪŋ]	*I find math class very challenging.* = *difficult*	schwierig
		theoretical [ˌθɪəˈretɪkl]	*My teacher likes it when we ask theoretical questions in class.*	theoretisch
		coaching [ˈkəʊtʃɪŋ]	*Students get expert coaching.*	Coaching

page	exercise	**Workshop 3**		
		process [ˈprəʊses]	They learn about the process of making an idea into a marketable product.	Prozess
		marketable [ˈmɑːkɪtəbl]	I didn't know what makes a product marketable before.	vermarktbar
		basically [ˈbeɪsɪkli]	That's basically what the program is about. = fundamentally	im Grunde
		to **sketch** [sketʃ]	Sometimes painters sketch before beginning a painting.	skizzieren; zeichnen
		marketing [ˈmɑːkɪtɪŋ]	The marketing people gave them advice on how to sell their product.	Marketing; Vermarktung
		session [ˈseʃn]	The first session was about brainstorming.	Session; Sitzung
		imagination [ɪˌmædʒɪˈneɪʃn]	Use your imagination to think about what life is like on the space station.	Vorstellung; Fantasie
		imaginary [ɪˈmædʒɪnəri]	Students play creative thinking games, like climbing an imaginary mountain.	imaginär; fiktiv
		to **get hit** [get hɪt]	In this game you have to try not to get hit by a water balloon.	getroffen sein; geschlagen sein
		athletic [æθˈletɪk]	≠ unathletic	athletisch; sportlich
		level [ˈlevl]	Everything is connected, and small things on a local level can have bigger effects on a global level.	Niveau; Stufe; Standard
		to **chill out** [tʃɪl aʊt]	After school, I chill out with my friends in the park. = relax	sich entspannen
	4c	**listener** [ˈlɪsnə]	A well-structured talk has clear 'signal phrases' that help the listener understand the information. ≠ talker	Hörer(in)
		to **rephrase** [ˌriːˈfreɪz]	Rephrase the main point to be sure your listeners understand it.	neu formulieren; umformulieren
		to **sum up** [sʌm ʌp]	Listen and decide which three statements sum up the conversation best.	zusammenfassen
	5b	**visual** [ˈvɪʒuəl]	Make sure you include visuals such as photos in your presentation.	Bildmaterial

page	exercise	**Workshop 3**		

Technology and innovations

artificial intelligence	künstliche	laptop [ˈlæptɒp]	Laptop
[ˌɑːtɪfɪʃl ɪnˈtelɪdʒəns]	Intelligenz	netbook [ˈnetbʊk]	Netbook
discovery [dɪˈskʌvəri]	Entdeckung	robot [ˈrəʊbɒt]	Roboter
gadget [ˈgædʒɪt]	Gerät; technische	solar power [ˌsəʊlə ˈpaʊə]	Solarenergie;
	Spielerei		Sonnenenergie
innovation [ˌɪnəˈveɪʃn]	Innovation; Neuheit	technological [ˌteknəˈlɒdʒɪkl]	technisch;
innovative [ˈɪnəveɪtɪv]	innovativ		technologisch
innovator [ˈɪnəveɪtə]	Innovator(in)	touchscreen [ˈtʌtʃskriːn]	Berührungs-
invention [ɪnˈvenʃn]	Erfindung		bildschirm

page	exercise	word	example	translation
86	S1a	**cyber bullying** [ˈsaɪbəbʊliŋ]	*I would like to see the end of cyberbullying, especially among young people.*	Cybermobbing
		nor [nɔː]	*I don't like the bus nor the train.*	noch; weder noch
		fuss [fʌs]	*We will show you how to bake without fuss.*	Aufregung
		pickpocket [ˈpɪkpɒkɪt]	*Pickpockets steal things out of people's pockets.*	Taschendieb(in)
	S2b	**shortlist** [ˈʃɔːtlɪst]	*Make a shortlist of the three best ideas.*	Auswahlliste
		weakness [ˈwiːknəs]	*Discuss the strengths and weaknesses of the posters in your group.* ≠ strength	Schwäche
		effectively [ɪˈfektɪvli]	≠ ineffectively ❗ Fr. 'efficacement'	wirksam
		aim [eɪm]	*The aim of a film trailer is to get people interested in the film.*	Absicht; Ziel
		input [ˈɪnpʊt]	*Focus everyone's ideas on the input from class.* ≠ output	Beitrag
		quantity [ˈkwɒləti]	*The quality of the sentences you write is more important than the quantity.*	Anzahl; Menge
		impractical [ɪmˈpræktɪkl]	*Be open to all ideas, even if they seem impossible or impractical.* ≠ practical	unpraktisch
		sticky [ˈstɪki]	*Use sticky notes on a wall to remind yourself.*	klebrig; klebend
87	S1	**luggage** [ˈlʌgɪdʒ]	*We were tired from carrying all our luggage onto the train.*	Gepäck
		sensor [ˈsensə]	*A small sensor alarm is attached to your bag.*	Sensor
		to attach [əˈtætʃ]	*Everything here has Velcro attached to it.*	befestigen
		to activate [ˈæktɪveɪt]	*Make sure to activate the device.*	aktivieren
		satellite connection [ˈsætəlaɪt kəˈnekʃn]	*A special band on your wrist activates a GPS satellite connection.*	Satellitenverbindung
		to separate [ˈseprət]	≠ connect	sich trennen

page	exercise	Workshop 3		
		wristband [ˈrɪstbænd]	*The wristband will come in different colours and styles for different fashion tastes.*	Armband
		taste [teɪst]	*What is your taste in music?*	Geschmack
		depression [dɪˈpreʃn]	*This can lead to depression and other illnesses.* = unhappiness	Depression
		illness [ˈɪlnəs]	*Depression is an illness.* = disease	Krankheit
		rental [ˈrentl]	*Our solution is a low-cost rental service for homes for the elderly.*	Miet...
88	2	**philosophy** [fəˈlɒsəfi]	*We like the Green Action Group's philosophy.*	Philosophie
		demonstration [ˌdemənˈstreɪʃn]	*That demonstration was a big success – after that, the city began cleaning up the river.*	Demonstration
		activism [ˈæktɪvɪzəm]	*Our focus is on environmental activism here at school.*	Aktivismus
		economic [ˌiːkəˈnɒmɪk]	*Pollution is not just an environmental problem, it's also a social and an economic problem.* = monetary	wirtschaftlich
	3	**scrap** [skræp]	*The cafeteria threw away 400 pounds of food scraps.*	Abfall
		straw [strɔː]	*All the food packaging, the plastic forks and straws – it's used once and then it's thrown away.*	Trinkhalm; Strohhalm; Stroh
89	7	**packaged food** [ˈpækɪdʒd fuːd]	*We eat better when mom cooks fresh food because a lot of packaged food is not healthy.*	verpacktes Essen
		junky [ˈdʒʌŋki]	*A lot of packaged food is junky snack food.*	schlecht; mangelhaft
		newsletter [ˈnjuːzletə]	*We could write an article for the parent newsletter, which they get every month by email.*	Mitteilungsblatt; Newsletter
		to measure [ˈmeʒə]	*Measure how much waste there is in your home.*	messen; ausmessen; abschätzen
		environmental [ɪnˌvaɪrənˈmentl]	*We are looking for a good environmental campaign slogan.*	ökologisch; Umwelt-
90	2a	**to spark** [spɑːk]	*Student action against climate change had already been growing, but Greta sparked a fire.* = kindle	entzünden
		global warming [ˌgləʊbl ˈwɔːmɪŋ]	*Global warming is our biggest challenge.*	Erderwärmung
		consequence [ˈkɒnsɪkwəns]	*We need to slow down global warming or face terrible consequences.*	Folge; Konsequenz

page	exercise	Workshop 3		
		radical [ˈrædɪkl]	*Radical changes were needed in areas such as energy, transport and food production.*	radikal; grundlegend
		Swedish [ˈswiːdɪʃ]	*Greta begun her school strike alone in front of the Swedish parliament.*	schwedisch
		tough [tʌf]	*= hard* *≠ easy*	hart
		to **voice** [vɔɪs]	*Her words voiced the feelings of a whole generation.* **⊞** *Fr. 'voix' (f.); Lat. 'vox, vocis' (f.)*	äußern; zum Ausdruck bringen
		strike [straɪk]	*Many students participated in the strike.*	Streik
	2b	to **involve** [ɪnˈvɒlv]	*Greta succeeded in involving many young people in organizing demonstrations.*	einbeziehen; umfassen
91	2d	to **demand** [dɪˈmɑːnd]	*≠ deny*	fordern; verlangen
92	1a	**partnership** [ˈpɑːtnəʃɪp]	*The International Space Station is a partnership between 16 countries.*	Partnerschaft; Kooperation
		Russian [ˈrʌʃn]	*American and Russian spaceships fly to the ISS.*	russisch
		spaceship [ˈspeɪsʃɪp]	*A spaceship carries astronauts into space.*	Raumschiff
		Iranian [ɪˈreɪniən]	*An Iranian-American woman was the first woman space tourist to visit the ISS.*	iranisch
	2	**hygiene** [ˈhaɪdʒiːn]	*Good hygiene in space is not easy. We don't have showers.*	Hygiene
		faucet [ˈfɔːsɪt]	*We don't have any faucets or a shower with running water.*	Wasserhahn
		wipe [waɪp]	*There are wet towels and wet wipes and dry towels that are used for cleaning yourself.*	Wischtuch
		quarter [ˈkwɔːtə]	*We live in close quarters and have to be kind to each other.*	Viertel; Quartier
		to **hydrate** [haɪˈdreɪt]	*We heat up a few cans and hydrate some freeze dried food.* *≠ dehydrate*	hydratisieren
		freeze-dried [ˈfriːz draɪd]	*We often eat freeze-dried food.*	gefriergetrocknet
		weightlessness [ˈweɪtləsnəs]	*Weightlessness in space has its wonderful advantages.* *≠ heaviness*	Schwerelosigkeit
93	3a	**commander** [kəˈmɑːndə]	*The commander of the ship took us on a tour.* *= commanding officer*	Kommandant(in)
		module [ˈmɒdjuːl]	*The space station is made up of different modules.*	Modul
		ceiling [ˈsiːlɪŋ]	*I painted stars on the ceiling in my bedroom.*	Decke

Workshop 3		
reference [ˈrefrəns]	*On the space station, your reference changes as you move around.*	Orientierung; Verweis
sensation [senˈseɪʃn]	*When you go to sleep on the ISS, you don't really have the sensation of lying.*	Gefühl
booth [buːð]	*Sleeping stations on the International Space Station are like little phone booths.*	Zelle
comfy [ˈkʌmfi]	*My bed is so comfy, it's difficult to get up in the morning.* ≠ *uncomfortable*	gemütlich
orientation [ˌɔːriənˈteɪʃn]	*It's easy to lose your orientation in a thick forest.*	Orientierung
upside [ˈʌpsaɪd]	*The upside of living in the city is all of the culture.* ≠ *downside*	Vorteil
density [ˈdensəti]	*Exercise is important for bone density and muscle mass.*	Dichte
muscle [ˈmʌsl]	*We train our muscles with exercise equipment.*	Muskel
gravity [ˈɡrævəti]	*We lose muscle mass because our bodies don't have to fight against gravity.*	Erdanziehungskraft; Schwerkraft
treadmill [ˈtredmɪl]	*We exercise using exercise equipment such as a treadmill.*	Laufband
weightlifting [ˈweɪtlɪftɪŋ]	*We have weightlifting equipment and an exercise bike in our basement.*	Gewichtheben
clip [klɪp]	*The movie clip got me interested in seeing the whole film.*	Ausschnitt
pedal [ˈpedl]	*Put your feet onto the bike's pedals.*	Pedal
to **pedal** [ˈpedl]	*On the International Space Station, you can pedal a bike to stay in shape.*	in die Pedale treten
essential [ɪˈsenʃl]	*We buy all the essential things, including milk, eggs and bread, at the grocery store.* = *necessary*	wichtig; wesentlich
toothpaste [ˈtuːθpeɪst]	*Don't put too much toothpaste on the toothbrush.*	Zahnpasta
luckily [ˈlʌkɪli]	*Luckily, toothpaste sticks to your toothbrush in space.* ≠ *unluckily*	glücklicherweise
bubble [ˈbʌbl]	*Water makes a bubble on a toothbrush on the ISS.*	Blase
tension [ˈtenʃn]	*Surface tension allows some insects to float on top of water.* ❗ *Fr. 'tension' (f.)*	Anspannung
to **swallow** [ˈswɒləʊ]	*Spit your toothpaste out, don't swallow it!*	schlucken; hinunterschlucken

page	exercise			
		Workshop 3		
		mouthwash [ˈmaʊθwɒʃ]	*After I brush my teeth I use mouthwash.*	Mundwasser
		gross [ɡrəʊs]	*Yuck, this mouthwash tastes a little gross.*	ätzend; ekelhaft
		to spit [spɪt]	*Try not to spit when you talk!*	spucken
		refrigerator [rɪˈfrɪdʒəreɪtə]	*Be sure to put the milk back into the refrigerator.*	Kühlschrank
		candy [ˈkændi]	*I love to eat candy, but it's not good for me.* = sweet	Süßigkeit
		dehydrated [ˌdiːhaɪˈdreɪtɪd]	*That plant is dehydrated. It needs water.* ≠ hydrated	dehydriert
		barbecued [ˈbɑːbɪkjuːd]	*My brother's favourite food is barbecued meat.*	gegrillt
		beef brisket [biːf ˈbrɪskɪt]	*My grandmother taught me to make beef brisket.*	Rinderbrust
		cupola [ˈkjuːpələ]	*You can see Earth from the cupola in the space station.*	Kuppel
		cloudy [ˈklaʊdi]	*On my birthday it was cloudy, but it didn't rain.* ≠ clear	wolkig; bewölkt; trüb
	4	**citizen** [ˈsɪtɪzn]	*A survey of US citizens showed most people aren't interested in space.* ❗Fr. 'citoyen' (m.), 'citoyenne' (f.)	Einwohner(in)
		to remain [rɪˈmeɪn]	*Buying a home will remain an impossible dream for most of us.* = stay	bleiben
	5b	**Arctic** [ˈɑːktɪk]	*By the year 2050, the Arctic ice sheet may have melted.*	arktisch; Arktis
		to melt [melt]	*Global warming is causing the Arctic ice sheet to melt.* ≠ freeze	schmelzen
	6a	**to settle** [ˈsetl]	*One day, humans will settle on Mars.*	sich ansiedeln
		extinct [ɪkˈstɪŋkt]	*There are more extinct animals every year.*	ausgestorben
94	1	**nut** [nʌt]	*Nuts are a healthy snack.*	Nuss
	2a	**nickname** [ˈnɪkneɪm]	*The nickname for Mars is the 'orange planet'.*	Spitzname
		proof [pruːf]	*Scientists have found proof of life on Mars.* = confirmation	Beweis
	2b	**microbe** [ˈmaɪkrəʊb]	*Scientists think it's possible that long ago there was already some form of life, such as tiny microbes.*	Mikrobe
		close [kləʊz]	*The fire is too close to the trees.* ≠ far	nah
		degree [dɪˈɡriː]	*Temperature can be measured in degrees.*	Grad; Abschluss

page	exercise	Workshop 3		
		centigrade [ˈsentɪɡreɪd]	*The average temperature is minus 81 degrees centigrade.*	Celsius
		pole [pəʊl]	*At the North and South Poles, the temperature can go down to minus 153 degrees.*	Pol; Stange
		frozen [ˈfrəʊzn]	*The only water on Mars today is frozen or underground.* *≠ melted*	gefroren
		to **drill** [drɪl]	*You would have to drill down under the ground to find it.*	bohren
		ground [ɡraʊnd]	*≠ sky*	Boden; Erde; Platz
	3	**mission** [ˈmɪʃn]	*I've been following the space missions, and I'm excited about the plans to send humans to Mars.*	Mission
	3a	**agency** [ˈeɪdʒənsi]	*What is the agenda of this government agency?* *= organization*	Agentur; Organisation
		to **achieve** [əˈtʃiːv]	*She believes that scientific objectives can best be achieved by using robots.* *≠ fail*	erreichen; schaffen
		rover [ˈrəʊvə]	*The Mars 2020 rover will test new technologies.*	Forschungsfahrzeug
		habitation [ˌhæbɪˈteɪʃn]	*NASA launched the Mars 2020 rover to test technologies necessary for human habitation.*	Bewohnbarkeit
		cargo [ˈkɑːɡəʊ]	*NASA will send a cargo ship to Mars in order to prepare for human settlement.*	Ladung
		crew [kruː]	*The crew of the spaceship will arrive on Mars.*	Mannschaft; Personal
		base [beɪs]	*They will set up a base on Mars where people can live.*	Basis
		crewed [kruːd]	*He was researching the possibility of rending a crewed mission to Mars.*	bemannt
		to **establish** [ɪˈstæblɪʃ]	*A mission to the moon will establish a base for humans.* *= found*	begründen
	3b	**crane** [kreɪn]	*There was a large crane at the construction site.*	Kran
		frame [freɪm]	*Do you think the plans are likely to succeed in this time frame?*	Rahmen
	4a	**space exploration** [ˈspeɪsˌekspləˈreɪʃn]	*I've been interested in space exploration since I was a kid.*	Weltraumforschung
		curiosity [ˌkjʊəriˈɒsəti]	*The main thing that drives me is my personal curiosity.*	Neugier
		frontier [ˈfrʌntɪə]	*Humans have always looked for new frontiers to explore.*	Grenzland
		ambition [æmˈbɪʃn]	*My ambition is to be one of the first people to visit another planet.*	Ziel; Ambition

page	exercise	Workshop 3		
		outback [ˈaʊtbæk]	*I grew up in Australia, in the outback.*	Hinterland
		correspondence [ˌkɒrəˈspɒndəns]	*I didn't go to school, my family lived too far away, so my schooling was by correspondence.*	Schriftverkehr
		physics [ˈfɪzɪks]	*My favourite subjects are science, maths and physics.*	Physik
95	4b	**adaptable** [əˈdæptəbl]	*To live on the International Space Station, you need to be adaptable.*	anpassungsfähig
		ambitious [æmˈbɪʃəs]	*She is an ambitious student who follows her dreams.* ≠ *unenthusiastic*	ehrgeizig
		resourceful [rɪˈsɔːsfl]	*If you are resourceful, you can solve problems well.*	erfinderisch
		tolerant [ˈtɒlərənt]	*People who work with children should be patient and tolerant.* ≠ *intolerant*	tolerant
	5b	**nun** [nʌn]	*Nuns are very religious and don't marry.*	Nonne
		to **starve** [stɑːv]	*There are many places in the world where children starve.*	hungern (lassen); verhungern (lassen)
		lens [lenz]	*He made small lenses from pieces of glass.*	Linse
		to **perfect** [ˈpɜːfɪkt]	*He spent all his time perfecting his gadgets.* ≠ *neglect*	perfektionieren
		microscope [ˈmaɪkrəskəʊp]	*A microscope is an important gadget in medicine.*	Mikroskop
		progress [ˈprəʊgres]	*The microscope has contributed enormously to the progress of medicine.*	Fortschritt
		doubt [daʊt]	*There's no doubt that space exploration is interesting.*	Zweifel
		planetary science [ˈplænətri ˈsaɪəns]	*The professor of planetary science thinks that sending crewed missions into space is unnecessary.*	planetarische Wissenschaft; Planetenforschung
		unnecessary [ʌnˈnesəsəri]	*I don't like to buy unnecessary things that I won't use.*	unnötig; überflüssig
		pointless [ˈpɔɪntləs]	*The flashlight is pointless if you forgot to bring batteries.*	sinnlos; zwecklos
		objective [əbˈdʒektɪv]	*She believes that scientific objectives can best be achieved by using robots.*	Ziel
		advanced [ədˈvɑːnst]	*Robots are so advanced, they can help achieve scientific objectives.*	fortgeschritten
		spacesuit [ˈspeɪssuːt]	*Astronauts are moving around slowly in spacesuits.*	Raumanzug
	6	**lyrics** [ˈlɪrɪks]	*Your teacher will give you the lyrics to the song.*	Liedtext
		ground control [ˈgraʊnd kəntrəʊl]	*Ground control keeps contact with the spaceship.*	Bodenstation

page	exercise	**Workshop 3**		
		oddity [ˈɒdəti]	= *strange thing*	Kuriosität
		protein [ˈprəʊtiːn]	*Eggs have a lot of protein.*	Protein; Eiweiß
		to **commence** [kəˈmens]	= *start*	anfangen
		countdown [ˈkaʊntdaʊn]	*Countdown always starts with ten.* = *start*	Countdown
		ignition [ɪgˈnɪʃn]	*She put the key in the ignition.*	Zündung
		capsule [ˈkæpsjuːl]	*The astronauts leave the capsule.*	Kapsel; Raumkapsel
		to **dare** [deə]	*It was so dark that I didn't dare to go out.*	sich trauen; wagen
		to **float** [fləʊt]	*Balloons were floating in the air.*	schweben; treiben
		still [stɪl]	= *calm*	ruhig
		circuit [ˈsɜːkɪt]	*The engineer works on an electric circuit.*	Schaltkreis
		limp [lɪmp]	≠ *strong*	schlaff

Space travel

commander [kəˈmɑːndə]	Kommandant(in)	**planetary sciene**	planetarische
crew [kruː]	Mannschaft; Personal	[ˈplænətri ˈsaɪəns]	Wissenschaft;
freeze-dried [ˈfriːz draɪd]	gefriergetrocknet		Planetenforschung
gravity [ˈgrævəti]	Erdanziehungskraft; Schwerkraft	**rover** [ˈrəʊvə]	Forschungsfahrzeug
		satellite [ˈsætəlaɪt]	Satellit
ground control	Bodenstation	**spacecraft** [ˈspeɪskrɑːft]	Raumfahrzeug
[ˈgraʊnd kəntrəʊl]		**space exploration**	Weltraumforschung
habitation [ˌhæbɪˈteɪʃn]	Bewohnbarkeit	[ˈspeɪsˌekspləˈreɪʃn]	
mission [ˈmɪʃn]	Mission	**spaceship** [ˈspeɪsʃɪp]	Raumschiff
module [ˈmɒdjuːl]	Modul	**spacesuit** [ˈspeɪssuːt]	Raumanzug
orbit [ˈɔːbɪt]	Orbit; Umlaufbahn	**weightlessness** [ˈweɪtləsnəs]	Schwerelosigkeit

page	exercise			
		Judgement Day [ˈdʒʌdʒmənt deɪ]	= *end of the world*	jüngste Gericht
		eternal [ɪˈtɜːnl]	= *never-ending*	ewig
		to **twinkle** [ˈtwɪŋkl]	*At night, the stars are twinkling.*	glitzern
96	S1a	to **demonstrate** [ˈdemənstreɪt]	*Demonstrate your product or service to your customers.* = *show how*	vorführen; zeigen
		whatever [wɒˈtevə]	*Don't forget to bring your backpack or whatever kind of bag you have.*	egal welche; gleichgültig welche
		to **prevent** [prɪˈvent]	*How can we prevent global warming from getting worse?*	verhindern; abhalten
		to **vibrate** [vaɪˈbreɪt]	*My wristband is vibrating, so I know that my phone is ringing.*	vibrieren; pulsieren
		navigating [ˈnævɪgeɪt]	*The wristband has a GPS system for navigating.*	Navigation
	S1b	to **recite** [rɪˈsaɪt]	*I recite my own poetry Friday night in the cafe.*	rezitieren; auswendig aufsagen
		poetry [ˈpəʊətri]	*It can dance, sing and recite poetry.*	Dichtung

page	exercise	**Workshop 3**		
		to **lease** [liːs]	Our plan is to lease the robots from the companies that make them – it's cheaper than buying them.	leasen; mieten
		competitor [kəmˈpetɪtə]	We don't have any competitors on the market yet. = challenger	Konkurrent(in); Mitbewerber(in)
	S2	to **hook** [hʊk]	Your presentation needs to be informative and entertaining, and it needs to 'hook' the audience.	haken
	S3	**cue card** [ˈkjuː kɑːd]	Use cue cards to help you remember important points.	Karteikarte
97	S1	**checklist** [ˈtʃeklɪst]	Your teacher will give you a copy of the checklist to complete while you are watching the presentations.	Checkliste
		enthusiastic [ɪnˌθjuːziˈæstɪk]	= interested ⚠ Fr. 'enthousiaste'	begeistert
100	3b	**previous** [ˈpriːviəs]	Ms Rice showed the class a few projects from the previous year. = earlier	bisherig; vorherig
103	4	**catastrophic** [ˌkætəˈstrɒfɪk]	Unless we become carbon neutral, the situation will be catastrophic.	katastrophal
		underwater [ˌʌndəˈwɔːtə]	A rise in the oceans will mean that cities such as Bangkok and London will disappear underwater.	unter Wasser; Unterwasser…
		flooding [ˈflʌdɪŋ]	By 2050, flooding will have had a drastic impact on many places in the world.	Fluten; Überflutung
		to **exaggerate** [ɪɡˈzædʒəreɪt]	Some people claim that experts are exaggerating the situation and that many of their predictions won't happen.	übertreiben
		hunger [ˈhʌŋɡə]	Today, around a billion people suffer from hunger, that's one in six people.	Hunger
104	3	**remote control** [rɪˌməʊt kənˈtrəʊl]	We sit on the sofa and use the remote control to turn on the TV.	Fernbedienung
105	8	**surely** [ˈʃʊəli]	Surely there are a lot more important things you can do with your time. = certainly	sicherlich
		homelessness [ˈhəʊmləsnəs]	Homelessness is a big problem in America's big cities.	Obdachlosigkeit
	9	to **refuse** [rɪˈfjuːz]	I think we should use the slogan 'If you can't reuse it, refuse it'. = decline	sich weigern
	10	**pessimistic** [ˌpesɪˈmɪstɪk]	Don't be so pessimistic about the future. There's still hope. ≠ optimistic	pessimistisch
	11	**driverless** [ˈdraɪvələs]	One day, all cars will be driverless.	führerlos

page	exercise	**Workshop 4**		
108	1	**archeologist** [ˌɑːkiˈɒlədʒɪst]	*An archeologist is someone who digs up and studies ancient buildings and objects.*	Archäologe / Archäologin
		librarian [laɪˈbreəriən]	*Ask the librarian if you can't find the book in the library.*	Bibliothekar(in)
		lifeguard [ˈlaɪfɡɑːd]	*He worked as a lifeguard at the beach during the summer.*	Rettungsschwimmer(in)
109	2a	**to memorize** [ˈmeməraɪz]	*I started out playing small parts, but I was good at memorizing my words and I got bigger roles to play.*	auswendig lernen; merken
		fascination [ˌfæsɪˈneɪʃn]	*I have a fascination with building things.* **!** *Fr. 'fascination' (f.)*	Faszination
	2b	**to specialize** [ˈspeʃəlaɪz]	*Jenny's company specializes in building small buildings.*	sich spezialisieren
		to fulfil [fʊlˈfɪl]	*Travis has fulfilled his childhood dream to become an inventor.* *= achieve*	verwirklichen; erfüllen
110	1a	**to be keen** [tə bi kiː]	*My schoolwork isn't great and I'm not very keen on studying.*	auf etw. scharf sein; auf etw. Lust haben
	2b	**spotlight** [ˈspɒtlaɪt]	*This week's spotlight is on two very different career ideas.*	Mittelpunkt des Interesses
		surfer [ˈsɜːfə]	*You could think about becoming a professional surfer or a lifeguard.*	Surfer(in)
		marine [məˈriːn]	*Marine biologists study the animals and plants that live in the ocean.*	Meeres...
		biologist [baɪˈɒlədʒɪst]	*If science is your thing, how about becoming a marine biologist?*	Biologe; Biologin
		in addition to [ɪn əˈdɪʃn tə]	*In addition to becoming experts in aquatic plants, they try to find solutions to different problems.* *= as well as*	zusätzlich zu; neben
		aquatic [əˈkwætɪk]	*They study the ocean and are experts in aquatic plants and animals.*	aquatisch; Wasser...
		passionate [ˈpæʃənət]	*These people are passionate about making a difference.*	leidenschaftlich
111		**imaginative** [ɪˈmædʒɪnətɪv]	*Are you creative and imaginative?* *≠ unimaginative*	fantasievoll
		to range [reɪndʒ]	*My work experience ranges from delivering pizzas to walking dogs.*	umfassen; reichen von ... bis
		catering service [ˈkeɪtərɪŋ ˈsɜːvɪs]	*To make money while studying, she started her own catering service.*	Verpflegungsservice
		to delegate [ˈdelɪɡət]	*As a manager, it's important to be good at delegating.*	delegieren; beauftragen
		to motivate [ˈməʊtɪveɪt]	*The boss motivates his team to work together.*	motivieren

page	exercise	Workshop 4		
		to **ensure** [ɪnˈʃʊə]	A monthly team meeting is a great way to motivate people and ensure they're all working together. = assure	sicherstellen
		blogpost [blɒgpəʊst]	To grow your company, you will probably have to spend a lot of time writing blogposts.	Blogeintrag
		vision [ˈvɪʒn]	So, if you have a vision, the right skills and qualities, you can work with us.	Vision
	4	**creature** [ˈkriːtʃə]	As a marine biologist, we get to study the ocean and all creatures that live in it.	Lebewesen; Wesen
		excitement [ɪkˈsaɪtmənt]	In his excitement he spilled his juice.	Aufregung
		wowed [waʊd]	It's the chance to be wowed and have a sense of wonder.	entzückt; begeistert
		to **pursue** [pəˈsjuː]	If you want to pursue your dream, you need to study hard. = follow	verfolgen
		biology [baɪˈɒlədʒi]	Biology is my favourite subject at school.	Biologie
		biodiversity [ˌbaɪəʊdaɪˈvɜːsəti]	I am interested in the ocean's biodiversity.	Artenvielfalt; Biodiversität
		to **observe** [əbˈzɜːv]	If you're interested in nature, get out and observe the environment. = watch	beobachten
	5b	**realistic** [ˌriːəˈlɪstɪk]	Discuss your dreams and how realistic they are.	realistisch
112	3	**versus** [ˈvɜːsəs]	I'm writing an article called 'Online Learning Versus School'.	versus
	3a	**bank teller** [bæŋk ˈtelə]	My mother works as a bank teller.	Kassierer(in)
		manufacture [ˌmænjuˈfæktʃə]	Thousands of manufacturing jobs have already been taken over by robots. = production	Herstellung; Produktion
		farmhand [ˈfɑːmhænd]	In the future, millions of farmhands could be replaced by intelligent machines.	Erntehelfer(in); Landarbeiter(in)
		to **automate** [ˈɔːtəmeɪt]	It is harder to automate jobs that involve strategic planning and making decisions.	automatisieren
		strategic [strəˈtiːdʒɪk]	Strategic planning is a difficult task to automate.	strategisch
		to **interact** [ˌɪntərˈækt]	Jobs where people need to interact with other people will be hard to replace with machines.	interagieren
		healthcare [ˈhelθkeə]	Healthcare and information technology are two of the fastest growing areas in the US.	Gesundheitswesen

page	exercise	Workshop 4		
		teamwork ['ti:mwɜ:k]	These jobs require teamwork and good communication skills.	Teamwork; Gruppenarbeit
113		cyber security ['saɪbə sɪ'kjʊərəti]	There will be many career opportunities for cyber security experts and scientists.	Cybersicherheit; Netzsicherheit
		to maintain [meɪn'teɪn]	Space workers who can develop and maintain equipment will be in demand in the future.	warten; pflegen
		demand [dɪ'mɑːnd]	Engineers are in high demand.	Nachfrage
		creativity [ˌkriːeɪ'tɪvəti]	Young people will need to develop skills that robots don't have, such as problem-solving and creativity. ⓘ Fr. 'créativité' (f.)	Kreativität
		portfolio [pɔːt'fəʊliəʊ]	In the future, many people are likely to have 'portfolio' careers, doing several part-time jobs at once.	Mappe; Portfolio
		initiative [ɪ'nɪʃətɪv]	Initiative is an important quality for leaders.	Initiative; Kampagne
		leadership ['liːdəʃɪp]	Qualities such as initiative, curiosity and leadership will be vital in the future.	Führung
		vital ['vaɪtl]	= essential ⓘ Fr. 'vital, vitale'	lebenswichtig
	6a	veterinarian [ˌvetərɪ'neəriən]	This week's spotlight is on being a veterinarian – a job many young animal-lovers dream of doing.	Tierarzt(in)
		vet [vet]	A vet is trained to take care of animals.	Tierarzt / -ärztin
		to diagnose ['daɪəgnəʊz]	A vet's duties range from diagnosing and looking after sick animals to performing operations.	diagnostizieren
114	1a	feature ['fiːtʃə]	Make a list of features that you like about this model. = aspect	Eigenschaft
		bakery ['beɪkəri]	We buy fresh bread from the bakery.	Bäckerei
	2a	shift [ʃɪft]	I work two shifts a week in a food truck.	Schicht
		takeout ['teɪkaʊt]	I love to get takeout from the restaurant.	Essen zum Mitnehmen
		counsellor ['kaʊnsələ]	The school counsellor says that students should apply to many universities.	Berater; psychologischer Betreuer
		Mexican ['meksɪkən]	You can get amazing Mexican food in America.	mexikanisch
		taco ['tækəʊ]	I work in a food truck selling tacos and burritos.	Taco
		burrito [bʊ'riːtəʊ]	In the restaurant you can order tacos, burritos and quesadillas.	Burrito
		quesadilla [ˌkeɪsə'diːə]	I love Mexican food like quesadillas.	Quesadilla

page	exercise	**Workshop 4**		
	3c	**babysitter** [ˈbeɪbisɪtə]	*I work as a babysitter for my neighbors.*	Babysitter(in)
		pizza deliverer [ˈpiːtsə dɪˈlɪvərə]	*Over summer vacation I work as a pizza deliverer.*	Pizzalieferant(in)
116	2a	**bulletin board** [ˈbʊlətɪn bɔːd]	*Look at the job ads posted on the school bulletin board.*	Anschlagtafel; Pinwand
	2b	**attractive** [əˈtræktɪv]	*Which of these job ads do you find the most interesting or attractive?*	anziehend; attraktiv; reizvoll
		wage [weɪdʒ]	*I got paid more than the minimum wage, so that was good.* = salary	Gehalt
		server [ˈsɜːvə]	*Fenelli's Creamery is looking for part-time ice cream servers.* = waiter	Kellner(in)
		to archive [ˈɑːkaɪv]	*With this computer programme you can scan, upload and archive texts and photos.*	archivieren
	3a	**to tutor** [ˈtjuːtə]	*You'll tutor students who need extra help.*	Nachhilfeunterricht geben
		alright [ɔːlˈraɪt]	*Is everything alright at home?*	in Ordnung
		to flip [flɪp]	*At work, I serve customers and flip burgers on the grill.*	umdrehen
		pushy [ˈpʊʃi]	*My boss is kind of pushy and loud.*	aufdringlich; penetrant
117	3c	**non-verbal** [ˌnɒn ˈvɜːbl]	*This time, pay attention to non-verbal communication.*	nonverbal
		tone of voice [təʊn əv vɔɪs]	*While you're listening, pay attention to the speaker's tone of voice.*	Tonfall; Artikulierung
		intonation [ˌɪntəˈneɪʃn]	*Does the intonation go up and down?*	Intonation
		monotone [ˈmɒnətəʊn]	*Do you think the intonation is good or is it flat and monotone?*	monoton
		facial expression [ˈfeɪʃl ɪkspreʃn]	*Pay attention to your listeners' facial expressions as you speak.*	Gesichtsausdruck
		eyebrow [ˈaɪbraʊ]	*Draw the eyebrows over the eyes.*	Augenbraue
		to slump [slʌmp]	*Does he or she sit up or slump in the chair?* ≠ ascent	zusammensacken
		gesture [ˈdʒestʃə]	*The speaker uses a lot of hand gestures.*	Geste
	4a	**to babysit** [ˈbeɪbisɪt]	*First school, then babysitting, then work, then home by midnight.*	babysitten
		perspective [pəˈspektɪv]	*For a long time, I hated the responsibility at home, but now my perspective has changed.*	Ansicht; Perspektive
	4c	**to admit** [ədˈmɪt]	*It's hard to admit your mistakes.* = confess	zugeben

page	exercise			

Workshop 4

The world of work

applicant [ˈæplɪkənt]	Bewerber(in)	**leadership** [ˈliːdəʃɪp]	Führung
application [ˌæplɪˈkeɪʃn]	Bewerbung; Antrag	**mentor** [ˈmentɔː]	Lehrmeister(in);
to **babysit** [ˈbeɪbɪsɪt]	babysitten		Mentor(in)
colleague [ˈkɒliːg]	Kollege, Kollegin;	**part-time** [ˌpɑːt ˈtaɪm]	Teilzeit…;
	Mitarbeiter(in)		nebenberuflich
demand [dɪˈmɑːnd]	Nachfrage	**portfolio** [pɔːtˈfəʊliəʊ]	Mappe; Portfolio
employee [ɪmˈplɔɪiː]	Angestellte	**shift** [ʃɪft]	Schicht
income / low-income	Einkommen /	**supervisor** [ˈsuːpəvaɪzə]	Leiter(in)
[ˈɪnkʌm] / [ˈləʊ ˈɪnkʌm]	einkommenschwach	**teamwork** [ˈtiːmwɜːk]	Teamwork;
initiative [ɪˈnɪʃətɪv]	Initiative; Kampagne		Gruppenarbeit
intern [ɪnˈtɜːn]	Praktikant(in);	to **tutor** [ˈtjuːtə]	Nachhilfeunterricht
	Volontär(in)		geben
internship [ˈɪntɜːnʃɪp]	Praktikum	**wage** [weɪdʒ]	Gehalt

page	exercise	word	example	translation
118	S1	**inclusive** [ɪnˈkluːsɪv]	*How inclusive is our school to students with disabilities?*	integrativ
		concept [ˈkɒnsept]	*You could also choose a concept to write about.*	Konzept; Begriff
119	S1	**storyboard** [ˈstɔːrɪbɔːd]	*A storyboard uses pictures – sketches or photos – to plan how each shot of the film should look.*	Storyboard; Szenenbuch
	S1a	**shot** [ʃɒt]	*Choose one of the two camera shots and describe it.*	Schuss; Schnappschuss
		sketch [sketʃ]	*A storyboard uses sketches or photos. = drawing*	Skizze; Sketch
		overview [ˈəʊvəvjuː]	*A storyboard is helpful during shooting because it gives you a visual overview of your story. = synopsis*	Überblick; Übersicht
		technical [ˈteknɪkl]	*Make a list of the technical details about each shot before you start shooting your film.*	technisch
	S2a	**template** [ˈtempleɪt]	*Copy the storyboard above or use the template that your teacher gives you.*	Vorlage
		blank [blæŋk]	*Keep a blank photocopy to fill in later. = empty*	leer
	S2b	**correction** [kəˈrekʃn]	*Make the changes or corrections that are needed.*	Korrektur
		dim [dɪm]	*I can't see. The light is too dim. ≠ bright*	trüb; schwach
120	1a	**showtime** [ˈʃəʊtaɪm]	*You can check the theatre's showtimes online.*	Vorstellungsbeginn
		usher [ˈʌʃə]	*My dream summer job is to work as an usher in the movie theatre.*	Platzanweiser(in)
	1b	**applicant** [ˈæplɪkənt]	*There are other applicants who are interested in the job.*	Bewerber(in)

page	exercise	Workshop 4		
	2	**worth** [wɜːθ]	*Are you sure this job is worth having less time to study?*	lohnenswert
122	1a	**abroad** [əˈbrɔːd]	*I am interested in volunteering abroad in the summer break.*	im Ausland
		plant [plɑːnt]	*My mother loves flowers and plants and grows them in our garden.* ▪ *Fr. 'plante' (f.)*	Pflanze
	2a	**freak** [friːk]	*I'm a nature freak – I really care about the earth.*	Begeisterte(r); Freak
	3	**dilemma** [dɪˈlemə]	*I have a big dilemma and need help.*	Dilemma
123	4a	**steward** [ˈstjuːəd]	*I found out that a steward is somebody who manages or looks after something.*	Verwalter
		conservation [ˌkɒnsəˈveɪʃn]	*My dream is to be a nature conservation officer one day.*	Schutz; Umwelterhaltung
		intern [ɪnˈtɜːn]	*I was one of eight interns and they gave us tools and gloves for work.*	Praktikant(in); Volontär(in)
		supervisor [ˈsuːpəvaɪzə]	*Our project supervisors showed us how to identify native plants and care for them.* = *boss*	Leiter(in)
		to **restore** [rɪˈstɔː]	*Together we worked to restore the natural habitat.* ▪ *Fr. 'restaurer'*	wiederherstellen
		habitat [ˈhæbɪtæt]	*They showed us how to identify native plants, and together we worked to restore the natural habitat.*	Habitat; Lebensraum
	4b	to **swap** [swɒp]	*Read about the robots and then swap information with another student.* = *exchange*	tauschen
	4c	**organizational** [ˌɔːgənaɪˈzeɪʃənl]	*The project manager spoke to the volunteers about organizational matters.*	organisatorisch
	5a	**webinar** [ˈwebɪnɑː]	*You're taking part in a webinar by a travel organization which offers two student projects.*	Webinar
		tropical [ˈtrɒpɪkl]	*It's a beautiful place, very green and tropical.*	tropisch
		to **clear** [klɪə]	*We cleared the table in order to play the game there.* ≠ *confusing* ▪ *Fr. 'clair, claire'*	räumen
		rewarding [rɪˈwɔːdɪŋ]	*It's physical work, but it is very rewarding.* = *gratifying*	lohnend
		villager [ˈvɪlɪdʒə]	*The villagers celebrate the festival on the main street.*	Dorfbewohner(in)
		paddling [ˈpædlɪŋ]	*On holiday we did a paddling tour through the jungle!*	Paddeln

page	exercise	Workshop 4		
		jungle [ˈdʒʌŋgl]	*It was very hot in the jungle.*	Dschungel
		township [ˈtaʊnʃɪp]	*The atmosphere in the townships is rich and full of life.*	Gemeinde
		mentor [ˈmentɔː]	*You'll be tutoring them, but you'll also be a mentor.*	Lehrmeister(in); Mentor(in)
		doorstep [ˈdɔːstep]	*Table Mountain National Park is right at our doorstep.*	direkt vor Ort; quasi vor der Haustür
	5b	**to confirm** [kənˈfɜːm]	*Check with your teacher to confirm understanding of the assignment.* ❗ *Fr. 'confirmer '*	bestätigen
		to clarify [ˈklærəfaɪ]	*Once you've listened to the instructions, be sure to clarify what you have heard.*	etw. klären
		repetition [ˌrepəˈtɪʃn]	*If you don't understand something, ask for repetition.*	Wiederholung
		clarification [ˌklærəfɪˈkeɪʃn]	*I didn't understand and asked my teacher for clarification.*	Abklärung
124	1	**convention** [kənˈvenʃn]	*Most countries in the world have signed the United Nations Convention on the Rights of the Child.*	Kongress; Konvention
		nutritious [njuˈtrɪʃəs]	*All children have a right to good health, including nutritious food and a clean, safe environment.*	nahrhaft
		to abduct [æbˈdʌkt]	*Governments must make sure that children are not abducted, sold or trafficked.* = *seize*	entführen
		to traffic [ˈtræfɪkt]	*Many teens were trafficked from their homes into the US illegally.*	verschleppen; illegalen Handel treiben
	2a	**dozen** [ˈdʌzn]	*This is the story of a major trafficking case which involved dozens of migrant workers.*	Dutzend
		migrant [ˈmaɪgrənt]	❗ *Lat. 'migrare (migro, migravi, migratum)' = to migrate*	herumziehend
		trafficker [ˈtræfɪktə]	*A trafficker promised them a better life in America if they paid him $15,000.*	Schlepper
		nightmare [ˈnaɪtmeə]	*But it was a lie: their dream turned into a nightmare.*	Albtraum
		cage [keɪdʒ]	*They worked twelve hours a day, six days a week cleaning the hens' cages at the egg farm.*	Käfig
		victim [ˈvɪktɪm]	*No one knows how many other victims of abuse there are in similar situations.* = *sufferer*	Opfer
		investigator [ɪnˈvestɪgeɪtə]	*Two of the victims spoke to investigators about the accident.*	Ermittler(in)

page	exercise	Workshop 4		
		dirt [dɜːt]	*You start sweating, and your eyes burn because of all the dirt.*	Dreck; Schmutz
		filthy [ˈfɪlθi]	*Your clothes get really dirty, completely filthy!* *= dirty*	dreckig
125		**authority** [ɔːˈθɒrəti]	*The uncle informed the authorities about the boys.*	Behörde; Autorität
		to rescue [ˈreskjuː]	*The authorities rescued the boys.*	retten
		educator [ˈedʒukeɪtə]	*According to a high school educator who works with immigrant teens, many of her students have jobs.* *= teacher*	Pädagoge; Pädagogin
		food processing [ˈfuːd ˈprəʊsesɪŋ]	*More than half of the students at her school have to work long shifts at local food processing plants to pay off their debt to traffickers.*	Lebensmittelverarbeitung
		debt [det]	*The children learned that they were 'debt slaves', forced to work to pay off their parents' debts.*	Schuld
		majority [məˈdʒɒrəti]	*The majority of children in the world go to school, but most of those who don't are girls.* *≠ minority*	Mehrheit
		abuse [əˈbjuːs]	*No one knows how many other victims of abuse there are in similar situations.*	Missbrauch
	3a	**migrant** [ˈmaɪgrənt]	*Most farm workers in the US are migrants.*	Migrant(in)
	3b	**farmworker** [ˈfɑːmwɜːkə]	*A large percentage of California's farmworkers are undocumented or illegal migrants.*	Landarbeiter(in); Farmarbeiter(in)
		undocumented [ˌʌnˈdɒkjumentɪd]	*Many of California's farmworkers are undocumented illegal migrants.* *≠ documented*	nicht erfasst
		agricultural [ˌægrɪˈkʌltʃərəl]	*There are many agricultural workers under the age of 18.*	landwirtschaftlich
126	2a	**essay** [ˈeseɪ]	*Use the notes to write a short essay.*	Aufsatz
		carpet [ˈkɑːpɪt]	*He worked in a factory that produces carpets.*	Teppich
		manufacturer [ˌmænjuˈfæktʃərə]	*His family sold him to a carpet manufacturer because they needed money.*	Hersteller(in)
		to enforce [ɪnˈfɔːs]	*Although there are laws against this in Pakistan, they are not enforced.* *= carry out*	durchsetzen
		freed [friːd]	*He started attending their school for freed child slaves.*	befreit

page	exercise	**Workshop 4**		
		lawyer [ˈlɔɪə]	*He dreamed of becoming a lawyer because he wanted to fight for children's rights.*	Rechtsanwalt / -anwältin
		injustice [ɪnˈdʒʌstɪs]	*He was brave and spoke up against injustice and exploitation.* ≠ *justice*	Ungerechtigkeit
		exploitation [ˌeksplɔɪˈteɪʃn]	*Child exploitation needs to be stopped.*	Ausbeutung
127	3a	**context** [ˈkɒntekst]	*Use the context to help you work out what they mean.*	Kontext; Zusammenhang
		inhumane [ˌɪnhjuːˈmeɪn]	*It is unfair and inhumane to treat children in this terrible way.* ≠ *humane*	inhuman; menschenunwürdig
		powerless [ˈpaʊələs]	*Young people have the power to change things: they are not powerless.* ≠ *powerfull*	kraftlos; machtlos
		to **eradicate** [ɪˈrædɪkeɪt]	*We must all work to eradicate child exploitation.*	ausmerzen; ausrotten
	3b	**unfairness** [ˌʌnˈfeənəs]	*It's an example of what one person can do to fight unfairness and injustice.* ≠ *fairness*	Ungerechtigkeit
		bonded laborer [ˌbɒndɪd ˈleɪbərə]	*I've met children sold as bonded laborers working 12 to 16 hours a day.*	Schuldknecht; Zwangsarbeiter(in)
		political clout [pəˈlɪtɪkl klaʊt]	*These children have no vote, no voice and no political clout.*	politischer Einfluss
		to **subject** [ˈsʌbdʒɪkt]	*Many of them are subjected to some of the most inhumane forms of exploitation.*	unterwerfen
		Pakistani [ˌpɑːkɪˈstɑːni]	*He read a newspaper article about a Pakistani boy who fought for children's rights.*	pakistanisch
		slavery [ˈsleɪvəri]	*The boy had been sold into slavery in the carpet industry at age four to pay off his family's debt.*	Sklaverei
		to **murder** [ˈmɜːdə]	*At the age of 12 he was murdered.* = *kill*	ermorden
		to **approach** [əˈprəʊtʃ]	*I didn't know that millions of children work long hours and in conditions approaching slavery.* ≠ *retreat*	näher kommen; sich nähern
		equal [ˈiːkwəl]	*All children are equal no matter where they come from and should be protected from child labour.*	gleich; gleichberechtigt
	3c	**headquarter** [ˌhedˈkwɔːtə]	*Using Craig's house as its headquarters, they set out with the goal of eradicating the exploitation of children.*	Headquarter; Hauptsitz

page	exercise	Workshop 4		
		throughout [θruːˈaʊt]	*We want to eradicate hunger throughout the world.*	durchweg
		to urge [ɜːdʒ]	*We sent a petition to world leaders urging them to end child labor.*	dringend bitten; drängen
	3d	**capable** [ˈkeɪpəbl]	*Young people are more capable than people think.* ≠ incapable	fähig
	4	**gunman** [ˈɡʌnmən]	*Malala was shot and nearly killed by a Taliban gunman.*	Schütze
		to recover [rɪˈkʌvə]	*She recovered in a hospital in England.* ❗ Lat. 'recuperare (recupero, recuperavi, recuperatum)	sich erholen
		sequence [ˈsiːkwəns]	*When you write about something, use time expressions and linking words to show the sequence of events.* ❗ Lat. 'sequentia, -ae' (f.)	Ablauf; Folge
	5a	**illiterate** [ɪˈlɪtərət]	*Many people around the world are still illiterate – they cannot read.* ≠ literate	analphabetisch
		to commit [kəˈmɪt]	*Much of the crime involving young people is committed by teenagers who did not have a good education.* ❗ Fr. 'commettre', Lat. 'committere (committo, commisi, commissum)'	begehen
128	S2	**close-up** [ˈkləʊsʌp]	*In this shot, there will be a close-up of the snack bar.*	Großaufnahme
		part-time [ˌpɑːt ˈtaɪm]	*He has a part-time job at the grocery store.* ≠ full time	Teilzeit...; nebenberuflich
		ditto [ˈdɪtəʊ]	*If you say "ditto" it means "another of the same".*	ditto; ebenfalls
129	S2a	**to delete** [dɪˈliːt]	*Delete the shots that you don't need.*	löschen
		to experiment [ɪkˈsperɪmənt]	*Experiment with alternative shots while making your film.*	experimentieren
	S2c	**rough** [rʌf]	*Choose one person in your group to put together a rough cut using the video editing app.* ≠ soft	rau
	S2d	**to combine** [kəmˈbaɪn]	*The next step is to combine and edit the film material.* ≠ divide ❗ Fr. 'combiner'	kombinieren; mischen
	S3	**desktop** [ˈdesktɒp]	*Download your finished film from your phone or tablet to a desktop computer or to another device.*	Desktop; Benutzeroberfläche
134	1	**fieldwork** [ˈfiːldwɜːk]	*Farm workers mainly do fieldwork.*	Geländearbeit
137	10	**declaration** [ˌdekləˈreɪʃn]	*Most of the articles in the declaration talk about the basic needs of children.*	Erklärung

Dictionary: English – German

3
3D printing [ˌθriːˈdiː prɪntɪŋ] 3D-Druck OT 1

A
a [eɪ] ein(e) OT 1
to **abduct** [æbˈdʌkt] entführen WS 4, 124
ability [əˈbɪləti] Können; Fähigkeit OT 2
   to **be able to** [bi ˈeɪbl tuː] können OT 2
aboard [əˈbɔːd] an Bord WS 1, 18
about [əˈbaʊt] über; ungefähr; um ... herum OT 1
above [əˈbʌv] oben; oberhalb OT 3
abroad [əˈbrɔːd] im Ausland WS 4, 122
to **abseil** [ˈæbseɪl] (sich) abseilen OT 2
absolute [ˈæbsəluːt] absolut OT 3
   absolutely [ˈæbsəluːtli] durchaus; total; wirklich; absolut OT 2
abuse [əˈbjuːs] Missbrauch WS 4, 125
accent [ˈæksənt] Akzent OT 1
to **accept** [əkˈsept] annehmen OT 3
access [ˈækses] Zugriff; Zugang WS 1, 31
accessible [əkˈsesəbl] zugänglich; barrierefrei OT 2
accessory [əkˈsesəri] Zubehör OT 3
accident [ˈæksɪdənt] Unfall OT 1
   Accident and Emergency [ˈæksɪdənt ənd iˌmɜːdʒənsi] Notaufnahme OT 1
accidentally [ˌæksɪˈdentəli] zufällig; versehentlich WS 3, 84
accompanied [əˈkʌmpənid] begleitet OT 3
according to [əˈkɔːdɪŋ tə] gemäß; nach OT 3
accordion [əˈkɔːdiən] Akkordeon OT 2
accurate [ˈækjərət] genau; präzise WS 1, 22
to **ache** [eɪk] schmerzen; wehtun OT 3
to **achieve** [əˈtʃiːv] erreichen; schaffen WS 3, 94
achievement [əˈtʃiːvmənt] Leistung OT 2
acoustic [əˈkuːstɪk] akustisch OT 2
acre [ˈeɪkə] Morgen WS 3, 80
across [əˈkrɒs] auf der anderen Seite; hinüber OT 1
to **act** [ækt] (sich) verhalten; Theater spielen OT 1
   to **act out** [ækt aʊt] vorführen OT 1
action [ˈækʃn] Aktion OT 1
   in action [ɪn ˈækʃn] im Einsatz OT 2

to **activate** [ˈæktɪveɪt] aktivieren WS 3, 87
active [ˈæktɪv] aktiv WS 2, 45
activism [ˈæktɪvɪzəm] Aktivismus WS 3, 88
activity [ækˈtɪvəti] Aktivität OT 1
actor [ˈæktə] Schauspieler(in) OT 1
actually [ˈæktʃuəli] eigentlich; sogar; tatsächlich OT 2
ad [æd] Werbung OT 2
adaptable [əˈdæptəbl] anpassungsfähig WS 3, 95
to **add** [æd] hinzufügen OT 1
addicted [əˈdɪktɪd] süchtig; abhängig OT 3
addition: in addition to [ɪn əˈdɪʃn tə] zusätzlich zu; neben WS 4, 110
address [əˈdres] Adresse OT 1
adjective [ˈædʒɪktɪv] Adjektiv OT 1
adjoining [əˈdʒɔɪnɪŋ] angrenzend OT 3
to **admit** [ədˈmɪt] zugeben WS 4, 117
adrenaline rush [əˈdrenəlɪn rʌʃ] Adrenalinstoß OT 1
adult [ˈædʌlt] Erwachsene(r) OT 1
advance [ədˈvɑːns] Fortschritt WS 3, 79
advanced [ədˈvɑːnst] fortgeschritten WS 3, 95
advantage [ədˈvɑːntɪdʒ] Vorteil OT 3
adventure [ədˈventʃə] Abenteuer OT 1
adventurous [ədˈventʃərəs] abenteuerlustig OT 2
adverb [ˈædvɜːb] Adverb; Umstandswort OT 1
advert [ˈædvɜːt] Inserat OT 1
to **advertise** [ˈædvətaɪz] Werbung machen für OT 2
advertisement [ədˈvɜːtɪsmənt] Werbung OT 1
advertiser [ˈædvətaɪzə] Werbeagentur; Werber OT 3
advertising [ˈædvətaɪzɪŋ] Werbung OT 2
advice [ədˈvaɪs] Rat OT 1
to **advise** [ədˈvaɪz] raten WS 2, 56
to **affect** [əˈfekt] sich auswirken auf OT 3
to **afford** [əˈfɔːd] (sich) leisten OT 2
affordable [əˈfɔːdəbl] bezahlbar WS 3, 77
afraid [əˈfreɪd] ängstlich OT 2
African [ˈæfrɪkən] afrikanisch OT 2
after [ˈɑːftə] nach OT 1
afternoon [ˌɑːftəˈnuːn] Nachmittag OT 1

afterwards [ˈɑːftəwədz] danach; nachher OT 3
again [əˈgen] wieder OT 1
against [əˈgenst] gegen OT 1
age [eɪdʒ] Alter OT 1
aged [eɪdʒd] im Alter von OT 1
agency [ˈeɪdʒənsi] Agentur; Organisation WS 3, 94
agenda [əˈdʒendə] Tagesordnung OT 3
aggressive [əˈgresɪv] aggressiv OT 3
agile [ˈædʒaɪl] beweglich OT 3
ago [əˈgəʊ] vor OT 1
to **agree** [əˈgriː] (sich) einig sein; zustimmen OT 1
agreement [əˈgriːmənt] Vereinbarung OT 3
agricultural [ˌægrɪˈkʌltʃərəl] landwirtschaftlich WS 4, 125
agriculture [ˈægrɪkʌltʃə] Landwirtschaft OT 2
ahead [əˈhed] voraus OT 3
aim [eɪm] Absicht; Ziel WS 3, 86
air [eə] Luft OT 1
airplane [ˈeəpleɪn] Flugzeug WS 3, 76
airport [ˈeəpɔːt] Flughafen OT 1
alarm [əˈlɑːm] Wecker; Alarm OT 2
alarmed [əˈlɑːmd] beunruhigt OT 3
Alaskan [əˈlæskən] alaskisch OT 2
album [ˈælbəm] Album OT 3
alcohol [ˈælkəhɒl] Alkohol OT 3
alcoholic [ˌælkəˈhɒlɪk] alkoholisch OT 3
to **alert** [əˈlɜːt] alarmieren OT 2
alien [ˈeɪliən] Außerirdische(r); Alien OT 2
alive [əˈlaɪv] lebendig WS 2, 49
all [ɔːl] alles; alle OT 1
   all over [ˈɔːl əʊvə] überall OT 2
   all right [ˌɔːl ˈraɪt] gut; in Ordnung OT 1
   all set [ɔːl ˈset] bereit OT 2
allergic [əˈlɜːdʒɪk] allergisch OT 2
allergy [ˈælədʒi] Allergie OT 1
to **allow** [əˈlaʊ] erlauben OT 3
allowance [əˈlaʊəns] Taschengeld OT 3
allowed [əˈlaʊd] erlaubt OT 3
   to **be allowed to** [bi əˈlaʊd tuː] dürfen; können OT 2
almost [ˈɔːlməʊst] fast OT 2
alone [əˈləʊn] allein OT 1
along [əˈlɒŋ] entlang OT 1
aloud [əˈlaʊd] laut; mit lauter Stimme OT 2
alpaca [ælˈpækə] Alpaka OT 2

alphabet [ˈælfəbet] Alphabet OT 1

alphabetical [ˌælfəˈbetɪkl] alphabetisch OT 2

already [ɔːlˈredi] schon; bereits OT 2

alright [ɔːlˈraɪt] in Ordnung OT 1

also [ˈɔːlsəʊ] auch OT 1

alternative [ɔːlˈtɜːnətɪv] Alternative OT 2

although [ɔːlˈðəʊ] obwohl OT 2

alumnus [əˈlʌmnaɪ] Absolvent(in); Ehemalige WS 2, 58

always [ˈɔːlweɪz] immer OT 1

amazed [əˈmeɪzd] erstaunt; überrascht OT 3

amazing [əˈmeɪzɪŋ] erstaunlich OT 1

ambition [æmˈbɪʃn] Ziel; Ambition WS 3, 94

ambitious [æmˈbɪʃəs] ehrgeizig WS 3, 95

ambulance [ˈæmbjələns] Krankenwagen OT 1

American [əˈmerɪkən] amerikanisch OT 1

among [əˈmʌŋ] unter; zwischen OT 3

amount [əˈmaʊnt] Menge OT 2

amphitheatre [ˈæmfɪθɪətə] Arena; Amphitheater OT 3

amplifier [ˈæmplɪfaɪə] Verstärker OT 2

amused [əˈmjuːzd] amüsiert OT 3

an [æn] ein(e) OT 1

to analyse [ˈænəlaɪz] analysieren OT 3

ancestor [ˈænsestə] Vorfahr(in) OT 3

to anchor [ˈæŋkə] ankern WS 1, 20

ancient [ˈeɪnʃənt] antik; uralt OT 2

and [ənd] und OT 1

anecdote [ˈænɪkdəʊt] Anekdote WS 1, 22

angel [ˈeɪndʒl] Engel OT 3

anger [ˈæŋgə] Ärger; Wut OT 3

angry [ˈæŋgri] böse OT 1
   angrily [ˈæŋgrəli] ärgerlich; böse; zornig OT 2

animal [ˈænɪml] Tier OT 1

ankle [ˈæŋkl] Fußknöchel OT 1

to announce [əˈnaʊns] ansagen; bekannt geben OT 2

announcement [əˈnaʊnsmənt] Bekanntgabe; Ansage OT 2

to annoy [əˈnɔɪ] ärgern OT 3

annoyed [əˈnɔɪd] genervt OT 2

annoying [əˈnɔɪɪŋ] ärgerlich; nervig OT 2

another [əˈnʌðə] noch ein(e); ein(e) andere(r, -s) OT 1

answer [ˈɑːnsə] Antwort OT 1

antenna [ænˈtenə] Antenne OT 2

antiseptic [ˌæntiˈseptɪk] antiseptisch; keimtötend OT 2

anxious [ˈæŋkʃəs] besorgt OT 2

any [ˈeni] irgendein(e) OT 1

anybody [ˈenibɒdi] irgendjemand OT 1

anymore [ˌeni ˈmɔː] mehr; länger; weiter OT 2

anyone [ˈeniwʌn] irgendjemand OT 2

anything [ˈeniθɪŋ] irgendetwas OT 1

anytime [ˈenitaɪm] jederzeit OT 3

anyway [ˈeniweɪ] trotzdem; sowieso; jedenfalls OT 1

anywhere [ˈeniweə] irgendwo OT 2

apart from [əˈpɑːt frəm] außer OT 3

apartment [əˈpɑːtmənt] Wohnung OT 1

to apologize [əˈpɒlədʒaɪz] (sich) entschuldigen OT 2

apology [əˈpɒlədʒi] Entschuldigung OT 2

app [æp] App WS 2, 48

apparently [əˈpærəntli] anscheinend WS 2, 70

appeal [əˈpiːl] Aufruf OT 2

to appear [əˈpɪə] erscheinen; scheinen; auftauchen OT 3

appearance [əˈpɪərəns] Aussehen OT 3

appetizing [ˈæpɪtaɪzɪŋ] appetitlich OT 3

to applaud [əˈplɔːd] applaudieren OT 2

applause [əˈplɔːz] Applaus OT 2

apple [ˈæpl] Apfel OT 1

appliance [əˈplaɪəns] Gerät; Haushaltsgerät OT 3

applicant [ˈæplɪkənt] Bewerber(in) WS 4, 120

application [ˌæplɪˈkeɪʃn] Bewerbung; Antrag WS 1, 17

to apply [əˈplaɪ] sich bewerben OT 3

to approach [əˈprəʊtʃ] näher kommen; sich nähern WS 4, 127

appropriate [əˈprəʊpriət] angemessen WS 1, 22

appropriately [əˈprəʊpriətli] passend; angemessen OT 3

to approve [əˈpruːv] genehmigen; zustimmen OT 3

April [ˈeɪprəl] April OT 1

aquatic [əˈkwætɪk] aquatisch; Wasser... WS 4, 110

aqueduct [ˈækwɪdʌkt] Aquädukt OT 3

archeologist [ˌɑːkiˈɒlədʒɪst] Archäologe / Archäologin WS 4, 108

architecture [ˈɑːkɪtektʃə] Architektur OT 2

to archive [ˈɑːkaɪv] archivieren WS 4, 116

Arctic [ˈɑːktɪk] arktisch; Arktis WS 3, 93

area [ˈeəriə] Gebiet; Gegend OT 1

arena [əˈriːnə] Arena OT 1

aeroplane [ˈeərəpleɪn] Flugzeug WS 3, 77

to argue [ˈɑːgjuː] streiten; argumentieren OT 2

argument [ˈɑːgjumənt] Streit; Auseinandersetzung OT 1

arm [ɑːm] Arm OT 1

armchair [ˈɑːmtʃeə] Sessel OT 1

army [ˈɑːmi] Armee OT 3

around [əˈraʊnd] um OT 1

to arrange [əˈreɪndʒ] planen; vereinbaren OT 2

arrangement [əˈreɪndʒmənt] Regelung; Vereinbarung OT 3

arrival [əˈraɪvl] Ankunft OT 2

to arrive [əˈraɪv] ankommen OT 1

arrow [ˈærəʊ] Pfeil OT 3

art [ɑːt] Kunst OT 1
   fine art [ˌfaɪn ˈɑːt] Kunstwissenschaft OT 2

article [ˈɑːtɪkl] Artikel; Geschlechtswort OT 1
   definite article [ˈdefɪnət ˌɑːtɪkl] bestimmter Artikel OT 1
   indefinite article [ɪnˌdefɪnət ˈɑːtɪkl] unbestimmter Artikel OT 1

artificial intelligence [ˌɑːtɪfɪʃl ɪnˈtelɪdʒəns] künstliche Intelligenz WS 3, 78

artificially [ˌɑːtɪˈfɪʃəli] künstlich OT 3

artist [ˈɑːtɪst] Künstler(in) OT 3

as [æz] als; wie OT 1

as well [əz wel] auch OT 1

ashamed [əˈʃeɪmd] beschämt OT 3

ashore [əˈʃɔːr] an Land WS 1, 20

Asian [ˈeɪʒn] asiatisch WS 1, 16

to ask [ɑːsk] fragen OT 1

aspect [ˈæspekt] Aspekt WS 2, 44

aspen [ˈæspən] Espe OT 2

assembly [əˈsembli] Versammlung OT 1
   assembly hall [əˈsembli ˌhɔːl] Aula OT 1

assertive [sʌlk] bestimmt OT 3

assignment [əˈsaɪnmənt] Aufgabe WS 3, 79

assimilation [əˌsɪməˈleɪʃn] Assimilation; Anpassung WS 1, 30

assistant [əˈsɪstənt] Assistent(in) OT 1

to associate [əˈsəʊsieɪt] assoziieren WS 1, 21

association [əˌsəʊʃiˈeɪʃn] Verein; Verband OT 2

asterisk [ˈæstərɪsk] Sternchen; Asterisk WS 1, 36

astonishingly [ə'stɒnɪʃɪŋli] erstaunlicherweise OT 3

astronaut ['æstrənɔːt] Astronaut(in) **WS 1**, 24

astronomy [ə'strɒnəmi] Astronomie OT 1

asylum seeker [ə'saɪləm siːkə] Asylbewerber(in) **WS 1**, 26

at [ət] an; in; bei OT 1

  at ... o'clock [æt ... ə'klɒk] um ... Uhr OT 1

  at the moment [ət ðə 'məʊmənt] momentan OT 2

athlete ['æθliːt] Sportler(in) OT 2

athletic [æθ'letɪk] athletisch; sportlich **WS 3**, 85

athletics [æθ'letɪks] Leichtathletik; Sport OT 1

atmosphere ['ætməsfɪə] Atmosphäre OT 3

to attach [ə'tætʃ] befestigen **WS 3**, 87

to attack [ə'tæk] angreifen OT 3

attacking [ə'tækɪŋ] angreifend OT 3

attempt [ə'tempt] Versuch OT 2

to attend [ə'tend] besuchen OT 2

attendant [ə'tendənt] Aufseher(in); Diener(in) OT 3

attention [ə'tenʃn] Aufmerksamkeit OT 2

  to pay attention [ˌpeɪ ə'tenʃn] aufpassen OT 2

attic ['ætɪk] Dachboden OT 3

attitude ['ætɪtjuːd] Haltung; Einstellung; Ansicht OT 3

to attract [ə'trækt] anziehen **WS 1**, 21

attraction [ə'trækʃn] Sehenswürdigkeit OT 2

attractive [ə'træktɪv] anziehend; attraktiv; reizvoll **WS 4**, 116

audience ['ɔːdiəns] Publikum OT 2

audio diary ['ɔːdiəʊ daɪəri] Audiotagebuch OT 2

audio file ['ɔːdiəʊ faɪl] Audiodatei OT 2

August [ɔː'ɡʌst] August OT 1

aunt [ɑːnt] Tante OT 1

auntie ['ɑːnti] Tantchen OT 2

Austrian ['ɒstriən] Österreicher(in) **WS 3**, 83

author ['ɔːθə] Autor(in) OT 2

authority [ɔː'θɒrəti] Behörde; Autorität **WS 4**, 125

to automate ['ɔːtəmeɪt] automatisieren **WS 4**, 112

automobile ['ɔːtəməbiːl] Automobil **WS 3**, 77

autonomous [ɔː'tɒnəməs] unabhängig; autonom **WS 3**, 78

autumn ['ɔːtəm] Herbst OT 2

available [ə'veɪləbl] verfügbar; erhältlich OT 3

avatar ['ævətɑː] Avatar OT 3

avenue ['ævənjuː] Allee OT 1

average ['ævərɪdʒ] durchschnittlich **WS 2**, 49

to avoid [ə'vɔɪd] vermeiden **WS 2**, 45

awake [ə'weik] wach OT 2

award [ə'wɔːd] Auszeichnung OT 2

  award-winning [ə'wɔːd wɪnɪŋ] preisgekrönt **WS 3**, 83

to award [ə'wɔːd] vergeben; verleihen **WS 3**, 83

away [ə'weɪ] weg OT 1

awesome ['ɔːsəm] toll; großartig OT 2

awful ['ɔːfl] fürchterlich; schrecklich OT 1

axis ['æksɪs] Achse **WS 2**, 64

aye [aɪ] ja OT 2

B

baby ['beɪbi] Säugling; Baby OT 1

to babysit ['beɪbisɪt] babysitten **WS 4**, 117

babysitter ['beɪbisɪtə] Babysitter(in) **WS 4**, 114

back [bæk] Rücken OT 1

backbone ['bækbəʊn] Rückgrat OT 2

background ['bækɡraʊnd] Hintergrund OT 3

backhand ['bækhænd] Rückhand OT 3

backpack ['bækpæk] Rucksack OT 2

to backpack ['bækpæk] mit dem Rucksack reisen OT 3

backup ['bækʌp] Backup; Unterstützung **WS 3**, 80

backwards ['bækwədz] nach hinten; rückwärts OT 3

backyard [ˌbæk'jɑːd] Garten (hinterm Haus) OT 2

bacon ['beɪkən] Speck; Bacon OT 1

bad [bæd] schlecht OT 1

  badly ['bædli] schlecht OT 2

badge [bædʒ] Abzeichen OT 1

badminton ['bædmɪntən] Badminton OT 1

bag [bæɡ] Tüte; Tasche OT 1

bagel ['beɪɡl] Bagel OT 1

baggage ['bæɡɪdʒ] Gepäck OT 2

  baggage claim ['bæɡɪdʒ kleɪm] Gepäckausgabe OT 2

bagpipe ['bæɡpaɪp] Dudelsack OT 3

to bake [beɪk] backen OT 1

baker ['beɪkə] Bäcker(in) OT 3

bakery ['beɪkəri] Bäckerei **WS 4**, 114

balance ['bæləns] Gleichgewicht OT 3

ball ['bɔːl] Ball OT 1

ballpoint pen ['bɔːlpɔɪnt pen] Kugelschreiber OT 1

ballet ['bæleɪ] Ballett OT 3

balloon [bə'luːn] Ballon OT 3

to ban [bæn] verbieten OT 3

banana [bə'nɑːnə] Banane OT 1

band [bænd] Band OT 1

bandage ['bændɪdʒ] Verband OT 2

Bangladeshi [ˌbæŋɡlə'deʃi] Bangladescher(in) **WS 1**, 25

bank [bæŋk] Ufer; Bank OT 3

  bank teller [bæŋk 'telə] Kassierer(in) **WS 4**, 112

bar [bɑː] Riegel; Bar OT 1

barbecued ['bɑːbɪkjuːd] gegrillt **WS 3**, 93

bargain ['bɑːɡən] Schnäppchen **WS 2**, 51

to bark [bɑːk] bellen OT 2

barn [bɑːn] Scheune OT 2

barrier ['bæriə] Barriere OT 3

base [beɪs] Basis **WS 3**, 94

to base on [beɪs ɒn] auf etw. basieren **WS 1**, 21

baseball ['beɪsbɔːl] Baseball OT 1

basic ['beɪsɪk] Grund-; grundsätzlich; einfach **WS 3**, 83

basically ['beɪsɪkli] im Grunde OT 3

basin ['beɪsn] Becken OT 3

basket ['bɑːskɪt] Korb OT 3

basketball ['bɑːskɪtbɔːl] Basketball OT 1

bat [bæt] Fledermaus; Schläger OT 1

  long-eared bat [ˌlɒŋɪəd 'bæt] Braunes Langohr OT 2

bath [bɑːθ] Badewanne; Bad OT 2

bathroom ['bɑːθruːm] Badezimmer OT 1

battery ['bætri] Batterie OT 2

battle ['bætl] Schlacht OT 1

Bavarian [bə'veəriən] bayerisch OT 2

bay [beɪ] Bucht OT 1

to be [biː] sein OT 1

beach [biːtʃ] Strand OT 1

beam [biːm] Balken OT 3

bean [biːn] Bohne OT 1

  baked beans [ˌbeɪkt 'biːnz] weiße Bohnen in Tomatensoße OT 1

bear [beə] Bär OT 1

to beat [biːt] schlagen; besiegen OT 2

beautiful ['bjuːtɪfl] schön OT 1

beauty ['bjuːti] Schönheit OT 3

because [bɪ'kɒz] weil OT 1

to **become** [bɪˈkʌm] werden OT 2

bed [bed] Bett; Beet OT 1

bedbug [ˈbedbʌg] Bettwanze OT 1

bedroom [ˈbedruːm] Schlafzimmer
OT 1

bee [biː] Biene OT 1

beef [biːf] Rindfleisch OT 2

  beef brisket [biːf ˈbrɪskɪt]
Rinderbrust **WS 3**, 93

beer [bɪə] Bier OT 3

beetroot [ˈbiːtruːt] Rote Bete **WS 1**, 26

before [bɪˈfɔː] vor OT 1

to **begin** [bɪˈgɪn] anfangen OT 1

beginning [bɪˈgɪnɪŋ] beginnend OT 1

to **behave** [bɪˈheɪv] (sich) benehmen
OT 2

behaviour [bɪˈheɪvjə] Benehmen OT 2

to **behead** [bɪˈhed] enthaupten OT 3

behind [bɪˈhaɪnd] hinter OT 1

belief [bɪˈliːf] Glaube **WS 1**, 32

to **believe** [bɪˈliːv] glauben OT 2

bell [bel] Glocke OT 1

to **belong** [bɪˈlɒŋ] gehören OT 2

belongings [bɪˈlɒŋɪŋz] persönliche
Sachen; Habe OT 3

below [bɪˈləʊ] unter OT 2

belt [belt] Gürtel OT 2

bench [bentʃ] Bank OT 3

beneficial [ˌbenɪˈfɪʃl] nützlich OT 2

benefit [ˈbenɪfɪt] Vorteil; Nutzen OT 2

to **benefit** [ˈbenɪfɪt] guttun; profitieren
OT 2

berry [ˈberi] Beere **WS 3**, 84

beside [bɪˈsaɪd] neben OT 2

best [best] beste(r, -s) OT 1

to **bet** [bet] wetten OT 1

better [ˈbetə] besser OT 1

between [bɪˈtwiːn] zwischen OT 1

biased [ˈbaɪəst] parteiisch **WS 2**, 54

bicycle [ˈbaɪsɪkəl] Fahrrad OT 2

big [bɪg] groß OT 1

bike [baɪk] Fahrrad OT 1

  bike lane [ˈbaɪk leɪn] Radstreifen
WS 1, 16

to **bike** [baɪk] Rad fahren OT 3

  mountain biking [ˈmaʊntən baɪkɪŋ]
Mountainbiken OT 2

bilingual [ˌbaɪˈlɪŋgwəl] bilingual;
zweisprachig OT 2

bill [bɪl] Rechnung OT 3

billion [ˈbɪljən] Milliarde OT 2

bin [bɪn] Eimer; Behälter OT 2

bingo [ˈbɪŋgəʊ] Bingo OT 1

binoculars [bɪˈnɒkjələz] Fernglas OT 2

biodiversity [ˌbaɪəʊdaɪˈvɜːsəti]
Artenvielfalt; Biodiversität **WS 4**, 111

biography [baɪˈɒgrəfi] Biografie
WS 1, 41

biologist [baɪˈɒlədʒɪst] Biologe;
Biologin **WS 4**, 110

biology [baɪˈɒlədʒi] Biologie OT 2

bird [bɜːd] Vogel OT 1

birth [bɜːθ] Geburt OT 2

  date of birth [ˌdeɪt əv ˈbɜːθ]
Geburtsdatum OT 2

birthday [ˈbɜːθdeɪ] Geburtstag OT 1

birthplace [ˈbɜːθpleɪs] Geburtsort
WS 1, 18

biscuit [ˈbɪskɪt] Keks OT 1

bit [bɪt] Stück OT 1

bite [baɪt] Biss OT 2

black [blæk] schwarz OT 1

blackberry [ˈblækbəri] Brombeere OT 1

blank [blæŋk] leer **WS 4**, 119

blanket [ˈblæŋkɪt] Decke OT 2

blazer [ˈbleɪzər] Blazer; Sportjacke OT 1

blind [blaɪnd] blind OT 2

blister [ˈblɪstə] Blase (Haut) OT 2

to **block** [blɒk] blockieren OT 3

blog [blɒg] Blog OT 1

blogger [ˈblɒgə] Blogger(in) OT 3

blogpost [ˈblɒgpəʊst] Blogeintrag
WS 4, 111

blonde [blɒnd] blond OT 1

blood [blʌd] Blut OT 2

to **blow** [bləʊ] blasen; pfeifen; wehen
OT 2

blubber [ˈblʌbə] Walspeck OT 2

blue [bluː] blau OT 1

bluebird [ˈbluːbɜːd] Hüttensänger OT 3

blues [bluːz] Blues OT 1

to **board** [bɔːd] an Bord gehen **WS 1**, 18

boat [bəʊt] Boot OT 1

body [ˈbɒdi] Körper OT 1

to **boil** [bɔɪl] kochen OT 2

boiling [ˈbɔɪlɪŋ] kochend heiß OT 1

bold [bəʊld] mutig; fettgedruckt OT 1

bomb: nuclear bomb [ˌnjuːkliər ˈbɒm]
Neutronenbombe OT 3

bonded: bonded laborer [ˌbɒndɪd
ˈleɪbərə] Schuldknecht;
Zwangsarbeiter(in) **WS 4**, 127

bone [bəʊn] Knochen OT 1

bong [bɒŋ] Klang (einer Glocke) OT 1

book [bʊk] Buch OT 1

bookcase [ˈbʊkkeɪs] Bücherregal OT 1

booking [ˈbʊkɪŋ] Buchung OT 2

  booking office [ˈbʊkɪŋ ˌɒfɪs]
Fahrkartenschalter OT 2

booklet [ˈbʊklət] Broschüre OT 2

to **bookmark** [ˈbʊkmɑːk] markieren
WS 1, 22

boot [buːt] Stiefel OT 1

booth [buːð] Zelle **WS 3**, 93

border [ˈbɔːdə] Grenze OT 3

bored [bɔːd] gelangweilt OT 1

boring [ˈbɔːrɪŋ] langweilig OT 1

to **be born** [bi ˈbɔːn] geboren sein OT 2

to **borrow** [ˈbɒrəʊ] leihen OT 2

boss [bɒs] Chef(in) OT 2

bossy [ˈbɒsi] herrisch OT 2

both [bəʊθ] beide OT 1

to **bother** [ˈbɒðə] stören **WS 1**, 29

bottle [ˈbɒtl] Flasche OT 1

bottled [ˈbɒtld] abgefüllt OT 3

bottom [ˈbɒtəm] unterster Teil; Boden
OT 1

bouquet [buˈkeɪ] Strauß; Bouquet
OT 3

bow [bəʊ] Bogen OT 2

bow-tie [ˌbəʊ ˈtaɪ] Fliege OT 2

bowl [bəʊl] Schüssel OT 1

box [bɒks] Kiste; Kästchen OT 1

boy [bɔɪ] Junge OT 1

boyband [ˈbɔɪbænd] Boygroup OT 2

bracket [ˈbrækɪt] Klammer OT 2

brain [breɪn] Gehirn OT 2

to **brainstorm** [ˈbreɪnstɔːm]
brainstormen OT 2

branch [brɑːntʃ] Ast OT 2

brand [brænd] Marke **WS 2**, 44

brand-new [ˌbrænd ˈnjuː] brandneu
OT 2

brave [breɪv] tapfer OT 1

Brazilian [brəˈzɪliən] brasilianisch
OT 2

bread [bred] Brot OT 1

breadcrumbs [ˈbredkrʌmz]
Brotkrumen; Paniermehl OT 3

break [breɪk] Pause OT 1

to **break** [breɪk] brechen OT 1

breakfast [ˈbrekfəst] Frühstück OT 1

breath [breθ] Atem(zug) OT 2

  out of breath [ˌaʊt əv ˈbreθ]
außer Atem OT 2

to **breathe** [briːð] atmen OT 2

breathless [ˈbreθləs] atemlos OT 3

breathtaking [ˈbreθteɪkɪŋ]
atemberaubend OT 3

breeze [briːz] Brise OT 3

bridge [brɪdʒ] Brücke OT 1

bright [braɪt] leuchtend OT 1

brill [brɪl] sehr gut OT 1

brilliant [ˈbrɪliənt] genial OT 1

to **bring** [brɪŋ] bringen OT 1

British [ˈbrɪtɪʃ] britisch OT 1

broccoli [ˈbrɒkəli] Broccoli OT 1

brochure [ˈbrəʊʃə] Broschüre OT 1

broken ['brəʊkən] gebrochen OT 1

brother ['brʌðə] Bruder OT 1

brown [braʊn] braun OT 1

browser ['braʊzər] Browser WS 1, 22

to **brush** [brʌʃ] bürsten; putzen WS 3, 78

bubble ['bʌbl] Blase OT 1

buddy ['bʌdi] Kumpel OT 2

budgie ['bʌdʒi] Wellensittich OT 1

buffalo ['bʌfələʊ] Büffel WS 1, 29

buffet ['bʌfeɪ] Buffet OT 3

buggy ['bʌgi] Pferdewagen; Kutsche WS 1, 32

bughouse ['bʌghaʊs] Insektenhaus OT 1

to **build** [bɪld] bauen OT 1

builder ['bɪldə] Bauarbeiter(in) OT 2

building ['bɪldɪŋ] Gebäude OT 1

bulb: LED bulb [‚el i: 'di: bʌlb] LED Birne OT 3

bulletin board ['bʊlətɪn bɔːd] Anschlagtafel; Pinwand WS 4, 116

bully ['bʊli] Mobbingtäter(in) OT 2

bullying ['bʊliɪŋ] Mobbing OT 2

to **bump** [bʌmp] stoßen OT 2

bumpy ['bʌmpi] holprig; uneben WS 1, 28

bungee jumping ['bʌndʒi dʒʌmpɪŋ] Bungee-Jumping OT 3

bunk bed [bʌŋk bed] Etagenbett; Stockbett OT 3

burger ['bɜːgə] Hamburger OT 1

to **burn** [bɜːn] brennen OT 2

burrito [bʊˈriːtəʊ] Burrito WS 4, 114

bus [bʌs] Bus OT 1

bus stop ['bʌs stɒp] Bushaltestelle OT 1

bush [bʊʃ] Busch OT 2

business ['bɪznəs] Geschäft(e) OT 3

businessman ['bɪznəsmæn] Unternehmer; Geschäftsmann WS 3, 83

businesswoman ['bɪznəswʊmən] Unternehmerin; Geschäftsfrau WS 3, 84

busy ['bɪzi] beschäftigt OT 1

but [bʌt] aber OT 1

butcher ['bʊtʃə] Fleischer(in); Metzger(in) WS 1, 20

butterfly ['bʌtəflaɪ] Schmetterling OT 2

button ['bʌtn] Knopf OT 1

to **buy** [baɪ] kaufen OT 1

buzzard ['bʌzəd] Bussard OT 2

by [faɪv] bei; neben; von OT 1

by accident [baɪ 'æksɪdənt] versehentlich OT 2

bye [baɪ] Tschüss! OT 1

C

cab [kæb] Taxi; Fahrerkabine; Führerhaus WS 1, 41

cabbage ['kæbɪdʒ] Kohl OT 1

caber ['keɪbə] Baumstamm OT 3

cabin ['kæbɪn] Kabine OT 2

café ['kæfeɪ] Café OT 1

cafeteria [‚kæfəˈtɪəriə] Cafeteria OT 2

cage [keɪdʒ] Käfig WS 4, 124

cake [keɪk] Kuchen OT 1

calendar ['kælɪndə] Kalender OT 1

call [kɔːl] Anruf OT 1

called [kɔːld] namens; mit dem Namen OT 1

caller ['kɔːlə] Anrufer(in) OT 2

calm [kɑːm] ruhig OT 2

calmly ['kɑːmli] ruhig OT 3

camera ['kæmərə] Fotoapparat; Kamera OT 1

camp [kæmp] Camp; Ferienlager OT 1

summer camp ['sʌmə kæmp] Ferienlager OT 2

campaign [kæmˈpeɪn] Kampagne; Aktion OT 3

camper ['kæmpə] Camper(in) OT 2

camper van ['kæmpə væn] Wohnmobil WS 3, 80

campfire ['kæmpfaɪə] Lagerfeuer OT 2

campground ['kæmpgraʊnd] Zeltplatz OT 2

camping ['kæmpɪŋ] Camping; Zelten OT 1

campsite ['kæmpsaɪt] Zeltplatz; Campingplatz OT 1

campus ['kæmpəs] Campus OT 2

can [kæn] Dose OT 2

canal [kəˈnæl] Kanal OT 3

to **cancel** ['kænsl] absagen WS 1, 41

cancer ['kænsə] Krebs WS 2, 52

candidate ['kændɪdət] Kandidat(in) WS 1, 13

candle ['kændl] Kerze OT 2

candlelight ['kændllaɪt] Kerzenlicht WS 3, 77

candy ['kændi] Süßigkeit WS 3, 93

canned [kænd] Dosen... OT 2

canoe [kəˈnuː] Kanu OT 1

canoeing [kəˈnuːɪŋ] Kanufahren OT 1

canteen [kænˈtiːn] Kantine OT 1

canyon ['kænjən] Schlucht; Canyon OT 3

canyoning ['kænjənɪŋ] Canyoning OT 3

cap [kæp] Mütze OT 1

capable ['keɪpəbl] fähig WS 4, 127

capital ['kæpɪtl] Hauptstadt OT 1

capital letter [‚kæpɪtl 'letə] Großbuchstabe OT 1

capsule ['kæpsjuːl] Kapsel; Raumkapsel WS 3, 95

captain ['kæptɪn] Spielführer(in); Kommandant(in) WS 1, 21

caption ['kæpʃn] Bildunterschrift; Bildtext; Untertitel OT 1

to **capture** ['kæptʃə] einfangen; festnehmen WS 1, 21

car [kɑː] Auto OT 1

car park ['kɑː pɑːk] Parkplatz OT 1

caramel ['kærəmel] Karamelle OT 3

caravan ['kærəvæn] Wohnwagen OT 1

carbon ['kɑːbən] Karbon OT 3

card [kɑːd] Karte OT 1

to **care** [keə] besorgt sein OT 1

to **care about** ['keə əˌbaʊt] (sich) interessieren; gern haben OT 2

career [kəˈrɪə] Karriere OT 3

careful ['keəfl] vorsichtig; sorgfältig OT 1

careless ['keələs] sorglos OT 2

carelessly ['keələsli] unvorsichtig; leichtsinnig OT 2

caretaker ['keəteɪkə] Hausmeister(in) OT 1

cargo ['kɑːgəʊ] Ladung OT 3

carpet ['kɑːpɪt] Teppich WS 4, 126

carriage ['kærɪdʒ] Wagen OT 1

carrier bag ['kæriə bæg] Tragetasche OT 2

carrot ['kærət] Karotte OT 1

to **carry** ['kæri] tragen OT 1

carsick ['kɑːsɪk] autokrank OT 2

carton ['kɑːtn] Karton OT 2

cartoon [kɑːˈtuːn] Zeichentrickfilm; Cartoon WS 1, 21

to **carve** [kɑːv] schnitzen OT 2

case [keɪs] Tasche; Koffer OT 1

cash [kæʃ] Kleingeld; Bargeld OT 1

cash register ['kæʃ redʒɪstə] Kasse OT 2

cashier [kæˈʃɪə] Kassierer(in) WS 3, 78

to **cast a spell** [kɑːst ə 'spel] einen Zauber bewirken OT 1

castle ['kɑːsl] Burg OT 1

cat [kæt] Katze OT 1

catastrophic [‚kætəˈstrɒfɪk] katastrophal WS 3, 103

to **catch** [kætʃ] fangen OT 1

category ['kætəgəri] Kategorie OT 3

catering service ['keɪtərɪŋ 'sɜːvɪs] Verpflegungsservice WS 4, 111

cathedral [kəˈθiːdrəl] Kathedrale OT 1

Catholic ['kæθlɪk] Katholik(in) OT 3

cause [kɔːz] Grund; Anliegen OT 2

to **cause** [kɔːz] verursachen OT 2

cave [keɪv] Höhle OT 1

ceiling [ˈsiːlɪŋ] Decke **WS 3**, 93

to **celebrate** [ˈselɪbreɪt] feiern OT 1

celebration [ˌselɪˈbreɪʃn] Feier OT 2

celebrity [səˈlebrəti] Prominente(r) OT 3

cell [sel] Zelle OT 1

cell phone [ˈsel fəʊn] Handy OT 2

cellar [ˈselə] Keller **WS 3**, 83

cellist [ˈtʃelɪst] Cellist(in) OT 2

cello [ˈtʃeləʊ] Cello OT 2

cent [sent] Cent OT 1

center [ˈsentə] Mitte; Zentrum OT 1

centigrade [ˈsentɪɡreɪd] Celsius **WS 3**, 94

centimetre (cm) [ˈsentɪmiːtə] Zentimeter OT 2

central [ˈsentrəl] Zentral... OT 1

centre [ˈsentə] Mitte; Zentrum OT 1

century [ˈsentʃəri] Jahrhundert OT 2

cereal [ˈsɪəriəl] Cornflakes; Frühstücksflocken OT 1

ceremonial [ˌserɪˈməʊniəl] zeremoniell; feierlich OT 3

ceremony [ˈserəməni] Feier OT 2

certain [ˈsɜːtn] sicher OT 3

certainly [ˈsɜːtnli] sicher; sicherlich OT 1

certificate [səˈtɪfɪkət] Zeugnis; Zertifikat OT 1

chain [tʃeɪn] Kette OT 2

chair [tʃeə] Stuhl OT 1

challenge [ˈtʃælɪndʒ] Herausforderung OT 2

challenging [ˈtʃælɪndʒɪŋ] schwierig **WS 3**, 85

chamber [ˈtʃeɪmbə] Kammer OT 2

chance [tʃɑːns] Zufall; Möglichkeit OT 2

change [tʃeɪndʒ] Wechselgeld; Änderung OT 1

to **change** [tʃeɪndʒ] ändern; wechseln OT 1

changing room [ˈtʃeɪndʒɪŋ ˌruːm] Umkleide OT 1

channel [ˈtʃænl] Programm OT 2

chapter [ˈtʃæptə] Kapitel OT 1

character [ˈkærəktə] Charakter OT 1

characteristic [ˌkærəktəˈrɪstɪk] charakteristisches Merkmal OT 2

charge: in charge [ɪn ˈtʃɑːdʒ] zuständig OT 1

   to **be in charge of** [tʃɑːdʒ] für etw. verantwortlich sein OT 3

to **charge** [tʃɑːdʒ] aufladen **WS 3**, 80

charity [ˈtʃærəti] Wohlfahrtsorganisation OT 2

charming [ˈtʃɑːmɪŋ] charmant OT 3

chart [tʃɑːt] Diagramm; Chart **WS 2**, 64

   bar chart [ˈbɑː tʃɑːt] Balkendiagramm **WS 2**, 64

   pie chart [ˈpaɪ tʃɑːt] Tortendiagramm; Kreisdiagramm **WS 2**, 64

to **chase** [tʃeɪs] jagen OT 1

chat [tʃæt] Unterhaltung OT 1

to **chatter** [ˈtʃætə] plaudern OT 2

chatty [ˈtʃæti] gesprächig OT 3

cheap [tʃiːp] billig OT 2

to **check** [tʃek] überprüfen OT 1

check-in desk [ˈtʃek ɪn desk] Abflugschalter OT 2

check-out [ˈtʃekaʊt] Kasse **WS 3**, 78

checker [ˈtʃekə] Prüfer(in) OT 3

checkers [ˈtʃekəz] Damespiel OT 1

checklist [ˈtʃeklɪst] Checkliste OT 1

cheeky [ˈtʃiːki] frech OT 1

to **cheer** [tʃɪə] jubeln OT 2

   cheer up [tʃɪə ʌp] Kopf hoch! OT 1

cheerleader [ˈtʃɪəliːdə] Cheerleader(in) OT 3

cheese [tʃiːz] Käse OT 1

chef [ʃef] Küchenchef; Küchenchefin; Koch / Köchin OT 1

chemical [ˈkemɪkl] Chemikalie OT 3

chemist [ˈkemɪst] Apotheker(in); Chemiker(in) OT 2

   chemist's shop [ˈkemɪsts ʃɒp] Apotheke OT 2

chess [tʃes] Schach OT 1

chessboard [ˈtʃesbɔːd] Schachbrett OT 1

chicken [ˈtʃɪkɪn] Huhn; Hähnchen OT 1

child [tʃaɪld] Kind OT 1

childhood [ˈtʃaɪldhʊd] Kindheit OT 3

chili [ˈtʃɪli] Chili OT 2

to **chill out** [tʃɪl aʊt] sich entspannen **WS 3**, 85

Chinese [ˌtʃaɪˈniːz] chinesisch OT 1

chip [tʃɪp] Fritte OT 1

chocoholic [ˌtʃɒkəˈhɒlɪk] Schokoladensüchtige(r) OT 3

chocolate [ˈtʃɒklət] Schokolade OT 1

choice [tʃɔɪs] Wahl OT 1

choir [ˈkwaɪə] Chor OT 1

cholera [ˈkɒlərə] Cholera **WS 1**, 28

to **choose** [tʃuːz] auswählen OT 1

to **chop** [tʃɒp] schneiden OT 3

chopped [tʃɒpt] gehackt OT 2

chopstick [ˈtʃɒpstɪk] Essstäbchen OT 1

chore [tʃɔːr] Hausarbeit **WS 1**, 13

chorizo [tʃəˈriːzəʊ] Chorizo OT 2

chowder [ˈtʃaʊdə] dickflüssige Fischsuppe OT 3

Christmas [ˈkrɪsməs] Weihnachten OT 1

   Christmas market [ˈkrɪsməs ˈmɑːkɪt] Weihnachtsmarkt OT 2

church [tʃɜːtʃ] Kirche OT 1

cinema [ˈsɪnəmə] Kino OT 1

circle [ˈsɜːkl] Kreis OT 1

circuit [ˈsɜːkɪt] Schaltkreis **WS 3**, 95

to **circulate** [ˈsɜːkjəleɪt] kursieren; zirkulieren **WS 2**, 55

citation [saɪˈteɪʃn] Anführung (einer Quelle) OT 2

to **cite** [saɪt] anführen; zitieren OT 2

citizen [ˈsɪtɪzn] Einwohner(in) OT 3

city [ˈsɪti] Stadt OT 1

   inner city [ˌɪnə ˈsɪti] Innenstadt **WS 2**, 63

clan [klæn] Klan OT 3

to **clap** [klæp] klatschen OT 1

clarification [ˌklærəfɪˈkeɪʃn] Abklärung **WS 4**, 123

to **clarify** [ˈklærəfaɪ] etw. klären **WS 4**, 123

clarinet [ˌklærəˈnet] Klarinette OT 2

to **clash** [klæʃ] klirren; nicht zusammenpassen OT 2

class [klɑːs] Unterricht; Klasse OT 1

classic [ˈklæsɪk] klassisch OT 2

classical [ˈklæsɪkl] klassisch OT 2

classmate [ˈklɑːsmeɪt] Klassenkamerad(in) OT 3

classroom [ˈklɑːsruːm] Klassenzimmer OT 1

clause [klɔːz] Satzteil OT 2

   relative clause [relətɪv ˈklɔːz] Relativsatz OT 2

clay [kleɪ] Ton **WS 3**, 82

clean [kliːn] sauber OT 1

cleaner [ˈkliːnə] Reinigungsmittel OT 3

   cleaning wipe [ˈkliːnɪŋ waɪp] Reinigungstuch OT 2

to **clear** [klɪə] räumen **WS 4**, 123

clear [klɪə] klar OT 2

   clearly [ˈklɪəli] deutlich OT 3

clever [ˈklevə] intelligent OT 1

to **click on** [klɪk] anklicken OT 3

climate [ˈklaɪmət] Klima OT 2

to **climb** [klaɪm] klettern; steigen OT 1

climber [ˈklaɪmə] Kletterer(in) OT 2

climbing [ˈklaɪmɪŋ] Klettern; Bergsteigen OT 1

to **cling** [klɪŋ] (sich) an etw. klammern; an etw. festhalten OT 2

clip [klɪp] Klammer; Ausschnitt; Klipp OT 1

cloak [kləʊk] Umhang OT 1

clock [klɒk] Uhr OT 1

   alarm clock [ə'lɑːm klɒk] Wecker OT 2

close [kləʊz] nah **WS 3**, 94

closed [kləʊzd] geschlossen OT 1

closely ['kləʊsli] eng OT 3

closet ['klɒzɪt] kleine Kammer; Wandschrank OT 2

close-up ['kləʊsʌp] Großaufnahme **WS 4**, 128

cloth [klɒθ] Lappen OT 2

clothes [kləʊðz] Kleidung; Kleider OT 1

clothing ['kləʊðɪŋ] Kleidung OT 3

cloud [klaʊd] Wolke OT 1

cloudy ['klaʊdi] wolkig; bewölkt; trüb **WS 3**, 93

club [klʌb] Klub; Verein OT 1

clue [kluː] Hinweis OT 1

clumsy ['klʌmzi] ungeschickt OT 2

co-ed [ˌkəʊ'ed] gemischtgeschlechtlich OT 2

co-educational [ˌkəʊedjə'keɪʃənl] gemischtgeschlechtlich OT 2

to co-found [kəʊfaʊnd] mitbegründen **WS 1**, 25

coach [kəʊtʃ] Reisebus; Trainer(in) OT 1

coaching ['kəʊtʃɪŋ] Coaching **WS 3**, 85

coal [kəʊl] Kohle OT 2

coast [kəʊst] Küste OT 1

coastal ['kəʊstl] Küsten... OT 1

coastguard ['kəʊstgɑːd] Küstenwache OT 2

coat [kəʊt] Mantel OT 1

code [kəʊd] Verschlüsselung OT 1

coffee ['kɒfi] Kaffee OT 1

coin [kɔɪn] Münze OT 1

cola ['kəʊlə] Cola OT 1

cold [kəʊld] kalt OT 1

collar ['kɒlə] Halsband OT 2

colleague ['kɒliːg] Kollege; Kollegin; MItarbelter(In) **WS 3**, 83

to collect [kə'lekt] sammeln OT 1

collection [kə'lekʃn] Sammlung OT 2

college ['kɒlɪdʒ] Hochschule OT 2

colonial [kə'ləʊniəl] kolonial **WS 1**, 18

colonist ['kɒlənɪst] Kolonist(in) OT 3

colony ['kɒləni] Kolonie **WS 1**, 12

colour ['kʌlə] Farbe OT 1

coloured ['kʌləd] farbig; bunt OT 1

colourful ['kʌləfl] farbenfroh OT 3

column ['kɒləm] Säule; Spalte OT 1

comb [kəʊm] Kamm OT 2

combination [ˌkɒmbɪ'neɪʃn] Kombination; Verbindung OT 3

to combine [kəm'baɪn] kombinieren; mischen **WS 4**, 129

to come [kʌm] kommen OT 1

   to come first / second / third [kʌm 'fɜːst / sekənd / θɜːd] den ersten / zweiten / dritten Platz belegen OT 2

   Come in! [kʌm 'ɪn] Herein! OT 2

comfortable ['kʌmftəbl] bequem OT 1

comfy ['kʌmfi] gemütlich **WS 3**, 93

comic ['kɒmɪk] Comicheft OT 1

comma ['kɒmə] Komma OT 3

commander [kə'mɑːndə] Kommandant(in) **WS 3**, 93

commanding [kə'mɑːndɪŋ] befehlshabend OT 2

to commence [kə'mens] anfangen **WS 3**, 95

comment ['kɒment] Kommentar OT 1

to comment ['kɒment] kommentieren OT 3

commercial [kə'mɜːʃl] kommerziell **WS 1**, 22

to commit [kə'mɪt] begehen **WS 4**, 127

committee [kə'mɪti] Ausschuss; Komitee OT 2

common ['kɒmən] normal; gewöhnlich **WW**, 10

to communicate [kə'mjuːnɪkeɪt] kommunizieren; etw. vermitteln **WS 1**, 32

community [kə'mjuːnəti] Gemeinschaft OT 2

commuter [kə'mjuːtə] Pendler(in) OT 2

   commuter rail [kəˌmjuːtə 'reɪl] Pendlerbahn OT 2

company ['kʌmpəni] Firma; Unternehmen OT 1

comparative [kəm'pærətɪv] Komparativ OT 2

to compare [kəm'peə] vergleichen OT 1

comparison [kəm'pærɪsn] Vergleich OT 2

compass ['kʌmpəs] Kompass OT 2

to compete [kəm'piːt] mit jmdm. / etw. konkurrieren OT 2

competition [ˌkɒmpə'tɪʃn] Konkurrenz; Wettbewerb OT 1

competitive [kəm'petətɪv] konkurrenzorientiert OT 3

   competitively [kəm'petətɪvli] konkurrierend; wetteifernd **WS 2**, 55

competitor [kəm'petɪtə] Konkurrent(in); Mitbewerber(in) **WS 3**, 96

to complain [kəm'pleɪn] sich beschweren OT 3

complaint [kəm'pleɪnt] Beschwerde OT 2

to complete [kəm'pliːt] vervollständigen OT 1

completely [kəm'pliːtli] ganz OT 2

complicated ['kɒmplɪkeɪtɪd] kompliziert OT 2

to compose [kəm'pəʊz] komponieren OT 3

composer [kəm'pəʊzə] Komponist(in) OT 2

compost ['kɒmpɒst] Kompost OT 3

composting ['kɒmpɒstɪŋ] Kompostierungs- **WS 3**, 80

computer [kəm'pjuːtə] Computer; Rechner OT 1

   computer lab [kəm'pjuːtə ˌlæb] Computerraum OT 2

computerized [kəm'pjuːtəraɪzd] computerbasiert; computergesteuert **WS 2**, 59

con [kɒn] Nachteil OT 2

to concentrate ['kɒnsntreɪt] konzentrieren OT 3

concentration [ˌkɒnsn'treɪʃn] Konzentration **WS 2**, 62

concept ['kɒnsept] Konzept; Begriff **WS 4**, 118

concert ['kɒnsət] Konzert OT 1

to conclude [kən'kluːd] schließen (aus etw.); beenden **WS 1**, 17

conclusion [kən'kluːʒn] Schluss OT 3

condition [kən'dɪʃn] Bedingung OT 3

condor ['kɒndɔː] Kondor OT 3

to conduct [kən'dʌkt] durchführen OT 3

conference ['kɒnfərəns] Konferenz **WS 1**, 13

   video conferencing ['vɪdiəʊ 'kɒnfərənsɪŋ] Videokonferenztechnik **WS 3**, 78

   web conference [web 'kɒnfərəns] Webkonferenz **WS 1**, 13

confident ['kɒnfɪdənt] selbstbewusst; zuversichtlich OT 2

   confidently ['kɒnfɪdəntli] selbstbewusst; zuversichtlich OT 2

to confirm [kən'fɜːm] bestätigen **WS 4**, 123

conflict ['kɒnflɪkt] Konflikt OT 2

confused [kən'fjuːzd] verwirrt OT 2

confusing [kən'fjuːzɪŋ] verwirrend OT 2

to congratulate [kən'grætʃuleɪt] gratulieren OT 2

congratulations [kənˌgrætʃu'leɪʃnz] Glückwünsche OT 2

to connect [kə'nekt] verbinden OT 2

connection [kə'nekʃn] Verbindung OT 2

consequence [ˈkɒnsɪkwəns] Folge; Konsequenz **WS 3**, 90

conservation [ˌkɒnsəˈveɪʃn] Schutz; Erhaltung OT 2

construction [kənˈstrʌkʃn] Bau **WS 1**, 31

contact [ˈkɒntækt] Kontakt OT 1
   to **be in contact with** [bi ɪn ˈkɒntækt wɪð] in Kontakt mit jmdm. sein OT 2

to **contain** [kənˈteɪn] beinhalten; enthalten OT 3

container [kənˈteɪnə] Behälter; Container OT 2

contemporary [kənˈtemprəri] zeitgenössisch OT 3

content [ˈkɒntents] Inhalt OT 2

context [ˈkɒntekst] Kontext; Zusammenhang **WS 4**, 127

continent [ˈkɒntɪnənt] Kontinent OT 3

to **continue** [kənˈtɪnjuː] andauern; weitermachen OT 1

contrast [ˈkɒntrɑːst] Gegenteil; Kontrast OT 3

contrasting [kənˈtrɑːstɪŋ] gegensätzlich **WS 1**, 33

to **contribute** [kənˈtrɪbjuːt] mitwirken **WS 1**, 24

contribution [ˌkɒntrɪˈbjuːʃn] Beitrag; Mitwirkung **WS 1**, 24

control [kənˈtrəʊl] Kontrolle OT 3

to **control** [kənˈtrəʊl] kontrollieren **WS 3**, 78

convenience [kənˈviːniəns] Bequemlichkeit; zweckmäßiges Gerät **WS 3**, 80

convenient [kənˈviːniənt] günstig; praktisch **WS 2**, 50

convention [kənˈvenʃn] Kongress; Konvention **WS 4**, 124

conversation [ˌkɒnvəˈseɪʃn] Gespräch OT 1

to **convince** [kənˈvɪns] überzeugen; überreden **WS 3**, 81

to **cook** [kʊk] kochen OT 1

cooker [ˈkʊkə] Herd OT 3

cookie [ˈkʊki] Keks OT 3

cooking [ˈkʊkɪŋ] Kochen OT 1

to **cool** [kuːl] kühlen OT 3

cooling [kuːlɪŋ] Kühl... OT 3

coop [kuːp] Hühnerstall **WS 3**, 80

copper [ˈkɒpə] Kupfer OT 1

to **copy** [ˈkɒpi] kopieren OT 1

core [kɔː] Kern; Haupt... **WS 3**, 80

corn [kɔːn] Mais OT 3

cornbread [ˈkɔːnbred] Maisbrot **WS 1**, 20

corner [ˈkɔːnə] Ecke OT 1

corporation [ˌkɔːpəˈreɪʃn] Unternehmen **WS 3**, 83

correct [kəˈrekt] richtig OT 1

correction [kəˈrekʃn] Korrektur **WS 4**, 119

correspondence [ˌkɒrəˈspɒndəns] Schriftverkehr **WS 3**, 94

corridor [ˈkɒrɪdɔː] Korridor OT 2

cost [kɒst] Kosten OT 1

to **cost** [kɒst] kosten OT 1

costume [ˈkɒstjuːm] Kostüm OT 2

cottage [ˈkɒtɪdʒ] Häuschen OT 3

cotton [ˈkɒtn] Baumwolle **WS 1**, 12

to **cough** [kɒf] husten OT 2

council [ˈkaʊnsl] Rat OT 3

counsellor [ˈkaʊnsələ] Jugendbetreuer(in); Berater(in); psychologischer Betreuer OT 2

to **count** [kaʊnt] zählen OT 1

countable [ˈkaʊntəbl] zählbar OT 1

countdown [ˈkaʊntdaʊn] Countdown **WS 3**, 95

counter [ˈkaʊntə] Theke OT 3

country [ˈkʌntri] Land OT 1
   country dancing [ˈkʌntri ˈdɑːnsɪŋ] Volkstanz OT 1

countryside [ˈkʌntrisaɪd] Land OT 1

couple [ˈkʌpl] Paar OT 2

coupon [ˈkuːpɒn] Gutschein OT 2

course [kɔːs] Kurs; Gang OT 1

court [kɔːt] Hof; Platz OT 3

courtyard [ˈkɔːtjɑːd] Hof; Innenhof OT 3

cousin [ˈkʌzn] Cousin(e) OT 1

cover [ˈkʌvə] Abdeckung; Hülle OT 1

to **cover** [ˈkʌvə] abdecken OT 2

cow [kaʊ] Kuh OT 1

cowboy word [ˈkaʊbɔɪ wɜːd] Wort, das im Englischen und Deutschen gleich ist OT 2

cozy [ˈkəʊzi] gemütlich OT 3

cracker [ˈkrækə] Cracker OT 3

cramp [kræmp] Krampf OT 2

cramped [kræmpt] beengt OT 3

cranberry [ˈkrænbəri] Cranberry; Moosbeere **WS 1**, 21

crane [kreɪn] Kran **WS 3**, 94

to **crash** [kræʃ] krachen OT 3

crate [kreɪt] Kiste **WS 1**, 18

crazy [ˈkreɪzi] verrückt OT 2

cream [kriːm] Sahne OT 1

to **create** [kriˈeɪt] schaffen; kreieren OT 2

creative [kriˈeɪtɪv] kreativ OT 2

creativity [ˌkriːeɪˈtɪvəti] Kreativität **WS 4**, 113

creature [ˈkriːtʃə] Lebewesen; Wesen **WS 4**, 111

credit card [ˈkredɪt kɑːd] Kreditkarte OT 1

creek [kriːk] Bach OT 3

creepy-crawly [ˌkriːpiˈkrɔːli] Krabbeltier OT 2

crescent [ˈkresnt] Sichel; sichelförmige Bauform OT 2

crew [kruː] Mannschaft; Personal OT 2

crewed [kruːd] bemannt **WS 3**, 94

cricket [ˈkrɪkɪt] Kricket OT 1

crime [kraɪm] Verbrechen **WS 2**, 49

criminal [ˈkrɪmɪnl] Kriminelle(r) OT 3

crisis [ˈkraɪsɪs] Krise OT 3

crisp [krɪsp] Chip OT 1

to **criticize** [ˈkrɪtɪsaɪz] kritisieren OT 3

crop [krɒp] Ernte; Getreide **WS 1**, 19

to **cross** [krɒs] überqueren; kreuzen OT 1
   to **cross out** [krɒs aʊt] ausstreichen OT 1

cross-country [ˌkrɒs ˈkʌntri] querfeldein OT 2

crossly [ˈkrɒsli] mürrisch OT 3

crossroads [ˈkrɒsrəʊdz] Kreuzung OT 1

crowd [kraʊd] Menge; Menschenmenge OT 1

crowded [ˈkraʊdɪd] überfüllt OT 2

crown [kraʊn] Krone OT 1

to **crown** [kraʊn] krönen OT 1

cruise [kruːz] Kreuzfahrt OT 2

to **cruise** [kruːz] mit dem Boot fahren; eine Kreuzfahrt machen OT 3

crush: to have a crush on [həv ə krʌʃ ɒn] in jmdn. verknallt sein **WS 2**, 47

crutch [krʌtʃ] Krücke OT 2

to **cry** [kraɪ] weinen OT 1

cuddly [ˈkʌdli] kuschelig; knuddelig OT 1

cue card [ˈkjuː kɑːd] Karteikarte **WS 3**, 96

cuisine [kwɪˈziːn] Küche OT 3

to **cultivate** [ˈkʌltɪveɪt] anbauen; bebauen **WS 2**, 63

cultural [ˈkʌltʃərəl] kulturell OT 3

culture [ˈkʌltʃə] Kultur OT 1

cultured [ˈkʌltʃəd] gebildet; kultiviert **WS 2**, 73

Cumbrian [ˈkʌmbriən] von / aus Cumbria OT 2

cup [kʌp] Tasse OT 1

cupboard [ˈkʌbəd] Schrank OT 1

cupola [ˈkjuːpələ] Kuppel **WS 3**, 93

to **cure** [kjʊə] heilen **WS 3**, 79

curfew [ˈkɜːfjuː] Ausgangssperre OT 3

curiosity [ˌkjʊəri'ɒsəti] Neugier
WS 3, 94

curious ['kjʊəriəs] neugierig; gespannt
WS 1, 29

curly ['kɜːli] gelockt OT 3

current ['kʌrənt] aktuell **WS 1**, 26

curry ['kʌri] Currygericht OT 1

curried ['kʌrid] mit Curry gewürzt OT 1

cursor ['kɜːsə] Mauszeiger OT 3

curtain ['kɜːtn] Vorhang OT 2

cushion ['kʊʃn] Kissen OT 1

custard ['kʌstəd] Vanillesoße OT 1

customer ['kʌstəmə] Kunde(-in) OT 3

customs ['kʌstəmz] Zoll OT 2

to **cut** [kʌt] schneiden OT 2

cute [kjuːt] niedlich OT 1

cutlery ['kʌtləri] Besteck OT 3

cyber bullying ['saɪbəbʊliŋ]
Cybermobbing **WS 3**, 86

cyber security ['saɪbə sɪ'kjʊərəti]
Cybersicherheit; Netzsicherheit
WS 4, 113

to **cycle** ['saɪkl] mit dem Fahrrad fahren
OT 1

cyclist ['saɪklɪst] Radfahrer(in) OT 3

D

dad [dæd] Papa OT 1

daily ['deɪli] täglich OT 2

to **damage** ['dæmɪdʒ] beschädigen;
schaden OT 2

dance [dɑːns] Tanz OT 1

dancer ['dɑːnsə] Tänzer(in) OT 3

dancing ['dɑːnsɪŋ] Tanzen OT 1

danger ['deɪndʒə] Gefahr OT 2

dangerous ['deɪndʒərəs] gefährlich
OT 1

to **dare** [deə] wagen; sich trauen OT 2

dark [dɑːk] dunkel OT 1

data ['deɪtə] Daten OT 3

date [deɪt] Datum OT 2

daughter ['dɔːtə] Tochter OT 1

dawn [dɔːn] Morgendämmerung
WS 1, 20

day [deɪ] Tag OT 1

day out [deɪ 'aʊt] Tagesausflug OT 2

day trip ['deɪ trɪp] Tagesausflug OT 2

daytime ['deɪtaɪm] Tageszeit OT 1

dead [ded] tot OT 1

deal [diːl] Geschäft; Deal **WS 2**, 52

to **deal with** [diːl wɪð] umgehen OT 2

dear [dɪə] liebe(r, -s) OT 1

death [deθ] Tod OT 2

date of death [deɪt əv 'deθ]
Todesdatum OT 2

debate [dɪ'beɪt] Debatte OT 3

debating club [dɪ'beɪtɪŋ klʌb]
Debattierklub **WS 2**, 53

debt [det] Schuld **WS 4**, 125

December [dɪ'sembə] Dezember OT 1

to **decide** [dɪ'saɪd] entscheiden OT 1

decision [dɪ'sɪʒn] Entscheidung OT 1

declaration [ˌdeklə'reɪʃn] Erklärung
WS 4, 137

to **declare** [dɪ'kleə] ausrufen;
verkünden **WS 1**, 39

to **decorate** ['dekəreɪt] dekorieren;
schmücken **WS 2**, 58

decorator ['dekəreɪtə] Dekorateur(in)
OT 3

deep [diːp] tief OT 1

default [dɪ'fɔːlt] Standard OT 3

to **defend** [dɪ'fend] verteidigen OT 3

defender [dɪ'fendə] Verteidiger(in) OT 3

to **define** [dɪ'faɪn] definieren;
bestimmen **WS 2**, 44

definite ['defɪnət] eindeutig; bestimmt
OT 1

definitely ['defɪnətli] eindeutig;
bestimmt; definitiv OT 1

definition [ˌdefɪ'nɪʃn] Definition OT 1

degree [dɪ'griː] Grad; Abschluss
WS 3, 94

dehydrated [ˌdiːhaɪ'dreɪtɪd] dehydriert
OT 2

to **delegate** ['delɪgət] delegieren;
beauftragen **WS 4**, 111

to **delete** [dɪ'liːt] löschen **WS 4**, 129

delicacy ['delɪkəsi] Delikatesse OT 3

delicious [dɪ'lɪʃəs] lecker OT 1

delighted [dɪ'laɪtɪd] entzückt; erfreut
OT 3

to **deliver** [dɪ'lɪvə] liefern **WS 3**, 78

delivery [dɪ'lɪvəri] Ausführung;
Lieferung OT 3

demand [dɪ'mɑːnd] Nachfrage
WS 4, 113

to **demand** [dɪ'mɑːnd] fordern;
verlangen **WS 3**, 91

democratic [ˌdemə'krætɪk]
demokratisch **WS 2**, 59

to **demonstrate** ['demənstreɪt]
vorführen; zeigen **WS 3**, 96

demonstration [ˌdemən'streɪʃn]
Demonstration **WS 3**, 88

demonstrative [dɪ'mɒnstrətɪv]
Demonstrativbegleiter OT 1

denim ['denɪm] Denim; Jeansstoff
WS 1, 25

density ['densəti] Dichte **WS 3**, 93

departure [dɪ'pɑːtʃə] Abfahrt; Abflug
OT 2

departure gate [dɪ'pɑːtʃə ˌgeɪt]
Abfluggate OT 2

to **depend** [dɪ'pend] (sich) verlassen
(auf); abhängen (von) OT 2

to **deport** [dɪ'pɔːt] ausweisen;
deportieren **WS 1**, 26

depressed [dɪ'prest] deprimiert **WS 2**, 62

depressing [dɪ'presɪŋ] deprimierend
WS 2, 49

depression [dɪ'preʃn] Depression
WS 3, 87

descendant [dɪ'sendənt] Nachkomme
WS 1, 18

to **describe** [dɪ'skraɪb] beschreiben OT 1

description [dɪ'skrɪpʃn] Beschreibung
OT 2

desert ['dezət] Wüste OT 3

to **deserve** [dɪ'zɜːv] verdienen OT 2

design [dɪ'zaɪn] Entwurf; Design OT 1

to **design** [dɪ'zaɪn] entwerfen OT 3

designer [dɪ'zaɪnə] Designer(in) OT 3

desk [desk] Schreibtisch OT 1

desktop ['desktɒp] Desktop;
Benutzeroberfläche **WS 4**, 129

desperately ['despərətli] verzweifelt
OT 3

dessert [dɪ'zɜːt] Nachtisch OT 1

destination [ˌdestɪ'neɪʃn] Reiseziel
WS 1, 27

to **destroy** [dɪ'strɔɪ] zerstören OT 2

detail ['diːteɪl] Detail OT 2

detailed ['diːteɪld] detailliert; genau
OT 3

determined [dɪ'tɜːmɪnd] entschlossen
OT 3

determiner [dɪ'tɜːmɪnə]
Bestimmungswort OT 1

detox ['diːtɒks] Entzugsprogramm OT 2

deuce [djuːs] Einstand OT 3

to **develop** [dɪ'veləp] entwickeln OT 2

development [dɪ'veləpmənt]
Entwicklung **WS 2**, 63

device [dɪ'vaɪs] Gerät OT 3

to **diagnose** ['daɪəgnəʊz]
diagnostizieren **WS 4**, 113

diagram ['daɪəgræm] Schaubild;
Diagramm OT 3

to **dial** ['daɪəl] wählen OT 2

dialogue ['daɪəlɒg] Dialog OT 1

diary ['daɪəri] Terminkalender;
Tagebuch OT 1

dictionary ['dɪkʃənri] Wörterbuch OT 1

to **die** [daɪ] sterben OT 1

diesel ['diːzl] Diesel OT 3

diet ['daɪət] Diät OT 3

difference ['dɪfrəns] Unterschied OT 1

different [ˈdɪfrənt] unterschiedlich OT 1

difficult [ˈdɪfɪkəlt] schwer; schwierig OT 1

difficulty [ˈdɪfɪkəlti] Schwierigkeit **WS 1**, 26

to **dig** [dɪg] graben OT 1

digit [ˈdɪdʒɪt] Ziffer OT 2

digital [ˈdɪdʒɪtl] digital OT 3

dilemma [dɪˈlemə] Dilemma **WS 4**, 122

dim [dɪm] trüb; schwach **WS 4**, 119

dimension [daɪˈmenʃn] Abmessung OT 2

dining room [ˈdaɪnɪŋ ruːm] Esszimmer OT 1

dinner [ˈdɪnə] Abendessen OT 1

dinosaur [ˈdaɪnəsɔː] Dinosaurier OT 1

to **dip** [dɪp] tauchen **WS 3**, 84

direct [dəˈrekt] direkt OT 3

direction [dəˈrekʃn] Anweisung; Richtung OT 3

director [dəˈrektə] Leiter(in) **WS 2**, 46

dirt [dɜːt] Dreck; Schmutz **WS 4**, 124

dirty [ˈdɜːti] schmutzig OT 1

disability [ˌdɪsəˈbɪləti] Behinderung OT 2

disadvantage [ˌdɪsədˈvɑːntɪdʒ] Nachteil OT 3

to **disagree** [ˌdɪsəˈgriː] anderer Meinung sein OT 2

disagreement [ˌdɪsəˈgriːmənt] Meinungsverschiedenheit OT 2

to **disappear** [ˌdɪsəˈpɪə] verschwinden OT 3

disappointed [ˌdɪsəˈpɔɪntɪd] enttäuscht OT 2

disappointingly [ˌdɪsəˈpɔɪntɪŋli] enttäuschend OT 3

disaster [dɪˈzɑːstə] Katastrophe OT 2

disaster area [dɪˈzɑːstər eərɪə] Katastrophengebiet OT 2

to **discover** [dɪˈskʌvə] entdecken OT 3

discovery [dɪˈskʌvəri] Entdeckung **WS 3**, 77

to **discuss** [dɪˈskʌs] besprechen OT 1

discussion [dɪˈskʌʃn] Besprechung; Diskussion OT 1

disease [dɪˈziːz] Krankheit OT 2

disgusting [dɪsˈgʌstɪŋ] ekelhaft OT 3

dish [dɪʃ] Gericht; Schale OT 2

dishes [ˈdɪʃɪz] Geschirr OT 2

to **do the dishes** [ˌduː ðə ˈdɪʃɪz] den Abwasch machen OT 2

dishwasher [ˈdɪʃwɒʃər] Geschirrspülmaschine **WS 1**, 15

to **dislike** [dɪsˈlaɪk] nicht mögen OT 3

disorganized [dɪsˈɔːgənaɪzd] chaotisch OT 2

display [dɪˈspleɪ] Ausstellung OT 3

disrespectful [ˌdɪsrɪˈspektfl] respektlos OT 3

distance [ˈdɪstəns] Entfernung OT 2

to **distribute** [dɪˈstrɪbjuːt] verteilen **WS 3**, 84

district [ˈdɪstrɪkt] Bezirk; Gegend OT 1

ditto [ˈdɪtəʊ] ditto; ebenfalls **WS 4**, 128

to **dive** [daɪv] tauchen OT 1

diverse [daɪˈvɜːs] vielfältig; verschieden **WS 2**, 73

diversity [daɪˈvɜːsəti] Vielfältigkeit **WS 1**, 26

to **divide** [dɪˈvaɪd] teilen OT 2

divided [dɪˈvaɪdɪd] getrennt; unterteilt OT 2

divorce [dɪˈvɔːs] Scheidung OT 3

to **do** [duː] tun; machen OT 1

to **do something about something** [ˌduː sʌmˈθɪŋ əˌbaʊt sʌmˈθɪŋ] etw. gegen etw. tun OT 2

dockyard [ˈdɒkjɑːd] Werft OT 3

doctor [ˈdɒktə] Arzt; Ärztin OT 1

document [ˈdɒkjumənt] Dokument **WS 1**, 26

documentary [ˌdɒkjuˈmentri] Dokumentation OT 2

dog [dɔːg] Hund OT 1

dog mess [ˈdɒg mes] Hundedreck OT 2

guide dog [ˈgaɪd dɒg] Blindenführhund OT 2

hot dog [ˈhɒt dɒg] Hotdog OT 2

service dog [ˈsɜːvɪs dɒg] Assistenzhund OT 2

doll [dɒl] Puppe OT 3

dollar [ˈdɒlə] Dollar OT 1

dolphin [ˈdɒlfɪn] Delfin OT 1

to **donate** [dəʊˈneɪt] spenden OT 2

donation [dəʊˈneɪʃn] Spende OT 2

to **make a donation** [ˌmeɪk ə dəʊˈneɪʃn] spenden OT 2

door [dɔː] Tür OT 1

doorbell [ˈdɔːbel] Klingel OT 2

doorstep [ˈdɔːstep] direkt vor Ort; quasi vor der Haustür **WS 4**, 123

double [ˈdʌbl] doppelt; Doppel... OT 1

double bass [ˌdʌbl ˈbeɪs] Kontrabass OT 2

doubles [ˈdʌblz] Doppel OT 3

doubt [daʊt] Zweifel **WS 3**, 95

dough [dəʊ] Knete; Teig OT 2

doughnut [ˈdəʊnʌt] Krapfen OT 2

down [daʊn] hinunter OT 1

downside [ˈdaʊnsaɪd] Nachteil OT 3

to **downsize** [ˈdaʊnsaɪz] reduzieren; sich einschränken OT 3

downstairs [ˈdaʊnsteəz] unten; im unteren Stockwerk OT 1

downtown [ˌdaʊnˈtaʊn] Innenstadt **WS 2**, 60

dozen [ˈdʌzn] Dutzend **WS 4**, 124

draft [drɑːft] Entwurf OT 2

dragon [ˈdrægən] Drache OT 1

to **drain** [dreɪn] abgießen OT 2

drained [dreɪnd] abgetropft OT 2

drama [ˈdrɑːmə] Drama OT 1

draughts [drɑːfts] Damespiel OT 1

to **draw** [drɔː] ziehen; zeichnen OT 1

drawer [drɔː] Schublade OT 3

drawing [ˈdrɔːɪŋ] Zeichen; Zeichnung OT 1

dream [driːm] Traum OT 1

to **dream** [driːm] träumen **WS 1**, 12

dreamer [ˈdriːmə] Träumer(in) OT 2

dress [dres] Kleid OT 3

dress code [ˈdres kəʊd] Kleiderordnung; Dresscode **WS 2**, 59

to **dress up** [dres ʌp] (sich) verkleiden OT 2

to **drill** [drɪl] bohren **WS 3**, 94

drink [drɪŋk] Getränk OT 1

to **drink** [drɪŋk] trinken OT 1

to **drip** [drɪp] tropfen OT 3

to **drive** [draɪv] fahren OT 1

driver [ˈdraɪvə] Fahrer(in) OT 1

driver's license [ˈdraɪvəz laɪsns] Führerschein; Fahrerlaubnis **WS 2**, 60

driverless [ˈdraɪvələs] führerlos **WS 3**, 105

driving licence [ˈdraɪvɪŋ laɪsns] Führerschein OT 2

drone [drəʊn] Drohne OT 3

to **drop** [drɒp] fallen lassen OT 1

to **drown** [draʊn] ertrinken OT 3

drug [drʌg] Droge OT 3

drugstore [ˈdrʌgstɔː] Apotheke; Drogerie OT 2

drums [drʌmz] Schlagzeug OT 1

dry [draɪ] trocken OT 2

duck [dʌk] Ente OT 2

dumpling [ˈdʌmplɪŋ] Kloß; Knödel **WS 1**, 26

during [ˈdjʊərɪŋ] während OT 2

duty free [ˌdjuːti ˈfriː] zollfrei OT 2

dweller [ˈdwelə] Bewohner(in) **WS 2**, 62

dye [daɪ] Färbemittel; Farbe **WS 2**, 52

E

each [iːtʃ] jede(r,-s) OT 1

eager [ˈiːgə] eifrig OT 2

eagle [ˈiːgl] Adler OT 2

ear [ɪə] Ohr OT 1

early [ˈɜːli] früh OT 1

to **earn** [ɜːn] verdienen OT 3

Earth [ɜːθ] Erde OT 2

earthquake [ˈɜːθkweɪk] Erdbeben OT 2

east [iːst] Ost- OT 1

Easter [ˈiːstər] Ostern OT 1

eastern [ˈiːstən] östlich OT 2

easy [ˈiːzi] einfach OT 1

  easily [ˈiːzəli] leicht OT 2

to **eat** [iːt] essen OT 1

eco-friendly [ˌiːkəʊ ˈfrendli] ökologisch OT 3

e-commerce [ˈiː kɒmɜːs] E-Commerce; Internethandel **WS 2**, 54

economic [ˌiːkəˈnɒmɪk] wirtschaftlich **WS 3**, 88

economy [ɪˈkɒnəmi] Wirtschaft; Ökonomie OT 3

ecotourism [ˈiːkəʊtʊərɪzəm] Ökotourismus OT 3

edge [edʒ] Rand OT 3

to **edit** [ˈedɪt] überarbeiten; redigieren OT 3

editor [ˈedɪtə] Redakteur(in); Herausgeber(in) OT 2

education [ˌedjʊˈkeɪʃən] Ausbildung OT 3

educational [ˌedʒuˈkeɪʃənl] Bildungs… OT 3

educator [ˈedʒukeɪtə] Pädagoge; Pädagogin **WS 4**, 125

eel [iːl] Aal **WS 1**, 20

effect [ɪˈfekt] Wirkung OT 3

effectively [ɪˈfektɪvli] wirksam **WS 3**, 86

efficient [ɪˈfɪʃnt] effizient **WS 3**, 84

  efficiently [ɪˈfɪʃntli] effizient OT 3

egg [eg] Ei OT 1

eggplant [ˈegplɑːnt] Aubergine OT 2

eight [eɪt] acht OT 1

eighteen [ˌeɪˈtiːn] achtzehn OT 1

eighty [ˈeɪti] achtzig OT 1

either [ˈaɪðə] auch nicht OT 1

elbow [ˈelbəʊ] Ellbogen OT 1

elderly [ˈeldəli] älter **WS 2**, 62

to **elect** [ɪˈlekt] wählen; auswählen **WS 2**, 58

election [ɪˈlekʃn] Wahl OT 3

elective [ɪˈlektɪv] Auswahlfach **WS 2**, 57

electric [ɪˈlektrɪk] elektrisch OT 1

electrical [ɪˈlektrɪkl] elektrisch **WS 1**, 41

electricity [ɪˌlekˈtrɪsəti] Strom OT 2

electronically [ɪˌlekˈtrɒnɪkli] elektronisch **WS 3**, 78

electronics [ɪˌlekˈtrɒnɪks] Elektronik OT 2

element [ˈelɪmənt] Bestandteil OT 2

  elementary school [ˌelɪˈmentri skuːl] Grundschule OT 2

elementary [ˌelɪˈmentri] Grund-; elementar OT 2

elephant [ˈelɪfənt] Elefant OT 1

eleven [ɪˈlevn] elf OT 1

elite sports [eɪˈliːt spɔːts] Spitzensport OT 3

else [els] sonst noch OT 1

email [ˈiːmeɪl] E-Mail OT 1

to **email** [ˈiːmeɪl] eine E-Mail schreiben OT 2

embarrassed [ɪmˈbærəst] verlegen; peinlich berührt OT 3

embarrassing [ɪmˈbærəsɪŋ] peinlich OT 2

emergency [ɪˈmɜːdʒənsi] Notfall OT 1

  emergency services [ɪˈmɜːdʒənsi ˌsɜːvɪsɪz] Rettungsdienste OT 2

emigrant [ˈemɪgrənt] Auswanderer; Auswanderin OT 3

to **emigrate** [ˈemɪgreɪt] auswandern **WS 1**, 18

emission [ɪˈmɪʃn] Ausstoss; Emission OT 3

emoji [ɪˈməʊdʒi] Emoji OT 3

emotion [ɪˈməʊʃn] Gefühl OT 3

employee [ɪmˈplɔɪiː] Angestellte(r) **WS 1**, 24

employer [ɪmˈplɔɪə] Arbeitgeber(in) OT 3

empty [ˈempti] leer OT 1

to **empty** [ˈempti] entleeren; leeren **WS 1**, 15

to **encourage** [ɪnˈkʌrɪdʒ] ermutigen OT 2

end [end] Ende OT 1

to **end** [end] enden OT 1

endangered [ɪnˈdeɪndʒəd] gefährdet OT 2

ending [ˈendɪŋ] Ende; Endung OT 2

endless [ˈendləs] endlos; unendlich **WS 1**, 12

endzone [ˈendzəʊn] Endzone OT 3

enemy [ˈenəmi] Feind OT 1

energetic [ˌenəˈdʒetɪk] aktiv; energisch OT 2

energy [ˈenədʒi] Energie OT 2

to **enforce** [ɪnˈfɔːs] durchsetzen **WS 4**, 126

to **engage** [ɪnˈgeɪdʒ] (sich) beschäftigen **WS 2**, 48

engine [ˈendʒɪn] Motor; Lokomotive OT 2

engineer [ˌendʒɪˈnɪə] Ingenieur(in); Lokführer(in) OT 3

engineering [ˌendʒɪˈnɪərɪŋ] Ingenieurwesen OT 1

English [ˈɪŋglɪʃ] englisch OT 1

to **engrave** [ɪnˈgreɪv] gravieren; eingravieren **WS 1**, 29

to **enjoy** [ɪnˈdʒɔɪ] genießen OT 1

enjoyable [ɪnˈdʒɔɪəbl] angenehm OT 2

enormous [ɪˈnɔːməs] riesig OT 1

enough [ɪˈnʌf] genug OT 1

to **ensure** [ɪnˈʃʊə] sicherstellen **WS 4**, 111

to **enter** [ˈentə] eintreten; eintragen OT 2

to **entertain** [ˌentəˈteɪn] unterhalten **WS 3**, 78

entertainer [ˌentəˈteɪnə] Künstler(in); Unterhalter(in) OT 3

entertaining [ˌentəˈteɪnɪŋ] unterhaltsam; amüsant OT 3

entertainment [ˌentəˈteɪnmənt] Unterhaltung OT 3

enthusiastic [ɪnˌθjuːziˈæstɪk] begeistert OT 3

entire [ɪnˈtaɪə] ganze(r, -s) OT 3

entrance [ˈentrəns] Eingang OT 1

  entrance hall [ˈentrəns ˌhɔːl] Eingangsbereich; Eingangshalle OT 1

entry [ˈentri] Eintrag; Einsendung OT 2

envelope [ˈenvələʊp] Briefumschlag OT 2

environment [ɪnˈvaɪrənmənt] Umfeld; Umwelt OT 2

environmental [ɪnˌvaɪrənˈmentl] Umwelt-; ökologisch OT 2

  environmentally [ɪnˌvaɪrənˈmentəli] umwelt… OT 3

environmentalist [ɪnˌvaɪrənˈmentəlɪst] Umweltschützer(in) OT 3

epidemic [ˌepɪˈdemɪk] Epidemie **WS 1**, 21

equal [ˈiːkwəl] gleich; gleichberechtigt **WS 4**, 127

equipment [ɪˈkwɪpmənt] Ausrüstung OT 2

  safety equipment [ˌseɪfti ɪˈkwɪpmənt] Sicherheitsausrüstung OT 2

equivalent [ɪˈkwɪvələnt] entsprechend **WS 2**, 56

era [ˈɪərə] Ära **WS 3**, 83

to **eradicate** [ɪˈrædɪkeɪt] ausmerzen; ausrotten **WS 4**, 127

to **escape** [ɪˈskeɪp] entkommen OT 2

escort [ˈeskɔːt] Begleiter(in) OT 3

especially [ɪˈspeʃəli] besonders OT 2

essay [ˈeseɪ] Aufsatz OT 2

essential [ɪˈsenʃl] wichtig; wesentlich **WS 3**, 93

to **establish** [ɪˈstæblɪʃ] begründen **WS 3**, 94

ETA (estimated time of arrival) [ˈestɪmeɪtɪd taɪm əv əˈraɪvl] geschätzte Ankunftszeit OT 2

etc. (et cetera) [ˌet ˈsetərə] und so weiter; usw. OT 1

eternal [ɪˈtɜːnl] ewig **WS 3**, 95

ethical [ˈeθɪkl] ethisch; moralisch vertretbar OT 3

etiquette [ˈetɪkət] Etikette OT 3

eureka moment [juˈriːkə ˈməʊmənt] Heureka-Erlebnis **WS 3**, 82

European [jʊərəˈpiːən] europäisch OT 3

to **evaluate** [ɪˈvæljueɪt] bewerten **WS 1**, 23

even [ˈiːvn] sogar OT 1

evening [ˈiːvnɪŋ] Abend OT 1

evenly [ˈiːvnli] ausgeglichen **WS 2**, 62

event [ɪˈvent] Ereignis OT 1

eventually [ɪˈventʃuəli] schließlich OT 3

ever [ˈevə] je OT 1

every [ˈevri] jede(r,-s) OT 1

everybody [ˈevrɪbɒdi] jeder; alle OT 1

everyday [ˈevrideɪ] alltäglich OT 3

everyone [ˈevriwʌn] jeder OT 1

everything [ˈevriθɪŋ] alles OT 1

everywhere [ˈevriweə] überall OT 1

to **evolve** [ɪˈvɒlv] (sich) entwickeln **WS 1**, 30

exact [ɪgˈzækt] genau OT 2

to **exaggerate** [ɪgˈzædʒəreɪt] übertreiben **WS 3**, 103

exam [ɪgˈzæm] Prüfung OT 1

example [ɪgˈzaːmpl] Beispiel OT 1

excellent [ˈeksələnt] ausgezeichnet OT 3

except [ɪkˈsept] außer OT 2

exchange [ɪksˈtʃeɪndʒ] Austausch OT 1

excited [ɪkˈsaɪtɪd] begeistert; aufgeregt OT 1

excitement [ɪkˈsaɪtmənt] Aufregung OT 3

exciting [ɪkˈsaɪtɪŋ] aufregend OT 1

to **excuse** [ɪkˈskjuːz] entschuldigen OT 1

to **execute** [ˈeksɪkjuːt] töten lassen; exekutieren OT 3

exercise [ˈeksəsaɪz] körperliche Bewegung; Übung OT 1

exercise book [ˈeksəsaɪz bʊk] Übungsheft OT 1

exhausted [ɪgˈzɔːstɪd] erschöpft OT 2

exhibit [ɪgˈzɪbɪt] Ausstellung OT 2

to **exhibit** [ɪgˈzɪbɪt] ausstellen OT 2

exhibition [ˌeksɪˈbɪʃn] Ausstellung OT 1

to **exist** [ɪgˈzɪst] existieren OT 3

exit [ˈeksɪt] Ausgang; Abfahrt OT 2

exotic [ɪgˈzɒtɪk] exotisch OT 2

to **expand** [ɪkˈspænd] erweitern; expandieren **WS 1**, 24

expanding [ɪkˈspænd] erweiternd OT 2

to **expect** [ɪkˈspekt] erwarten OT 2

expedition [ˌekspəˈdɪʃn] Expedition OT 2

expensive [ɪkˈspensɪv] teuer OT 1

experience [ɪkˈspɪəriəns] Erfahrung OT 2

experienced [ɪkˈspɪəriənst] erfahren OT 3

experiment [ɪkˈsperɪmənt] Experiment OT 1

to **experiment** [ɪkˈsperɪmənt] experimentieren **WS 4**, 129

expert [ˈekspɜːt] Experte(-in) OT 3

to **explain** [ɪkˈspleɪn] erklären OT 1

explanation [ˌekspləˈneɪʃn] Erklärung OT 1

to **exploit** [ɪkˈsplɔɪt] ausbeuten OT 3

exploitation [ˌeksplɔɪˈteɪʃn] Ausbeutung **WS 4**, 126

to **explore** [ɪkˈsplɔː] erforschen; erkunden OT 1

explorer [ɪkˈsplɔːrə] Forscher(in) OT 3

to **express** [ɪkˈspres] ausdrücken OT 3

expression [ɪkˈspreʃn] Ausdruck OT 1

facial expression [ˈfeɪʃl ɪksˈpreʃn] Gesichtsausdruck **WS 4**, 117

extinct [ɪkˈstɪŋkt] ausgestorben OT 2

extra [ˈekstrə] Extra... OT 1

extract [ɪkˈstrækt] Auszug **WS 1**, 32

extreme [ɪkˈstriːm] extrem OT 3

extremely [ɪkˈstriːmli] extrem OT 3

eye [aɪ] Auge OT 1

eyebrow [ˈaɪbraʊ] Augenbraue **WS 4**, 117

eyelid [ˈaɪlɪd] Augenlid OT 2

F

fabulous [ˈfæbjələs] fabelhaft OT 2

face [feɪs] Gesicht OT 1

face paint [ˈfeɪs peɪnt] Schminke OT 2

to **face** [feɪs] begegnen **WS 1**, 26

facility [fəˈsɪləti] Anlage **WS 1**, 30

fact [fækt] Tatsache; Fakt OT 1

factory [ˈfæktri] Fabrik **WS 2**, 52

factual [ˈfæktʃuəl] sachlich **WS 1**, 22

to **fade** [feɪd] verwelken; verblassen OT 2

to **fail** [feɪl] scheitern OT 2

failure [ˈfeɪljə] Misserfolg **WS 3**, 84

faint [feɪnt] schwindlig OT 2

fair [feə] Jahrmarkt **WS 1**, 20

fairground [ˈfeəgraʊnd] Jahrmarkt OT 2

fairy [ˈfeəri] Fee OT 2

fairy tale [ˈfeəri ˌteɪl] Märchen OT 1

to **fall** [fɔːl] fallen; stürzen OT 1

to **fall apart** [fɔːl əˈpaːt] auseinanderfallen **WS 2**, 53

to **fall asleep** [fɔːl əˈsliːp] einschlafen OT 2

to **fall over** [fɔːl ˈəʊvə] hinfallen; umfallen OT 2

falls [fɔːls] Wasserfall OT 1

false [fɔːls] falsch OT 1

false friend [ˌfɔːls ˈfrend] falscher Freund; Übersetzungsfalle OT 2

fame [feɪm] Ruhm; Ruf OT 3

familiar [fəˈmɪliə] vertraut; bekannt OT 2

family [ˈfæməli] Familie OT 1

famine [ˈfæmɪn] Hungersnot **WS 1**, 24

famous [ˈfeɪməs] berühmt OT 1

fan [fæn] Fan OT 1

fancy [ˈfænsi] schick; einfallsreich OT 2

fancy dress [ˌfænsi ˈdres] Kostüm- OT 2

fantastic [fænˈtæstɪk] fantastisch OT 1

fantasy [ˈfæntəsi] Fantasy; Fantasie OT 2

FAQ (frequently asked questions) [ˌef eɪ ˈkjuː] häufig gestellte Fragen OT 1

far [faː] weit OT 1

far-off [ˈfaː ɒf] fern OT 2

so far [səʊ ˈfaː] bisher OT 2

faraway [ˈfaːrəweɪ] fern **WS 2**, 53

farm [faːm] Bauernhof OT 1

farmer [ˈfaːmə] Bauer / Bäuerin OT 2

farmhand [ˈfaːmhænd] Erntehelfer(in); Landarbeiter(in) **WS 4**, 112

farmhouse [ˈfaːmhaʊs] Bauernhaus OT 3

farming [ˈfaːmɪŋ] Landwirtschaft OT 2

farmland [ˈfaːmlænd] Ackerland **WS 1**, 12

farmworker [faːmwɜːkə] Landarbeiter(in); Farmarbeiter(in) **WS 4**, 125

fascinating [ˈfæsɪneɪtɪŋ] faszinierend OT 3

fascination [ˌfæsɪˈneɪʃn] Faszination **WS 4**, 109

fashion [ˈfæʃn] Trend; Mode OT 1

fast [faːst] schnell OT 1

to **fasten** [ˈfaːsn] anschließen; festmachen OT 1

fat [fæt] Fett OT 2

father [ˈfɑːðə] Vater OT 1
faucet [ˈfɔːsɪt] Wasserhahn WS 3, 92
fault [fɔːlt] Fehler OT 2
faulty [ˈfɔːlti] defekt OT 2
favourite [ˈfeɪvərɪt] Lieblings... OT 1
fear [fɪə] Angst; Furcht OT 3
feast [fiːst] Fest; Festmahl WS 1, 18
feather [ˈfeðə] Feder OT 2
feature [ˈfiːtʃə] Sonderbeitrag; Eigenschaft; Merkmal OT 1
to feature [ˈfiːtʃə] aufweisen; präsentieren WS 1, 21
February [ˈfebruəri] Februar OT 1
fee [fiː] Gebühr OT 3
to feed [fiːd] füttern OT 2
feedback [ˈfiːdbæk] Feedback OT 1
feeding [ˈfiːdɪŋ] Füttern OT 2
to feel [fiːl] (sich) fühlen; fühlen; anfassen OT 1
feeling [ˈfiːlɪŋ] Gefühl OT 2
fell [fel] Berg (in Nordengland) OT 2
female [ˈfiːmeɪl] weiblich OT 2
ferris wheel [ˈferɪs wiːl] Riesenrad WS 2, 61
ferry [ˈferi] Fähre OT 2
fertilizer [ˈfɜːtəlaɪzə] Dünger OT 3
festival [ˈfestɪvl] Festival; Festspiele; Fest OT 1
festivity [feˈstɪvəti] Festlichkeit WS 2, 58
to fetch [fetʃ] holen; abholen WS 1, 20
few [fjuː] wenige OT 1
fiction [ˈfɪkʃn] Fiktion; Romanliteratur OT 2
fictional [ˈfɪkʃənl] erfunden OT 2
field [fiːld] Feld OT 1
fieldwork [ˈfiːldwɜːk] Geländearbeit WS 4, 134
fifteen [ˌfɪfˈtiːn] fünfzehn OT 1
fifth [fɪfθ] fünfte(r, -s) OT 1
fifty [ˈfɪfti] fünfzig OT 1
fight [faɪt] Kampf OT 1
figure [ˈfɪgə] Zahl; Figur OT 3
flle [faɪl] Datei OT 3
to fill [fɪl] füllen OT 2
film [fɪlm] Film OT 1
film director [fɪlm dəˈrektə] Regisseur(in) OT 2
filthy [ˈfɪlθi] dreckig WS 4, 124
final [ˈfaɪnl] endgültig OT 1
finally [ˈfaɪnəli] schließlich OT 1
to find [faɪnd] finden OT 1
to find out [ˈfaɪnd aʊt] herausfinden OT 1
finding [ˈfaɪndɪŋ] Ergebnis; Befund WS 1, 30

fine [faɪn] gut; prima OT 1
finger [ˈfɪŋgə] Finger OT 1
fingers crossed [ˈfɪŋgəz krɒst] Daumen gedrückt OT 1
fingernail [ˈfɪŋgəneɪl] Fingernagel OT 2
to finish [ˈfɪnɪʃ] abschließen; aufhören OT 1
fire [ˈfaɪə] Feuer OT 2
fire station [ˈfaɪə steɪʃn] Feuerwache OT 2
firefighter [ˈfaɪəfaɪtə] Feuerwehrmann / -frau OT 2
firefighting [ˌfaɪəˈfaɪtɪŋ] Brandbekämpfung OT 2
fireplace [ˈfaɪəpleɪs] Kamin OT 1
firewood [ˈfaɪəwʊd] Brennholz WS 1, 20
fireworks [ˈfaɪəwɜːks] Feuerwerk OT 3
firework display [ˈfaɪəwɜːk dɪˈspleɪ] Feuerwerk WS 1, 21
first [fɜːst] erste(r, -s) OT 1
first aid [ˌfɜːst ˈeɪd] Erste Hilfe OT 2
first aid kit [ˌfɜːst ˈeɪd kɪt] Verbandkasten; Erstehilfekasten OT 2
fish [fɪʃ] Fisch OT 1
fish finger [ˌfɪʃ ˈfɪŋgə] Fischstäbchen OT 1
fishing [ˈfɪʃɪŋ] Angeln OT 2
fit [fɪt] in Form; geeignet OT 2
fitness [ˈfɪtnəs] Fitness OT 2
five [faɪv] fünf OT 1
to fix [fɪks] korrigieren OT 2
fizzy [ˈfɪzi] kohlensäurehaltig OT 2
flag [flæg] Fahne OT 1
flagship [ˈflægʃɪp] Flaggschiff OT 3
flamingo [fləˈmɪŋgəʊ] Flamingo OT 2
flammable [ˈflæməbl] brennbar OT 2
flashlight [ˈflæʃlaɪt] Taschenlampe OT 2
flask [flɑːsk] Thermosflasche OT 3
flat [flæt] Wohnung OT 1
flavour [ˈfleɪvə] Geschmack OT 2
flesh [fleʃ] Fleisch OT 2
flexible [ˈfleksəbl] anpassungsfähig; flexibel WS 3, 82
flight [flaɪt] Flug OT 2
flight crew [ˈflaɪt kruː] Flugpersonal OT 2
to flip [flɪp] umdrehen WS 4, 116
float [fləʊt] Umzugswagen; Parade-Wagen WS 1, 21
flood [flʌd] Hochwasser; Flut OT 2
flooding [ˈflʌdɪŋ] Fluten; Überflutung WS 3, 103
floor [flɔː] Boden; Stockwerk OT 1
flour [ˈflaʊə] Mehl OT 3
flower [ˈflaʊə] Blume OT 1
fluent [ˈfluːənt] fließend OT 3

fluffy [ˈflʌfi] flauschig OT 2
flute [fluːt] Querflöte OT 2
to fly [flaɪ] fliegen OT 1
flyer [ˈflaɪə] Flyer WS 3, 83
flying [ˈflaɪɪŋ] Fliegen OT 1
focus [ˈfəʊkəs] Fokus OT 1
to focus [ˈfəʊkəs] fokussieren WS 2, 71
focused [ˈfəʊkəst] fokussiert WS 2, 73
to fold [fəʊld] falten OT 2
folk [fəʊk] Volks... OT 2
folk hero [ˈfəʊk hɪərəʊ] Volksheld WS 1, 21
folks [fəʊks] Leute OT 2
to follow [ˈfɒləʊ] folgen OT 2
to follow a journey [ˈfɒləʊ ə ˌdʒɜːni] eine Reise verfolgen OT 2
follower [ˈfɒləʊə] Anhänger(in) OT 3
fond: to be fond of [bi fɒnd] etw. mögen WS 1, 21
food [fuːd] Essen OT 1
food poisoning [ˈfuːd ˌpɔɪzənɪŋ] Lebensmittelvergiftung OT 2
foot [fʊt] Fuß OT 1
square foot [skweə fʊt] Quadratfuß OT 2
football [ˈfʊtbɔːl] Fußball OT 1
footpath [ˈfʊtpɑːθ] Fußpfad OT 1
footprint [ˈfʊtprɪnt] Fußabdruck OT 3
for [fər] für OT 1
force [fɔːs] Kraft OT 1
to force [fɔːs] zwingen OT 2
forecast [ˈfɔːkɑːst] Prognose OT 3
foreground [ˈfɔːgraʊnd] Vordergrund OT 3
forehand [ˈfɔːhænd] Vorhand OT 3
foreign [ˈfɒrən] ausländisch; fremd OT 1
foreigner [ˈfɒrənə] Fremde(r) OT 3
forest [ˈfɒrɪst] Wald OT 1
forever [fərˈevə] für immer OT 2
to forget [fəˈget] vergessen OT 1
to forgive [fəˈgɪv] vergeben OT 2
fork [fɔːk] Gabel OT 2
form [fɔːm] Form OT 1
to form [fɔːm] gründen; bilden WS 1, 29
former [ˈfɔːmə] ehemalig WS 2, 58
to formulate [ˈfɔːmjuleɪt] formulieren WS 2, 44
fort [fɔːt] Festung OT 2
fortnight [ˈfɔːtnaɪt] zwei Wochen OT 2
fortress [ˈfɔːtrəs] Zitadelle; Festung OT 3
fortune [ˈfɔːtʃuːn] Glück; Reichtum OT 3
forty [ˈfɔːti] vierzig OT 1
fossil [ˈfɒsl] fossil OT 3
to foul [faʊl] foulen OT 3

to **found** [faʊnd] begründen; gründen **WS 1**, 18

fountain [ˈfaʊntən] Springbrunnen OT 1

four [fɔː] vier OT 1

fourteen [ˌfɔːˈtiːn] vierzehn OT 1

fox [fɒks] Fuchs OT 1

frame [freɪm] Rahmen **WS 3**, 94

frantic [ˈfræntɪk] hektisch; aufgeregt OT 3

freak [friːk] Begeisterte(r); Freak **WS 4**, 122

freckle [ˈfrekl] Sommersprose OT 2

free [friː] frei; kostenlos OT 1

freed [friːd] befreit **WS 4**, 126

freedom [ˈfriːdəm] Freiheit OT 3

freeze-dried [ˈfriːz draɪd] gefriergetrocknet **WS 3**, 92

freezer [ˈfriːzə] Gefrierschrank OT 3

freezing [ˈfriːzɪŋ] kalt OT 2

French [frentʃ] französisch; Französisch OT 1

  French fries [ˌfrentʃˈfraɪz] Pommes frites OT 2

  French horn [ˌfrentʃˈhɔːn] Waldhorn OT 1

frequency [ˈfriːkwənsi] Häufigkeit OT 1

frequently [ˈfriːkwəntli] häufig OT 3

fresh [freʃ] frisch OT 2

freshman [ˈfreʃmən] Student im ersten Jahr; Studienanfänger(in) **WS 2**, 49

Friday [ˈfraɪdeɪ] Freitag OT 1

fridge [frɪdʒ] Kühlschrank OT 1

friend [frend] Freund(in) OT 1

  to **make friends** [meɪk ˈfrendz] (sich) anfreunden OT 2

friendly [ˈfrendli] freundlich OT 1

friendship [ˈfrendʃɪp] Freundschaft OT 3

fries [fraɪz] Pommes frites OT 2

to **frighten** [ˈfraɪtn] erschrecken OT 3

frightened [ˈfraɪtnd] verängstigt OT 1

frightening [ˈfraɪtnɪŋ] erschreckend OT 1

frisbee [ˈfrɪzbi] Frisbee OT 1

frizzy [ˈfrɪzi] kraus OT 3

from [frəm] von; aus OT 1

  from around the world [frəm əˌraʊnd ði ˈwɜːld] aus aller Welt OT 1

front [frʌnt] Vorderseite; Vorderteil OT 1

  in front of [ɪn frʌnt əv] vor OT 1

frontier [ˈfrʌntɪə] Grenzland **WS 3**, 94

frozen [ˈfrəʊzn] gefroren **WS 3**, 94

fruit [fruːt] Obst OT 1

frustrated [frʌˈstreɪtɪd] frustriert OT 3

to **fry** [fraɪ] braten; frittieren OT 2

fuel [ˈfjuːəl] Brennstoff OT 2

to **fulfil** [fʊlˈfɪl] verwirklichen; erfüllen **WS 4**, 109

full [fʊl] voll OT 1

fun [fʌn] Spaß OT 1

  good fun [ɡʊdˈfʌn] ziemlich spaßig OT 2

function [ˈfʌŋkʃn] Funktion **WS 1**, 22

to **fund** [fʌnd] finanzieren OT 3

fundraiser [ˈfʌndreɪzə] Spendensammler(in) OT 2

fundraising [ˈfʌndreɪzɪŋ] Spendensammlung OT 2

funny [ˈfʌni] lustig; merkwürdig OT 1

furniture [ˈfɜːnɪtʃə] Möbel OT 1

further [ˈfɜːðə] weiter **WS 1**, 12

fuss [fʌs] Aufregung **WS 3**, 86

fussy [ˈfʌsi] pingelig; wählerisch OT 2

future [ˈfjuːtʃə] Zukunft OT 2

fuzz [fʌz] Fussel; Belag **WS 3**, 84

G

gadget [ˈɡædʒɪt] Gerät; technische Spielerei **WS 3**, 79

to **gain** [ɡeɪn] erlangen OT 1

galaxy [ˈɡæləksi] Galaxie OT 1

gallery [ˈɡæləri] Galerie OT 1

gallon [ˈɡælən] Gallone OT 3

game [ɡeɪm] Spiel OT 1

  game console [ˈɡeɪm kɒnsəʊl] Spielekonsole **WS 3**, 78

gaming [ˈɡeɪmɪŋ] Spielen **WS 2**, 48

gap [ɡæp] Lücke OT 3

garage [ˈɡærɑːʒ] Garage; Werkstatt **WS 3**, 84

garbage [ˈɡɑːbɪdʒ] Abfall OT 2

  garbage collector [ˈɡɑːbɪdʒ kəˈlektə] Müllarbeiter(in) **WS 1**, 16

garden [ˈɡɑːdn] Garten OT 1

gardener [ˈɡɑːdnə] Gärtner(in) **WS 2**, 63

gardening [ˈɡɑːdnɪŋ] Gartenarbeit OT 1

gas [ɡæs] Gas; Benzin OT 3

to **gasp** [ɡɑːsp] keuchen OT 2

gate [ɡeɪt] Tor OT 1

to **gather** [ˈɡæðə] sammeln **WS 1**, 20

gel [dʒel] Gel OT 1

gender [ˈdʒendə] Geschlecht; Gender **WS 2**, 55

general [ˈdʒenrəl] allgemein OT 3

generally [ˈdʒenrəli] im Allgemeinen; hauptsächlich **WS 2**, 45

to **generate** [ˈdʒenəreɪt] erzeugen **WS 3**, 80

generation [ˌdʒenəˈreɪʃn] Generation **WS 1**, 30

generous [ˈdʒenərəs] großzügig OT 3

genre [ˈʒɒrə] Genre **WS 2**, 44

gentleman [ˈdʒentlmən] Herr; Gentleman OT 3

gently [ˈdʒentli] sanft OT 3

geocache [ˈdʒiːəʊkæʃ] Geocache OT 2

geocaching [ˈdʒiːəʊkæʃɪŋ] Geocaching OT 2

geographical [ˌdʒiːəˈɡræfɪkl] geografisch **WS 1**, 25

geography [dʒiˈɒɡrəfi] Erdkunde; Geografie OT 1

geology [dʒiˈɒlədʒi] Geologie OT 2

German [ˈdʒɜːmən] deutsch OT 1

gesture [ˈdʒestʃə] Geste **WS 4**, 117

to **get** [ɡet] bekommen OT 1

  to **get down** [ɡet daʊn] hinunterkommen OT 2

  to **get hit** [ɡet hɪt] getroffen sein; geschlagen sein **WS 3**, 85

  to **get off** [ɡetˈɒf] aussteigen OT 2

  to **get on** [ɡetˈɒn] zusteigen OT 2

  to **get ready** [ɡetˈredi] vorbereiten OT 1

  to **get rid of** [ɡet rɪd əv] loswerden OT 3

  to **get up** [ɡet ʌp] aufstehen OT 1

ghost [ɡəʊst] Geist OT 2

giant [ˈdʒaɪənt] riesig OT 2

gift [ɡɪft] Geschenk OT 1

  gift voucher [ˈɡɪft vaʊtʃə] Geschenkgutschein OT 1

ginormous [dʒaɪˈnɔːməs] gigantisch OT 2

giraffe [dʒəˈrɑːf] Giraffe OT 1

girl [ɡɜːl] Mädchen OT 1

to **give** [ɡɪv] geben OT 1

  to **give a talk** [ɡɪv əˈtɔːk] einen Vortrag / Referat halten OT 2

  to **give up** [ɡɪvˈʌp] aufgeben OT 2

glad [ɡlæd] froh OT 1

gladiator [ˈɡlædieɪtə] Gladiator(in) OT 3

glamorous [ˈɡlæmərəs] glamourös **WS 3**, 83

glass [ɡlɑːs] Glas OT 1

glasses [ˈɡlɑːsɪz] Brille OT 1

to **glitter** [ˈɡlɪtə] glitzern OT 2

global [ˈɡləʊbl] global; weltweit **WS 2**, 52

  global warming [ˌɡləʊblˈwɔːmɪŋ] Klimaerwärmung; Erderwärmung OT 3

glove [ɡlʌv] Handschuh OT 1

glue [ɡluː] Klebstoff OT 1

to **gnaw** [nɔː] abnagen OT 2

go: a go [əˈɡəʊ] ein Versuch OT 2

to **go** [ɡəʊ] gehen; fahren OT 1

to **go ahead** [ˌgəʊ əˈhed]
weitermachen **WS 1**, 13

to **go to sleep** [ˌgəʊ tə ˈsliːp]
einschlafen OT 1

to **go out** [gəʊ aʊt] ausgehen OT 1

goal [gəʊl] Tor OT 1

goalkeeper [ˈgəʊlkiːpə] Torwart(in)
OT 3

goat [gəʊt] Ziege **WS 1**, 20

God [gɒd] Gott **WS 1**, 20

gold [gəʊld] Gold OT 2

gold rush [ˈgəʊld rʌʃ] Goldrausch
WS 1, 25

golden [ˈgəʊldən] golden OT 3

to **gongoozle** [gɒŋˈguːzl] gaffen OT 3

gongoozler [gɒŋˈguːzlə] Gaffer OT 3

goodbye [gʊdˈbaɪ] Auf Wiedersehen
OT 1

goodies [ˈgʊdiz] tolle Kleinigkeiten
OT 2

goods [gʊdz] Güter **WS 1**, 28

goose [guːs] Gans **WS 1**, 21

gospel [ˈgɒspl] Gospel OT 2

to **govern** [ˈgʌvn] regieren OT 3

government [ˈgʌvənmənt] Regierung
OT 3

GPS (global positioning system)
[ˌdʒiː piː ˈes] Navigationssystem;
Globales Positionsbestimmungs-
system OT 2

to **grab** [græb] greifen OT 3

grade [greɪd] Klassenstufe OT 2

to **graduate** [ˈgrædʒuət] einen
akademischen Grad erlangen OT 3

gram [græm] Gramm OT 2

grammar [ˈgræmə] Grammatik OT 1

gramophone [ˈgræməfəʊn] Grammofon
WS 3, 83

grandchild [ˈgræntʃaɪld] Enkel(in);
Enkelkind OT 3

granddad [ˈgrændæd] Opa OT 1

grandfather [ˈgrænfɑːðə] Großvater
OT 2

grandma [ˈgrænmɑː] Oma OT 1

grandmother [ˈgrænmʌðə] Großmutter
OT 1

grandpa [ˈgrænpɑː] Opa OT 1

grandparents [ˈgrænpeərənts]
Großeltern OT 1

grandson [ˈgrænsʌn] Enkel OT 1

graphic [ˈgræfɪks] Grafik OT 3

grass [grɑːs] Gras OT 1

gravity [ˈgrævəti] Erdanziehungskraft;
Schwerkraft **WS 3**, 93

gravy [ˈgreɪvi] Bratensoße OT 1

great [greɪt] groß; toll OT 1

Greek [griːk] griechisch OT 2

green [griːn] grün OT 1

greenhouse [ˈgriːnhaʊs] Treibhaus OT 1

grey [greɪ] grau OT 1

to **grin** [grɪn] grinsen OT 2

groceries [ˈgrəʊsəriz] Lebensmittel
WS 3, 80

grocery store [ˈgrəʊsəri stɔː]
Lebensmittelladen **WS 1**, 25

gross [grəʊs] ätzend; ekelhaft OT 3

ground [graʊnd] Boden; Erde; Platz
OT 1

ground control [ˈgraʊnd kəntrəʊl]
Bodenstation **WS 3**, 95

group [gruːp] Gruppe OT 1

to **grow** [grəʊ] wachsen; anbauen OT 1

grubby [ˈgrʌbi] dreckig OT 2

to **grumble** [ˈgrʌmbl] mosern; murren;
schimpfen OT 2

guardian [ˈgɑːdiən] Betreuer(in) OT 2

to **guess** [ges] schätzen OT 1

guessing game [ˈgesɪŋ geɪm]
Rätselraten OT 1

guest [gest] Gast OT 2

guide [gaɪd] Führer(in) OT 1

guidebook [ˈgaɪdbʊk] Reiseführer OT 1

guideline [ˈgaɪdlaɪn] Richtlinie; Regel
OT 3

guitar [gɪˈtɑː] Gitarre OT 1

guitarist [gɪˈtɑːrɪst] Gitarrist(in) OT 1

gun [gʌn] Schusswaffe **WS 1**, 29

gunman [ˈgʌnmən] Schütze **WS 4**, 127

gurning [ˈgɜːnɪŋ] Grimassieren OT 2

guys [gaɪz] Leute OT 2

gym [dʒɪm] Fitnesscenter; Turnhalle
OT 3

gymnasium [dʒɪmˈneɪziəm] Sporthalle;
Turnhalle **WS 1**, 30

gymnastics [dʒɪmˈnæstɪks] Gymnastik
OT 1

H

habit [ˈhæbɪt] Gewohnheit **WS 2**, 48

habitat [ˈhæbɪtæt] Habitat;
Lebensraum **WS 4**, 123

habitation [ˌhæbɪˈteɪʃn] Bewohnbarkeit
WS 3, 94

hair [heə] Haare OT 1

haircut [ˈheəkʌt] Haarschnitt OT 2

halal [həˈlæl] halal OT 3

half-time [ˈhɑːf ˌtaɪm] Halbzeit OT 2

half [hɑːf] halbe(r,-s); halb OT 1

half past [ˈhɑːf pɑːst] eine halbe
Stunde nach OT 1

halfway [ˌhɑːfˈweɪ] halb; halbwegs OT 3

hall [hɔːl] Diele; Halle OT 1

Halloween [ˌhæləʊˈiːn] Halloween OT 2

halt [hɔːlt] Haltestelle OT 2

ham [hæm] Schinken OT 3

hamburger [ˈhæmbɜːgə] Hamburger
OT 2

hamster [ˈhæmstə] Hamster OT 1

hand [hænd] Hand OT 1

to **hand in** [hænd ɪn] einreichen OT 2

handbag [ˈhændbæg] Handtasche OT 3

handbook [ˈhændbʊk] Handbuch OT 3

handle [ˈhændl] Griff OT 2

handout [ˈhændaʊt] Handout; Flugblatt
WS 2, 55

handset [ˈhændset] Mobilteil OT 2

handsome [ˈhænsəm] gut aussehend
OT 1

handwriting [ˈhændraɪtɪŋ] Handschrift
OT 2

handy [ˈhændi] praktisch; nützlich
OT 2

to **hang on** [ˌhæŋˈɒn] warten OT 2

to **hang out** [hæŋ aʊt] abhängen;
rumhängen; herumhängen OT 1

to **happen** [ˈhæpən] geschehen;
passieren OT 1

to **happen upon** [ˈhæpən əˈpɒn]
zufällig entdecken **WS 3**, 84

happy [ˈhæpi] glücklich OT 1

happily [ˈhæpɪli] glücklich;
glücklicherweise OT 2

harbour [ˈhɑːbə] Hafen OT 2

hard [hɑːd] hart OT 1

hardly [ˈhɑːdli] kaum OT 3

to **harm** [hɑːm] verletzen; schaden
OT 2

harmful [ˈhɑːmfl] schädlich OT 3

harness [ˈhɑːnɪs] Sicherheitsgurt; Gurt
OT 1

harp [hɑːp] Harfe OT 1

harpist [ˈhɑːpɪst] Harfenist(in) OT 3

harvest [ˈhɑːvɪst] Ernte **WS 1**, 20

hash browns [ˌhæʃ ˈbraʊnz]
kleine gebratene Kartoffelwürfel,
wie Rösti OT 3

hat [hæt] Hut; Mütze OT 1

to **hate** [heɪt] hassen OT 1

to **have** [həv] haben OT 1

to **have a son** [həv ə ˈsʌn] einen Sohn
bekommen OT 1

have got [ˈhæv gɒt] haben OT 1

to **have to** [ˈhæv tə] müssen OT 1

hazard [ˈhæzəd] Gefahr; Risiko OT 2

he [hiː] er OT 1

head [hed] Kopf OT 1

head teacher [ˌhed ˈtiːtʃə]
Schulleiter(in) OT 1

to **head: to head out** [hed aʊt]
aufbrechen; losfahren **WS 2**, 62

headache [ˈhedeɪk] Kopfschmerzen
OT 1

headband [ˈhedbænd] Stirnband;
Kopfband OT 3

heading [ˈhedɪŋ] Überschrift OT 1

headline [ˈhedlaɪn] Schlagzeile OT 2

headquarter [ˌhedˈkwɔːtə]
Headquarter; Hauptsitz **WS 4**, 127

headset [ˈhedset] Headset **WS 3**, 78

headword [ˈhedwɜːd] Stichwort OT 2

health [helθ] Gesundheit OT 2

healthcare [ˈhelθkeə]
Gesundheitswesen **WS 4**, 112

healthy [ˈhelθi] gesund OT 2

heap [hiːp] Haufen **WS 3**, 80

to **hear** [hɪə] hören OT 1

heart [hɑːt] Herz OT 2

by heart [baɪ hɑːt] auswendig OT 2

heartland [ˈhɑːtlænd] Kernland
WS 1, 12

hearty [ˈhɑːti] herzhaft OT 2

to **heat** [hiːt] heizen OT 3

heater [ˈhiːtə] Heizung OT 2

heating [ˈhiːtɪŋ] Heizung OT 3

heavy [ˈhevi] schwer OT 1

hectic [ˈhektɪk] hektisch **WS 2**, 73

hedgehog [ˈhedʒhɒg] Igel OT 1

height [haɪt] Höhe OT 1

helicopter [ˈhelɪkɒptə] Hubschrauber
OT 2

hello [həˈləʊ] hallo OT 1

helmet [ˈhelmɪt] Helm OT 1

to **help** [help] helfen OT 1

helper [ˈhelpə] Helfer(in) OT 3

helpful [ˈhelpfl] hilfreich OT 1

helpless [ˈhelpləs] hilflos **WS 1**, 26

helpline [ˈhelplaɪn] Hotline OT 2

hen [hen] Henne OT 2

heptathlon [hepˈtæθlən] Siebenkampf
OT 2

her [hə] sie; ihr OT 1

herb [hɜːb] Kraut OT 3

herd [hɜːd] Herde **WS 1**, 29

here [hɪə] hier OT 1

hero [ˈhɪərəʊ] Held(in) OT 3

hers [hɜːz] ihre(r, -s) OT 2

herself [hɜːˈself] sich (selbst) OT 3

to **hesitate** [ˈhezɪteɪt] zögern OT 3

hesitation [ˌheziˈteɪʃn] Zögern OT 3

Hey! [heɪ] He! OT 1

hi [haɪ] hallo OT 1

hiccup [ˈhɪkʌp] Schluckauf OT 2

to **hide** [haɪd] sich verstecken OT 3

high [haɪ] hoch OT 1

to **highlight** [ˈhaɪlaɪt] hervorheben OT 3

highway [ˈhaɪweɪ] Highway;
Landstrasse OT 3

hike [haɪk] Wanderung OT 2

hiker [ˈhaɪkə] Wanderer; Wanderin OT 2

hiking [ˈhaɪkɪŋ] Wandern OT 1

hiking boot [ˈhaɪkɪŋ buːt]
Wanderstiefel OT 2

hill [hɪl] Hügel OT 1

hilly [ˈhɪli] hügelig OT 2

him [hɪm] ihn; ihm OT 1

himself [hɪmˈself] (sich) selbst OT 1

Hindu [ˈhɪnduː] hinduistisch OT 1

hip [hɪp] Hüfte OT 3

hip hop [ˈhɪp hɒp] Hip-Hop OT 1

hippopotamus [ˌhɪpəˈpɒtəməs] Nilpferd
OT 2

to **hire** [haɪə] mieten OT 3

his [hɪz] seine(r, -s) OT 1

Hispanic [hɪˈspænɪk] hispanisch OT 3

historian [hɪˈstɔːriən] Historiker(in)
OT 3

historic [hɪˈstɒrɪk] historisch OT 3

historical [hɪˈstɒrɪkl] geschichtlich OT 2

history [ˈhɪstri] Geschichte OT 1

to **hit** [hɪt] schlagen OT 1

hob [hɒb] Kochfeld OT 3

hobby [ˈhɒbi] Hobby OT 1

hockey [ˈhɒki] Hockey OT 1

to **hold** [həʊld] halten OT 1

hole [həʊl] Loch OT 1

holiday [ˈhɒlədeɪ] Urlaub OT 1

holidaymaker [ˈhɒlədeɪmeɪkə]
Urlauber(in) OT 3

home [həʊm] Zuhause OT 1

homecoming [ˈhəʊmkʌmɪŋ]
Absol“ententreffen an Schulen oder
Universitäten **WS 2**, 58

homeland [ˈhəʊmlænd] Heimat
WS 1, 20

homeless [ˈhəʊmləs] heimatlos;
obdachlos OT 3

homelessness [ˈhəʊmləsnəs]
Obdachlosigkeit **WS 3**, 105

homemade [ˈhəʊmmeɪd] selbst
gemacht; selbst zubereitet OT 3

homepage [ˈhəʊmpeɪdʒ] Startseite OT 1

homeschooled [ˌhəʊmˈskuːld] zu Hause
unterrichtet **WS 3**, 80

homesick [ˈhəʊmsɪk] voll Heimweh
OT 2

homesickness [ˈhəʊmsɪknəs] Heimweh
WS 1, 17

hometown [ˈhəʊmtaʊn] Heimatstadt
WS 1, 12

homework [ˈhəʊmwɜːk] Hausaufgaben
OT 1

honest [ˈɒnɪst] ehrlich OT 3

honey [ˈhʌni] Honig; Schatz (als
Kosename) OT 2

hoodie [ˈhʊdi] Kapuzenpullover OT 1

to **hook** [hʊk] haken **WS 3**, 96

to **hope** [həʊp] hoffen OT 1

hopefully [ˈhəʊpfəli] hoffentlich
WS 2, 70

hopeless [ˈhəʊpləs] hoffnungslos;
hilflos **WS 1**, 26

horizontal [ˌhɒrɪˈzɒntl] horizontal
WS 2, 64

horn [hɔːn] Horn OT 2

horrible [ˈhɒrəbl] furchtbar OT 2

horror [ˈhɒrə] Horror; Grauen OT 2

horse [hɔːs] Pferd OT 1

horse-drawn [ˈhɔːs drɔːn]
pferdebespannt OT 1

horse riding [ˈraɪdɪŋ] Reiten OT 1

hospital [ˈhɒspɪtl] Krankenhaus OT 1

hospitality [ˌhɒspɪˈtæləti]
Gastfreundschaft OT 2

to **host** [həʊst] ausrichten OT 3

hostel [ˈhɒstl] Hostel OT 2

hot [hɒt] heiß; scharf OT 1

hotel [həʊˈtel] Hotel OT 1

hound [haʊnd] Spürhund OT 2

hour [ˈaʊə] Stunde OT 1

house [haʊs] Haus OT 1

houseboat [ˈhaʊsbəʊt] Hausboot OT 3

household [ˈhaʊshəʊld] häuslich;
Haushalts- **WS 3**, 78

housekeeper [ˈhaʊskiːpə]
Haushälter(in) OT 3

housework [ˈhaʊswɜːk] Hausarbeit OT 1

housing [ˈhaʊzɪŋ] Wohnraum;
Unterkunft OT 3

how [haʊ] wie OT 1

however [haʊˈevə] jedoch OT 2

hug [hʌg] Umarmung OT 1

to **hug** [hʌg] (sich) umarmen **WS 1**, 14

huge [hjuːdʒ] riesig OT 2

human [ˈhjuːmən] menschlich OT 3

humour [ˈhjuːmə] Humor OT 3

hundred [ˈhʌndrəd] hundert OT 1

Hungarian [hʌŋˈgeəriən] ungarisch
OT 2

hunger [ˈhʌŋgə] Hunger **WS 3**, 103

hungry [ˈhʌŋgri] hungrig OT 1

to **hunt** [hʌnt] jagen OT 2

to **hurry** [ˈhʌri] (sich) beeilen OT 1

hurt [hɜːt] verletzt OT 1

husband [ˈhʌzbənd] Ehemann; Mann
OT 2

to **hydrate** [haɪˈdreɪt] hydratisieren
WS 3, 92

hygiene [ˈhaɪdʒiːn] Hygiene WS 3, 92

hyper-connected [ˈhaɪpə kəˈnektɪd]
angeschlossen WS 2, 48

hyperlink [ˈhaɪpəlɪŋk] Hyperlink OT 3

hypothermia [ˌhaɪpəˈθɜːmiə]
Unterkühlung OT 2

I

I [aɪ] ich OT 1

ice [aɪs] Eis OT 1

ice cream [ˌaɪsˈkriːm] Eis; Eiscreme
OT 1

ice lolly [aɪs ˈlɒli] Eis am Stiel OT 1

iceberg [ˈaɪsbɜːg] Eisberg OT 3

iconic [aɪˈkɒnɪk] ikonisch; Kult… OT 3

**ICT (information and communications
technology)** [ˌaɪ siːˈtiː] Informations-
und Kommunikationstechnologie OT 1

idea [aɪˈdɪə] Idee OT 1

ideal [aɪˈdiːəl] ideal OT 2

to **identify** [aɪˈdentɪfaɪ] identifizieren
OT 3

identity [aɪˈdentəti] Identität OT 3

if [ɪf] falls OT 1

ignition [ɪgˈnɪʃn] Zündung WS 3, 95

to **ignore** [ɪgˈnɔː] ignorieren WS 1, 31

ill [ɪl] krank OT 2

illegal [ɪˈliːgl] illegal OT 3

illiterate [ɪˈlɪtərət] analphabetisch
WS 4, 127

illness [ˈɪlnəs] Krankheit OT 2

to **illustrate** [ˈɪrɪtəbl] darstellen;
illustrieren OT 3

illustration [ˌɪləˈstreɪʃn] Illustration OT 2

image [ˈɪmɪdʒ] Bild OT 1

imaginary [ɪˈmædʒɪnəri] imaginär;
fiktiv WS 3, 85

imagination [ɪˌmædʒɪˈneɪʃn]
Vorstellung; Fantasie WS 3, 85

imaginative [ɪˈmædʒɪnətɪv] fantasievoll
WS 4, 111

to **imagine** [ɪˈmædʒɪn] sich etwas
vorstellen; sich einbilden; glauben
OT 1

immediately [ɪˈmiːdiətli] sofort OT 1

immigrant [ˈɪmɪgrənt] Einwanderer;
Einwanderin OT 3

immigration [ˌɪmɪˈgreɪʃn]
Einwanderungskontrolle OT 2

impact [ˈɪmpækt] Auswirkung OT 3

to **impart** [ɪmˈpɑːt] vermitteln WS 1, 30

impatient [ɪmˈpeɪʃnt] ungeduldig OT 3

imperative [ɪmˈperətɪv] Imperativ;
Befehlsform OT 1

to **import** [ˈɪmpɔːt] importieren;
einführen OT 3

importance [ɪmˈpɔːtəns] Bedeutung;
Wichtigkeit OT 2

important [ɪmˈpɔːtnt] wichtig OT 1

impossible [ɪmˈpɒsəbl] unmöglich OT 2

impractical [ɪmˈpræktɪkl] unpraktisch
WS 3, 86

impressed [ɪmˈprest] beindruckt
WS 1, 39

to **improve** [ɪmˈpruːv] verbessern OT 2

improvement [ɪmˈpruːvmənt]
Verbesserung OT 3

improvisation [ˌɪmprəvaɪˈzeɪʃn]
Improvisation OT 2

to **improvise** [ˈɪmprəvaɪz] improvisieren
OT 2

in [ɪn] im OT 1

inaccessible [ˌɪnækˈsesəbl]
unzugänglich OT 3

inch [ɪntʃ] Zoll (2,54 cm) OT 2

to **include** [ɪnˈkluːd] einschließen OT 1

included [ɪnˈkluːdɪd] inklusive OT 1

including [ɪnˈkluːdɪŋ] inklusive OT 1

inclusive [ɪnˈkluːsɪv] integrativ
WS 4, 118

income [ˈɪnkʌm] Einkommen WS 2, 63

increase [ˈɪnkriːs] Zunahme OT 3

to **increase** [ɪnˈkriːs] anwachsen;
erhöhen OT 3

incredible [ɪnˈkredəbl] unglaublich
OT 2

incredibly [ɪnˈkredəbli] unglaublich
OT 3

indefinite [ɪnˈdefɪnət] unbestimmt OT 1

independence [ˌɪndɪˈpendəns]
Unabhängigkeit OT 2

independent [ˌɪndɪˈpendənt]
selbstständig OT 3

index [ˈɪndeks] Index; Register WS 2, 62

indexer [ˈɪndeksə] Indexer(in) WS 2, 62

Indian [ˈɪndiən] indisch OT 2

individual [ˌɪndɪˈvɪdʒuəl] Einzelne(r)
WS 1, 32

individual [ˌɪndɪˈvɪdʒuəl] individuell
OT 3

individually [ˌɪndɪˈvɪdʒuəli] einzeln
WS 2, 49

indoor [ˈɪndɔː] Innen… OT 2

indoors [ˌɪnˈdɔːz] drinnen OT 3

industrial [ɪnˈdʌstriəl] Industrie… OT 2

industry [ˈɪndəstri] Industrie OT 2

inexpensive [ˌɪnɪkˈspensɪv] billig;
preiswert WS 3, 83

infection [ɪnˈfekʃn] Entzündung OT 2

infinite [ˈɪnfɪnət] unendlich WS 2, 49

infinitive [ɪnˈfɪnətɪv] Infinitiv OT 2

influence [ˈɪnfluəns] Einfluss WS 1, 30

infographic [ˌɪnfəʊˈgræfɪk] Infografik
OT 3

information [ˌɪnfəˈmeɪʃn] Information
OT 1

informative [ɪnˈfɔːmətɪv] informativ;
instruktiv OT 3

to **inform** [ɪnˈfɔːm] informieren
WS 1, 26

ingredient [ɪnˈgriːdiənt] Zutat OT 2

inhumane [ˌɪnhjuːˈmeɪn] inhuman;
menschenunwürdig WS 4, 127

initiative [ɪˈnɪʃətɪv] Initiative;
Kampagne WS 4, 113

to **injure** [ˈɪndʒə] verletzen OT 2

injury [ˈɪndʒəri] Verletzung OT 2

injustice [ɪnˈdʒʌstɪs] Ungerechtigkeit
WS 4, 126

inn [ɪn] Gasthaus OT 2

innovation [ˌɪnəˈveɪʃn] Innovation;
Neuheit WS 3, 78

innovative [ˈɪnəveɪtɪv] innovativ
WS 3, 84

innovator [ˈɪnəveɪtə] Innovator(in)
WS 3, 84

input [ˈɪnpʊt] Beitrag WS 3, 86

insect [ˈɪnsekt] Insekt OT 1

inside [ˌɪnˈsaɪd] in; innerhalb OT 1

insides [ˌɪnˈsaɪdz] Innereien OT 3

inspiration [ˌɪnspəˈreɪʃn] Inspiration;
Eingebung WS 3, 84

to **inspire** [ɪnˈspaɪə] inspirieren OT 3

to **get inspired** [get ɪnˈspaɪəd]
inspiriert werden WS 2, 50

to **install** [ɪnˈstɔːl] installieren WS 3, 80

instead [ɪnˈsted] stattdessen OT 2

institution [ˌɪnstɪˈtjuːʃn] Einrichtung
WS 1, 22

instruction [ɪnˈstrʌkʃn] Anweisung OT 1

instructor [ɪnˈstrʌktə] Lehrer(in) OT 3

instrument [ˈɪnstrəmənt] Instrument
OT 1

intelligent [ɪnˈtelɪdʒənt] intelligent
OT 2

to **interact** [ˌɪntərˈækt] interagieren
WS 4, 112

interaction [ˌɪntərˈækʃn] Interaktion
WS 1, 32

interest [ˈɪntrəst] Interesse OT 1

interested [ˈɪntrəstɪd] interessiert OT 1

interesting [ˈɪntrəstɪŋ] interessant OT 1

intern [ɪnˈtɜːn] Praktikant(in);
Volontär(in) WS 4, 123

internal combustion [ɪnˈtɜːnl
kəmˈbʌstʃən] Verbrennungs… WS 3, 77

international [ˌɪntəˈnæʃnəl] international OT 1

internet [ˈɪntənet] Internet OT 1

internship [ˈɪntɜːnʃɪp] Praktikum **WS 1**, 30

to **interpret** [ɪnˈtɜːprət] interpretieren **WS 1**, 26

interpreter [ɪnˈtɜːprɪtə] Dolmetscher(in) **WS 1**, 21

to **interrupt** [ˌɪntəˈrʌpt] unterbrechen OT 2

interview [ˈɪntəvjuː] Vorstellungsgespräch; Interview OT 1

to **interview** [ˈɪntəvjuː] ein Vorstellungsgespräch führen mit; interviewen OT 1

interviewer [ˈɪntəvjuːə] Interviewer(in) OT 1

into [ˈɪntuː] in OT 1

intonation [ˌɪntəˈneɪʃn] Intonation **WS 4**, 117

to **introduce** [ˌɪntrəˈdjuːs] vorstellen OT 2

introduction [ˌɪntrəˈdʌkʃn] Vorstellung; Einführung OT 2

to **invade** [ɪnˈveɪd] einmarschieren OT 3

to **invent** [ɪnˈvent] erfinden OT 2

invention [ɪnˈvenʃn] Erfindung **WS 3**, 76

inventor [ɪnˈventə] Erfinder(in) OT 2

to **invest** [ɪnˈvest] investieren OT 3

investigator [ɪnˈvestɪgeɪtə] Ermittler(in) **WS 4**, 124

investment [ɪnˈvestmənt] Investition OT 3

investor [ɪnˈvestə] Investor(in); Geldgeber(in) **WS 3**, 83

invitation [ˌɪnvɪˈteɪʃn] Einladung; Aufforderung OT 1

to **invite** [ɪnˈvaɪt] einladen OT 2

to **invite along** [ɪnˈvaɪt əˈlɒŋ] mit einladen OT 2

to **involve** [ɪnˈvɒlv] einbeziehen; umfassen **WS 3**, 90

involved [ɪnˈvɒlvd] involviert; teilnehmend OT 3

Iranian [ɪˈreɪniən] iranisch **WS 3**, 92

Irish [ˈaɪrɪʃ] irisch OT 1

irregular [ɪˈregjələ] unregelmäßig OT 1

irritable [ˈɪrɪtəbl] reizbar OT 3

irritated [ˈɪrɪteɪtɪd] verärgert OT 2

island [ˈaɪlənd] Insel OT 2

Israeli [ɪzˈreɪli] israelisch OT 2

issue [ˈɪsjuː] Thema; Angelegenheit; Ausgabe OT 2

it [ɪt] es / ihm OT 1

Italian [ɪˈtæliən] italienisch OT 2

itchy [ˈɪtʃi] juckend OT 2

item [ˈaɪtəm] Gegenstand OT 2

its [ɪts] sein; ihr OT 1

itself [ɪtˈself] sich (selbst) OT 3

ivory [ˈaɪvəri] Elfenbein OT 3

J

jack-o-lantern [ˌdʒæk əˈlæntən] Kürbislaterne OT 2

jacket [ˈdʒækɪt] Jacke OT 1

jam [dʒæm] Marmelade OT 2

Jamaican [dʒəˈmeɪkən] jamaikanisch OT 1

January [ˈdʒænjuəri] Januar OT 1

Japanese [ˌdʒæpəˈniːz] japanisch OT 1

jar [dʒɑː] Einweckglas OT 2

jazz [dʒæz] Jazz OT 2

jeans [dʒiːnz] Jeanshose OT 1

jewelry [ˈdʒuːəlri] Schmuck OT 2

jewel [ˈdʒuːəl] Juwel OT 1

job [dʒɒb] Stelle; Job; Aufgabe OT 1

to **do a good / great job** [duː ə gʊd / greɪt dʒɒb] gute Arbeit leisten OT 2

to **jog** [dʒɒg] traben; joggen OT 2

to **join** [dʒɔɪn] Mitglied werden in; eintreten in OT 1

joke [dʒəʊk] Witz OT 2

to **joke** [dʒəʊk] Witze machen OT 2

journalist [ˈdʒɜːnəlɪst] Journalist(in) OT 2

journey [ˈdʒɜːni] Reise; Fahrt OT 1

judge [dʒʌdʒ] Richter(in); Preisrichter(in) OT 2

to **judge** [dʒʌdʒ] einschätzen; beurteilen OT 2

Judgement Day [ˈdʒʌdʒmənt deɪ] jüngste Gericht **WS 3**, 95

judging [ˈdʒʌdʒɪŋ] Beurteilung OT 2

judo [ˈdʒuːdəʊ] Judo OT 1

juice [dʒuːs] Saft OT 1

July [dʒuˈlaɪ] Juli OT 1

jumbled [ˈdʒʌmbld] durcheinander OT 2

to **jump** [dʒʌmp] springen OT 2

jumper [ˈdʒʌmpə] Pullover OT 1

June [dʒuːn] Juni OT 1

jungle [ˈdʒʌŋgl] Dschungel **WS 4**, 123

junior [ˈdʒuːniə] Junior(in) OT 2

junky [ˈdʒʌŋki] schlecht; mangelhaft **WS 3**, 89

just [dʒʌst] genau; nur OT 1

justice [ˈdʒʌstɪs] Gerechtigkeit **WS 2**, 50

K

karate [kəˈrɑːti] Karate OT 1

kart racing [kɑːt reɪsɪŋ] Kartrennen OT 3

kayaking [ˈkaɪækɪŋ] Kajakfahren OT 2

keen: to be keen [tə bi kiː] auf etw. scharf sein; auf etw. Lust haben **WS 4**, 110

to **keep** [kiːp] bleiben; behalten; aufbewahren OT 2

to **keep away** [kiːp əˈweɪ] fernbleiben; fernhalten OT 2

to **keep in touch** [ˌkiːp ɪn ˈtʌtʃ] in Kontakt bleiben OT 2

keeper [ˈkiːpə] Hüter(in) **WS 1**, 31

ketchup [ˈketʃəp] Ketchup OT 1

kettle [ˈketl] Kessel; Wasserkocher OT 2

key [kiː] Schlüssel OT 1

to **key in** [kiː ɪn] eintippen OT 2

keyboard [ˈkiːbɔːd] Tastatur; Keyboard OT 1

keyword [ˈkiːwɜːd] Stichwort **WS 1**, 22

to **kick** [kɪk] treten OT 1

kickball [ˈkɪkbɔːl] Kickball **WS 3**, 79

kid [kɪd] Kind OT 1

kidnapper [ˈkɪdnæpə] Entführer(in) OT 2

kidney bean [ˈkɪdni biːn] Kidneybohne OT 2

to **kill** [kɪl] töten OT 1

kilometre [ˈkɪləmiːtə] Kilometer OT 1

kimchi [ˈkɪmtʃi] Kimchi OT 1

kind [kaɪnd] Art OT 1

kind [kaɪnd] freundlich; nett OT 1

kindly [ˈkaɪndli] netterweise OT 2

king [kɪŋ] König OT 1

kingdom [ˈkɪŋdəm] Königreich **WS 1**, 25

kiss [kɪs] Kuss OT 3

kit [kɪt] Ausrüstung OT 2

kitchen [ˈkɪtʃɪn] Küche OT 1

kiwi [ˈkiːwiː] Kiwi OT 1

knee [niː] Knie OT 1

to **kneel** [niːl] knien OT 1

knife [naɪf] Messer OT 2

knight [naɪt] Ritter OT 3

to **knight** [naɪt] zum Ritter schlagen OT 3

knock [nɒk] Klopfen OT 2

to **knock over** [nɒk ˈəʊvə] umstoßen OT 2

to **know** [nəʊ] wissen OT 1

well known [ˌwel ˈnəʊn] bekannt OT 2

knowledge [ˈnɒlɪdʒ] Wissen **WS 1**, 19

knowledgeable [ˈnɒlɪdʒəbl] kenntnisreich OT 3

Korean [kəˈriən] koreanisch OT 1

L

lab [læb] Labor OT 2

label [ˈleɪbl] Etikett OT 1

labor [ˈleɪbə] Arbeitskraft; Arbeit **WS 2**, 52

laboratory [ləˈbɒrətri] Labor **WS 3**, 83

lack [læk] Mangel OT 3

ladder [ˈlædə] Leiter OT 2

lady [ˈleɪdi] Dame OT 1

laid-back [ˌleɪd ˈbæk] locker; entspannt **WS 2**, 73

lake [leɪk] See OT 1

lakefront [ˈleɪkfrʌnt] Seeufer **WS 2**, 61

lakeside [ˈleɪksaɪd] Seeufer **WS 2**, 63

lamb [læm] Lamm OT 1

lamp [læmp] Lampe OT 1

to **land** [lænd] landen OT 1

landfill [ˈlændfɪl] Mülldeponie OT 3

landline [ˈlændlaɪn] Festnetz **WS 3**, 79

landmark [ˈlændmɑːk] Wahrzeichen **WS 1**, 25

landscape [ˈlændskeɪp] Landschaft OT 2

lane [leɪn] Fahrspur; Gasse OT 2

language [ˈlæŋgwɪdʒ] Sprache OT 1

lantern [ˈlæntən] Laterne OT 2

laptop [ˈlæptɒp] Laptop OT 1

large [lɑːdʒ] groß OT 2

lasagna [ləˈzænjə] Lasagne OT 1

laser [ˈleɪzə] Laser OT 3

last [lɑːst] letzte(r,-s) OT 1

to **last** [lɑːst] andauern OT 2

late [leɪt] spät OT 1

later [ˈleɪtə] später OT 1

Latin [ˈlætɪn] lateinisch OT 1

Latino [læˈtiːnəʊ] lateinamerikanisch OT 2

to **laugh** [lɑːf] lachen OT 1

to **launch** [lɔːntʃ] starten; auf den Markt bringen **WS 3**, 76

laundry [ˈlɔːndri] Wäsche **WS 1**, 20

law [lɔː] Gesetz OT 3

lawyer [ˈlɔɪə] Rechtsanwalt / -anwältin **WS 4**, 126

to **lead** [liːd] führen OT 3

leader [ˈliːdə] Leiter(in) OT 1

leadership [ˈliːdəʃɪp] Führung **WS 4**, 113

leaf [liːf] Blatt **WS 2**, 46

leaflet [ˈliːflət] Reklamezettel OT 2

league [liːg] Liga OT 2

to **lean** [liːn] lehnen OT 3

to **learn** [lɜːn] lernen OT 1

learner [ˈlɜːnə] Lernende(r); Fahranfänger(in) OT 3

to **lease** [liːs] leasen; mieten **WS 3**, 96

least [liːst] wenigste(r, -s) OT 2

leather [ˈleðə] Leder OT 3

to **leave** [liːv] verlassen OT 1

to **leave behind** [ˌliːv bɪˈhaɪnd] hinterlassen OT 2

left [left] linke(r, -s) OT 1

leg [leg] Bein OT 1

legal [ˈliːgl] rechtlich; legal **WS 1**, 26

legend [ˈledʒənd] Legende OT 2

leisure [ˈleʒə] Freizeit OT 3

lemonade [ˌleməˈneɪd] Zitronenlimonade OT 1

to **lend** [lend] leihen OT 2

length [leŋθ] Länge OT 2

lens [lenz] Linse **WS 3**, 95

leopard [ˈlepəd] Leopard OT 2

less [les] weniger OT 2

lesson [ˈlesn] Unterricht OT 1

to **let** [let] lassen OT 1

let's [lets] lass / lasst uns **WS 1**, 13

letter [ˈletə] Brief; Buchstabe OT 1

introductory letter [ˌɪntrəˈdʌktəri ˈletə] Einführungsbrief **WS 1**, 17

lettuce [ˈletɪs] Kopfsalat OT 2

level [ˈlevl] Niveau; Stufe; Standard OT 2

liberty [ˈlɪbəti] Freiheit OT 1

librarian [laɪˈbreəriən] Bibliothekar(in) **WS 4**, 108

library [ˈlaɪbrəri] Bibliothek OT 1

licence [ˈlaɪsns] Erlaubnis OT 3

to **lick** [lɪk] lecken OT 3

lid [lɪd] Deckel OT 2

to **lie** [laɪ] liegen OT 1

life [laɪf] Leben OT 1

life-threatening [ˈlaɪf ˌθretnɪŋ] lebensbedrohlich OT 2

lifeguard [ˈlaɪfgɑːd] Rettungsschwimmer(in) **WS 4**, 108

lifestyle [ˈlaɪfstaɪl] Lebensstil; Lifestyle **WS 1**, 14

lifetime [ˈlaɪftaɪm] Lebenszeit; Leben OT 2

to **lift** [lɪft] anheben; hochheben; heben OT 3

light [laɪt] Licht OT 1

light [laɪt] leicht OT 3

lightbulb [ˈlaɪtbʌlb] Glühbirne OT 3

lighting [ˈlaɪtɪŋ] Beleuchtung **WS 3**, 80

like [laɪk] irgendwie; also; wie; als ob OT 1

likely [ˈlaɪkli] wahrscheinlich OT 3

to **like** [laɪk] gernhaben; mögen OT 1

would like / love [wʊd laɪk / lʌv] hätte(n) gern; möchte(n) OT 1

to **limit** [ˈlɪmɪt] einschränken; begrenzen OT 3

limp [lɪmp] schlaff **WS 3**, 95

line [laɪn] Linie; Text (eines Schauspielers); Seil OT 1

link [lɪŋk] Verbindung OT 2

linking verb [ˈlɪŋkɪŋ vɜːb] Kopula OT 2

linking word [ˈlɪŋkɪŋ wɜːd] Verbindungswort **WS 1**, 33

linked [lɪŋkt] verbunden OT 2

lion [ˈlaɪən] Löwe; Löwin OT 1

lip [lɪp] Lippe OT 2

liquid [ˈlɪkwɪd] flüssig OT 2

list [lɪst] Liste OT 1

to **list** [lɪst] auflisten OT 3

to **listen** [ˈlɪsn] hören; zuhören OT 1

listener [ˈlɪsənə] Zuhörer(in); Hörer(in) OT 1

liter [ˈliːtə] Liter **WS 2**, 52

literature [ˈlɪtrətʃə] Literatur **WS 2**, 57

litter [ˈlɪtə] herumliegende Abfälle OT 2

little [ˈlɪtl] klein OT 1

to **live** [lɪv] leben; wohnen OT 1

liveable [ˈlɪvəbl] bewohnbar **WS 2**, 63

living room [ˈlɪvɪŋ ruːm] Wohnzimmer OT 1

loads of [ˈləʊdz əv] eine Menge OT 3

local [ˈləʊkl] Einheimische(r) OT 2

local [ˈləʊkl] einheimisch OT 2

locally [ˈləʊkəli] hier; am Ort OT 3

location [ləʊˈkeɪʃn] Standort OT 2

loch [lɒx] See OT 1

lock [lɒk] Schloss OT 2

locker [ˈlɒkə] Spind; Schließfach OT 2

lodge [lɒdʒ] Gasthaus OT 2

log [lɒg] Holzscheit OT 3

logo [ˈləʊgəʊ] Logo OT 1

lonely [ˈləʊnli] einsam OT 3

long [lɒŋ] lang OT 1

loo [luː] Klo OT 2

loo break [ˈluː breɪk] Klopause OT 2

to **look** [lʊk] sehen OT 1

to **look after** [lʊk ɑːftə] aufpassen auf OT 1

to **look at** [lʊk æt] anschauen; ansehen OT 1

to **look forward to** [ˌlʊk ˈfɔːwəd tə] (sich) auf etwas freuen OT 1

to **look lost** [lʊk lɒst] verloren aussehen **WS 1**, 13

to **lose** [luːz] verlieren OT 1

lot: a lot [ə lɒt] viel; sehr OT 1

lots [lɒts] viel OT 1

lottery [ˈlɒtəri] Lotterie OT 3

loud [laʊd] laut OT 1

loudspeaker [ˈlaʊd ˌspiːkə] Lautsprecher OT 2

to **love** [lʌv] lieben OT 1

lovely [ˈlʌvli] hübsch; schön OT 1

lover [ˈlʌvə] Liebhaber(in) OT 3

low [ləʊ] tief OT 1

low-income [ləʊ ˈɪnkʌm] einkommensschwach **WS 2**, 63

luck [lʌk] Glück OT 1

  good luck [gʊd 'lʌk] Alles Gute! OT 2

lucky ['lʌki] glücklich; glückbringend OT 2

  luckily ['lʌkɪli] glücklicherweise **WS 3**, 93

luggage ['lʌgɪdʒ] Gepäck **WS 3**, 87

lunch [lʌntʃ] Mittagessen OT 1

  lunch break ['lʌntʃ breɪk] Mittagspause OT 1

  lunchtime ['lʌntʃtaɪm] Mittagszeit OT 1

lung [lʌŋ] Lunge OT 3

luxurious [lʌg'ʒʊəriəs] luxuriös OT 2

lynx [lɪŋks] Luchs OT 2

lyrics ['lɪrɪks] Songtext; Liedtext OT 2

M

ma'am [mæm] gnädige Frau OT 2

machine [mə'ʃiːn] Maschine OT 1

machinery [mə'ʃiːnəri] Maschinen OT 2

mad [mæd] verrückt; böse OT 2

madam ['mædəm] gnädige Frau OT 1

made of [meɪd əv] gemacht aus OT 2

madman ['mædmən] Irrer; Verrückter **WS 1**, 16

magazine [ˌmægə'ziːn] Zeitschrift OT 1

magic ['mædʒɪk] Zauber OT 1

magical ['mædʒɪkl] magisch OT 2

magician [mə'dʒɪʃn] Zauberer; Zauberin OT 1

magnetic [mæg'netɪk] magnetisch OT 2

magnet ['mægnət] Magnet OT 1

mail [meɪl] Post OT 1

  mailbox ['meɪlbɒks] Briefkasten; Mailbox **WS 2**, 49

  mail carrier ['meɪl kæriə] Postbote; Postbotin **WS 1**, 16

  snail mail ['sneɪl meɪl] Schneckenpost; traditioneller Brief **WS 3**, 79

main [meɪn] Haupt... OT 1

  main course ['meɪn kɔːs] Hauptgang OT 1

mainland ['meɪnlænd] Festland OT 3

mainly ['meɪnli] hauptsächlich OT 2

to maintain [meɪn'teɪn] warten; pflegen **WS 4**, 113

maintenance ['meɪntənəns] Wartung OT 3

major ['meɪdʒə] bedeutend OT 2

majority [mə'dʒɒrəti] Mehrheit **WS 4**, 125

to make [meɪk] kochen; machen OT 1

  to make a mess [meɪk ə 'mes] ein Chaos anrichten OT 2

maker ['meɪkə] Macher(in) OT 3

malamute ['mælə‚mjuːt] Malamut OT 2

male [meɪl] männlich OT 2

mall [mɔːl] Einkaufszentrum OT 3

malware ['mælweə] Malware OT 3

mammal ['mæml] Säugetier OT 2

man [mæn] Mann OT 1

  man-made [ˌmæn 'meɪd] menschengemacht; künstlich OT 1

to manage ['mænɪdʒ] leiten; managen OT 1

manager ['mænɪdʒə] Geschäftsführer(in); Manager(in); Leiter(in) OT 1

manner ['mænə] Weise OT 2

manufacture [ˌmænju'fæktʃə] Herstellung; Produktion **WS 4**, 112

manufacturer [ˌmænju'fæktʃərə] Hersteller(in) **WS 4**, 126

manure [mə'njʊə] Dung OT 3

many ['meni] viele OT 1

  many times ['meni taɪmz] häufig; oftmals **WS 1**, 26

Maori ['maʊri] Maori OT 1

map [mæp] Landkarte OT 1

maple ['meɪpl] Ahorn OT 3

marathon ['mærəθən] Marathon OT 2

  half marathon ['haːf ˌmærəθən] Halbmarathon OT 2

marbles ['maːblz] Murmelspiel **WS 1**, 20

March [maːtʃ] März OT 1

march [maːtʃ] Marsch OT 3

  marching band ['maːtʃɪŋ bænd] Blaskapelle **WS 1**, 21

marine [mə'riːn] Meeres... **WS 4**, 110

maritime ['mærɪtaɪm] Marine... OT 3

to mark [maːk] korrigieren OT 2

marker ['maːkə] Markierung; Filzstift OT 1

market ['maːkɪt] Markt OT 1

marketable ['maːkɪtəbl] vermarktbar **WS 3**, 85

marketing ['maːkɪtɪŋ] Marketing; Vermarktung **WS 3**, 85

marquee [maːˈkiː] Markise; Zelt OT 2

to marry ['mæri] heiraten OT 1

mask [maːsk] Maske OT 3

mass [mæs] Massen... **WS 3**, 77

massacre ['mæsəkə] Massaker OT 3

massive ['mæsɪv] riesig OT 3

master ['maːstə] Meister(in) **WS 2**, 59

match [mætʃ] Spiel; Wettkampf OT 1

material [mə'tɪəriəl] Material; Stoff OT 3

math [mæθ] Mathe OT 1

mathematician [ˌmæθəmə'tɪʃn] Mathematiker(in) OT 3

mathematics [ˌmæθə'mætɪks] Mathematik OT 1

maths [mæθs] Mathematik OT 1

matter ['mætə] Angelegenheit; Problem OT 2

  What's the matter? [wɒts ðə 'mætə] Was ist los? OT 2

maximum ['mæksɪməm] Maximum OT 2

may [meɪ] könnte(n) OT 1

maybe ['meɪbi] vielleicht OT 1

mayonnaise [ˌmeɪə'neɪz] Mayonnaise OT 1

mayor [meə] Bürgermeister(in) OT 3

me [miː] mich; mir OT 1

meadow ['medəʊ] Wiese OT 2

meal [miːl] Mahlzeit OT 1

to mean [miːn] bedeuten OT 1

meaning ['miːnɪŋ] Sinn; Bedeutung OT 1

to measure ['meʒə] messen; ausmessen; abschätzen **WS 3**, 89

measurement ['meʒəmənt] Maß; Maßeinheit OT 2

meat [miːt] Fleisch OT 1

meatball ['miːtbɔːl] Fleischklößchen; Hackfleischbällchen OT 1

meatloaf ['miːt ləʊf] Hackbraten OT 3

meaty ['miːti] Fleisch... OT 3

medal ['medl] Medaille OT 2

media ['miːdiə] Medien OT 2

  social media [ˌsəʊʃl 'miːdiə] soziale Medien OT 2

mediation [ˌmiːdi'eɪʃn] Mediation; Vermittlung OT 1

medical ['medɪkl] ärztliche Untersuchung; medizinisch OT 1

  medical science ['medɪkl 'saɪəns] Heilkunde; Medizin **WS 3**, 79

medicine ['medsn] Medikament; Medizin OT 2

medium ['miːdiəm] mittelgroß OT 1

  medium-sized ['miːdiəm saɪzd] mittelgroß OT 2

to meet [miːt] treffen OT 1

meeting ['miːtɪŋ] Besprechung; Treffen OT 1

meetinghouse ['miːtɪŋhaʊs] Andachtshaus; Gebetshaus **WS 1**, 32

melody ['melədi] Melodie OT 2

to melt [melt] schmelzen **WS 3**, 93

member ['membə] Mitglied OT 1

memorable ['memərəbl] unvergesslich OT 3

to memorize ['meməraɪz] auswendig lernen; merken **WS 4**, 109

memory [ˈmeməri] Gedächtnis OT 1

mental [ˈmentl] geistig; mental **WS 1**, 30

to **mention** [ˈmenʃn] erwähnen OT 3

mentor [ˈmentɔː] Lehrmeister(in); Mentor(in) **WS 4**, 123

menu [ˈmenjuː] Speisekarte OT 1

mess [mes] Unordnung OT 3

to **mess up** [ˌmesˈʌp] in Unordnung bringen; vergeigen OT 2

message [ˈmesɪdʒ] Nachricht OT 1

to **message** [ˈmesɪdʒɪŋ] texten OT 3

messy [ˈmesi] unordentlich; chaotisch OT 2

metal [ˈmetl] Metall OT 1

method [ˈmeθəd] Methode OT 1

metre [ˈmiːtə] Meter OT 1

metro [ˈmetrəʊ] U-Bahn OT 1

Mexican [ˈmeksɪkən] mexikanisch **WS 4**, 114

microbe [ˈmaɪkrəʊb] Mikrobe **WS 3**, 94

microphone [ˈmaɪkrəfəʊn] Mikrofon **WS 1**, 13

microscope [ˈmaɪkrəskəʊp] Mikroskop **WS 3**, 95

mid [mɪd] in der Mitte; mittel **WS 1**, 24

midday [ˌmɪdˈdeɪ] Mittag **WS 3**, 80

middle [ˈmɪdl] Mitte OT 1

middle school [ˈmɪdl skuːl] Mittelschule OT 2

midfielder [ˌmɪdˈfiːldə] Mittelfeldspieler(in) OT 3

midge [mɪdʒ] Mücke OT 3

midnight [ˈmɪdnaɪt] Mitternacht OT 1

midwest [ˌmɪdˈwest] mittlerer Westen **WS 1**, 25

midwestern [ˌmɪdˈwestən] mittlerer Westen **WS 1**, 31

might [maɪt] könnte(n) OT 1

mighty [ˈmaɪti] sehr; mächtig OT 3

migrant [ˈmaɪɡrənt] Migrant(in) **WS 4**, 125

migrant [ˈmaɪɡrənt] herumziehend **WS 4**, 124

to **migrate** [maɪˈɡreɪt] migrieren OT 3

migration [maɪˈɡreɪʃn] Migration OT 3

mile [maɪl] Meile OT 1

military [ˈmɪlətri] Militär **WS 3**, 83

milk [mɪlk] Milch OT 1

millennial [mɪˈleniəl] die Generation der Jahrtausendwende **WS 2**, 64

million [ˈmɪljən] Million OT 1

to **mime** [maɪm] pantomimisch darstellen OT 2

mind [maɪnd] Verstand OT 1

mind-expanding [maɪnd ɪkˈspænd] sinneserweiternd OT 2

mind map [ˈmaɪnd mæp] Gedankenkarte; Mindmap OT 1

to **mind** [maɪnd] etw. macht jmdm. etwas aus **WS 1**, 12

mine [maɪn] meine(r, -s) OT 2

miner [ˈmaɪnə] Bergarbeiter **WS 1**, 25

mini [ˈmɪni] klein OT 2

miniature [ˈmɪnətʃə] sehr klein OT 3

minibus [ˈmɪnibʌs] Kleinbus OT 2

minimum [ˈmɪnɪməm] Mindest... OT 1

mining [ˈmaɪnɪŋ] Bergbau... OT 3

mint [mɪnt] Minze OT 2

minute [ˈmɪnɪt] Minute OT 1

mirror [ˈmɪrə] Spiegel OT 1

miserable [ˈmɪzrəbl] unglücklich OT 2

misfit [ˈmɪsfɪt] Außenseiter(in) **WS 2**, 49

misleading [ˌmɪsˈliːdɪŋ] irreführend OT 3

mismatched [ˌmɪsˈmætʃ] nicht zusammenpassend **WS 2**, 58

to **miss** [mɪs] vermissen OT 2

missing [ˈmɪsɪŋ] fehlend OT 1

mission [ˈmɪʃn] Mission **WS 3**, 94

mistake [mɪˈsteɪk] Fehler OT 2

by mistake [baɪ mɪˈsteɪk] versehentlich OT 2

to **make a mistake** [ˌmeɪk ə mɪˈsteɪk] einen Fehler machen OT 2

misunderstanding [ˌmɪsʌndəˈstændɪŋ] Missverständnis **WS 1**, 26

misunderstood [ˌmɪsʌndəˈstʊd] verkannt; missverstanden **WS 3**, 83

to **mix** [mɪks] mischen OT 2

to **mix up** [mɪks ʌp] vermischen; durcheinanderbringen OT 2

mixed up [ˌmɪkst ˈʌp] durcheinander OT 2

mixture [ˈmɪkstʃə] Mischung OT 3

mobile [ˈməʊbaɪl] mobil OT 1

mobile phone [ˈməʊbaɪl] Handy OT 1

modal [ˈməʊdl] Modalverb OT 2

model [ˈmɒdl] Modell OT 1

modern [ˈmɒdn] modern OT 1

module [ˈmɒdjuːl] Modul **WS 3**, 93

mom [mɒm] Mama OT 1

moment [ˈməʊmənt] Moment OT 1

monastery [ˈmɒnəstri] Kloster OT 3

Monday [ˈmʌndeɪ] Montag OT 1

money [ˈmʌni] Geld OT 1

monk [mʌŋk] Mönch OT 3

monkey [ˈmʌŋki] Affe OT 2

monotone [ˈmɒnətəʊn] monoton **WS 4**, 117

monster [ˈmɒnstə] Monster OT 1

month [mʌnθ] Monat OT 1

monument [ˈmɒnjumənt] Denkmal OT 1

moon [muːn] Mond **WS 1**, 24

to **moor** [mɔː] vertäuen; anlegen OT 3

mooring [ˈmɔːrɪŋ] Anlegeplatz OT 3

more [mɔː] mehr OT 1

morning [ˈmɔːnɪŋ] Morgen OT 1

mosque [mɒsk] Moschee OT 1

mosquito [məˈskiːtəʊ] Stechmücke OT 2

most [məʊst] der / die / das meiste; die meisten OT 1

motel [məʊˈtel] Motel OT 3

mother [ˈmʌðə] Mutter OT 1

motion picture [ˌməʊʃn ˈpɪktʃə] Film; Spielfilm **WS 3**, 83

to **motivate** [ˈməʊtɪveɪt] motivieren **WS 4**, 111

to **motor** [ˈməʊtə] fahren OT 3

mountain [ˈmaʊntən] Berg OT 1

mountain range [ˈmaʊntən reɪndʒ] Bergkette; Gebirgszug **WS 1**, 25

mouse [maʊs] Maus OT 2

mouth [maʊθ] Mund OT 1

mouthguard [ˈmaʊθɡɑːd] Mundschutz OT 2

mouthwash [ˈmaʊθwɒʃ] Mundwasser **WS 3**, 93

to **move** [muːv] bewegen; umziehen OT 1

to **move on** [muːv ɒn] weitergehen **WS 1**, 13

movie [ˈmuːvi] Film OT 1

moving van [ˈmuːvɪŋ ˌvæn] Umzugswagen OT 2

Mr [ˈmɪstə] Herr OT 1

Mrs [ˈmɪsɪz] Frau OT 1

Ms [mɪz] Frau OT 1

much [mʌtʃ] viel OT 1

muffin [ˈmʌfɪn] Muffin OT 1

mug [mʌɡ] Becher; Tasse OT 3

mule [mjuːl] Maultier OT 3

multi [mʌlti] multi... OT 3

multiple choice [ˌmʌltɪpl ˈtʃɔɪs] Multiple-Choice OT 2

mum [mʌm] Mutti OT 1

mummy [ˈmʌmi] Mumie OT 2

mural [ˈmjʊərəl] Wandgemälde OT 2

to **murder** [ˈmɜːdə] ermorden **WS 4**, 127

murky [ˈmɜːki] trübe **WS 3**, 84

muscle [ˈmʌsl] Muskel **WS 3**, 93

museum [mjuːˈziːəm] Museum OT 1

mushroom [ˈmʌʃrʊm] Pilz; Champignon OT 1

music [ˈmjuːzɪk] Musik... OT 1

musical [ˈmjuːzɪkl] Musik-; musikalisch OT 2

   extra-musical [ˈekstrəˈmjuːzɪkl] außermusikalisch OT 2

   musical instrument [ˌmjuːzɪkl ˈɪnstrəmənt] Musikinstrument OT 2

musician [mjuˈzɪʃn] Musiker(in) OT 2

Muslim [ˈmʊzlɪm] Muslim OT 3

mussel [ˈmʌsl] Muschel WS 1, 20

must [mʌst] müssen OT 1

mustard [ˈmʌstəd] Senf OT 2

my [maɪ] mein OT 1

myself [maɪˈself] ich (selbst) OT 3

mystery [ˈmɪstri] Rätsel; Mysterium OT 2

N

name [neɪm] Name OT 1

   first name [ˈfɜːst neɪm] Vorname OT 2

   last name [ˈlɑːst neɪm] Nachname OT 2

to name [neɪm] benennen WS 1, 28

nappy [ˈnæpi] Windel OT 3

narrow [ˈnærəʊ] eng OT 2

narrowboat [ˈnærəʊbəʊt] schmales Kanalboot; Hausboot OT 3

nasty [ˈnɑːsti] unangenehm OT 2

nation [ˈneɪʃn] Nation OT 2

national [ˈnæʃnəl] national OT 1

nationality [ˌnæʃəˈnæləti] Staatsangehörigkeit OT 2

native [ˈneɪtɪv] einheimisch OT 3

natural [ˈnætʃrəl] natürlich OT 1

nature [ˈneɪtʃə] Natur OT 2

navigating [ˈnævɪgeɪt] Navigation WS 3, 96

navy [ˈneɪvi] Marine OT 3

near [nɪə] nahe; in der Nähe von OT 1

nearby [ˌnɪəˈbaɪ] in der Nähe OT 3

nearly [ˈnɪəli] fast OT 1

neat [niːt] ordentlich WS 1, 29

necessary [ˈnesəsəri] notwendig OT 3

neck [nek] Hals OT 1

to need [niːd] brauchen OT 1

negative [ˈnegətɪv] Verneinung; Negativ OT 1

neighbourhood [ˈneɪbəhʊd] Nachbarschaft WS 1, 14

neighbour [ˈneɪbə] Nachbar(in) OT 2

neither [ˈnaɪðə] auch nicht; weder OT 2

nerve [nɜːv] Nerv OT 3

nervous [ˈnɜːvəs] nervös OT 2

   nervously [ˈnɜːvəsli] nervös OT 2

nest [nest] Nest OT 3

net [net] Netz OT 3

netball [ˈnetbɔːl] Netzball OT 1

netbook [ˈnetbʊk] Netbook WS 3, 78

neutral [ˈnjuːtrəl] neutral OT 3

never [ˈnevə] nie OT 1

new [njuː] neu OT 1

news [njuːz] Neuigkeit(en) OT 1

newsletter [ˈnjuːzletə] Mitteilungsblatt; Newsletter WS 3, 89

newspaper [ˈnjuːzpeɪpə] Zeitung OT 1

next [nekst] nächste(r, -s) OT 1

   next to [ˈnekst tuː] neben OT 1

nice [naɪs] schön; nett OT 1

nickname [ˈnɪkneɪm] Spitzname WS 3, 94

night [naɪt] Nacht OT 1

nightmare [ˈnaɪtmeə] Albtraum WS 4, 124

nine [naɪn] neun OT 1

nineteen [ˌnaɪnˈtiːn] neunzehn OT 1

ninety [ˈnaɪnti] neunzig OT 1

no [nəʊ] nein OT 1

nobody [ˈnəʊbədi] niemand OT 1

to nod [nɒd] nicken OT 2

noise [nɔɪz] Geräusch; Lärm OT 1

noisy [ˈnɔɪzi] laut OT 1

to nominate [ˈnɒmɪneɪt] nominieren WS 1, 27

nomination [ˌnɒmɪˈneɪʃn] Nominierung; Ernennung WS 1, 27

none [nʌn] keine(r, -s) OT 2

non-profit [ˌnɒnˈprɒfɪt] gemeinnützig WS 1, 22

non-verbal [ˌnɒn ˈvɜːbl] nonverbal WS 4, 117

noon [nuːn] Mittag WS 2, 47

nor [nɔː] noch; weder noch WS 3, 86

normal [ˈnɔːml] normal OT 1

   normally [ˈnɔːməli] gewöhnlich; normalerweise OT 1

north [nɔːθ] Nord...- OT 1

northern [ˈnɔːðən] nördlich OT 2

nose [nəʊz] Nase OT 2

not [nɒt] nicht OT 1

note [nəʊt] Notiz; Schein OT 1

notebook [ˈnəʊtbʊk] Notizbuch OT 2

nothing [ˈnʌθɪŋ] nichts OT 1

to notice [ˈnəʊtɪs] bemerken OT 1

noticeboard [ˈnəʊtɪsbɔːd] Anschlagbrett OT 1

noun [naʊn] Substantiv; Nomen; Hauptwort OT 1

novel [ˈnɒvl] Roman OT 2

November [nəʊˈvembə] November OT 1

now [naʊ] jetzt OT 1

nowadays [ˈnaʊədeɪz] heutzutage OT 3

nowhere [ˈnəʊweə] nirgendwo OT 2

nuclear [ˈnjuːkliə] Atom...; Nuklear... OT 3

number [ˈnʌmbə] Zahl; Nummer OT 1

nun [nʌn] Nonne WS 3, 95

nurse [nɜːs] Krankenschwester / -pfleger OT 1

nut [nʌt] Nuss WS 3, 94

nutrition [njuˈtrɪʃn] Ernährung WS 2, 63

nutritious [njuˈtrɪʃəs] nahrhaft WS 4, 124

O

oats [əʊts] Haferflocken OT 3

object [ˈɒbdʒɪkt] Gegenstand; Objekt OT 1

   object pronoun [ˌɒbdʒekt ˈprəʊnaʊn] Objektpronomen OT 1

objection [əbˈdʒekʃn] Einwand OT 3

objective [əbˈdʒektɪv] Ziel WS 3, 95

obligation [ˌɒblɪˈgeɪʃn] Verpflichtung OT 2

observation [ˌɒbzəˈveɪʃn] Beobachtung OT 3

to observe [əbˈzɜːv] beobachten WS 4, 111

obvious [ˈɒbviəs] offensichtlich OT 3

   obviously [ˈɒbviəsli] offenbar; offensichtlich OT 1

occasionally [əˈkeɪʒnəli] gelegentlich OT 2

occupation [ˌɒkjuˈpeɪʃn] Tätigkeit; Beschäftigung WS 1, 32

ocean [ˈəʊʃn] Ozean OT 3

October [ɒkˈtəʊbə] Oktober OT 1

octopus [ˈɒktəpəs] Krake; Oktopus OT 1

odd [ɒd] eigenartig OT 2

   odd one out [ɒd wʌn aʊt] Außenseiter(in); etwas, was nicht in die Reihe passt OT 2

oddity [ˈɒdəti] Kuriosität WS 3, 95

of [əv] von OT 1

   of course [əv ˈkɔːs] natürlich OT 1

off [ɒf] von; aus; weg OT 1

   off the grid [ɒf ðə grɪd] vom Netz WS 3, 80

   Off you go! [ˌɒf ju ˈgəʊ] Fort mit dir! OT 2

to offend [əˈfend] beleidigen OT 3

offer [ˈɒfə] Angebot OT 1

to offer [ˈɒfə] anbieten OT 2

office [ˈɒfɪs] Büro OT 1

   office park [ˈɒfɪs pɑːk] Büropark OT 2

officer [ˈɒfɪsə] Offizier(in) OT 2

official [əˈfɪʃl] Amtsperson OT 3

official [əˈfɪʃl] offiziell WS 1, 21

offstage [ˈɒfˌsteɪdʒ] aus dem Off OT 2

often [ˈɒfn] oft OT 1

oil [ɔɪl] Öl OT 1

OK [əʊˈkeɪ] in Ordnung OT 1

old [əʊld] alt OT 1

  old-fashioned [ˌəʊldˈfæʃnd] altmodisch WS 2, 62

Olympic [əˈlɪmpɪk] olympisch OT 1

omelette [ˈɒmlət] Omelett OT 2

on [ɒn] auf; an; in OT 1

once [wʌns] einmal OT 2

  Once upon a time ... [ˈwʌns əpɒn ə ˈtaɪm] Es war einmal... OT 1

one [wʌn] eins OT 1

onion [ˈʌnjən] Zwiebel OT 2

  onion ring [ˈʌnjən rɪŋ] Zwiebelring OT 2

online [ˌɒnˈlaɪn] online OT 1

  online forum [ˌɒnlaɪn ˈfɔːrəm] Online-Forum WS 1, 22

only [ˈəʊnli] nur OT 1

onscreen [ˌɒnˈskriːn] auf dem Bildschirm; auf der Leinwand OT 2

onto [ˈɒntuː] auf OT 1

open [ˈəʊpən] offen OT 1

to open [ˈəʊpən] aufmachen; öffnen OT 1

opening times [ˈəʊpnɪŋ ˌtaɪmz] Öffnungszeiten OT 1

operation [ˌɒpəˈreɪʃn] Operation OT 3

operator [ˈɒpəreɪtə] Leitstellendisponent(in); Telefonist(in) OT 2

opinion [əˈpɪnjən] Meinung OT 3

opponent [əˈpəʊnənt] Gegner(in) OT 2

opportunity [ˌɒpəˈtjuːnəti] Gelegenheit OT 2

opposing [əˈpəʊzɪŋ] gegnerisch OT 3

opposite [ˈɒpəzɪt] Gegenteil OT 1

optimistic [ˌɒptɪˈmɪstɪk] optimistisch OT 2

option [ˈɒpʃn] Wahl OT 2

optional [ˈɒpʃənl] optional OT 2

or [ɔː] oder OT 1

orange [ˈɒrɪndʒ] orange OT 1

  orange juice [ˈɒrɪndʒ dʒuːs] Orangensaft OT 1

orbit [ˈɔːbɪt] Orbit; Umlaufbahn WS 3, 76

orchestra [ˈɔːkɪstrə] Orchester OT 1

order [ˈɔːdə] Bestellung; Reihenfolge OT 1

ordinary [ˈɔːdnri] normal OT 2

organ [ˈɔːgən] Orgel; Organ OT 3

organic [ɔːˈgænɪk] biologisch (angebaut) OT 2

organization [ˌɔːgənaɪˈzeɪʃn] Organisation OT 2

organizational [ˌɔːgənaɪˈzeɪʃənl] organisatorisch WS 4, 123

to organize [ˈɔːgənaɪz] organisieren OT 1

organizer [ˈɔːgənaɪzə] Organisator(in) OT 3

oriental [ˌɔːriˈentl] orientalisch OT 1

orientation [ˌɔːriənˈteɪʃn] Orientierung WS 3, 93

origin [ˈɒrɪdʒɪn] Ursprung OT 3

original [əˈrɪdʒənl] ursprünglich; Original... OT 3

  originally [əˈrɪdʒənəli] ursprünglich OT 2

other [ˈʌðə] andere(r, -s) OT 1

Ouch! [aʊtʃ] Aua! OT 1

our [ˈaʊə] unser OT 1

ours [ɑːz] unsere(r, -s) OT 2

ourselves [ɑːˈselvz, ˌaʊəˈselvz] uns OT 3

out [aʊt] heraus; aus OT 1

outback [ˈaʊtbæk] Hinterland WS 3, 94

outdoor [ˈaʊtdɔː] draußen OT 3

outdoors [ˈaʊtdɔːz] draußen OT 2

to outline [ˈaʊtlaɪn] skizzieren OT 3

outside [ˌaʊtˈsaɪd] draußen OT 1

outstanding [aʊtˈstændɪŋ] herausragend OT 3

outward journey [ˈaʊtwəd ˈdʒɜːni] Hinfahrt OT 3

oven [ˈʌvn] Ofen WS 1, 21

over [ˈəʊvə] über OT 1

overboard [ˈəʊvəbɔːd] über Bord OT 3

overgrown [ˌəʊvəˈgrəʊn] überwuchert; überwachsen WS 2, 63

to overhear [ˌəʊvəˈhɪə] hören; mithören OT 3

overnight [ˌəʊvəˈnaɪt] über Nacht OT 2

overseas [ˌəʊvəˈsiːz] ausländisch OT 2

to oversee [ˌəʊvəˈsiː] überwachen; beaufsichtigen WS 3, 83

to overuse [ˌəʊvəˈjuːs] zu oft verwenden OT 2

overview [ˈəʊvəvjuː] Überblick; Übersicht WS 4, 119

Ow! [aʊ] Au! OT 1

own [əʊn] eigene(r, -s) OT 1

  on one's own [ɒn wʌnz ˈəʊn] allein OT 2

to own [əʊn] besitzen WS 3, 82

owner [ˈəʊnə] Besitzer(in) OT 2

P

PA (public address) system [piː ˈeɪ ˌsɪstəm] Lautsprecheranlage OT 2

to pack [pæk] packen OT 2

package [ˈpækɪdʒ] Paket OT 3

packaged food [ˈpækɪdʒd fuːd] verpacktes Essen WS 3, 89

packaging [ˈpækɪdʒɪŋ] Verpackung OT 3

packet [ˈpækɪt] Paket OT 2

paddle [ˈpædl] Paddel OT 3

  paddle-boarding [ˈpædlbɔːdɪŋ] Paddle-Boarding OT 1

paddling [ˈpædlɪŋ] Paddeln WS 4, 123

page [peɪdʒ] Seite OT 1

pain [peɪn] Schmerz OT 2

painful [ˈpeɪnfl] schmerzhaft OT 2

  painfully [ˈpeɪnfəli] schmerzhaft OT 2

painkiller [ˈpeɪnkɪlə] Schmerzmittel OT 2

paint [peɪnt] Farbe OT 2

to paint [peɪnt] malen OT 1

painted [ˈpeɪntɪd] gestrichen OT 1

painting [ˈpeɪntɪŋ] Malen; Gemälde OT 1

pair [peə] Paar OT 1

pajamas [pəˈdʒɑːmə] Schlafanzug; Pyjama WS 2, 58

Pakistani [ˌpɑːkɪˈstɑːni] pakistanisch WS 4, 127

palace [ˈpæləs] Palast OT 1

pan [pæn] Pfanne OT 2

pancake [ˈpænkeɪk] Pfannkuchen WS 1, 24

panda [ˈpændə] Pandabär OT 1

to panic [ˈpænɪk] in Panik geraten OT 2

panoramic [ˌpænəˈræmɪk] Panorama... OT 3

panther [ˈpænθə] Panther OT 2

paper [ˈpeɪpə] Papier OT 1

parade [pəˈreɪd] Umzug; Parade OT 2

paradise [ˈpærədaɪs] Paradies WS 1, 13

paragraph [ˈpærəgrɑːf] Absatz OT 1

Paralympics [ˌpærəˈlɪmpɪks] paralympische Spiele OT 3

paramedic [ˌpærəˈmedɪk] Rettungssanitäter(in) OT 1

parcel [ˈpɑːsl] Paket WS 3, 78

parent [ˈpeərənt] Elternteil OT 1

park [pɑːk] Park OT 1

  park ranger [ˈpɑːk ˌreɪndʒə] Forstbeamter / -beamtin OT 2

to park [pɑːk] parken OT 1

parking ticket [ˈpɑːkɪŋ tɪkɪt] Parkzettel OT 1

parliament [ˈpɑːləmənt] Parlament OT 1

part [pɑːt] Teil OT 1

  part of speech [ˌpɑːt əv ˈspiːtʃ] Wortart OT 2

part-time [ˌpɑːt ˈtaɪm] Teilzeit...; nebenberuflich **WS 4**, 128

participle [pɑːˈtɪsɪpl] Partizip OT 2

particular: in particular [pəˈtɪkjələ] besonders **WS 2**, 70

partly [ˈpɑːtli] teilweise OT 3

partner [ˈpɑːtnə] Partner(in) OT 1

partnership [ˈpɑːtnəʃɪp] Partnerschaft; Kooperation **WS 3**, 92

party [ˈpɑːti] Party; Feier OT 1

to **pass** [pɑːs] zuspielen; an etw. vorbeifahren OT 3

to **pass an exam** [ˌpɑːs ən ɪɡˈzæm] eine Prüfung bestehen OT 2

passenger [ˈpæsɪndʒə] Passagier(in); Fahrgast OT 2

passionate [ˈpæʃənət] leidenschaftlich **WS 4**, 110

passport [ˈpɑːspɔːt] Pass OT 2

passport control [ˈpɑːspɔːt kənˌtrəʊl] Passkontrolle OT 2

password [ˈpɑːswɜːd] Kennwort; Passwort **WS 1**, 13

past [pɑːst] nach OT 1

past participle [ˌpɑːst pɑːˈtɪsɪpl] Partizip Perfekt OT 2

past progressive [pɑːst prəˈɡresɪv] Verlaufsform der Vergangenheit OT 2

pasta [ˈpæstə] Nudeln OT 1

to **paste** [peɪst] kleben; einfügen OT 2

pastor [ˈpɑːstə] Pfarrer(in) OT 2

pat [pæt] Klaps OT 3

pâté [ˈpæteɪ] Pastete OT 1

patent [ˈpætnt] Patent **WS 3**, 83

to **patent** [ˈpætnt] patentieren **WS 3**, 76

path [pɑːθ] Weg OT 1

patient [ˈpeɪʃnt] Patient(in) OT 1

patriot [ˈpeɪtriət] Patriot(in) OT 2

pattern [ˈpætn] Muster OT 1

pause [pɔːz] Pause OT 3

to **pause** [pɔːz] eine Pause machen OT 3

pavement [ˈpeɪvmənt] Gehweg; Bürgersteig OT 1

to **pay** [peɪ] bezahlen OT 1

payment [ˈpeɪmənt] Bezahlung OT 2

PE (physical education) [ˌpiːˈiː] Sportunterricht OT 1

pea [piː] Erbse OT 1

peaceful [ˈpiːsfl] friedlich; einträchtig OT 2

pear [peə] Birne OT 1

pedal [ˈpedl] Pedal **WS 3**, 93

pedigree [ˈpedɪɡriː] Rasse... OT 3

pen [pen] Stift OT 1

penalty [ˈpenəlti] Strafe; Strafstoß OT 3

pencil [ˈpensl] Bleistift OT 1

pencil case [ˈpensl ˌkeɪs] Federtasche OT 1

pencil sharpener [ˈpensl ʃɑːpnə] Anspitzer OT 1

penguin [ˈpeŋgwɪn] Pinguin OT 1

penicillin [ˌpenɪˈsɪlɪn] Penizillin OT 2

penny [ˈpeni] Penny OT 1

people [ˈpiːpl] Leute OT 1

pepper [ˈpepə] Paprika; Pfeffer OT 2

percent [pəˈsent] Prozent **WS 1**, 21

percentage [pəˈsentɪdʒ] Prozent OT 3

perfect [ˈpɜːfɪkt] perfekt OT 1

to **perfect** [pɜːˈfɪkt] perfektionieren **WS 3**, 95

to **perform** [pəˈfɔːm] auftreten OT 2

performance [pəˈfɔːməns] Aufführung OT 2

performer [pəˈfɔːmə] Künstler(in); Darsteller(in); Interpret(in) OT 2

perhaps [pəˈhæps] vielleicht OT 3

period [ˈpɪəriəd] Zeit; Epoche OT 3

permission [pəˈmɪʃn] Erlaubnis OT 2

permit [pəˈmɪt] Erlaubnis OT 3

persecution [ˌpɜːsɪˈkjuːʃn] Verfolgung **WS 1**, 24

person [ˈpɜːsn] Person; Mensch OT 1

personal [ˈpɜːsənl] persönlich OT 2

personality [ˌpɜːsəˈnæləti] Persönlichkeit **WS 1**, 17

perspective [pəˈspektɪv] Ansicht; Perspektive **WS 4**, 117

to **persuade** [pəˈsweɪd] überreden; überzeugen OT 3

pessimistic [ˌpesɪˈmɪstɪk] pessimistisch **WS 3**, 105

pest [pest] Schädling; Plage; Plagegeist OT 2

pesticide [ˈpestɪsaɪd] Pestizid **WS 2**, 52

pet [pet] Haustier OT 1

petition [pəˈtɪʃn] Antrag OT 3

petrol [ˈpetrəl] Benzin **WS 3**, 77

pharmacist [ˈfɑːməsɪst] Apotheker(in) OT 2

pharmacy [ˈfɑːməsi] Apotheke OT 2

philosophy [fəˈlɒsəfi] Philosophie **WS 3**, 88

phone [fəʊn] Telefon OT 1

phone call [ˈfəʊn kɔːl] Telefonat OT 2

to **phone** [fəʊn] telefonieren OT 2

phonograph [ˈfəʊnəɡrɑːf] Phonograph **WS 3**, 83

photo [ˈfəʊtəʊ] Foto OT 1

to **photocopy** [ˈfəʊtəʊkɒpi] fotokopieren **WS 2**, 55

photograph [ˈfəʊtəɡrɑːf] Foto OT 1

photographer [fəˈtɒɡrəfə] Fotograf(in) OT 3

photography [fəˈtɒɡrəfi] Fotografie **WS 1**, 13

phrase [freɪz] Wendung OT 1

physical [ˈfɪzɪkl] körperlich OT 2

physics [ˈfɪzɪks] Physik **WS 3**, 94

pianist [ˈpɪənɪst] Pianist(in) OT 2

piano [piˈænəʊ] Klavier OT 1

to **pick** [pɪk] pflücken; auswählen OT 1

to **pick up** [pɪk ʌp] aufheben OT 2

picker [ˈpɪkə] Sammler(in) OT 3

pickle [ˈpɪkl] Gurke; Gewürzgurke OT 1

pickpocket [ˈpɪkpɒkɪt] Taschendieb(in) **WS 3**, 86

picnic [ˈpɪknɪk] Picknick OT 1

picture [ˈpɪktʃə] Bild OT 1

pie [paɪ] (gedeckter) Obstkuchen OT 1

piece [piːs] Stück; Teil OT 1

in one piece [ɪn ˌwʌn ˈpiːs] heil OT 2

pierced [pɪəst] durchstochen OT 3

pig [pɪɡ] Schwein OT 1

pilgrimage [ˈpɪlɡrɪmɪdʒ] Pilgerfahrt OT 3

pill [pɪl] Pille OT 1

pillow [ˈpɪləʊ] Kopfkissen OT 2

pilot [ˈpaɪlət] Pilot(in) OT 3

to **pilot** [ˈpaɪlət] steuern **WS 3**, 76

pin [pɪn] Stecknadel OT 1

pineapple [ˈpaɪnæpl] Ananas OT 3

ping-pong [ˈpɪŋ pɒŋ] Tischtennis OT 1

pink [pɪŋk] rosa OT 1

pioneer [ˌpaɪəˈnɪə] Pionier(in) **WS 1**, 28

pipeline [ˈpaɪplaɪn] Pipeline **WS 1**, 31

pirate [ˈpaɪrət] Pirat(in) OT 3

pitch [pɪtʃ] Spielfeld OT 3

pizza [ˈpiːtsə] Pizza OT 1

pizza deliverer [ˈpiːtsə dɪˈlɪvərə] Pizzalieferant(in) **WS 4**, 114

place [pleɪs] Ort OT 1

place mat [ˈpleɪs mæt] Platzdeckchen OT 2

plagiarism [ˈpleɪdʒərɪzəm] Plagiat OT 2

to **plagiarize** [ˈpleɪdʒəraɪz] plagiieren OT 2

plain [pleɪn] nicht besonders; gutbürgerlich **WS 1**, 32

to **plan** [plæn] planen OT 1

plane [pleɪn] Flugzeug OT 1

planet [ˈplænɪt] Planet OT 2

planetarium [ˌplænɪˈteəriəm] Planetarium OT 1

planner [ˈplænə] Planer(in) OT 3

plant [plɑːnt] Pflanze OT 2

plaster [ˈplɑːstə] Verputz; Gips; Pflaster OT 1

plastic [ˈplæstɪk] Kunststoff OT 2

plate [pleɪt] Teller OT 1

platform [ˈplætfɔːm] Bahnsteig OT 1

play [pleɪ] Theaterstück OT 1

player [ˈpleɪə] Spieler(in) OT 1

playground [ˈpleɪɡraʊnd] Spielplatz; Schulhof OT 1

playlist [ˈpleɪlɪst] Playlist; Wiedergabeliste **WS 2**, 44

please [pliːz] bitte OT 1

pleased [pliːzd] zufrieden OT 1

pleasure [ˈpleʒə] Freude OT 1

plenty [ˈplenti] reichlich; viel OT 2

plot [plɒt] Handlung **WS 2**, 49

plum [plʌm] Pflaume OT 1

plural [ˈplʊərəl] Plural; Mehrzahl OT 1

poacher [ˈpəʊtʃə] Wilderer / Wilderin OT 3

poaching [ˈpəʊtʃɪŋ] Wilderei OT 3

pocket [ˈpɒkɪt] Tasche OT 2

   pocket money [ˈpɒkɪt mʌni] Taschengeld OT 2

pocketknife [ˈpɒkɪtnaɪf] Taschenmesser OT 2

podcast [ˈpɒdkɑːst] Podcast OT 1

podium [ˈpəʊdiəm] Podium OT 3

poem [ˈpəʊɪm] Gedicht OT 1

poet [ˈpəʊɪt] Dichter(in) OT 3

poetry [ˈpəʊətri] Poesie; Dichtung OT 1

point [pɔɪnt] Punkt OT 1

pointless [ˈpɔɪntləs] sinnlos; zwecklos **WS 3**, 95

poison [ˈpɔɪzən] Gift OT 1

pole [pəʊl] Stange; Pol OT 3

police [pəˈliːs] Polizei OT 1

   police officer [pəˈliːs ɒfɪsə] Polizist(in) OT 1

policy [ˈpɒləsi] Politik; Regel OT 3

Polish [ˈpəʊlɪʃ] polnisch OT 2

polite [pəˈlaɪt] höflich OT 1

political [pəˈlɪtɪkl] politisch **WS 1**, 24

   political clout [pəˈlɪtɪkl klaʊt] politischer Einfluss **WS 4**, 127

politician [ˌpɒləˈtɪʃn] Politiker(in) OT 3

pollution [pəˈluːʃn] Umweltverschmutzung OT 2

polo [ˈpəʊləʊ] Polo OT 3

polyurethane [ˌpɒliˈjʊərəθeɪn] Polyurethan (Kunststoff) **WS 3**, 82

pond [pɒnd] Teich **WS 3**, 80

pony [ˈpəʊni] Pony OT 3

pool [puːl] Lache; Schwimmbecken OT 1

poor [pʊə] arm OT 1

pop [pɒp] Pop OT 2

popcorn [ˈpɒpkɔːn] Popcorn OT 2

Pope [pəʊp] Papst OT 3

popular [ˈpɒpjələ] beliebt OT 1

population [ˌpɒpjəˈleɪʃən] Bevölkerung OT 3

porch [pɔːtʃ] Veranda **WS 1**, 14

pork [pɔːk] Schweinefleisch OT 2

porridge [ˈpɒrɪdʒ] Haferbrei OT 3

port [pɔːt] Hafen OT 2

portable [ˈpɔːtəbl] tragbar **WS 3**, 77

portfolio [pɔːtˈfəʊliəʊ] Mappe; Portfolio **WS 4**, 113

portion [ˈpɔːʃn] Portion; Menge **WS 1**, 13

position [pəˈzɪʃn] Position OT 3

positive [ˈpɒzətɪv] Positiv OT 1

possessive [pəˈzesɪv] besitzanzeigend; Possessiv... OT 1

   possessive determiner [pəˌzesɪv dɪˈtɜːmɪnə] Possessivbegleiter OT 1

possibility [ˌpɒsəˈbɪləti] Möglichkeit OT 2

possible [ˈpɒsəbl] möglich OT 2

post [pəʊst] Post OT 1

   post box [ˈpəʊst bɒks] Briefkasten OT 1

to post [pəʊst] posten OT 3

postcard [ˈpəʊstkɑːd] Postkarte OT 1

postcode [ˈpəʊstkəʊd] Postleitzahl OT 1

poster [ˈpəʊstə] Plakat OT 1

potato [pəˈteɪtəʊ] Kartoffel OT 1

   jacket potato [ˌdʒækɪt pəˈteɪtəʊ] Ofenkartoffel OT 1

   mashed potato [ˌmæʃt pəˈteɪtəʊ] Kartoffelbrei OT 1

   sweet potato [ˌswiːt pəˈteɪtəʊ] Süßkartoffel **WS 1**, 21

poultry [ˈpəʊltri] Geflügel OT 2

pound [paʊnd] Pfund OT 1

to pour [pɔː] gießen OT 1

poverty [ˈpɒvəti] Armut OT 3

powered [ˈpaʊəd] angetrieben **WS 3**, 76

powerless [ˈpaʊələs] kraftlos; machtlos **WS 4**, 127

practical [ˈpræktɪkl] praktisch OT 3

practice [ˈpræktɪs] Praxis; Übung OT 2

to practise [ˈpræktɪs] üben OT 1

prayer [preə] Gebet **WS 1**, 28

to predict [prɪˈdɪkt] vorhersagen **WS 1**, 20

prediction [prɪˈdɪkʃn] Vorhersage OT 2

to prefer [prɪˈfɜː] vorziehen OT 1

preference [ˈprefrəns] Vorliebe OT 3

pregnant [ˈpregnənt] schwanger **WS 1**, 28

premier [ˈpremiə] erste(r, -s) OT 2

preparation [ˌprepəˈreɪʃn] Vorbereitung OT 2

to prepare [prɪˈpeə] vorbereiten OT 1

   well prepared [ˌwel prɪˈpeəd] gut vorbereitet OT 2

preposition [ˌprepəˈzɪʃn] Präposition; Verhältniswort OT 2

present [ˈpreznt] Geschenk; Gegenwart OT 1

   present perfect [ˌpreznt ˈpɜːfɪkt] vollendete Gegenwart OT 2

   present progressive [ˈpreznt prəˌgresɪv] Verlaufsform des Präsens OT 1

to present [prɪˈzent] präsentieren; vorstellen OT 1

presentation [ˌpreznˈteɪʃn] Präsentation OT 1

to preserve [prɪˈzɜːv] erhalten OT 3

president [ˈprezɪdənt] Präsident(in) **WW**, 10

to press [pres] drücken OT 1

pressure [ˈpreʃə] Druck OT 3

to pretend [prɪˈtend] vorgeben; so tun, als ob OT 2

pretty [ˈprɪti] hübsch OT 1

to prevent [prɪˈvent] verhindern; abhalten **WS 3**, 96

prevention [prɪˈvenʃn] Vermeidung OT 2

previous [ˈpriːviəs] bisherig; vorherig **WS 3**, 100

   previously [ˈpriːviəsli] früher OT 3

price [praɪs] Preis OT 1

pride [praɪd] Stolz **WS 2**, 58

primary [ˈpraɪməri] Haupt...; Grund... OT 1

prince [prɪns] Prinz OT 1

principal [ˈprɪnsəpl] Rektor(in) OT 2

to print [prɪnt] (aus)drucken OT 2

prison [ˈprɪzn] Gefängnis OT 1

privacy [ˈprɪvəsi] Privatsphäre OT 3

private [ˈpraɪvət] privat OT 3

privateer [ˌpraɪvəˈtɪə] Freibeuter(in) OT 3

prize [praɪz] Preis; Gewinn OT 1

probably [ˈprɒbəbli] wahrscheinlich OT 2

problem [ˈprɒbləm] Problem OT 1

   problem-solver [ˈprɒbləm sɒlvə] Problemlöser(in) **WS 3**, 84

   problem-solving [ˈprɒbləm sɒlvɪŋ] problemlösend **WS 2**, 63

process [ˈprəʊses] Prozess **WS 3**, 85

   food processing [ˈfuːd ˈprəʊsesɪŋ] Lebensmittelverarbeitung **WS 4**, 125

procession [prəˈseʃn] Umzug OT 2

to produce [prəˈdjuːs] erzeugen OT 3

product ['prɒdʌkt] Produkt OT 2

production [prə'dʌkʃn] Produktion; Herstellung **WS 2**, 52

professional [prə'feʃənl] professionell OT 2

professor [prə'fesə] Professor(in) **WS 1**, 39

profile ['prəʊfaɪl] Steckbrief; Profil OT 3

profit ['prɒfɪt] Profit; Gewinn **WS 1**, 22

program ['prəʊɡræm] Programm; Kurs OT 3

programme ['prəʊɡræm] Programm; Sendung OT 2

to **programme** ['prəʊɡræm] programmieren OT 2

programmer ['prəʊɡræmə] Programmierer(in) OT 3

progress ['prəʊɡres] Fortschritt **WS 3**, 95

progressive [prə'ɡresɪv] fortschrittlich; progressiv OT 1

project ['prɒdʒekt] Projekt OT 1

projector [prə'dʒektə] Projektor; Beamer OT 1

prom [prɒm] Schulball OT 3

promise ['prɒmɪs] Versprechen OT 2

to **promise** ['prɒmɪs] versprechen OT 2

prompt [prɒmpt] Stichwort; Aufforderung **WS 2**, 73

pronoun ['prəʊnaʊn] Pronomen; Fürwort OT 1

   relative pronoun [ˌrelətɪv 'prəʊnaʊn] Relativpronomen OT 2

to **pronounce** [prə'naʊns] aussprechen OT 3

pronunciation [prəˌnʌnsi'eɪʃn] Aussprache OT 2

proof [pruːf] Beweis **WS 3**, 94

prop [prɒp] Stütze; Requisite OT 1

proper ['prɒpə] richtig; anständig OT 3

   properly ['prɒpəli] ordentlich; in richtiger Art und Weise OT 2

pro [prəʊ] Vorteil OT 2

to **protect** [prə'tekt] schützen OT 2

protein ['prəʊtiːn] Protein; Eiweiß **WS 3**, 95

protest ['prəʊtest] Protest OT 3

to **protest** [prəʊ'test] protestieren OT 3

prototype ['prəʊtətaɪp] Prototyp **WS 3**, 83

proud [praʊd] stolz OT 2

to **prove** [pruːv] beweisen OT 3

to **provide** [prə'vaɪd] zur Verfügung stellen; versorgen (mit) **WS 3**, 80

psycho ['saɪkəʊ] Psychopath(in) **WS 2**, 49

pub [pʌb] Kneipe OT 2

public ['pʌblɪk] öffentlich OT 2

to **publish** ['pʌblɪʃ] veröffentlichen OT 2

pueblo ['pwebləʊ] Pueblo OT 3

to **pull** [pʊl] ziehen OT 1

pulse [pʌls] Hülsenfrucht **WS 3**, 80

to **pump** [pʌmp] pumpen **WS 3**, 80

pumpkin ['pʌmpkɪn] Kürbis OT 2

punctual ['pʌŋktʃuəl] pünktlich **WS 2**, 57

to **punctuate** ['pʌŋktʃueɪt] mit Satzzeichen versehen OT 3

punctuation [ˌpʌŋktʃu'eɪʃn] Zeichensetzung OT 1

to **punish** ['pʌnɪʃ] bestrafen OT 3

puppy ['pʌpi] Welpe OT 2

purchase ['pɜːtʃəs] Kauf; Ankauf **WS 3**, 78

purple ['pɜːpl] lila OT 1

purpose ['pɜːpəs] Zweck **WS 3**, 80

to **pursue** [pə'sjuː] verfolgen **WS 4**, 111

to **push** [pʊʃ] stoßen OT 2

pushy ['pʊʃi] aufdringlich; penetrant **WS 4**, 116

to **put** [pʊt ʌp] tun; stellen OT 1

   to **put away** [pʊt' əweɪ] wegräumen OT 2

   to **put on** ['pʊt ɒn] aufführen; veranstalten OT 2

   to **put out** [pʊt aʊt] löschen OT 2

   to **put up** [pʊt] heben; errichten OT 1

puzzle ['pʌzl] Puzzle; Rätsel OT 2

pyjamas [pə'dʒɑːməz] Schlafanzug OT 3

Q

quack! [kwæk] Quak! (Ente) OT 2

quad biking [kwɒd 'baɪkɪŋ] Vierradfahrzeug fahren OT 2

quality ['kwɒləti] Eigenschaft; Qualität OT 3

quantity ['kwɒləti] Anzahl; Menge **WS 3**, 86

quarry ['kwɒri] Steinbruch OT 1

quarter ['kwɔːtə] Viertel; Quartier OT 1

   quarter to ['kwɔːtə tə] viertel vor OT 1

quarterback ['kwɔːtəbæk] Quarterback OT 2

queen [kwiːn] Königin OT 1

quesadilla [ˌkeɪsə'diːə] Quesadilla **WS 4**, 114

question ['kwestʃən] Frage OT 1

questionnaire [ˌkwestʃə'neə] Fragebogen OT 1

queue [kjuː] Schlange; Warteschlange OT 1

to **queue** [kjuː] anstehen; Schlange stehen **WS 1**, 15

quick [kwɪk] schnell OT 2

   quickly ['kwɪkli] schnell OT 2

quiet ['kwaɪət] still; ruhig OT 1

quilt [kwɪlt] Steppdecke **WS 1**, 32

to **quit** [kwɪt] kündigen; verlassen **WS 3**, 80

quite [kwaɪt] ziemlich OT 2

quiz [kwɪz] Quiz OT 2

quotation mark [kwəʊ'teɪʃn mɑːk] Anführungszeichen OT 2

to **quote** [kwəʊt] zitieren OT 2

R

rabbit ['ræbɪt] Kaninchen OT 1

race [reɪs] Rennen OT 2

racing ['reɪsɪŋ] Rennsport OT 2

racist ['reɪsɪst] rassistisch **WS 1**, 16

racket ['rækɪt] Schläger OT 2

radical ['rædɪkl] radikal; grundlegend **WS 3**, 90

radio ['reɪdiəʊ] Radio OT 1

   radio station ['reɪdiəʊ ˌsteɪʃn] Radiosender OT 2

radius ['reɪdiəs] Radius OT 2

rafting: white water rafting [waɪt 'wɔːtə 'rɑːftɪŋ] Wildwasser fahren OT 3

rail [reɪl] Schiene; Eisenbahn OT 2

railway ['reɪlweɪ] Bahn; Eisenbahn OT 1

   railway line ['reɪlweɪ laɪn] Eisenbahnlinie OT 2

to **rain** [reɪn] regnen OT 1

rainbow ['reɪnbəʊ] Regenbogen OT 1

raincoat ['reɪnkəʊt] Regenmantel OT 3

rainforest ['reɪnfɒrɪst] Regenwald OT 2

rainwater ['reɪnwɔːtə] Regenwasser **WS 3**, 80

to **raise** [reɪz] heben; erheben OT 2

rally ['ræli] Treffen; Kundgebung **WS 2**, 58

ramp [ræmp] Rampe OT 2

to **range** [reɪndʒ] umfassen; reichen von ... bis **WS 4**, 111

ranger ['reɪndʒə] Aufseher(in); Förster(in) OT 3

to **rank** ['ræŋk] in eine Rangfolge bringen **WS 2**, 54

ranking ['ræŋkɪŋ] Rangfolge **WS 2**, 54

rap [ræp] Rap OT 1

rapping ['ræpɪŋ] Rappen OT 1

rare [reə] selten OT 2

raspberry ['rɑːzbəri] Himbeere OT 1

to **rate** [reɪt] bewerten OT 2

rather ['rɑːðə] ziemlich OT 3

raw [rɔː] roh OT 3

to **reach** [riːtʃ] erreichen OT 3

to **react** [riˈækt] reagieren OT 3

reaction [riˈækʃn] Reaktion **WS 1**, 26

to **read** [riːd] lesen OT 1

reader [ˈriːdə] Leser(in) OT 3

reading [ˈriːdɪŋ] Lesen OT 1

ready [ˈredi] bereit OT 1

   Ready, set, go! [ˌredi set ˈɡəʊ] Auf die Plätze, fertig, los! OT 1

real [rɪəl] echt OT 1

realistic [ˌriːəˈlɪstɪk] realistisch **WS 4**, 111

reality [riˈæləti] Realität **WS 3**, 78

to **realize** [ˈriːəlaɪz] erkennen OT 2

really [ˈriːəli] wirklich; sehr OT 1

reason [ˈriːzn] Grund OT 1

to **rebell** [rebl] rebellieren **WS 1**, 18

rebellion [rɪˈbeljən] Aufstand **WS 1**, 20

to **receive** [rɪˈsiːv] erhalten OT 2

recent [ˈriːsnt] neueste(r); jüngst **WS 1**, 19

   recently [ˈriːsntli] neulich OT 3

reception [rɪˈsepʃn] Rezeption; Empfang OT 1

receptionist [rɪˈsepʃənɪst] Empfangschef(in); Rezeptionist(in) OT 1

recipe [ˈresəpi] Rezept OT 2

to **recite** [rɪˈsaɪt] rezitieren; auswendig aufsagen **WS 3**, 96

to **recognize** [ˈrekəɡnaɪz] erkennen OT 2

to **recommend** [ˌrekəˈmend] empfehlen OT 2

to **record** [rɪˈkɔːd] aufnehmen OT 1

to **recover** [rɪˈkʌvə] sich erholen **WS 4**, 127

re-creation [ˌriːkriˈeɪʃn] Nachstellung; Neugestaltung **WS 1**, 18

recreational [ˌrekriˈeɪʃənl] Freizeit... OT 3

rectangular [rekˈtæŋɡjələ] rechteckig OT 2

to **recycle** [ˌriːˈsaɪkl] wiederverwerten OT 2

recycler [ˌriːˈsaɪklə] Wiederverwerter(in) OT 3

recycling [ˌriːˈsaɪklɪŋ] Recycling OT 2

red [red] rot OT 1

to **reduce** [rɪˈdjuːs] reduzieren; verringern OT 2

re-enactment [ɪˈnæktmənt] Nachstellung **WS 1**, 20

to **refer** [rɪˈfɜː] sich beziehen OT 3

referee [ˌrefəˈriː] Schiedsrichter(in) OT 3

reference [ˈrefrəns] Orientierung; Verweis **WS 3**, 93

to **refine** [rɪˈfaɪn] verfeinern **WS 1**, 23

reformation [ˌrefəˈmeɪʃn] Reformation **WS 1**, 32

refreshment [rɪˈfreʃmənt] Erfrischungsgetränk OT 2

refrigerator [rɪˈfrɪdʒəreɪtə] Kühlschrank **WS 3**, 93

refugee [ˌrefjuˈdʒiː] Flüchtling **WS 1**, 26

   refugee camp [ˌrefjuˈdʒiː kæmp] Flüchtlingslager **WS 1**, 26

refuse [ˈrefjuːs] Müll OT 2

   refuse collector [ˈrefjuːs kəlektə] Müllmann / -frau OT 2

to **refuse** [rɪˈfjuːz] sich weigern **WS 3**, 105

reggae [ˈreɡeɪ] Reggae OT 2

region [ˈriːdʒən] Region **WS 1**, 12

to **register** [ˈredʒɪstə] (sich) anmelden; registrieren **WS 1**, 26

to **regret** [rɪˈɡret] bereuen OT 2

regular [ˈreɡjələ] regelmäßig OT 1

   regularly [ˈreɡjələli] regelmäßig OT 2

rehearsal [rɪˈhɜːsl] Probe OT 2

to **rehearse** [rɪˈhɜːs] proben OT 3

reign [reɪn] Herrschaft OT 3

to **reign** [reɪn] herrschen OT 3

reindeer [ˈreɪndɪə] Rentier OT 2

to **reinvent** [ˌriːɪnˈvent] wieder erfinden **WS 3**, 82

to **relate** [rɪˈleɪt] sich beziehen auf OT 3

   related to [rɪˈleɪtɪd tə] in Bezug auf **WS 1**, 13

relation [rɪˈleɪʃn] Verwandte(r) OT 2

relationship [rɪˈleɪʃnʃɪp] Beziehung OT 3

relative [ˈrelətɪv] Verwandte; Angehörige OT 1

to **relax** [rɪˈlæks] sich entspannen; loslassen OT 2

   relaxed [rɪˈlæks] entspannt **WS 1**, 13

relaxation [ˌriːlækˈseɪʃn] Erholung OT 3

relaxing [rɪˈlæksɪŋ] erholsam OT 2

to **release** [rɪˈliːs] veröffentlichen; auf den Markt bringen **WS 3**, 76

relevant [ˈreləvənt] wichtig; relevant **WS 1**, 32

reliable [rɪˈlaɪəbl] verlässlich **WS 1**, 22

relief [rɪˈliːf] Erleichterung; Hilfe **WS 3**, 83

relieved [rɪˈliːvd] erleichtert OT 2

religion [rɪˈlɪdʒən] Religion OT 3

religious [rɪˈlɪdʒəs] religiös OT 1

   religious studies [rɪˈlɪdʒəs ˈstʌdiz] Religionsunterricht OT 1

to **relive** [riːˈlɪv] wieder erleben **WS 1**, 18

to **remain** [rɪˈmeɪn] bleiben **WS 3**, 93

remains [rɪˈmeɪnz] Überreste OT 3

to **remember** [rɪˈmembə] (sich) erinnern an OT 1

to **remind** [rɪˈmaɪnd] erinnern OT 2

remotely [rɪˈməʊtli] aus der Ferne **WS 3**, 78

removal van [rɪˈmuːvəl væn] Umzugswagen OT 2

to **remove** [rɪˈmuːv] entfernen OT 2

to **rent** [rent] mieten **WS 2**, 61

rental [ˈrentl] Miet... **WS 3**, 87

to **repaint** [ˌriːˈpeɪnt] übermalen **WS 3**, 81

to **repair** [rɪˈpeə] reparieren OT 2

to **repeat** [rɪˈpiːt] wiederholen OT 1

repetition [ˌrepəˈtɪʃn] Wiederholung **WS 4**, 123

to **rephrase** [ˌriːˈfreɪz] neu formulieren; umformulieren **WS 3**, 85

to **replace** [rɪˈpleɪs] ersetzen OT 3

replica [ˈreplɪkə] Kopie **WS 1**, 18

to **reply** [rɪˈplaɪ] antworten OT 1

report [rɪˈpɔːt] Bericht OT 2

reporter [rɪˈpɔːtə] Reporter(in) OT 1

reptile [ˈreptaɪl] Reptil OT 2

republic [rɪˈpʌblɪk] Republik **WS 1**, 25

request [rɪˈkwest] Bitte OT 2

to **require** [rɪˈkwaɪə] verlangen; fordern **WS 2**, 57

rescue [ˈreskjuː] Rettung OT 2

to **rescue** [ˈreskjuː] retten **WS 4**, 125

research [rɪˈsɜːtʃ] Forschung OT 2

to **research** [rɪˈsɜːtʃ] forschen OT 2

researcher [rɪˈsɜːtʃə] Forscher(in) OT 2

reservation [ˌrezəˈveɪʃn] Reservierung; Reservat OT 1

to **reserve** [rɪˈzɜːv] reservieren OT 3

   reserved [rɪˈzɜːvd] reserviert OT 2

resettlement [ˌriːˈsetlmənt] Umsiedlung **WS 1**, 26

resident [ˈrezɪdənt] Bewohner(in) OT 3

resort [rɪˈzɔːt] Urlaubsort; Zuflucht OT 2

resource [rɪˈsɔːs] Ressource; Mittel **WS 2**, 48

resourceful [rɪˈsɔːsfl] erfinderisch **WS 3**, 95

to **respect** [rɪˈspekt] achten OT 3

respectful [rɪˈspektfl] respektvoll OT 3

to **respond** [rɪˈspɒnd] reagieren; antworten OT 3

responsibility [rɪˌspɒnsəˈbɪləti] Verantwortung OT 3

responsible [rɪˈspɒnsəbl] verantwortlich OT 3

rest [rest] Rest; Pause OT 1

to **rest** [rest] ausruhen OT 1

restaurant [ˈrestrɒnt] Restaurant OT 1

to **restore** [rɪˈstɔː] wiederherstellen **WS 4**, 123

result [rɪˈzʌlt] Ergebnis OT 2

retailer [ˈriːteɪlə] Händler(in); Einzelhändler(in) **WS 2**, 64

to **retell** [ˌriːˈtel] nacherzählen **WS 3**, 83

retirement home [rɪˈtaɪəmənt həʊm] Seniorenheim OT 3

to **return** [rɪˈtɜːn] zurückkehren OT 2

reusable [ˌriːˈjuːzəbl] wiederverwendbar OT 3

to **reuse** [ˌriːˈjuːs] wiederverwenden OT 2

review [rɪˈvjuː] Rückblick OT 1

to **revise** [rɪˈvaɪz] revidieren; überarbeiten OT 2

revolting [rɪˈvəʊltɪŋ] abstoßend OT 2

revolution [ˌrevəˈluːʃn] Revolution OT 2

to **revolutionize** [ˌrevəˈluːʃənaɪz] revolutionieren **WS 3**, 78

rewarding [rɪˈwɔːdɪŋ] lohnend **WS 4**, 123

to **rewrite** [ˌriːˈraɪt] neu schreiben; umschreiben OT 1

rhinoceros [raɪˈnɒsərəs] Nashorn OT 2

rhyme [raɪm] Reim OT 1

rice [raɪs] Reis OT 1

rich [rɪtʃ] reich OT 1

ride [raɪd] Fahrt OT 1

to **ride** [raɪd] fahren; reiten OT 1

rider [ˈraɪdə] Fahrer(in); Reiter(in) OT 1

rifle [ˈraɪfl] Gewehr **WS 1**, 20

right [raɪt] rechte(r, -s); richtig OT 1

rights [raɪt] Rechte OT 3

rim [rɪm] Rand OT 3

to **ring** [rɪŋ] klingeln OT 1

ripe [raɪp] reif **WS 1**, 20

ripped [rɪpt] gerissen **WS 2**, 59

to **rise** [raɪz] aufsteigen OT 3

risk [rɪsk] Risiko; Gefahr OT 3

risky [ˈrɪski] gefährlich OT 3

river [ˈrɪvə] Fluss OT 1

road [rəʊd] Straße OT 1

roast [rəʊst] gebraten OT 1

robot [ˈrəʊbɒt] Roboter **WS 3**, 78

rock [rɒk] Stein; Rockmusik OT 2

  rock and roll [ˌrɒk ən ˈrəʊl] Rock and Roll OT 2

  rock climbing [ˈrɒk klaɪmɪŋ] Felsklettern OT 2

to **rock** [rɒk] schaukeln OT 3

rocket [ˈrɒkɪt] Rakete **WS 1**, 24

role [rəʊl] Rolle OT 1

roll [rəʊl] Rolle; Filmrolle OT 2

roller skate [ˈrəʊlə skeɪt] Rollschuh **WS 3**, 82

Roman [ˈrəʊmən] römisch OT 2

roof [ruːf] Dach OT 1

room [ruːm] Raum OT 1

root [ruːt] Wurzel OT 3

rope [rəʊp] Seil OT 1

rose [rəʊz] Rose **WS 1**, 16

rough [rʌf] rau **WS 4**, 129

round [raʊnd] rund; um ... herum OT 1

route [ruːt] Strecke OT 2

routine [ruːˈtiːn] Routine; Tagesablauf **WS 1**, 20

rover [ˈrəʊvə] Forschungsfahrzeug **WS 3**, 94

row [rəʊ] Reihe OT 1

rowing boat [ˈrəʊɪŋ bəʊt] Ruderboot OT 1

royal [ˈrɔɪəl] königlich OT 1

to **rub** [rʌb] reiben OT 3

rubber [ˈrʌbə] Gummi; Radiergummi OT 1

rubbish [ˈrʌbɪʃ] Müll OT 2

  rubbish bin [ˈrʌbɪʃ ˌbɪn] Mülleimer OT 2

  rubbish collection [ˈrʌbɪʃ kəˌlekʃn] Müllabfuhr OT 2

rucksack [ˈrʌksæk] Rucksack OT 1

rude [ruːd] unhöflich OT 1

rugby [ˈrʌgbi] Rugby OT 1

ruin [ˈruːɪn] Ruine OT 2

rule [ruːl] Regel OT 1

rulebook [ˈruːl bʊk] Regelwerk OT 2

ruler [ˈruːlə] Lineal OT 1

rummy [ˈrʌmi] Rommee OT 2

run [rʌn] Punkte OT 1

to **run** [rʌn] laufen; rennen OT 1

  to **run out** [rʌnˈaʊt] zur Neige gehen; zu Ende gehen OT 2

runner [ˈrʌnə] Läufer(in) OT 2

rural [ˈrʊərəl] ländlich **WS 2**, 62

to **rush** [rʌʃ] eilen OT 2

  to **rush off** [rʌʃ ɒf] losstürzen; wegrennen OT 2

  rush hour [ˈrʌʃ aʊə] Hauptverkehrszeit OT 1

Russian [ˈrʌʃn] russisch OT 2

S

sack [sæk] Sack OT 2

sacred [ˈseɪkrɪd] heilig **WS 1**, 31

sad [sæd] traurig OT 1

saddle [ˈsædl] Sattel OT 3

safari [səˈfɑːri] Safari OT 2

safe [seɪf] sicher OT 1

safety [ˈseɪfti] Sicherheit OT 2

to **sail** [seɪl] mit dem Schiff fahren; segeln OT 2

sailing [ˈseɪlɪŋ] Segeln OT 1

sailor [ˈseɪlə] Matrose OT 1

salad [ˈsæləd] Salat OT 1

sale [seɪl] Sale; Ausverkauf **WS 2**, 51

salmon [ˈsæmən] Lachs OT 1

salt [sɔːlt] Salz OT 3

same [seɪm] gleich OT 1

sample [ˈsɑːmpl] Probe **WS 3**, 84

sand [sænd] Sand OT 1

sandal [ˈsændl] Sandale **WS 2**, 59

sandwich [ˈsænwɪtʃ] Sandwich OT 1

sandy [ˈsændi] sandig OT 1

sassafras [ˈsæsəfræs] Sassafras OT 3

satellite [ˈsætəlaɪt] Satellit **WS 3**, 77

  satellite connection [ˈsætəlaɪt kəˈnekʃn] Satellitenverbindung **WS 3**, 87

Saturday [ˈsætədeɪ] Samstag OT 1

sauce [sɔːs] Soße OT 1

sausage [ˈsɒsɪdʒ] Wurst OT 1

sauté [ˈsəʊteɪ] geröstet OT 3

to **save** [seɪv] retten; sparen OT 2

savings [ˈseɪvɪŋz] Erspartes OT 3

savoury [ˈseɪvəri] pikant OT 3

saxophone [ˈsæksəfəʊn] Saxofon OT 2

to **say** [seɪ] sagen OT 1

to **scan** [skæn] überfliegen; scannen OT 3

to **scare** [skeə] Angst machen OT 2

scared [skeəd] verängstigt OT 1

scarf [skɑːf] Schal OT 2

scary [ˈskeəri] unheimlich OT 1

scene [siːn] Szene OT 2

scenery [ˈsiːnəri] Landschaft OT 2

schedule [ˈʃedjuːl] Stundenplan OT 2

school [skuːl] Schule OT 1

  school bag [ˈskuːl bæg] Schultasche OT 1

  school day [ˈskuːl deɪ] Schultag OT 1

schooling [ˈskuːlɪŋ] Schulausbildung **WS 3**, 80

schoolmate [ˈskuːlmeɪt] Schulkamerad(in) **WS 3**, 80

science [ˈsaɪəns] Wissen; Naturwissenschaften OT 1

  planetary science [ˈplænətri ˈsaɪəns] planetarische Wissenschaft; Planetenforschung **WS 3**, 95

  science fiction [ˌsaɪəns ˈfɪkʃn] Science-Fiction OT 2

scientific [ˌsaɪənˈtɪfɪk] wissenschaftlich OT 3

scientist [ˈsaɪəntɪst] Naturwissenschaftler(in) OT 1

scissors [ˈsɪzəz] Schere OT 1

scone [skəʊn] brötchenartiges, süßes Gebäck OT 3

to score [skɔː] punkten OT 1

scoring [ˈskɔːɪŋ] Treffen; Erzielen OT 1

Scottish [ˈskɒtɪʃ] schottisch OT 3

scout [skaʊt] Pfadfinder(in) OT 3

scrap [skræp] Abfall WS 3, 88

scrapple [skræpl] Scrapple OT 3

to scratch [skrætʃ] kratzen OT 2

to scream [skriːm] schreien; kreischen OT 3

screen [skriːn] Bildschirm; Leinwand OT 1

script [skrɪpt] Drehbuch OT 1

sculpture [ˈskʌlptʃə] Skulptur OT 2

sea [siː] Meer OT 1

seabed [ˈsiːbed] Meeresboden OT 3

seafood [ˈsiːfuːd] Meeresfrüchte OT 3

seal [siːl] Robbe OT 1

to search [sɜːtʃ] suchen OT 2

seaside [ˈsiːsaɪd] Küste OT 1

season [ˈsiːzn] Jahreszeit OT 3

seasoning [ˈsiːzənɪŋ] Gewürz OT 2

seat [siːt] Sitzplatz OT 1

seating [ˈsiːtɪŋ] Sitzplätze OT 2

second [ˈsekənd] Sekunde OT 1

second [ˈsekənd] zweite(r, -s) OT 1

secondary [ˈsekəndri] weiterführend; sekundär OT 1

secondary school [ˈsekəndri ˌskuːl] Sekundarschule; weiterführende Schule OT 1

secondly [ˈsekəndli] zweitens OT 2

secret [ˈsiːkrət] Geheimnis OT 2

secretary [ˈsekrətri] Sekretär(in) OT 1

section [ˈsekʃn] Teil OT 2

security [sɪˈkjʊərəti] Sicherheit OT 3

to see [siː] sehen OT 1

to seem [siːm] scheinen OT 2

to select [sɪˈlekt] wählen; auswählen WS 1, 32

self: by one's self [baɪ wʌnz ˈself] allein OT 2

self-catering [ˌself ˈkeɪtərɪŋ] mit Selbstversorgung OT 3

self-checkout [ˌself ˈtʃekaʊt] Selbstzahlerkasse WS 3, 78

self-motivated [ˌself ˈməʊtɪveɪtɪd] motiviert WS 3, 84

self-sufficient [ˌself səˈfɪʃnt] unabhängig; autark WS 3, 80

selfie [ˈselfiː] Selfie OT 1

selfish [ˈselfɪʃ] egoistisch OT 3

to sell [sel] verkaufen OT 1

semester [sɪˈmestə] Halbjahr; Semester OT 3

to send [send] schicken OT 1

sender [ˈsendə] Absender(in) OT 3

senior [ˈsiːniə] Oberstufenschüler(in); Senior(in) WS 2, 46

senior citizen [ˌsiːniə ˈsɪtɪzn] Senior(in) OT 3

sensation [senˈseɪʃn] Gefühl WS 3, 93

sense [sens] Sinn OT 2

sensible [ˈsensəbl] vernünftig OT 3

sensor [ˈsensə] Sensor WS 3, 87

sentence [ˈsentəns] Satz OT 1

separate [ˈseprət] getrennt OT 2

to separate [ˈseprət] sich trennen WS 3, 87

September [sepˈtembə] September OT 1

sequence [ˈsiːkwəns] Ablauf; Folge WS 4, 127

to sequence [ˈsiːkwəns] in eine Reihenfolge bringen OT 3

sequencing [ˈsiːkwənsɪŋ] Sequenzierung; Reihenfolge OT 3

sequentially [sɪˈkwenʃəli] folgend; nacheinander WS 2, 48

series [ˈsɪəriːz] Serie OT 1

serious [ˈsɪəriəs] ernst OT 2

seriously [ˈsɪəriəsli] ernst; im Ernst OT 2

to serve [sɜːv] servieren; bedienen OT 1

server [ˈsɜːvə] Aufschläger(in); Servierer(in); Kellner(in) OT 3

service [ˈsɜːvɪs] Dienst OT 2

session [ˈseʃn] Sitzung; Session; Einheit OT 2

set [set] Satz OT 3

to set [set] setzen; stellen OT 1

to set the stage [set ðə steɪdʒ] die Bühne vorbereiten OT 2

setting [ˈsetɪŋ] Einstellung OT 3

to settle [ˈsetl] sich ansiedeln WS 3, 93

to settle down [ˌsetl ˈdaʊn] (sich) beruhigen OT 2

settlement [ˈsetlmənt] Siedlung WS 1, 18

settler [ˈsetlə] Siedler(in) OT 3

seven [ˈsevn] sieben OT 1

seventeen [ˌsevnˈtiːn] siebzehn OT 1

seventy [ˈsevnti] siebzig OT 1

several [ˈsevrəl] mehrere; einige OT 2

sewing machine [ˈsəʊɪŋ məʃiːn] Nähmaschine OT 3

to shake [ʃeɪk] schütteln OT 2

to shake hands [ʃeɪk ˈhændz] jdm. die Hand geben OT 2

shaky [ˈʃeɪki] wackelig OT 3

shall [ʃæl] werden OT 2

shame: That's a shame. [ðæts ə ˈʃeɪm] Das ist schade. OT 2

shampoo [ʃæmˈpuː] Shampoo OT 3

shape [ʃeɪp] Form OT 1

to shape [ʃeɪp] formen OT 3

shaped [ʃeɪpt] geformt WS 1, 21

to share [ʃeə] teilen OT 1

she [ʃi] sie OT 1

shed [ʃed] Schuppen OT 1

sheep [ʃiːp] Schaf OT 1

sheepdog [ˈʃiːpdɒg] Hütehund OT 2

sheet [ʃiːt] Blatt OT 1

shelf [ʃelf] Regal OT 1

shelter [ˈʃeltə] Unterschlupf OT 2

shepherd [ˈʃepəd] Schäfer(in) OT 2

shift [ʃɪft] Schicht WS 4, 114

to shine [ʃaɪn] scheinen OT 1

ship [ʃɪp] Schiff OT 2

tall ship [ˌtɔːl ˈʃɪp] Großsegler OT 2

shipbuilding [ˈʃɪpbɪldɪŋ] Schiffbau OT 3

shirt [ʃɜːt] Hemd OT 1

shocked [ʃɒkt] schockiert WS 1, 13

shoe [ʃuː] Schuh OT 1

shoebox [ˈʃuːbɒks] Schuhschachtel OT 3

to shoot [ʃuːt] schießen OT 3

shop [ʃɒp] Laden OT 1

to shop [ʃɒp] kaufen; einkaufen OT 1

shopping [ˈʃɒpɪŋ] Einkaufen OT 1

shopper [ˈʃɒpə] Käufer(in) WS 2, 53

shore [ʃɔː] Küste OT 2

short [ʃɔːt] kurz OT 1

shortlist [ˈʃɔːtlɪst] Auswahlliste OT 2

shorts [ʃɔːts] kurze Hose; Shorts OT 1

shot [ʃɒt] Schuss; Schnappschuss WS 4, 119

should [ʃəd] sollte(n) OT 1

shoulder [ˈʃəʊldə] Schulter OT 1

shoulder pad [ˈʃəʊldə pæd] Schulterpolster OT 2

to shout [ʃaʊt] laut rufen OT 1

shovel [ˈʃʌvl] Schaufel OT 2

show [ʃəʊ] Vorstellung; Ausstellung OT 1

to show [ʃəʊ] zeigen OT 1

show-and-tell [ˌʃəʊ ən ˈtel] Kurzvortrag über einen mitgebrachten Gegenstand OT 1

shower [ˈʃaʊə] Dusche OT 2

showground [ˈʃəʊgraʊnd] Ausstellungsgelände OT 2

showtime ['ʃəʊtaɪm]
Vorstellungsbeginn **WS 4**, 120

shredded ['ʃredɪd] gerieben;
geschnetzelt OT 2

to **shut** [ʃʌt] zumachen; schließen OT 2

shy [ʃaɪ] schüchtern OT 2

sick [sɪk] krank OT 1

side [saɪd] Seite OT 1

sidewalk ['saɪdwɔːk] Bürgersteig
WS 1, 14

sigh [saɪ] Seufzer OT 2

to **sigh** [saɪ] seufzen OT 3

sight [saɪt] Sehvermögen;
Sehenswürdigkeit OT 1

sightseeing ['saɪtsiːɪŋ] Besichtigungen
OT 1

sign [saɪn] Schild OT 1

to **sign** [saɪn] unterschreiben OT 2

signal ['sɪgnəl] Signal OT 2

sign-up sheet ['saɪn ʌp ʃiːt]
Anmeldeliste OT 2

silence ['saɪləns] Stille OT 2

silly ['sɪli] dumm; albern OT 1

silver ['sɪlvə] Silber...; silbern OT 1

similar ['sɪmələ] ähnlich OT 2

similarity [ˌsɪmə'lærəti] Ähnlichkeit
OT 3

to **simmer** ['sɪmə] köcheln OT 2

simple ['sɪmpl] einfach OT 1

simple present [ˌsɪmpl 'preznt]
einfaches Präsens; einfache
Gegenwart OT 1

since [sɪns] seit OT 3

sincerely [sɪn'sɪəli] aufrichtig; mit
freundlichen Grüßen **WS 1**, 31

to **sing** [sɪŋ] singen OT 1

singer ['sɪŋə] Sänger(in) OT 1

single ['sɪŋgl] Einzel... OT 3

singular ['sɪŋgjələ] Einzahl; Singular
OT 1

sink [sɪŋk] Spülbecken OT 3

to **sink** [sɪŋk] sinken OT 3

sir [sɜː] Herr OT 1

siren ['saɪrən] Sirene OT 3

sister ['sɪstə] Schwester OT 1

to **sit** [sɪt] sitzen OT 1

to **sit down** [sɪt daʊn] hinsetzen OT 1

site [saɪt] Platz OT 2

situation [ˌsɪtʃu'eɪʃn] Lage; Situation
OT 1

six [sɪks] sechs OT 1

sixteen [ˌsɪks'tiːn] sechzehn OT 1

sixty ['sɪksti] sechzig OT 1

size [saɪz] Größe OT 1

to **skate** [skeɪt] Schlittschuh laufen
OT 2

skateboard ['skeɪtbɔːd] Skateboard
WS 3, 82

to **skateboard** ['skeɪtbɔːd]
Skateboardfahren gehen **WS 3**, 82

skeleton ['skelɪtn] Skelett OT 1

sketch [sketʃ] Skizze; Sketch **WS 4**, 119

to **sketch** [sketʃ] skizzieren; zeichnen
WS 3, 85

to **ski** [skiː] Ski laufen OT 3

skier ['skiːə] Skiläufer(in) OT 3

skiing ['skiːɪŋ] Skifahren OT 2

skilful ['skɪlfl] geschickt OT 3

skill [skɪl] Geschick; Fähigkeit OT 2

skilled [skɪld] geschickt; ausgebildet
WS 1, 24

to **skim** [skɪm] querlesen OT 3

skin [skɪn] Haut OT 2

skirt [skɜːrt] Rock OT 1

skit [skɪt] Sketch OT 2

sky [skaɪ] Himmel OT 1

skyscraper ['skaɪskreɪpə]
Wolkenkratzer OT 3

slave [sleɪv] Sklave; Sklavin **WS 1**, 21

slavery ['sleɪvəri] Sklaverei **WS 4**, 127

to **sleep** [sliːp] schlafen OT 1

sleeping bag ['sliːpɪŋ bæg] Schlafsack
OT 2

sleepover ['sliːpəʊvə] Pyjama-Party
OT 1

sleeve [sliːv] Ärmel OT 3

sleeveless ['sliːvləs] ärmellos **WS 2**, 59

slice [slaɪs] Scheibe OT 1

slide ['slaɪd] Folie OT 1

slideshow ['slaɪdʃəʊ] Präsentation;
Diashow OT 3

slogan ['sləʊgən] Slogan OT 2

slope [sləʊp] Piste OT 3

slow [sləʊ] langsam OT 2

slowly ['sləʊli] langsam OT 2

to **slow down** [sləʊ daʊn] (sich)
verlangsamen **WS 1**, 24

slum [slʌm] Slum OT 3

to **slump** [slʌmp] zusammensacken
WS 4, 117

small [smɔːl] klein OT 1

smallpox ['smɔːlpɒks] Pocken **WS 1**, 21

smart [smɑːt] intelligent; schlau
WS 2, 59

smartphone ['smɑːtfəʊn] Smartphone
OT 3

to **smell** [smel] riechen OT 1

to **smile** [smaɪl] lächeln OT 1

smoke [sməʊk] Rauch OT 2

smooth [smuːð] glatt OT 3

smoothly ['smuːðli] glatt OT 3

snack [snæk] Snack OT 1

snake [sneɪk] Schlange OT 1

snakes and ladders [ˌsneɪks ən 'lædəz]
Leiterspiel OT 2

sneaker ['sniːkər] Turnschuh **WS 1**, 15

snore [snɔː] Schnarcher OT 1

snow [snəʊ] Schnee OT 1

snowboarding ['snəʊbɔːdɪŋ]
Snowboard fahren OT 3

snowy ['snəʊi] verschneit OT 3

so [səʊ] also OT 1

soaked [səʊkd] durchnässt OT 3

soap [səʊp] Seife OT 2

to **soar** [sɔː] schweben OT 3

soccer ['sɒkə] Fußball OT 2

social ['səʊʃl] sozial OT 2

to **socialize** ['səʊʃəlaɪz] Kontakte
pflegen; unter die Leute kommen
WS 2, 58

society [sə'saɪəti] Gesellschaft **WS 1**, 32

sock [sɒk] Socke OT 2

sofa ['səʊfə] Sofa OT 1

soft [sɒft] weich OT 3

software ['sɒftweə] Software OT 1

soil [sɔɪl] Erdboden; Erde; Erdreich
OT 2

solar ['səʊlə] Sonnen... OT 3

solar power [ˌsəʊlə 'paʊə]
Solarenergie; Sonnenenergie **WS 3**, 80

soldier ['səʊldʒə] Soldat(in) OT 1

solo ['səʊləʊ] Solo **WS 2**, 46

solution [sə'luːʃn] Lösung OT 2

to **solve** [sɒlv] lösen OT 3

some [sʌm] etwas; einige OT 1

somebody ['sʌmbədi] jemand OT 1

someone ['sʌmwʌn] jemand OT 1

something ['sʌmθɪŋ] etwas OT 1

sometimes ['sʌmtaɪmz] manchmal
OT 1

somewhere ['sʌmweər] irgendwo OT 1

son [sʌn] Sohn OT 1

song [sɒŋ] Lied OT 1

songwriter ['sɒŋraɪtə] Songwriter(in)
OT 2

soon [suːn] bald OT 1

sore [sɔː] schmerzend OT 2

sorry ['sɒri] Entschuldigung OT 1

sort [sɔːt] Art OT 2

sound [saʊnd] Geräusch OT 1

to **sound** [saʊnd] klingen; ertönen OT 2

soup [suːp] Suppe OT 1

source [sɔːs] Quelle OT 2

south [saʊθ] Süd... OT 1

southern ['sʌðən] südlich OT 3

southwest [ˌsaʊθ'west] Südwesten OT 3

souvenir [suːvə'nɪə] Reiseandenken
OT 1

spa [spɑː] Heilbad OT 3

space [speɪs] Platz; Feld; Weltraum OT 2

  space exploration [ˈspeɪsˌekspləˈreɪʃn] Weltraumforschung **WS 3**, 94

spacecraft [ˈspeɪskrɑːft] Raumfahrzeug **WS 3**, 76

spaceship [ˈspeɪsʃɪp] Raumschiff **WS 3**, 92

spacesuit [ˈspeɪssuːt] Raumanzug **WS 3**, 95

spaghetti [spəˈgeti] Spaghetti OT 1

spaniel [ˈspænjəl] Spaniel OT 2

Spanish [ˈspænɪʃ] spanisch OT 1

to **spark** [spɑːk] entzünden **WS 3**, 90

sparkling [ˈspɑːklɪŋ] sprudelnd OT 1

to **speak** [spiːk] sprechen OT 1

speaker [ˈspiːkə] Sprecher(in) OT 1

speaking [ˈspiːkɪŋ] Sprechen OT 1

special [ˈspeʃl] Tagesgericht OT 1

special [ˈspeʃl] besondere(r,-s) OT 1

to **specialize** [ˈspeʃəlaɪz] sich spezialisieren **WS 4**, 109

specific [spəˈsɪfɪk] bestimmt; konkret; spezifisch OT 3

spectacular [spekˈtækjələ] spektakulär OT 2

spectator [spekˈteɪtə] Zuschauer(in) OT 3

to **speculate** [ˈspekjuleɪt] spekulieren; nachdenken **WS 1**, 26

speech [spiːtʃ] Rede OT 1

  speech bubble [ˈspiːtʃ bʌbl] Sprechblase OT 2

speed [spiːd] Geschwindigkeit OT 2

to **spell** [spel] buchstabieren OT 1

spelling [ˈspelɪŋ] Rechtschreibung; Schreibweise OT 1

to **spend** [spend] ausgeben; verbringen OT 1

spice [spaɪs] Gewürz OT 3

spiced [spaɪst] gewürzt **WS 3**, 84

spider [ˈspaɪdə] Spinne OT 1

to **spill** [spɪl] verschütten OT 2

spirit [ˈspɪrɪt] Geist OT 2

to **spit** [spɪt] spucken **WS 3**, 93

split [splɪt] Riss OT 3

to **spoil** [spɔɪl] verderben OT 2

spoilage [ˈspɔɪlɪdʒ] Verderben; Abfall **WS 3**, 84

spokeswoman [ˈspəʊkswʊmən] Sprecherin OT 2

sponsor [ˈspɒnsə] Sponsor(in); Geldgeber(in) OT 2

sponsored [ˈspɒnsəd] gesponsert; gestiftet OT 2

sponsorship [ˈspɒnsəʃɪp] finanzielle Unterstützung OT 2

spoon [spuːn] Löffel OT 2

spoonful [ˈspuːnfʊl] Löffel (Maßangabe) OT 2

sport [spɔːt] Sport OT 1

  to **be a good sport** [bi ə gʊd spɔːt] kein(e) Spielverderber(in) sein OT 2

  mass sport [mæs spɔːt] Massensport OT 3

sportsman [ˈspɔːtsmən] Sportler OT 3

sportspeople [ˈspɔːts piːpl] Sportler(innen) OT 3

sportswoman [ˈspɔːtswʊmən] Sportlerin OT 2

to **spot** [spɒt] erspähen OT 1

spotlight [ˈspɒtlaɪt] Mittelpunkt des Interesses **WS 4**, 110

to **sprain** [spreɪn] verstauchen OT 2

to **spread (out)** [spred] verbreiten **WS 1**, 27

spring [sprɪŋ] Frühling; Quelle OT 2

  hot spring [ˈhɒt sprɪŋ] Thermalquelle OT 2

  spring clean [ˌsprɪŋ ˈkliːn] Frühjahrsputz OT 2

to **sprinkle** [ˈsprɪŋkl] streuen OT 2

sprint [sprɪnt] Sprint OT 3

sprinter [ˈsprɪntə] Sprinter(in) OT 3

square [skweə] Quadrat; Feld; Platz OT 1

squash [skwɒʃ] Kürbis **WS 1**, 21

squirrel [ˈskwɪrəl] Eichhörnchen OT 1

to **stack** [stæk] stapeln **WS 3**, 80

stadium [ˈsteɪdiəm] Stadion OT 1

staff [stɑːf] Personal OT 3

stage [steɪdʒ] Phase; Bühne OT 2

  stage directions [ˈsteɪdʒ dərekʃnz] Bühnenanweisungen OT 2

stairs [ˈsteəz] Treppe, Treppenstufen OT 1

stalactite [ˈstæləktaɪt] Stalaktit OT 1

stalagmite [ˈstæləgmaɪt] Stalagmit OT 1

stall [stɔːl] Bude; Stall OT 2

to **stand** [stænd] stehen OT 1

  to **stand up** [ˈstænd ʌp] aufstehen OT 1

standard [ˈstændəd] normal; Standard... OT 3

stapler [ˈsteɪplə] Tacker OT 2

star [stɑː] Stern; Star OT 1

to **stare** [steə] starren OT 2

start [stɑːt] Anfang OT 1

to **start** [stɑːt] anfangen; beginnen OT 1

starter [ˈstɑːtə] Vorspeise OT 1

to **starve** [stɑːv] hungern (lassen); verhungern (lassen) OT 1

state [steɪt] Staat OT 1

statement [ˈsteɪtmənt] Aussage OT 1

station [ˈsteɪʃn] Station; Bahnhof OT 1

statistic [stəˈtɪstɪk] Statistik OT 3

statue [ˈstætʃuː] Statue OT 1

status [ˈsteɪtəs] Status; Stand **WS 1**, 26

to **stay** [steɪ] bleiben OT 1

steady [ˈstedi] ruhig; stabil OT 3

steak [steɪk] Steak OT 1

to **steal** [stiːl] klauen OT 2

steam [stiːm] Dampf OT 2

steel [stiːl] Stahl OT 2

steep [stiːp] steil OT 2

to **steer** [stɪə] steuern OT 3

stegosaurus [ˌstegəˈsɔːrəs] Stegosaurus OT 1

step [step] Schritt; Stufe OT 1

to **step** [step] treten **WS 1**, 16

  to **step in** [step ˈɪn] eintreten **WS 2**, 46

stew [stjuː] Eintopf OT 2

steward [ˈstjuːəd] Verwalter **WS 4**, 123

to **stick** [stɪk] kleben OT 1

sticky [ˈstɪki] klebrig; klebend **WS 3**, 86

still [stɪl] ruhig **WS 3**, 95

sting [stɪŋ] Stich OT 2

to **sting** [stɪŋ] stechen OT 2

to **stir** [stɜː] rühren OT 2

stock [stɒk] Viehbestand; Bestand OT 2

stomach [ˈstʌmək] Magen OT 2

stone [stəʊn] Stein OT 1

stop [stɒp] Halt; Haltestelle OT 2

storage [ˈstɔːrɪdʒ] Lagerung; Aufbewahrung OT 3

store [stɔː] Laden OT 1

storm [stɔːm] Sturm OT 2

story [ˈstɔːri] Geschichte OT 1

storyboard [ˈstɔːrɪbɔːd] Storyboard; Szenenbuch **WS 4**, 119

storybook [ˈstɔːrɪbʊk] Geschichtenbuch OT 2

stove [stəʊv] Ofen OT 3

straight [streɪt] gerade; direkt OT 3

  straight away [streɪt əˈweɪ] sofort; gleich OT 2

strange [streɪndʒ] seltsam OT 1

strategic [strəˈtiːdʒɪk] strategisch **WS 4**, 112

strategy [ˈstrætədʒi] Strategie **WS 1**, 33

straw [strɔː] Trinkhalm; Strohhalm; Stroh **WS 3**, 88

strawberry [ˈstrɔːbəri] Erdbeere OT 1

stream [striːm] Bach OT 2

streamer [ˈstriːmə] Luftschlangen **WS 2**, 58

street [striːt] Straße OT 1

  street collection [ˈstriːt kəlekʃn] Straßensammlung OT 2

strength [streŋθ] Stärke OT 2

stress [stres] Stress; Betonung OT 1

stressed [strest] gestresst; angestrengt OT 2

stressful [ˈstresfl] stressig **WS 2**, 61

to **stretch** [stretʃ] dehnen OT 2

strict [strɪkt] streng OT 2

strike [straɪk] Streik **WS 3**, 90

to **strike** [straɪk] schlagen; zuschlagen; streiken OT 1

striker [ˈstraɪkə] Stürmer(in) OT 3

string [strɪŋ] Schnur; Saite OT 2

stroke [strəʊk] Schlag OT 3

strong [strɒŋ] stark OT 2

structure [ˈstrʌktʃə] Struktur OT 1

student [ˈstjuːdnt] Student(in); Schüler(in) OT 1

  student council [ˈstjuːdnt ˈkaʊnsl] Schülerrat OT 2

studies [stʌdiz] Studium; Wissenschaft OT 1

to **study** [ˈstʌdi] studieren OT 1

stuff [stʌf] Zeug OT 2

stupid [ˈstjuːpɪd] dumm OT 2

  stupidly [ˈstjuːpɪdli] dumm OT 2

style [staɪl] Stil OT 2

stylish [ˈstaɪlɪʃ] schick **WS 3**, 85

sub-heading [ˈsʌb ˌhedɪŋ] Unterüberschrift OT 2

to **subject** [ˈsʌbdʒɪkt] unterwerfen **WS 4**, 127

subject [ˈsʌbdʒɪkt] Thema; Fach; Subjekt OT 1

  subject pronoun [ˌsʌbdʒekt ˈprəʊnaʊn] Subjektpronomen OT 1

submarine [ˌsʌbməˈriːn] U-Boot OT 3

substitute [ˈsʌbstɪtjuːt] Ersatz OT 3

substitution [ˌsʌbstɪˈtjuːʃn] Ersatz OT 3

subway [ˈsʌbweɪ] U-Bahn OT 1

to **succeed** [səkˈsiːd] erfolgreich sein OT 2

success [səkˈses] Erfolg OT 3

successful [səkˈsesfl] erfolgreich OT 2

such [sʌtʃ] so OT 2

sudden [ˈsʌdn] plötzlich OT 2

  suddenly [ˈsʌdənli] plötzlich OT 1

sugar [ˈʃʊgə] Zucker OT 3

to **suggest** [səˈdʒest] vorschlagen OT 1

suggestion [səˈdʒestʃən] Vorschlag OT 1

suit [suːt] Anzug OT 1

suitable [ˈsuːtəbl] geeignet **WS 2**, 64

suitcase [ˈsuːtkeɪs] Koffer OT 2

to **sulk** [sʌlk] schmollen OT 3

to **sum up** [sʌm ʌp] zusammenfassen **WS 3**, 85

to **summarize** [ˈsʌməraɪz] zusammenfassen OT 2

summary [ˈsʌməri] Zusammenfassung OT 3

summer [ˈsʌmə] Sommer OT 1

sun [sʌn] Sonne OT 1

sunburn [ˈsʌnbɜːn] Sonnenbrand OT 2

Sunday [ˈsʌndeɪ] Sonntag OT 1

sunglasses [ˈsʌnglɑːsɪz] Sonnenbrille OT 2

sunny [ˈsʌni] sonnig OT 1

sunscreen [ˈsʌnskriːn] Sonnenschutzmittel OT 2

sunset [ˈsʌnset] Sonnenuntergang OT 3

sunshine [ˈsʌnʃaɪn] Sonnenschein OT 3

sunstroke [ˈsʌnstrəʊk] Sonnenstich OT 2

superlative [suˈpɜːlətɪv] Superlativ OT 2

supermarket [ˈsuːpəmɑːkɪt] Supermarkt OT 1

to **supervise** [ˈsuːpəvaɪz] beaufsichtigen OT 3

supervisor [ˈsuːpəvaɪzə] Leiter(in) **WS 4**, 123

supply [səˈplaɪ] Vorrat OT 3

to **support** [səˈpɔːt] unterstützen OT 1

supporter [səˈpɔːtə] Befürworter(in); Fan OT 2

to **suppose** [səˈpəʊz] vermuten; annehmen OT 1

sure [ʃʊə] sicher OT 1

  to **make sure** [meɪk ʃʊə] sichergehen; sicherstellen OT 2

surely [ˈʃʊəli] sicherlich **WS 3**, 105

surface [ˈsɜːfɪs] Oberfläche OT 3

surfer [ˈsɜːfə] Surfer(in) **WS 4**, 110

surfing [ˈsɜːfɪŋ] Surfen OT 1

surgeon [ˈsɜːdʒən] Chirurg(in) OT 3

surprise [səˈpraɪz] Überraschung OT 1

surprised [səˈpraɪzd] überrascht OT 1

surprising [səˈpraɪzɪŋ] überraschend OT 2

survey [ˈsɜːveɪ] Umfrage OT 1

survival [səˈvaɪvl] Überleben OT 2

to **survive** [səˈvaɪv] überleben OT 3

sushi [ˈsuːʃi] Sushi OT 1

sustainability [səˌsteɪnəˈbɪləti] Nachhaltigkeit OT 3

sustainable [səˈsteɪnəbl] nachhaltig **WS 3**, 80

to **swallow** [ˈswɒləʊ] schlucken; hinunterschlucken **WS 3**, 93

swamp [swɒmp] Sumpf OT 2

to **swap** [swɒp] tauschen OT 1

to **swear** [sweə] schwören **WS 2**, 49

to **sweat** [swet] schwitzen OT 2

sweatshirt [ˈswetʃɜːt] Sweatshirt OT 1

Swedish [ˈswiːdɪʃ] schwedisch **WS 3**, 90

to **sweep** [swiːp] fegen **WS 1**, 14

sweet [swiːt] süß OT 1; Bonbon OT 2

  sweet corn [ˈswiːt kɔːn] Zuckermais OT 1

swelling [ˈswelɪŋ] Schwellung OT 2

to **swim** [swɪm] schwimmen OT 1

swimmer [ˈswɪmə] Schwimmer(in) OT 2

swimming [ˈswɪmɪŋ] Schwimmen OT 1

switch [swɪtʃ] Schalter OT 3

to **switch on** [swɪtʃ ɒn] anschalten OT 1

swollen [ˈswəʊln] geschwollen OT 2

sword [sɔːd] Schwert OT 1

syllable [ˈsɪləbəl] Silbe OT 2

symbol [ˈsɪmbl] Symbol OT 1

sympathetic [ˌsɪmpəˈθetɪk] mitfühlend OT 3

synaesthesia [ˌsɪnəsˈθiːziə] Synästhesie OT 2

synagogue [ˈsɪnəgɒg] Synagoge OT 1

synonym [ˈsɪnənɪm] Synonym OT 2

synthetic [sɪnˈθetɪk] synthetisch **WS 2**, 53

syrup [ˈsɪrəp] Sirup OT 3

system [ˈsɪstəm] System OT 1

T

tab [tæb] Tab OT 3

table [ˈteɪbl] Tisch OT 1

tablespoon [ˈteɪblspuːn] Esslöffel OT 2

tablet [ˈtæblət] Tablette OT 2

to **tackle** [ˈtækl] angreifen OT 3

taco [ˈtækəʊ] Taco OT 1

tactic [ˈtæktɪk] Taktik OT 2

tag [tæg] Etikett; kurze Schnur, die gelochte Blätter zusammenhält OT 2

tail [teɪl] Schwanz OT 2

Taiwanese [taɪwɑːnˈniːz] taiwanisch **WS 1**, 25

to **take** [teɪk] nehmen OT 1

  to **take a call** [teɪk ə kɔːl] einen Anruf entgegennehmen OT 2

  to **take a joke** [teɪk ə dʒəʊk] Spaß verstehen OT 2

  to **take a photo** [ˌteɪk ə ˈfəʊtəʊ] ein Foto machen OT 1

  to **take charge** [teɪk tʃɑːdʒ] die Leitung übernehmen OT 2 to **take for granted** [teɪk fə ˈɡrɑːntɪd] für selbstverständlich halten **WS 3**, 78

to **take out** [ˈteɪk aʊt] rausbringen **WS 1**, 15

to **take part** [teɪk ˈpɑːt] teilnehmen OT 2

to **take turns** [teɪk tɜːnz] (sich) abwechseln OT 1

to **take up** [teɪk ʌp] mit etw. anfangen; aufnehmen OT 1

takeout [ˈteɪkaʊt] Essen zum Mitnehmen **WS 4**, 114

tale [teɪl] Geschichte OT 2

talent [ˈtælənt] Talent; Begabung OT 2

talented [ˈtæləntɪd] talentiert OT 3

to **talk** [tɔːk] reden OT 1

tall [tɔːl] groß; hoch OT 1

tally [ˈtæli] Gesamtliste **WS 2**, 64

tank [tæŋk] Tank OT 3

to **tap** [tæp] tippen; klopfen OT 2

tape [teɪp] Klebeband OT 1

target [ˈtɑːɡɪt] Ziel OT 2

task [tɑːsk] Aufgabe OT 1

taste [teɪst] Geschmack **WS 3**, 87

tasty [ˈteɪsti] schmackhaft OT 2

tattoo [təˈtuː] Tätowierung OT 3

tax [tæks] Steuer **WS 1**, 18

taxi [ˈtæksi] Taxi OT 1

tea [tiː] Tee OT 1

tea light [ˈtiː laɪt] Teelicht OT 2

to **teach** [tiːtʃ] unterrichten OT 1

teacher [ˈtiːtʃə] Lehrer(in) OT 1

team [tiːm] Mannschaft OT 1

teammate [ˈtiːmmeɪt] Mitspieler(in) OT 2

teamwork [ˈtiːmwɜːk] Teamwork; Gruppenarbeit **WS 4**, 112

tear [tɪə] Träne OT 2

to **tease** [tiːz] ärgern OT 1

tech [tek] technisch OT 2

technical [ˈteknɪkl] technisch **WS 4**, 119

technique [tekˈniːk] Technik; Methode **WS 2**, 49

technological [ˌteknəˈlɒdʒɪkl] technisch; technologisch **WS 3**, 77

technology [tekˈnɒlədʒi] Technologie OT 1

teen [tiːn] Teenager OT 2

teenage [ˈtiːneɪdʒ] Teenager... **WS 1**, 16

teenager [ˈtiːneɪdʒə] Teenager; Jugendliche(r) OT 2

teleconference [ˈtelikɒnfrəns] Telefonkonferenz OT 3

telegraph [ˈteligrɑːf] Telegraf **WS 3**, 83

television [ˈtelivɪʒn] Fernseher OT 2

to **tell** [tel] erzählen OT 1

temperature [ˈtemprətʃə] Temperatur OT 2

template [ˈtempleɪt] Vorlage **WS 4**, 119

temple [ˈtempl] Tempel OT 1

ten [ten] zehn OT 1

tennis [ˈtenɪs] Tennis OT 1

tense [tens] Zeitform; Tempus OT 1

tension [ˈtenʃn] Anspannung **WS 3**, 93

tent [tent] Zelt OT 1

term [tɜːm] Semester OT 2

terrible [ˈterəbl] schrecklich OT 1

terrier [ˈteriə] Terrier OT 2

terrified [ˈterɪfaɪd] verängstigt OT 3

test [test] Test OT 1

text [tekst] SMS; Text OT 1

to **text** [tekst] texten; simsen OT 1

than [ðən] als OT 1

to **thank** [θæŋk] danken OT 1

thanks [θæŋks] danke OT 1

Thanksgiving [ˌθæŋksˈɡɪvɪŋ] amerikanisches Erntedankfest OT 2

that [ðæt] diese(r, -s); jene(r, -s) OT 1

That'll be ... [ðætl bi] Das macht... OT 2

the [ðiː] der; die; das OT 1

theatre [ˈθiːətər] Theater OT 1

their [ðeə] ihr OT 1

theirs [ðeəz] ihre(r, -s) OT 2

them [ðem] sie; ihnen OT 1

theme [θiːm] Thema **WS 2**, 58

themselves [ðəmˈselvz] sich (selbst) OT 3

then [ðen] dann OT 1

theoretical [ˌθɪəˈretɪkl] theoretisch **WS 3**, 85

theory [ˈθɪəri] Theorie OT 1

there [ðeə] da; dort OT 1

there is / are [ðeə ɪz / ɑ] es gibt OT 1

therefore [ˈðeəfɔː] deshalb OT 3

these [ðiːz] diese OT 1

they [ðeɪ] sie OT 1

thick [θɪk] dick OT 1

thigh [θaɪ] Oberschenkel OT 1

thin [θɪn] dünn OT 1

thing [θɪŋ] Ding OT 1

to **think** [θɪŋk] denken OT 1

to **think about** [ˈθɪŋk əbaʊt] denken an; nachdenken über OT 1

to **think of** [ˈθɪŋk əv] denken an; sich erinnern an OT 1

good thinking [ˈɡʊd ˈθɪŋkɪŋ] Gut mitgedacht! OT 2

third [θɜːd] dritte(r, -s) OT 1

thirsty [ˈθɜːsti] durstig OT 1

thirteen [ˌθɜːˈtiːn] dreizehn OT 1

thirty [ˈθɜːti] dreißig OT 1

this [ðɪs] diese(r, -s) OT 1

thorn [θɔːn] Stachel OT 2

those [ðəʊz] diese; jene dort OT 1

though [ðəʊ] obwohl; jedoch OT 2

thought [θɔːt] Gedanke **WS 1**, 15

thoughtful [ˈθɔːtfl] nachdenklich; rücksichtsvoll OT 3

thoughtless [ˈθɔːtləs] gedankenlos; rücksichtslos OT 2

thousand [ˈθaʊznd] Tausend OT 1

three [θri] drei OT 1

thrifting [θrɪftɪŋ] Secondhand shoppen **WS 2**, 50

thrift store [ˈθrɪft stɔː] Secondhandladen **WS 2**, 44

throat [θrəʊt] Hals OT 2

throng [θrɒŋ] Menschenmenge OT 2

through [θruː] durch OT 1

throughout [θruːˈaʊt] während; durchweg OT 3

to **throw** [θrəʊ] werfen OT 1

to **throw away** [ˌθrəʊ əˈweɪ] wegwerfen OT 2

to **throw up** [θrəʊ ʌp] (sich) übergeben OT 2

thumb [θʌm] Daumen **WS 2**, 46

thunderstorm [ˈθʌndəstɔːm] Gewitter OT 2

Thursday [ˈθɜːzdeɪ] Donnerstag OT 1

tick [tɪk] Haken; Häkchen OT 2

ticket [ˈtɪkɪt] Eintrittskarte; Fahrkarte OT 1

ticket office [ˈtɪkɪt ˌɒfɪs] Fahrkartenschalter OT 2

tidy [ˈtaɪdi] aufgeräumt OT 2

tie [taɪ] Krawatte OT 1

to **tie** [taɪ] binden; anbinden OT 2

tiger [ˈtaɪɡə] Tiger OT 1

till [tɪl] bis OT 2

to **tilt** [tɪlt] sich neigen OT 3

time [taɪm] Zeit OT 1

all the time [ɔːl ðiː taɪm] die ganze Zeit OT 2

timeline [ˈtaɪmlaɪn] Zeitachse OT 2

timely [ˈtaɪmli] rechtzeitig; passend OT 3

timetable [ˈtaɪmteɪbl] Fahrplan; Stundenplan OT 1

timing [ˈtaɪmɪŋ] Zeitpunkt OT 3

tin [tɪn] Zinn; Dose OT 2

tinder [ˈtɪndə] Zunder OT 2

tinned [tɪnd] in Dosen OT 2

tiny [ˈtaɪni] winzig OT 1

tip [tɪp] Spitze; Hinweis OT 1

tired [ˈtaɪəd] müde OT 1

title [ˈtaɪtl] Titel OT 1

to [tu:] zu OT 1
toad [təʊd] Kröte OT 2
toast [təʊst] Toast OT 2
tobacco [təˈbækəʊ] Tabak OT 3
today [təˈdeɪ] heute OT 1
toe [təʊ] Zeh OT 1
together [təˈgeðə] zusammen OT 1
toilet [ˈtɔɪlət] Toilette OT 2
  composting toilet [ˈkɒmpɒstɪŋ ˈtɔɪlət] Biotoilette OT 3
tolerant [ˈtɒlərənt] tolerant WS 3, 95
tomato [təˈmɑːtəʊ] Tomate OT 1
tomorrow [təˈmɒrəʊ] morgen OT 1
ton [tʌn] Tonne OT 2
tongue [tʌŋ] Zunge OT 3
tonight [təˈnaɪt] heute Abend OT 1
too [tu:] zu; auch OT 1
tool [tu:l] Werkzeug OT 2
tooth [tu:θ] Zahn OT 2
toothbrush [ˈtuːθbrʌʃ] Zahnbürste WS 3, 78
toothpaste [ˈtuːθpeɪst] Zahnpasta WS 3, 93
top [tɒp] obere(r, -s); Spitze OT 1
to top [tɒp] belegen OT 3
topic [ˈtɒpɪk] Thema OT 1
torch [tɔːtʃ] Taschenlampe OT 1
torchlight [ˈtɔːtʃlaɪt] Licht der Taschenlampe OT 1
tortoise [ˈtɔːtəs] Schildkröte OT 1
to toss [tɒs] werfen OT 3
total [ˈtəʊtl] gesamt OT 1
to touch [tʌtʃ] berühren; anfassen OT 1
touchdown [ˈtʌtʃdaʊn] Touchdown OT 2
touchscreen [ˈtʌtʃskriːn] Berührungsbildschirm WS 3, 77
tough [tʌf] hart WS 3, 90
tour [tʊə] Reise; Rundgang OT 1
tourism [ˈtʊərɪzəm] Tourismus OT 2
tourist [ˈtʊərɪst] Tourist(in) OT 1
tournament [ˈtɔːnəmənt] Turnier OT 3
towards [təˈwɔːdz] in Richtung OT 2
towel [ˈtaʊəl] Handtuch OT 2
tower [ˈtaʊə] Turm OT 1
town [taʊn] Stadt OT 1
township [ˈtaʊnʃɪp] Gemeinde WS 4, 123
townspeople [ˈtaʊnzpiːpl] Stadtbewohner(innen) WS 1, 20
towpath [ˈtəʊpɑːθ] Treidelpfad OT 3
toxic [ˈtɒksɪk] toxisch; giftig WS 2, 52
toy [tɔɪ] Spielzeug OT 2
track [træk] Weg OT 1
tractor [ˈtræktə] Traktor OT 2
tradition [trəˈdɪʃn] Tradition OT 2

traditional [trəˈdɪʃənl] traditionell OT 1
traffic [ˈtræfɪk] Verkehr OT 1
  traffic jam [ˈtræfɪk dʒæm] Stau OT 2
to traffic [ˈtræfɪkt] verschleppen; illegalen Handel treiben WS 4, 124
trafficker [ˈtræfɪktə] Schlepper WS 4, 124
trail [treɪl] Pfad; Spur OT 2
trailer [ˈtreɪlə] Trailer WS 2, 49
train [treɪn] Zug OT 1
  steam train [ˈstiːm treɪn] Dampfzug OT 2
to train [treɪn] trainieren OT 2
trainer [ˈtreɪnə] Turnschuh; Trainer(in) OT 1
training [ˈtreɪnɪŋ] Ausbildung OT 2
  training course [ˈtreɪnɪŋ kɔːs] Ausbildungslehrgang; Weiterbildungslehrgang OT 2
tram [træm] Straßenbahn OT 1
transatlantic [ˌtrænzətˈlæntɪk] transatlantisch OT 3
to transfer [trænsˈfɜː] transferieren; übertragen WS 1, 26
to transform [trænsˈfɔːm] verändern WS 2, 63
transformation [ˌtrænsfəˈmeɪʃn] Veränderung; Verwandlung WS 2, 63
to translate [trænsˈleɪt] übersetzen OT 1
transplant [trænsˈplɑːnt] Transplantation OT 3
transport [ˈtrænspɔːt] Verkehr; Verkehrsmittel OT 2
  public transport [ˌpʌblɪk ˈtrænspɔːt] öffentliche Verkehrsmittel OT 2
trash [træʃ] Abfall OT 2
  trash can [ˈtræʃ kæn] Mülleimer OT 2
travel [ˈtrævl] Reisen OT 1
travel agent [ˈtrævl eɪdʒənt] Reisekauffrau / -mann OT 3
to travel [ˈtrævl] reisen OT 1
traveller [ˈtrævələ] Reisende(r) OT 3
tray [treɪ] Tablett OT 2
treadmill [ˈtredmɪl] Laufband WS 3, 93
treasure [ˈtreʒə] Schatz OT 3
to treat [triːt] behandeln WS 2, 49
tree [triː] Baum OT 1
to trek [trek] trecken OT 2
to tremble [ˈtrembl] zittern OT 2
trend [trend] Trend WS 2, 44
trial [ˈtraɪəl] Prozess OT 2
triangle [ˈtraɪæŋgl] Dreieck; Triangel OT 2
triangular [traɪˈæŋgjələ] dreieckig OT 3
tribal [ˈtraɪbl] Stammes... OT 3

tribe [traɪb] Stamm OT 3
tricky [ˈtrɪki] kompliziert WS 1, 19
trip [trɪp] Reise; Ausflug OT 1
to trip [trɪp] stolpern OT 2
trolley [ˈtrɒli] Wagen OT 1
trophy [ˈtrəʊfi] Pokal OT 2
tropical [ˈtrɒpɪkl] tropisch WS 4, 123
to trot [trɒt] traben OT 2
trouble [ˈtrʌbl] Schwierigkeit; Ärger OT 2
  to be in trouble [ˌbi ɪn ˈtrʌbl] in Schwierigkeiten sein; Ärger bekommen OT 2
trousers [ˈtraʊzəz] Hose OT 1
truck [trʌk] Laster; Lastkraftwagen OT 1
true [truː] wahr; richtig OT 1
trumpet [ˈtrʌmpɪt] Trompete OT 2
trunk [trʌŋk] Kofferraum OT 2
to trust [trʌst] vertrauen OT 3
truth [truːθ] Wahrheit OT 3
to try [traɪ] versuchen OT 1
  to try out [traɪ aʊt] ausprobieren OT 2
tube [tjuːb] Schlauch; Londoner U-Bahn OT 1
Tuesday [ˈtjuːzdeɪ] Dienstag OT 1
tuna [ˈtjuːnə] Thunfisch OT 1
tunnel [ˈtʌnl] Tunnel OT 3
turbine [ˈtɜːbaɪn] Turbine WS 3, 80
turkey [ˈtɜːki] Truthahn OT 1
turn: It's your turn. [ˌɪts ˈjɔː tɜːn] Du bist dran. OT 1
to turn [tɜːn] drehen OT 2
  to turn off [tɜːn ɒf] ausschalten OT 2
turntable [ˈtɜːnteɪbl] Drehscheibe OT 2
turtle [ˈtɜːtl] Schildkröte OT 2
  leatherback turtle [ˈleðəbæk ˌtɜːtl] Lederrückenschildkröte OT 2
tusk [tʌsk] Stoßzahn OT 3
tutor [ˈtjuːtə] Tutor(in) WS 2, 59
TV [ˌtiːˈviː] Fernsehen OT 1
tweezers [ˈtwiːzəz] Pinzette OT 2
twelve [twelv] zwölf OT 1
twenty [ˈtwenti] zwanzig OT 1
twenty-four [ˈtwenti fɔː] vierundzwanzig OT 1
twenty-one [ˈtwenti wʌn] einundzwanzig OT 1
twenty-three [ˈtwenti θri] dreiundzwanzig OT 1
twenty-two [ˈtwenti tu] zweiundzwanzig OT 1
twice [twaɪs] zweimal OT 2
twig [twɪg] Zweig OT 2
twin [twɪn] Zwilling OT 1

to **twinkle** ['twɪŋkl] glitzern **WS 3**, 95
twisted ['twɪstɪd] verdreht OT 1
two [tu:] zwei OT 1
type [taɪp] Art OT 2
typical ['tɪpɪkl] typisch OT 2
tyrannosaurus rex [tɪˌrænəˈsɔːrəs reks]
Tyrannosaurus rex OT 1

U
ugly ['ʌgli] hässlich OT 1
umbrella [ʌmˈbrelə] Regenschirm OT 1
unaccompanied minor [ˌʌnəkʌmpənɪd
ˈmaɪnə] alleinreisendes Kind OT 2
unbelievable [ˌʌnbɪˈliːvəbl] unglaublich
OT 2
uncle ['ʌŋkl] Onkel OT 1
uncomfortable [ʌnˈkʌmftəbl]
unbequem OT 3
uncountable [ʌnˈkaʊntəbl] unzählbar
OT 1
to **uncover** [ʌnˈkʌvə] freilegen OT 3
under ['ʌndə] unter OT 1
underground ['ʌndəgraʊnd] U-Bahn
OT 1
to **underline** [ˌʌndəˈlaɪn] unterstreichen
OT 1
underneath [ˌʌndəˈniːθ] darunter OT 3
to **understand** [ˌʌndəˈstænd] verstehen
OT 1
underwater [ˌʌndəˈwɔːtə]
Unterwasser-; unter Wasser OT 2
undocumented [ˌʌnˈdɒkjumentɪd] nicht
erfasst **WS 4**, 125
undrained [ˌʌnˈdreɪnd] nicht abgetropft
OT 2
unemployment [ˌʌnɪmˈplɔɪmənt]
Arbeitslosigkeit OT 3
unexpectedly [ˌʌnɪkˈspektɪdli]
unerwarteterweise OT 3
unfair [ˌʌnˈfeə] nicht fair OT 2
unfairness [ˌʌnˈfeənəs]
Ungerechtigkeit; Unfairness **WS 4**, 127
unfortunately [ʌnˈfɔːtʃənətli] leider
OT 3
unfriendly [ʌnˈfrendli] unfreundlich
WS 1, 26
unhappy [ʌnˈhæpi] unglücklich OT 1
unhealthy [ʌnˈhelθi] ungesund OT 1
uni ['juːni] Uni OT 3
uniform ['juːnɪfɔːm] Uniform OT 1
unique [juˈniːk] einzigartig OT 2
university [ˌjuːnɪˈvɜːsəti] Universität
OT 1
unknown [ˌʌnˈnəʊn] unbekannt OT 3
unless [ənˈles] außer wenn **WS 2**, 51
unlike [ˌʌnˈlaɪk] anders als OT 3

unlikely [ʌnˈlaɪkli] unwahrscheinlich
WS 2, 51
to **unlock** [ˌʌnˈlɒk] aufschließen;
entriegeln OT 1
unlucky [ʌnˈlʌki] glücklos OT 2
unnecessary [ʌnˈnesəsəri] unnötig;
überflüssig **WS 3**, 95
to **unpack** [ˌʌnˈpæk] auspacken OT 2
unpredictability [ˌʌnprɪˌdɪktəˈbɪləti]
Unberechenbarkeit OT 2
unsafe [ʌnˈseɪf] gefährlich OT 3
unspoilt [ˌʌnˈspɔɪlt] unberührt OT 3
unsurprisingly [ˌʌnsəˈpraɪzɪŋli]
erwartungsgemäß OT 3
until [ʌnˈtɪl] bis OT 3
unusual [ʌnˈjuːʒuəl] ungewöhnlich
OT 2
unwell [ʌnˈwel] krank OT 2
up [ʌp] hinauf; nach oben OT 1
to **update** ['ʌpdeɪt] aktualisieren OT 3
to **upload** ['ʌpləʊd] hochladen OT 3
upset [ʌpˈset] verärgert; traurig OT 2
upside ['ʌpsaɪd] Vorteil **WS 3**, 93
upstairs [ʌpˈsteəz] oben; im oberen
Stockwerk OT 1
upwards ['ʊpwədz] aufwärts; nach
oben OT 3
urban ['ɜːbən] städtisch; urban
WS 2, 63
to **urge** [ɜːdʒ] dringend bitten; drängen
WS 4, 127
us [ʌs] uns OT 1
to **use** [juːz] benutzen OT 1
useful ['juːsfl] nützlich OT 1
user ['juːzə] Benutzer(in) OT 2
usher ['ʌʃə] Platzanweiser(in) **WS 4**, 120
usual ['juːʒuəl] üblich OT 2
usually ['juːʒuəli] normalerweise
OT 1

V
vacation [veɪˈkeɪʃn] Urlaub OT 2
to **vacuum** ['vækjuːm] staubsaugen
WS 1, 15
vacuum cleaner ['vækjuːm kliːnə]
Staubsauger **WS 3**, 78
valley ['væli] Tal OT 1
valuable ['væljuəbl] wertvoll OT 2
value ['væljuː] Wert **WS 1**, 32
vampire ['væmpaɪə] Vampir(in) OT 2
van [væn] Transporter; Lieferwagen
WS 3, 80
vanilla [vəˈnɪlə] Vanille OT 1
vegan ['viːgən] Veganer(in); vegan
OT 1
vegetable ['vedʒtəbl] Gemüse OT 1

vegetarian [ˌvedʒəˈteəriən]
Vegetarier(in); vegetarisch OT 1
veggie ['vedʒi] vegetarisch OT 2
vehicle ['viːəkl] Fahrzeug OT 1
off-road vehicle ['ɒf rəʊd ˌviːəkl]
Geländefahrzeug OT 1
velvety ['velvəti] samtartig OT 2
vending machine ['vendɪŋ məʃiːn]
Automat OT 1
venue ['venjuː] Veranstaltungsort
OT 3
verb [vɜːb] Verb; Zeitwort OT 1
versatile ['vɜːsətaɪl] vielseitig OT 3
verse [vɜːs] Strophe OT 1
version ['vɜːʒn] Version OT 3
versus ['vɜːsəs] versus **WS 4**, 112
vertical ['vɜːtɪkl] senkrecht; vertikal
WS 2, 64
very ['veri] sehr OT 1
vest [vest] Weste; Unterhemd OT 2
vet [vet] Tierarzt / -ärztin **WS 4**, 113
veterinarian [ˌvetərɪˈneəriən]
Tierarzt / -ärztin **WS 4**, 113
via ['viːə] über OT 2
to **vibrate** [vaɪˈbreɪt] vibrieren;
pulsieren **WS 3**, 96
victim ['vɪktɪm] Opfer **WS 4**, 124
video ['vɪdiəʊ] Videokassette; Video
OT 1
video clip ['vɪdiəʊ klɪp] Videoclip
OT 2
video game ['vɪdiəʊ geɪm] Videospiel
OT 2
view [vjuː] Sicht; Aussicht OT 1
viewer ['vjuːə] Zuschauer(in) OT 3
viewing gallery ['vjuːɪŋ ˈgæləri]
Aussichtsgalerie OT 1
viewpoint ['vjuːpɔɪnt] Aussichtspunkt
OT 3
village ['vɪlɪdʒ] Dorf OT 1
villager ['vɪlɪdʒə] Dorfbewohner(in)
WS 4, 123
violence ['vaɪələns] Gewalt **WS 2**, 61
non-violence [ˌnɒn ˈvaɪələns]
Gewaltlosigkeit OT 3
violet ['vaɪələt] violett OT 1
violin [ˌvaɪəˈlɪn] Geige OT 1
virtual ['vɜːtʃuəl] virtuell **WS 2**, 59
visa ['viːzə] Visum **WS 1**, 26
vision ['vɪʒn] Vision **WS 4**, 111
to **visit** ['vɪzɪt] besuchen OT 1
visitor ['vɪzɪtə] Besucher(in) OT 1
visual ['vɪʒuəl] Bildmaterial **WS 3**, 85
visual ['vɪʒuəl] visuell OT 2
visual aid [ˌvɪʒuəl ˈeɪd]
Anschauungsmaterial **WS 2**, 53

visual art [ˈvɪʒuəl ˈɑːt] bildende Kunst OT 2

visualization [ˌvɪʒuəlaɪˈzeɪʃn] Visualisierung OT 3

vital [ˈvaɪtl] lebenswichtig WS 4, 113

vlog [ˈvlɒg] Vlog; Video-Blog OT 3

vlogger [ˈvlɒgə] Vlogger(in) OT 3

vocals [ˈvəʊklz] Gesang OT 2

voice [vɔɪs] Stimme OT 2

tone of voice [təʊn əv vɔɪs] Tonfall; Artikulierung WS 4, 117

to **voice** [vɔɪs] äußern; zum Ausdruck bringen WS 3, 90

volleyball [ˈvɒlibɔːl] Volleyball OT 3

volunteer [ˌvɒlənˈtɪə] Freiwillige(r); Ehrenamtliche(r) OT 2

to **vote** [vəʊt] wählen OT 1

vowel [ˈvaʊəl] Vokal; Selbstlaut OT 1

voyage [ˈvɔɪɪdʒ] Reise OT 3

W

wacky [ˈwæki] verrückt; verdreht WS 2, 58

waffle [ˈwɒfl] Waffel OT 3

wage [weɪdʒ] Gehalt WS 4, 116

wagon [ˈwægən] Wagen WS 1, 28

wagon train [ˈwægən treɪn] Treck; Wagenzug WS 1, 28

to **wait** [weɪt] warten OT 1

waiter [ˈweɪtə] Kellner(in) OT 1

to **wake up** [weɪk ʌp] aufwachen OT 1

walk [wɔːk] Spaziergang; Wanderung OT 2

walker [ˈwɔːkə] Wanderer / Wanderin OT 3

wall [wɔːl] Wand OT 1

wall display [wɔːl dɪˈspleɪ] Wandzeitung OT 2

wallet [ˈwɒlɪt] Brieftasche OT 1

to **want** [wɒnt] wollen OT 1

war [wɔː] Krieg OT 2

wardrobe [ˈwɔːdrəʊb] Kleiderschrank OT 1

warm [wɔːm] warm OT 2

warm-up [ˈwɔːm ʌp] Aufwärmübung OT 2

to **warm up** [wɔːm ʌp] aufwärmen OT 2

to **warn** [wɔːn] warnen OT 3

warrior [ˈwɒriə] Krieger(in) OT 2

warship [ˈwɔːʃɪp] Kriegsschiff OT 3

to **wash** [wɒʃ] waschen OT 2

washing up [ˌwɒʃɪŋ ʌp] Geschirrspülen OT 2

wasp [wɒsp] Wespe OT 3

waste [weɪst] Abfall OT 3

to **watch** [wɒtʃ] beobachten OT 1

water [ˈwɔːtə] Wasser OT 1

waterbus [ˈwɔːtə bʌs] Wasserbus OT 3

waterfall [ˈwɔːtəfɔːl] Wasserfall OT 1

waterproof [ˈwɔːtəpruːf] wasserdicht OT 2

waterproofs [ˈwɔːtəpruːfs] wasserdichte Kleidung OT 3

wave [weɪv] Welle OT 1

to **wave** [weɪv] winken OT 2

way [weɪ] Weg OT 1

waypoint [ˈweɪpɔɪnt] Zwischenstation OT 2

we [wi] wir OT 1

weak [wiːk] schwach OT 3

weakness [ˈwiːknəs] Schwäche WS 3, 86

wealth [welθ] Reichtum; Vermögen WS 1, 24

weapon [ˈwepən] Waffe OT 3

to **wear** [weə] tragen OT 1

weather [ˈweðə] Wetter OT 1

webinar [ˈwebɪnɑː] Webinar WS 4, 123

website [ˈwebsaɪt] Webseite OT 1

to **wed** [wedɪd] heiraten OT 3

wedding [ˈwedɪŋ] Hochzeit OT 3

Wednesday [ˈwenzdeɪ] Mittwoch OT 1

week [wiːk] Woche OT 1

weekday [ˈwiːkdeɪ] Wochentag OT 3

weekend [ˈwiːkend] Wochenende OT 1

weekly [ˈwiːkli] wöchentlich OT 3

to **weigh** [weɪ] wiegen OT 3

weight [weɪt] Gewicht WS 1, 29

weightlessness [ˈweɪtləsnəs] Schwerelosigkeit WS 3, 92

weightlifting [ˈweɪtlɪftɪŋ] Gewichtheben WS 3, 93

weird [wɪəd] seltsam OT 1

welcome [ˈwelkəm] willkommen OT 1

well [wel] also OT 1

well done [wel ˈdʌn] gut gemacht OT 1

wellness [ˈwelnəs] Wellness; Wohlbefinden WS 1, 30

Welsh [welʃ] walisisch OT 1

west [west] West- OT 1

westward [ˈwestwəd] westwärts WS 1, 24

wet [wet] nass OT 2

wetsuit [ˈwetsuːt] Taucheranzug; Neoprenanzug OT 1

whale [weɪl] Wal OT 1

whaling [ˈweɪlɪŋ] Walfang OT 2

what [wɒt] was OT 1

whatever [wɒˈtevə] was auch immer; egal welche OT 3

wheel [wiːl] Rad OT 1

wheelchair [ˈwiːltʃeə] Rollstuhl OT 2

wheelchair user [ˈwiːltʃeə ˌjuːzə] Rollstuhlfahrer(in) OT 2

when [wen] wann OT 1

whenever [wenˈevə] wann auch immer WS 2, 45

where [weə] wo OT 1

wherever [weərˈevə] wo (auch) immer OT 3

whether [ˈweðə(r)] ob; falls; wann OT 1

which [wɪtʃ] welche(r, -s) OT 1

while [waɪl] während OT 1

whistle [ˈwɪsl] Pfeife OT 2

white [waɪt] weiß OT 1

to **whizz** [wɪz] zischen OT 2

who [huː] wer / wen / wem OT 1

whoever [huːˈevə] wer auch immer WS 1, 28

whole [həʊl] ganz OT 1

whose [huːz] wessen; dessen / deren OT 2

why [waɪ] warum OT 1

wicket [ˈwɪkɪt] Wicket; Törchen OT 1

wide [waɪd] weit OT 2

wife [waɪf] Frau; Ehefrau OT 1

wild [waɪld] wild OT 2

wilderness [ˈwɪldənəs] Wildnis OT 2

wildfire [ˈwaɪldfaɪə] Waldbrand OT 2

wildlife [ˈwaɪldlaɪf] Tierwelt; Pflanzenwelt OT 2

willing: to be willing [bi ˈwɪlɪŋ] bereit sein WS 1, 24

to **win** [wɪn] gewinnen OT 1

wind [wɪnd] Wind OT 2

windlass [ˈwɪndləs] Winsch OT 3

window [ˈwɪndəʊ] Fenster OT 1

to **windsurf** [ˈwɪndsɜːf] windsurfen OT 1

windsurfer [ˈwɪndsɜːfə] Windsurfer(in) OT 1

windy [ˈwɪndi] windig OT 2

wine [waɪn] Wein OT 1

wing [wɪŋ] Flügel OT 1

winner [ˈwɪnə] Gewinner(in); Sieger(in) OT 1

winter [ˈwɪntə] Winter OT 1

wipe [waɪp] Wischtuch WS 3, 92

to **wish** [wɪʃ] wünschen OT 3

witch [wɪtʃ] Hexe OT 2

with [wɪð] mit OT 1

within [wɪˈðɪn] innerhalb WS 1, 30

without [wɪˈðaʊt] ohne OT 2

woman [ˈwʊmən] Frau OT 1

to **wonder** [ˈwʌndə] sich fragen OT 3

wonderful [ˈwʌndəfl] wunderbar OT 1

wood [wʊd] Holz OT 2

wood-burning [ˈwʊdˈbɜ:nɪŋ] holzverbrennend **WS 3**, 80

wooden [ˈwʊdn] hölzern OT 1

wool [wʊl] Wolle OT 2

woolly [ˈwʊli] wollig; aus Wolle OT 2

word [wɜ:d] Wort OT 1

to **work** [wɜ:k] arbeiten OT 1

   to **work out** [wɜ:k aʊt] herausfinden OT 2

workbook [ˈwɜ:kbʊk] Arbeitsheft OT 1

worker [ˈwɜ:kə] Arbeiter(in) OT 2

workman [ˈwɜ:kmən] Arbeiter OT 3

workplace [ˈwɜ:kpleɪs] Arbeitsplatz OT 2

workshop [ˈwɜ:kʃɒp] Werkstatt OT 1

world [wɜ:ld] Welt OT 1

worldwide [ˌwɜ:ldˈwaɪd] weltweit OT 3

worm [wɜ:m] Wurm OT 1

worried [ˈwʌrid] besorgt OT 1

to **worry** [ˈwʌri] (sich) Sorgen machen OT 1

   No worries. [nəʊ ˈwʌriz] Keine Sorge. OT 2

to **worship** [ˈwɜ:ʃɪp] eine Religion ausüben; anbeten **WS 1**, 20

worth [wɜ:θ] lohnenswert **WS 4**, 120

   to **be worth it** [wɜ:θ ɪt] (sich) lohnen OT 1

worthwhile [ˌwɜ:θˈwaɪl] lohnend OT 2

Wow! [waʊ] Toll! OT 1

wowed [waʊd] entzückt; begeistert **WS 4**, 111

to **wrap** [ræp] einwickeln OT 2

wreath [ri:θ] Kranz OT 3

wreck [rek] Wrack OT 3

wrestling [ˈreslɪŋ] Ringen OT 2

to **wriggle** [ˈrɪgl] schlängeln OT 2

wrist [rɪst] Handgelenk OT 1

wristband [ˈrɪstbænd] Armband **WS 3**, 87

to **write** [raɪt] schreiben OT 1

   to **write down** [ˌraɪt ˈdaʊn] aufschreiben OT 2

writer [ˈraɪtə] Autor(in); Schriftsteller(in) OT 2

writing [ˈraɪtɪŋ] Schreiben OT 1

wrong [rɒŋ] falsch OT 1

   What's wrong? [wɒts ˈrɒŋ] Was ist los? OT 2

X

X-ray [ˈeks reɪ] Röntgen OT 1

Y

yacht [jɒt] Jacht OT 2

yachting: land yachting [ˈlænd jɒtɪŋ] Strandsegeln OT 3

yard [jɑ:d] Garten OT 2

yeah [jeə] ja OT 1

year [jɪə] Jahr OT 1

yellow [ˈjeləʊ] gelb OT 1

yes [jes] ja OT 1

yesterday [ˈjestədeɪ] gestern OT 1

yet [jet] noch; schon OT 2

yoghurt [ˈjɒgət] Joghurt OT 1

you [ju] du / Sie; man OT 1

young [jʌŋ] jung OT 1

your [jɔ:] dein / Ihr; euer / Ihr OT 1

yours [jɔ:z] deine(r, -s); eure(r, -s); ihre(r, -s) OT 2

yourself [ˌjəˈself] dich / sich; dich / sich (selbst) OT 1

yourselves [jɔ:ˈselvz, jəˈselvz] euch (selbst) OT 3

youth [ju:θ] Jugend OT 1

   youth hostel [ˈju:θ hɒstl] Jugendherberge OT 2

yuck [jʌk] Igitt! OT 3

Z

zebra [ˈzebrə] Zebra OT 1

   zebra crossing [ˌzebrə ˈkrɒsɪŋ] Zebrastreifen OT 1

zero [ˈzɪərəʊ] null OT 1

zip [zɪp] Reißverschluss OT 1

   zip line [ˈzɪp laɪn] Seilrutsche OT 1

zombie [ˈzɒmbi] Zombie OT 2

zone [zəʊn] Zone OT 2

   end zone [ˈend zəʊn] Endzone OT 2

zoo [zu:] Zoo OT 1

zucchini [zuˈki:ni] Zucchini OT 3

Dictionary: German – English

3
3D-Druck 3D printing OT 1

A
Aal eel **WS 1**, 20
abdecken to cover OT 2
Abdeckung cover OT 1
Abend evening OT 1
Abendessen dinner OT 1
Abenteuer adventure OT 1
abenteuerlustig adventurous OT 2
aber but OT 1
Abfahrt exit; departure OT 2
Abfall garbage; trash OT 2; waste OT 3; spoilage **WS 3**, 84; scrap **WS 3**, 88
   herumliegende Abfälle litter OT 2
Abflug departure OT 2
Abfluggate departure gate OT 2
Abflugschalter check-in desk OT 2
abgefüllt bottled OT 3
abgetropft drained OT 2
abgießen to drain OT 2
abhalten to prevent **WS 3**, 96
abhängen to hang out OT 1
   abhängen (von) to depend OT 2
abhängig addicted OT 3
abholen to fetch **WS 1**, 20
Abklärung clarification **WS 4**, 123
Ablauf sequence **WS 4**, 127
Abmessung dimension OT 2
abnagen to gnaw OT 2
absagen to cancel **WS 1**, 41
Absatz paragraph OT 1
abschätzen to measure **WS 3**, 89
abschließen to finish OT 1; to lock OT 2
Abschluss degree **WS 3**, 94
abseilen to abseil OT 2
Absender(in) sender OT 3
Absicht aim **WS 3**, 86
absolut absolute OT 3
Absolvent(in) alumnus **WS 2**, 58
abstoßend revolting OT 2
abtropfen: nicht abgetropft undrained OT 2
Abwasch: den Abwasch machen to do the dishes OT 2
abwechseln to take turns OT 1
Abzeichen badge OT 1
Achse axis **WS 2**, 64
acht eight OT 1
achten to respect OT 3
achtzehn eighteen OT 1
achtzig eighty OT 1

Ackerland farmland **WS 1**, 12
Adjektiv adjective OT 1
Adler eagle OT 2
Adrenalinstoß adrenaline rush OT 1
Adresse address OT 1
Adverb adverb OT 1
Affe monkey OT 2
afrikanisch African OT 2
Agentur agency **WS 3**, 94
aggressiv aggressive OT 3
ähnlich similar OT 2
Ähnlichkeit similarity OT 3
Ahorn maple OT 3
akademisch: einen akademischen Grad erlangen to graduate OT 3
Akkordeon accordion OT 2
Aktion action OT 1; campaign OT 3
aktiv energetic OT 2; active **WS 2**, 45
aktivieren to activate **WS 3**, 87
Aktivismus activism **WS 3**, 88
Aktivität activity OT 1
aktualisieren to update OT 3
aktuell current **WS 1**, 26
akustisch acoustic OT 2
Akzent accent OT 1
Alarm alarm OT 2
alarmieren to alert OT 2
alaskisch Alaskan OT 2
albern silly OT 1
Albtraum nightmare **WS 4**, 124
Album album OT 3
Alkohol alcohol OT 3
alkoholisch alcoholic OT 3
alle all; everybody OT 1
Allee avenue OT 1
allein by one's self OT 2
   alleinreisendes Kind unaccompanied minor OT 2
Allergie allergy OT 1
allergisch allergic OT 2
alles all; everything OT 1
allgemein general OT 3
   im Allgemeinen generally **WS 2**, 45
alltäglich everyday OT 3
Alpaka alpaca OT 2
Alphabet alphabet OT 1
alphabetisch alphabetical OT 2
als as; than OT 1
also like; so; well OT 1
alt old OT 1
Alter age OT 1
   im Alter von aged OT 1
älter elderly **WS 2**, 62

Alternative alternative OT 2
altmodisch old-fashioned **WS 2**, 62
Ambition ambition **WS 3**, 94
amerikanisch American OT 1
Amphitheater amphitheatre OT 3
Amtsperson official OT 3
amüsant entertaining OT 3
amüsiert amused OT 3
an at; on OT 1
analphabetisch illiterate **WS 4**, 127
analysieren to analyse OT 3
Ananas pineapple OT 3
anbauen to grow OT 1; to cultivate **WS 2**, 63
anbeten to worship **WS 1**, 20
anbieten to offer OT 2
anbinden to tie OT 2
Andachtshaus meetinghouse **WS 1**, 32
andauern to continue OT 1; to last OT 2
andere(r, -s) other OT 1
ändern to change OT 1
anders als unlike OT 3
Änderung change OT 1
Anekdote anecdote **WS 1**, 22
Anfang start OT 1
anfangen to start; to take up; to begin OT 1; to commence **WS 3**, 95
anfassen to feel; to touch OT 1
anfreunden to make friends OT 2
anführen to cite OT 2
Anführung (einer Quelle) citation OT 2
Anführungszeichen quotation mark OT 2
Angebot offer OT 1
Angehörige relative OT 1
Angelegenheit issue; matter OT 2
Angeln fishing OT 2
angemessen appropriately OT 3; appropriate **WS 1**, 22
angenehm enjoyable OT 2
angeschlossen hyper-connected **WS 2**, 48
Angestellte(r) employee **WS 1**, 24
angestrengt stressed OT 2
angetrieben powered **WS 3**, 76
angreifen to attack; to tackle OT 3
angrenzend adjoining OT 3
Angst fear OT 3
   Angst machen to scare OT 2
ängstlich afraid OT 2
anhalten to stop OT 1

Anhänger(in) follower OT 3
anheben to lift OT 3
Ankauf purchase **WS 3**, 78
ankern to anchor **WS 1**, 20
anklicken to click on OT 3
ankommen to arrive OT 1
Ankunft arrival OT 2
Ankunftszeit: geschätzte Ankunftszeit
    ETA (estimated time of arrival) OT 2
Anlage facility **WS 1**, 30
anlegen to moor OT 3
Anlegeplatz mooring OT 3
Anliegen cause OT 2
Anmeldeliste sign-up sheet OT 2
anmelden to register **WS 1**, 26
annehmen to supose OT 1;
    to accept OT 3
Anpassung assimilation **WS 1**, 30
anpassungsfähig flexible **WS 3**, 82;
    adaptable **WS 3**, 95
Anruf call OT 1
    einen Anruf entgegennehmen to
    take a call OT 2
anrufen to call OT 1
Anrufer(in) caller OT 2
Ansage announcement OT 2
ansagen to announce OT 2
anschalten to switch on OT 1
anschauen to look at OT 1
Anschauungsmaterial visual aid
    WS 2, 53
anscheinend apparently **WS 2**, 70
Anschlagbrett noticeboard OT 1
Anschlagtafel bulletin board **WS 4**, 116
anschließen to fasten OT 1
ansehen to look at OT 1
Ansicht attitude OT 3
ansiedeln to settle **WS 3**, 93
Anspannung tension **WS 3**, 93
Anspitzer pencil sharpener OT 1
anständlg proper OT 3
anstehen to queue **WS 1**, 15
anstoßen to bump into OT 2
Antenne antenna OT 2
antik ancient OT 2
antiseptisch antiseptic OT 2
Antrag petition OT 3; application
    WS 1, 17
Antwort answer OT 1
antworten to reply OT 1
anwachsen to increase OT 3
Anweisung instruction OT 1; direction
    OT 3
Anzahl quantity **WS 3**, 86
anziehen to attract **WS 1**, 21
    anziehend attractive **WS 4**, 116

Anzug suit OT 1
Apfel apple OT 1
Apotheke chemist's shop; drugstore;
    pharmacy OT 2
Apotheker(in) chemist; pharmacist
    OT 2
App app **WS 2**, 48
appetitlich appetizing OT 3
applaudieren to applaud OT 2
Applaus applause OT 2
April April OT 1
Aquädukt aqueduct OT 3
aquatisch aquatic **WS 4**, 110
Ära era **WS 3**, 83
Arbeit labor **WS 2**, 52
arbeiten to work OT 1
Arbeiter workman OT 3
Arbeiter(in) worker OT 2
Arbeitgeber(in) employer OT 3
Arbeitsheft workbook OT 1
Arbeitskraft labor **WS 2**, 52
Arbeitslosigkeit unemployment OT 3
Arbeitsplatz workplace OT 2
Archäologe / Archäologin archeologist
    WS 4, 108
Architektur architecture OT 2
archivieren to archive **WS 4**, 116
Arena arena OT 1; amphitheatre OT 3
Ärger trouble OT 2; anger OT 3
    Ärger bekommen to be in trouble
    OT 2
ärgerlich annoying; angrily OT 2
ärgern to tease OT 1; to annoy OT 3
argumentieren to argue OT 2
Arktis Arctic **WS 3**, 93
arktisch Arctic **WS 3**, 93
Arm arm OT 1
arm poor OT 1
Armband wristband **WS 3**, 87
Armee army OT 3
Ärmel sleeve OT 3
ärmellos sleeveless **WS 2**, 59
Armut poverty OT 3
Art kind OT 1; type; sort OT 2
Artikel article OT 1
Artikulierung tone of voice **WS 4**, 117
Arzt; Ärztin doctor OT 1
asiatisch Asian **WS 1**, 16
Aspekt aspect **WS 2**, 44
Assimilation assimilation **WS 1**, 30
Assistent(in) assistant OT 1
Assistenzhund service dog OT 2
assoziieren to associate **WS 1**, 21
Ast branch OT 2
Asterisk asterisk **WS 1**, 36
Astronaut(in) astronaut **WS 1**, 24

Astronomie astronomy OT 1
Asylbewerber(in) asylum seeker
    WS 1, 26
Atem(zug) breath OT 2
    außer Atem out of breath OT 2
atemberaubend breathtaking OT 3
atemlos breathless OT 3
athletisch athletic **WS 3**, 85
atmen to breathe OT 2
Atmosphäre atmosphere OT 3
Atom… nuclear OT 3
attraktiv attractive **WS 4**, 116
ätzend gross OT 3
Au! Ow! OT 1
Aua! Ouch! OT 1
Aubergine eggplant OT 2
auch too; also; as well OT 1
    auch nicht either OT 1; neither
    OT 2
Audiodatei audio file OT 2
Audiotagebuch audio diary OT 2
auf on; onto OT 1
aufbewahren to keep OT 2
Aufbewahrung storage OT 3
aufbrechen to head out **WS 2**, 62
aufdringlich pushy **WS 4**, 116
Aufforderung invitation OT 1; prompt
    WS 2, 73
aufführen to put on OT 2
Aufführung performance OT 2
Aufgabe task; job OT 1; assignment
    WS 3, 79
aufgeben to give up OT 2
aufgeräumt tidy OT 2
aufgeregt excited OT 1; frantic OT 3
aufheben to pick up OT 2
aufhören to finish; to stop OT 1
aufladen to charge **WS 3**, 80
auflisten to list OT 3
aufmachen to open OT 1
Aufmerksamkeit attention OT 2
aufmuntern cheer up OT 1
aufnehmen to take up; to record OT 1
aufpassen to pay attention OT 2
    aufpassen auf to look after OT 1
aufräumen to tidy OT 1
aufregend exciting OT 1
Aufregung excitement OT 3; fuss
    WS 3, 86
aufrichtig sincerely **WS 1**, 31
Aufruf appeal OT 2
Aufsatz essay OT 2
Aufschläger(in) server OT 3
aufschließen to unlock OT 1
aufschreiben to write down OT 2
Aufseher(in) attendant; ranger OT 3

Aufstand rebellion **WS 1**, 20

aufstehen to stand up; to get up OT 1

aufsteigen to rise OT 3

auftauchen to appear OT 3

auftreten to perform OT 2

aufwachen to wake up OT 1

aufwärmen to warm up OT 2

Aufwärmübung warm-up OT 2

aufwärts upwards OT 3

Auge eye OT 1

Augenbraue eyebrow **WS 4**, 117

Augenlid eyelid OT 2

August August OT 1

Aula assembly hall OT 1

aus from; out; off OT 1

ausbeuten to exploit OT 3

Ausbeutung exploitation **WS 4**, 126

Ausbildung training OT 2; education OT 3

Ausbildungslehrgang training course OT 2

Ausdruck expression OT 1

   zum Ausdruck bringen to voice **WS 3**, 90

ausdrucken to print OT 2

ausdrücken to express OT 3

auseinanderfallen to fall apart **WS 2**, 53

Auseinandersetzung argument OT 1

Ausflug trip OT 1

Ausführung delivery OT 3

Ausgabe issue OT 2

Ausgang exit OT 2

Ausgangssperre curfew OT 3

ausgeben to spend OT 1

ausgebildet skilled **WS 1**, 24

ausgeglichen evenly **WS 2**, 62

ausgehen to go out OT 1

ausgestorben extinct OT 2

ausgezeichnet excellent OT 3

Ausland abroad **WS 4**, 122

ausländisch foreign OT 1; overseas OT 2

ausmachen: etw. macht jmdm. etw. aus to mind **WS 1**, 12

ausmerzen to eradicate **WS 4**, 127

ausmessen to measure **WS 3**, 89

auspacken to unpack OT 2

ausprobieren to try out OT 2

ausrichten to host OT 3

ausrotten to eradicate **WS 4**, 127

ausrufen to declare **WS 1**, 39

ausruhen to rest OT 1

Ausrüstung kit; equipment OT 2

Aussage statement OT 1

ausschalten to turn off OT 2

Ausschnitt clip OT 1

Ausschuss committee OT 2

Aussehen appearance OT 3

Außenseiter(in) odd one out OT 2; misfit **WS 2**, 49

außer except OT 2; apart from OT 3

   außer wenn unless **WS 2**, 51

Außerirdische(r) alien OT 2

außermusikalisch extra-musical OT 2

äußern to voice **WS 3**, 90

Aussicht view OT 1; perspective **WS 4**, 117

Aussichtsgalerie viewing gallery OT 1

Aussichtspunkt viewpoint OT 3

Aussprache pronunciation OT 2

aussprechen to pronounce OT 3

aussteigen to get off OT 2

ausstellen to exhibit OT 2

Ausstellung show; exhibition OT 1; display OT 3

Ausstellungsgelände showground OT 2

Ausstoss emission OT 3

ausstreichen to cross out OT 1

Austausch exchange OT 1

Ausverkauf sale **WS 2**, 51

auswählen to choose OT 1

Auswahlfach elective **WS 2**, 57

Auswahlliste shortlist OT 2

Auswanderer; Auswanderin emigrant OT 3

auswandern to emigrate **WS 1**, 18

ausweisen to deport **WS 1**, 26

auswendig by heart OT 2

   auswendig aufsagen to recite **WS 3**, 96

auswirken: sich auswirken auf to affect OT 3

Auswirkung impact OT 3

Auszeichnung award OT 2

Auszug extract **WS 1**, 32

autark self-sufficient **WS 3**, 80

Auto car OT 1

autokrank carsick OT 2

Automat vending machine OT 1

automatisieren to automate **WS 4**, 112

Automobil automobile **WS 3**, 77

autonom autonomous **WS 3**, 78

Autor(in) writer; author OT 2

Autorität authority **WS 4**, 125

Avatar avatar OT 3

B

Baby baby OT 1

babysitten to babysit **WS 4**, 117

Babysitter(in) babysitter **WS 4**, 114

Bach stream OT 2; creek OT 3

backen to bake OT 1

Bäcker(in) baker OT 3

Bäckerei bakery **WS 4**, 114

Backup backup **WS 3**, 80

Bad bath OT 2

Badewanne bath OT 2

Badezimmer bathroom OT 1

Badminton badminton OT 1

Bagel bagel OT 1

Bahn railway OT 1

Bahnhof station OT 1

Bahnsteig platform OT 1

bald soon OT 1

Balken beam OT 3

Balkendiagramm bar chart **WS 2**, 64

Ball ball OT 1

Ballett ballet OT 3

Ballon balloon OT 3

Banane banana OT 1

Band band OT 1

Bank bench; bank OT 3

Bar bar OT 1

Bär bear OT 1

Bargeld cash OT 1

Barriere barrier OT 3

barrierefrei accessible OT 2

Baseball baseball OT 1

basieren to base on **WS 1**, 21

Basis base **WS 3**, 94

Basketball basketball OT 1

Batterie battery OT 2

Bau construction **WS 1**, 31

Bauarbeiter(in) builder OT 2

bauen to build OT 1

Bauer / Bäuerin farmer OT 2

Bauernhaus farmhouse OT 3

Bauernhof farm OT 1

Baum tree OT 1

Baumstamm caber OT 3

Baumwolle cotton **WS 1**, 12

bayerisch Bavarian OT 2

beabsichtigen to aim **WS 2**, 58

Beamer projector OT 1

beantworten to answer OT 1

beaufsichtigen to supervise OT 3; to oversee **WS 3**, 83

beauftragen to delegate **WS 4**, 111

bebauen to cultivate **WS 2**, 63

Becher mug OT 3

Becken basin OT 3

bedeuten to mean OT 1

bedeutend major OT 2

Bedeutung meaning OT 1; importance OT 2

bedienen to serve OT 1

Bedingung condition OT 3

beeilen to hurry OT 1

beeinflussen to influence **WS 2**, 50

beenden to conclude **WS 1**, 17

beengt cramped OT 3

Beere berry **WS 3**, 84

Beet bed OT 1

befehlen to order OT 1

Befehlsform imperative OT 1

befehlshabend commanding OT 2

befestigen to attach **WS 3**, 87

befreit freed **WS 4**, 126

Befund finding **WS 1**, 30

Befürworter(in) supporter OT 2

Begabung talent OT 2

begegnen to face **WS 1**, 26

begehen to commit **WS 4**, 127

begeistert excited OT 1; enthusiastic OT 3; wowed **WS 4**, 111

beginnen to start; to begin OT 1

Begleiter(in) escort OT 3

begleitet accompanied OT 3

begrenzen to limit OT 3

Begriff concept **WS 4**, 118

begründen to found **WS 1**, 18; to establish **WS 3**, 94

behalten to keep OT 2

Behälter bin; container OT 2

behandeln to treat **WS 2**, 49

Behinderung disability OT 2

bei at; by OT 1

beide both OT 1

Bein leg OT 1

beindruckt impressed **WS 1**, 39

beinhalten to contain OT 3

Beispiel example OT 1

Beitrag contribution **WS 1**, 24; input **WS 3**, 86

bekannt well known; familiar OT 2

bekannt geben to announce OT 2

Bekanntgabe announcement OT 2

bekommen to get OT 1

Belag fuzz **WS 3**, 84

belegen to top OT 3

beleidigen to offend OT 3

Beleuchtung lighting **WS 3**, 80

beliebt popular OT 1

bellen to bark OT 2

bemannt crewed **WS 3**, 94

bemerken to notice OT 1

Benehmen behaviour OT 2

benehmen to behave OT 2

benennen to name **WS 1**, 28

benutzen to use OT 1

Benutzer(in) user OT 2

Benutzeroberfläche desktop **WS 4**, 129

Benzin gas OT 3; petrol **WS 3**, 77

beobachten to watch OT 1; to observe **WS 4**, 111

Beobachtung observation OT 3

bequem comfortable OT 1

Bequemlichkeit convenience **WS 3**, 80

Berater(in) counsellor OT 2

bereit ready OT 1; all set OT 2

bereit sein to be willing **WS 1**, 24

bereits already OT 2

bereuen to regret OT 2

Berg mountain OT 1; fell OT 2

Bergarbeiter(in) miner **WS 1**, 25

Bergbau... mining OT 3

Bergkette mountain range **WS 1**, 25

Bergsteigen climbing OT 1

Bergwerk mine OT 2

Bericht report OT 2

berichten to report OT 1

beruhigen to settle down OT 2

berühmt famous OT 1

berühren to touch OT 1

beschädigen to damage OT 2

beschäftigen to engage **WS 2**, 48

beschäftigt busy OT 1

Beschäftigung occupation **WS 1**, 32

beschämt ashamed OT 3

beschreiben to describe OT 1

Beschreibung description OT 2

Beschwerde complaint OT 2

beschweren to complain OT 3

Besichtigungen sightseeing OT 1

besiegen to beat OT 2

besitzanzeigend possessive OT 1

besitzen to own **WS 3**, 82

Besitzer(in) owner OT 2

besondere(r, -s) special OT 1

besonders especially OT 2; in particular **WS 2**, 70

nicht besonders plain **WS 1**, 32

besorgt worried OT 1; anxious OT 2

besorgt sein to care OT 1

besprechen to discuss OT 1

Besprechung discussion; meeting OT 1

besser better OT 1

Bestand stock OT 2

Bestandteil element OT 2

bestätigen to confirm **WS 4**, 123

beste(r, -s) best OT 1

Besteck cutlery OT 3

Bestellung order OT 1

bestimmen to define **WS 2**, 44

bestimmt definite OT 1; assertive; specific OT 3

bestimmter Artikel definite article OT 1

Bestimmungswort determiner OT 1

bestrafen to punish OT 3

besuchen to attend; to visit OT 2

Besucher(in) visitor OT 1

Betonung stress OT 1

Betreuer(in) guardian OT 2

Bett bed OT 1

beunruhigt alarmed OT 3

beurteilen to judge OT 2

Beurteilung judging OT 2

Bevölkerung population OT 3

bewegen to move OT 1

beweglich agile OT 3

Beweis proof **WS 3**, 94

beweisen to prove OT 3

bewerben to apply OT 3

Bewerber(in) applicant **WS 4**, 120

Bewerbung application **WS 1**, 17

bewerten to rate OT 2; to evaluate **WS 1**, 23

bewohnbar liveable **WS 2**, 63

Bewohnbarkeit habitation **WS 3**, 94

Bewohner(in) resident OT 3; dweller **WS 2**, 62

bewölkt cloudy **WS 3**, 93

bezahlbar affordable **WS 3**, 77

bezahlen to pay OT 1

Bezahlung payment OT 2

beziehen to refer OT 3

sich beziehen auf to relate OT 3

Beziehung relationship OT 3

Bezirk district OT 1

Bezug: in Bezug auf related to **WS 1**, 13

Bibliothek library OT 1

Bibliothekar(in) librarian **WS 4**, 108

Biene bee OT 1

Bier beer OT 3

Bild picture; image OT 1

bilden to form **WS 1**, 29

Bildmaterial visual **WS 3**, 85

Bildschirm screen OT 1

Bildtext caption OT 1

Bildungs... educational OT 3

Bildunterschrift caption OT 1

bilingual bilingual OT 2

billig cheap OT 2; inexpensive **WS 3**, 83

binden to tie OT 2

Bingo bingo OT 1

Biodiversität biodiversity **WS 4**, 111

Biografie biography **WS 1**, 41

Biologe; Biologin biologist **WS 4**, 110

Biologie biology OT 2

biologisch angebaut organic OT 2

Biotoilette composting toilet OT 3

Birne pear OT 1

bis till OT 2; until OT 3

bisher so far OT 2

bisherig previous **WS 3**, 100

Biss bite OT 2

Bitte request OT 2
bitte please OT 1
bitten to ask OT 1; urge **WS 4**, 127
Blase bubble OT 1; blister OT 2
blasen to blow OT 2
Blaskapelle marching band **WS 1**, 21
Blatt sheet OT 1; leaf **WS 2**, 46
blau blue OT 1
Blazer blazer OT 1
bleiben to stay OT 1; to keep OT 2;
    to remain **WS 3**, 93
Bleistift pencil OT 1
blind blind OT 2
Blindenführhund guide dog OT 2
blockieren to block OT 3
Blog blog OT 1
Blogeintrag blogpost **WS 4**, 111
Blogger(in) blogger OT 3
blond blonde OT 1
Blues blues OT 1
Blume flower OT 1
Blut blood OT 2
Boden ground; bottom; floor OT 1
Bodenstation ground control **WS 3**, 95
Bogen bow OT 2
Bohne bean OT 1
    Bohnen in Tomatensoße baked
    beans OT 1
bohren to drill **WS 3**, 94
Bonbon sweet OT 2
Boot boat OT 1
    Boot fahren to cruise OT 3
Bord aboard **WS 1**, 18
    an Bord gehen to board **WS 1**, 18
böse angry OT 1; mad OT 2
Bouquet bouquet OT 3
Boygroup boyband OT 2
brainstormen to brainstorm OT 2
Brandbekämpfung firefighting OT 2
brandneu brand-new OT 2
brasilianisch Brazilian OT 2
braten to fry OT 2
Bratensoße gravy OT 1
brauchen to need OT 1
braun brown OT 1
brechen to break OT 1
brennbar flammable OT 2
brennen to burn OT 2
Brennholz firewood **WS 1**, 20
Brennstoff fuel OT 2
Brett board OT 1
Brief letter OT 1
Briefkasten post box OT 1; mailbox
    WS 2, 49
Brieftasche wallet OT 1
Briefumschlag envelope OT 2

Brille glasses OT 1
bringen to bring OT 1
Brise breeze OT 3
britisch British OT 1
Broccoli broccoli OT 1
Brombeere blackberry OT 1
Broschüre brochure OT 1; booklet OT 2
Brot bread OT 1
Brotkrumen breadcrumbs OT 3
Browser browser **WS 1**, 22
Brücke bridge OT 1
Bruder brother OT 1
Buch book OT 1
buchen to book OT 2
Bücherregal bookcase OT 1
Buchstabe letter OT 1
buchstabieren to spell OT 1
Bucht bay OT 1
Buchung booking OT 2
Bude stall OT 2
Büffel buffalo **WS 1**, 29
Buffet buffet OT 3
Bühne stage OT 2
Bühnenanweisungen stage directions
    OT 2
Bungee-Jumping bungee jumping OT 3
bunt coloured OT 1
Burg castle OT 1
Bürgermeister(in) mayor OT 3
Bürgersteig pavement OT 1; sidewalk
    WS 1, 14
Büro office OT 1
Büropark office park OT 2
Bürste brush OT 2
Bus bus OT 1
Busch bush OT 2
Bushaltestelle bus stop OT 1
Bussard buzzard OT 2

C

Café café OT 1
Cafeteria cafeteria OT 2
Camp camp OT 1
Camper(in) camper OT 2
Camping camping OT 1
Campingplatz campsite OT 1
Campus campus OT 2
Canyon canyon OT 3
Cartoon cartoon **WS 1**, 21
Cellist(in) cellist OT 2
Cello cello OT 2
Celsius centigrade **WS 3**, 94
Cent cent OT 1
Champignon mushroom OT 1
Chaos: ein Chaos anrichten to make a
    mess OT 2

chaotisch disorganized; messy OT 2
Charakter character OT 1
charmant charming OT 3
Chart chart **WS 2**, 64
Checkliste checklist OT 1
Cheerleader(in) cheerleader OT 3
Chef(in) boss OT 2
Chemikalie chemical OT 3
Chemiker(in) chemist OT 2
Chili chili OT 2
chinesisch Chinese OT 1
Chip crisp OT 1
Chirurg(in) surgeon OT 3
Cholera cholera **WS 1**, 28
Chor choir OT 1
Chorizo chorizo OT 2
Coaching coaching **WS 3**, 85
Cola cola OT 1
Comicheft comic OT 1
Computer computer OT 1
computerbasiert computerized
    WS 2, 59
computergesteuert computerized
    WS 2, 59
Computerraum computer lab OT 2
Container container OT 2
cool cool OT 1
Cornflakes cereal OT 1
Countdown countdown **WS 3**, 95
Cousin(e) cousin OT 1
Cracker cracker OT 3
Cranberry cranberry **WS 1**, 21
Curry(gericht) curry OT 1
    mit Curry gewürzt curried OT 1
Cybermobbing cyber bullying **WS 3**, 86
Cybersicherheit cyber security
    WS 4, 113

D

da there OT 1
Dach roof OT 1
Dachboden attic OT 3
Dame lady OT 1
Damespiel checkers; draughts OT 1
Dampf steam OT 2
Dampfzug steam train OT 2
danach afterwards OT 3
danke thanks OT 1
danken to thank OT 1
dann then OT 1
darstellen to illustrate OT 3
Darsteller(in) performer OT 2
darunter underneath OT 3
das the OT 1
Datei file OT 3
Daten data OT 3

Datum date OT 2

Daumen thumb **WS 2**, 46

   Daumen gedrückt fingers crossed OT 1

Deal deal **WS 2**, 52

Debatte debate OT 3

Debattierklub debating club **WS 2**, 53

Decke blanket OT 2; ceiling **WS 3**, 93

Deckel lid OT 2

defekt faulty OT 2

definieren to define **WS 2**, 44

Definition definition OT 1

definitiv definitely OT 1

dehnen to stretch OT 2

dehydriert dehydrated OT 2

dein your OT 1

deine(r, -s) yours OT 2

Dekorateur(in) decorator OT 3

dekorieren to decorate **WS 2**, 58

delegieren to delegate **WS 4**, 111

Delfin dolphin OT 1

Delikatesse delicacy OT 3

demokratisch democratic **WS 2**, 59

Demonstration demonstration **WS 3**, 88

Demonstrativbegleiter demonstrative OT 1

Denim denim **WS 1**, 25

denken to think OT 1

   denken an to think about; to think of OT 1

Denkmal monument OT 1

deportieren to deport **WS 1**, 26

Depression depression **WS 3**, 87

deprimierend depressing **WS 2**, 49

deprimiert depressed **WS 2**, 62

der the OT 1

deshalb therefore OT 3

Design design OT 1

Designer(in) designer OT 3

Desktop desktop **WS 4**, 129

dessen / deren whose OT 2

Detail detail OT 2

detailliert detailed OT 3

deutlich clearly OT 3

deutsch German OT 1

Dezember December OT 1

diagnostizieren to diagnose **WS 4**, 113

Diagramm diagram OT 3; chart **WS 2**, 64

Dialog dialogue OT 1

Diashow slideshow OT 3

Diät diet OT 3

dich / sich yourself OT 1

Dichte density **WS 3**, 93

Dichter(in) poet OT 3

Dichtung poetry OT 1

dick thick OT 1

die the OT 1

   die meisten most OT 1

Diele hall OT 1

Diener(in) attendant OT 3

Dienst service OT 2

Dienstag Tuesday OT 1

diese these; those OT 1

diese(r, -s) this; that OT 1

Diesel diesel OT 3

digital digital OT 3

Dilemma dilemma **WS 4**, 122

Ding thing OT 1

Dinosaurier dinosaur OT 1

direkt straight; direct OT 3

Diskussion discussion OT 1

ditto ditto **WS 4**, 128

Dokument document **WS 1**, 26

Dokumentation documentary OT 2

Dollar dollar OT 1

Dolmetscher(in) interpreter **WS 1**, 21

Donnerstag Thursday OT 1

Doppel doubles OT 3

Doppel... double OT 1

doppelt double OT 1

Dorf village OT 1

Dorfbewohner(in) villager **WS 4**, 123

dort there OT 1

Dose can; tin OT 2

   in Dosen tinned; canned OT 2

Drache dragon OT 1

Drama drama OT 1

dran: Du bist dran. It's your turn OT 1

drängen to urge **WS 4**, 127

draußen outside OT 1; outdoor(s) OT 2

Dreck dirt **WS 4**, 124

dreckig grubby OT 2; filthy **WS 4**, 124

Drehbuch script OT 1

drehen to turn OT 2

Drehscheibe turntable OT 2

drei three OT 1

Dreieck triangle OT 2

dreieckig triangular OT 3

dreißig thirty OT 1

dreiundzwanzig twenty-three OT 1

dreizehn thirteen OT 1

Dresscode dress code **WS 2**, 59

drinnen indoors OT 3

dritte(r, -s) third OT 1

Droge drug OT 3

Drogerie drugstore OT 2

Drohne drone OT 3

Druck pressure OT 3

drücken to press OT 1

Dschungel jungle **WS 4**, 123

du / Sie you OT 1

Dudelsack bagpipe OT 3

dumm silly OT 1; stupid OT 2

Dung manure OT 3

Dünger fertilizer OT 3

dunkel dark OT 1

dünn thin OT 1

durch through OT 1

durchaus absolutely OT 2

durcheinander jumbled; mixed up OT 2

durcheinanderbringen to mix up OT 2

durchführen to conduct OT 3

durchnässt soaked OT 3

durchschnittlich average **WS 2**, 49

durchsetzen to enforce **WS 4**, 126

durchstochen pierced OT 3

durchweg throughout OT 3

dürfen to be allowed to OT 2

durstig thirsty OT 1

Dusche shower OT 2

Dutzend dozen **WS 4**, 124

E

ebenfalls ditto **WS 4**, 128

echt real OT 1

Ecke corner OT 1

E-Commerce e-commerce **WS 2**, 54

effizient efficient **WS 3**, 84

egal welche whatever OT 3

egoistisch selfish OT 3

Ehefrau wife OT 1

ehemalig former **WS 2**, 58

Ehemalige(r) alumnus **WS 2**, 58

Ehemann husband OT 2

Ehrenamt: ein Ehrenamt haben to volunteer OT 2

Ehrenamtliche(r) volunteer OT 2

ehrgeizig ambitious **WS 3**, 95

ehrlich honest OT 3

Ei egg OT 1

Eichhörnchen squirrel OT 1

eifrig eager OT 2

eigenartig odd OT 2

eigene(r, -s) own OT 1

Eigenschaft feature OT 1; quality OT 3

eigentlich actually OT 2

eilen to rush OT 2

Eimer bin OT 2

ein(e) a, an OT 1

   ein(e) andere(r, -s) another OT 1

einbeziehen to involve **WS 3**, 90

Einbildung imagination **WS 3**, 85

eindeutig definitely OT 1

einfach easy OT 1

einfallsreich fancy OT 2

einfangen to capture **WS 1**, 21

Einfluss influence **WS 1**, 30

einfügen to paste OT 2

einführen to import OT 3

Einführung introduction OT 2

Einführungsbrief introductory letter **WS 1**, 17

Eingang entrance OT 1

Eingangsbereich entrance hall OT 1

Eingangshalle entrance hall OT 1

Eingebung inspiration **WS 3**, 84

eingravieren to engrave **WS 1**, 29

einheimisch local OT 2; native OT 3

Einheimische(r) local OT 2

Einheit session OT 2

einig: sich einig sein to agree OT 1

einige some OT 1; several OT 2

einkaufen to shop OT 1

Einkaufen shopping OT 1

Einkaufszentrum mall OT 3

Einkommen income **WS 2**, 63

einkommensschwach low-income **WS 2**, 63

einladen to invite OT 2

   mit einladen to invite along OT 2

Einladung invitation OT 1

einloggen to log on OT 3

einmal once OT 2

   Es war einmal... Once upon a time ... OT 1

einmarschieren to invade OT 3

einreichen to hand in OT 2

Einrichtung institution **WS 1**, 22

eins one OT 1

einsam lonely OT 3

Einsatz in action OT 2

einschätzen to judge OT 2

einschlafen to go to sleep OT 1; to fall asleep OT 2

einschließen to include OT 1

einschränken to limit OT 3

   sich einschränken to downsize OT 3

Einsendung entry OT 2

Einstand deuce OT 3

Einstellung setting; attitude OT 3

eintippen to key in OT 2

Eintopf stew OT 2

einträchtig peaceful OT 2

Eintrag entry OT 2

eintragen to enter OT 2

eintreten to enter OT 2; to step in **WS 2**, 46

   eintreten in to join OT 1

Eintrittskarte ticket OT 1

einundzwanzig twenty-one OT 1

Einwand objection OT 3

Einwanderer; Einwanderin immigrant OT 3

Einwanderungskontrolle immigration OT 2

Einweckglas jar OT 2

einwickeln to wrap OT 2

Einwohner(in) citizen OT 3

Einzahl singular OT 1

Einzel... single OT 3

Einzelhändler(in) retailer **WS 2**, 64

einzeln individually **WS 2**, 49

Einzelne(r) individual **WS 1**, 32

einzigartig unique OT 2

Eis ice; ice cream OT 1

   Eis am Stiel ice lolly OT 1

Eisberg iceberg OT 3

Eiscreme ice cream OT 1

Eisenbahn rail OT 2

Eisenbahnlinie railway line OT 2

Eiweiß protein **WS 3**, 95

ekelhaft disgusting; gross OT 3

Elefant elephant OT 1

elektrisch electric OT 1; electrical **WS 1**, 41

Elektronik electronics OT 2

elektronisch electronically **WS 3**, 78

elementar elementary OT 2

elf eleven OT 1

Elfenbein ivory OT 3

Ellbogen elbow OT 1

Elternteil parent OT 1

E-Mail email OT 1

   E-Mail schreiben to email OT 2

Emission emission OT 3

Emoji emoji OT 3

Empfang reception OT 1

Empfangschef(in) receptionist OT 1

empfehlen to recommend OT 2

Ende end OT 1; ending OT 2

enden to end OT 1

endgültig final OT 1

endlos endless **WS 1**, 12

Endung ending OT 2

Endzone end zone OT 2

Energie energy OT 2

energisch energetic OT 2

eng narrow OT 2; close OT 3

Engel angel OT 3

englisch English OT 1

Enkel grandson OT 1

Enkelin granddaughter OT 3

Enkelkind grandchild OT 3

entdecken to discover OT 3

   entdecken to happen upon **WS 3**, 84

Entdeckung discovery **WS 3**, 77

Ente duck OT 2

entfernen to remove OT 2

Entfernung distance OT 2

entführen to abduct **WS 4**, 124

Entführer(in) kidnapper OT 2

enthalten to contain OT 3

enthaupten to behead OT 3

entkommen to escape OT 2

entlang along OT 1

entleeren to empty **WS 1**, 15

entriegeln to unlock OT 1

entscheiden to decide OT 1

Entscheidung decision OT 1

entschlossen determined OT 3

entschuldigen to excuse OT 1; to apologize OT 2

Entschuldigung sorry OT 1; apology OT 2

entspannen to relax OT 2; to chill out **WS 3**, 85

entspannt relaxed **WS 1**, 13; laid-back **WS 2**, 73

entsprechend equivalent **WS 2**, 56

enttäuschend disappointingly OT 3

enttäuscht disappointed OT 2

entwerfen to design OT 3

entwickeln to develop OT 2

   sich entwickeln to evolve **WS 1**, 30

Entwicklung development **WS 2**, 63

Entwurf design OT 1; draft OT 2

entzückt delighted OT 3; wowed **WS 3**, 90

Entzugsprogramm detox OT 2

entzünden to spark **WS 3**, 90

Entzündung infection OT 2

Epidemie epidemic **WS 1**, 21

Epoche period OT 3

er he OT 1

Erbse pea OT 1

Erdanziehungskraft gravity **WS 3**, 93

Erdbeben earthquake OT 2

Erdbeere strawberry OT 1

Erdboden soil OT 2

Erde ground OT 1; earth OT 2

Erderwärmung global warming OT 3

Erdkunde geography OT 1

Ereignis event OT 1

erfahren experienced OT 3

Erfahrung experience OT 2

erfasst: nicht erfasst undocumented **WS 4**, 125

erfinden to invent OT 2

   wieder erfinden to reinvent **WS 3**, 82

Erfinder(in) inventor OT 2

erfinderisch resourceful **WS 3**, 95

Erfindung invention **WS 3**, 76

Erfolg success OT 3

erfolgreich successful OT 2

   erfolgreich sein to succeed OT 2

erforderlich to require **WS 2**, 57

erforschen to explore OT 1

erfreut delighted OT 3

Erfrischungsgetränk refreshment OT 2

erfüllen to fulfil **WS 4**, 109

erfunden fictional OT 2

Ergebnis result OT 2; finding **WS 1**, 30

erhalten to receive OT 2; to preserve
OT 3

erhältlich available OT 3

Erhaltung conservation OT 2

erheben to raise OT 2

erhöhen to raise OT 2; to increase OT 3

erholen to recover **WS 4**, 127

erholsam relaxing OT 2

Erholung relaxation OT 3

erinnern to remind OT 2

   sich erinnern an to remember;
to think of OT 1

erkennen to realize; to recognize OT 2

erklären to explain OT 1

Erklärung explanation OT 1; declaration
WS 4, 137

erkunden to explore OT 1

erlangen to gain OT 1

erlauben to allow OT 3

Erlaubnis permission OT 2; permit;
licence OT 3

erlaubt allowed OT 3

erleben to relive **WS 1**, 18

erleichtert relieved OT 2

Erleichterung relief **WS 3**, 83

Ermittler(in) investigator **WS 4**, 124

ermorden to murder **WS 4**, 127

ermutigen to encourage OT 2

Ernährung nutrition **WS 2**, 63

Ernennung nomination **WS 1**, 27

ernst serious OT 2

Ernte crop **WS 1**, 19; harvest **WS 1**, 20

Erntedankfest Thanksgiving OT 2

Erntehelfer(in) farmhand **WS 4**, 112

ernten to harvest **WS 3**, 84

erreichen to reach OT 3; to achieve
WS 1, 94

errichten to put up OT 1

Ersatz substitution; substitute OT 3

erscheinen to appear OT 3

erschöpft exhausted OT 2

erschrecken to frighten OT 3

erschreckend frightening OT 1

ersetzen to replace OT 3

erspähen to spot OT 1

Erspartes savings OT 3

erstaunlich amazing OT 1

erstaunlicherweise astonishingly OT 3

erstaunt amazed OT 3

erste(r, -s) first OT 1; premier OT 2

Erste Hilfe first aid OT 2

ertönen to sound OT 2

ertrinken to drown OT 3

Erwachsene(r) adult OT 1

erwähnen to mention OT 3

erwarten to expect OT 2

erwartungsgemäß unsurprisingly OT 3

erweitern to expand **WS 1**, 24

erweiternd expanding OT 2

erzählen to tell OT 1

erzeugen to produce OT 3; to generate
WS 3, 80

Erzielen scoring OT 1

es it OT 1

   es gibt there is / are OT 1

Essen food OT 1

   Essen zum Mitnehmen takeout
WS 4, 114

Esslöffel tablespoon OT 2

Essstäbchen chopstick OT 1

Esszimmer dining room OT 1

Etagenbett bunk bed OT 3

ethisch ethical OT 3

Etikett label OT 1; tag OT 2

Etikette etiquette OT 3

etwas some; something OT 1

euch (selbst) yourselves OT 3

euer / Ihr your OT 1

eure(r, -s) yours OT 2

europäisch European OT 3

ewig eternal **WS 3**, 95

exekutieren to execute OT 3

existieren to exist OT 3

exotisch exotic OT 2

expandieren to expand **WS 1**, 24

Expedition expedition OT 2

Experiment experiment OT 1

experimentieren to experiment
WS 4, 129

Experte / Expertin expert OT 3

Extra... extra OT 1

extrem extreme OT 3

F

fabelhaft fabulous OT 2

Fabrik factory **WS 2**, 52

Fach subject OT 1

fähig capable **WS 4**, 127

Fähigkeit skill; ability OT 2

Fahne flag OT 1

Fahranfänger(in) learner OT 3

Fähre ferry OT 2

fahren to go; to drive; to ride OT 1;
to motor OT 3

Fahrer(in) rider; driver OT 1

Fahrerkabine cab **WS 1**, 41

Fahrerlaubnis driver's license **WS 2**, 60

Fahrgast passenger OT 2

Fahrkarte ticket OT 1

Fahrkartenschalter booking office;
ticket office OT 2

Fahrplan timetable OT 1

Fahrrad bike OT 1; bicycle OT 2

   Fahrrad fahren to cycle OT 1

Fahrspur lane OT 2

Fahrt journey; ride OT 1

Fahrzeug vehicle OT 1

fair unfair OT 2

Fakt fact OT 1

fallen to fall OT 1

   fallen lassen to drop OT 1

falls whether; if OT 1

falsch false; wrong OT 1

falsch wrong OT 1

   falscher Freund false friend OT 2

falten to fold OT 2

Familie family OT 1

Fan fan OT 1; supporter OT 2

fangen to catch OT 1

Fantasie fantasy OT 2; imagination
WS 3, 85

fantasievoll imaginative **WS 4**, 111

fantastisch fantastic OT 1

Fantasy fantasy OT 2

Farbe colour OT 1; paint OT 2; dye
WS 2, 52

Färbemittel dye **WS 2**, 52

farbenfroh colourful OT 3

farbig coloured OT 1

Farmarbeiter(in) farmworker **WS 4**, 125

fast nearly OT 1; almost OT 2

Faszination fascination **WS 4**, 109

faszinierend fascinating OT 3

Februar February OT 1

Feder feather OT 2

Federtasche pencil case OT 1

Fee fairy OT 2

Feedback feedback OT 1

fegen to sweep **WS 1**, 14

fehlend missing OT 1

Fehler fault; mistake OT 2

   Fehler machen to make a mistake
OT 2

Feier party OT 1; celebration; ceremony
OT 2

feierlich ceremonial OT 3

feiern to celebrate OT 1; to feast **WS 1**, 21

Feind enemy OT 1

Feld field; square OT 1; space OT 2

Fels rock OT 2

Fenster window OT 1

Ferienlager camp OT 1

fern far-off OT 2; faraway **WS 2**, 53

Fernbedienung remote control **WS 3**, 104

fernbleiben to keep away OT 2

Ferne remotely **WS 3**, 78

Fernglas binoculars OT 2

fernhalten to keep away OT 2

Fernsehen TV OT 1; television OT 2

Fest festival OT 1; feast **WS 1**, 18

festhalten: an etw. festhalten to cling to OT 2

Festival festival OT 1

Festland mainland OT 3

Festlichkeit festivity **WS 2**, 58

festmachen to fasten OT 1

Festmahl feast **WS 1**, 18

festnehmen to capture **WS 1**, 21

Festnetz landline **WS 3**, 79

Festung fort OT 2; fortress OT 3

Fett fat OT 2

fettgedruckt bold OT 1

Feuer fire OT 2

Feuerwache fire station OT 2

Feuerwehrmann / -frau firefighter OT 2

Feuerwerk fireworks OT 3; firework display **WS 1**, 21

Figur figure OT 3

Fiktion fiction OT 2

fiktiv imaginary **WS 3**, 85

Film film; movie OT 1; motion picture **WS 3**, 83

Filmrolle roll OT 2

Filzstift marker OT 1

finanziell: finanziell unterstützen to sponsor OT 2

  finanzielle Unterstützung sponsorship OT 2

finanzieren to fund OT 3

finden to find OT 1

Finger finger OT 1

Fingernagel fingernail OT 2

Firma company OT 1

Fisch fish OT 1

Fischstäbchen fish finger OT 1

Fischsuppe chowder OT 3

Fitness fitness OT 2

Fitnesscenter gym OT 3

Flaggschiff flagship OT 3

Flamingo flamingo OT 2

Flasche bottle OT 1

flauschig fluffy OT 2

Fleisch meat OT 1; flesh OT 2

  Fleisch... meaty OT 3

Fleischer(in) butcher **WS 1**, 20

Fleischklößchen meatball OT 1

flexibel flexible **WS 3**, 82

Fliege bow-tie OT 2

fliegen to fly OT 1

fließend fluent OT 3

Flüchtling refugee **WS 1**, 26

Flüchtlingslager refugee camp **WS 1**, 26

Flug flight OT 2

Flugblatt handout **WS 2**, 55

Flügel wing OT 1

Flughafen airport OT 1

Flugpersonal flight crew OT 2

Flugzeug plane OT 1; airplane **WS 3**, 76; aeroplane **WS 3**, 77

Fluss river OT 1

flüssig liquid OT 2

Flut flood OT 2

Fluten flooding **WS 3**, 103

Flyer flyer **WS 3**, 83

Fokus focus OT 1

fokussieren to focus **WS 2**, 71

Folge consequence **WS 3**, 90; sequence **WS 4**, 127

folgen to follow OT 2

folgend sequentially **WS 2**, 48

Folie slide OT 1

fordern to require **WS 2**, 57; to demand **WS 3**, 91

Form form; shape OT 1

  in Form fit OT 2

formen to shape OT 3

formulieren to formulate **WS 2**, 44

  neu formulieren to rephrase **WS 3**, 85

forschen to research OT 2

Forscher(in) researcher OT 2; explorer OT 3

Forschung research OT 2

Forstbeamter / -beamtin park ranger OT 2

Förster(in) ranger OT 3

fortgeschritten advanced **WS 3**, 95

Fortschritt advance **WS 3**, 79; progress **WS 3**, 95

fortschrittlich progressive OT 1

fossil fossil OT 3

Foto photo; photograph OT 1

  ein Foto machen to take a photo OT 1

Fotoapparat camera OT 1

Fotograf(in) photographer OT 3

Fotografie photography **WS 1**, 13

fotokopieren to photocopy **WS 2**, 55

foulen to foul OT 3

Frage question OT 1

Fragebogen questionnaire OT 1

fragen to ask OT 1

  sich fragen to wonder OT 3

französisch French OT 1

Frau Mrs; Ms; woman; wife OT 1

Freak freak **WS 4**, 122

frech cheeky OT 1

frei free OT 1

Freibeuter(in) privateer OT 3

Freiheit liberty OT 1; freedom OT 3

freilegen to uncover OT 3

Freitag Friday OT 1

melden to volunteer OT 2

Freiwillige(r) volunteer OT 2

Freizeit leisure OT 3

  Freizeit... recreational OT 3

fremd foreign OT 1

Fremde(r) foreigner OT 3

Freude pleasure OT 1

freuen to look forward to OT 1

Freund(in) friend OT 1

freundlich friendly; kind OT 1

Freundschaft friendship OT 3

friedlich peaceful OT 2

Frisbee frisbee OT 1

frisch fresh OT 2

Fritte chip OT 1

frittieren to fry OT 2

froh glad OT 1

früh early OT 1

früher previously OT 3

Frühling spring OT 2

Frühjahrsputz spring clean OT 2

Frühstück breakfast OT 1

Frühstücksflocken cereal OT 1

frustriert frustrated OT 3

Fuchs fox OT 1

fühlen to feel OT 1

führen to lead OT 3

Führer(in) guide OT 1

Führerhaus cab **WS 1**, 41

führerlos driverless **WS 3**, 105

Führerschein driving licence OT 2; driver's license **WS 2**, 60

Führung leadership **WS 4**, 113

füllen to fill OT 2

fünf five OT 1

fünfte(r, -s) fifth OT 1

fünfzehn fifteen OT 1

fünfzig fifty OT 1

Funke spark OT 2

Funktion function **WS 1**, 22

für for OT 1

Furcht fear OT 3

furchtbar horrible OT 2

fürchterlich awful OT 1

Fürwort pronoun OT 1

Fuß foot OT 1

Fußabdruck footprint OT 3

Fußball football OT 1; soccer OT 2

Fussel fuzz **WS 3**, 84
Fußknöchel ankle OT 1
Fußpfad footpath OT 1
Füttern feeding OT 2
füttern to feed OT 2

G
Gabel fork OT 2
gaffen to gongoozle OT 3
Gaffer gongoozler OT 3
Galaxie galaxy OT 1
Galerie gallery OT 1
Gallone gallon OT 3
Gamer(in) gamer **WS 2**, 49
Gang course OT 1
Gans goose **WS 1**, 21
ganz whole OT 1; completely OT 2
  ganze(r, -s) entire OT 3
Garage garage **WS 3**, 84
Garten garden OT 1; yard OT 2
  Garten hinterm Haus backyard OT 2
Gartenarbeit gardening OT 1
Gärtner(in) gardener **WS 2**, 63
Gas gas OT 3
Gasse lane OT 2
Gast guest OT 2
Gastfreundschaft hospitality OT 2
Gasthaus lodge; inn OT 2
Gebäude building OT 1
geben to give OT 1
Gebet prayer **WS 1**, 28
Gebetshaus meetinghouse **WS 1**, 32
Gebiet area OT 1
gebildet cultured **WS 2**, 73
Gebirgszug mountain range **WS 1**, 25
geboren sein to be born OT 2
gebraten roast OT 1
gebrochen broken OT 1
Gebühr fee OT 3
Geburt birth OT 2
Geburtsdatum date of birth OT 2
Geburtsort birthplace **WS 1**, 18
Geburtstag birthday OT 1
Gedächtnis memory OT 1
Gedanke thought **WS 1**, 15
gedankenlos thoughtless OT 2
Gedicht poem OT 1
geeignet fit OT 2; suitable **WS 2**, 64
Gefahr danger; hazard OT 2; risk OT 3
gefährdet endangered OT 2
gefährlich dangerous OT 1; risky;
  unsafe OT 3
Gefängnis prison OT 1
Geflügel poultry OT 2
geformt shaped **WS 1**, 21
gefriergetrocknet freeze-dried **WS 3**, 92

Gefrierschrank freezer OT 3
gefroren frozen **WS 3**, 94
Gefühl feeling OT 2; emotion OT 3;
  sensation **WS 3**, 93
gegen against OT 1
Gegend area; district OT 1
gegensätzlich contrasting **WS 1**, 33
Gegenstand object OT 1; item OT 2
Gegenteil opposite OT 1; contrast OT 3
Gegenwart present OT 1
  vollendete Gegenwart present
  perfect OT 2
Gegner(in) opponent OT 2
gegnerisch opposing OT 3
gegrillt barbecued **WS 3**, 93
gehackt chopped OT 2
Gehalt wage **WS 4**, 116
Geheimnis secret OT 2
gehen to go OT 1
  zu Fuß gehen to walk OT 1
Gehirn brain OT 2
gehören to belong OT 2
Gehweg pavement OT 1
Geige violin OT 1
Geist spirit; ghost OT 2
geistig mental **WS 1**, 30
gekocht boiled OT 1
Gel gel OT 1
Geländearbeit fieldwork **WS 4**, 134
Geländefahrzeug off-road vehicle OT 1
gelangweilt bored OT 1
gelb yellow OT 1
Geld money OT 1
Geldgeber(in) sponsor OT 2; investor
  WS 3, 83
Gelegenheit opportunity OT 2
gelegentlich occasionally OT 2
gelockt curly OT 3
Gemälde painting OT 1
gemäß according to OT 3
gemein mean OT 2
Gemeinde township **WS 4**, 123
gemeinnützig non-profit **WS 1**, 22
Gemeinschaft community OT 2
gemischtgeschlechtlich co-ed;
  co-educational OT 2
Gemüse vegetable OT 1
gemütlich cozy OT 3; comfy **WS 3**, 93
genau just OT 1; exact OT 2; detailed
  OT 3; accurate **WS 2**, 55
genehmigen to approve OT 3
Generation generation **WS 1**, 30
  die Generation der Jahrtausend-
  wende millennial **WS 2**, 64
genervt annoyed OT 2
genial brilliant OT 1

genießen to enjoy OT 1
Genre genre **WS 2**, 44
Gentleman gentleman OT 3
genug enough OT 1
Geocache geocache OT 2
Geocaching geocaching OT 2
Geografie geography OT 1
geografisch geographical **WS 1**, 25
Geologie geology OT 2
Gepäck baggage OT 2; luggage **WS 3**, 87
Gepäckausgabe baggage claim OT 2
gerade straight OT 3
Gerät appliance; device OT 3;
  gadget **WS 3**, 79
Geräusch sound; noise OT 1
gerecht fair OT 2
Gerechtigkeit justice **WS 2**, 50
Gericht dish OT 2
  jüngstes Gericht Judgement Day
  WS 3, 95
gerissen ripped **WS 2**, 59
gernhaben to like OT 1; to care about
  OT 2
  hätte(n) gern would like / love OT 1
geröstet sauté OT 3
gesamt total OT 1
Gesamtliste tally **WS 2**, 64
Gesang vocals OT 2
Geschäft business OT 3; deal **WS 2**, 52
Geschäftsfrau businesswoman **WS 3**, 84
Geschäftsführer(in) manager OT 1
Geschäftsmann businessman **WS 3**, 83
geschehen to happen OT 1
Geschenk gift OT 1
Geschenkgutschein gift voucher OT 1
Geschichte history; story OT 1; tale OT 2
Geschichtenbuch storybook OT 2
geschichtlich historical OT 2
Geschick skill OT 2
geschickt skilful OT 3; skilled **WS 1**, 24
Geschirr dishes OT 2
Geschirrspülen washing up OT 2
Geschirrspülmaschine dishwasher
  WS 1, 15
Geschlecht gender **WS 2**, 55
Geschlechtswort article OT 1
geschlossen closed OT 1
Geschmack flavour OT 2; taste **WS 3**, 87
geschnetzelt shredded OT 2
Geschwindigkeit speed OT 2
geschwollen swollen OT 2
Gesellschaft society **WS 1**, 32
Gesetz law OT 3
Gesicht face OT 1
Gesichtsausdruck facial expression
  WS 4, 117

gespannt curious **WS 1**, 29

gesponsert sponsored OT 2

Gespräch conversation OT 1

gesprächig chatty OT 3

Geste gesture **WS 4**, 117

gestern yesterday OT 1

gestiftet sponsored OT 2

gestresst stressed OT 2

gestrichen painted OT 1

gesund healthy OT 2

Gesundheit health OT 2

Gesundheitswesen healthcare **WS 4**, 112

Getränk drink OT 1

Getreide crop **WS 1**, 19

getrennt divided; separate OT 2

Gewalt violence **WS 2**, 61

Gewaltlosigkeit non-violence OT 3

Gewehr rifle **WS 1**, 20

Gewicht weight **WS 1**, 29

Gewichtheben weightlifting **WS 3**, 93

Gewinn prize OT 1; profit **WS 1**, 22

gewinnen to win OT 1

Gewinner(in) winner OT 1

Gewitter thunderstorm OT 2

Gewohnheit habit **WS 2**, 48

gewöhnlich normally OT 1; common **WW**, 10

Gewürz seasoning OT 2; spice OT 3

Gewürzgurke pickle OT 1

gewürzt spiced **WS 3**, 84

gießen to pour OT 1

Gift poison OT 1

giftig toxic **WS 2**, 52

gigantisch ginormous OT 2

Gips plaster OT 1

Giraffe giraffe OT 1

Gitarre guitar OT 1

Gitarrist(in) guitarist OT 1

Gladiator(in) gladiator OT 3

glamourös glamorous **WS 3**, 83

Glas glass OT 1

glatt smooth OT 3

Glaube belief **WS 1**, 32

glauben to believe OT 2

gleich same OT 1

gleichberechtigt equal **WS 4**, 127

Gleichgewicht balance OT 3

glitzern to glitter OT 2; to twinkle **WS 3**, 95

global global **WS 2**, 52

Glocke bell OT 1

Glück luck OT 1; fortune OT 3

glückbringend lucky OT 2

glücklich happy OT 1; lucky OT 2

glücklos unlucky OT 2

Glückwünsche congratulations OT 2

Glühbirne lightbulb OT 3

Gold gold OT 2

golden golden OT 3

Goldrausch gold rush **WS 1**, 25

Gospel gospel OT 2

Gott God **WS 1**, 20

graben to dig OT 1

Grad degree **WS 3**, 94

Grafik graphic OT 3

Gramm gram OT 2

Grammatik grammar OT 1

Grammofon gramophone **WS 3**, 83

Gras grass OT 1

gratulieren to congratulate OT 2

grau grey OT 1

Grauen horror OT 2

gravieren to engrave **WS 1**, 29

greifen to grab OT 3

Grenze border OT 3

Grenzland frontier **WS 3**, 94

griechisch Greek OT 2

Griff handle OT 2

Grillen barbecue OT 2

grinsen to grin OT 2

groß tall; big; great OT 1; large OT 2

großartig awesome OT 2

Großaufnahme close-up **WS 4**, 128

Großbuchstabe capital letter OT 1

Größe size OT 1

Großeltern grandparents OT 1

Großmutter grandmother OT 1

Großsegler tall ship OT 2

Großvater grandfather OT 2

großzügig generous OT 3

grün green OT 1

Grund reason OT 1; cause OT 2

Grund... primary OT 1; elementary OT 2; basic **WS 3**, 17

gründen to found **WS 1**, 18; to form **WS 1**, 29

grundlegend radical **WS 3**, 90

grundsätzlich basic **WS 3**, 83

Grundschule elementary school OT 2

Gruppe group OT 1

Gruppenarbeit teamwork **WS 4**, 112

Gruß: mit freundlichen Grüßen sincerely **WS 1**, 31

günstig convenient **WS 2**, 50

Gurke pickle OT 1

Gurt harness OT 1

Gürtel belt OT 2

gut fine; good; all right OT 1

    gut aussehend handsome OT 1

    gutbürgerlich plain **WS 1**, 32

    gut gemacht well done OT 1

    gute Arbeit leisten to do a good / great job OT 2

Güter goods **WS 1**, 28

Gutschein coupon OT 2

guttun to benefit OT 2

Gymnastik gymnastics OT 1

H

Haare hair OT 1

Haarschnitt haircut OT 2

Habe belongings OT 3

haben feature OT 1

Habitat habitat **WS 4**, 123

Hackbraten meatloaf OT 3

Hackfleischbällchen meatball OT 1

Hafen port; harbour OT 2

Haferbrei porridge OT 3

Haferflocken oats OT 3

Hähnchen chicken OT 1

Häkchen tick OT 2

haken to hook **WS 3**, 96

halal halal OT 3

halb half OT 1; halfway OT 3

    eine halbe Stunde nach half past OT 1

Halbjahr semester OT 3

Halbmarathon half marathon OT 2

halbwegs halfway OT 3

Halbzeit half-time OT 2

Halle hall OT 1

hallo hello; hi OT 1

Halloween Halloween OT 2

Hals neck OT 1; throat OT 2

Halsband collar OT 2

Halt stop OT 2

halten to hold OT 1

Haltestelle stop; halt OT 2

Haltung attitude OT 3

Hamburger burger OT 1; hamburger OT 2

Hamster hamster OT 1

Hand hand OT 1

    jmdm. die Hand geben to shake hands OT 2

Handbuch handbook OT 3

Handel: illegalen Handel treiben to traffic **WS 4**, 124

Handgelenk wrist OT 1

Händler(in) retailer **WS 2**, 64

Handlung plot **WS 2**, 49

Handout handout **WS 2**, 55

Handschrift handwriting OT 2

Handschuh glove OT 1

Handtasche handbag OT 3

Handtuch towel OT 2

Handy mobile phone OT 1; cell phone OT 2

Harfe harp OT 1

Harfenist(in) harpist OT 3

hart hard OT 1; tough **WS 3**, 90

hassen to hate OT 1

hässlich ugly OT 1

Haufen heap **WS 3**, 80

häufig frequently OT 3; many times **WS 1**, 26

> **häufig gestellte Fragen** FAQ (frequently asked questions) OT 1

Häufigkeit frequency OT 1

Haupt... primary; main OT 1; core **WS 3**, 80

Hauptgang main course OT 1

hauptsächlich mainly OT 2; generally **WS 3**, 77

Hauptsitz headquarter **WS 4**, 127

Hauptstadt capital OT 1

Hauptverkehrszeit rush hour OT 1

Hauptwort noun OT 1

Haus house OT 1

Hausarbeit housework OT 1; chore **WS 1**, 13

Hausaufgaben homework OT 1

Hausboot narrowboat; houseboat OT 3

Häuschen cottage OT 3

Haushälter(in) housekeeper OT 3

Haushalts... household **WS 3**, 78

Haushaltsgerät appliance OT 3

häuslich household **WS 3**, 78

Hausmeister(in) caretaker OT 1

Haustier pet OT 1

Haut skin OT 2

Headquarter headquarter **WS 4**, 127

Headset headset **WS 3**, 78

heben to raise OT 2; to lift OT 3

heften to pin OT 1

heil in one piece OT 2

Heilbad spa OT 3

heilen to cure **WS 3**, 79

heilig sacred **WS 1**, 31

Heilkunde medical science **WS 3**, 79

Heimat homeland **WS 1**, 20

heimatlos homeless OT 3

Heimatstadt hometown **WS 1**, 12

Heimweh homesickness **WS 1**, 17

heiraten to marry OT 1; to wed OT 3

heiß hot OT 1

heizen to heat OT 3

Heizung heater OT 2; heating OT 3

hektisch frantic OT 3; hectic **WS 3**, 73

Held(in) hero OT 3

helfen to help OT 1

Helfer(in) helper OT 3

Helm helmet OT 1

Hemd shirt OT 1

Henne hen OT 2

heraus out OT 1

herausfinden to find out OT 1; to work out OT 2

Herausforderung challenge OT 2

Herausgeber(in) editor OT 2

herausragend outstanding OT 3

Herbst autumn OT 2

Herd cooker OT 3

Herde herd **WS 1**, 29

Herein! Come in! OT 2

Herr Mr; Sir OT 1; gentleman OT 3

herrisch bossy OT 2

Herrschaft reign OT 3

herrschen to reign OT 3

Hersteller(in) manufacturer **WS 4**, 126

Herstellung production **WS 2**, 52; manufacture **WS 4**, 112

herumhängen to hang out OT 1

herumziehend migrant **WS 4**, 124

hervorheben to highlight OT 3

Herz heart OT 2

herzhaft hearty OT 2

Heureka-Erlebnis eureka moment **WS 3**, 82

heute today OT 1

> **heute Abend** tonight OT 1

heutzutage nowadays OT 3

Hexe witch OT 2

hier here OT 1; locally OT 3

Highway highway OT 3

Hilfe relief **WS 3**, 83

hilflos helpless **WS 1**, 26; hopeless **WS 1**, 26

hilfreich helpful OT 1

Himbeere raspberry OT 1

Himmel sky OT 1

hinauf up OT 1

hinduistisch Hindu OT 1

Hinfahrt outward journey OT 3

hinfallen to fall over OT 2

hinsetzen to sit down OT 1

hinter behind OT 1

Hintergrund background OT 3

Hinterland outback **WS 3**, 94

hinterlassen to leave behind OT 2

hinüber across OT 1

hinunter down OT 1

hinunterkommen to get down OT 2

hinunterschlucken to swallow **WS 3**, 93

Hinweis tip; clue OT 1

hinzufügen to add OT 1

Hip-Hop hip hop OT 1

hispanisch Hispanic OT 3

Historiker(in) historian OT 3

historisch historic OT 3

Hobby hobby OT 1

hoch high; tall OT 1

hochheben to lift OT 3

hochladen to upload OT 3

Hochschule college OT 2

Hochwasser flood OT 2

Hochzeit wedding OT 3

Hockey hockey OT 1

Hof court; courtyard OT 3

hoffen to hope OT 1

hoffentlich hopefully **WS 2**, 70

hoffnungslos hopeless **WS 1**, 26

höflich polite OT 1

Höhe height OT 1

Höhle cave OT 1

holen to fetch **WS 1**, 20

holprig bumpy **WS 1**, 28

Holz wood OT 2

hölzern wooden OT 1

Holzscheit log OT 3

Honig honey OT 2

hören to hear OT 1

Hörer(in) listener OT 1

horizontal horizontal **WS 2**, 64

Horn horn OT 2

Horror horror OT 2

Hose trousers OT 1

> **kurze Hose** shorts OT 1

Hostel hostel OT 2

Hotdog hot dog OT 2

Hotel hotel OT 1

Hotline helpline OT 2

hübsch lovely; pretty OT 1

Hubschrauber helicopter OT 2

Hüfte hip OT 3

Hügel hill OT 1

hügelig hilly OT 2

Huhn chicken OT 1

Hühnerstall coop **WS 3**, 80

Hülle cover OT 1

Hülsenfrucht pulse **WS 3**, 80

Humor humour OT 3

Hund dog OT 1

Hundedreck dog mess OT 2

hundert hundred OT 1

Hunger hunger **WS 3**, 103

hungern (lassen) to starve OT 1

Hungersnot famine **WS 1**, 24

hungrig hungry OT 1

husten to cough OT 2

Hut hat OT 1

Hütehund sheepdog OT 2

Hüter(in) keeper **WS 1**, 31

hydratisieren to hydrate **WS 3**, 92

Hygiene hygiene **WS 3**, 92

Hyperlink hyperlink OT 3

I
ich I OT 1
ich (selbst) myself OT 3
ideal ideal OT 2
Idee idea OT 1
identifizieren to identify OT 3
Identität identity OT 3
Igel hedgehog OT 1
Igitt! yuck OT 3
ignorieren to ignore WS 1, 31
ihm him OT 1
ihn him OT 1
ihnen them OT 1
ihr their; her OT 1
ihre(r, -s) hers; theirs; yours OT 2
ikonisch iconic OT 3
illegal illegal OT 3
Illustration illustration OT 2
illustrieren to illustrate OT 3
imaginär imaginary WS 3, 85
immer always OT 1
   für immer forever OT 2
   immer noch still OT 1
Imperativ imperative OT 1
importieren to import OT 3
Improvisation improvisation OT 2
improvisieren to improvise OT 2
in at; on; into; inside OT 1
Index index WS 2, 62
Indexer(in) indexer WS 2, 62
indisch Indian OT 2
individuell individual OT 3
Industrie industry OT 2
Industrie... industrial OT 2
Infinitiv infinitive OT 2
Infografik infographic OT 3
Information information OT 1
informativ informative OT 3
informieren to inform WS 1, 26
Ingenieur(in) engineer OT 3
Ingenieurwesen engineering OT 1
Inhalt content OT 2
inhuman inhumane WS 4, 127
Initiative initiative WS 4, 113
inklusive including; include OT 1
innen indoor(s) OT 2
Innenhof courtyard OT 3
Innenstadt downtown WS 2, 60; inner
   city WS 2, 63
Innereien insides OT 3
innerhalb inside OT 1; within WS 1, 30
Innovation innovation WS 3, 78
innovativ innovative WS 3, 84
Innovator(in) innovator WS 3, 84
Insekt insect OT 1
Insektenhaus bughouse OT 1

Insel island OT 2
Inserat advert OT 1
Inspiration inspiration WS 3, 84
inspirieren to inspire OT 3
   inspiriert werden to get inspired
   WS 2, 50
installieren to install WS 3, 80
instruktiv informative OT 3
Instrument instrument OT 1
integrativ inclusive WS 4, 118
intelligent clever OT 1; intelligent OT 2;
   smart WS 2, 59
interagieren to interact WS 4, 112
Interaktion interaction WS 1, 32
interessant interesting OT 1
Interesse interest OT 1
interessieren: sich interessieren to
   care about OT 2
interessiert interested OT 1
international international OT 1
Internet internet OT 1
Internethandel e-commerce WS 2, 54
Interpret(in) performer OT 2
interpretieren to interpret WS 1, 26
Interview interview OT 1
interviewen to interview OT 1
Interviewer(in) interviewer OT 1
Intonation intonation WS 4, 117
investieren to invest OT 3
Investition investment OT 3
Investor(in) investor WS 3, 83
involviert involved OT 3
iranisch Iranian WS 3, 92
irgendein(e) any OT 1
irgendetwas anything OT 1
irgendjemand anybody; anyone OT 2
irgendwie like OT 1
irgendwo somewhere OT 1; anywhere
   OT 2
irisch Irish OT 1
Irre madman WS 1, 16
irreführend misleading OT 3
israelisch Israeli OT 2
italienisch Italian OT 2

J
ja yes; yeah OT 1
Jacht yacht OT 2
Jacke jacket OT 1
jagen to chase OT 1; to hunt OT 2
Jahr year OT 1
Jahreszeit season OT 3
Jahrhundert century OT 2
Jahrmarkt fairground OT 2; fair WS 1, 20
jamaikanisch Jamaican OT 1
Januar January OT 1

japanisch Japanese OT 1
Jazz jazz OT 2
je ever OT 1
Jeanshose jeans OT 1
Jeansstoff denim WS 1, 25
jede(r, s) everybody; every; each;
   everyone OT 1
jederzeit anytime OT 3
jedoch though; however OT 2
jemand someone; somebody OT 1
jene(r, -s) that OT 1
   jene dort those OT 1
jetzt now OT 1
Job job OT 1
joggen to jog OT 2
Joghurt yoghurt OT 1
Journalist(in) journalist OT 2
jubeln to cheer OT 2
juckend itchy OT 2
Judo judo OT 1
Jugend youth OT 1
Jugendbetreuer(in) counsellor OT 2
Jugendherberge youth hostel OT 2
Jugendliche(r) teenager OT 2
Juli July OT 1
jung young OT 1
Junge boy OT 1
jüngst recent WS 1, 19
Juni June OT 1
Junior(in) junior OT 2
Juwel jewel OT 1

K
Kabine cabin OT 2
Kaffee coffee OT 1
Käfig cage WS 4, 124
Kajakfahren kayaking OT 2
Kalender calendar OT 1
kalt cold OT 1; freezing OT 2
Kamera camera OT 1
Kamin fireplace OT 1
Kamm comb OT 2
Kammer chamber OT 2
   kleine Kammer closet OT 2
Kampagne campaign OT 3; initiative
   WS 4, 113
Kampf fight OT 1
kämpfen to fight OT 1
Kanal canal OT 3
Kanalboot narrowboat OT 3
Kandidat(in) candidate WS 1, 13
Kaninchen rabbit OT 1
Kantine canteen OT 1
Kanu canoe OT 1
Kanufahren canoeing OT 1
Kapitel chapter OT 1

Kapsel capsule **WS 3**, 95

Kapuzenpullover hoodie OT 1

Karamelle caramel OT 3

Karate karate OT 1

Karbon carbon OT 3

Karotte carrot OT 1

Karriere career OT 3

Karte card OT 1

Karteikarte cue card **WS 3**, 96

Kartoffel potato OT 1

Kartoffelbrei mashed potato OT 1

Karton carton OT 2

Kartrennen kart racing OT 3

Käse cheese OT 1

Kasse cash register OT 2; check-out **WS 3**, 78

Kassierer(in) cashier **WS 3**, 78; bank teller **WS 4**, 112

Kästchen box OT 1

katastrophal catastrophic **WS 3**, 103

Katastrophe disaster OT 2

Katastrophengebiet disaster area OT 2

Kategorie category OT 3

Kathedrale cathedral OT 1

Katholik(in) Catholic OT 3

Katze cat OT 1

Kauf purchase **WS 3**, 78

kaufen to buy; to shop OT 1

Käufer(in) shopper **WS 2**, 53

kaum hardly OT 3

keimtötend antiseptic OT 2

keine(r, -s) none OT 2

Keks biscuit OT 1; cookie OT 3

Keller cellar **WS 3**, 83

Kellner(in) waiter OT 1

kenntnisreich knowledgeable OT 3

Kennwort password **WS 1**, 13

Kerl guy OT 2

Kern core **WS 3**, 80

Kernland heartland **WS 1**, 12

Kerze candle OT 2

Kerzenlicht candlelight **WS 3**, 77

Kessel kettle OT 2

Ketchup ketchup OT 1

Kette chain OT 2

keuchen to gasp OT 2

Keyboard keyboard OT 1

Kickball kickball **WS 3**, 79

Kidneybohne kidney bean OT 2

Kilometer kilometre OT 1

Kind child; kid OT 1

Kindheit childhood OT 3

Kino cinema OT 1

Kirche church OT 1

Kissen cushion OT 1

Kiste box OT 1; crate **WS 1**, 18

Kiwi kiwi OT 1

Klammer clip OT 1; bracket OT 2

klammern to cling OT 2

Klan clan OT 3

Klang (einer Glocke) bong OT 1

Klaps pat OT 3

klar clear OT 2

klären to clarify **WS 4**, 123

Klarinette clarinet OT 2

Klasse class OT 1

Klassenkamerad(in) classmate OT 3

Klassenstufe grade OT 2

Klassenzimmer classroom OT 1

klassisch classic; classical OT 2

klatschen to clap OT 1

klauen to steal OT 2

Klavier piano OT 1

Klebeband tape OT 1

kleben to stick OT 1; to paste OT 2

klebend sticky **WS 3**, 86

klebrig sticky OT 1

Klebstoff glue OT 1

Kleid dress OT 3

Kleider clothes OT 1

Kleiderordnung dress code **WS 2**, 59

Kleiderschrank wardrobe OT 1

Kleidung clothes OT 1; clothing OT 3

klein small; little OT 1

sehr klein miniature OT 3

Kleinbus minibus OT 2

Kleingeld cash OT 1

Kletterer(in) climber OT 2

klettern to climb OT 1

Klima climate OT 2

Klimaerwärmung global warming OT 3

Klingel doorbell OT 2

klingeln to ring OT 1

klingen to sound OT 2

klirren to clash OT 2

Klo loo OT 2

Klopfen knock OT 2

Kloß dumpling **WS 1**, 26

Kloster monastery OT 3

Klub club OT 1

Kneipe pub OT 2

Knete dough OT 2

Knie knee OT 1

knien to kneel OT 1

Knochen bone OT 1

Knödel dumpling **WS 1**, 26

Knopf button OT 1

knuddelig cuddly OT 1

Koch / Köchin chef OT 1

köcheln to simmer OT 2

kochen to make; to cook OT 1; to boil OT 2

kochend heiß boiling OT 1

Kochfeld hob OT 3

Koffer case OT 1; suitcase OT 2

Kofferraum trunk OT 2

Kohl cabbage OT 1

Kohle coal OT 2

kohlensäurehaltig fizzy OT 2

Kollege; Kollegin colleague **WS 3**, 83

kolonial colonial **WS 1**, 18

Kolonie colony **WS 1**, 12

Kolonist(in) colonist OT 3

Kombination combination OT 3

kombinieren to combine **WS 4**, 129

Komitee committee OT 2

Komma comma OT 3

Kommandant(in) captain **WS 1**, 21; commander **WS 3**, 93

kommen: näher kommen to approach **WS 4**, 127

kommen to come OT1

Kommentar comment OT 1

kommentieren to comment OT 3

kommerziell commercial **WS 1**, 22

kommunizieren to communicate **WS 1**, 32

Komparativ comparative OT 2

Kompass compass OT 2

kompliziert complicated OT 2; tricky **WS 1**, 19

komponieren to compose OT 3

Komponist(in) composer OT 2

Kompost compost OT 3

Kondor condor OT 3

Konferenz conference **WS 1**, 13

Konflikt conflict OT 2

Kongress convention **WS 4**, 124

König king OT 1

Königin queen OT 1

königlich royal OT 1

Königreich kingdom **WS 1**, 25

konkret specific OT 3

Konkurrent(in) competitor **WS 3**, 96

Konkurrenz competition OT 1

konkurrenzorientiert competitive OT 3

konkurrieren to compete OT 2

Können ability OT 2

können can OT 1; to be able to; to be allowed to OT 2

könnte might; may OT 1

Konsequenz consequence **WS 3**, 90

Kontakt contact OT 1

in Kontakt bleiben to keep in touch OT 2

Kontakte pflegen to socialize **WS 2**, 58

Kontext context **WS 4**, 127

Kontinent continent OT 3
Kontrabass double bass OT 2
Kontrast contrast OT 3
Kontrolle control OT 3
kontrollieren to control **WS 3**, 78
Konvention convention **WS 4**, 124
Konzentration concentration **WS 2**, 62
konzentrieren to concentrate OT 3
Konzept concept **WS 4**, 118
Konzert concert OT 1
Kooperation partnership **WS 3**, 92
Kopf head OT 1
  Kopf hoch! cheer up OT 1
Kopfband headband OT 3
Kopfkissen pillow OT 2
Kopfsalat lettuce OT 2
Kopfschmerzen headache OT 1
Kopie replica **WS 1**, 18
kopieren to copy OT 1
Korb basket OT 3
koreanisch Korean OT 1
Körper body OT 1
körperlich physical OT 2
Korrektur correction **WS 4**, 119
Korridor corridor OT 2
korrigieren to correct OT 1; to fix;
  to mark OT 2
Kosten cost OT 1
kosten to cost OT 1
kostenlos free OT 1
Kostüm costume; fancy dress OT 2
Krabbeltier creepy-crawly OT 2
krachen to crash OT 3
Kraft force OT 1
kraftlos powerless **WS 4**, 127
Krake octopus OT 1
Krampf cramp OT 2
Kran crane **WS 3**, 94
krank sick OT 1; unwell; ill OT 2
Krankenhaus hospital OT 1
Krankenschwester / -pfleger nurse
  OT 1
Krankenwagen ambulance OT 1
Krankheit disease; illness OT 2
Kranz wreath OT 3
Krapfen doughnut OT 2
kratzen to scratch OT 2
kraus frizzy OT 3
Kraut herb OT 3
Krawatte tie OT 1
kreativ creative OT 2
Kreativität creativity **WS 4**, 113
Krebs cancer **WS 2**, 52
Kreditkarte credit card OT 1
kreieren to create OT 2
Kreis circle OT 1

kreischen to scream OT 3
Kreisdiagramm pie chart **WS 2**, 64
kreuzen to cross OT 1
Kreuzfahrt cruise OT 2
  eine Kreuzfahrt machen to cruise
  OT 3
Kreuzung crossroads OT 1
Kricket cricket OT 1
Krieg war OT 2
Krieger(in) warrior OT 2
Kriegsschiff warship OT 3
Kriminelle(r) criminal OT 3
Krise crisis OT 3
kritisieren to criticize OT 3
Krone crown OT 1
krönen to crown OT 1
Kröte toad OT 2
Krücke crutch OT 2
Küche kitchen OT 1; cuisine OT 3
Kuchen cake OT 1
Küchenchef; Küchenchefin chef OT 1
Kugelschreiber ballpoint pen OT 1
Kuh cow OT 1
kühl cool OT 1
kühlen to cool OT 3
Kühlschrank fridge OT 1; refrigerator
  WS 3, 93
Kult... iconic OT 3
kultiviert cultured **WS 2**, 73
Kultur culture OT 1
kulturell cultural OT 3
Kumpel buddy OT 2
Kunde / Kundin customer OT 3
Kundgebung rally **WS 2**, 58
kündigen to quit **WS 3**, 80
Kunst art OT 1
  bildende Kunst visual art OT 2
Künstler(in) performer OT 2;
  entertainer; artist OT 3
künstlich man-made OT 1; artifical
  OT 3
  künstliche Intelligenz artificial
  intelligence **WS 3**, 78
Kunststoff plastic OT 2
Kunstwissenschaft fine art OT 2
Kupfer copper OT 1
Kuppel cupola **WS 3**, 93
Kürbis pumpkin OT 2; squash **WS 1**, 21
Kürbislaterne jack-o-lantern OT 2
Kuriosität oddity **WS 3**, 95
Kurs course OT 1; program OT 3
kursieren to circulate **WS 2**, 55
kurz short OT 1
kuschelig cuddly OT 1
Kuss kiss OT 3
Küste seaside; coast OT 1; shore OT 2

Küsten... coastal OT 1
Küstenwache coastguard OT 2
Kutsche buggy **WS 1**, 32
Kutschfahrten carriage driving OT 2

L
Labor lab OT 2; laboratory **WS 3**, 83
Lache pool OT 1
lächeln to smile OT 1
lachen to laugh OT 1
Lachs salmon OT 1
Laden shop; store OT 1
Ladung cargo OT 3
Lage situation OT 1
Lagerfeuer campfire OT 2
Lagerung storage OT 3
Lamm lamb OT 1
Lampe lamp OT 1
Land countryside OT 1
  an Land ashore **WS 1**, 20
Landarbeiter(in) farmhand **WS 4**, 112;
  farmworker **WS 4**, 125
landen to land OT 1
Landkarte map OT 1
ländlich rural **WS 2**, 62
Landschaft landscape; scenery OT 2
Landstrasse highway OT 3
Landwirtschaft farming; agriculture
  OT 2
landwirtschaftlich agricultural
  WS 4, 125
lang long OT 1
Länge length OT 2
langsam slow OT 2
langweilig boring OT 1
Lappen cloth OT 2
Laptop laptop OT 1
Lärm noise OT 1
Lasagne lasagna OT 1
Laser laser OT 3
lassen to let OT 1
  lass / lasst uns let's **WS 1**, 13
Laster truck OT 1
Lastkraftwagen truck OT 1
lateinamerikanisch Latino OT 2
lateinisch Latin OT 1
Laterne lantern OT 2
Laufband treadmill **WS 3**, 93
laufen to walk; to run OT 1
Läufer(in) runner OT 2
laut loud; noisy OT 1; aloud OT 2
  laut rufen to shout OT 1
Lautsprecher loudspeaker OT 2
Lautsprecheranlage PA (public
  address) system OT 2
leasen to lease **WS 3**, 96

Leben life OT 1; lifetime OT 2
leben to live OT 1
lebendig alive **WS 2**, 49
lebensbedrohlich life-threatening OT 2
Lebensmittel groceries **WS 3**, 80
Lebensmittelladen grocery store **WS 1**, 25
Lebensmittelverarbeitung food processing **WS 4**, 125
Lebensmittelvergiftung food poisoning OT 2
Lebensraum habitat **WS 4**, 123
Lebensstil lifestyle **WS 1**, 14
lebenswichtig vital **WS 4**, 113
Lebenszeit lifetime OT 2
Lebewesen creature **WS 4**, 111
lecken to lick OT 3
lecker delicious OT 1
LED Birne LED bulb OT 3
Leder leather OT 3
leer empty OT 1; blank **WS 4**, 119
leeren to empty **WS 1**, 15
legal legal **WS 1**, 26
Legende legend OT 2
lehnen to lean OT 3
Lehrer(in) teacher OT 1; instructor OT 3
Lehrmeister(in) mentor **WS 4**, 123
leicht easy OT 2; light OT 3
Leichtathletik athletics OT 1
leichtsinnig carelessly OT 2
leidenschaftlich passionate **WS 4**, 110
leider unfortunately OT 3
leihen to lend; to borrow OT 2
Leinwand screen OT 1
   auf der Leinwand onscreen OT 2
leisten to afford OT 2
Leistung achievement OT 2
leiten to manage OT 1
Leiter ladder OT 2
Leitung: die Leitung übernehmen to take charge OT 2
Leopard leopard OT 2
lernen to lern OT 1
   auswendig lernen to memorize **WS 4**, 109
Lernende(r) learner OT 3
Lesen reading OT 1
lesen to read OT 1
Leser(in) reader OT 3
Lesezeichen marker OT 1
letzte(r, -s) last OT 1
leuchtend bright OT 1
Leute people OT 1; folks; guys OT 2
Licht light OT 1
liebe(r, -s) dear OT 1
lieben to love OT 1

Liebhaber(in) lover OT 3
Lieblings... favourite OT 1
Lied song OT 1
Liedtext lyrics OT 2
liefern to deliver **WS 3**, 78
Lieferung delivery OT 3
Lieferwagen van **WS 3**, 80
liegen to lie OT 1
Lifestyle lifestyle **WS 1**, 14
Liga league OT 2
lila purple OT 1
Lineal ruler OT 1
Linie line OT 1
linke(r, -s) left OT 1
Linse lens **WS 3**, 95
Lippe lip OT 2
Liste list OT 1
Liter liter **WS 2**, 52
Literatur literature **WS 2**, 57
Loch hole OT 1
locker laid-back **WS 2**, 73
Löffel spoon OT 2
   Löffel (Maßangabe) spoonful OT 2
Logo logo OT 1
lohnen to be worth it OT 1
lohnend worthwhile OT 2; rewarding **WS 4**, 123
lohnenswert worth **WS 4**, 120
Lokführer(in) engineer OT 3
Lokomotive engine OT 2
löschen to put out OT 2; to delete **WS 4**, 129
lösen to solve OT 3
losfahren to head out **WS 2**, 62
loslassen to relax OT 2
losstürzen to rush off OT 2
Lösung solution OT 2
loswerden to get rid of OT 3
Lotterie lottery OT 3
Löwe; Löwin lion OT 1
Luchs lynx OT 2
Lücke gap OT 3
Luft air OT 1
Luftschlangen streamer **WS 2**, 58
Lunge lung OT 3
Lust: auf etw. Lust haben to be keen on sth. **WS 4**, 110
lustig funny OT 1
luxuriös luxurious OT 2

M
machen to make; to do OT 1
   das macht... That'll be ... OT 2
Macher(in) maker OT 3
mächtig mighty OT 3
machtlos powerless **WS 4**, 127

Mädchen girl OT 1
Magen stomach OT 2
magisch magical OT 2
Magnet magnet OT 1
magnetisch magnetic OT 2
Mahlzeit meal OT 1
Mai May OT 1
Mailbox mailbox **WS 2**, 49
Mais corn OT 3
Maisbrot cornbread **WS 1**, 20
malen to paint OT 1
Mama mum OT 1
man you OT 1
managen to manage OT 1
Manager(in) manager OT 1
manchmal sometimes OT 1
Mangel lack OT 3
mangelhaft junky **WS 3**, 89
Mann man OT 1; husband OT 2
männlich male OT 2
Mannschaft team OT 1; crew OT 2
Mannschaft crew OT 2
Mantel coat OT 1
Mappe portfolio **WS 4**, 113
Marathon marathon OT 2
Märchen fairy tale OT 1
Marine navy OT 3
   Marine... maritime OT 3
Marke brand **WS 2**, 44
Marketing marketing **WS 3**, 85
markieren to bookmark **WS 1**, 22
Markise marquee OT 2
Markt market OT 1
   auf den Markt bringen to launch **WS 3**, 76; to release **WS 3**, 76
Marmelade jam OT 2
Marsch march OT 3
März March OT 1
Maschine machine OT 1
   Maschinen machinery OT 2
Maske mask OT 3
Maß measurement OT 2
Massaker massacre OT 3
Maßeinheit measurement OT 2
Massen... mass **WS 3**, 77
Massensport mass sport OT 3
Material material OT 3
Mathe math OT 1
Mathematik maths OT 1; mathematics OT 3
Mathematiker(in) mathematician OT 3
Matrose sailor OT 1
Maultier mule OT 3
Maus mouse OT 2
Mauszeiger cursor OT 3
Maximum maximum OT 2

Mayonnaise mayonnaise OT 1
Medaille medal OT 2
Mediation mediation OT 1
Medien media OT 2
Medikament medicine OT 2
Medizin medicine OT 2; medical science
WS 3, 79
medizinisch medical OT 1
Meer sea OT 1
Meeres... marine WS 4, 110
Meeresboden seabed OT 3
Meeresfrüchte seafood OT 3
Mehl flour OT 3
mehr more OT 1; anymore OT 2
mehrere several OT 2
Mehrheit majority WS 4, 125
Mehrzahl plural OT 1
Meile mile OT 1
mein my OT 1
meine(r, -s) mine OT 2
Meinung opinion OT 3
anderer Meinung sein to disagree
OT 2
Meinungsverschiedenheit
disagreement OT 2
meiste most OT 1
Meister(in) master WS 2, 59
Melodie melody OT 2
Menchenmenge throng OT 2
Menge crowd OT 1; amount OT 2;
portion WS 1, 13; quantity WS 3, 86
eine Menge loads of OT 3
Mensch person OT 1
menschengemacht man-made OT 1
Menschenmenge crowd OT 1
menschenunwürdig inhumane
WS 4, 127
menschlich human OT 3
mental mental WS 1, 30
Mentor(in) mentor WS 4, 123
merken: sich merken to memorize
WS 4, 109
Merkmal feature OT 1
merkwürdig funny OT 1
messen to measure WS 3, 89
Messer knife OT 2
Metall metal OT 1
Meter metre OT 1
Methode method OT 1; technique
WS 2, 49
Metzger(in) butcher WS 1, 20
mexikanisch Mexican WS 4, 114
mich me OT 1
Miet... rental WS 3, 87
mieten to rent WS 2, 61
Migrant(in) migrant WS 4, 125

Migration migration OT 3
migrieren to migrate OT 3
Mikrobe microbe WS 3, 94
Mikrofon microphone WS 1, 13
Mikroskop microscope WS 3, 95
Milch milk OT 1
Militär military WS 3, 83
Milliarde billion OT 2
Million million OT 1
Mindest... minimum OT 1
Mindmap mind map OT 1
Mine mine OT 2
Minute minute OT 1
Minze mint OT 2
mir me OT 1
mischen to mix OT 2; to combine
WS 4, 129
Mischung mixture OT 3
Missbrauch abuse WS 4, 125
Misserfolg failure WS 3, 84
Mission mission WS 3, 94
Missverständnis misunderstanding
WS 1, 26
mit with OT 1
Mitarbeiter(in) colleague WS 3, 83
mitbegründen to co-found WS 1, 25
Mitbewerber(in) competitor WS 3, 96
mitfühlend sympathetic OT 3
Mitglied member OT 1
Mitglied werden in to join OT 1
mithören to overhear OT 3
Mitspieler(in) teammate OT 2
Mittag noon WS 2, 47; midday WS 3, 80
Mittagessen lunch OT 1
Mittagspause lunch break OT 1
Mittagszeit lunchtime OT 1
Mitte centre OT 1, middle OT 1
in der Mitte mid WS 1, 24
Mitteilungsblatt newsletter WS 3, 89
Mittel resource WS 2, 48
Mittelfeldspieler(in) midfielder OT 3
mittelgroß medium OT 1; medium-sized
OT 2
Mittelschule middle school OT 2
Mitternacht midnight OT 1
Mittwoch Wednesday OT 1
mitwirken to contribute WS 1, 24
Mitwirkung contribution WS 1, 24
Mobbing bullying OT 2
Möbel furniture OT 1
mobil mobile OT 1
Mobilteil handset OT 2
möchte(n) would like / love OT 1
Modalverb modal OT 2
Mode fashion OT 1
Modell model OT 1

modern modern OT 1
Modul module WS 3, 93
mögen to like OT 1; to be fond of WS 1, 21
nicht mögen to dislike OT 3
möglich possible OT 2
Möglichkeit chance; possibility OT 2
Moment moment OT 1
momentan at the moment OT 2
Monat month OT 1
Mönch monk OT 3
Mond moon WS 1, 24
monoton monotone WS 4, 117
Monster monster OT 1
Montag Monday OT 1
Moosbere cranberry WS 1, 21
moralisch ethical OT 3
Morgen morning OT 1; acre WS 3, 80
morgen tomorrow OT 1
Morgendämmerung dawn WS 1, 20
Moschee mosque OT 1
mosern to grumble OT 2
Motel motel OT 3
motivieren to motivate WS 4, 111
motiviert self-motivated WS 3, 84
Motor engine OT 2
Mountainbiken mountain biking OT 2
Mücke midge OT 3
müde tired OT 1
Muffin muffin OT 1
Müll rubbish; refuse OT 2
Müllabfuhr rubbish collection OT 2
Müllarbeiter(in) garbage collector
WS 1, 16
Mülldeponie landfill OT 3
Mülleimer rubbish bin; trash can OT 2
Müllmann / -frau refuse collector
OT 2
Mumie mummy OT 2
Mund mouth OT 1
Mundschutz mouthguard OT 2
Mundwasser mouthwash WS 3, 93
Münze coin OT 1
Murmelspiel marbles WS 1, 20
murren to grumble OT 2
mürrisch crossly OT 3
Muschel mussel WS 1, 20
Museum museum OT 1
Musik music OT 1
musikalisch musical OT 2
Musiker(in) musician OT 2
Musikinstrument musical instrument
OT 2
Muskel muscle WS 3, 93
Muslim Muslim OT 3
müssen must; to have to OT 1
Muster pattern OT 1

mutig bold OT 1
Mutter mother OT 1
Mutti mum OT 1
Mütze hat; cap OT 1
Mysterium mystery OT 2

N
nach after; past OT 1; according to OT 3
   nach hinten backwards OT 3
   nach oben up OT 1; upwards OT 3
   nach Christus AD (Anno Domini) OT 2
Nachbar(in) neighbour OT 2
Nachbarschaft neighbourhood WS 1, 14
nachdenken to speculate WS 1, 26
   nachdenken über to think about OT 1
nachdenklich thoughtful OT 3
nacheinander sequentially WS 2, 48
nacherzählen to retell WS 3, 83
Nachfrage demand WS 4, 113
nachhaltig sustainable WS 3, 80
Nachhaltigkeit sustainability OT 3
nachher afterwards OT 3
Nachhilfe geben to tutor WS 4, 116
Nachkomme descendant WS 1, 18
Nachmittag afternoon OT 1
Nachname last name OT 2
Nachricht message OT 1
nächste(r, -s) next OT 1
Nachstellung re-creation WS 1, 18;
   re-enactment WS 1, 20
Nachstellung re-enactment WS 1, 20
Nacht night OT 1
Nachteil con OT 2; disadvantage;
   downside OT 3
Nachtisch dessert OT 1
nah close WS 3, 94
nahe near OT 1
Nähe: in der Nähe nearby OT 3
nähern to approach WS 4, 127
Nähmaschine sewing machine OT 3
nahrhaft nutritious WS 4, 124
Name name OT 1
   mit dem Namen called OT 1
namens called OT 1
Nase nose OT 2
Nashorn rhinoceros OT 2
nass wet OT 2
Nation nation OT 2
national national OT 1
Natur nature OT 2
natürlich of course; natural OT 1
Naturwissenschaften science OT 1
Naturwissenschaftler(in) scientist OT 1
Navigation navigating WS 3, 96
neben by; next to OT 1; beside OT 2; in
   addition to WS 4, 110

nebenberuflich part-time WS 4, 128
Negativ negative OT 1
nehmen to take OT 1
Neige: zur Neige gehen to run out OT 2
neigen to tilt OT 3
nein no OT 1
nennen to call OT 1
Neoprenanzug wetsuit OT 1
Nerv nerve OT 3
nervig annoying OT 2
nervös nervous OT 2
Nest nest OT 3
Netbook netbook WS 3, 78
nett nice; kind OT 1
Netz net OT 3
   vom Netz off the grid WS 3, 80
Netzball netball OT 1
Netzsicherheit cyber security WS 4, 113
neu new OT 1
   neu schreiben to rewrite OT 1
neueste(r) recent WS 1, 19
Neugestaltung re-creation WS 1, 18
Neugier curiosity WS 3, 94
neugierig curious WS 1, 29
Neuheit innovation WS 3, 78
Neuigkeit(en) news OT 1
neulich recently OT 3
neun nine OT 1
neunzehn nineteen OT 1
neunzig ninety OT 1
neutral neutral OT 3
Neutronenbombe nuclear bomb OT 3
Newsletter newsletter WS 3, 89
nicht not OT 1
nichts nothing OT 1
nicken to nod OT 2
nie never OT 1
niedlich cute OT 1
niemand nobody OT 1
Nilpferd hippopotamus OT 2
nirgendwo nowhere OT 2
Niveau level OT 2
noch yet OT 2; nor WS 3, 86
   noch ein(e) another OT 1
Nomen noun OT 1
nominieren to nominate WS 1, 27
Nominierung nomination WS 1, 27
Nonne nun WS 3, 95
nonverbal non-verbal WS 4, 117
Nord... north OT 1
nördlich northern OT 2
normal normal OT 1; ordinary OT 2;
   standard OT 3; common WW, 10
Notaufnahme Accident and Emergency
   OT 1
Notfall emergency OT 1

Notiz note OT 1
Notizbuch notebook OT 2
notwendig necessary OT 3
November November OT 1
Nudeln pasta OT 1
Nuklear... nuclear OT 3
null zero OT 1
Nummer number OT 1
nur just; only OT 1
Nuss nut WS 3, 94
Nutzen benefit OT 2
nützlich useful OT 1; beneficial;
   handy OT 2

O
ob whether OT 1
obdachlos homeless OT 3
Obdachlosigkeit homelessness
   WS 3, 105
oben upstairs OT 1; above OT 3
obere(r, -s) top OT 1
   im oberen Stockwerk upstairs OT 1
Oberfläche surface OT 3
oberhalb above OT 3
Oberschenkel thigh OT 1
Oberstufenschüler(in) senior WS 2, 46
Objekt object OT 1
Obst fruit OT 1
Obstkuchen pie OT 1
obwohl although; though OT 2
oder or OT 1
Ofen stove OT 3; oven WS 1, 21
Ofenkartoffel jacket potato OT 1
Off: aus dem Off offstage OT 2
offen open OT 1
offenbar obviously OT 1
offensichtlich obvious OT 1
öffentlich public OT 2
   öffentliche Verkehrsmittel public
   transport OT 2
offiziell official WS 1, 21
Offizier(in) officer OT 2
öffnen to open OT 1
Öffnungszeiten opening times OT 1
oft often OT 1
oftmals many times WS 1, 26
ohne without OT 2
ohnmächtig werden to faint OT 2
Ohr ear OT 1
ökologisch environmental OT 2;
   eco-friendly OT 3
Ökonomie economy OT 3
Ökotourismus ecotourism OT 3
Oktober October OT 1
Oktopus octopus OT 1
Öl oil OT 1

olympisch Olympic OT 1
Oma grandma OT 1
Omelett omelette OT 2
Onkel uncle OT 1
online online OT 1
Opa grandpa; granddad OT 1
Operation operation OT 3
Opfer victim WS 4, 124
optimistisch optimistic OT 2
optional optional OT 2
orange orange OT 1
Orangensaft orange juice OT 1
Orbit orbit WS 3, 76
Orchester orchestra OT 1
ordentlich properly OT 2; neat WS 1, 29
Ordnung: in Ordnung OK; all right OT 1
Organ organ OT 3
Organisation organization OT 2; agency
  WS 3, 94
Organisator(in) organizer OT 3
organisatorisch organizational
  WS 4, 123
organisieren to organize OT 1
Orgel organ OT 3
orientalisch oriental OT 1
Orientierung reference WS 3, 93;
  orientation WS 3, 93
Original original OT 3
Ort place OT 1
  am Ort locally OT 3
  direkt vor Ort on the doorstep
  WS 4, 123
Osten east OT 1
Ostern Easter OT 1
Österreicher(in) Austrian WS 3, 83
östlich eastern OT 2
Ozean ocean OT 3

P
Paar pair OT 1; couple OT 2
packen to pack OT 2
Pädagoge / Pädagogin educator
  WS 4, 125
Paddel paddle OT 3
Paddle-Boarding paddle-boarding OT 1
paddeln to paddle WS 4, 123
Paket packet OT 2; package OT 3; parcel
  WS 3, 78
pakistanisch Pakistani WS 4, 127
Palast palace OT 1
Pandabär panda OT 1
Paniermehl breadcrumbs OT 3
Panik: in Panik geraten to panic OT 2
Panorama... panoramic OT 3
Panther panther OT 2
pantomimisch darstellen to mime OT 2

Papa dad OT 1
Papier paper OT 1
Paprika pepper OT 2
Papst Pope OT 3
Parade parade OT 2
  Parade-Wagen float WS 1, 21
Paradies paradise WS 1, 13
paralympische Spiele Paralympics OT 3
Park park OT 1
parken to park OT 1
Parkplatz car park OT 1
Parkzettel parking ticket OT 1
Parlament parliament OT 1
parteiisch biased WS 2, 54
Partizip participle OT 2
  Partizip Perfekt past participle OT 2
Partner(in) partner OT 1
Partnerschaft partnership WS 3, 92
Party party OT 1
Pass passport OT 2
Passagier(in) passenger OT 2
passen to fit OT 1
passend timely; appropriately OT 3
passieren to happen OT 1
Passkontrolle passport control OT 2
Passwort password WS 1, 13
Pastete pâté OT 1
Patent patent WS 3, 83
patentieren to patent WS 3, 76
Patient(in) patient OT 1
Patriot(in) patriot OT 2
Pause break; rest OT 1; pause OT 3
  Pause machen to pause OT 3
Pedal pedal WS 3, 93
peinlich embarrassing OT 2
Pendler(in) commuter OT 2
penetrant pushy WS 4, 116
Penizillin penicillin OT 2
Penny penny OT 1
perfekt perfect OT 1
perfektionieren to perfect WS 3, 95
Personal crew OT 2; staff OT 3
persönlich personal OT 2
  persönliche Sachen belongings OT 3
Persönlichkeit personality WS 1, 17
Perspektive perspective WS 4, 117
pessimistisch pessimistic WS 3, 105
Pestizid pesticide WS 2, 52
Pfad trail OT 2
Pfadfinder(in) scout OT 3
Pfanne pan OT 2
Pfannkuchen pancake WS 1, 24
Pfarrer(in) pastor OT 2
Pfeffer pepper OT 2
Pfeife whistle OT 2
pfeifen to blow; to whistle OT 2

Pfeil arrow OT 3
Pferd horse OT 1
pferdebespannt horse-drawn OT 1
Pferdewagen buggy WS 1, 32
Pflanze plant OT 2
Pflanzenwelt wildlife OT 2
Pflaster plaster OT 1
Pflaume plum OT 1
pflegen to maintain WS 4, 113
pflücken to pick OT 1
Pfund pound OT 1
Phase stage OT 2
Philosophie philosophy WS 3, 88
Phonograph phonograph WS 3, 83
Physik physics WS 3, 94
Pianist(in) pianist OT 2
Picknick picnic OT 1
pikant savoury OT 3
Pilgerfahrt pilgrimage OT 3
Pille pill OT 1
Pilot(in) pilot OT 3
Pilz mushroom OT 1
pingelig fussy OT 2
Pinguin penguin OT 1
Pinsel brush OT 2
Pinwand bulletin board WS 4, 116
Pinzette tweezers OT 2
Pionier(in) pioneer WS 1, 28
Pipeline pipeline WS 1, 31
Pirat(in) pirate OT 3
Piste slope OT 3
Pizza pizza OT 1
Plage pest OT 2
Plagegeist pest OT 2
Plagiat plagiarism OT 2
plagiieren to plagiarize OT 2
Plakat poster OT 1
planen to plan OT 1; to arrange OT 2
Planer(in) planner OT 3
Planet planet OT 2
planetarisch planetary WS 3, 95
Planetarium planetarium OT 1
Planetenforschung planetary science
  WS 3, 95
Platz square; ground OT 1; site; space
  OT 2; court OT 3
  Auf die Plätze, fertig, los! Ready, set,
  go! OT 1
  einen ... Platz belegen to come ...
  OT 2
Platzanweiser(in) usher WS 4, 120
Platzdeckchen place mat OT 2
plaudern to chatter OT 2
Playlist playlist WS 2, 44
plötzlich suddenly OT 1; sudden OT 2
Plural plural OT 1

Pocken smallpox **WS 1**, 21
Podcast podcast OT 1
Podium podium OT 3
Poesie poetry OT 1
Pokal trophy OT 2
Pol pole OT 3
Politik policy OT 3
Politiker(in) politician OT 3
politisch political **WS 1**, 24
Polizei police OT 1
Polizist(in) police officer OT 1
polnisch Polish OT 2
Polo polo OT 3
Polyurethan (Kunststoff) polyurethane **WS 3**, 82
Pommes frites (French) fries OT 2
Pony pony OT 3
Pop pop OT 2
Popcorn popcorn OT 2
Portfolio portfolio **WS 4**, 113
Portion portion **WS 1**, 13
Position position OT 3
Possessivbegleiter possessive determiner OT 1
Post post; mail OT 1
Postbote / -botin mail carrier **WS 1**, 16
posten to post OT 3
Postkarte postcard OT 1
Postleitzahl postcode OT 1
Praktikant(in) intern **WS 4**, 123
Praktikum internship **WS 1**, 30
praktisch handy OT 2; practical OT 3; convenient **WS 2**, 50
Präposition preposition OT 2
Präsentation presentation OT 1; slideshow OT 3
präsentieren to present OT 1; to feature **WS 1**, 21
Präsident(in) president **WW**, 10
Praxis practice OT 2
präzise accurate **WS 1**, 22
Preis prize; price OT 1
preisgekrönt award-winning **WS 3**, 83
Preisrichter(in) judge OT 2
preiswert inexpensive **WS 3**, 83
prima fine OT 1
Prinz prince OT 1
privat private OT 3
Privatsphäre privacy OT 3
Probe rehearsal OT 2; sample **WS 3**, 84
proben to rehearse OT 3
Problem problem OT 1; matter OT 2
Problemlöser(in) problem-solver **WS 3**, 84
Produkt product OT 2

Produktion production **WS 2**, 52; manufacture **WS 4**, 112
Produktion manufacture **WS 4**, 112
professionell professional OT 2
Professor(in) professor **WS 1**, 39
Profil profile OT 3
Profit profit **WS 1**, 22
profitieren to benefit OT 2
Prognose forecast OT 3
Programm programme; channel OT 2; program OT 3
programmieren to programme OT 2
Programmierer(in) programmer OT 3
progressiv progressive OT 1
Projekt project OT 1
Projektor projector OT 1
Prominente(r) celebrity OT 3
Pronomen pronoun OT 1
Protein protein **WS 3**, 95
Protest protest OT 3
protestieren to protest OT 3
Prototyp prototype **WS 3**, 83
Prozent percentage OT 3; percent **WS 1**, 21
Prozess trial OT 2; process **WS 3**, 85
Prüfer(in) checker OT 3
Prüfung exam OT 1
psychologische(r) Betreuer(in) counsellor OT 2
Psychopath(in) psycho **WS 2**, 49
Publikum audience OT 2
Pullover jumper OT 1
pulsieren to vibrate **WS 3**, 96
pumpen to pump **WS 3**, 80
Punkt point OT 1
punkten to score OT 1
pünktlich punctual **WS 2**, 57
Puppe doll OT 3
putzen to brush **WS 3**, 78
Puzzle puzzle OT 2
Pyjama pajamas **WS 2**, 58
Pyjama-Party sleepover OT 1

Q

Quadrat square OT 1
Quadratfuß square foot OT 2
Qualität quality OT 3
Quarterback quarterback OT 2
Quartier quarter OT 1
Quelle spring; source OT 2
querfeldein cross-country OT 2
Querflöte flute OT 2
querlesen to skim OT 3
Quiz quiz OT 2

R

Rad wheel OT 1
Rad fahren to bike OT 3
Radfahrer(in) cyclist OT 3
Radiergummi rubber OT 1
radikal radical **WS 3**, 90
Radio radio OT 1
Radiosender radio station OT 2
Radius radius OT 2
Radweg bike lane **WS 1**, 16
Rahmen frame **WS 3**, 94
Rakete rocket **WS 1**, 24
Rampe ramp OT 2
Rand edge; rim OT 3
Rangfolge ranking **WS 2**, 54
in eine Rangfolge bringen to rank **WS 2**, 54
Rap rap OT 1
Rasse... pedigree OT 3
rassistisch racist **WS 1**, 16
Rat advice OT 1; council OT 3
raten to advise **WS 2**, 56
Rätsel puzzle; mystery OT 2
Rätselraten guessing game OT 1
rau rough **WS 4**, 129
Rauch smoke OT 2
Raum room OT 1
Raumanzug spacesuit **WS 3**, 95
räumen to clear **WS 4**, 123
Raumfahrzeug spacecraft **WS 3**, 76
Raumkapsel capsule **WS 3**, 95
Raumschiff spaceship **WS 3**, 92
rausbringen to take out **WS 1**, 15
reagieren to react; to respond OT 3
Reaktion reaction **WS 1**, 26
realistisch realistic **WS 4**, 111
Realität reality **WS 3**, 78
rebellieren to rebel **WS 1**, 18
Rechner computer OT 1
Rechnung bill OT 3
Rechte rights OT 3
rechte(r, -s) right OT 1
rechteckig rectangular OT 2
rechtlich legal **WS 1**, 26
Rechtsanwalt / -anwältin lawyer **WS 4**, 126
Rechtschreibung spelling OT 1
rechtzeitig timely OT 3
Recycling recycling OT 2
Redakteur(in) editor OT 2
Rede speech OT 1; talk OT 2
reden to talk OT 1
redigieren to edit OT 3
reduzieren to reduce OT 2; to downsize OT 3
Reformation reformation **WS 1**, 32

Regal shelf OT 1

Regel rule OT 1; guideline; policy OT 3

regelmäßig regular OT 1

Regelung arrangement OT 3

Regelwerk rulebook OT 2

Regenbogen rainbow OT 1

Regenmantel raincoat OT 3

Regenschirm umbrella OT 1

Regenwald rainforest OT 2

Regenwasser rainwater **WS 3**, 80

Reggae reggae OT 2

regieren to govern OT 3

Regierung government OT 3

Region region **WS 1**, 12

Regisseur(in) film director OT 2

Register index **WS 2**, 62

regnen to rain OT 1

reiben to rub OT 3

reich rich OT 1

reichen (von ... bis) to range **WS 4**, 111

reichlich plenty OT 2

Reichtum fortune OT 3; wealth **WS 1**, 24

reif ripe **WS 1**, 20

Reihe row OT 1

Reihenfolge order OT 1; sequencing OT 3

   in eine Reihenfolge bringen to sequence OT 3

Reim rhyme OT 1

Reinigungsmittel cleaner OT 3

Reinigungstuch cleaning wipe OT 2

Reis rice OT 1

Reise journey; trip; tour OT 1; voyage OT 3

Reiseandenken souvenir OT 1

Reisebus coach OT 1

Reiseführer guidebook OT 1

Reisekauffrau / -mann travel agent OT 3

reisen to travel OT 1

Reisende(r) traveller OT 3

Reiseziel destination **WS 1**, 27

reißen to tear OT 2

Reißverschluss zip OT 1

reiten to ride OT 1

Reiter(in) rider OT 1

reizbar irritable OT 3

reizvoll attractive **WS 4**, 116

Reklamezettel leaflet OT 2

Rektor(in) principal OT 2

Relativpronomen relative pronoun OT 2

Relativsatz relative clause OT 2

relevant relevant **WS 1**, 32

Religion religion OT 3

eine Religion ausüben to worship **WS 1**, 20

Religionsunterricht religious studies OT 1

religiös religious OT 1

Rennen race OT 2

Rennsport racing OT 2

Rentier reindeer OT 2

reparieren to repair OT 2

Reporter(in) reporter OT 1

Reptil reptile OT 2

Republik republic **WS 1**, 25

Requisite prop OT 1

Reservat reservation OT 1

reservieren to reserve OT 3

Reservierung reservation OT 1

respektlos disrespectful OT 3

respektvoll respectful OT 3

Ressource resource **WS 2**, 48

Rest rest OT 1

Restaurant restaurant OT 1

retten to save OT 2; to rescue **WS 4**, 125

Rettung rescue OT 2

Rettungsdienste emergency services OT 2

Rettungssanitäter(in) paramedic OT 1

Rettungsschwimmer(in) lifeguard **WS 4**, 108

revidieren to revise OT 2

Revolution revolution OT 2

revolutionieren to revolutionize **WS 3**, 78

Rezept recipe OT 2

Rezeption reception OT 1

Rezeptionist(in) receptionist OT 1

rezitieren to recite **WS 3**, 96

Richter(in) judge OT 2

richtig correct; right; true OT 1; proper OT 3

Richtlinie guideline OT 3

Richtung direction OT 3

   in Richtung towards OT 2

riechen to smell OT 1

Riesenrad ferris wheel **WS 2**, 61

riesig enormous OT 1; huge; giant OT 2; massive OT 3

Rinderbrust beef brisket **WS 3**, 93

Rindfleisch beef OT 2

Ringen wrestling OT 2

Risiko hazard OT 2; risk OT 3

Riss split OT 3

Ritter knight OT 3

Robbe seal OT 1

Roboter robot **WS 3**, 78

Rock skirt OT 1

Rockmusik rock OT 2

roh raw OT 3

Rolle role OT 1; roll OT 2

Rollschuh roller skate **WS 3**, 82

Rollstuhl wheelchair OT 2

Rollstuhlfahrer(in) wheelchair user OT 2

Roman novel OT 2

Romanliteratur fiction OT 2

römisch Roman OT 2

Rommee rummy OT 2

Röntgen X-ray OT 1

rosa pink OT 1

Rose rose **WS 1**, 16

rot red OT 1

   Rote Bete beetroot **WS 1**, 26

Routine routine **WS 1**, 20

Rückblick review OT 1

Rücken back OT 1

Rückgrat backbone OT 2

Rückhand backhand OT 3

Rucksack rucksack OT 1; backpack OT 2

   mit Rucksack reisen to backpack OT 3

rücksichtslos thoughtless OT 2

rücksichtsvoll thoughtful OT 3

rückwärts backwards OT 3

Ruderboot rowing boat OT 1

Ruf fame OT 3

Rugby rugby OT 1

ruhig quiet OT 1; calm OT 2; steady OT 3; still **WS 3**, 95

Ruhm fame OT 3

rühren to stir OT 2

Ruine ruin OT 2

rumhängen to hang out OT 1

rund round OT 1

Rundgang tour OT 1

russisch Russian OT 2

S

sachlich factual **WS 1**, 22

Sack sack OT 2

Safari safari OT 2

Saft juice OT 1

sagen to say OT 1

Sahne cream OT 1

Saite string OT 2

Salat salad OT 1

Salz salt OT 3

sammeln to collect OT 1

Sammler(in) picker OT 3

Sammlung collection OT 2

Samstag Saturday OT 1

samtig velvety OT 2

Sand sand OT 1

Sandale sandal **WS 2**, 59

sandig sandy OT 1

Sandwich sandwich OT 1

sanft gently OT 3

Sänger(in) singer OT 1

Satellit satellite WS 3, 77

Sattel saddle OT 3

Satz sentence OT 1; set OT 3

Satzteil clause OT 2

sauber clean OT 1

Säugetier mammal OT 2

Säugling baby OT 1

Säule column OT 1

Saxofon saxophone OT 2

scannen to scan OT 3

Schach chess OT 1

Schachbrett chessboard OT 1

schade: Das ist schade. That's a shame. OT 2

schaden to harm; to damage OT 2

schädlich harmful OT 3

Schädling pest OT 2

Schaf sheep OT 1

Schäfer(in) shepherd OT 2

schaffen to create OT 2; to achieve WS 3, 94

Schal scarf OT 2

Schale dish OT 2

Schalter switch OT 3

Schaltkreis circuit WS 3, 95

scharf hot OT 1

    auf etw. scharf sein to be keen on sth. WS 4, 110

Schatz treasure OT 3

    Schatz (als Kosename) honey OT 2

schätzen to guess OT 1

Schaubild diagram OT 3

Schaufel shovel OT 2

schaukeln to rock OT 3

Schauspieler(in) actor OT 1

Scheibe slice OT 1

scheiden: sich scheiden lassen to divorce OT 3

Scheidung divorce OT 3

Schein note OT 1

scheinen to shine OT 1; to seem OT 2; to appear OT 3

scheitern to fail OT 2

Schere scissors OT 1

Scheune barn OT 2

Schicht shift WS 4, 114

schick fancy OT 2; stylish WS 3, 85

schicken to send OT 1

Schiedsrichter(in) referee OT 3

Schiene rail OT 2

schießen to shoot OT 3

Schiff ship OT 2

mit dem Schiff fahren to sail OT 2

Schiffbau shipbuilding OT 3

Schild sign OT 1

Schildkröte tortoise OT 1; turtle OT 2

schimpfen to grumble OT 2

Schinken ham OT 3

Schlacht battle OT 1

Schlafanzug pyjamas OT 3; pajamas WS 2, 58

schlafen to sleep OT 1

schlaff limp WS 3, 95

Schlafsack sleeping bag OT 2

Schlafzimmer bedroom OT 1

Schlag stroke OT 3

Schläger bat OT 1; racket OT 2

Schlagzeile headline OT 2

Schlagzeug drums OT 1

Schlange queue; snake OT 1

    Schlange stehen to queue WS 1, 15

schlängeln to wriggle OT 2

schlau smart WS 2, 59

Schlauch tube OT 1

schlecht bad OT 1; junky WS 3, 89

schlemmen to feast WS 1, 21

Schlepper trafficker WS 4, 124

schließen to close OT 1; to shut OT 2

    schließen (aus etw.) to conclude WS 1, 17

Schließfach locker OT 2

schließlich finally OT 1; eventually OT 3

Schlittschuh laufen to skate OT 2

Schloss lock OT 2

Schlucht canyon OT 3

Schluckauf hiccup OT 2

schlucken to swallow WS 3, 93

Schluss conclusion OT 3

Schlüssel key OT 1

schmackhaft tasty OT 2

schmecken to taste OT 1

schmelzen to melt WS 3, 93

Schmerz pain OT 2

schmerzen to hurt OT 1; to ache OT 3

schmerzend sore OT 2

schmerzhaft painful OT 2

Schmerzmittel painkiller OT 2

Schmetterling butterfly OT 2

Schminke face paint OT 2

schmollen to sulk OT 3

Schmuck jewelry OT 2

schmücken to decorate WS 2, 58

Schmutz dirt WS 4, 124

schmutzig dirty OT 1

Schnäppchen bargain WS 2, 51

Schnappschuss shot WS 4, 119

Schneckenpost snail mail WS 3, 79

Schnee snow OT 1

schneiden to cut OT 2; to chop OT 3

schnell fast OT 1; quick OT 2

schnitzen to carve OT 2

schockiert shocked WS 1, 13

Schokolade chocolate OT 1

schon already; yet OT 2

schön beautiful; nice; lovely OT 1

Schönheit beauty OT 3

schottisch Scottish OT 3

Schrank cupboard OT 1

schrecklich terrible; awful OT 1

schreiben to write OT 1

Schreibtisch desk OT 1

Schreibweise spelling OT 1

schreien to scream OT 3

Schriftsteller(in) writer OT 2

Schriftverkehr correspondence WS 3, 94

Schritt step OT 1

Schublade drawer OT 3

schüchtern shy OT 2

Schuh shoe OT 1

Schuhschachtel shoebox OT 3

Schulausbildung schooling WS 3, 80

Schulball prom OT 3

Schuld debt WS 4, 125

Schuldknecht bonded laborer WS 4, 127

Schule school OT 1

Schüler(in) student OT 1

Schülerrat student council OT 2

Schulhof playground OT 1

Schulkamerad(in) schoolmate WS 3, 80

Schulleiter(in) head teacher OT 1

Schultag school day OT 1

Schultasche school bag OT 1

Schulter shoulder OT 1

Schulterpolster shoulder pad OT 2

Schuppen shed OT 1

Schuss shot WS 4, 119

Schüssel bowl OT 1

Schusswaffe gun WS 1, 29

schütteln to shake OT 2

Schutz conservation OT 2

Schütze gunman WS 4, 127

schützen to protect OT 2

schwach weak OT 3; dim WS 4, 119

Schwäche weakness WS 3, 86

schwanger pregnant WS 1, 28

Schwanz tail OT 2

schwarz black OT 1

schweben to float OT 3; to soar OT 3

schwedisch Swedish WS 3, 90

Schwein pig OT 1

Schweinefleisch pork OT 2

Schwellung swelling OT 2

schwer difficult; heavy OT 1

Schwerelosigkeit weightlessness WS 3, 92

Schwerkraft gravity WS 3, 93

Schwert sword OT 1

Schwester sister OT 1

schwierig difficult; challenging OT 1

Schwierigkeit trouble OT 2; difficulty WS 1, 26

Schwimmbecken pool OT 1

schwimmen to swim OT 1

Schwimmer(in) swimmer OT 2

schwindlig faint OT 2

schwitzen to sweat OT 2

schwören to swear WS 2, 49

Science-Fiction science fiction OT 2

sechs six OT 1

sechzehn sixteen OT 1

sechzig sixty OT 1

Secondhandladen thrift store WS 2, 44

See lake; loch OT 1

Seeufer lakefront WS 2, 61; lakeside WS 2, 63

segeln to sail OT 2

sehen to look; to see OT 1

Sehenswürdigkeit sight OT 1; attraction OT 2

sehr very; really; a lot OT 1; mighty OT 3

   sehr gut brill OT 1

Sehvermögen sight OT 1

Seife soap OT 2

Seil line; rope OT 1

Seilrutsche zip line OT 1

seine(r, -s) his; its OT 1

sein to be OT 1

seit since OT 3

Seite page OT 1, side OT 1

   auf der anderen Seite across OT 1

Sekretär(in) secretary OT 1

sekundär secondary OT 1

Sekundarschule secondary school OT 1

Sekunde second OT 1

selbst: (sich) selbst himself OT 1; themselves; herself; itself OT 3

   selbst gemacht homemade OT 3

selbstbewusst confident OT 2

Selbstlaut vowel OT 1

selbstständig independent OT 3

Selbstversorgung self-catering OT 3

selbstverständlich: für selbstverständlich halten to take for granted WS 3, 78

Selbstzahlerkasse self-checkout WS 3, 78

Selfie selfie OT 1

selten rare OT 2

seltsam strange; weird OT 1

Semester term OT 2; semester OT 3

Sendung programme OT 2

Senf mustard OT 2

Senior(in) senior citizen OT 3; senior WS 2, 46

Seniorenheim retirement home OT 3

senkrecht vertical WS 2, 64

Sensor sensor WS 3, 87

September September OT 1

Sequenzierung sequencing OT 3

Serie series OT 1

servieren to serve OT 1

Sessel armchair OT 1

Session session OT 2

setzen to set OT 1

seufzen to sigh OT 3

Seufzer sigh OT 2

Shampoo shampoo OT 3

Shorts shorts OT 1

Sichel crescent OT 2

sicher sure; safe; certainly OT 1; certain OT 3

sichergehen to make sure OT 2

Sicherheit safety OT 2; security OT 3

Sicherheitsausrüstung safety equipment OT 2

Sicherheitsgurt harness OT 1

sicherlich certainly OT 1; surely WS 3, 111

sicherstellen to make sure OT 2; to ensure WS 4, 111

Sicht view OT 1

sie they; her; them; she OT 1

sieben seven OT 1

Siebenkampf heptathlon OT 2

siebzehn seventeen OT 1

siebzig seventy OT 1

Siedler(in) settler OT 3

Siedlung settlement WS 1, 18

Sieger(in) winner OT 1

Signal signal OT 2

Silbe syllable OT 2

Silber... silver OT 1

simsen to text OT 1

singen to sing OT 1

Singular singular OT 1

sinken to sink OT 3

Sinn meaning OT 1; sense OT 2

sinneserweiternd mind-expanding OT 2

sinnlos pointless WS 3, 95

Sirene siren OT 3

Sirup syrup OT 3

Situation situation OT 1

sitzen to sit OT 1

Sitzplatz seat OT 1

Sitzung session OT 2

Skateboard skateboard WS 3, 82

Skelett skeleton OT 1

Sketch skit OT 2; sketch WS 4, 119

Ski laufen to ski OT 3

Skiläufer(in) skier OT 3

Skizze sketch WS 4, 119

skizzieren to outline OT 3; to sketch WS 3, 85

Sklave; Sklavin slave WS 1, 21

Sklaverei slavery WS 4, 127

Skulptur sculpture OT 2

Slogan slogan OT 2

Slum slum OT 3

Smartphone smartphone OT 3

SMS text OT 1

Snack snack OT 1

Snowboard fahren snowboarding OT 3

so such OT 2

   so tun, als ob to pretend OT 2

Socke sock OT 2

Sofa sofa OT 1

sofort immediately OT 1; straight away OT 2

Software software OT 1

sogar even OT 1; actually OT 2

Sohn son OT 1

Solarenergie solar power WS 3, 80

Soldat(in) soldier OT 1

sollte(n) should OT 1

Solo solo WS 2, 46

Sommer summer OT 1

Sommersprose freckle OT 2

Songtext lyrics OT 2

Songwriter(in) songwriter OT 2

Sonne sun OT 1

Sonnen... solar OT 3

Sonnenbrand sunburn OT 2

Sonnenbrille sunglasses OT 2

Sonnenenergie solar power WS 3, 80

Sonnenkollektor solar panel OT 3

Sonnenschein sunshine OT 3

Sonnenschutzmittel sunscreen OT 2

Sonnenstich sunstroke OT 2

Sonnensystem solar system OT 1

Sonnenuntergang sunset OT 3

sonnig sunny OT 1

Sonntag Sunday OT 1

sonst noch else OT 1

Sorge: keine Sorge no worries OT 2

   sich Sorgen machen to worry OT 1

sorgfältig careful OT 1

sorglos careless OT 2

Soße sauce OT 1

sozial social OT 2

Spaghetti spaghetti OT 1

Spalte column OT 1

Spaniel spaniel OT 2

spanisch Spanish OT 1

sparen to save OT 2

Spaß fun OT 1

    Spaß verstehen to take a joke OT 2

spät late OT 1

Spaziergang walk OT 2

Speck bacon OT 1

Speisekarte menu OT 1

spektakulär spectacular OT 2

spekulieren to speculate WS 1, 26

Spende donation OT 2

spenden to make a donation; to donate OT 2

Spendensammler(in) fundraiser OT 2

Spendensammlung fundraising OT 2

spezialisieren to specialize WS 4, 109

spezifisch specific OT 3

Spiegel mirror OT 1

Spiel game; match OT 1

Spielekonsole game console WS 3, 78

spielen to play OT 1

Spieler(in) player OT 1; gamer WS 2, 49

Spielfeld pitch OT 3

Spielfilm motion picture WS 3, 83

Spielführer(in) captain WS 1, 21

Spielplatz playground OT 1

Spielverderber(in): kein Spielverderber sein to be a good sport OT 2

Spielzeug toy OT 2

Spind locker OT 2

Spinne spider OT 1

Spitze tip; top OT 1

Spitzensport elite sports OT 3

Spitzname nickname WS 3, 94

Sponsor(in) sponsor OT 2

Sport sport; athletics OT 1

Sporthalle gymnasium WS 1, 30

Sportjacke blazer OT 1

Sportler(in) sportsman OT 3

    Sportler(innen) sportspeople OT 3

sportlich athletic WS 3, 85

Sportunterricht PE (physical education) OT 1

Sprache language OT 1

Sprechblase speech bubble OT 2

sprechen to speak OT 1

Sprecher(in) speaker OT 1; spokesman; spokeswoman OT 2

Springbrunnen fountain OT 1

springen to jump OT 2

Sprint sprint OT 3

Sprinter(in) sprinter OT 3

sprudelnd sparkling OT 1

spucken to spit WS 3, 93

Spülbecken sink OT 3

Spur trail OT 2

Spürhund hound OT 2

Staat state OT 1

Staatsangehörigkeit nationality OT 2

stabil steady OT 3

Stachel thorn OT 2

Stadion stadium OT 1

Stadt town; city OT 1

Stadtbewohner(innen) townspeople WS 1, 20

städtisch urban WS 2, 63

Stahl steel OT 2

Stalagmit stalagmite OT 1

Stalaktit stalactite OT 1

Stall stall OT 2

Stamm tribe OT 3

Stammes... tribal OT 3

Stand status WS 1, 26

Standard level OT 2, default OT 3

Standard... standard OT 3

Standort location OT 2

Stange pole OT 3

stapeln to stack WS 3, 80

Star star OT 1

stark strong OT 2

Stärke strength OT 2

starren to stare OT 2

starten to launch WS 3, 76

Startseite homepage OT 1

Station station OT 1

Statistik statistic OT 3

stattdessen instead OT 2

Statue statue OT 1

Status status WS 1, 26

Stau traffic jam OT 2

staubsaugen to vacuum WS 1, 15

Staubsauger vacuum cleaner WS 3, 78

Steak steak OT 1

stechen to sting OT 2

Stechmücke mosquito OT 2

Steckbrief profile OT 3

Stecknadel pin OT 1

Stegosaurus stegosaurus OT 1

stehen to stand OT 1

    jdm. stehen to suit sb. OT 1

steigen to climb OT 1

steil steep OT 2

Stein stone OT 1; rock OT 2

Steinbruch quarry OT 1

Stelle job OT 1

stellen to put; to set OT 1

Steppdecke quilt WS 1, 32

sterben to die OT 1

Stern star OT 1

Sternchen asterisk WS 1, 36

Steuer tax WS 1, 18

steuern to steer OT 3; to pilot WS 3, 76

Stich sting OT 2

Stichwort headword OT 2; keyword WS 1, 22; prompt WS 2, 73

Stiefel boot OT 1

Stift pen OT 1

Stil style OT 2

still quiet OT 1

Stille silence OT 2

Stimme voice OT 2

Stirnband headband OT 3

Stockbett bunk bed OT 3

Stockwerk floor OT 1

    im unteren Stockwerk downstairs OT 1

Stoff material OT 3

stolpern to trip OT 2

Stolz pride WS 2, 58

stolz proud OT 2

stören to bother WS 1, 29

Storyboard storyboard WS 4, 119

stoßen to bump; to push OT 2

Stoßzahn tusk OT 3

Strafe penalty OT 3

Strafstoß penalty OT 3

Strand beach OT 1

Strandsegeln land yachting OT 3

Straße road; street OT 1

Straßenbahn tram OT 1

Straßensammlung street collection OT 2

Strategie strategy WS 1, 33

strategisch strategic WS 4, 112

Strauß bouquet OT 3

Strecke route OT 2

Streik strike WS 3, 90

streiken to strike OT 1

Streit argument OT 1

streiten to argue OT 2

streng strict OT 2

Stress stress OT 1

stressig stressful WS 2, 61

streuen to sprinkle OT 2

Stroh straw WS 3, 88

Strohhalm straw WS 3, 88

Strom electricity OT 2

Strophe verse OT 1

Struktur structure OT 1

Stück piece; bit OT 1

Student(in) student OT 1

    Student im ersten Jahr freshman WS 2, 49

Studienanfänger(in) freshman WS 2, 49

studieren to study OT 1

Studium studies OT 1

Stufe step OT 1; level OT 2

Stuhl chair OT 1

Stunde hour OT 1

Stundenplan timetable OT 1; schedule OT 2

Sturm storm OT 2

Stürmer(in) striker OT 3

stürzen to fall OT 1

Stütze prop OT 1

Subjekt subject OT 1

Subjektpronomen subject pronoun OT 1

Substantiv noun OT 1

Suche search OT 2

suchen to search OT 2

süchtig addicted OT 3

Süd… south OT 1

südlich southern OT 3

Südwesten southwest OT 3

Sumpf swamp OT 2

Superlativ superlative OT 2

Supermarkt supermarket OT 1

Suppe soup OT 1

Surfen surfing OT 1

Surfer(in) surfer WS 4, 110

Sushi sushi OT 1

süß sweet OT 1

Süßigkeit candy WS 3, 93

Süßkartoffel sweet potato WS 1, 21

Sweatshirt sweatshirt OT 1

Symbol symbol OT 1

Synagoge synagogue OT 1

Synästhesie synaesthesia OT 2

Synonym synonym OT 2

synthetisch synthetic WS 2, 53

System system OT 1

Szene scene OT 2

Szenenbuch storyboard WS 4, 119

T

Tab tab OT 3

Tabak tobacco OT 3

Tablett tray OT 2

Tablette tablet OT 2

Tacker stapler OT 2

Tafel board OT 1

Tag day OT 1

Tagebuch diary OT 1

Tagesablauf routine WS 1, 20

Tagesausflug day trip; day out OT 2

Tagesgericht special OT 1

Tagesordnung agenda OT 3

Tageszeit daytime OT 1

täglich daily OT 2

taiwanisch Taiwanese WS 1, 25

Takt beat OT 1

Taktik tactic OT 2

Tal valley OT 1

Talent talent OT 2

talentiert talented OT 3

Tank tank OT 3

Tante aunt OT 1

Tanz dance OT 1

tanzen to dance OT 1

Tänzer(in) dancer OT 3

tapfer brave OT 1

Tasche case; bag OT 1; pocket OT 2

Taschendieb(in) pickpocket WS 3, 86

Taschengeld pocket money OT 2; allowance OT 3

Taschenlampe torch OT 1; flashlight OT 2

Taschenmesser pocketknife OT 2

Tasse cup OT 1; mug OT 3

Tastatur keyboard OT 1

Tätigkeit occupation WS 1, 32

Tätowierung tattoo OT 3

Tatsache fact OT 1

tatsächlich actually OT 2

tauchen to dive OT 1; to dip WS 3, 84

Taucheranzug wetsuit OT 1

tauschen to swap OT 1

Tausend thousand OT 1

Taxi taxi OT 1; cab WS 1, 41

Teamwork teamwork WS 4, 112

Technik technique WS 2, 49

technisch tech OT 2; technological WS 3, 77; technical WS 4, 119

technische Spielerei gadget WS 3, 79

Technologie technology OT 1

technologisch technological WS 3, 77

Tee tea OT 1

Teelicht tea light OT 2

Teenager teenager; teen OT 2

Teich pond WS 3, 80

Teig dough OT 2

Teil piece; part OT 1; section OT 2

teilen to share OT 1; to divide OT 2

teilnehmen to take part OT 2

teilweise partly OT 3

Teilzeit… part-time WS 4, 128

Telefon phone OT 1

Telefonat phone call OT 2

telefonieren to phone OT 2

Telefonist(in) operator OT 2

Telefonkonferenz teleconference OT 3

Telegraf telegraph WS 3, 83

Teller plate OT 1

Tempel temple OT 1

Temperatur temperature OT 2

Tempus tense OT 1

Tennis tennis OT 1

Teppich carpet WS 4, 126

Terminkalender diary OT 1

Terrier terrier OT 2

Test test OT 1

teuer expensive OT 1

Text text OT 1

Text (eines Schauspielers) line OT 1

texten to message OT 3

Theater theatre OT 1

Theater spielen to act OT 1

Theaterstück play OT 1

Theke counter OT 3

Thema subject OT 1

theoretisch theoretical WS 3, 85

Theorie theory OT 1

Thermalquelle hot spring OT 2

Thermosflasche flask OT 3

Thunfisch tuna OT 1

tief low; deep OT 1

Tier animal OT 1

Tierarzt / -ärztin veterinarian WS 4, 113; vet WS 4, 113

Tierwelt wildlife OT 2

Tiger tiger OT 1

tippen to tap OT 2

Tisch table OT 1

Tischtennis ping-pong OT 1

Titel title OT 1

Toast toast OT 2

Tochter daughter OT 1

Tod death OT 2

Todesdatum date of death OT 2

Toilette toilet OT 2

tolerant tolerant WS 3, 95

toll great OT 1; awesome OT 2

Toll! Wow! OT 1

Tomate tomato OT 1

Ton clay WS 3, 82

Tonne ton OT 2

Tor goal; gate OT 1

Tortendiagramm pie chart WS 2, 64

Torwart(in) goalkeeper OT 3

tot dead OT 1

total absolutely OT 2

töten to kill OT 1

töten lassen to execute OT 3

Touchdown touchdown OT 2

Tourismus tourism OT 2

Tourist(in) tourist OT 1

toxisch toxic WS 2, 52

traben to trot OT 2

Tradition tradition OT 2

traditionell traditional OT 1

tragbar portable WS 3, 77

tragen to wear; to carry OT 1

Tragetasche carrier bag OT 2

Trailer trailer **WS 2**, 49
Trainer(in) coach; trainer OT 1
trainieren to train OT 2
Traktor tractor OT 2
Träne tear OT 2
transatlantisch transatlantic OT 3
transferieren to transfer **WS 1**, 26
Transplantation transplant OT 3
trauen: sich trauen to dare OT 2
Traum dream OT 1
träumen to dream **WS 1**, 12
Träumer(in) dreamer OT 2
traurig sad OT 1; upset OT 2
Treck wagon train **WS 1**, 28
trecken to trek OT 2
treffen to meet OT 1
Treffen meeting; scoring OT 1; rally **WS 2**, 58
treiben to herd OT 2; to float OT 3
Treibhaus greenhouse OT 1
Treidelpfad towpath OT 3
Trend fashion OT 1; trend **WS 2**, 44
trennen to separate **WS 3**, 87
Treppe stairs OT 1
Treppenstufen stairs OT 1
treten to kick OT 1; to step **WS 1**, 16
Triangel triangle OT 2
trinken to drink OT 1
Trinkhalm straw **WS 3**, 88
trocken dry OT 2
Trompete trumpet OT 2
tropisch tropical **WS 4**, 123
tropfen to drip OT 3
trotzdem anyway OT 1
trüb cloudy **WS 3**, 93; murky **WS 3**, 84; dim **WS 4**, 119
Truthahn turkey OT 1
Tschüss! bye OT 1
tun to put; to do OT 1
Tunnel tunnel OT 3
Tür door OT 1
Turbine turbine **WS 3**, 80
Turm tower OT 1
Turnhalle gym OT 3
Turnier tournament OT 3
Turnschuh trainer OT 1
Tüte bag OT 1
Tutor(in) tutor **WS 2**, 59
typisch typical OT 2
Tyrannosaurus rex tyrannosaurus rex OT 1

U
U-Bahn metro; subway; underground OT 1
U-Boot submarine OT 3

üben to practise OT 1
über about; over OT 1; via OT 2
    über Bord overboard OT 3
    über Nacht overnight OT 2
überall everywhere OT 1; all over OT 2
überarbeiten to revise OT 2; to edit OT 3
Überblick overview **WS 4**, 119
überfliegen to scan OT 3
überflüssig unnecessary **WS 3**, 95
Überflutung flooding **WS 3**, 103
überfüllt crowded OT 2
übergeben to throw up OT 2
übergenau fussy OT 2
überleben to survive OT 3
übermalen to repaint **WS 3**, 81
überprüfen to check OT 1
überqueren to cross OT 1
überraschend surprising OT 2
überrascht surprised OT 1; amazed OT 3
Überraschung surprise OT 1
überreden to persuade OT 3; to convince **WS 3**, 81
Überreste remains OT 3
Überschrift heading OT 1
übersetzen to translate OT 1
Übersetzungsfalle false friend OT 2
Übersicht overview **WS 4**, 119
übertragen to transfer **WS 1**, 26
übertreiben to exaggerate **WS 3**, 103
überwachen to oversee **WS 3**, 83
überwachsen overgrown **WS 2**, 63
überwuchert overgrown **WS 2**, 63
überzeugen to persuade OT 3; to convince **WS 3**, 81
üblich usual OT 2
Übung exercise OT 1; practice OT 2
Übungsheft exercise book OT 1
Ufer bank OT 3
Uhr clock OT 1
    um ... Uhr at ... o'clock OT 1
um around OT 1
    um ... herum about; round OT 1
umarmen: (sich) umarmen to hug **WS 1**, 14
Umarmung hug OT 1
umdrehen to flip **WS 4**, 116
umfallen to fall over OT 2
umfassen to involve **WS 3**, 90; to range **WS 4**, 111
Umfeld environment OT 2
umformulieren to rephrase **WS 3**, 85
Umfrage survey OT 1
umgehen to deal with OT 2
Umhang cloak OT 1
Umkleide changing room OT 1
Umlaufbahn orbit **WS 3**, 76

umschreiben to rewrite OT 1
Umsiedlung resettlement **WS 1**, 26
Umstandswort adverb OT 1
umstoßen to knock over OT 2
Umwelt environment OT 2
    Umwelt... environmental OT 2
Umweltschützer(in) environmentalist OT 3
Umweltverschmutzung pollution OT 2
umziehen to move OT 1
Umzug procession; parade OT 2
Umzugswagen moving van; removal van OT 2
unabhängig autonomous **WS 3**, 78
Unabhängigkeit independence OT 2
unangenehm nasty OT 2
unbekannt unknown OT 3
unbequem uncomfortable OT 3
Unberechenbarkeit unpredictability OT 2
unberührt unspoilt OT 3
unbestimmt indefinite OT 1
und and OT 1
    und so weiter etc. (et cetera) OT 1
uneben bumpy **WS 1**, 28
unendlich endless **WS 1**, 12; infinite **WS 2**, 49
unerwarteterweise unexpectedly OT 3
Unfairness unfairness **WS 4**, 127
Unfall accident OT 1
unfreundlich unfriendly **WS 1**, 26
ungarisch Hungarian OT 2
ungeduldig impatient OT 3
ungefähr about OT 1
Ungerechtigkeit injustice **WS 4**, 126; unfairness **WS 4**, 127
ungeschickt clumsy OT 2
ungesund unhealthy OT 1
ungewöhnlich unusual OT 2
unglaublich incredible; unbelievable OT 2
unglücklich unhappy OT 1
unheimlich scary OT 1
unhöflich rude OT 1
Uni uni OT 3
Uniform uniform OT 1
Universität university OT 1
unmöglich impossible OT 2
unnötig unnecessary **WS 3**, 95
unordentlich messy OT 2
Unordnung mess OT 3
    in Unordnung bringen to mess up OT 2
unpraktisch impractical **WS 3**, 86
unregelmäßig irregular OT 1
uns us OT 1; ourselves OT 3

unsere(r, -s) our OT 1; ours OT 2

unter under OT 1; below OT 2; among OT 3

   unter die Leute kommen to socialize **WS 2**, 58

   unter Wasser underwater OT 2

unterbrechen to interrupt OT 2

unterhalten to entertain **WS 3**, 78

Unterhalter(in) entertainer OT 3

unterhaltsam entertaining OT 3

Unterhaltung chat OT 1; entertainment OT 3

Unterhemd vest OT 2

Unterkühlung hypothermia OT 2

Unterkunft housing OT 3

Unternehmen company OT 1; corporation **WS 3**, 83

Unternehmer(in) businessman **WS 3**, 83; businesswoman **WS 3**, 83

Unterricht class; lesson OT 1

unterrichten to teach OT 1

Unterschied difference OT 1

unterschiedlich different OT 1

Unterschlupf shelter OT 2

unterschreiben to sign OT 2

unterstreichen to underline OT 1

unterstützen to support OT 1

Unterstützung backup **WS 3**, 80

unterteilt divided OT 2

Untertitel caption OT 1

Unterüberschrift sub-heading OT 2

unterwerfen to subject **WS 4**, 127

unvergesslich memorable OT 3

unvorsichtig carelessly OT 2

unwahrscheinlich unlikely **WS 2**, 51

unzählbar uncountable OT 1

unzugänglich inaccessible OT 3

uralt ancient OT 2

urban urban **WS 2**, 63

Urlaub holiday OT 1; vacation OT 2

Urlauber(in) holidaymaker OT 3

Urlaubsort resort OT 2

Ursprung origin OT 3

ursprünglich originally OT 2; original OT 3

usw. etc. (et cetera) OT 1

V

Vampir(in) vampire OT 2

Vanille vanilla OT 1

Vanillesoße custard OT 1

Vater father OT 1

vegan vegan OT 1

Veganer(in) vegan OT 1

Vegetarier(in) vegetarian OT 1

vegetarisch vegetarian OT 1; veggie OT 2

Veranda porch **WS 1**, 14

verändern to transform **WS 2**, 63

Veränderung transformation **WS 2**, 63

verängstigt scared; frightened OT 1; terrified OT 3

veranstalten to put on OT 2

Veranstaltungsort venue OT 3

verantwortlich responsible OT 3

Verantwortung responsibility OT 3

verärgert upset; irritated OT 2

Verb verb OT 1

Verband association; bandage OT 2

Verbandkasten first aid kit OT 2

verbessern to improve OT 2

Verbesserung improvement OT 3

verbieten to ban OT 3

verbinden to connect OT 2

Verbindung connection; link OT 2; combination OT 3

Verbindungswort linking word **WS 1**, 33

verblassen to fade OT 2

Verbrechen crime **WS 2**, 49

verbreiten to spread (out) **WS 1**, 27

Verbrennungs... internal combustion **WS 3**, 77

verbringen to spend OT 1

verbunden connected OT 1

Verderben spoilage **WS 3**, 84

verdienen to deserve OT 2; to earn OT 3

verdreht twisted OT 1; wacky **WS 2**, 58

Verein club OT 1; association OT 2

vereinbaren to arrange OT 2

Vereinbarung arrangement; agreement OT 3

verfeinern to refine **WS 1**, 23

verfolgen to pursue **WS 4**, 111

Verfolgung persecution **WS 1**, 24

verfügbar available OT 3

Verfügung: zur Verfügung stellen to provide **WS 3**, 80

vergeben to forgive OT 2; to award **WS 3**, 83

vergeigen to mess up OT 2

vergessen to forget OT 1

Vergleich comparison OT 2

vergleichen to compare OT 1

verhalten to act OT 1

Verhältniswort preposition OT 2

verhindern to prevent **WS 3**, 96

verhungern (lassen) to starve OT 1

verkannt misunderstood **WS 3**, 83

verkaufen to sell OT 1

Verkehr traffic OT 1; transport OT 2

Verkehrsmittel transport OT 2

verkleiden to dress up OT 2

verknallt: in jmdn. verknallt sein to have a crush on **WS 2**, 47

verkünden to declare **WS 1**, 39

verlangen to demand **WS 3**, 91

verlangsamen to slow down **WS 1**, 24

verlassen to leave OT 1

   sich verlassen auf to depend OT 2

verlässlich reliable **WS 1**, 22

verlegen embarrassed OT 3

verleihen to award **WS 3**, 83

verletzen to harm OT 2

Verletzung injury OT 2

verlieren to lose OT 1

vermarktbar marketable **WS 3**, 85

Vermarktung marketing **WS 3**, 85

vermeiden to avoid **WS 2**, 45

Vermeidung prevention OT 2

vermischen to mix up OT 2

vermissen to miss OT 2

vermitteln to impart **WS 1**, 30

   etw. vermitteln to communicate **WS 1**, 32

Vermittlung mediation OT 1

Vermögen wealth **WS 1**, 24

vermuten to suppose OT 1

Verneinung negative OT 1

vernünftig sensible OT 3

veröffentlichen to publish OT 2; to release **WS 3**, 76

Verpackung packaging OT 3

Verpflegungsservice catering service **WS 4**, 111

Verpflichtung obligation OT 2

Verputz plaster OT 1

verringern to reduce OT 2

verrückt crazy OT 2; wacky **WS 2**, 58

Verrückter madman **WS 1**, 16

Versammlung assembly OT 1

verschieden diverse **WS 2**, 73

Verschlüsselung code OT 1

verschneit snowy OT 3

verschütten to spill OT 2

verschwenden to waste OT 3

verschwinden to disappear OT 3

versehentlich by accident; by mistake OT 2; accidentally OT 3

Version version OT 3

versorgen (mit) to provide **WS 3**, 80

Versprechen promise OT 2

versprechen to promise OT 2

Verstand mind OT 1

Verstärker amplifier OT 2

verstauchen to sprain OT 2

verstecken to hide OT 3

verstehen to understand OT 1

Versuch attempt OT 2

einen Versuch machen to have a go OT 2

versuchen to try OT 1

versus versus **WS 4**, 112

vertäuen to moor OT 3

verteidigen to defend OT 3

Verteidiger(in) defender OT 3

verteilen to distribute **WS 3**, 84

vertikal vertical **WS 2**, 64

vertrauen to trust OT 3

vertraut familiar OT 2

verursachen to cause OT 2

vervollständigen to complete OT 1

Verwalter(in) steward **WS 4**, 123

Verwandlung transformation **WS 2**, 63

Verwandte(r) relative OT 1; relation OT 2

Verweis reference **WS 3**, 93

verwelken to fade OT 2

verwirklichen to fulfil **WS 4**, 109

verwirrend confusing OT 2

verwirrt confused OT 2

verzweifelt desperately OT 3

vibrieren to vibrate **WS 3**, 96

Video video OT 1

Video-Blog vlog OT 3

Videoclip video clip OT 2

Videokassette video OT 1

Videokonferenztechnik video conferencing **WS 3**, 78

Videospiel video game OT 2

Viehbestand stock OT 2

viel lots; a lot; much OT 1; plenty OT 2

viele many OT 1

vielfältig diverse **WS 2**, 73

Vielfältigkeit diversity **WS 1**, 26

vielleicht maybe OT 1; perhaps OT 3

vielseitig versatile OT 3

vier four OT 1

Viertel quarter OT 1

viertel vor quarter to OT 1

vierundzwanzig twenty-four OT 1

vierzehn fourteen OT 1

vierzig forty OT 1

violett violet OT 1

virtuell virtual **WS 2**, 59

Vision vision **WS 4**, 111

Visualisierung visualization OT 3

visuell visual OT 2

Visum visa **WS 1**, 26

Vlog vlog OT 3

Vlogger(in) vlogger OT 3

Vogel bird OT 1

Vokal vowel OT 1

Volks... folk OT 2

Volksheld folk hero **WS 1**, 21

Volkstanz country dancing OT 1

voll full OT 1

Volleyball volleyball OT 3

Volontär(in) intern **WS 4**, 123

von of; from; by; off OT 1

vor ago; before; in front of OT 1

voraus ahead OT 3

vorbeifahren to pass OT 3

vorbereiten to prepare; to get ready OT 1

Vorbereitung preparation OT 2

Vordergrund foreground OT 3

Vorderseite front OT 1

Vorderteil front OT 1

Vorfahr(in) ancestor OT 3

vorführen to act out OT 1; to demonstrate **WS 3**, 96

vorgeben to pretend OT 2

Vorhand forehand OT 3

Vorhang curtain OT 2

vorherig previous **WS 3**, 100

Vorhersage prediction OT 2

vorhersagen to predict **WS 1**, 20

Vorlage template **WS 4**, 119

Vorliebe preference OT 3

Vorname first name OT 2

Vorrat supply OT 3

Vorschlag suggestion OT 1

vorschlagen to suggest OT 1

vorsichtig careful OT 1

Vorspeise starter OT 1

vorstellen to imagine; to present OT 1; to introduce OT 2

Vorstellung show OT 1; introduction OT 2

Vorstellungsbeginn showtime **WS 4**, 120

Vorstellungsgespräch interview OT 1

ein Vorstellungsgespräch führen mit to interview OT 1

Vorteil benefit; pro OT 2; advantage OT 3

Vortrag talk OT 2

vorziehen to prefer OT 1

W

wach awake OT 2

wachsen to grow OT 1

wackelig shaky OT 3

Waffe weapon OT 3

Waffel waffle OT 3

Wagen trolley; carriage OT 1; wagon **WS 1**, 28

wagen to dare OT 2

Wagenzug wagon train **WS 1**, 28

Wahl choice OT 1; option OT 2; election OT 3

wählen to vote OT 1; to dial OT 2; to select **WS 1**, 32; to elect **WS 2**, 58

wählerisch fussy OT 2

wahr true OT 1

während while OT 1; during OT 2; throughout OT 3

Wahrheit truth OT 3

wahrscheinlich probably OT 2; likely OT 3

Wahrzeichen landmark **WS 1**, 25

Wal whale OT 1

Wald forest OT 1

Waldbrand wildfire OT 2

Waldhorn French horn OT 1

Walfang whaling OT 2

walisisch Welsh OT 1

Walspeck blubber OT 2

Wand wall OT 1

Wanderer; Wanderin hiker OT 2; walker OT 3

wandern to hike OT 1

Wanderstiefel hiking boot OT 2

Wanderung walk; hike OT 2

Wandgemälde mural OT 2

Wandschrank closet OT 2

Wandzeitung wall display OT 2

wann when OT 1

wann auch immer whenever **WS 2**, 45

warm warm OT 2

warnen to warn OT 3

warten to wait OT 1; to hang on OT 2

Warteschlange queue OT 1

Wartung maintenance OT 3

warum why OT 1

was what OT 1

was auch immer whatever OT 3

Wäsche laundry **WS 1**, 20

waschen to wash OT 2

Wasser water OT 1

Wasser... aquatic **WS 4**, 110

Wasserbus waterbus OT 3

wasserdicht waterproof OT 2

Wasserfall falls; waterfall OT 1

Wasserhahn faucet **WS 3**, 92

Wasserkocher kettle OT 2

Webinar webinar **WS 4**, 123

Webkonferenz web conference **WS 1**, 13

Webseite website OT 1

Wechselgeld change OT 1

wechseln to change OT 1

Wecker alarm; alarm clock OT 2

weder neither OT 2

weder noch nor **WS 3**, 86

Weg track; way; path OT 1

weg off; away OT 1

wegräumen to put away OT 2

wegrennen to rush off OT 2

wegwerfen to throw away OT 2

wehen to blow OT 2

wehtun to hurt OT 1; to ache OT 3

weiblich female OT 2

weich soft OT 3

weigern to refuse **WS 3**, 105

Weihnachten Christmas OT 1

Weihnachtsmarkt Christmas market OT 2

weil because OT 1

Wein wine OT 1

weinen to cry OT 1

Weise manner OT 2

weiß white OT 1

weit far OT 1; wide OT 2

weiter anymore OT 2; further **WS 1**, 12

Weiterbildungslehrgang training course OT 2

weiterführende Schule secondary school OT 1

weitergehen to move on **WS 1**, 13

weitermachen to continue OT 1; to go ahead **WS 1**, 13

welche(r, -s) which OT 1

Welle wave OT 1

Wellensittich budgie OT 1

Wellness wellness **WS 1**, 30

Welpe puppy OT 2

Welt world OT 1

    aus aller Welt from around the world OT 1

Weltraum space OT 2

Weltraumforschung space exploration **WS 3**, 94

weltweit worldwide OT 3; global **WS 2**, 52

Wendung phrase OT 1

wenige few OT 1

    weniger less OT 2

    wenigste(r, -s) least OT 2

wer who OT 1

    wer auch immer whoever **WS 1**, 28

Werbeagentur advertiser OT 3

Werber advertiser OT 3

Werbung advertisement OT 1; ad; advertising OT 2

    Werbung machen für to advertise OT 2

werden to become; shall; will OT 2

werfen to throw OT 1; to toss OT 3

Werft dockyard OT 3

Werkstatt workshop OT 1; garage **WS 3**, 84

Werkzeug tool OT 2

Wert value **WS 1**, 32

wertvoll valuable OT 2

Wesen creature **WS 4**, 111

wesentlich essential **WS 3**, 93

Wespe wasp OT 3

wessen whose OT 2

Weste vest OT 2

Westen west OT 1

    mittlerer Westen midwest **WS 1**, 25; midwestern **WS 1**, 31

westwärts westward **WS 1**, 24

Wettbewerb competition OT 1

wetteifernd competitively **WS 2**, 55

wetten to bet OT 1

Wetter weather OT 1

Wettkampf match OT 1

wichtig important OT 1; relevant **WS 1**, 32; essential **WS 3**, 93

Wichtigkeit importance OT 2

wie how; as OT 1

wieder again OT 1

Wiedergabeliste playlist **WS 2**, 44

wiederherstellen to restore **WS 4**, 123

wiederholen to repeat OT 1

Wiederholung repetition **WS 4**, 123

Wiedersehen goodbye OT 1

wiederverwendbar reusable OT 3

wiederverwenden to reuse OT 2

wiederverwerten to recycle OT 2

Wiederverwerter(in) recycler OT 3

wiegen to weigh OT 3

Wiese meadow OT 2

wild wild OT 2

Wilderei poaching OT 3

Wilderer / Wilderin poacher OT 3

Wildnis wilderness OT 2

Wildwasser fahren white water rafting OT 3

willkommen welcome OT 1

Wind wind OT 2

Windel nappy OT 3

windig windy OT 2

windsurfen to windsurf OT 1

Windsurfer(in) windsurfer OT 1

winken to wave OT 2

Winsch windlass OT 3

Winter winter OT 1

winzig tiny OT 1

wir we OT 1

wirklich really OT 1

wirksam effectively **WS 3**, 86

Wirkung effect OT 3

Wirtschaft economy OT 3

wirtschaftlich economic **WS 3**, 88

Wischtuch wipe **WS 3**, 92

wissen to know OT 1

Wissen science OT 1; knowledge **WS 1**, 19

Wissenschaft studies OT 1

wissenschaftlich scientific OT 3

Witz joke OT 2

wo where OT 1

    wo (auch) immer wherever OT 3

Woche week OT 1

Wochenende weekend OT 1

Wochentag weekday OT 3

wöchentlich weekly OT 3

Wohlbefinden wellness **WS 1**, 30

Wohlfahrtsorganisation charity OT 2

wohnen to live OT 1

Wohnmobil camper van **WS 3**, 80

Wohnraum housing OT 3

Wohnung flat; apartment OT 1

Wohnwagen caravan OT 1

Wohnzimmer living room OT 1

Wolke cloud OT 1

Wolkenkratzer skyscraper OT 3

wolkig cloudy **WS 3**, 93

Wolle wool OT 2

    aus Wolle woolly OT 2

wollen to want OT 1

wollig woolly OT 2

Wort word OT 1

Wortart part of speech OT 2

Wörterbuch dictionary OT 1

Wrack wreck OT 3

wunderbar wonderful OT 1

wünschen to wish OT 3

Wurm worm OT 1

Wurst sausage OT 1

Wurzel root OT 3

Wüste desert OT 3

Wut anger OT 3

Z

Zahl number OT 1; figure OT 3

zählbar countable OT 1

zählen to count OT 1

Zahn tooth OT 2

Zahnbürste toothbrush **WS 3**, 78

Zahnpasta toothpaste **WS 3**, 93

Zauber magic OT 1

Zauberer; Zauberin magician OT 1

Zebra zebra OT 1

Zebrastreifen zebra crossing OT 1

Zeh toe OT 1

zehn ten OT 1

Zeichen drawing OT 1

Zeichensetzung punctuation OT 1

Zeichentrickfilm cartoon **WS 1**, 21

zeichnen to draw OT 1; to sketch **WS 3**, 85

Zeichnung drawing OT 1

zeigen to show OT 1

Zeit time OT 1; period OT 3

Zeitachse timeline OT 2

Zeitform tense OT 1

zeitgenössisch contemporary OT 3

Zeitpunkt timing OT 3

Zeitrechnung: unserer Zeitrechnung
AD (Anno Domini) OT 2

Zeitschrift magazine OT 1

Zeitung newspaper OT 1

Zeitwort verb OT 1

Zelle cell OT 1; booth **WS 3**, 93

Zelt tent OT 1; marquee OT 2

zelten to camp OT 1

Zeltplatz campsite OT 1; campground
OT 2

Zentimeter centimetre (cm) OT 2

Zentral… central OT 1

Zentrum centre OT 1

zeremoniell ceremonial OT 3

zerkleinert shredded OT 2

zerstören to destroy OT 2

Zertifikat certificate OT 1

Zeug stuff OT 2

Zeugnis certificate OT 1

Ziege goat **WS 1**, 20

ziehen to draw; to pull OT 1

Ziel target OT 2; aim **WS 3**, 86; ambition
WS 3, 94; objective **WS 3**, 95

zielen to aim **WS 2**, 58

ziemlich quite OT 2; rather OT 3

Ziffer digit OT 2

Zinn tin OT 2

zirkulieren to circulate **WS 2**, 55

zischen to whizz OT 2

Zitadelle fortress OT 3

zitieren to quote; to cite OT 2

Zitronenlimonade lemonade OT 1

zittern to tremble OT 2

zögern to hesitate OT 3

Zoll customs OT 2

Zoll (2,54 cm) inch OT 2

zollfrei duty free OT 2

Zombie zombie OT 2

Zone zone OT 2

Zoo zoo OT 1

zornig angrily OT 2

zu too; to OT 1

Zubehör accessory OT 3

Zucchini zucchini OT 3

Zucker sugar OT 3

Zuckermais sweet corn OT 1

Zufall chance OT 2

zufällig accidentally OT 3

Zuflucht resort OT 2

zufrieden pleased OT 1

Zug train OT 1

Zugang access **WS 1**, 31

zugänglich accessible OT 2

zugeben to admit **WS 4**, 117

zugreifen auf to access **WS 2**, 48

Zugriff access **WS 1**, 31

Zuhause home OT 1

zuhören to listen OT 1

Zuhörer(in) listener OT 1

Zukunft future OT 2

zumachen to shut OT 2

Zunahme increase OT 3

Zunder tinder OT 2

Zündung ignition **WS 3**, 95

Zunge tongue OT 3

zurück back OT 1

zurückkehren to return OT 2

zusammen together OT 1

zusammenfassen to summarize OT 2;
to sum up **WS 3**, 85

Zusammenfassung summary
OT 3

Zusammenhang context **WS 4**, 127

**zusammenpassen: nicht
zusammenpassen** to clash OT 2

**zusammenpassend: nicht
zusammenpassend** mismatched
WS 2, 58

zusammensacken to slump **WS 4**, 117

zusammenstoßen to bump into OT 2

zusätzlich in addition to **WS 4**, 110

Zuschauer(in) spectator; viewer OT 3

zuschlagen to strike OT 1

zuspielen to pass OT 3

zuständig in charge OT 1

zusteigen to get on OT 2

zustimmen to approve OT 3

Zutat ingredient OT 2

zuversichtlich confident OT 2

Zwangsarbeiter(in) bonded laborer
WS 4, 127

zwanzig twenty OT 1

Zweck purpose **WS 3**, 80

zwecklos pointless **WS 3**, 95

zweckmäßiges Gerät convenience
WS 3, 80

zwei two OT 1
zwei Wochen fortnight OT 2

Zweifel doubt **WS 3**, 95

Zweig twig OT 2

zweimal twice OT 2

zweisprachig bilingual OT 2

zweite(r, -s) second OT 1

zweitens secondly OT 2

zweiundzwanzig twenty-two OT 1

Zwiebel onion OT 2

Zwiebelring onion ring OT 2

Zwilling twin OT 1

Dictionary: Names

A

Abraham Lincoln [ˌeɪbrəhæm ˈlɪŋkən] 16th president of the USA, during the Civil War period **WW**, 10

Afghanistan [æfˈɡænəstɑːn] country in Asia **WS 1**, 41

Alexander Hamilton [ˌæliɡzɑːndə ˈhæmltən] American statesman and politician, known as one of America's Founding Fathers **WS 1**, 19

Alisha [əˈlɪsə] girl's name **WS 2**, 46

Alma [ˌælmə] girl's name **WS 2**, 60

Amish [ˈɑːmɪʃ] Christian religious group **WS 1**, 27

Andrea Sreshta [ˈændrɪə sreʃtɑː] co-inventor of the solar lantern **WS 3**, 83

Anna Stork [ˌænə stɔːk] co-inventor of the solar lantern **WS 3**, 83

Anousheh Ansari [ænuːˈʃɛ ænsɔːˈriː] American businesswoman who was the first female space tourist **WS 3**, 92

Arctic Circle [ˌɑːktɪk ˈsɜːkl] northerly polar circle **WS 3**, 103

Arizona [ˌærəˈzəʊnə] state in the southwest of the USA **WS 1**, 13

Arnold Schwarzenegger [ˈɑːnəld ˈʃwɔːtsənegə] US actor born in Austria **WS 1**, 39

Atlanta [ətˈlæntə] capital city of the state of Georgia, USA **WW**, 11

Austria [ˈɒstriə] country in central Europe **WS 1**, 39

Aziz [ˈazɪz] boy's name **WS 4**, 122

B

Bangkok [bæŋˈkɒk] capital city of Thailand **WS 3**, 103

Bangladesh [ˌbæŋɡləˈdeʃ] country in South Asia **WS 2**, 52

Bavaria [bəˈveəriə] province in southeast Germany **WS 1**, 25

Bessie [ˈbesi] girl's name **WS 1**, 29

Beth [beθ] girl's name **WS 4**, 117

Boston [ˈbɒstən] capital city of the state of Massachusetts, USA **WS 1**, 20

Brazil [brəˈzɪl] country in South America **WS 4**, 127

Bridgeport [ˈbrɪdʒpɔːt] city in Connecticut, USA **WS 3**, 82

Brooklyn [ˈbrʊklɪn] area in New York City, USA **WS 2**, 59

Buzz Aldrin [bʌz ɔːldrɪn] American astronaut who was the second man to step onto the Moon **WS 3**, 92

C

Cambodia [kæmˈbəʊdiə] country in southeast Asia **WS 2**, 52

Cape Canaveral [ˌkeɪp kəˈnævərəl] cape in Florida, USA which is famous for the Kennedy Space Center **WS 4**, 136

Cape Town [ˈkeɪptaʊn] city in South Africa **WS 4**, 123

Captain Weymouth [ˈkæptɪn ˈweɪməθ] English explorer **WS 1**, 21

Cedar Rapids [ˌsiːdə ˈræpɪdz] city in the state of Iowa, USA **WS 1**, 12

Charleston [ˈtʃɑːlstən] city in South Carolina, USA **WS 1**, 13

Chernivtsi [ˌtʃɪrnɪftˈsi] city in Ukraine **WS 1**, 41

Cheyenne [ʃaɪˈæn] a Native American group from the states of Wyoming and Montana, USA **WS 1**, 29

Chicago [ʃəˈkɑːɡəʊ] the third largest city in the USA, located in Illinois **WW**, 11

China [ˈtʃaɪnə] largest country in eastern Asia **WS 1**, 24

Cindy [ˈsɪndi] girl's name **WS 2**, 73

Clark Gable [ˌklɑːk ˈɡeɪbl] US film actor **WS 3**, 82

Clarke [ˈklɑːk] surname **WS 1**, 16

Cole [ˌkəʊl] surname **WS 1**, 29

Colorado [ˌkɒləˈrɑːdəʊ] state in the USA **WS 1**, 12

Connecticut [kəˈnetɪkət] state in the USA **WS 3**, 82

Conor [ˈkɒnə] boy's name **WS 1**, 13

Constance [kɒnstəns] girl's name **WS 1**, 20

Costa Rica [ˌkɒstə ˈriːkə] country in Central America **WS 4**, 123

Craig Kielburger [ˈkreɪg kiːlˈbɜːɡə] Canadian human rights activist and social entrepreneur **WS 4**, 126

Cuba [ˈkjuːbə] island country in the Caribbean off the southeastern coast of the USA **WW**, 11

D

Daisy [ˈdeɪzi] girl's name **WS 1**, 16

Dan [dæn] boy's name **WS 2**, 46

Dana [ˈdeɪnə] girl's name **WS 2**, 73

Detroit [dɪˈtrɔɪt] city in Michigan, USA **WS 1**, 12

Dodd [dɒd] surname **WS 1**, 14

Dundee [dʌnˈdiː] city in Scotland **WS 1**, 14

E

Ellie [ˈeli] girl's name **WS 1**, 13

Emily [ˈeməli] girl's name **WS 1**, 12

Emma [ˈemə] girl's name **WS 2**, 58

Empire State Building [ˌempaɪə ˈsteɪt bɪldɪŋ] building in Manhattan, New York City, USA **WS 1**, 24

Ernst Stuhlinger [ɜːnst stuːlɪŋə] German-American atomic, electrical and rocket scientist **WS 3**, 95

F

Ferdinando Gorges [ˈfɜːd(ə)nændəʊ ˈɡɔːdʒɪz] man who Squanto lived with in England **WS 1**, 21

Florida [ˈflɒrɪdə] state in the USA **WS 1**, 12

Fran Bagenal [fræn bægəˈnɑːl] Professor of Planetary Science at Colorado University, USA **WS 3**, 95

Frank Nasworthy [ˈfræŋk ˈnæzwɜːði] inventor of the skateboard **WS 3**, 82

Frazier [freɪziə] surname **WS 4**, 117

Fritz Mandl [ˈfrɪts mændl] Austrian buisnessman who sold weapons to the Nazis **WS 3**, 83

G

Genevieve [ˈdʒɛn əˌviv] girl's name **WS 1**, 30

George Antheil [ˈdʒɔːdʒ ænˈtʰaɪl] American composer **WS 3**, 83

George Washington [ˌdʒɔːdʒ ˈwɒʃɪŋtən] first president of the USA, general during the American Revolution **WW**, 10

Georgia [ˈdʒɔːdʒə] state in the USA **WS 1**, 27

Germaine [dʒəˈmeɪn] girl's name **WS 1**, 12

Glasgow [ˈɡlɑːzɡəʊ] largest city in Scotland **WS 1**, 13

Greta Thunberg [ˈɡrɛt ə toonˌburg] Swedish environmental activist who has mobilized youth around the world **WS 3**, 90

Guatemala [ˌɡwɑːtəˈmɑːlə] country in Central America **WS 4**, 124

zwischen between **WS 4**, 124; among **OT 3**

Bursche boy's name **WS 2**, 47; **OT 2**

zwölf twelve **OT 1**

H

Haiti [ˈheɪti] country in the Caribbean Sea **WS 3**, 83

Hamburg [ˈhæmbɜːɡ] city in Germany **WS 1**, 24

Hedy Lamarr [ˈheɪdi ləˈmɑː] Hollywood film star born in Austria **WS 3**, 83

Houston [ˈhjuːstən] city in Texas, USA **WS 1**, 13

I

Illinois [ˌɪlɪˈnɔɪ] state in the USA **WS 1**, 13

Independence Rock [ˌɪndɪˈpendəns rɑːk] landmark in Wyoming, USA **WS 1**, 28

Indonesia [ˌɪndəʊˈniːziə] country in the southeast Indian Ocean **WS 2**, 52

Iowa [ˈaɪəwə] state in the USA **WS 1**, 12

Iqbal Masih [ˈɪkbəl mæzi] Pakistani Christian boy who became a symbol of child labour in Pakistan **WS 4**, 126

J

Jackie [ˈdʒæki] girl's name **WS 1**, 13

Jamaica [dʒəˈmeɪkə] island in the West Indies in the Caribbean Sea **WS 1**, 14

Jan Koum [dʒæn kuːm] co-founder of a messenger **WS 1**, 25

Janet [ˈdʒænɪt] girl's name **WS 4**, 123

Jarvis [ˈdʒɑːvɪs] boy's name **WS 2**, 63

Jawed Karim [dʒɔːd ˈkærɪm] co-founder of a video streaming platform **WS 1**, 25

Jerry Yang [ˈdʒerɪ ˈjæŋ] founder of a famous search engine **WS 1**, 41

Jimmy Stewart [ˈdʒɪmɪ ˈstjuːət] US film actor **WS 3**, 83

John [dʒɒn] boy's name **WS 1**, 31

Jonesy [ˈdʒəʊnzɪ] boy's name **WS 1**, 16

Jordan [ˈdʒɔːdən] boy's name **WS 2**, 46

Joseph Swan [ˌdʒəʊzəf swɒn] inventor of a simple electric light bulb **WS 3**, 77

Joshua [ˈdʒɒʃuə] boy's name **WS 1**, 13

Julia [ˈdʒuːliə] girl's name **WS 1**, 13

K

Kabul [ˈkɑːbʊl] capital city of Afghanistan **WS 1**, 41

Karl Benz [kɑːl benz] German engine designer and automotive engineer **WS 3**, 77

Kavita Shukla [kæˈvaɪtə ʃʊklə] inventor of 'fresh paper' **WS 3**, 84

Kenya [ˈkenjə] country in East Africa **WS 1**, 26

Khaled Hosseini [kælɛd huːseɪniː] American author **WS 1**, 41

Khayelitsha [ˌkʌɪjəˈlɪtʃə] township in the southeast of Cape Town, South Africa **WS 4**, 123

Kim [kɪm] surname **WS 1**, 16

Kutztown [ˈkʌtˌstaʊn] borough in Pennsylvania, USA **WS 1**, 27

L

Lake Michigan [ˌleɪk ˈmɪʃɪɡən] lake in the USA **WS 1**, 25

Lakota [ləˈkəʊtə] a group of Native American tribes **WS 1**, 30

Lancaster [ˈlæŋkəstə] city in Pennsylvania, USA **WS 1**, 32

Larry Page [ˈlærɪ ˈpeɪdʒ] co-founder of the most famous search engine **WS 1**, 39

Latino [læˈtiːnəʊ] man in the US whose family comes from Latin America **WS 1**, 16

Leonardo Da Vinci [liːəˌnɑːdəʊ də ˈvɪntʃi] Italian painter, inventor and scientist **WS 3**, 84

Levi Strauss [ˈliːvaɪ straʊs] founder of a company for denim jeans **WS 1**, 25

Lily [ˈlɪli] girl's name **WS 3**, 80

Liverpool [ˈlɪvəpuːl] city in the northwest of England **WS 1**, 24

Luis [luːˈiːs] boy's name **WS 1**, 13

M

Mahatma Gandhi [məˈhætmə ˈɡændiː] Indian lawyer and politician who led the fight for India's independence from the British **WS 3**, 112

Malala Yousafzai [məˈlaːlə jusəf ˈzəj] Pakistani Nobel Prize laureate who advocates for female education **WS 4**, 127

Manchester [ˈmæntʃəstə] city in the northwest of England **WS 1**, 13

Martha [ˈmɑːθə] girl's name **WS 1**, 28

Martian [ˈmɑːʃən] relating to the planet Mars **WS 3**, 94

Mayflower [ˈmeɪflaʊə] the ship the Pilgrims took from England to America **WS 1**, 18

Mennonites [ˈmenənaɪt] member of a Protestant religious group **WS 1**, 27

Mexico [ˈmeksɪkəʊ] country in the southern part of North America **WW**, 11

Mia [ˈmiːə] girl's name **WS 2**, 51

Miami [maɪˈæmi] city in Florida, USA **WS 3**, 103

Mila Kunis [mˈiːlə kˈuːniz] American actress **WS 1**, 41

Milan [mɪˈlæn] city in Italy **WS 3**, 83

Miller [ˈmɪlə] surname **WS 2**, 47

Mina [ˈmiːnə] girl's name **WS 1**, 13

Minnesota [ˌmɪnəˈsəʊtə] state in the USA **WS 1**, 26

Mississippi [ˌmɪsɪˈsɪpi] state in the USA **WS 1**, 12

Missouri [məˈsʊəri] state in the USA **WS 1**, 24

Moscow [ˈmɒskəʊ] capital of Russia **WS 1**, 39

Mother Teresa [ˌmʌðə təˈriːzə] Albanian Roman Catholic nun who lived and worked in India **WS 4**, 127

Mount Everest [ˌmaʊnt ˈevərəst] mountain in the Himalayas **WS 1**, 25

N

NASA [ˈnæsə] US government organization, National Aeronautics and Space Administration **WS 1**, 39

Nashville [ˈnæʃvɪl] capital city of the state of Tennessee, USA **WS 1**, 12

Natalie [ˈnætəli] girl's name **WS 2**, 50

Navajo [ˈnævəhəʊ] member of the Navajo tribe, one of the largest tribes of Native Americans **WW**, 10

Neil Armstrong [niːl ˈɑːmstrɒŋ] American astronaut who was the first man to step onto the Moon **WS 3**, 92

Nevada [nəˈvaːdə] state in the USA **WS 1**, 12

New Jersey [ˌnjuː ˈdʒɜːzi] state in the USA **WS 3**, 83

New Orleans [ˌnjuː ɔːˈliːnz] city in the state of Louisiana **WS 1**, 24

Nicky [ˈnɪki] girl's name **WS 4**, 123

O

O'Brien [əʊˈbraɪən] surname **WS 1**, 46

Ohio [əʊˈhaɪəʊ] state in the USA **WS 1**, 24

Olivia [əˈlɪviə] girl's name **WS 4**, 122

Oregon Trail [ˌɒrəɡən ˈtreɪl] path from the middle part to the western part of the USA **WS 1**, 28

Oxford University [ˌɒksfəd juːnɪˈvɜːsəti] oldest university in Britain **WS 4**, 127

P

Pablo [ˈpɑbloʊ] boy's name **WS 1**, 16
Pakistan [ˌpɑːkɪˈstɑːn] country in Asia **WS 4**, 126
Patuxet [pəˈtʌksət] tribe of Native Americans **WS 1**, 21
Pennsylvania [ˌpensəlˈveɪniə] state in the USA **WS 1**, 27
Pereira [pəˈreərə] surname **WS 4**, 123
Philadelphia [ˌfɪləˈdelfiə] city in Pennsylvania, USA **WS 2**, 59
Phoenix [ˈfiːnɪks] city in the state of Arizona, USA **WS 1**, 13
Pilgrim Fathers [ˌpɪlgrɪm ˈfɑːðəz] the group of English people who arrived to settle in the US in 1620 **WS 1**, 18
Platte River [plat ˈrɪvə] river in the USA **WS 1**, 28
Plimoth Plantation [ˈplɪməθ plɑːnˈteɪʃn] a history museum in Plymouth, Massachusetts, USA that recreates the Plymouth Colony **WS 1**, 18
Pocahontas [ˌpɒkəˈhɒntəs] a Native American woman who saved the life of Captain John Smith **WS 1**, 22
Port Huron [pɔːtˈhjʊərɒn] city in Michigan, USA **WS 3**, 83
Portland [ˈpɔːtlənd] city in the state of Oregon, USA **WS 1**, 29
Price [praɪs] surname **WS 3**, 79
Protestant [ˈprɒtəstənt] member of a part of the Christian Church **WS 1**, 32

Q

Quinn [kwɪn] surname **WS 1**, 13

R

Reed [riːd] surname **WS 1**, 16
Rhonda [ˈrɒndə] girl's name **WS 4**, 117
Rifa [ˈrifːə] girl's name **WS 2**, 53
Roscoe [ˈrɒskəʊ] dog's name **WS 1**, 16
Roscosmos [rɒsˈkɒzmɒs] Russian space agency **WS 3**, 94
Roy [rɔɪ] boy's name **WS 2**, 47
Ruby [ˈruːbi] girl's name **WS 3**, 81
Russian [ˈrʌʃən] a person who comes from Russia **WS 3**, 94
Rusty [ˈrʌsti] boy's name **WS 4**, 123

S

Sam [ˈsæm] boy's name **WS 4**, 123
Samuel Adams [ˈsæm yu əl ˈæd əmz] American political philosopher, known as one of America's Founding Fathers **WS 1**, 18

San Francisco [ˌsæn frənˈsɪskəʊ] city in California, USA **WS 1**, 12
Sergey Brin [sɜːˈgeɪ brɪn] co-founder of the most famous search engine **WS 1**, 39
Shanghai [ʃæŋˈhaɪ] city in East China **WS 3**, 103
Silicon Valley [ˌsɪlɪkən ˈvæli] area in California known for the technology industry **WS 1**, 24
Somali [səˈmɑːli] sb. who comes from Somalia **WS 1**, 26
Somalia [səˈmɑːliə] country in East Africa **WS 1**, 26
South Carolina [ˌsaʊθ kærəˈlaɪnə] state in the USA **WS 1**, 13
South Dakota [ˌsaʊθ dəˈkəʊtə] state in the USA **WS 1**, 29
Squanto [ˈskwɒntəʊ] a Native American who helped the Pilgrim Fathers **WS 1**, 21
St Kitts [sənt ˌkɪts] island in the West Indies in the Caribbean Sea **WS 1**, 24
Stacy [ˈsteɪsi] girl's name **WS 4**, 123
Stanford University [ˌstænfəd juːnɪˈvɜːsəti] private university in California, USA **WS 1**, 41
Statue of Liberty [ˌstætʃuː əv ˈlɪbəti] statue in New York Harbor, given to the US by France in 1884 **WW**, 11
Sterling [ˈstɜːlɪŋ] city in Illinois, USA **WS 1**, 13
Steve Chen [stiːv ˈʃən] co-founder of a video streaming platform **WS 1**, 25
Steven [ˈstiːvən] boy's name **WS 3**, 79
Sunita Williams [suːniːtə ˈwɪljəmz] American astronaut **WS 3**, 93
Sykes [saɪks] surname **WS 2**, 46

T

Taipei [ˈtaɪˈpeɪ] largest city of Taiwan **WS 1**, 41
Taiwan [ˌtaɪˈwɑːn] island off the southeast coast of China **WS 1**, 41
Taliban [ˈtɑːlɪˌbɑːn] group which took control of most of Afghanistan after the civil war in 1997 **WS 4**, 127
Tennessee [ˌtenəˈsiː] state in the USA **WS 1**, 12
Texas [ˈteksəs] state in the USA **WS 1**, 26
Thailand [ˈtaɪlænd] country in southeast Asia **WS 4**, 127
Thomas Edison [ˌtɒməs ˈedɪsən] American inventor who created the first light bulb **WS 3**, 76

Thomas Jefferson [ˌtɒməs ˈdʒefəsən] 3rd president of the USA, main author of the Declaration of Independence **WW**, 10
Tim Berners-Lee [tɪm ˌbɜːnəz ˈliː] British computer scientist who invented the World Wide Web **WS 3**, 77
Trent [trent] boy's name **WS 4**, 122
Tucson [ˈtuːsɒn] city in the state of Arizona, USA **WS 1**, 13

U

Ukraine [juːˈkreɪn] country in eastern Europe **WS 1**, 14

V

Vienna [viˈenə] capital city of Austria **WS 3**, 83
Viking [ˈvaɪkɪŋ] Scandinavian pirates from the 9th to 11th centuries **WW**, 10

W

Walker Bear [ˈwɔːkə beə] surname **WS 1**, 31
Wampanoag [ˌwɑm pəˈnoʊ æg] a Native American group from the American northeast **WS 1**, 18
West Indies [ˌwest ˈɪndiz] islands of the Caribbean sea **WS 1**, 24
White [waɪt] surname **WS 2**, 63
William Morrison [ˌwɪljəm ˈmɒrɪsən] developer of the plastic frisbee **WS 3**, 82
Withers [ˈwɪðəz] surname **WS 2**, 46
Wright [ˈraɪt] surname **WS 3**, 76
Wyoming [waɪˈoʊ mɪŋ] state in the USA **WS 1**, 28

Y

Yale University [jeɪl juːnɪˈvɜːsəti] university in Connecticut, USA **WS 3**, 82
Yuri Gagarin [ˈjuːri gəˈgɑːrɪn] first person to travel into outer space **WS 3**, 76

Acknowledgements

Text credits

p. 34: © 2019 Boudin Bakery, San Fransisco; **p. 35:** © hamburg.de GmbH & Co. KG, „Schönste Stadt der Welt – Hoher Wohlfühlfaktor in Hamburg", https://www.hamburg.de/sehenswuerdigkeiten-architektur/3607488/schoenste-stadt-deutschlands/; **p. 37:** © by Ludlow Music, Ltd., D/A/CH: essex Musikvertrieb GmbH, Hamburg ; **p. 66:** "Statistiken zur Mediennutzung von Jugendlichen", https://de.statista.com/themen/2662/mediennutzung-von-jugendlichen/; **p. 69:** Simon Mason, *Hey Sherlock!* (The Garvie Smith Mysteries), David Fickling Books Ltd., Oxford, UK; **p. 98:** © Verlagsgruppe Random House GmbH, München; **p. 101:** "Across the Universe", © Razorbill: London, 2011; **p. 131:** © Church of the Holy Apostles, New York; © Holy Apostles Soup Kitchen, New York; **p. 133:** "Soup kitchen", taken from Walter Dean Meyers, *All the Right Stuff*, New York: HarperCollins Publishers, 2012; pp. 13–17; **p. 145:** Elizabeth Acevedo, *Poet X*, New York: HarperTeen (HarperCollins Publishers), 2018; pp. 96–98

Picture credits

|Alamy Stock Photo, Abingdon/Oxfordshire: AB Forces News Collection 131.1; AGENZIA SINTESI 142.1; ALIKI SAPOUNTZI / aliki image library 134.1; Allenden, Ian 45.3; Alpegor 81.1; Archive Image 92.2; B.A.E. Inc. 84.1; BA LaRue 80.1; bilwissedition Ltd. & Co. KG 24.1; Blue Jean Images 82.1; brt COMM 33.1; Carr, Eric 103.1; CHANDARA TUBCHAND 86.2; Charles Stirling (Travel) 14.1, 16.2; cineclassico 83.3; Cole, David 83.2, 122.2; Corban, Tom 108.2; Cultura Creative (RF) 51.2; Daemmrich, Bob 85.1; Dagnall, Ian 60.1; David L. Moore - Education 85.2; David L. Moore - OR 26.7; Denkou Images 120.1; dotted zebra 95.1; Drobot, Vadym 50.1; FORGET Patrick/SAGAPHOTO.COM 59.1; Foto: Junger Mann mit seiner Garderobe 52.1; GALA Images 61.1; Gorodenkov, Aleksei 109.2; Grossman, David 63.1, 122.3; Guy, Greg 143.1; Helfman, Yuval 123.2; HEX LLC. 122.6; Holden, Jim 81.2; Iakobchuk, Viacheslav 122.4; Image navi - QxQ images 86.1; Image Source 110.1, 122.7; imageBROKER 20.2, 126.5; Ink Drop 90.2; Jeffrey Isaac Greenberg 3+ 27.1; Johner Images 48.1; Khabliuk, Iryna 135.2; Kippe, Fredrick 108.1; Kliapitski, Dzmitry 122.8; LightField Studios Inc. 50.4; Longhurst, Melvyn 18.3; Lumi Images 114.1; M&N 24.2; Marmaduke St. John 114.4; Martin, Montgomery 108.4; MBI 62.1; Megapress 14.2; Mojzes, Igor 33.3; moyceeey 135.1; NASA Photo 92.4; Olson, Tyler 120.3; Pavone, Sean 27.2; Phanie 122.5; PhotoAlto 59.2; PhotoMagicWorld 80.4; Pixel-shot 114.3; PR images 94.4; Prostock-studio 51.1; rakus 87.1; Ramos, Giuseppe / Alamy Vektorgrafik 104.1; Realy Easy Star 84.2; Reinholds, Aigars 114.2; Ringuette, Chantal 108.3; robertharding 60.2, 83.1; Roberts, Frances 63.2; Rout, Chris 130.1; Saz. Alfredo Garcia 62.2; Science Photo Library 94.2; Shafiqul Alam 52.7; Skjold, Steve 45.2; Smythe, Danny 11.4; Steward, Gordon 10.1; Stillman Rogers 20.1; Stocktrek Images, Inc 94.3; Sykes, Homer 81.3; TaniaL 111.1; Tetra Images 45.1; Tholpady, Ashok 109.1; VStock 121.1; Wavebreak Media ltd 109.3; WENN Rights Ltd 126.2, 144.1; West, Jim 122.1, 123.1; Westend61 GmbH 35.1; ZUMA Press 11.3; ZUMA Press, Inc. 120.2. |Alamy Stock Photo (RMB), Abingdon/Oxfordshire: Alba, Natali 91.1; ALEXANDROS MICHAILIDIS 90.4; Ammentorp Photography 48.3; Berkut, Anna 76.5; Callaert, Ed 37.4; christian ouellet 37.5; Douglas Peebles Photography 33.2; Foto: Mars Rover 94.1; Fox, Nick 37.3; GL Archive 76.4; Granger Historical Picture Archive 21.1; Ianni Dimitrov Pictures 48.2; Jenny, Andre 28.1; John Warburton-Lee Photography 11.2; Kalytta, Ralf 10.2; Kerrison, Mark 90.5; Koehler, Thomas/photothek images UG 66.1; LightField Studios Inc. 5.2, 56.1; LOC Photo 77.3; MacDonald, Dennis 76.1; Maumus, Ninette 37.1; MBI 12.2; McAllister, Neil 11.1; National Geographic Image Collection 30.3; Norbert-Zsolt Suto 84.4; North Wind Picture Archives 10.3; Oleksii Afanasiev 48.4, 48.5, 48.6, 48.7, 48.8; Pluto 133.1; Rodgers, Gina 18.4; Science History Images 76.3; Seitan, Florin 30.2; Shakirov, Albert 59.3; Shipunov, Denis 84.3; Tsuni 33.4; venimo 77.1; Vetre Antanaviciute-Meskauskiene 91.2; Volgutova, Tatiana 82.2; ZUMA Press, Inc. 99.1. |Bridgeman Images, Berlin: Granger 28.3. |CartoonStock.com, Bath: Sizemore, Jim 113.2. |Creative Listening, Newick: 80.2, 96.1, 96.2, 97.1, 116.1, 116.2, 116.3, 143.2. |Domke, Franz-Josef, Hannover: 3.1, 3.2, 5.1, 28.4, 52.2, 52.3, 52.5, 52.6, 52.8, 64.1, 125.1, 137.1, 259.1. |Donnelly, Karen, Brighton: 13.3, 15.1, 16.1, 17.1, 31.1, 31.2, 31.3, 31.4, 38.1, 44.1, 44.2, 44.3, 45.4, 45.5, 45.6, 45.7, 46.1, 46.2, 47.1, 54.1, 55.1, 55.2, 55.3, 55.4, 58.1, 58.4, 60.3, 65.1, 65.2, 65.3, 78.1, 88.1, 89.1, 94.5, 94.6, 94.7, 100.1, 112.1, 114.5, 115.1, 119.1, 119.2, 119.3, 119.4, 119.5, 120.4, 150.1, 150.2, 258.1, 258.2, 293.1, 293.2, 293.3. |Getty Images, München: AFP/MAXIM MARMUR 92.3; Andersen, Ulf 98.1; Pettersson, Per-Anders 9.1, 126.3; Sullivan, Brian / Barcroft Media 80.3; Universal History Archive 92.1; van Hasselt, John - Corbis 126.4. |Interfoto, München: Science & Society 7.1, 77.2. |iStockphoto.com, Calgary: Antonio_Diaz 129.2; bgwalker 50.2; bluejayphoto 37.2; Branimir76 150.3; dulezidar 34.2; elenab 78.2; FatCamera 57.1; filo 12.5; izusek 151.1; LauriPatterson 34.5; ma-k 34.1; monkeybusinessimages 24.3; OlegAlbinsky 18.2; omersukrugoksu 18.1; Portugal2004 34.4; seb_ra 154.1; Steer, Chris 90.1; subjug 34.3; tupungato 50.3. |Picture-Alliance GmbH, Frankfurt/M.: REUTERS/Boylan, Desmond 126.1. |Shutterstock.com, New York: Alexander Image 26.6; Algol 95.2; Allard One 159.1; ananaline 102.1; BG-Studio 124.2; Bruev, Grisha 82.4; Digital Media Pro 30.1; Edreff, Steve 26.4, 26.5; ESB Professional 23.3; FabrikaSimf 26.1; Foltin, Anton 28.2; G Diaz, Diego 31.5; GagliardiPhotography 23.2; Gorodenkoff 67.1; Guillem, Antonio 161.1; Habich, Arina P 156.1; Hogan Imaging 117.1, 132.2; Hurelych, Mariia 90.3; IgorGolovniov 39.1; JStone 127.1; Keifer, Kenneth 13.2; Kelleher Photography 22.1; Konstantin, Yuganov 39.3; Luciano Mortula - LGM 13.4; lzf 82.3; mangostock 72.1; MaxyM 12.6; Monica Garza 73 26.2; Monkey Business I 71.3; Monkey Business Images 12.4, 71.2; Motortion Films 164.1; philophoto 13.1; polya_olya 12.7; Pressmaster 113.1, 132.1; Rattanapon Ninlapoom 58.3; Salcedo, Jorge 23.1; Shahrin, Djohan 124.1; Sk Hasan Ali 52.4; SNEHIT PHOTO 71.1; Sohm, Joseph 58.2; spyarm 39.2; Symchych, Maria 118.1, 129.1; Vec.

Stock 49.2; ventdusud 12.1; Ward, Dana 53.1, 68.1; Zaiets, Roman 12.3; Zaskochenko, Olena 13.5. |Shutterstock.com (RM), New York: Summit Entertainment/Kobal 49.4. |stock.adobe.com, Dublin: coco 80.5; denisgorelkin 15.2, 15.3, 15.4, 15.5, 15.6, 49.1, 49.3; niroworld 76.2; PhotoSpirit 32.1; Ranta Images 26.3. |Williamson, Pete, Kent, Southborough, Tunbridge Wells: 42.1, 42.2, 43.1, 43.2, 74.1, 74.2, 75.1, 106.1, 106.2, 107.1, 107.2, 138.1, 138.2, 139.1, 140.1, 141.1, 141.2, 141.3.

Audio credits

dialogues, words and phrases: recorded and mixed at Air-Edel Recording Studios London; recording engineer Mark Smith. Produced by Anne Rosenfeld for RBA Productions; Music in Track 19: http://www.gemalos.de; Music in Track 59: David Bowie "Space Oddity", Onward Music Ltd., Essex Musikvertrieb GmbH; Music in Track 60: Zager and Evans "In the Year 2525", Chelsea-Music Publishing Co. Ltd, Budde Music International GmbH, Budde Music Publishing GmbH

Video credits

video 1, 4, 6, 7, 12, 13, 15, 16, 17: procuded by James Vyner and Luke Vyner for Creative Listening, London (www.creativelistening. co.uk); **video 1:** stills: Funwithfood / iStockphoto.com; Everett Historical / Shutterstock.com; fstop123 / iStockphoto.com; a katz / Shutterstock.com; KarSol / stock.adobe.com; **video 4:** stills: eddie linssen / Alamy Stock Photo; WoodysPhotos / Shutterstock. com; Shawn, Joel / Shutterstock.com; Crowe, John / Alamy Stock Photo; ZUMA Press, Inc. / Alamy Stock Photo; Photo by Leonard Ortiz / Digital First Media / Orange County Register via Getty Images / Getty Images; **video 6:** stills: Mays, Buddy / Alamy Stock Photo; Napuri, Juan / Alamy Stock Photo; Citizen of the Planet / Alamy Stock Photo; XXLPhoto / Alamy Stock Photo; rsdphotography / Alamy Stock Photo; coco/stock.adobe.com; Sullivan, Brian / Barcroft Media / Getty Images; Rawpixel.com / stock.adobe.com; **video 8, 9:** edited by David Rafique; texts for voiceovers: Heather Jones, Marc Proulx; voiceovers recorded at Air-Edel Studios, London; recording engineer Mark Smith; produced by Anne Rosenfeld for RBA Productions (www.rbaproductions.co.uk); **video 8:** stills: Cole, David / Alamy Stock Photo; World History Archive / Alamy Stock Photo; Pictorial Press Ltd / Alamy Stock Photo; B Christopher / Alamy Stock Photo; Dinodia Photos / Alamy Stock Photo; agefotostock / Alamy Stock Photo; Granger / Bridgeman Images; Duchaine, Randy / Alamy Stock Photo; Granger Historical Picture Archive / Alamy Stock Photo; **video 9:** stills: Archive PL/Alamy Stock Photo; Moviestore/Shutterstock. com (RM); ScreenProd / Photononstop / Alamy Stock Photo; Elekta / Kobal / Shutterstock.com (RM); IMAGNO / Votava / akg-images GmbH; Snap / Shutterstock.com (RM); Granger Historical Picture Archive / Alamy Stock Photo; Pictorial Press Ltd / Alamy Stock Photo; cineclassico / Alamy Stock Photo; **video 19, 20, 21:** Wildfang GbR Video & Audio Produktion; **video 20:** stills: Pixel-shot / Alamy Stock Foto

Medienbildung

Folgende **Kompetenzen** werden in *On Track 4* abgedeckt:

1.	**Suchen, Verarbeiten und Aufbewahren**	
1.1	Suchen und Filtern	S. 14 – 16; S. 20 – 23; S. 32 – 33; S. 48; S. 54 – 55; S. 66; S. 82; S. 98; S. 116 – 117
1.2	Auswerten und Bewerten	S. 14 – 16; S. 22 – 24; S. 28; S. 32 – 33; S. 48; S. 52; S. 62; S. 64 – 65; S. 112; S. 116; S. 125; S. 137
1.3	Speichern und Abrufen	S. 18; S. 20; S. 22 – 23; S. 32; S. 53, S. 64, S. 125
2.	**Kommunizieren und Kooperieren**	
2.1	Interagieren	S. 16; S. 28; S. 48 – 49; S. 56; S. 50; S. 78 – 79; S. 94; S. 116 – 117
2.2	Teilen	S. 22 – 23; S. 32
2.3	Zusammenarbeiten	S. 12 – 13; S. 17; S. 21; S. 56 – 59; S. 67; S. 98
2.4	Umgangsregeln kennen und einhalten (Netiquette)	S. 48; S. 59, S. 66; S. 90 – 91
2.5	An der Gesellschaft aktiv teilhaben	S. 14 – 15; S. 24 – 25; S. 48; S. 50 – 51; S. 90 – 91; S. 122 – 123; S. 126
3.	**Produzieren und Präsentieren**	
3.1	Entwickeln und Produzieren	S. 17; S. 19; S. 23; S. 27; S. 33; S. 53; S. 55; S. 59; S. 63; S. 65; S. 81; S. 85 – 87; S. 91; S. 93; S. 97; S. 119; S. 121; S. 129
3.2	Weiterverarbeiten und Integrieren	S. 14; S. 19; S. 20; S. 49; S. 50; S. 58 – 59; S. 62 – 63; S. 84; S. 90; S. 94; S. 113; S. 116 – 117; S. 127
3.3	Rechtliche Vorgaben beachten	S. 32; S. 128 – 129
4.	**Schützen und sicher agieren**	
4.1	Sicher in digitalen Umgebungen agieren	S. 48 – 49; S. 66; S. 76 – 79; S. 102 – 105; S. 112 – 113
4.2	Persönliche Daten und Privatsphäre schützen	S. 44 – 45; S. 48 – 49; S. 66; S. 80 – 81
4.3	Gesundheit schützen	S. 52 – 53; S. 62 – 63; S. 99; S. 124 – 125; S. 137
4.4	Natur und Umwelt schützen	S. 44 – 45; S. 50 – 54; S. 65; S. 80; S. 88 – 91; S. 102 – 105; S. 110; S. 122 – 123
5.	**Problemlösen und Handeln**	
5.1	Technische Probleme lösen	S. 79; S. 80 – 81; S. 86 – 87; S. 88
5.2	Werkzeuge bedarfsgerecht einsetzen	S. 22 – 23; S. 32; S. 54 – 55; S. 56; S. 64 – 65; S. 86; S. 96 – 97; S. 118 – 119; S. 128 – 129
5.3	Eigene Defizite ermitteln und nach Lösungen suchen	S. 22; S. 32 – 33; S. 54, S. 128
5.4	Digitale Werkzeuge und Medien zum Lernen, Arbeiten und Problemlösen nutzen	S. 22 – 23; S. 32 – 33; S. 54 – 55; S. 64; S. 96
5.5	Algorithmen erkennen und formulieren	
6.	**Analysieren und Reflektieren**	
6.1	Medien analysieren und bewerten	S. 44 – 45; S. 48 – 49; S. 55; S. 66
6.2	Medien in der digitalen Welt verstehen und reflektieren	S. 48; S. 50 – 51; S. 66; S. 76 – 77; S. 78; S. 80 – 81; S. 90 – 91; S. 100; S. 102 – 105

Classroom phrases

What your teacher can say
Can anyone remember … from our last session?
Who would like to explain?
What did you find out?
Don't interrupt each other.
Remember the advice about …
Can you think of any other tips?
Check your spelling in the dictionary.
Read and comment on each other's texts.
Compare your answers / solutions with a partner.
Make some notes about key points.
Give reasons for your opinion.
Read the text about … and be ready to talk about it in the next lesson.
Practise your talk at home or in front of your friends.

What you can say
What page are we on?
Can you write it on the board, please?
What does … mean?
What do you mean by …?
What's this in German / English?
Can you spell it, please?
Can you repeat the task, please?
I haven't finished the task yet.
I've already finished the task.
I've got something different.
Are we allowed to use our phones?
Can we do research on the internet?
Can we work with a partner / group?

Working with a partner / in a group / in class
Would you like to join us?
Let's go through our notes.
I'd like to make a suggestion.
Do you have a spare pen?
Can I borrow your book for a second?
Is there anything you would like to add?
I disagree. / I don't agree.
I agree (but …).
I see what you mean, but …
How do you fel about …?
That's a good point.
It's my turn / your turn.
You have a point, but …
Could I just say …
Sorry to interrupt …
Go ahead.
I'm sorry, what did you say?
When you say …, what exactly do you mean?
So what you're saying is …
What I mean is …
Just let me explain …
Whose turn is it?

Giving feedback
You did a great job.
I liked the part where you …
I had a feeling you really knew …
The visual aids were helpful.
The sound quality of your video is really clear.
I like the way you added …
What I really liked about your talk was that …
My favourite part was … because …
I think your presentation is good / interesting / funny because …
I like the way you used …
It really impressed me when you …
Can you say more about …, please?
My tip for you is to …
It would be better if you …
How about …?
Next time you should speak more clearly / loudly / slowly …
One suggestion would be …
Perhaps you should add …
Maybe you could include more information about …
You could also talk about …
I would like more descriptions of … / more information about … / more conversations between …

Media use	
Let's make a new document / slide.	Type the website address into the browser.
Copy / Insert the photo / text …	We need to refine our search.
Mark the text and copy it …	Let's read the information on the website …
Delete / Save the file.	Can you scroll up / down?
Let's share / post our blog / vlog online.	Click on the link.
We can drag and drop the files …	Let's watch the video.
Let's search for information online.	We should check the terms and conditions.
Let's go to the website.	We should bookmark our sources.

The English alphabet

a [eɪ]		**g** [dʒi:]		**m** [em]		**s** [es]		**y** [waɪ]	
b [bi:]		**h** [eɪtʃ]		**n** [en]		**t** [ti:]		**z** [zed]	
c [si:]		**i** [aɪ]		**o** [əʊ]		**u** [ju:]			
d [di:]		**j** [dʒeɪ]		**p** [pi]		**v** [vi:]			
e [i:]		**k** [keɪ]		**q** [kju:]		**w** [ˈdʌbl ju:]			
f [ef]		**l** [el]		**r** [a:]		**x** [eks]			

Consonants

Vowels

Consonants		Vowels	
[p]	**p**rivacy	[i]	colon**y**
[b]	responsi**b**ility	[e]	p**e**nalty
[t]	**t**iller	[æ]	b**a**rrier
[d]	**d**esigner	[ɒ]	w**a**sp
[k]	**c**ouncil	[ʌ]	t**u**nnel
[g]	**g**uidebook	[ʊ]	f**oo**tball
[f]	**f**reckles	[ə]	bott**o**m
[v]	**v**ote	[ɪ]	**e**lection
[θ]	sou**th**west	[u:]	concl**u**sion
[ð]	fea**th**er	[i:]	refer**ee**
[s]	re**c**ycling	[a:]	c**a**st
[z]	ma**z**e	[ɔ:]	div**o**rce
[ʃ]	flag**sh**ip	[u]	infl**u**ence
[ʒ]	vi**s**ualization	[ɜ:]	reh**ea**rsal
[h]	**h**istorian	[eɪ]*	s**ai**lor
[x]	lo**ch**	[aɪ]*	**i**sland
[tʃ]	**ch**allenge	[ɔɪ]*	lifeb**uoy**
[dʒ]	ob**j**ection	[əʊ]*	r**o**pe
[m]	**m**igration	[aʊ]*	ch**ow**der
[n]	questio**nn**aire	[ɪə]*	f**ea**r
[ŋ]	timi**ng**	[eə]*	c**a**re
[w]	ki**w**i	[ʊə]*	sec**u**re
[l]	**l**ocker	[uə]*	event**ua**l
[r]	**r**egular		
[j]	vo**y**age		

* Diphthongs: two vowel sounds in one syllable.
  The mouth moves from one sound to another.

Finland

Moscow

Belarus

Ukraine

Romania

Crimea

Georgia
Armenia
Azerbaijan

Turkey

Greece

Syria

Lebanon
Israel

Jordan

Iraq

Kuwait

Egypt

Saudi Arabia

Bahrain
Qatar
United Arab Emirates

Oman

Sudan

Eritrea

Yemen

Djibouti

Central African Republic

South Sudan

Ethiopia

Somalia

Uganda

Democratic Republic of the Congo

Rwanda
Burundi

Kenya

Tanzania

Zambia

Malawi

Mozambique

Zimbabwe

Botswana

Pretoria

Swaziland

Lesotho

South Africa

Seychelles

Comoros

Madagascar

Mauritius

Russia

Kazakhstan

Mongolia

Uzbekistan

Kyrgyzstan

Turkmenistan

Tajikistan

Iran

Afghanistan

Pakistan

New Delhi

Nepal

Bhutan

Bangladesh

India

Myanmar

Sri Lanka

Maldives

Beijing

China

North Korea

South Korea

Japan

Tokyo

Taiwan

Laos

Thailand

Vietnam

Cambodia

Philippines

Brunei

Malaysia

Singapore

Indonesia

Timor-Leste

Papua New Guinea

Australia

Canberra

New Zealand

Wellington

Pacific Ocean

Indian Ocean

Europe inset:

Iceland

Reykjavik

Norway

Sweden

Finland

Russia

Oslo

Stockholm

Helsinki

Tallinn

Estonia

North Sea

Baltic Sea

Moscow

Riga

Latvia

Denmark

Copenhagen

Lithuania

Vilnius

Minsk

Ireland

Dublin

United Kingdom

Irish Sea

London

Netherlands

Amsterdam

Berlin

Warsaw

Belarus

Kiev

English Channel

Brussels

Belgium

Germany

Poland

Ukraine

Luxembourg

Paris

Prague

Czechia

Slovakia

Bratislava

Moldova

Chișinău

France

Liechtenstein

Vienna

Austria

Budapest

Hungary

Romania

Bern

Switzerland

Vaduz

Slovenia

Ljubljana

Zagreb

Belgrade

Bucharest

Monaco

San Marino

Croatia

BIH

Serbia

Bulgaria

Black Sea

Portugal

Lisbon

Madrid

Andorra

Rome

MNE

RKS

Sofia

Ankara

Spain

Italy

Tirana
Albania

North Macedonia

Turkey

Gibraltar (UK)

Greece

Athens

Mediterranean Sea

Cyprus

Valletta
Malta

0   250   500   750 km

Alaska
(state
of the USA)

Greenland
(Denmark)

Iceland

Norway   Sweden

Canada

Denmark

Ireland   United
           Kingdom

Germany

*Great
Lakes*

Ottawa

France

Italy

**United States of America
(USA)**

Washington, D.C.

Spain

Portugal

Tunisia

Morocco

A t l a n t i c

Canary Islands

Mexico

Algeria   **Libya**

Western
Sahara

Bahamas

Cuba

Dominican
Republic

Puerto Rico (USA)

Mauritania

Mali

Niger

Belize

Haiti

Antigua and Barbuda

Cape Verde

Chad

Guatemala **Honduras** Jamaica

Dominica

Senegal

El Salvador

Saint Kitts
and Nevis

Saint Lucia

Barbados

Gambia

Burkina
Faso

Nicaragua

Grenada Saint Vincent
         and the Grenadines

Guinea-Bissau

Benin

Nigeria

Costa Rica

Trinidad and Tobago

Guinea

Côte
d'Ivoire

Togo

Panama

Venezuela

Sierra Leone

Ghana

Cameroon

Liberia

Colombia

Guyana

Suri-
name

French
Guiana

Equatorial Guinea
São Tomé and

Equator

Príncipe

Gabon

Ecuador

Congo

O c e a n

Peru

Pacific

B r a z i l

Angola

Bolivia

Paraguay

Namibia

Argentina

Uruguay

Chile

O c e a n

Falkland Islands
(UK)

A n t a r c t i c a

Hawaii
(state
of the USA)

Abbreviations:

BIH   Bosnia and
      Herzegovina

UK   United Kingdom

USA   United States of America

MNE   Montenegro

RKS   Kosovo

0   500 1,000 1,500 2,000 2,500

km